Upper
West
Side

Central Park

Upper
East
Side

Upper
Midtown

Lower
Midtown

East River

Central Park
Pages 198–203

Upper East Side
Pages 178–197

Upper Midtown
Pages 162–177

Lower Midtown
Pages 146–161

**Gramercy and the
Flatiron District**
Pages 118–125

East Village
Pages 112–117

Lower East Side
Pages 86–95

Brooklyn
Pages 226–241

EYEWITNESS TRAVEL

NEW
YORK
CITY

EYEWITNESS TRAVEL

NEW
YORK
CITY

Main Contributor **Eleanor Berman**

DK

A7 019 022 4

DK Penguin Random House

Project Editor Fay Franklin

Art Editor Tony Foo

Editors Donna Dailey, Ellen Dupont, Esther Labi

Designers Steve Bere, Louise Parsons, Mark Stevens

Editorial Assistant Fiona Morgan

Contributors Lester Brooks, Patricia Brooks,
Susan Farewell, Stephen Keeling

Photographers
Max Alexander, Dave King, Michael Moran

Illustrators
Richard Draper, Robbie Polley, Hamish Simpson

This book was produced with the assistance of
Websters International Publishers.

Printed and bound in China

First published in Great Britain in 1993
by Dorling Kindersley Limited
80 Strand, London WC2R 0RL

16 17 18 19 10 9 8 7 6 5 4 3 2 1

Reprinted with revisions 1994, 1995 (twice), 1997, 1999, 2000, 2001, 2002,
2003, 2004, 2005, 2006, 2007, 2008, 2009, 2010, 2011, 2012, 2013, 2014,
2015, 2016

Copyright 1993, 2016 © Dorling Kindersley Limited, London

A Penguin Random House Company

A CIP catalogue record is available from the British Library.

ISBN: 978-0-24120-942-4

Throughout this book, floors are referred to in accordance with
American usage, ie the "first floor" is at ground level.

MIX
Paper from
responsible sources
FSC
www.fsc.org   FSC™ C018179

**The information in this
DK Eyewitness Travel Guide is checked annually.**
Every effort has been made to ensure that this book is as up-to-date as possible
at the time of going to press. Some details, however, such as telephone numbers,
opening hours, prices, gallery hanging arrangements, and travel information, are
liable to change. The publishers cannot accept responsibility for any consequences
arising from the use of this book, nor for any material on third-party websites, and
cannot guarantee that any website address in this book will be a suitable source of
travel information. We value the views and suggestions of our readers very highly.
Please write to: Publisher, DK Eyewitness Travel Guides, Dorling Kindersley,
80 Strand, London, WC2R 0RL, UK, or email: travelguides@dk.com.

Front cover main image: The Empire State Building as seen from the Top of the Rock

◀ Towering skyscrapers in central New York

Contents

New York
Yankees Baseball
star Babe Ruth
(1895–1948)

Introducing
New York City

Iconic yellow taxis in New York City

Fresh produce and fish for sale in Chinatown

Classic New York dining at the Oyster Bar in Grand Central Terminal

The New York City Ballet

Solomon R. Guggenheim Museum, Upper East Side

HOW TO USE THIS GUIDE

This Eyewitness Travel Guide helps you get the most from your stay in New York with the minimum of practical difficulty. The opening section, *Introducing New York City*, locates the city geographically, sets modern New York in its historical context and describes the highlights of the year. *New York City at a Glance* is an overview of the city's attractions. Section two, *New York City Area by Area*, guides you through the city's sightseeing areas. It describes all the main

sights with maps, photographs, and detailed illustrations. In addition, seven planned walks take you step-by-step through standout areas.

Well-researched tips on where to stay, eat, shop, and on sports and entertainment, are in section three, *Travelers' Needs*. *Children's New York City* lists highlights for young visitors, and section four, *Survival Guide*, shows you how to do everything from mailing a letter to using the subway.

New York City Area by Area

New York City has been divided into 15 sightseeing areas, each described separately. Each area opens with a portrait, summing up the area's character and

history and listing all the sights to be covered. Sights are numbered and clearly located on an *Area Map*. After this comes a large-scale *Street-by-Street Map* focusing on the most interesting

part of the area. Finding your way around each area is made simple by the numbering system. This refers to the order in which sights are described on the pages that follow.

Color-coding on each page makes the area easy to find in the book.

Recommended restaurants in the area are listed and plotted on the map.

Numbered circles pinpoint all the listed sights on the area map. The Roosevelt Island, for example, is ⑰

A locator map shows you where you are in relation to surrounding areas. The area of the *Street-by-Street Map* is highlighted.

1 Area Map
For easy reference, the sights in each area are numbered and located on an area map. To help the visitor, the map also shows subway stations, heliports, and ferry embarkation points.

Stars indicate the sights that no visitor should miss.

The Paley Center for Media ⑥ is shown on this map as well.

A suggested route for a walk takes in the most attractive and interesting streets in the area.

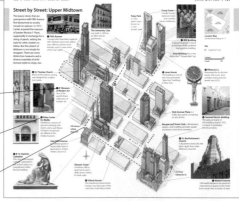

2 The Street-by-Street Map
This gives a bird's-eye view of the heart of each sightseeing area. The numbering of the sights ties in with the area map and the fuller descriptions on the pages that follow.

New York City at a Glance

Each map in this section concentrates on a specific theme: *Museums, Architecture, Multicultural New York,* and *Remarkable New Yorkers*. The top sights are shown on the map; other sights are described on the following two pages.

Each sightseeing area is color-coded.

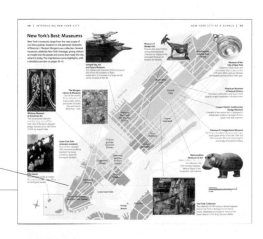

Practical Information lists all the information you need to visit every sight, including a map reference to the Street Finder at the back of the book.

Numbers refer to each sight's position on the area map and its place in the chapter.

3 Detailed information on each sight
All important sights in each area are described in depth in this section. They are listed in order, following the numbering on the *Area Map*. Practical information on opening hours, telephone numbers, websites, admission charges, and facilities available is given for each sight. The key to the symbols used can be found on the back flap.

The Visitors' Checklist provides the practical information you will need to plan your visit.

The facade of each major sight is shown to help you spot it quickly.

Stars indicate the most interesting architectural details of the building, and the most important works of art or exhibits on view inside.

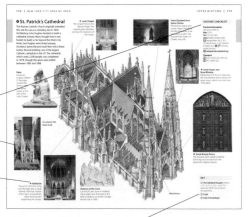

4 New York's major sights
These are given two or more full pages in the sightseeing area in which they are found. Notable buildings are dissected to reveal their interiors; and museums and galleries have color-coded floor plans to help you find particular exhibits.

Numbered circles point out key features of the sight listed in a key.

INTRODUCING NEW YORK CITY

GREAT DAYS IN NEW YORK CITY

New York is a city packed with treasures of things to see and do. Whether you are here for several days, or just wanting a flavor of this great metropolis, you need to make the most of your time. Over the following pages, you'll find itineraries for some of the best attractions New York has to offer, arranged first by theme and then by length of stay. There's a mix of activities, and the schedules are not meant to be rigid – you'll find ample time to explore places that catch your fancy too. Price guides show the cost for two adults or for a family of two adults and two children including lunch.

City Landmarks

Two adults
allow at least $140

- A tour of the UN
- Modern, Art Deco, and Beaux Arts edifices
- Lights of Times Square
- Empire State Building

Morning
Start at the **Flatiron Building** *(see p123)* and stroll through Madison Square toward the East River. Join a guided tour of the **United Nations headquarters** *(see pp156–9)*, with its striking modern architecture. Then head to 42nd Street, and drop in to admire the Art Deco interior of the **Chrysler Building** *(see p151)*. Next is **Grand Central Terminal**, a great Beaux Arts landmark *(see pp152–3)*. Admire the Main Concourse and explore the shopping gallery, colorful food market, and a food court with everything from sushi to Southern barbecue to New York cheesecake. Another lunchtime option is chowder or a platter of Long Island oysters at the **Grand Central Oyster Bar** *(see p302)*.

Afternoon
Back on 42nd Street is another Beaux Arts creation, the **New York Public Library** *(see p142; free 1-hour tours at 11am and 2pm Tue–Thu)*. The marble halls, stairways, Main Reading Room and Periodicals Room are highlights. Check your e-mail for free in the Bill Blass Public Catalog Room. Look out also for current exhibits. Behind the library is **Bryant Park** *(see p141)*, a welcome oasis of green in Midtown. Ahead is New York's most famous crossroads, **Times Square** *(see p142–3)*, gateway to the glittering neon of Broadway. Just beyond is 42nd Street, now a bright avenue of restored theaters, giant movie palaces, and Madame Tussauds wax museum, with many true-to-life celebrities. Hail a cab to the **Empire State Building** *(see pp132–3)* and end the day with a fine twilight view of the city from the 86th-floor observatory.

Glistening Prometheus Statue and Lower Plaza at Rockefeller Center

Art and Shopping

Two adults
allow at least $135

- A morning of modern art
- Lunch at Rockefeller Center
- St. Patrick's Cathedral
- Fifth Avenue shopping

Morning
The spectacular **Museum of Modern Art** (MoMA) *(see pp168–71)* will easily fill your morning with its wonderful art. Allow a couple of hours to enjoy its great works, including Vincent van Gogh's *The Starry Night* and Claude Monet's *Water Lilies*, as well as Pablo Picasso's *Les Demoiselles d'Avignon*, to name just a few. Don't miss the design exhibits on floor three; one of MoMA's best-known facets. Leave the museum and stroll over to **Rockefeller Center** *(see p140)* for lunch at the Rock Center Café, where you can watch the ice skaters in winter. In summer the rink is transformed into a leafy garden, where you can dine at the Rink Bar.

The neon lights of Times Square, the city's famous crossroads

◀ The tip of Manhattan in 1942

Afternoon

After lunch, head for **St. Patrick's Cathedral** *(see pp174–5)*, the largest Catholic cathedral in the US and one of the city's finest places of worship. Then continue along **Fifth Avenue** for an afternoon of window shopping. Saks Fifth Avenue is just across the street from St. Patrick's at 50th Street. Heading uptown, the temptations on Fifth Avenue include a dizzying variety of glitzy shops, such as Cartier (52nd St), Henri Bendel (55–56th sts), Prada, Tiffany (57th St), and Bergdorf Goodman (57 st). For more affordable shopping, head to **Macy's** *(see pp130–31)* or **Bloomingdale's** *(see p177)*.

Historic New York

Two adults
allow at least $120

- **A boat trip to Ellis Island and the Statue of Liberty**
- **Lunch at Fraunces Tavern**
- **A tour of Old New York**

Morning

At Battery Park, board the ferry to the **Statue of Liberty** *(see pp78–9)* or on to **Ellis Island** *(see pp82–3)*, the point of arrival for many immigrants (round trip includes both stops). If you have time on your return, exit the park at **Bowling Green**, the city's oldest park *(see p76–7)*. Walk to the **Fraunces Tavern Museum** *(see p80)*, New York's last remaining block of 18th-century commercial buildings. The recreated Tavern includes a museum of the revolutionary period and a restaurant that is the perfect choice for an atmospheric lunch.

Afternoon

A block away is Stone Street Historic District, rebuilt after a fire in 1835. Look for **India House** *(see p58)*, once the New York Cotton Exchange, now **Harry's Café**. Take William Street to Wall Street and **Federal Hall** *(see p70)*, with exhibits on the US Constitution. Nearby is the **New York Stock Exchange**

(see pp72–3) and **Trinity Church** *(see p71)*, built in 1839. Go up Broadway to **St. Paul's Chapel** *(see p85)*, miraculously unscathed after the World Trade Center fell behind it. Ahead is **City Hall** *(see p84)*. Finally, head for the **South Street Seaport historic district**, heart of the 19th-century port *(see p84)*, with a view of the awesome **Brooklyn Bridge** *(see pp232–5)*.

A Family Fun Day

Family of four
allow at least $225

- **A morning in Central Park**
- **The Marionette Theater**
- **Dinosaurs at the American Museum of Natural History**

Morning

Central Park *(see pp198–203)* was made for family fun. Ride the vintage Carousel, watch model boats in action at Conservatory Pond, visit the Zoo, where you can also watch the animal parade on the Delacorte Clock on the half-hour. There are themed playgrounds to please all ages: Safari at West 91st Street (2–5 years); Adventure at West 67th Street (6–12 years). The Swedish

Central Park, a vast area of fun activities, animals, and places to play

Cottage Marionette Theater, at West 79th, presents classic fairy tales at 10:30am and noon Tue–Fri (Wed also 2:30pm) and 1pm Sat; book ahead. Rent bikes or take a boat out on the lake, then picnic near the Boathouse, which has a view of the lake. In winter, you can ice skate at the Wollman Rink.

Afternoon

Depending on ages and interests, choose between the interactive **Children's Museum of Manhattan** *(see p213)*, or the famous dinosaurs and dioramas at the **American Museum of Natural History** *(see pp210–11)*. Finish up on West 73rd Street for a "wee tea" at Alice's Tea Cup.

Ellis Island, the view greeting early immigrants to New York

2 days in New York City

* Marvel at the masterpieces in the Met
* Ascend the Empire State Building for iconic views
* Take a boat to the Statue of Liberty and Ellis Island

View uptown over the vast expanse of Central Park

Day 1

Morning Start with a 1-hour guided tour of the city's vast **Metropolitan Museum of Art** *(pp186–93)*, known as the Met, daily at 10am. Follow this with a walk through neighboring **Central Park** *(pp198–203)*, with views of the lake and the skyline beyond.

Afternoon Hop on the Fifth Avenue bus to 59th Street and Grand Army Plaza, then walk on down **Fifth Avenue** *(p166)* to **Rockefeller Center** *(p140)* at 49th Street, passing shopping meccas such as Bergdorf Goodman, Tiffany, Trump Tower, and Saks Fifth Avenue, as well as the striking **St. Patrick's Cathedral** *(pp174–5)*. Visit the 86th-floor observatory at the **Empire State Building** *(pp132–3)* for the legendary panorama of the city. For souvenir shopping, the "world's largest store," **Macy's** *(pp130–31)*, is a block west. After dark, enjoy the bright lights of **Times Square** *(p142–3)*, and take in a **Broadway** *(p338)* show. Check the TKTS booth on Times Square for discount seats.

Day 2

Morning To avoid long lines head to **Battery Park** *(p81)* early to catch the boat to the **Statue of Liberty** *(pp78–9)* and **Ellis Island** *(pp82–3)*, the symbol of America's immigrant heritage. There will be time on your return to visit the moving **National September 11 Memorial and Museum** *(p74)*, in Lower Manhattan. Book in advance.

Afternoon Stroll down Wall Street, taking in the monumental Neo-Classical facade of the **New York Stock Exchange** *(pp72–3)* on the corner of Broad Street. Next,

head to historic **South Street Seaport** *(p84)*, once the hub of New York's seafaring activity. Spend a couple of hours wandering this cobblestone neighborhood, now home to historic ships, museums, food stalls, and shops. End the day with a sunset walk across **Brooklyn Bridge** *(pp232–5)*.

3 days in New York City

* Enjoy modern art at MoMA
* Visit the National September 11 Memorial and Museum
* See a show on Broadway

Day 1

Morning Take in city views from the top of the **Empire State Building** *(pp132–3)*, then stroll up **Fifth Avenue** *(p166)* with its luxury stores. Detour along 42nd Street to see the beautiful interiors of the **Grand Central Terminal** *(pp152–3)*, then continue on to **Rockefeller Center** *(p140)* for an exploratory wander. **St. Patrick's Cathedral** *(pp174–5)* is across the street.

Afternoon See masterpieces at **The Museum of Modern Art** *(pp168–71)* and shop for souvenirs at the MoMA store or **Macy's** *(pp130–31)*. At night, the bright lights of **Broadway** *(p338)* beckon.

Day 2

Morning After a stroll through **Central Park** *(pp198–203)*, visit the **Metropolitan Museum of Art** *(pp186–93)*. Step into the

lobby of Frank Lloyd Wright's **Solomon R. Guggenheim Museum** *(pp184–5)* to admire the amazing architecture, and linger to see some modern art.

Afternoon Take a walk on the **High Line** *(p134)*, the city's park in the sky, then stroll around the leafy lanes of trendy **Greenwich Village** *(pp102–11)* and browse its many stores. At night, sample the lively cafés of **SoHo** *(pp96–101)*, or opt for a show at **Lincoln Center for the Performing Arts** *(p208)*.

Day 3

Morning Start with the city's symbol of freedom, the **Statue of Liberty** *(pp78–9)*, and a visit to the fascinating **Ellis Island** *(pp82–3)*; arrive early at **Battery Park** *(p81)* for shorter lines for the boat ride. Afterward, take time to visit the **National September 11 Memorial and Museum** *(p74)*.

The spiral rotunda of Frank Lloyd Wright's Solomon R. Guggenheim Museum

Afternoon Visit the fascinating **Museum of Jewish Heritage** *(p76)*, then wander down Wall Street to see the grand **New York Stock Exchange** *(pp72–3)*. End the day with a stroll and an early dinner in **South Street Seaport** *(p84)*, from where there are also great views of **Brooklyn Bridge** *(pp232–5)*.

5 days in New York City

- **Take a walk in Central Park**
- **Explore Greenwich Village, SoHo, and Chelsea**
- **View the city from across beautiful Brooklyn Bridge**

Day 1

Morning Head to **Fifth Avenue** *(p166)* to browse its famous stores and nearby sights, including **St. Patrick's Cathedral** *(pp174–5)* and **Rockefeller Center** *(p140)* with its Art Deco sky-scrapers and beautiful gardens.

Afternoon Enjoy the open spaces of **Central Park** *(pp198–203)*, the masterpieces at **The Metropolitan Museum of Art** *(pp186–93)*, and great views from atop the **Empire State Building** *(pp132–3)*. In the evening, take in the lights of **Broadway** *(p338)*.

Day 2

Morning The boat ride to the **Statue of Liberty** *(pp78–9)* and **Ellis Island** *(pp82–3)* is a thrill, offering remarkable photo opportunities. Take the boat back late morning and visit the **National September 11 Memorial and Museum** *(p74)*, a very poignant experience.

Afternoon Visit the vibrant **Museum of Jewish Heritage** *(p76)*, then make your way to Wall Street for a stroll through the skyscraper canyons and to see the **New York Stock Exchange** *(pp72–3)*. Look out for the **Federal Hall** *(p70)* along the way. Next, spend a couple of hours exploring **South Street Seaport** *(p84)*, the city's old maritime center and now a lively complex with museums, shops, and restaurants.

Day 3

Morning Spend the morning exploring two major museums, the **Museum of Modern Art** *(pp168–71)* and Frank Lloyd Wright's **Solomon R. Guggenheim Museum** *(pp184–5)*, both with exciting modern art collections.

Afternoon Explore Manhattan's neighborhoods: the quaint, historic streets and lively cafés of **Greenwich Village** *(pp102–11)*, the shops and classic cast-iron buildings of **SoHo** *(pp98–9)*, or peruse a few of the many art galleries of **Chelsea** *(pp126–35)*. Take a walk along the city's most unusual park, the **High Line** *(p134)*, ending with the upscale boutiques on 14th Street in the trendy **Meat Packing District** *(pp106–107)*.

Day 4

Morning Explore the **Upper West Side** *(pp204–13)*, walking down to **Columbus Circle** *(p209)*. Then head east to take a tour of the **United Nations** *(pp156–9)* headquarters, then explore the **Lower East Side** *(pp86–95)*, where the **Lower East Side Tenement Museum** *(p92)* tells the tale of life in the city's old tenements. **Orchard Street** *(p93)*, a mix of bargain stores and hip boutiques, serves the newest generation of residents.

Afternoon Check out some big-name stores, such as **Lord & Taylor** *(p313)* and **Bloomingdale's** *(p177)*, or take in at least one more museum. The **Frick Collection** *(pp196–7)*, housed in

The Immigration Museum on Ellis Island, where 12 million US immigrants arrived

a palatial gilded-age mansion, has an outstanding collection of Old Masters. Alternatively, visit the **Whitney Museum** *(pp108–9)*, home to the entire range of 20th-century American art. In the evening, head to **Harlem** *(pp214–225)* for a jazz club or to see a show at the famous **Apollo Theater** *(p224)*.

Day 5

Morning Walk across **Brooklyn Bridge** *(pp232–5)* to **Brooklyn Heights Promenade** *(p270–271)* for views of Manhattan. A subway ride leads to Brooklyn's impressive **Grand Army Plaza** *(p236)* and the world-class **Brooklyn Museum** *(pp238–41)*.

Afternoon Spend some time admiring the lovely **Brooklyn Botanic Garden** *(p237)*, famous for its Japanese Garden, and **Prospect Park** *(pp236–7)*, laid out by Central Park's designers. Visit the **Brooklyn Academy of Music** *(p231)* for avant-garde theater and dance.

Elevated walkway on the Brooklyn Bridge, the world's first steel-wire suspension bridge

Putting New York City on the Map

New York is a city of over eight million people, covering 301 sq miles (780 sq km). The city gets its name from the state of New York, the capital of which is Albany, 156 miles (251 km) to the north. New York is also a good base from which to visit the historic cities of Boston and Philadelphia, as well as the nation's capital, Washington, DC.

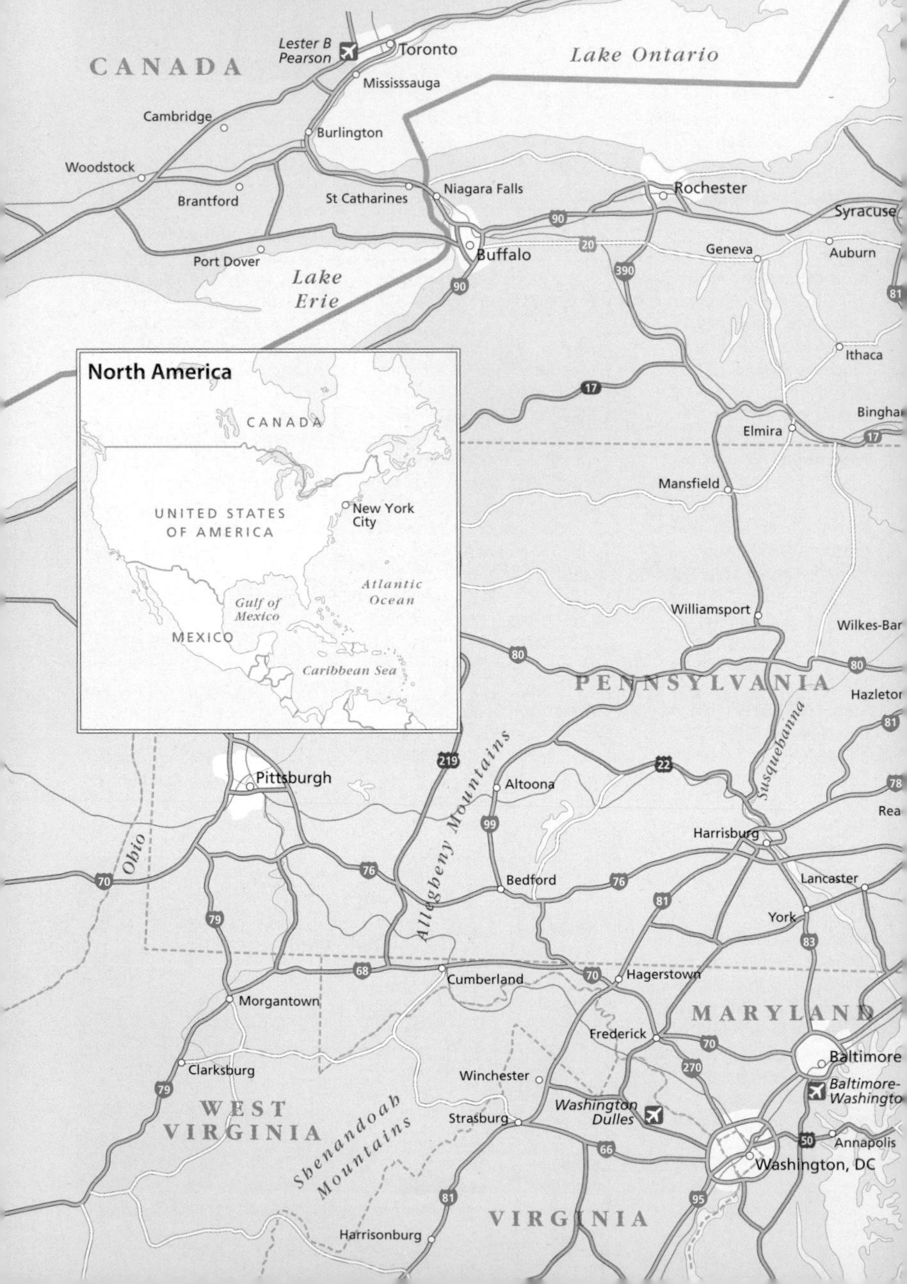

Watertc

CANADA

Lester B Pearson ✈ Toronto

Mississsauga

Lake Ontario

Cambridge

Burlington

Woodstock

Brantford

St Catharines

Niagara Falls

Rochester

Syracuse

90

Geneva

Auburn

Port Dover

Lake Erie

90

Buffalo

20

390

81

Ithaca

North America

CANADA

17

UNITED STATES OF AMERICA

New York City

Elmira

Bingha

17

Mansfield

Atlantic Ocean

Williamsport

Wilkes-Bar

Gulf of Mexico

80

80

MEXICO

Caribbean Sea

PENNSYLVANIA

Hazleton

81

Pittsburgh

219

Altoona

22

78

Allegheny Mountains

Susquehanna

Rea

99

Harrisburg

70

Ohio

76

Bedford

76

81

Lancaster

79

York

83

68

Cumberland

70

Hagerstown

MARYLAND

Morgantown

Frederick

70

Baltimore

Clarksburg

270

Baltimore-Washingto

79

Winchester

WEST VIRGINIA

Shenandoah Mountains

Strasburg

Washington Dulles ✈

66

50

Annapolis

Washington, DC

81

95

Harrisonburg

VIRGINIA

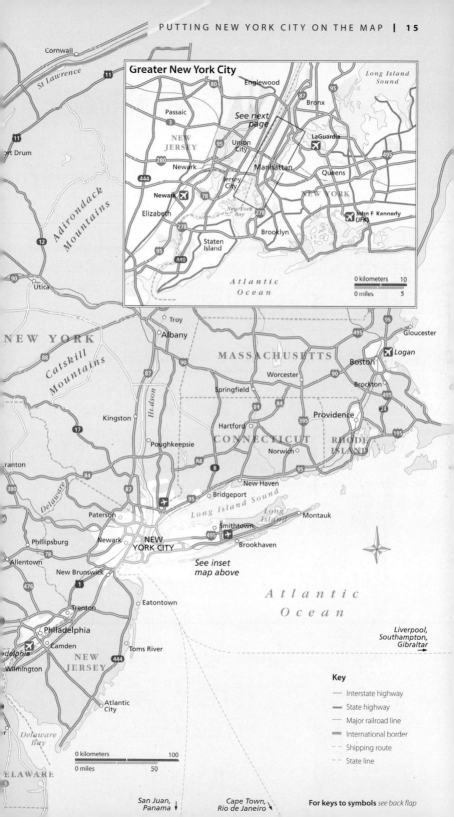

Greater New York City

Cornwall

St Lawrence

11

11

rt Drum

Adirondack Mountains

12

90

Utica

NEW YORK

88

Catskill Mountains

17

ranton

380

Delaware

84

87

Phillipsburg

Allentown

78

476

Paterson

Newark

NEW YORK CITY

See inset map above

New Brunswick

1

Trenton

Philadelphia

Camden

delphia

Wilmington

NEW JERSEY

444

Toms River

Atlantic City

Delaware Bay

ELAWARE

3

Troy

Albany

90

87

Kingston

Poughkeepsie

R4

8

95

Hudson

MASSACHUSETTS

Worcester

Springfield

91

84

Hartford

CONNECTICUT

Norwich

395

New Haven

Bridgeport

95

Boston

Logan

Brockton

495

24

Providence

195

RHODE ISLAND

Montauk

Long Island Sound

Long Island

495

Smithtown

Brookhaven

05

Gloucester

Atlantic Ocean

Liverpool, Southampton, Gibraltar →

San Juan, Panama ↓

Cape Town, Rio de Janeiro ↘

Inset – Greater New York City

80

Englewood

95

Long Island Sound

Passaic

3

87

Bronx

NEW JERSEY

95

Union City

See next page

LaGuardia

280

Newark

444

Manhattan

Jersey City

Queens

Newark

78

NEW YORK

Elizabeth

278

New York Bay

278

John F Kennedy (JFK)

95

Brooklyn

278

440

Staten Island

Atlantic Ocean

0 kilometers 10

0 miles 5

Key

— Interstate highway

— State highway

⋯ Major railroad line

— International border

-- Shipping route

-- State line

0 kilometers 100

0 miles 50

For keys to symbols *see back flap*

Manhattan

This guide divides Manhattan into 14 areas, with a further chapter dedicated to Brooklyn. Many of New York's oldest and newest buildings rub shoulders in Lower Manhattan. It is from here, too, that you can take the Staten Island ferry, for breath-taking views of the city's skyline and the Statue of Liberty. Midtown includes the Theater District and Fifth Avenue's glittering shops. Museum Mile, alongside Central Park on the Upper East Side, is a cultural paradise. To the north lies Harlem, the US's most famous African-American community.

Grand Central Terminal
This Beaux Arts station has been a gateway to the city since 1913. Its concourse is a vast pedestrian area with a high-vaulted roof *(see pp152–3)*.

The Morgan Library & Museum
One of the world's finest collections of rare manuscripts, prints, and books is on display in this palazzo-style building *(see pp160–61)*.

Cathedral of St. John the Divine
When it is finished, at some time after the mid-21st century, this great cathedral will be the largest in the world. It is also a theater and music venue *(see pp220–21)*.

Statue of Liberty
Presented as a gift from the French to the American people in 1886, this towering statue has become a symbol of freedom throughout the world *(see pp78–9)*.

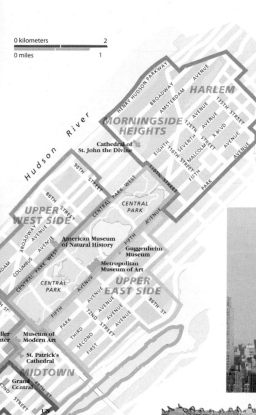

United Nations (UN)
New York is the headquarters of the global organization set up to preserve world peace and security *(see pp156–9)*.

Empire State Building
This is one of America's tallest buildings and a symbol of New York City. Built in the 1930s, it has since attracted more than 110 million visitors *(see pp132–3)*.

The Metropolitan Museum of Art
With a stunning collection of artifacts dating from prehistoric times to the present, this is one of the world's greatest museums *(see pp186–93)*.

Brooklyn Bridge
This bridge spans the East River between Manhattan and Brooklyn. Built in 1883, it was the largest suspension bridge and the first to be constructed of steel *(see pp232–5)*.

Solomon R. Guggenheim Museum
A masterpiece of architecture by Frank Lloyd Wright, this unique building contains a fine collection of 19th- and 20th-century painting *(see pp184–5)*.

THE HISTORY OF NEW YORK CITY

From its first sighting almost 500 years ago by Giovanni da Verrazano, New York's harbor was the prize that all of Europe wanted to capture. The Dutch first sent fur traders to the area in 1621, but they lost the colony they called New Amsterdam to the English in 1664. The settlement was re-christened New York, and the name stayed, even after the English lost the colony in 1783, at the end of the Revolutionary War.

The Growing City

In the 19th century, New York grew rapidly and became a major port. Ease of shipping spawned manufacturing, commerce was king, and great fortunes were made. In 1898, Manhattan was joined with the four outer boroughs to form the world's second largest city. From 1800 to 1900, the population grew from 79,000 to 3 million people. New York City became the country's cultural and entertainment mecca as well as its business center.

The Melting Pot

The city continued to grow, as thousands of immigrants came seeking a better life. Overpopulation meant that many at first lived in slums. Today, the mix of cultures has enriched the city and become its defining quality. Its eight million inhabitants speak some 100 languages.

Manhattan's skyline took shape as the city grew skyward to make space for its ever-increasing population. Throughout its history, the city has experienced alternating periods of economic decline and growth, but it remains one of the world's most vital cities.

The following pages illustrate significant periods in New York's history.

A deed signed by New Amsterdam's last Dutch governor, Peter Stuyvesant, in 1664

◀ The southern half of Manhattan and part of Brooklyn in 1767

Early New York City

Manhattan was a forested land populated by Algonquian-speaking Natives when the Dutch West India Company established a fur-trading post called New Amsterdam in 1625. The first settlers built houses helter-skelter, so even today the streets of Lower Manhattan still twist. Broadway, then called by the Dutch name *Breede Wegh,* began as an Indian trail known as the Weekquaesgeek Trail. Harlem has also kept its Dutch name. The town was unruly until Peter Stuyvesant arrived to bring order. But the colony did not produce the expected revenues, and in 1664 the Dutch let it fall to the English, who renamed it New York.

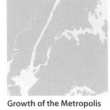

Growth of the Metropolis
1664   Today

Seal of New Netherland
The beaver pelt and wampum (Indian shell beads) on the seal were the currency of the colony of New Netherland.

The First New Yorkers
Algonquian-speaking Natives were the first inhabitants of Manhattan.

First View of Manhattan (1626)

The southern tip of Manhattan resembled a Dutch town, down to the windmill. Although a fort shown here, it had not yet been built.

Dutch ships

Iroquois Pot
Iroquois Indians were frequent visitors to early Manhattan.

Native American Village
Some Algonquians lived in longhouses on Manhattan before the Dutch arrived.

Native canoe

1524 Giovanni da Verrazano sails into New York harbor

1626 Peter Minuit buys Manhattan from the Natives

1625 Dutch establish first permanent trading post

1653 Wall is built for protection from attack; adjacent street is called Wall Street

1600

1620

1640

1609 Henry Hudson sails up the now Hudson River in search of the Northwest Passage

1625 First black slaves brought from Africa

1643–45 Native American Indian skirmishes end with temporary peace treaty

1654 First Jewish settlers arrive

1647 Peter Stuyvesant becomes colonial governor

Dutch Delftware
Colonists brought this popular tin-glazed earthenware pottery from Holland.

Manhattan Skyline
The Strand, now Whitehall Street, was the site of the city's first brick house.

Tiger timbers

Where to See Dutch New York

Dug up by workmen in 1916, these remnants of a Dutch ship, the *Tiger*, which burned in 1613, are the earliest artifacts of the period and are now in the Museum of the City of New York (*see p195*). Rooms in this museum, as well as in the Morris-Jumel Mansion (*see p245*) and the Vorleezer's House in Richmond Town (*see p258*), give a good idea of life in Dutch New York.

Purchase of Manhattan
Peter Minuit bought the island from the Natives in 1626 for a bucket of trade goods worth 60 guilders.

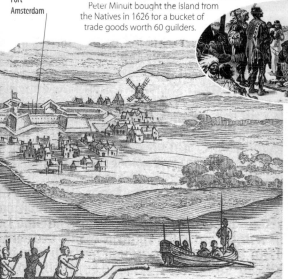

Fort Amsterdam

Peter Stuyvesant
The last Dutch governor was a tyrant who imposed strict laws – such as an edict closing all the city's taverns at 9 o'clock.

1660 First city hospital established

1664 British forces oust Dutch without a fight and change city's name to New York

1676 Great Dock built on East River

1698 Trinity Church dedicated

1660

1680

1700

The surrender of New Amsterdam to the British

1680s Bolting Laws give New York exclusive right to process and ship grain

1683 First New York city charter established

1689 Merchant Jacob Leisler leads a revolt against taxes and takes over the city for two years

1693 Ninety-two cannons installed for protection; area becomes known as the Battery

1691 Leisler sentenced to death for treason

Colonial New York City

Under British rule, New York prospered, and the population grew rapidly. The bolting of flour (grinding grain) was the main commercial enterprise. Shipbuilding also flourished. As the city prospered, an elite emerged that could afford a more refined way of life, and fine furniture and household silver were made for use in their homes during the Colonial period. During more than a century of governing New York, Britain proved more interested in profit than in the welfare of the colony. The Crown imposed hated taxes, and the spirit of rebellion grew, although loyalties were divided, especially in New York. On the eve of Revolution, New York was the second-largest city in the 13 colonies, with 20,000 citizens.

Growth of the Metropolis
1760   Today

Colonial currency
This early paper money was based on the British pound.

Bedroom

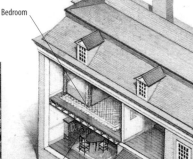

Colonial Street
Pigs and dogs roamed free on the streets of Colonial New York.

Dining room

Shipping
Trade with the West Indies and Britain helped New York prosper. In some years, 200 or more vessels visited the port.

Kas
This Dutch-style pine wardrobe was made in New York's Hudson River valley around 1720.

1702 Lord Cornbury, known for often wearing women's clothes, appointed Colonial governor

1711 Slave market set up at the foot of Wall Street

1720 First shipyard opens

1734 John Pet Zenger's libel tri upholds freedo of the pre

1700	1710	1720	1730

1710 Iroquois chief Hendrick visits England

1725 *New York Gazette*, city's first newspaper, is established

1732 First city theater opens

1733 Bowling Green becomes first city park; first ferries to Brooklyn

Captain Kidd
The Scottish pirate William Kidd was a respected citizen, lending a block and tackle to help build the Trinity Church *(see p71)*.

Van Cortlandt House
Frederick Van Cortlandt (1699–1749) built this Georgian style house in 1748 on a wheat plantation in what is now the Bronx. Today a museum, it shows how a well-to-do Dutch-English family once lived.

West parlor

Where to See Colonial New York

Colonial buildings are open to the public at Historic Richmond Town on Staten Island *(see p258)*. Fine examples of Colonial silver and furniture are on display at the Museum of the City of New York *(see p195)*.

Richmond Town General Store

Colonial Kitchen
Plain white cheese, called "white meat," was often served in place of meat. Waffles, introduced by the Dutch, were popular. Fresh fruit was rare, but preserved fruits were eaten.

Pewter baby bottle

Cheese mold

Waffle iron

Decorative Carvings
A face carved in stone peers over each of the front windows.

Sucket fork, for eating preserved fruits

1741 Slave uprising creates hysteria; 31 slaves are executed, and 150 imprisoned

1754 French and Indian War begins; King's College (now Columbia University) founded

British soldier

1759 First jail built

1740

1750

1760

King's College

1762 First paid police force established

1763 War ends; the British gain control of North America

Revolutionary New York City

Dug up into trenches for defense, heavily shelled by British troops, and scarred by recurring fires, New York suffered during the American Revolution. But, despite the hardships, many continued to enjoy cricket games, horse races, balls, and boxing matches. After the British took the city in 1776, it became their headquarters. The Continental army did not return to Manhattan until November 25, 1783, two years after the fighting ended.

Growth of the Metropolis
◻ 1776   ◻ Today

Battle Dress
The Continental (Patriot) army wore blue uniforms, while the British wore red.

British soldier

Soldier's Haversack
American soldiers in the War of Independence carried their supplies in haversacks.

Continental soldier

Toppling the King
New Yorkers tore down the statue of King George III in Bowling Green and melted it down to make ammunition.

Patriot

Battle of Harlem Heights
Washington won this battle on September 16, 1776. However, he did not have enough troops to hold New York, so retreated, leaving it to the British.

Death of a Patriot
While working behind British lines in 1776, Nathan Hale was captured and hanged by the British without trial for spying.

1765 British pass Stamp Act; New Yorkers protest; Sons of Liberty formed

1767 New duties imposed with Townshend Act; after protests, the act is repealed

1770 Sons of Liberty fight British in the "Battle of Golden Hill"

1774 Rebels dump tea in New York harbor to protest against taxes

1760

1770

17

St. Paul's Chapel

1766 St. Paul's Chapel completed; Stamp Act repealed; Statue of George III erected on Bowling Green

General William Howe, commander-in-chief of the British troops

1776 War begins; 500 ships under General Howe assemble in New York harbor

Firefighters

Fires had long threatened the city, but during the war a series of fires nearly destroyed it. In the wake of the Patriot retreat, on September 21, 1776, a devastating fire razed the Trinity Church and 1,000 houses.

Leather fire bucket

General Washington Returns
Washington received a hero's welcome when he re-entered New York on November 25, 1783, after the British withdrawal.

Statue of George III

Cheering patriots

Flags of the Revolution

Washington's army flew the Continental colors, with a stripe for each of the 13 colonies and a Union Jack in the corner. The Stars and Stripes became the official flag in 1777.

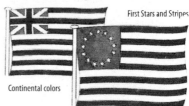

First Stars and Stripes

Continental colors

Where to See the Revolutionary City

In 1776, George Washington used the Morris-Jumel Mansion in Upper Manhattan as a headquarters (see p245). He also slept at the Van Cortlandt House (see pp22–3). After the war he bade farewell to his officers at the Fraunces Tavern (see p80).

Morris-Jumel Mansion

1783 Treaty of Paris grants US independence; the British evacuate New York

1785 New York named US capital

1784 Bank of New York chartered

1789 George Washington inaugurated as first president at Federal Hall

Washington's inauguration

1790 US capital is moved to Philadelphia

1794 Bellevue Hospital opens on the East River

1790

1792 Tontine Coffee House, first home of the Stock Exchange, built

1791 New York Hospital, city's oldest, opens

1801 *New York Post* founded by Alexander Hamilton

1800

1804 Vice President Aaron Burr kills political rival Alexander Hamilton in a duel

New York City in the 19th Century

Firmly established as the nation's largest city and preeminent seaport, New York grew increasingly wealthy. Manufacturing increased due to the ease of shipping; tycoons such as John Jacob Astor made millions. The rich moved uptown; public transportation followed. With rapid growth came fires, epidemics, and financial panics. Immigrants from Ireland, Germany, and other nations arrived. Some found prosperity; others crowded into slums in Lower Manhattan.

Growth of the Metropolis
▨ 1840   ▨ Today

Sheet Music
The Stephen Foster ballad *Jeanie with the Light Brown Hair* was popular at this time.

Croton Distributing Reservoir was built in 1842. Until then, New Yorkers had no fresh drinking water – they relied on deliveries of bottled water.

Keeping Fit
Gymnasia such as Dr. Rich's Institute for Physical Education were established in New York in the 1830s and 1840s.

Omnibus
The horse-drawn omnibus was introduced for public transportation in 1832 and remained on New York streets until World War I.

1805 First free state schools established in New York

1811 Randel Plan divides Manhattan into grid pattern above 14th Street

1812–14 War of 1812; British blockade New York harbor

The Constitution, most famous ship in War of 1812

1835 Much of old New York razed in city's worst fire

1810   **1820**   **1830**

1807 Robert Fulton launches first steamboat, on the Hudson River

1822 Yellow fever epidemic; people evacuate to Greenwich Village

1823 New York surpasses Boston and Philadelphia to become nation's largest city

1827 New York abolishes slavery

1837 New Yorker Samuel Morse sends first telegraph message

The Brownstone

Many brownstone row houses were built in the first half of the century. The raised stoop allowed separate entry to the parlor and ground-floor servants' quarters.

Crystal Palace was an iron-and-glass exhibition hall erected for the 1853 World's Fair.

The Port of New York

New York's importance as a port city grew by leaps and bounds in the early 19th century. Robert Fulton launched his first steamboat, the *Clermont*, in 1807. Steamboats made travel much quicker – it now took 72 hours to reach Albany, which was both the state capital and the gateway to the West. Trade with the West by steamboat and canal boat, and with the rest of the world by clipper ship, made the fortunes of many New Yorkers.

The steamboat *Clermont*

New York in 1855

Looking south from 42nd Street, Crystal Palace and the Croton Distributing Reservoir stood where the main public library and Bryant Park are today.

Crystal Palace in Flames

On October 5, 1858, New York's Crystal Palace exhibition hall burned to the ground, just as its predecessor in London did.

Grand Canal Celebration

Ships in New York harbor lined up to celebrate the 1825 Erie Canal opening. In connecting the Great Lakes with Albany, the state capital, on the Hudson River, the canal opened a water link between the Midwest and the Port of New York. The city realized huge profits.

1849 Astor Place riots; ships set sail for California Gold Rush	**1851** *The New York Times* first published	**1861** Civil War begins	**1863** Draft riots last four days, many die
	1853 New York hosts World's Fair	**1857** Financial panic and depression	**1865** Abraham Lincoln lies in state in City Hall

1840   **1850**   **1860**

Early baseball player

1845 New York Knickerbockers, first organized baseball team, chartered

Clipper ship card

FOR SAN FRANCISCO

FREE TRADE

1858 Vaux and Olmsted design Central Park; Macy's founded

Crowds in Central Park

1842 Croton Reservoir built

The Age of Extravagance

As New York's merchant princes grew ever wealthier, the city entered a gilded era during which many of its most opulent buildings went up. Luxury hotels such as the Plaza and the original Waldorf-Astoria were built, and elegant department stores arose to serve the wealthy while crime, poverty, and disease were rife in the slums. Even so, political and social reform did emerge. In 1900, the International Ladies' Garment Workers' Union was founded to fight for the rights of women and children, working at low wages in hazardous factories.

Growth of the Metropolis
◻ 1890 ◻ Today

Gateway to America
Almost five times as crowded as the rest of New York, the Lower East Side was the most densely populated place in the world at this time.

Crowded Conditions
Tenements were unhealthy and overcrowded. They often lacked windows, air shafts, or proper sanitary facilities.

Overlooking the Park
The Dakota (1880) was the first grand luxury apartment house on the Upper West Side (see p212).

Inside a Sweatshop
Workers toiled long hours for low wages in the overcrowded sweatshops of the garment district. This view of Moe Levy's shop was taken in 1912.

Streetcars on Broadway

1872 Bloomingdale's opens

1876 Central Park opens to a design by Fredrick Law Olmsted and Calvert Vaux

1877 A.G. Bell demonstrates the telephone in New York

1880 Canned fruits and meats first appear in stores; Metropolitan Museum of Art opens; streets lit by electricity

1865　　1870　　1875　　1880　　1885

The interior of the Stock Exchange

1873 Banks fail: Stock Exchange panics

1879 St. Patrick's Cathedral completed; first city telephone exchange opened on Nassau Street

1883 Metropolitan Opera opens on Broadway; Brooklyn Bridge completed

1886 Statue of Liberty unveiled

Flatiron Building

Overlooking Madison Square, where Broadway, Fifth Avenue, and 23rd Street meet, the 21-story tower was one of the city's first skyscrapers (1902). Triangle-shaped, it was dubbed the Flatiron Building (see p123).

Underlying steel structure

Elaborate limestone facade

Only 6 ft (185 cm) wide at the apex of triangle

Where to See the Age of Extravagance

The Morgan Library *(see pp160–61)*, once home to the legendary merchant banker Pierpont Morgan, is a good place to experience the city's opulent past. The Museum of the City of New York also has period rooms *(p195)*.

Mark Twain's Birthday

Twain (1835–1910), whose 1873 novel *The Gilded Age* portrayed the decadent lifestyle of New Yorkers, celebrated his birthday at Delmonico's.

Fashion City

Lord & Taylor built a new store on Broadway's Ladies' Mile; 6th Avenue between 14th and 23rd streets was known as Fashion Row.

BATHING SUITS.

A GREAT SPECIALTY AT
LORD & TAYLOR'S, Broadway and 20th Street, N. Y.

Palatial Living

Fifth Avenue was lined with glorious mansions. When it was built in 1882, W.K. Vanderbilt's Italianate palace at 660 Fifth Avenue, was one of the farthest north.

1897 Waldorf-Astoria Hotel opens – the largest hotel in the world

1898 Five boroughs merge to form world's second-largest city

1913 Woolworth Building is world's tallest; new Grand Central Terminal opens; Harlem's Apollo Theater opens

1895　**1900**　**1905**　**1910**

1891 Carnegie Hall opens

1900 Mayor Robert Van Wyck breaks ground for city's first subway with silver shovel

1901 Macy's opens Broadway department store

1903 Lyceum Theater opens – oldest Broadway house still in use

1911 Triangle Shirtwaist Factory fire kills 146 sweatshop workers; New York Public Library completed

New York City Between the Wars

The 1920s were a time of high living for many New Yorkers. Mayor Jimmy Walker set the pace, whether squiring chorus girls, drinking in speakeasies, or watching the Yankees. But the good times ended with the 1929 stock market crash. By 1932, Walker had resigned, charged with corruption, and one-quarter of New Yorkers were unemployed. With Mayor Fiorello La Guardia's 1933 election, New York began to recover and thrive.

Growth of the Metropolis
■ 1933   ■ Today

Exotic Costumes
Chorus girls were a major Cotton Club attraction.

The Cotton Club
This Harlem nightclub was host to the best jazz in town, as first Duke Ellington and then Cab Calloway led the band. People flocked from all over the city to hear them.

Defying Prohibition
Although alcohol was outlawed, speakeasies – semi-secret illegal drinking dens – still sold it.

Home-Run Hitter
In 1927, baseball star Babe Ruth hit a then-record 60 home runs for the Yankees. Yankee Stadium *(see p251)* became known as "the house that Ruth built."

Sawed-off shotgun concealed in violin case

Gangsters
Dutch Schultz was the kingpin of an illegal booze racket.

1918 End of World War I
1919 18th Amendment bans alcohol and launches Prohibition Era
1920 US women get the vote

Opening of the Holland Tunnel

1926 Jimmy Walker becomes mayor

1931 Empire State Building becomes world's tallest

1920

1925

1930

1924 Novelist James Baldwin is born in Harlem

1925 *The New Yorker* magazine is launched

1927 Lindbergh flies across the Atlantic; first talking movie, *The Jazz Singer*, opens; Holland Tunnel opens

1929 Stock market crash; Great Depression begins

1930 Chrysler Building completed

Big Band Leaders
Banned from many downtown clubs, black artists such as Cab Calloway starred at the Cotton Club.

Broadway Melodies
The 1920s were the heyday of the Broadway musical, with a record number of plays opening.

The Great Depression
The Roaring Twenties ended with the stock market crash of October 29, 1929, which set off the Depression. New York was hard hit: squatters' shacks sprang up in Central Park, and thousands were out of work. But art flourished, as artists toiled for the Works Projects Administration (WPA), creating outstanding murals and artworks throughout the city.

Waiting to receive benefits in 1931

Breakfast menu

Lindbergh's plane, *Spirit of St. Louis*

Lindbergh's Flight
New Yorkers celebrated Lindbergh's nonstop solo flight across the Atlantic in 1927 in a variety of ways, including a breakfast in his honor.

Rockefeller Center
Millionaire John D. Rockefeller drove the final rivet to celebrate the opening of Rockefeller Center on May 1, 1939.

Mass Event
Forty-five million people visited the 1939 World's Fair in New York.

1933 Prohibition ends; Fiorello La Guardia begins three terms as mayor

1940 Queens–Midtown Tunnel opens

1942 Times Square blacked out during World War II; Idlewild International Airport (now JFK) opens

1935

1940

1945

1936 Parks Department headed by Robert Moses; new parks created

1939 Rockefeller Center is completed

1941 US enters World War II

1944 Black leader Adam Clayton Powell elected to Congress

Postwar New York City

Since World War II, New York has seen both the best of times and the worst. In the 1940s, the city became the headquarters of the United Nations (UN) and, in the1950s, saw major movements in art, poetry, and jazz. The 1960s witnessed the Stonewall Riots and the birth of the American Gay Rights Movement. Although always a dynamic cultural center, the city has seen ups and downs with its economy. In 1975, New York almost went bankrupt under a mountain of debt. Despite a recovery, led by Wall Street in the early 1980s, the tough times continued, culminating in the recession of 1989.

1959
Guggenheim Museum opens

1945 End of World War II

1946 UN headquarters established in New York

1951 Jack Kerouac writes seminal Beat novel *On the Road* in his Manhattan apartment

1963 Pennsylvania Station razed

1945	1950	1955	1960
MAYORS:	Impelliteri	Wagner	
1945	1950	1955	1960

1954 Ellis Island closes

1953 Merce Cunningham founds dance company

1947 Jackie Robinson, first black baseball player in the major leagues, signs with Brooklyn Dodgers

1964 New York World's Fair; race riots in Harlem and Bedford-Stuyvesant; Verrazano Narrows Bridge links Brooklyn and Staten Island; the Beatles play at Shea Stadium

Souvenir scarf

1967 Hippie musical *Hair* opens on Off-Broadway, then transfers to the Biltmore Theater

1968 20,000 anti-establishment hippies gather in Central Park; student sit-ins at Columbia University

1983 Economic boom: property prices skyrocket; Trump Tower completed by real-estate tycoon Donald Trump, who symbolizes the "yuppie" wealth of the 1980s

1971 Pop artist Andy Warhol has a retrospective show of his work at the Whitney Museum

1977 New York City Blackout, which lasts 25 hours, triggers civil unrest

1988 Twenty-five per cent of New Yorkers live below the poverty line

1965	1970	1975	1980	1985
Lindsay		Beame	Koch	
1965	1970	1975	1980	1985

1969 The Stonewall Riots

1975 Federal loan saves New York from bankruptcy

1981 New York regains solvency

1973 World Trade Center completed

1980 John Lennon is shot outside his apartment on the Upper West Side

1986 Shock of corruption scandals rocks Mayor Koch's administration; Centennial of Statue of Liberty

1987 Black Monday; the stock market crashes

Modern New York City

Since the 1990s, New York has seen a dramatic drop in the crime rate and an increase in gentrification, with areas such as Harlem, Lower Manhattan, and Brooklyn undergoing redevelopment. Tourism and the economy are booming as never before, even in the face of the terrorist attacks of September 2001 which destroyed the iconic Twin Towers, the financial crisis of 2008, and Hurricane Sandy in 2012. This constant regeneration is emblematic of New York's position as an important international cultural and financial center.

1996 Times Square is redeveloped, and the city becomes one of the safest and statistically most crime-free cities in the US

1997 Giuliani re-elected mayor

2005 Bloomberg is re-elected mayor

2000 Population reaches just over 8 million

2002 Tribeca Film Festival established with the support of Robert De Niro

1990 David Dinkins, New York's first black mayor, takes office

1990	1995	2000	2005
Dinkins	Giuliani		Bloomberg
1990	1995	2000	2005

1990 Ellis Island reopens as an immigration museum

1994 New York Rangers win the Stanley Cup, ice hockey's biggest prize

1993 A truck bomb detonates in the basement of World Trade Center, killing six people

2003 Mayor Bloomberg bans smoking in bars, clubs, and restaurants

2001 Terrorist attack on the World Trade Center; both towers collapse. Mayor Giuliani is a great support to the people of New York

2002 The lights go on in a regenerated 42nd Street, which crosses Broadway at Times Square

2008 US mortgage crisis hits Wall Street: the Dow Jones slumps 500 points, and, after more than 150 years, Lehman Brothers merchant bank goes bankrupt

2013 One World Trade Center (formerly the Freedom Tower) opens

2009 Michael Bloomberg is re-elected mayor for a third time

2014 The National September 11 Museum opens

2011 National September 11 Monument opens on tenth anniversary of 9/11

2015 The new Whitney Museum of American Art, designed by architect Renzo Piano, opens on the High Line

2010   2015   2020

De Blasio

2010   2015   2020

2007 New York Giants win Superbowl XLII

2010 One of the largest snowstorms in the city's history

Mayor Bill de Blasio

2013 Bill de Blasio becomes the first Democratic mayor since 1993

2012 Hurricane Sandy hits New York, causing widespread flooding, damage, and power outage across the city

2009 US Airways Airbus flight 1549 crash-lands in the Hudson River after a bird strike. All 155 passengers survive

NEW YORK CITY AT A GLANCE

There are hundreds of places of interest in the Area by Area section of this book. They range from the bustling New York Stock Exchange *(see pp72–3)* to Central Park's peaceful Strawberry Fields *(see p202)*, and from historic synagogues to dazzling skyscrapers. The following 14 pages provide a time-saving guide to New York's most noteworthy sights. Museums and architecture each have a section, and there are guides to the people and cultures that have given the city its unique character. Each sight is cross-referenced to its own full entry. Below are the top ten tourist attractions to start you off.

New York's Top Ten Tourist Attractions

Ellis Island
See pp82–3

Empire State Building
See pp132–3

9/11 Memorial
See p74

One World Trade Center
See pp74–5

Museum of Modern Art (MoMA)
See pp168–71

Central Park
See pp198–203

Statue of Liberty
See pp78–9

Metropolitan Museum of Art
See pp186–93

Brooklyn Bridge
See pp232–5

The High Line
See p134

◀ Iconic Chrysler Building, illuminated at night

New York's Best: Museums

New York's museums range from the vast scope of
the Metropolitan Museum to the personal treasures
of financier J. Pierpont Morgan's own collection. Several
museums celebrate New York's heritage, giving visitors
an insight into the people and events that made the city
what it is today. This map features some highlights, with
a detailed overview on pages 40–41.

Intrepid Sea, Air
and Space Museum
This military and maritime history museum
also traces the progress of flight
exploration. It is housed in a large aircraft
carrier situated at Pier 86.

**The Morgan
Library & Museum**
One of the world's
finest collections of
manuscripts, prints,
and books includes
this rare French
Bible from 1230.

**Whitney Museum
of American Art**
This exceptional collection
includes many views of New
York. One of the best is *Brooklyn
Bridge: Variation on an Old Theme*
(1939), by Joseph Stella.

**Lower East Side
Tenement Museum**
Tours of this cramped
1863 tenement building
highlight the living
conditions faced by
immigrant families.

Ellis Island
This museum vividly re-creates
the experiences of many millions
of immigrant families.

Hudson River

Midtown
West and
the Theater
District

Chelsea
and the
Garment
District

Gramercy
and the
Flatiron
District

Greenwich
Village

East
Village

SoHo and
TriBeCa

Lower East Side

Lower Manhattan
and the Civic Center

Brooklyn
Museum

Museum of Modern Art

Picasso's *She-Goat* (1950) is among the impressive collection on display in the renovated Museum of Modern Art (MoMA).

Morningside Heights and Harlem

Museum of the City of New York

Costumes, works of art, and household objects (such as this 1725 silver dish) create an intricate and detailed picture of New York's past.

Upper West Side

Central Park

American Museum of Natural History

Dinosaurs, meteorites, and much more have fascinated generations of visitors here.

Cooper Hewitt, Smithsonian Design Museum

A wealth of decorative arts is displayed in industrialist Andrew Carnegie's former Upper East Side mansion.

Upper East Side

Solomon R. Guggenheim Museum

Painting and sculpture by almost all major avant-garde artists of the late 19th and 20th centuries fill Frank Lloyd Wright's stunningly renovated building.

Upper Midtown

Lower Midtown

Metropolitan Museum of Art

Of the millions of works in its collection, this 12th-dynasty Egyptian faïence hippo is the museum's own mascot.

East River

0 kilometers   2

0 miles   1

Brooklyn

The Frick Collection

The collection of 19th-century railroad magnate Henry Clay Frick is displayed in his former home. Masterpieces include *St. Francis in the Desert* (about 1476–8) by Giovanni Bellini.

Exploring New York's Museums

You could devote months to New York's museums and still not do them justice. There are more than 60 museums in Manhattan alone, and half as many again in the other boroughs. The wealth of art and the huge variety of offerings – from Old Masters to old fire engines, dinosaurs to dolls, Tibetan tapestries to African masks – are equal to that of any city in the world. Some museums close on Monday, as well as on another day. Many stay open late one or two evenings a week, and some have one evening when entry is free. Most museums charge for admission; for some, this is a suggested donation rather than a mandatory fee.

Painting and Sculpture

New York is best known for its art museums. The **Metropolitan Museum of Art** houses an extensive collection of American art, as well as world-famous masterpieces. **The Cloisters**, a branch of the "Met" in Upper Manhattan, is a treasury of medieval art and architecture. The **Frick Collection** has a superb display of Old Masters. In contrast, the **Museum of Modern Art (MoMA)** houses Impressionist and modern paintings. The **Whitney Museum of American Art** and the **Solomon R. Guggenheim Museum** also specialize in modern art, with the Whitney's biennial show being the foremost display of work by living artists. Today's cutting-edge art is at the **New Museum of Contemporary Art**, while the work of craft artists can be seen at the **American Folk Art Museum**. The **National Academy Museum** displays a collection of 19th- and 20th-century art, donated by academy members. In Harlem, the **Studio Museum** shows the work of black artists.

Crafts and Design

If you are interested in textiles, porcelain and glass, embroideries and laces, wallpaper, and prints, visit the **Cooper Hewitt, Smithsonian Design Museum**, the decorative arts outpost of Washington's Smithsonian Institution. The collections at **MoMA** trace the history of design from clocks to couches. The **Museum of Arts and Design** offers the finest work of today's skilled artisans in mediums from furniture to pottery, and the **American Folk Art Museum** presents folk forms, from quilts to canes. Silver collections are notable at the **Museum of the City of New York**. The fine displays of native art at the **National Museum of the American Indian** include jewelry, rugs and pottery.

Prints and Photography

The **International Center of Photography** is the only museum in New York that is totally devoted to this medium. Collections can also be seen at the **Metropolitan Museum of Art** and **MoMA**, and there are many examples of early photography at the **Museum of the City of New York** and **Ellis Island**.

Prints and drawings by such great book illustrators as Kate Greenaway and Sir John Tenniel are featured at **The Morgan Library & Museum**. The **Cooper Hewitt, Smithsonian Design Museum** has examples of the use of prints in the decorative arts.

Furniture and Costumes

The annual exhibition of the Costume Institute at the **Metropolitan Museum of Art** is always worth a visit. Also impressive is the American Wing, with its 24 rooms of original furnishings tracing life from 1640 to the 20th century. Period rooms depicting New York in various settings, beginning with the 17th-century Dutch, are on display

Corn husk doll, American Museum of Natural History

at the **Museum of the City of New York**.

There are also some house museums that give a realistic picture of life and furnishings in old New York. The **Merchant's House Museum**, a preserved residence from 1832, was occupied by the same family for 98 years. **Gracie Mansion** was the residence of mayor Archibald Gracie, who bought it in 1798 from a shipping merchant, and it is open periodically for public tours. The **Theodore Roosevelt Birthplace** is the brownstone where the 26th president of the United States grew up, and the **Mount Vernon Hotel Museum** was an early 19th-century resort.

The Peaceable Kingdom (c.1833–4) by Edward Hicks, at the Brooklyn Museum

---

Exhibit from the National Museum of the American Indian

History

American history unfolds at **Federal Hall**, the United States' first capitol, where George Washington took his oath as America's first president on the balcony in April 1789.

Visit the **Frances Tavern Museum** for a glimpse of colonial New York. **Ellis Island** and **Lower East Side Tenement Museum** re-create the hardships faced by immigrants. The **Museum of Jewish Heritage** in Battery City is a living memorial to the Holocaust. The **New York City Fire Museum** chronicles heroism and tragedy, while the **South Street Seaport Museum** re-creates early maritime history.

Technology and Natural History

Forest-dwelling bonga, American Museum of Natural History

Science museums hold exhibitions from nature to space-age technology. The **American Museum of Natural History** has vast collections covering flora, fauna, and cultures from around the world. Its Rose Center/Hayden Planetarium offers a unique view of space. The *Intrepid* Sea, Air & Space **Museum** is a repository of technology that chronicles

military progress, all based on the decks of an aircraft carrier. If you missed a classic Lucille Ball sitcom or footage of the first man on the moon, the place to visit is the **Paley Center for Media**, which holds these and many other classics of TV and radio.

Art from Other Cultures

Artwork of other nations is the focus of several special collections. Oriental art is the specialty of the **Asia Society** and the **Japan Society**. The **Jewish Museum** features major collections of Judaica and has changing exhibitions of various aspects of Jewish life. The **Museo del Barrio** is dedicated to the arts of Puerto Rico, including many Pre-Columbian Taino artifacts. For an impressive review of African-American art and history, visit the **Schomburg Center for Research in Black Culture**. Finally, the **Metropolitan Museum of Art** excels in its multicultural displays, ranging from the art of ancient Egypt to that of contemporary Africa.

Egyptian mummy, Brooklyn Museum

Libraries

New York's notable libraries, such as **The Morgan Library & Museum**, offer superb art collections as well as a chance to view pages from ancient manuscripts and rare books. The **New York Public Library's** collection includes historic documents and manuscripts of many famous works.

Beyond Manhattan

Other museums worth a visit include the **Brooklyn Museum of Art**, with a huge collection of artifacts from across the world and over one million

paintings. The **Museum of the Moving Image** in Queens has a unique collection of motion-picture history. The **Jacques Marchais Museum of Tibetan Art** is a rare find on Staten Island, as is **Historic Richmond Town**, a well-restored village dating from the 1600s.

New York's Best: Architecture

Even when following world trends, New York has given its own twist to the turns of architectural fashion, the style of its buildings influenced by both geography and economy. An island city, with space at a premium, must look upward to grow. This trend was reflected early on with tall, narrow town houses and later with the city's apartment buildings and skyscrapers. Building materials such as cast-iron and brownstone were chosen for their local availability and low cost. The result is a city that has developed by finding flamboyant answers to practical needs. A more detailed overview of New York's architecture is on pages 44–5.

Apartment Buildings
The Majestic is one of five Art Deco twin-towered apartment buildings on Central Park West.

Cast-Iron Architecture
Mass-produced cast iron was often used for building facades. SoHo has many of the best examples, such as this building at 28–30 Greene Street.

Post-Modernism
The quirky, yet elegant, shapes of buildings like the World Financial Center, built in 1985 *(see p71)*, mark a bold departure from the sleek steel-and-glass boxes of the 1950s and 1960s.

Hudson River

Midtown West and the Theatre District

Chelsea and the Garment District

Greenwich Village

Gramercy and the Flatiron District

East Village

SoHo and TriBeCa

Lower East Side

Lower Manhattan and the Civic Center

Brownstones
Built from local sandstone, brownstones were favored by the 19th-century middle classes. India House, built in a Florentine palazzo style on Wall Street, is typical of many brownstone commercial buildings.

Morningside
Heights and
Harlem

Upper
West
Side

Central
Park

Upper
East Side

Upper
Midtown

Lower
Midtown

East River

0 kilometers 2
0 miles 1

Brooklyn

19th-Century Mansions
The Jewish Museum (see p182), formerly the home of the banker Felix M. Warburg, is a fine example of the French Renaissance style that typified these mansions.

Beaux Arts
Opulent style, created for the richest of owners, is exemplified by the Beaux Arts grandeur of the Frick mansion.

Modernism
The Seagram Building's sleek bronze-and-glass walls, scant decoration and the monumental scale typify postwar architecture (see p173).

The Skyscraper
The glory of New York architecture, these buildings expressed a perfect blend of practical engineering skill and fabulous decoration, such as this gargoyle on the Chrysler Building.

Federal Architecture
Federal style was popular in civic architecture of the 19th century; City Hall combines it with French Renaissance influences.

Tenements
Constructed as an economic form of housing, these buildings were for many a stark introduction to new lives. Mainly built on the Lower East Side, the apartments were hopelessly over-crowded. In addition, the buildings' design, with inadequate air shafts, resulted in apartments with little or no ventilation.

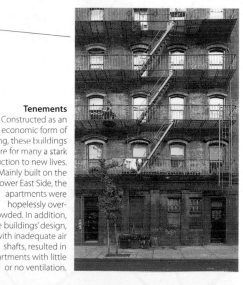

Exploring New York's Architecture

During its first 200 years, New York, like all of America, looked to Europe for architectural inspiration. None of the buildings from the Dutch colonial period survives in Manhattan today; most were lost in the great fire of 1776 or torn down to make way for new developments in the early 1800s. Throughout the 18th and 19th centuries, the city's major architectural trends followed those of Europe. With the advent of cast-iron architecture in the 1850s, the Art Deco period and the ever-higher rise of the skyscraper, New York's architecture came into its own.

Federal Architecture
This American adaptation of the Neo-Classical Adam style flowered in the early decades of the new nation, featuring square buildings two or three stories tall, with low hipped roofs, balustrades, and decorative elements – all carefully balanced. **City Hall** (1811, John McComb, Jr. and Joseph François Mangin) is a blend of Federal and French Renaissance influences. The restored warehouses of **Schermerhorn Row** (c.1812) in the Seaport district are also in Federal style.

Brownstones
Plentiful and cheap, the brown sandstone found in the nearby Connecticut River Valley and along the banks of the Hackensack River in New Jersey was the most common building material in the 1800s. It is found all over the city's residential neighborhoods, used for small homes or small apartments – some of the best examples of brownstone can be found in **Chelsea**. Because street space was limited, these buildings were very narrow in width, but also very deep. A typical brownstone has a flight of steps, called a stoop, leading up to the living floors. Separate stairs lead down to the basement, which was originally used for the servants' quarters.

Tenements
Tenements were built to house the huge influx of immigrants who arrived from the 1840s up to World War I. The six-story blocks, 100 ft (30 m) long and 25 ft (8 m) wide, offered very little light and air except from tiny sidewall air shafts and windows at each end, leaving the middle rooms in darkness. The tiny apartments were called railroad flats after their similarity to railroad cars. Later designs had air shafts between buildings, but these helped the spread of fire. The **Lower East Side Tenement Museum** has scale models of the old tenements.

Cast-Iron Architecture
An American architectural innovation of the 19th century, cast iron was cheaper than stone or brick and allowed ornate features to be prefabricated in foundries from molds and used as building facades. Today, New York has the world's largest concentration of full and partial cast-iron facades. The best, built in the 1870s, are in the **SoHo Cast-Iron Historic District**.

The original cast-iron facade of 72–76 Greene Street, SoHo

Beaux Arts
This French school of architecture dominated the design of public buildings and wealthy residential properties during New York's gilded age. This era (from 1880 to about 1920) produced many of the city's most prominent architects, including Richard Morris Hunt (**Carnegie Hall**, 1891; **Metropolitan Museum of Art**, 1895), who in 1845 was the first American architect to study in Paris; Cass Gilbert (**National Museum of the American Indian**, 1907; **New York Life**

A typical brownstone with stoop leading up to the main entrance

Architectural Disguises
Some of the most fanciful forms on the New York skyline were devised by clever architects to disguise the city's essential but utilitarian – and rather unattractive – rooftop water tanks. Look skyward to discover the ornate cupolas, spires, and domes that transform the most mundane of features into veritable castles in the air. Examples that are easy to spot are atop two neighboring Fifth Avenue hotels: the Sherry Netherland at 60th Street and the Pierre at 61st Street.

Standard water tower

The Dakota Apartments, built in 1884, on the Upper West Side across from Central Park

Insurance Company Building, 1928; **United States Courthouse**, 1936); the teams of Warren & Wetmore (**Grand Central Terminal**, 1913; **Helmsley Building**, 1929); Carrère & Hastings (**New York Public Library**, 1911; **Frick Mansion**, 1914); and McKim, Mead & White, the city's most famous firm of architects (**Villard Houses**, 1884; **James A. Farley Post Office Building**, 1913.

Apartment Buildings
As the city's population grew and space became ever more precious, family homes in Manhattan became much too expensive for most New Yorkers, and even the wealthy joined the trend toward communal living. In 1884 Henry Hardenbergh's Dakota (see p212), one of the first luxury apartment buildings, started a spate of turn-of-the-century construction on the Upper West Side. Many of the buildings resembled castles

and châteaux, and were built around courtyards not visible from the street. Favorite landmarks are the five **Twin Towers** on Central Park West, the San Remo, Eldorado, Century, the Beresford, and the Majestic. Built during the peak of Art Deco (1929 to 1931), they create the distinctive skyline seen from the park.

Skyscrapers
In 1902, Daniel Burnham, a Chicago architect, built the **Flatiron Building**, so tall at 300 ft (91 m) that skeptics said it would collapse. By 1913, the **Woolworth Building** had risen to 792 ft (241 m). New zoning laws demanded that skyscrapers be built in such a way as to allow light to reach street level. This suited the Art Deco style. The **Chrysler Building** (1930) was the world's tallest until the **Empire State Building** (1931) was completed. Both are Art Deco classics, but it was Raymond Hood's

Art Deco arched pattern on the spire of the Chrysler Building

McGraw-Hill Building
that represented New York in 1932 in the International Style architectural survey.
The World Trade Center was New York's tallest building until September 2001 (see p56). It represented the Modernist style, now superseded by the Post-Modern style, such as the **Citigroup Center** (1977). In 2013, One World Trade Center became the Western world's tallest building, reaching 1,776 ft (541 m), a reference to the year of American Independence.

DIRECTORY

Where to Find the Buildings

245 Fifth Avenue
(Apartment Building)

60 Gramercy Park North
(Brownstone)

The Pierre
(Beaux Arts)

Sherry Netherland
Hotel (Beaux Arts)

Multicultural New York City

Wherever you go in New York, even in pockets of the hectic high-rise downtown, you will find evidence of the richly ethnic flavor of the city. A bus ride can take you from Madras to Moscow, Hong Kong to Haiti. Immigrants are still coming to New York, though numbers are fewer than in the peak years from 1880 to 1910, when 17 million people arrived. In the 1980s, a million newcomers, largely from Caribbean countries and Asia, arrived and found their own special corner of the city. Throughout the year you will encounter crowds celebrating one of many festivals. To find out more about national celebrations and parades, see pages 52–5.

Hell's Kitchen
For a while called "Clinton" to reflect a new neighborhood mix, this was the first home of early Irish immigrants.

Little Korea
Not far from Herald Square is a small Korean enclave with a variety of restaurants.

Little Ukraine
Services are held at T. Shevchenko Place as part of the May 17 festivities to mark the Ukrainians' conversion to Christianity.

Midtown West and the Theater District

Chelsea and the Garment District

Greenwich Village

Gramercy and the Flatiron District

East Village

Little Italy
For 11 days in September, the Italian community gathers around the Mulberry Street area, and the streets are taken over by the celebrations of the Festa di San Gennaro.

SoHo and TriBeCa

Lower East Side

Lower Manhattan and the Civic Center

0 kilometers   2

0 miles   1

Chinatown
Every year, in January or February, Mott Street is packed as residents celebrate the Chinese New Year.

The Lower East Side
The synagogues around Rivington and Eldridge streets reflect the religious traditions of this old Jewish area.

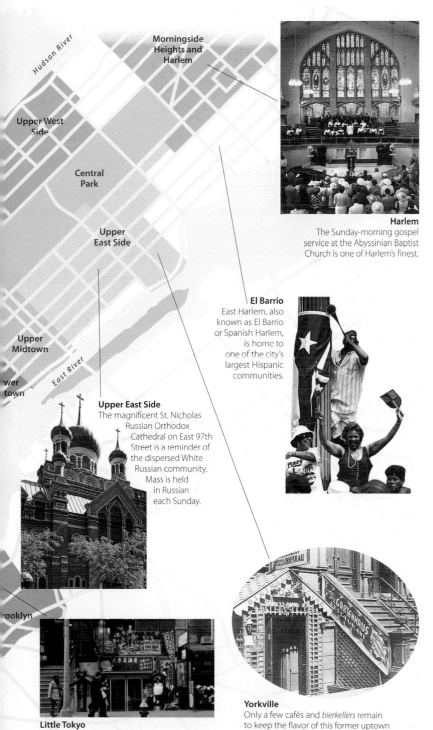

Harlem
The Sunday-morning gospel service at the Abyssinian Baptist Church is one of Harlem's finest.

Morningside Heights and Harlem

Upper West Side

Central Park

Upper East Side

El Barrio
East Harlem, also known as El Barrio or Spanish Harlem, is home to one of the city's largest Hispanic communities.

Upper Midtown

Upper East Side
The magnificent St. Nicholas Russian Orthodox Cathedral on East 97th Street is a reminder of the dispersed White Russian community. Mass is held in Russian each Sunday.

Little Tokyo
This tiny locality is peppered with Japanese stores, noodle shops, supermarkets, and sushi bars.

Yorkville
Only a few cafés and *bierkellers* remain to keep the flavor of this former uptown German district. The Steuben Day Parade is still held here each September.

Exploring New York's Many Cultures

Even "native" New Yorkers have ancestral roots in other countries. Throughout the 17th century, the Dutch and English settled here, establishing trade colonies in the New World. Soon America became a symbol of hope for the downtrodden elsewhere in Europe. Many flocked across the ocean, some penniless and with little knowledge of the language. The potato famine of the 1840s led to the first wave of Irish immigrants, followed by German and other European workers displaced by political unrest and the Industrial Revolution. Immigrants continue to enrich New York in countless ways, and today an estimated 100 languages are spoken.

Turkish immigrants arriving at former Idlewild Airport in 1963

The Jews

There has been a Jewish community in New York since 1654. The city's first synagogue, Shearith Israel, was established by refugees from a Dutch colony in Brazil and is still active today. These first settlers, Sephardic Jews of Spanish descent, included such prominent families as the Baruchs. They were followed by the German Jews, who set up successful retailing enterprises, including the Straus brothers at Macy's. Russian persecution led to the mass immigration that began in the late 1800s. By the start of World War I, 600,000 Jews were living on the Lower East Side. Today, this area is more Hispanic and Asian than Jewish, but it holds reminders of its role as a place of refuge and new beginnings.

The Germans

In the 18th century the Germans began to settle in New York. From John Peter Zenger onward (see p22), the city's German community has championed the freedom to express ideas and opinions. It has also produced giants of industry, such as John Jacob Astor, the city's first millionaire.

The Italians

Italians first came to New York in the 1830s and 1840s. Many came from northern Italy to escape the failing revolution at home. In the 1870s, poverty in southern Italy drove many more Italians across the ocean. In time, Italians became a potent political force in the city, exemplified by Fiorello La Guardia and Rudy Giuliani, two of New York's most popular mayors.

The Chinese

The Chinese were late arrivals to New York. In 1880, the population of the Mott Street district was a mere 700. By the

Eastern States Buddhist Temple, in central Chinatown (see p91)

1940s, they were the city's fastest-growing and most upwardly mobile ethnic group, extending the old boundaries of Chinatown and establishing new neighborhoods in parts of Brooklyn and Queens. Once a closed community, Chinatown now bustles with tourists exploring the streets and markets, and sampling the creative cuisine.

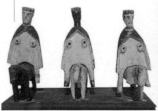

Hispanic religious carving at the Museo del Barrio (see p225)

The Hispanic Americans

Puerto Ricans were in New York as early as 1838, but it was not until after World War II that they arrived in large numbers in search of work. Most live in the Bronx, parts of Brooklyn, and El Barrio, formerly known as Spanish Harlem. Professionals who fled Fidel Castro's Cuba have moved out of the city itself but are still influential in Hispanic commerce and culture. Parts of Washington Heights have large Dominican and Colombian communities, as well as those from Mexico, Ecuador, and El Salvador.

The Irish

First arriving in New York in the 1840s, the Irish had to overcome harsh odds. Starving and with barely a penny to their names, they labored hard to escape the slums of Five Points and Hell's Kitchen, helping to build the modern city in the process. Many joined the police and fire-fighting forces, rising to high rank through dedication to duty. Others set up successful businesses, such as the Irish bars that act as a focus for the now-scattered New York Irish community.

The African Americans

Perhaps the best-known black inner-city community in the Western world, Harlem is noted for the Harlem Renaissance *(see pp30–31)* as much as it is for great entertainment, gospel music, and soul food. The move of black African Americans from the South to the North began with emancipation in the 1860s and increased markedly in the 1920s, when Harlem's black population rose from 83,000 to 204,000. Today Harlem is undergoing revitalization in many areas. The African-American population has also dispersed throughout the city, with the largest community in Brooklyn's Bedford-Stuyvesant.

The Melting Pot

Other New York cultures are not distinctly defined but are still easily found. Ukrainians gather in the East Village, around St. George's Ukrainian Catholic Church on East 7th Street. Little Tokyo can be spotted by the ramen noodle bars along East 9th Street. Koreans own many of the small grocery stores in Manhattan, but most tend to live in the Flushing area of Queens. The religious diversity of New York can be seen in the Islamic Center on Riverside Drive; the Islamic Cultural Center on

A woman celebrating at the Greek Independence Day parade

96th Street – Manhattan's first major mosque; and the Russian Orthodox Cathedral on East 97th Street *(see p195).*

The Outer Boroughs

Brooklyn and Queens are by far the most culturally diverse boroughs of New York. In Brooklyn, Caribbean newcomers from Jamaica and Haiti are among the fastest-growing immigrant groups. West Indians tend to cluster along Eastern Parkway between Grand Army Plaza and Utica Avenue, the route of the lavish, exotically costumed West Indian Day Parade in September. Recently arrived Russian Jewish immigrants have turned Brighton Beach into "Little Odessa by the Sea," and the Scandinavians and Lebanese have settled in Bay Ridge and the Finns in Sunset Park. Borough Park and Williamsburg are home to Orthodox Jews, and Midwood has an Israeli-Middle East accent. Italians live in the Bensonhurst area. Greenpoint is little Poland, and Atlantic Avenue is home to the largest Arab community in America.

The Irish were among the earliest groups to cross the Harlem River into the Bronx. Japanese executives favor the more exclusive Riverdale area. One of the most distinctive ethnic areas is Astoria, Queens, which has the largest Greek population outside the motherland. Jackson Heights is home to a large Latin American quarter, including hundreds of thousands of Colombians. Indians also favor this area and nearby Flushing, a lively neighborhood also populated by thousands of expats from China, Korea, and other Asian countries.

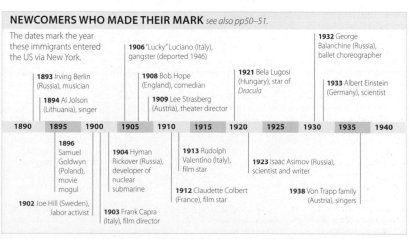

The New York police, a haven for Irish Americans

NEWCOMERS WHO MADE THEIR MARK *see also pp50–51.*

The dates mark the year these immigrants entered the US via New York.

1893 Irving Berlin (Russia), musician

1894 Al Jolson (Lithuania), singer

1896 Samuel Goldwyn (Poland), movie mogul

1902 Joe Hill (Sweden), labor activist

1903 Frank Capra (Italy), film director

1904 Hyman Rickover (Russia), developer of nuclear submarine

1906 "Lucky" Luciano (Italy), gangster (deported 1946)

1908 Bob Hope (England), comedian

1909 Lee Strasberg (Austria), theater director

1912 Claudette Colbert (France), film star

1913 Rudolph Valentino (Italy), film star

1921 Bela Lugosi (Hungary), star of *Dracula*

1923 Isaac Asimov (Russia), scientist and writer

1932 George Balanchine (Russia), ballet choreographer

1933 Albert Einstein (Germany), scientist

1938 Von Trapp family (Austria), singers

1890	1895	1900	1905	1910	1915	1920	1925	1930	1935	1940

Remarkable New Yorkers

New York has nourished some of the best creative talents since the beginning of the 20th century. Pop Art began here, and Manhattan is still the world center for modern art. The alternative writers of the 1950s and 1960s – known as the Beat Generation – took inspiration from the city's jazz clubs. And, as New York is the financial capital, many leading world financiers have made it their home.

Pop artist Andy Warhol

Novelist James Baldwin

Writers

Much great American literature was created in New York. *Charlotte Temple, A Tale of Truth*, first published in 1791 by Susanna Rowson (c.1762–1824), was a tale of seduction in the city and a bestseller for 50 years.

American literature won international recognition with Washington Irving's (1783–1859) satire, *A History of New York* (1809). Irving coined the names "Gotham" for New York and "Knickerbockers" for New Yorkers. He and James Fenimore Cooper (1789–1851), whose books gave birth to the "Western" novel, formed the Knickerbocker group of US writers. Edgar Allan Poe (1809–49), the pioneer of the modern detective story, lived in the Bronx, while Herman Melville (1819–91), author of *Moby Dick* (1851), was born in Lower Manhattan. Henry James (1843–1916) published *Washington Square* (1880) and became the master of the psychological novel, and his friend Edith Wharton (1861–1937) was known for her satirical novels about New York society, such as *The Age of Innocence* (1920).

By the end of World War I, Greenwich Village had become New York's Left Bank. Poet Edna St. Vincent Millay, playwright Eugene O'Neill, and the writer E. E. Cummings all lived here. Henry Miller (1891–1980) wrote about his experiences in the book *Tropic of Capricorn* (1939), which was banned until 1961. Jack Kerouac (1922–69), Allen Ginsberg, and William Burroughs all went to Columbia University and drank at the San Remo Café in Greenwich Village. James Baldwin (1924–87), born in Harlem, wrote *Another Country* (1963) on his return to New York from Europe. Ralph Ellison (1914–94) penned *Invisible Man* (1952) in Harlem, while Richard Wright (1908–60) wrote *Native Son* in Fort Greene. The city's current list of writers is strong: Jonathan Franzen, Joshua Ferris, Téa Obreht, and Jennifer Egan, among others. High-profile émigrés like Martin Amis and Salman Rushdie also call the city home.

Artists

The New York School of Abstract Expressionists founded the first influential American art movement. It was launched by Hans Hofmann (1880–1966) with Franz Kline and Willem de Kooning, whose first job in America was as a housepainter. Adolph Gottlieb, Mark Rothko (1903–70), and Jackson Pollock (1912–56) went on to popularize this style. Pollock, Kline, and de Kooning all had their studios on the Lower East Side.

Pop Art began in New York in the 1960s with Roy Lichtenstein and Andy Warhol (1926–87), who made some of his cult films at 33 Union Square. Keith Haring (1958–90) was a very prolific graffiti artist who gained fame for his Pop Art murals and sculptures. Robert Mapplethorpe (1946–89) acquired notoriety for his homoerotic photos of men. Jeff Koons (1955–) was part of the Neo-Pop or Post-Pop Movement of the 1980s, while street artist Jean-Michel Basquiat (1960–88) still retains a cult following for his Neo-Expressionist works.

Actors

In 1849 the British actor Charles Macready started a riot by saying Americans were vulgar. A mob stormed the Astor Place Opera House, where Macready was playing Macbeth, police opened fire, and 22 rioters were killed. In 1927 Mae West (1893–1980) spent 10 days in a workhouse on Roosevelt Island and was fined $500 for giving a lewd performance in her Broadway show *Sex*.

The musical has been New York's special contribution to the theater. Florenz Ziegfeld's (1869–1932) *Follies* ran from 1907 to 1931. The opening of *Oklahoma!* on Broadway in 1943 began

Vaudeville actress Mae West

the age of musicals by the famous duo Richard Rodgers (1902–79) and Oscar Hammerstein, Jr. (1895–1960).

Thousands of movies and TV shows have been filmed in the city since the 1930s. Audrey Hepburn moved audiences with her role in *Breakfast at Tiffany's* (1961), as did Al Pacino in *Dog Day Afternoon* (1975), and Robert De Niro in *Taxi Driver* (1976). The 1980s saw classics such as *Fame*, *Ghostbusters*, and *When Harry Met Sally*. In 2006, *The Devil Wears Prada* offered a critical look at the city's fashion industry, while more recently, Amy Schumer's *Trainwreck* (2015) was a break from the traditional romantic comedy. Iconic TV shows, such as *Friends*, *Sex and the City*, *Gossip Girl*, and Lena Dunham's *Girls*, have all been based and often filmed on location in New York.

Musicians

Leonard Bernstein (1918–90) followed a long line of great conductors at the New York Philharmonic, including Bruno Walter (1876–1962), Arturo Toscanini (1867–1957), and Leopold Stokowski (1882–1977). The soprano Maria Callas (1923–77) was born in New York but moved to Europe.

Harlem's Cotton Club featured Duke Ellington and other greats in the 1920s, while the Village Vanguard opened in the 1930s. Sonny Rollins made a legendary recording here in 1957, and John Coltrane followed in 1961. Bob Dylan had his first professional gig at Gerde's Folk City in 1961, while Jimi Hendrix began his career at Café Wha? in Greenwich Village and Lady Gaga was a regular on the Lower East Side.

Musical producer Florenz Ziegfeld

In the early 1970s, hip-hop emerged in the South Bronx, with pioneers such as DJ Kool Herc and Afrikaa Bambaataa. Mos Def, Nas, 50 Cent, and Jay-Z are all still based here. Live rock venue CBGB opened in 1973, launching the careers of punk bands including the Ramones as well as Blondie and the Talking Heads. In the early 1980s Madonna lived in the East Village and by 2001 the neighborhood was the epicentre of the garage rock revival scene, led by groups such as The Strokes, Interpol, and the Yeah Yeah Yeahs.

Tycoon Cornelius Vanderbilt

Industrialists and Entrepreneurs

Andrew Carnegie (1835–1919), "the steel baron with a heart of gold," started with nothing and died having given away $350 million. His beneficiaries included public libraries and universities throughout America. Many other foundations are the legacies of wealthy philanthropists. Some, such as Cornelius Vanderbilt (1794–1877), tried to shake off their rough beginnings by patronizing the arts. In business, New York's "robber barons" did what they liked with apparent impunity. Financiers Jay Gould (1836–92) and James Fisk (1834–72) beat Vanderbilt in the war for the Erie Railroad by manipulating stock. In September 1869 they caused Wall Street's first "Black Friday" when they tried to corner the gold market, but fled when their fraud was discovered. Gould died a happy billionaire, while Fisk was killed in a fight over a woman. J. P. Morgan (1837–1918) was referred to

American rapper 50 Cent at the Billboard Music Awards, Las Vegas

as the grandfather of Wall Street, while property magnate John Jacob Astor (1763–1848) was once the richest man in America.

Modern entrepreneurs include Donald Trump, owner of Trump Tower, Michael Bloomberg, three-time mayor of the city, and George Soros, well-known hedge-fund manager.

Architects

Cass Gilbert (1858–1934), who built such Neo-Gothic skyscrapers as the Woolworth Building of 1913 *(see p85)*, was one of the men who literally shaped the city. His caricature can be seen in the lobby, clutching a model of his masterpiece. Stanford White (1853–1906) was as well-known for his scandalous private life as for his fine Beaux Arts buildings, such as The Players club *(p124)*. For most of his life, Frank Lloyd Wright (1867–1959) spurned city architecture. When he was persuaded to leave his mark on the city, it was in the form of the Soloman R. Guggenheim Museum *(pp184–5)*. German-born Ludwig Mies van der Rohe (1886–1969), who built the Seagram Building *(p173)*, did not believe in "inventing a new architecture every Monday morning," although some might argue that this is just what New York has always done best.

NEW YORK CITY THROUGH THE YEAR

Springtime in New York sees Park Avenue filled with blooms, while Fifth Avenue goes green for St. Patrick's Day, the first of the year's many big parades. Summer in the city is hot and humid, but it is worth forsaking an air-conditioned interior to step outside, where parks and squares are the setting for free open-air music and theater. The first Monday in September marks Labor Day and the advent of the orange-red colors of autumn. Then, as Christmas nears, the shops and streets begin to sparkle with dazzling window displays.

Dates of the events on the following pages may vary. For details, consult the listings magazines *(see p371)*. NYC & Co., the city's official tourism and marketing organization *(see p362–3)*, maintains a useful calendar of events on its website.

Spring

Every season in New York brings its own tempo and temptations. In spring, the city shakes off the winter with tulips and cherry blossoms in the parks and spring fashions in the stores. Everyone window-shops and gallery-hops. The hugely popular St. Patrick's Day Parade draws the crowds, and thousands don their finery for the Easter Parade down Fifth Avenue.

Inventive Easter bonnets in New York's Easter Parade

March
St. Patrick's Day Parade *(Mar 17)*, Fifth Ave, from 44th to 86th St. Green clothes, beer, and flowers, plus bagpipes.
Greek Independence Day Parade *(Mar 25)*, Fifth Ave, from 49th to 59th St. Greek dancing and food.

Easter
Easter Flower Show
(week before Easter), Macy's department store. Annual floral extravaganza with a different theme each year *(pp130–31)*.

Yellow tulips and cabs shine on Park Avenue

Easter Parade *(Easter Sun)*, Fifth Ave, from 44th to 59th St. Paraders in costumes and outrageous millinery gather around St. Patrick's Cathedral.

April
Cherry Blossom Festival *(late Mar–Apr)*, Brooklyn Botanic Garden. Famous for Japanese cherry trees and beautifully laid-out ornamental gardens.
Tribeca Film Festival *(Apr)*. Celebrates film, music, and culture with more than 100 films from around the world *(p342)*.
New York City Ballet Spring Season *(Apr–Jun)*, New York State Theater and Metropolitan Opera House in Lincoln Center *(pp208–9)*.
Baseball *(Apr–late Sep/early Oct)*. Major league season starts for Yankees and Mets *(p354)*.

May
Five Boro Bike Tour *(first Sun May)*, a 42-mile (68-km) ride ending with a festival with live music, food and exhibitions.
Cuban Day Parade *(first Sun May)*, a carnival on Sixth Ave, between 44th St and Central Park South.

Parading in national costume on Greek Independence Day

Ninth Avenue International Food Festival *(mid-May)*, from W 37th to W 57th St. Ethnic foods, music, and dance.
Washington Square Outdoor Art Exhibit *(usually last two weekends May; also Sep)*.
Memorial Day Activities *(last weekend May)*. A parade down Fifth Ave, and festivities at South Street Seaport.

Average Daily Hours of Sunshine

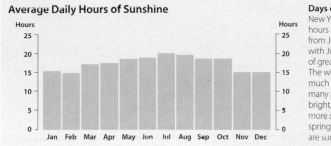

Days of Sunshine
New York enjoys long hours of summer sun from June to August, with July the month of greatest sunshine. The winter days are much shorter, but many are clear and bright. Autumn has more sunshine than spring, although both are sunny.

Summer

New Yorkers escape the hot city streets when possible, for picnics, boat rides, and the beaches. Macy's fireworks light up the Fourth of July skies, and more sparks fly when the New York Yankees and Mets baseball teams are in town. Summer also brings street fairs, outdoor concerts, and free Shakespeare and opera in Central Park.

Policeman dancing in the Puerto Rican Day Parade

June

Puerto Rican Day Parade
(early Jun), Fifth Ave, from 44th to 86th St. Floats and marching bands celebrate people of Puerto Rican descent living in the US.
Museum Mile Festival *(second Tue)*, Fifth Ave, from 82nd to 105th St. Free entry (usually 6–9pm) to the several museums located along this stretch of Fifth Ave.
American Crafts Festival *(mid-Jun–early Jul)*, Lincoln Center *(p208)*. Displays of high-quality crafts.
Central Park SummerStage *(Jun–Aug)*, Central Park. Music and dance of every variety, almost daily, rain or shine.

Metropolitan Opera Parks Concerts. Free evening concerts in parks throughout the city *(p345)*
Shakespeare in the Park *(Jun–Sep)*. Star actors take on the Bard at Delacorte Theater, Central Park *(p341)*.
NYC Pride March *(late Jun)*. The annual parade sets off from 36th St and goes along Fifth Ave to Christopher St past the Stonewall Inn *(p349)*.

July

Macy's Firework Display *(Jul 4)*, usually the East River. This is the undisputed high point of the city's Independence Day celebrations, featuring the best fireworks in town.
Mostly Mozart Festival *(end Jul–end Aug)*, Avery Fisher Hall, Lincoln Center *(p344)*.
NY Philharmonic Parks Concerts *(late Jul–early Aug)*. Free concerts in parks

Festivities at a summer street fair in Greenwich Village

throughout the city *(p345)*.
Lincoln Center Festival *(Jul)*. Dance, opera, and other arts from around the world.

August

Harlem Week *(mid-Aug)*. Films, art, music, dance, fashion, sports, and tours.
Out-of-Doors Festival *(Aug)*, Lincoln Center. Free dance and theater performances *(p208)*.
US Open Tennis Championships *(late Aug–early Sep)*, Flushing Meadows *(pp354–5)*.

Crowds of spectators flock to the US Open Tennis Championships

Average Monthly Temperature

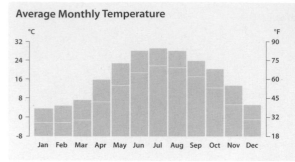

Temperature
The chart shows the average minimum and maximum temperatures for each month in New York. With top temperatures averaging 84° F (29° C), the city can become hot and humid. In contrast, the months of winter, although rarely below freezing, can seem bitterly cold.

Autumn

Labor Day marks the end of the summer. The Giants and the Jets kick off the football season, the Broadway season begins, and the Festa di San Gennaro in Little Italy is the high point in a succession of fun neighborhood fairs. Macy's Thanksgiving Day Parade is the nation's symbol that the holiday season has arrived.

September

Richmond County Fair *(Labor Day weekend)*, in the grounds of Historic Richmond Town, Staten Island *(p258)*. New York's only authentic county fair.
West Indian Carnival *(Labor Day weekend)*, Brooklyn. Parade, floats, music, dancing, and food.
Brazilian Festival *(early Sep)*, E 46th St, between Times Sq and Madison Ave. Brazilian music, food, and crafts.
Festa di San Gennaro *(third week)*, Little Italy *(p90)*. Ten

days of festivities and processions.
New York Film Festival *(mid-Sep–early Oct)*, Lincoln Center *(p208)*. American films and international art films.
Von Steuben Day Parade *(third week)*, Upper Fifth Ave. German-American celebrations.
African-American Day Parade *(late Sep)*, Adam Clayton Powell Jr. Blvd, from 111th to 136th Sts. The largest African-American parade in the country.
American Football *(season begins)*, MetLife Stadium, home to the Giants and the Jets *(pp354–5)*.

October

Columbus Day Parade *(second Mon)*, Fifth Ave, from 44th to 86th Sts. Parades and music to celebrate Columbus's first sighting of America.
Pulaski Day Parade *(Sun closest to Oct 5)*, Fifth Ave, from 26th to 52nd Sts. Celebrations for Polish-American hero Casimir Pulaski.
Rockefeller Center Ice Skating Rink *(Oct–Mar)*. Skate beneath the famous Christmas tree.
Halloween Parade *(Oct 31)*, Sixth Avenue, Greenwich Village. Brilliant event with fantastic costumes.
Big Apple Circus *(Oct–Jan)*, Damrosch Park, Lincoln Center. Special themes are presented each year *(p359)*.
Basketball *(season begins)*, Madison Square Garden. Local team is the Knicks *(pp354–5)*.

Huge Superman balloon floating above Macy's Thanksgiving Day Parade

November

New York City Marathon *(first Sun)*. From Staten Island through all the city boroughs.
Macy's Thanksgiving Day Parade *(fourth Thu)*, from Central Park West and W 79th St to Broadway and W 34th St. A joy for children, this famous parade features floats, huge balloons, and even an appearance from Santa.
Christmas Spectacular *(Nov–Dec)*, Radio City Music Hall. Variety show, with the Rockettes.

Revelers in Greenwich Village's Halloween Parade

Exotic Caribbean carnival costume in the streets of Brooklyn

Average Monthly Rainfall

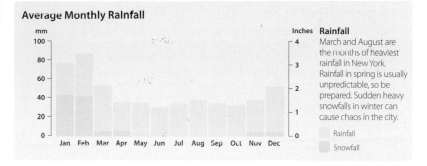

Rainfall
March and August are the months of heaviest rainfall in New York. Rainfall in spring is usually unpredictable, so be prepared. Sudden heavy snowfalls in winter can cause chaos in the city.

Rainfall
Snowfall

Winter

New York is a magical place at Christmas – even the stone lions at the Public Library don wreaths for the occasion, and shops become works of art. From Times Square to Chinatown, New Year celebrations punctuate the season, and Central Park becomes a winter sports arena.

Statue of Alice in Wonderland in Central Park

December

Tree-Lighting Ceremony *(early Dec)*, Rockefeller Center *(p140)*. Lighting of the giant Christmas tree in front of the RCA Building.
Messiah Sing-In *(mid-Dec)*, Lincoln Center *(p208)*. The audience rehearses and performs under the guidance of various conductors.
Hanukkah Menorah *(mid-late Dec)*, Grand Army Plaza, Brooklyn. Lighting of the huge menorah (candelabra) every night during the eight-day Festival of Lights.
New Year's Eve. Fireworks display in Central Park *(pp198-203)*; festivities in Times Square *(p142-3)*; 5-mile (8-km) run in Central Park; poetry reading in St. Mark's Church.

January

National Boat Show *(Jan)*, Jacob K. Javits Convention Center *(p134)*.
Chinese New Year *(late Jan/Feb)*, Chinatown *(p91)*. Dragons, fireworks, and food.
Winter Antiques Show *(Jan)*, Seventh Regiment Armory. NYC's most prestigious antiques fair.

February

Black History Month. African-American events take place throughout the city.
Empire State Building Run-Up *(early Feb)*. Runners race to the 102nd floor *(pp132-3)*.
Presidents' Day Holiday Sales *(Feb 12-22)* Big department stores sales throughout the city.
Westminster Kennel Club Dog Show *(mid-Feb)*, Madison Square Garden *(p131)*. America's most prestigious dog show.

Chinese New Year celebrations in Chinatown

PUBLIC HOLIDAYS

New Year's Day (Jan 1)
Martin Luther King Jr. Day (3rd Mon, Jan)
Presidents' Day (3rd Mon, Feb)
Memorial Day (last Mon, May)
Independence Day (Jul 4)
Labor Day (1st Mon, Sep)
Columbus Day (2nd Mon, Oct)
Election Day (1st Tue, Nov)
Veterans Day (Nov 11)
Thanksgiving Day (4th Thu, Nov)
Christmas Day (Dec 25)

The giant Christmas tree and decorations at Rockefeller Center

The Manhattan Skyline: Southern Tip

Lower Manhattan, as seen from the Hudson River, encompasses some of the most striking modern additions to the city skyline, such as the distinctively topped quartet of the World Financial Center. You will also catch glimpses of earlier Manhattan: Castle Clinton set against the green space of Battery Park and, behind it, Custom House. From 1973 until September 2001 the area also boasted the World Trade Center. Its landmark towers were destroyed in a terrorist attack on the city. The One World Trade Center building (formerly known as Freedom Tower), on the northwest corner of the National September 11 Memorial and Museum site, was completed in 2013.

Locator Map
◻ The Southern Tip

9/11 Memorial and Memorial Museum
Built on the site of the former World Trade Center, the 9/11 Memorial and Memorial Museum pay tribute to the nearly 3,000 people who died in a terrorist attack on the city (*see p74*).

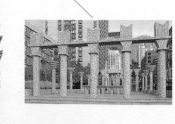

The Upper Room
This walk-around sculpture by Ned Smyth is one of many works of art in Battery Park City (*see p81*).

Detail from The *Upper Room*

An Earlier View
This 1898 photograph shows a skyline that is now changed beyond recognition.

KEY

① **Brookfield Place** has at the heart of its complex the Winter Garden – a place to shop, dine, be entertained, plus great views of the Hudson River (see p71).

② **One World Trade Center** was completed in 2013. Numerous other skyscrapers are still being built on the complex.

③ **Liberty View**

④ **Liberty Plaza**

⑤ **Bank of New York**

⑥ **East Coast War Memorial**

⑦ **26 Broadway**

⑧ **17 State Street**

⑨ **Castle Clinton**

⑩ **US Custom House**

26 Broadway
The tower of the former Standard Oil Building resembles an oil lamp. The interior is still decorated with company symbols.

East Coast War Memorial
In Battery Park, a huge bronze eagle by Albino Manca honors the dead of World War II

American Merchant Mariners' Memorial (1991)
This sculpture by Marisol is on Pier A, the last of Manhattan's old piers. The pier also has a restaurant, an oyster bar, and an outdoor deck.

Shrine of Mother Seton
The first US-born saint lived here (see p77).

Lower Manhattan from the East River

At first sight, this stretch of East River shoreline, running up from the tip of Manhattan Island, is a seamless array of 20th-century office buildings. But from sea level, streets and slips are still visible, offering glimpses of old New York and the Financial District to the west. On the skyline itself, a few of the district's early skyscrapers still proudly display their ornate crowns above their more anonymous modern counterparts.

Locator Map
◼ East River View

Vietnam Veterans' Plaza
An engraved green-glass memorial dominates the former Coenties Slip, a wharf filled in to make a park in the late 19th century *(see p80)*.

Hanover Square
The Queen Elizabeth II September 11th Garden commemorates the lives of the British and Commonwealth citizens killed during the 9/11 attacks.

India House
The handsome brownstone at One Hanover Square was completed for the Hanover Bank in 1853.

Battery Maritime Building
This historic ferry terminal serves only Governors Island *(see p80)*.

Downtown Heliport
Air-Sea Rescue and sightseeing flights operate from here.

Delmonico's
This upscale steakhouse draws many carnivores.

New York Stock Exchange
Although hidden from view by more modern edifices, this is still the hub of the hectic Financial District (see pp72–3).

40 Wall Street
In the 1940s, the pyramid-topped tower of the former Bank of Manhattan was hit by a light aircraft.

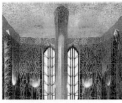

Bank of New York
This serene 1928 interior is part of the bank set up in 1784 by Alexander Hamilton (see p25).

70 Pine Street
Replicas of this elegant Gothic-style tower can be seen near the Pine and Cedar street entrances.

100 Old Slip
Now in the shadow of One Financial Square, the small palazzo-style First Precinct Police Department was the city's most modern police station when it was built in 1911.

Carved medallion, 100 Old Slip

Queen Elizabeth Monument
The ocean liner that sank in 1972 is remembered here.

South Street Seaport

Where the Financial District ends, the skyline, as seen from the East River or Brooklyn, changes dramatically. The corporate headquarters are replaced by the piers, low-rise streets, and warehouses of the old seaport area, now restored as the South Street Seaport *(see p84)*. The Civic Center lies not far inland, and a few of its monumental buildings can be seen. The Brooklyn Bridge marks the end of this stretch of skyline. Between here and Midtown, apartment blocks make up the majority of riverside features.

Locator Map
☐ South Street Area

Pier 17
A focal point of the Seaport, this leisure pier is undergoing renovations, which are due to be completed in 2017.

Stonework on the Woolworth Building

Woolworth Building
The handsomely decorated spire marks the headquarters of F. W. Woolworth's empire. It is still the finest "cathedral of commerce" ever built *(see p85)*.

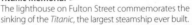

Pier 15
With two floors of observation decks, offering brilliant East River views, Pier 15 is also home to the Maritime Crafts Center.

***Titanic* Memorial**
The lighthouse on Fulton Street commemorates the sinking of the *Titanic*, the largest steamship ever built.

Police Plaza
5 in 1 (1971–4), in Police Plaza, is a sculpture by Bernard Rosenthal. It represents the five boroughs of New York.

Surrogate's Courthouse (Hall of Records)
Archives dating back to 1664 are stored and displayed here.

Municipal Building
Until 2009, this building was where weddings "at City Hall" actually took place. The copper statue on the skyline is *Civic Fame* by Adolph Weinman.

United States Courthouse
The Civic Center is marked on the skyline by the golden pyramid of architect Cass Gilbert's courthouse.

Con Edison Mural
In 1975, artist Richard Haas re-created the Brooklyn Bridge on the sidewall of a former electrical substation.

Brooklyn Bridge
Views of, and from, the bridge have made it one of New York's best-loved landmarks *(see pp232–5)*.

Midtown Manhattan

The skyline of Midtown Manhattan is graced with some of the city's most spectacular towers and spires – from the familiar beauty of the Empire State Building's Art Deco pinnacle to the dramatic wedge shape of Citibank's modern headquarters. As the shoreline progresses uptown, so the architecture becomes more varied; the United Nations complex dominates a long stretch, and then Beekman Place begins a strand of exclusive residential enclaves that offer the rich and famous some seclusion in this busy part of the city.

Locator Map
■ Midtown

Empire State Building
At 1,250 ft (381 m), this was the tallest building in the world for many years (see pp132–3).

Grand Central Terminal
Now dwarfed by its neighbors, this landmark building is full of period details, such as this fine clock (see pp152–3).

Chrysler Building
Glinting in the sun by day or lit up by night, this stainless-steel spire is, for many, the ultimate New York skyscraper (see p151).

Tudor City
Built in the 1920s, this complex is mock Tudor on a grand scale, with over 3,000 apartments.

United Nations
Works of art from member countries include this Barbara Hepworth sculpture, a gift from Britain (see pp156–9).

1 and 2 UN Plaza
Angular glass towers house offices and the ONE UN New York Hotel.

General Electric Building
Built of brick in 1931, this Art Deco
building has a tall spiked crown that
resembles radio waves (see p172).

KEY

① The Highpoint
② MetLife Building
③ Trump World Tower
④ 100 UN Plaza
⑤ General Electric Building
⑥ 866 United Nations Plaza
⑦ Citigroup Center (601 Lexington)

Rockefeller Center
The outdoor skating
rink and walkways of
this complex of office
buildings, shops, and
eateries are great
for people-watching
(see p140).

Waldorf-Astoria
The splendid interior of one
of the city's most historic hotels
lies beneath twin copper-
capped towers (see p173).

The Nail
This exterior cross designed by
Arnaldo Pomodoro resides in
St. Peter's Church, which is
located in one corner of the
Citigroup Center (see p173).

Japan Society
Japanese culture, from ancient
art to avant-garde plays, can be
seen here (see pp154–5).

St. Mary's Garden
The garden at Holy
Family Church is a
peaceful haven.

Beekman Tower
Now a complex of
corporate apartments,
this Art Deco tower
was built in 1928 as a
hotel for women who
were members of US
college sororities.

Queensboro Bridge and Midtown Manhattan skyline at dusk ▶

NEW YORK CITY AREA BY AREA

LOWER MANHATTAN AND THE CIVIC CENTER

The old and the new converge in Lower Manhattan, where Colonial churches and early American monuments stand in the shadow of skyscrapers. New York was born here in the 1620s, and, with the emergence of Wall Street, it has remained at the heart of the world's financial markets. Since the September 11 attacks, there has been startling regeneration:

the new One World Trade Center soars 1,776 ft (541 m) above the city, with a spate of modern office towers, hotels, and transport hubs dotting the area. To the north, the Civic Center is the axis of the police department and the federal goverment's court systems, while nearby South Street Seaport is a restored dock area of shops, restaurants, and old ships.

Sights at a Glance

Historic Streets, Buildings, and Important Sites
1. Federal Reserve Bank
2. Federal Hall
3. *New York Stock Exchange pp72–3*
7. 9/11 Memorial
9. 9/11 Tribute Center
21. Governors Island
26. Schermerhorn Row
27. South Street Seaport
28. Criminal Courthouses
29. City Hall
32. Woolworth Building

Museums and Galleries
4. Museum of American Finance
8. 9/11 Memorial Museum
12. Museum of Jewish Heritage
13. Skyscraper Museum
16. National Museum of the American Indian
18. Fraunces Tavern Museum
23. *Ellis Island pp82–3*

Monuments and Statues
14. Charging Bull
22. *Statue of Liberty pp78–9*
25. Castle Clinton National Monument
33. African Burial Ground National Monument

Parks and Squares
15. Bowling Green
19. Vietnam Veterans' Plaza
24. Battery Park
30. City Hall Park and Park Row

Boat Trips
20. Staten Island Ferry

Churches
5. Trinity Church
17. Saint Elizabeth Ann Seton Shrine
31. St. Paul's Chapel

Modern Architecture
6. Brookfield Place
10. One World Trade Center
11. Battery Park City & Irish Hunger Memorial

Restaurants *see pp294–9*
1. Adrienne's Pizza Bar
2. Battery Gardens
3. Fraunces Tavern
4. Les Halles
5. SUteiShi

See also Street Finder maps 1, 2

◀ Statue of Liberty monument, Liberty Island

For keys to symbols *see back flap*

Street by Street: Wall Street

No intersection has been of greater importance to the city, past or present, than the one at Wall and Broad streets. Three important sites are located near here. Federal Hall National Monument marks the place where, in 1789, George Washington was sworn in as president. The New York Stock Exchange, founded in 1817, is to this day a financial nerve center whose ups and downs cause tremors globally. Nearby, Trinity Church is one of the nation's oldest Anglican parishes. The surrounding buildings are the very heart of New York's famous financial district.

The Marine Midland Building rises straight up 55 stories. This dark glass tower occupies only 40 per cent of its site. The other 60 per cent is a plaza in which a large red sculpture by Isamu Noguchi, *Cube*, balances on one of its points.

Trinity Building, an early 20th-century Gothic skyscraper, was designed to complement nearby Trinity Church.

The Equitable Building (1915) deprived its neighbors of light, prompting a change in the law: skyscrapers had to be set back from the street.

❺ ★ Trinity Church
Built in 1846 in a Gothic style, this is the third church on this site. Once the tallest structure in the city, the bell tower is now dwarfed by the skyscrapers that surround it. Many famous early New Yorkers are buried in the churchyard.

Wall Street subway
(lines 4, 5)

One Wall Street, built in 1932, has an outer wall patterned to look like fabric. In the lobby is an Art Deco mosaic in shades of flame red and gold.

BROADWAY

EXCHANGE PLACE

NEW STREET

BROAD STREET

26 Broadway was built as the home of the Standard Oil Trust. An oil lamp rests on top of it.

NEW YORK STOCK EXCHANGE

❸ ★ New York Stock Exchange
The hub of the world's financial markets is housed in a 17-story building constructed in 1903.

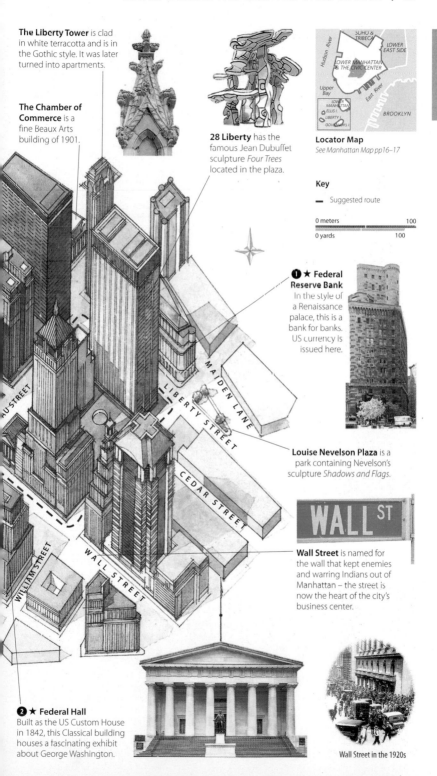

The Liberty Tower is clad in white terracotta and is in the Gothic style. It was later turned into apartments.

The Chamber of Commerce is a fine Beaux Arts building of 1901.

28 Liberty has the famous Jean Dubuffet sculpture *Four Trees* located in the plaza.

Locator Map
See Manhattan Map pp16–17

Key

— Suggested route

0 meters   100
0 yards   100

❶ ★ **Federal Reserve Bank**
In the style of a Renaissance palace, this is a bank for banks. US currency is issued here.

Louise Nevelson Plaza is a park containing Nevelson's sculpture *Shadows and Flags*.

WALL ST

Wall Street is named for the wall that kept enemies and warring Indians out of Manhattan – the street is now the heart of the city's business center.

❷ ★ **Federal Hall**
Built as the US Custom House in 1842, this Classical building houses a fascinating exhibit about George Washington.

Wall Street in the 1920s

Entrance to the Federal Reserve Bank, built in 1924

❶ Federal Reserve Bank

33 Liberty St. **Map** 1 C2. **Tel** (212) 720-6130. Ⓜ Fulton St–Broadway Nassau. 🕒 11:15am–3pm Mon–Fri (tours only). Free (register in advance). **Closed** pub hols. ✉ ♿ ⓦ **newyorkfed.org**

This is a government bank for banks – it is one of the 12 Federal Reserve banks, and therefore issues US currency. You can identify bills originating from this branch by the letter B in the Federal Reserve seal on each note.

Five stories below ground is one of the largest storehouses for international gold. Each nation's hoard is stored in its own compartment within the subterranean vault, guarded by 90-ton doors. Payments between nations used to be made by physical transfers of gold, until

1971 when President Nixon ended the trading of gold at a fixed price. Designed by York & Sawyer in the Italian Renaissance style, the 1924 building occupies a full block and is adorned with fine wrought-iron grillwork.

❷ Federal Hall

26 Wall St. **Map** 1 C3. **Tel** (212) 825-6888. Ⓜ Wall St. **Open** 9am–5pm Mon–Fri. **Closed** public hols. ♿ 🕒 10am, 1pm, 2pm, 3pm Mon–Fri. 📷 ⓦ **nps.gov/feha**

A bronze statue of George Washington on the steps of Federal Hall marks the site where the nation's first president took his oath of office in 1789. Thousands of New Yorkers jammed Wall and Broad streets for the occasion. They roared their approval when the Chancellor of the State of New York shouted, "Long live George Washington, President of the United States."

The present structure, renovated in 2006, was built between 1834 and 1842 as the US Customs House. It is one of the finest Greek Revival designs in the city. Display rooms off the Rotunda pay tribute to the Washington connection, and include the Bill of Rights Room.

❸ New York Stock Exchange

See pp72–3.

Exterior of the Museum of American Finance, Wall Street

❹ Museum of American Finance

48 Wall St. **Map** 1 C3. **Tel** (212) 908-4110. Ⓜ Wall St. **Open** 10am–4pm Tue–Sat. ⓦ **moaf.org.**

Completed in 1929, this museum sits in the former main hall of the lavish Bank of New York & Trust building. An ideal place to gain an understanding of the city's financial trading rooms, the museum explains stocks, bonds, and future trading. Multimedia presentations and exhibits explain all there is to know, and there are several rare artifacts on display, including a bond signed by George Washington in 1792, a gold ingot from the 1850s, and ticker tape from the opening moments of the Great Crash in 1929.

The first Secretary of the Treasury, Alexander Hamilton (c. 1755–1604), was a financial pioneer in his time, and there is an entire gallery dedicated to him at the museum. Documentary films on Wall Street are shown through the day as well.

Marble-columned rotunda within Federal Hall

The beautiful gardens at
Trinity Church

❺ Trinity Church

79 Broadway at Wall St. **Map** 1 C3.
Tel (212) 602-0800. Ⓜ Wall St,
Rector St. **Open** 7am–6pm Mon–
Fri, 8am–4pm Sat, 7am–4pm Sun
✝ 12:05pm Mon–Fri, 9am &
11:15am Sun, except during services.
📷 2pm daily; also Sun after
11:15am service. Concerts: see details
online. 📷 📷
Ⓦ **trinitywallstreet.org**

This square-towered Episcopal
church at the head of Wall
Street is the third one on this
site. Designed in 1846 by
Richard Upjohn, it was among
the grandest churches of its
day, marking the beginning
of the best period of Gothic
Revival architecture in America.
Richard Morris Hunt's design
for the sculpted brass doors
was inspired by Lorenzo
Ghiberti's *Gates of Paradise* at
the Baptistery in Florence.
Restoration has uncovered
the original rosy sandstone,
long buried beneath layers
of city grime. The 280-ft (85-m)
steeple, the tallest structure
in New York until 1890, still
commands respect despite
its towering neighbors.
Many prominent early
New Yorkers are buried in
the graveyard: statesman
Alexander Hamilton; steamboat
inventor Robert Fulton; and
William Bradford, founder
of New York's first newspaper
in 1725, to name but a few.

❻ Brookfield Place

230 Vesey St. **Map** 1 A2. **Tel** (212)
945-2600. Ⓜ Fulton St, Cortlandt St,
Rector St. 📷 📷 📷 📷
Ⓦ **brookfieldplaceny.com**

A model of urban design by
Cesar Pelli & Associates in
the 1980s, Brookfield Place
(formerly known as the
World Financial Center), is
an imposing 14-acre (6-ha)
shopping, dining, and
business complex. When it
was first inaugurated in 1988,
the building was hailed as the
Rockefeller Center of the 21st
century. Thereafter, following
9/11, an ambitious $250-million
renovation took place, which
was finally completed in 2014.
Today, there are four office
towers that soar skyward, and
house the headquarters of
some of the biggest financial
companies in the world,
such as Merrill Lynch and
American Express.
Located within the
Brookfield Place complex is
the dazzling Winter Garden, a
magnificent, 10-story public
plaza. The ceiling is made
entirely of glass, of which
2,000 panes were replaced
after the attacks of 9/11. The
plaza is further complemented
by 16 *Washingtonia robusta*
palms from Florida, each
standing at a height of 45 ft
(14 m) and replacing the palm
court tradition of yesteryear.
A sweeping marble staircase

Main floor of the magnificent Winter
Garden, Brookfield Place

leads down to the Winter
Garden, but this often doubles
as picturesque seating for
free events. There are a variety
of shows held at the plaza,
ranging from concerts in
classical and contemporary
music to dance and theater
performances, all of which are
listed on the website.
There are two food halls
that both adjoin the Winter
Garden plaza – Hudson Eats
offers modern and popular
eateries, while Le District is a
French-themed food court.
The plaza then opens out
onto the North Cove yacht
harbor and promenade by the
Hudson River.

Brookfield Place viewed from the Hudson River

❸ New York Stock Exchange

In 1790, trading in stocks and shares took place haphazardly on or around Wall Street, but in 1792 24 brokers who traded at 68 Wall Street signed an agreement to deal only with one another: the basis of the New York Stock Exchange (NYSE) was formed. The NYSE has weathered a succession of alternating slumps ("bear markets") and booms ("bull markets"), growing from a local marketplace into a financial center of global importance. Membership is strictly limited. In 1817, a "seat" cost $25; in the "bullish" years of the late 1990s, the prices ran as high as $4 million. In 2006, the NYSE became a for-profit public company, and all the seats were exchanged for cash and stock settlements. Traders now buy one-year licenses.

A Guide to Trading Posts

The 17 trading posts each consist of 22 groups, or "sections," of traders and technology, each buying and selling the stock of up to 10 listed companies. Commission brokers work for brokerage firms, and rush between booth and trading post, buying and selling securities (stocks and bonds) for the public. A specialist trades in just one stock at a time, quoting bids to other brokers, and independent floor brokers handle orders for busy brokerage firms. Clerks process the orders that come into the trading post via SuperDOT computer into the Exchange's Market Data System. The pages help on the busy exchange floor, bringing orders from the booths to the brokers and specialists. Post display units show stock prices, and flat screens show prices and trades for the specialist. As of January 24, 2007, all NYSE stocks have been traded via an electronic hybrid market.

Trading post

KEY

① **Computerized stock tickers** flash a steady stream of prices as fast as the human eye is able to read them.

② **Visitors' gallery**

③ **Trading post**

Ticker-Tape Machine
Introduced around 1870, these machines printed out up-to-the-minute details of purchase prices on ribbons of paper tape.

The 48-Hour Day
During the 1929 Crash, Stock Exchange clerks worked nonstop for 48 hours. Their mood stayed cheerful despite the panic outside.

Members' entrance, Wall Street

Trading Floor
On a typical day, some 3.5 billion shares are traded for more than 2,000 listed companies. The advanced electronics that support the Designated Order Turnaround (SuperDOT) computer are carried above the chaos of the trading floor in a web of gold piping.

Great Crash of 1929
On Tuesday, October 29, over 16 million shares changed hands as the stock market crashed. Investors thronged Wall Street in bewilderment, but, contrary to popular myth, traders did not leap from windows in panic.

1792 Buttonwood Agreement signed on May 17

1844 Invention of the telegraph allows trading nationwide

1867 Ticker-tape machines introduced

1903 Present Stock Exchange building opens

1987 "Black Monday" crash, October 19. Dow Jones Index drops 508 points

2015 Dow Jones Index hits 18,351 in May, an all-time peak

| 1750 | 1800 | 1850 | 1900 | 1950 | 2000 | 2050 |

1817 New York Stock & Exchange Board created

1865 New Exchange Building opens at Wall and Broad streets

1869 "Black Friday" gold crash, September 24

1929 Wall St. Crash, October 29

2001 After 8 years of bull markets, economy falters after September 11

2006 The NYSE merges with Archipelago Holdings to become a for-profit public company

2009 Dow Jones Index hits 6,547, a 12-year low

Offerings for victims of the attacks at the 9/11 Memorial

❶ 9/11 Memorial

Greenwich St, between Fulton and Liberty Sts. **Map** 1 B2. **Tel** (212) 266-5211. Ⓜ Fulton St, World Trade Center, Cortland St, Rector St. **Open** 7:30am–9pm daily. 🚶Ⓦ **911memorial.org**

The moving 9/11 Memorial was built to commemorate the 10-year anniversary of the terrorist attacks of September 11 2001. The process began in 2003, when the Lower Manhattan Development Corporation launched an international competition to design the memorial. A year later, the Israeli architect Michael Arad, employed at the landscape-architecture firm Peter Walker & Partners, was selected for his work *Reflecting Absence*.

The two vast memorial pools represent the footprints of the original towers, each almost one acre (0.40 ha) in extent. To mute the sounds of the city, 30-ft (9-m) waterfalls were contructed on either side. The brónze parapets that encircle the pools display the names of 2,977 victims of the attacks, along with the additional six killed during the 1993 attack on the World Trade Center.

The surrounding plaza is studded with 400 swamp white oak trees, intended to provide a meditative oasis within the city for later years; the trees can grow up to a height of 80 ft (24 m) at maturity, and live between 300 to 350 years. The plaza is also home to a callery pear tree, better known as the Survivor Tree,

which miraculously survived the collapse of the World Trade Center. The tree was originally planted in the 1970s, and suffered grave damage during the September 11 attacks. It was replanted in the Van Cortlandt Park in the Bronx, where it slowly recovered, before it was returned to its original spot by the memorial, in 2010.

❽ 9/11 Memorial Museum

Greenwich St, between Fulton and Liberty Sts. **Map** 1 B2. **Tel** (212) 266-5211. Ⓜ Fulton St, World Trade Center, Cortland St, Rector St. **Open** 9am–8pm Sun–Thu (last entry 6pm), 9am–9pm Fri & Sat (last entry 7pm). 🚶🅿️Ⓦ **911memorial.org**

Designed by the New York-based architectural firm David Brody Bond, this underground

M27 steel impact display at the 9/11 Memorial Museum

museum opened in 2014, and is a thorough testament to the events of 9/11. With poignant exhibits, personal accounts and videos, and countless artifacts recovered from Ground Zero, the museum details the events of September 11, 2001 informing visitors of both the happenings that led up to the attacks, and after.

The cavernous Foundation Hall sits at the exhibition level, and contains the structural remains of the Twin Towers. A section of slurry wall remains, which today protects the site from the Hudson River. There is also a crushed FDNY fire truck, and the iconic final piece of structural steel to be removed from Ground Zero, referred to as the Last Column.

The September 11, 2001 Historical Exhibition is at the center of the museum, and contains a host of images, recordings, and videos that cover the events of September 11 almost minute by minute. There are phone calls made by passengers from Flight 93, which crashed in Pennsylvania, photographs of the burning towers, and radio recordings of firemen in the towers just before the collapse.

Tickets to the 9/11 Memorial Museum can be purchased three months in advance, or visitors can queue for entry on the day. Note queues can be long.

❾ One World Trade Center

285 Fulton St. **Map** 1 B2. **Tel** (844) 696-1776. Ⓜ World Trade Center, Cortland St, Rector St. **Open** Late May–early Sep: 9am–midnight daily (last entry 11:15pm); early Sep–early May 9am–8pm daily (last entry 7:15pm). ℹ️🚶🅿️ Ⓦ **oneworldobservatory.com**

The tallest skyscraper in the United States, One World Trade Center stands at an epic height of 1,776 ft (541 m), and is a grand pinnacle of steel and glass. The construction of the building began in 2006, supervised by architect

The remarkable One World Trade Center against the Manhattan skyline

stands at 741 ft (226 m); and Fumihiko Maki's 4 World Trade Center, which opened in 2013, and stands at 978 ft (298 m).

⑩ 9/11 Tribute Center

120 Liberty St. **Map** 1 B2. **Tel** (866) 737-1184. **M** World Trade Center, Cortland St, Rector St. 🅸 ⓘ 🅲
W tributewtc.org

The 9/11 Tribute Center was established by the September 11th Families' Association, an organisation set up by the victims' families, and aims to give a personal understanding of the attacks and its victims. Opened in 2006, while the nearby 9/11 Memorial was still under development, the center stands separately and houses just five small galleries.

Among its exhibits, the center offers a model of the 1974 Twin Towers, and has a section dedicated to the day of the attacks. There are also several videos and recorded accounts of the survivors of the attacks. The center offers daily walking tours for visitors, led by family members, rescue and recovery workers, survivors, civilian volunteers, and residents of Lower Manhattan. The tours take visitors through the 9/11 Memorial.

David Childs. The structure incorporated the *Tower of Freedom* design, originally created by Polish architect, Daniel Libeskind.

At the ground level of the building, there is a multimedia show entitled "Voices", which takes visitors through the lives and stories of the people who built the tower. The Foundations exhibit, which is located here as well, lays out the bedrock of the land beneath the building. Five high-speed elevators, known as Sky Pods, transport visitors to the top of the building in just 60 seconds. From here, there are beautiful views of the harbor, Staten Island, and Mahattan.

The One World Trade Center Observatory occupies the 100th, 101st, and 102nd floors and offers visitors an array of activities. The See Forever Theater on the 102nd floor screens a two-minute video

with bird's-eye images of New York on loop. On the 100th floor, the Main Observatory features the Sky Portal, a 14-ft (4-m) wide circular disc that provides dazzling views of the drop below. There are also several dining options for visitors with a ticket to the Observatory.

The site surrounding One World Trade Center swarms with workers involved in construction projects, which can be seen at various stages of development. Although seven buildings were destroyed during the 2001 attacks, the area has seen a massive boom and much investment, thanks to the focus on regenerating Lower Manhattan. The entire World Trade complex, which includes five towers and an arts center, is estimated to be completed by 2019. Structures that have so far seen fruition include 7 World Trade Center, which opened in 2006, and

A model of the Twin Towers, highlighting the lives of victims

Arturo Di Modica's iconic bull statue, at the southern end of Broadway

⓫ Battery Park City & Irish Hunger Memorial

7 Battery Park City. **Map** 1 A3.
Ⓜ Rector St. Ⓦ **batteryparkcity.org**

Construction of the former World Trade Center resulted in a million cubic yards of landfill, which was poured into the Hudson River to form a lovely neighborhood of restaurants, apartments, sculptures, and gardens. The 1.2-mile (2-km) esplanade along the river offers spectacular views of the Statue of Liberty.

Overlooking the Hudson at the end of Vesey Street, the Irish Hunger Memorial is a monument dedicated to the Irish who starved to death during the Great Famine of 1845–52. The centerpiece, an abandoned stone cottage from Ireland, is set on a raised, grassy embankment.

⓬ Museum of Jewish Heritage

36 Battery Pl. **Map** 1 B4. **Tel** (646) 437-4200. Ⓜ Bowling Green, South Ferry.
🚌 M5, M15, M20. **Open** 10am–5:45pm Sun–Thu (to 8pm Wed), 10am–5pm Fri (to 3pm Nov–Mar) and eve of Jewish hols. **Closed** Sat, Jewish holidays, Thanksgiving. 🎁 ♿ 📷 📷 💻 Lectures. Ⓦ **mjhnyc.org**

This museum stands as a memorial to the victims of the Holocaust. The core exhibition, which covers three floors, is

housed in a remarkable six-sided building, symbolizing the six million Jews who died under the Nazis, as well as the six points of the Star of David. The poignant and informative collection begins with the practicalities and rituals of everyday Eastern European Jewish life, pre-1930. It then moves on to the horrors of the Holocaust, and ends with the establishment of Israel and subsequent Jewish achievements. The audio guides are narrated by Meryl Streep and Itzhak Perlman.

⓭ Skyscraper Museum

39 Battery Pl. **Map** 1 A3. **Tel** (212) 968-1961. Ⓜ Bowling Green, Rector St. **Open** noon–6pm Wed–Sun. 🎁 📷 Ⓦ **skyscraper.org**

Adjacent to the Ritz-Carlton hotel, this museum celebrates New York's architectural heritage and examines the historical forces and individuals that shaped the city's skyline. There is a permanent exhibition on the World Trade Center and a digital reconstruction of how Manhattan has changed over time, as well as temporary exhibitions that analyze the various definitions of tall buildings: as objects of design, products of technology, sites of construction, real-estate investments, and places of work and residence.

⓮ Charging Bull

Broadway at Bowling Green.
Map 1 C4. Ⓜ Bowling Green.

At 1am on December 15, 1989, sculptor Arturo Di Modica (b. 1941) and 30 friends unloaded his 7,000-lb (3,200-kg) *Charging Bull* bronze statue in front of the New York Stock Exchange. The group had eight minutes between police patrols to place the sculpture, but they managed to in just five. The bull was later taken away for obstructing traffic and lacking a permit. Public outcry ensued and the Parks Department gave it a "temporary" stomping ground on Broadway, where it remains to this day as the unofficial mascot of Wall Street.

Di Modica created the sculpture after the 1987 stock-market crash, to symbolize the "strength, power, and hope of the American people for the future." It took him two years to complete, at a personal cost of $350,000.

The charming fountain at Bowling Green, Battery Park

⓯ Bowling Green

Map 1 C4. Ⓜ Bowling Green.

This triangular plot north of Battery Park was the city's earliest park, used first as a cattle market and later as a bowling ground. A statue of King George III stood here until the signing of the Declaration of Independence, when, as a symbol of British rule, the

An exhibit at the National Museum of the American Indian

statue was hacked to pieces and smelted for ammunition *(see pp24–5)*. The wife of the governor of Connecticut is said to have melted down enough pieces to mold 42,000 bullets.

The fence, erected in 1771, is still standing, but minus the royal crowns that once adorned it – they met the same fate as the statue. The Green was once surrounded by elegant homes. Beyond it is the start of Broadway, which runs the length of Manhattan and, under its formal name of Route 9, all the way north to the State capital in Albany.

⓰ National Museum of the American Indian

1 Bowling Green. **Map** 1 C4.
Ⓜ Bowling Green. National Museum of the American Indian. **Tel** (212) 514-3700. **Open** 10am–5pm daily (to 8pm Thu). **Closed** Dec 25. & 🖰
Ⓦ nmai.si.edu

Cass Gilbert's stately US Custom House now houses the Smithsonian National Museum of the American Indian. The museum's outstanding collection of about a million artifacts, along with an archive of many thousands of photographs, spans the breadth of the native cultures of North, Central, and South America. Exhibitions include works by contemporary Native American artists as well as changing

displays drawn from the permanent collection. The National Archives, on the third floor, contains a small exhibition featuring a selection of original documents from the National Archives based in Washington, D. C.

Completed in 1907, and in use until 1973, the Beaux Arts Custom House is also a part of the attraction. The impressive facade, adorned with elaborate statuary by Daniel Chester French, depicts the major continents, and some of the world's great commercial centers. The magnificent marble Great Hall, and rotunda located inside, are beautifully decorated. The 16 murals covering the 135-ft (41-m) dome were painted by Reginald Marsh in 1937 and show the progress of ships into the harbor.

⓱ Saint Elizabeth Ann Seton Shrine

7 State St. **Map** 1 C4. **Tel** (212) 269-6865. Ⓜ Whitehall, South Ferry. **Open** 7am–5pm daily.
✝ 8:05am, 12:15pm Mon–Fri; 11am Sun. Ⓦ setonheritage.org

Elizabeth Ann Seton (1774–1821), the first native-born American to be canonized by the Catholic Church, lived here from 1801 to 1803. Mother Seton founded the American Sisters of Charity, the first order of nuns in the United States. After the Civil War, the Mission of Our Lady of the Rosary turned the building into a shelter for homeless Irish immigrant women – 170,000 passed through on their way to a new life in America. The adjoining church was built in 1965. The Mission established and maintains the shrine to Mother Seton.

Front facade of Saint Elizabeth Ann Seton Shrine

㉒ Statue of Liberty

A gift from the French to the American people, the statue was the brainchild of sculptor Frédéric-Auguste Bartholdi and has become a symbol of freedom throughout the world. In Emma Lazarus's poem, which is engraved on the base, Lady Liberty says: "Give me your tired, your poor, Your huddled masses yearning to breathe free." Unveiled by President Grover Cleveland on October 28, 1886, the statue was restored in time for its 100th anniversary in 1986. Public access to the balcony surrounding the torch has been barred for safety reasons since 1916.

★ **Golden Torch**
In 1986, a new torch replaced the corroded original. The replica's flame is coated in 24-carat gold leaf.

The Statue
With a height of 305 ft (93 m) from ground to torch, the Statue of Liberty dominates New York harbor.

From Her Toes to Her Torch
Three hundred molded copper sheets riveted together make up Lady Liberty.

KEY

① **The original torch** now stands in the main lobby.

② **Museum**

③ **The pedestal** is set within the walls of an army fort. It was the largest concrete mass ever poured.

④ **354 steps** lead from the entrance to the crown.

⑤ **Observation deck**

⑥ **A central pylon** anchors the 200-ton statue to its base.

⑦ **The frame** was designed by Gustave Eiffel, who later built the Eiffel Tower. The copper shell hangs on bars from a central iron pylon.

⑧ **The crown**'s seven rays represent the world's seas and continents.

★ **Statue of Liberty Museum**
Posters featuring the statue are among the items on display.

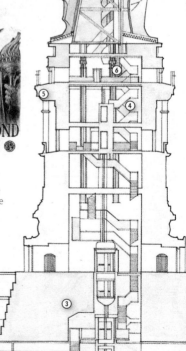

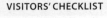

★ **Ferries to Liberty Island**
Ferries cross New York harbor to Liberty Island, where the Statue offers some of the city's finest views.

Portrait of Liberty
Bartholdi's mother was the model for Liberty. The seven rays of her crown represent the seven seas and seven continents.

Making the Hand
To mold the copper shell, the hand was made first in plaster, then wood.

A Model Figure
A series of graduated scale models enabled Bartholdi to build the largest metal statue ever constructed.

Frédéric-Auguste Bartholdi

The French sculptor who designed the Statue of Liberty intended it as a monument to the freedom he found lacking in his own country. He said, "I will try to glorify the Republic and Liberty over there, in the hope that someday I will find it again here." Bartholdi devoted 21 years of his life to making the statue a reality, even traveling to America in 1871 to talk President Ulysses S. Grant and others into funding it and installing it in New York's harbor.

Restoration Celebration
On July 3, 1986, after a $100-million restoration, the statue was unveiled. The $2-million fireworks display was the largest ever seen in America.

The 18th-century Fraunces Tavern Museum and restaurant

⓲ Fraunces Tavern Museum

54 Pearl St. **Map** 1 C4. **Tel** (212) 425-1778. Ⓜ Wall St, Broad St, Bowling Green. **Open** noon–5pm daily. **Closed** public hols. 📧 🏛 groups only. Lectures, films. 🔗 📷 📶 **frauncestavern museum.org**

New York's only remaining block of 18th-century commercial buildings contains an exact replica of the 1719 Fraunces Tavern where George Washington said farewell to his officers in 1783. The tavern had been an early casualty of the Revolution: the British ship *Asia* shot a cannonball through its roof in August 1775. The building was bought in 1904 by the Sons of the Revolution. Its restoration in 1907 was one of the first efforts to preserve the nation's heritage. The ground-floor restaurant has wood-burning fires and great charm. An upstairs museum has changing exhibits interpreting the history and culture of early America.

George Washington's famous farewell speech took place in the Long Room, which has been recreated in the manner of the time. The adjacent Federal-style Clinton Room is a dining room, decorated in rare French wallpaper from 1838. There are galleries of art pertaining to the Revolution, such as the Sons of the Revolution gallery, which explains much of the society's history.

⓳ Vietnam Veterans' Plaza

Between Water St and South St. **Map** 2 D4. Ⓜ Whitehall, South Ferry.

This multilevel brick plaza features, in its center, an enormous wall of translucent green glass, engraved with excerpts from speeches, news stories, and moving letters to families from servicemen and women who died in the Vietnam war between 1959 and 1975.

⓴ Staten Island Ferry

Whitehall St. **Map** 2 D5. **Tel** 311. Ⓜ South Ferry. **Open** 24 hrs. Free. ♿ 📶 **siferry.com**

The first business venture of a promising Staten Island boy named Cornelius Vanderbilt, who later became the railroad magnate, the ferry has operated since 1810, carrying island commuters to and from the city and offering visitors an unforgettable close-up of the harbor, the Statue of Liberty, Ellis Island, and lower Manhattan's incredible skyline. The fare is still the city's best bargain: it's free.

㉑ Governors Island

.Governors Island, New York Harbor. **Map** 1 A5–B. Ⓜ South Ferry, Bowling Green. **Open** late May–late Sep: 10am–6pm Mon–Fri, 10am–7pm Sat & Sun. 📶 **govisland.com**

With its village greens and colonial halls reminiscent of a college campus, this 172-acre (70-ha) island in New York Harbor makes for a great day-trip. Between 1794 and 1966, the US Army occupied the island, and for the next thirty years it was the US Coast Guard's largest base. Since 2003, the island has been shared between the city and the National Park Service.

Along with a visitors center, there is an artificial beach and a small museum. On the north-west corner of the island, Castle Williams was built in 1811 to complement the near-identical Castle Clinton in Battery Park *(see p81)*. Used as a prison until 1966, its cramped cells held up to 1,000 Confederate soldiers during the Civil War. The island also boasts plenty of green spaces in which to laze in the sun plus a breezy promenade.

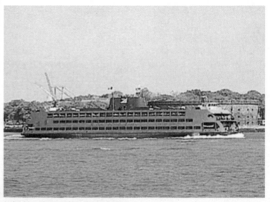

Staten Island Ferry, which is free to travel on

Castle Clinton National Monument in Battery Park

㉒ Statue of Liberty

See pp78–9.

㉓ Ellis Island

See pp82–3.

Beaux Arts subway entrance at the corner of Battery Park

㉔ Battery Park

Map 1 B4. **M** South Ferry, Bowling Green.

Named for the British cannons that once protected New York, the park is one of the best places in the city for views of the harbor. The park is rimmed with statues and monuments, such as the Netherlands Memorial Monument and memorials to New York's first Jewish immigrants and the Coast Guard. The newer attractions include the Pier A Harbor House, headquarters of the New York Harbor Police in 1886, which now hosts bars and restaurants; the SeaGlass Carousel, an aquatic-themed merry-go-round; and Battery Farm, which contains plots for fruits, vegetables, and herbs.

㉕ Castle Clinton National Monument

Battery Park. **Map** 1 B4. **Tel** (212) 344-7220. **M** Bowling Green, South Ferry. **Open** 8am–5pm daily. **Closed** Dec 25. 🅰 🗹 Concerts. 🏠 **W** nps.gov/cacl

Castle Clinton was built in 1811 as an artillery defense post some 300 ft (91 m) offshore, connected to Battery Park by a causeway; but landfill gradually linked it to the mainland. None of its 28 guns was ever used in battle.

The fort was enclosed in 1824 to become a fashionable theater, where Phineas T. Barnum introduced "Swedish nightingale" Jenny Lind in 1850. In 1855 it preceded Ellis Island as the city's immigration point, and, by 1890, it had processed over 8 million newcomers. In 1896, it became the New York Aquarium, which moved to Coney Island in 1941 (see p259).

A small exhibit on the history of the site is open to visitors, and a section of the original "Battery Wall" can be viewed here as well. Tickets to Ellis Island (see pp82–3) and the Statue of Liberty (see pp78–9) are also available.

㉖ Schermerhorn Row

Fulton and South sts. **Map** 2 D3. **M** Fulton St.

This is Seaport's architectural showpiece. Constructed in 1811 by shipowner and chandler Peter Schermerhorn on land reclaimed from the river, the buildings were originally warehouses and counting-houses. With the opening of the Brooklyn Ferry terminus in 1814 and then of Fulton Market in 1822, the block became desirable property.

The Row has been restored as part of the South Street development, and it now houses museum galleries, as well as shops, and restaurants.

Restored buildings on Schermerhorn Row

㉓ Ellis Island

Around half of America's population can trace its roots to Ellis Island, which served as the country's immigration depot from 1892 until 1954. Nearly 12 million people passed through its gates and dispersed across the country in the greatest wave of migration the world has ever known. Centered on the Great Hall or Registry Room, the site today houses the three-story Ellis Island Immigration Museum. Much of this story is told with photographs and the voices of actual immigrants, and an electronic database traces ancestors. Outside, the American Immigrant Wall of Honor is the largest wall of names in the world. No other place explains so well the "melting pot" that formed the character of the nation. Visit early to avoid the crowds.

Main building

★ Baggage Room
The immigrants' meager possessions were checked here on arrival.

Rail Ticket
A special fare for immigrants led many on to California.

★ Dormitory
There were separate sleeping quarters for male and female detainees.

★ Great Hall
Immigrant families were made to wait for "processing" in the Registry Room. The old metal railings were replaced with wooden benches in 1911.

KEY

① **The ferry office** sold tickets to New Jersey.

② **The railroad office** sold tickets onward to the final destination.

③ **The metal-and-glass awning** is a re-creation of the original.

The Restoration

In 1990 a $156-million project by the Statue of Liberty-Ellis Island Foundation, Inc., renewed several ruined buildings, replacing the copper domes and restoring the interior with original fixtures.

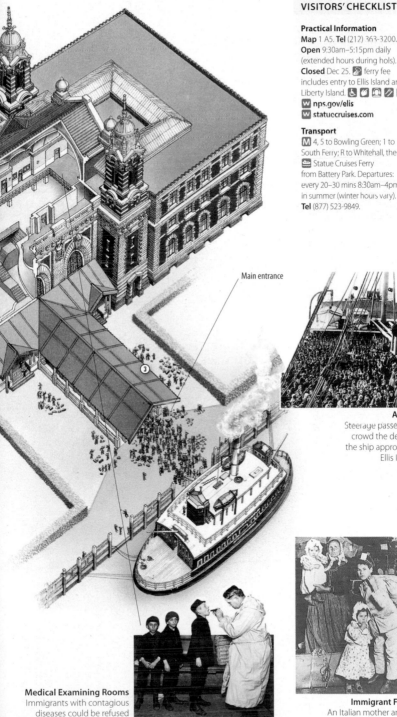

Main entrance

VISITORS' CHECKLIST

Practical Information
Map 1 A5. **Tel** (212) 363-3200.
Open 9:30am–5:15pm daily
(extended hours during hols).
Closed Dec 25. 🎟 ferry fee
includes entry to Ellis Island and
Liberty Island. 👤 📷 🎧 🚻 🛍
W nps.gov/elis
W statuecruises.com

Transport
Ⓜ 4, 5 to Bowling Green; 1 to
South Ferry; R to Whitehall, then
🚢 Statue Cruises Ferry
from Battery Park. Departures:
every 20–30 mins 8:30am–4pm
in summer (winter hours vary).
Tel (877) 523-9849.

Arrival
Steerage passengers
crowd the deck, as
the ship approaches
Ellis Island.

Medical Examining Rooms
Immigrants with contagious
diseases could be refused
entry and sent back home.

Immigrant Family
An Italian mother and her
children arrive in 1905.

The *Ambrose* lightship at a South Street Seaport pier on the East River

㉗ South Street Seaport

19 Fulton St. **Map** 2 E2. **Tel** (212) 732-8257. Ⓜ Fulton St. **Open** 10am–9pm Mon–Sat, 11am–8pm Sun. ♿ 🅿 Concerts. 🟦 📷 🆆 **southstreetseaport.com**. South Street Seaport Museum: 12 Fulton St. **Tel** (212) 748-8600. **Open** Apr–Oct: 11am–5pm Wed–Sun. 🎭 ♿ 🅿 Lectures, exhibits, films. 🟦 📷 🆆 **southstreetseaportmuseum.org**

This district of cobbled streets offers spectacular views of Brooklyn Bridge and the East River. Part of New York's original dockyards, South Street Seaport has been nestled here since 1966, with a multitude of restaurants and shops. Since Hurricane Sandy hit the area in 2012, the site has been undergoing a multi-year redevelopment project. Plans include the opening of the iPic Theaters in the Fulton Market building and a new shopping mall on Pier 17.

The **South Street Seaport Museum** has a large collection of maritime art and artifacts, as well as Federal-style warehouses that date back to 1812. The main ticket office and galleries are located on Schermerhorn Row (*see p81*), Fulton Street.

The museum owns six historic ships that stand at nearby Pier 16. Those open to visitors include the *Ambrose*, a lightship from 1908, and the *Peking*, a massive German merchant ship that

later served as a British training vessel in the 1930s. The museum also owns the schooner *Pioneer*, which cruises the harbor in the summer. To enjoy views of the Brooklyn Bridge, visit the upper deck of Pier 15.

㉘ Criminal Courthouses

New York Court District: Centre St and Chambers St. **Map** 1 C1–2 D1. Ⓜ Brooklyn Bridge-City Hall. **Open** 9am–5pm Mon–Fri. ♿

Grand Neo-Classical buildings dominate New York's court district. The pyramid-topped Thurgood Marshall US Courthouse, designed by Cass Gilbert in 1936, soars at 590 ft (180 m), and serves as a federal courthouse today. The adjacent New York County Courthouse, opened in 1927, is one of the state's supreme courts. Its elaborate rotunda has Tiffany lighting fixtures, and murals on themes of law and justice by Attilio Pusterla.

Surrogate's Court, completed in 1907, stands on Chambers Street. With an ornate-columned facade of white Maine granite, the roof area has figures by Henry K. Bush-Brown, representing the different stages of life from childhood to old age. The ceiling mosaic of the stunning central hall was designed by William de Leftwich Dodge, and features the signs of the zodiac.

㉙ City Hall

City Hall Park. **Map** 1 C1. **Tel** 311. Ⓜ Brooklyn Br-City Hall Park Pl. **Open** 10am Thu (free tours, book in advance). ♿ 🅿 (212) 788-2656.

A gleaming marble palace, City Hall features columns, arches, and furnishings practically unchanged since 1812. A stately Federal-style building (with some influences from the French Renaissance), it was designed by John McComb, Jr., the first prominent American-born architect, and the French émigré Joseph Mangin.

Marble cladding was not used for the building's rear, since it was not expected that the city would ever develop farther to the north. In 1954, a program of restoration remedied this, and the interior was refurbished.

Mangin is usually given credit for designing the exterior, and McComb for the beautiful interior with its fine domed rotunda encircled by 10 columns. The space beneath it opens onto elegant marble stairways, leading to the splendid second-floor City Council chambers and the Governor's Room, which houses a portrait gallery of early New York leaders. This magnificent entrance has welcomed rulers and heroes for nearly 200 years. In 1865 Abraham Lincoln's body lay in state in this hall.

Stand on the steps and look to your right to see a statue of Nathan Hale, a US soldier hanged by the British as a spy

City Hall's magnificent early 19th-century facade

in September 1776 during the Revolutionary War. His last words – "My only regret is that I have not more lives than one to offer in the service of my country" – won him a permanent place in the history books and hearts of America.

⑳ City Hall Park and Park Row

Map 1 C2.
Ⓜ Brooklyn Br-City Hall Park Pl.

Once a communal pasture in the 17th century, City Hall has been the seat of New York's government since 1812. An almshouse for the poor stood on the site between 1736–97, and it was later home to protests against British rule. During the Revolutionary War (1775–83), the British used the nearby debtors' prison to capture and hang 250 prisoners. Today, a memorial in honor of the "Liberty Poles" (symbols of revolt) stands in City Hall's west lawn.

The Park Row Building was completed in 1899. At 391 ft (119 m), it became one of the tallest office buildings in the world. Originally, behind the limestone-and-brick facade sat the offices of the Associated Press. Park Row runs along the east side of City Hall Park. Once called "Newspaper Row," it was lined with the lofty offices of the *Sun, World, Tribune,* and other papers. Printing House Square has a statue of Benjamin Franklin with his *Pennsylvania Gazette.*

㉛ St. Paul's Chapel

209–211 Broadway. **Map** 1 C2.
Tel (212) 602-0800. Ⓜ Fulton St
Open 10am–6pm Mon–Sat,
7am–6pm Sun. **Closed** most public hols. 🕐 12:30pm Wed; 8am, 10am Sun. 📷 by appt. Concerts 1pm Mon.

Miraculously untouched when the World Trade Center towers collapsed in 2001, St. Paul's is Manhattan's only extant church built before the Revolutionary War. It is a Georgian gem that dates back to 1766. One of the main attractions here is Unwavering Spirit, a moving exhibition on the September 11 attacks. For eight months after the episode, the chapel acted as a sanctuary for rescue workers at Ground Zero. The pew where George Washington prayed between 1789–90 is also part of the exhibition as well. The shrine-like pew has been preserved since the time New York was the capital of the US, and even served as a foot-treatment chair for firefighters during the attacks.

㉜ Woolworth Building

233 Broadway. **Map** 1 C2.
Tel (203) 966-9663. Ⓜ City Hall
Park Pl. **Open** daily for tours
(book in advance).
Ⓦ woolworthtours.com

In 1879, salesclerk Frank W. Woolworth opened a new kind of store, where shoppers could see and touch the goods, and everything cost five cents. The chain of stores that followed made him a fortune and changed retailing forever.

The 1913 Gothic headquarters of his empire was New York's tallest building until 1929. It set the standard for the great skyscrapers. Architect Cass Gilbert's soaring two-tiered design, adorned with gargoyles of bats and other wildlife, is topped with a pyramid roof, flying buttresses, pinnacles, and four small towers.

The marble interior is rich with filigree, sculptured reliefs, and painted decoration, and has a high glass-tile mosaic ceiling that almost seems to glow. The lobby is one of the city's treasures. Gilbert showed his sense of humor here, in bas-relief caricatures of the founder counting out his fortune in nickels and dimes; of the real-estate broker closing a deal; and of Gilbert cradling a large model of the building. Paid for with $13.5 million in cash, the building has never been mortgaged. Woolworth's went out of business in 1997. After several years of the building being closed to the pubic, guided tours resumed in 2014.

㉝ African Burial Ground

Duane St. **Map** 1 C1. **Tel** (212) 637-2019.
Ⓜ Chambers St, City Hall. **Open** 9am–5pm Mon–Sat. Ⓦ nps.gov/afbg
African Burial Ground Visitor Center: 290 Broadway. **Open** 10am–4pm Tue–Sat.

This elegant, black granite monument occupies a portion of a cemetery that previously lay outside the city. Once the only place African slaves could be buried, the site was accidentally discovered in 1991, with the exhumation of 419 skeletons. After being examined, the remains were reinterred here in 2003.

The Visitor Center, located around the corner, offers an interactive exhibition that traces the history of slavery in New York.

The Georgian interior of St. Paul's Chapel

LOWER EAST SIDE

Nowhere does the strong ethnic flavor of New York come through more tangibly than in the Lower East Side, where immigrants began to settle in the late 19th century. Here Italians, Chinese, Jews, and, more recently, Dominicans established distinct neighborhoods, preserving their languages, customs, foods, and religions in the midst of a strange land. Since the 1980s, Chinatown – Manhattan's most densely populated ethnic neighborhood – has pushed into Little Italy, now a narrow strip along Mulberry Street. Both are colorful neighborhoods with a host of fun places to eat. To the north is the Nolita, home to chic boutiques, restaurants, and bars.

Sights at a Glance

Historic Streets and Buildings
1 Bowery Savings Bank
2 Old Police Headquarters
3 Little Italy and Nolita
5 Chinatown
11 Orchard Street
14 East Houston Street

Parks and Squares
7 Columbus Park

Museums and Galleries
4 Museum of Chinese in America
9 Museum at Eldridge Street
10 Lower East Side Tenement Museum
16 New Museum of Contemporary Art
17 FusionArts Museum
21 International Center of Photography

Shops and Markets
6 Ten Ren Tea
12 The Pickle Guys
18 Economy Candy
20 Essex Street Market

Churches and Synagogues
8 Mahayana Buddhist Temple
13 Bialystoker Synagogue
15 Basilica of St. Patrick's Old Cathedral
19 Angel Orensanz Center

Restaurants *see pp294–9*
1 Beauty & Essex
2 Congee Village
3 Freemans
4 Joe's Shanghai
5 Katz's Delicatessen
6 Lombardi's
7 Nom Wah Tea Parlor
8 Mission Cantina
9 Pho Pasteur
10 Public
11 Russ & Daughters Cafe
12 Sammy's Roumanian
13 Stanton Social

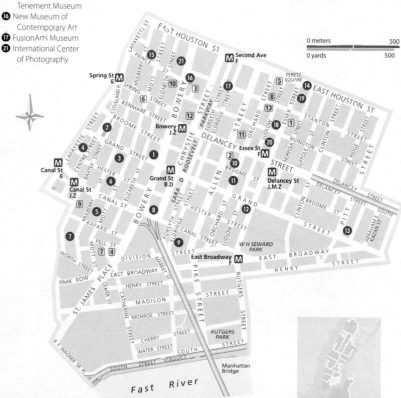

See also Street Finder maps 4, 5

◀ Striking facade of the New Museum of Contemporary Art

For keys to symbols *see back flap*

Street by Street: Little Italy and Chinatown

Manhattan's largest and most colorful ethnic neighborhood is Chinatown, which is growing so rapidly that it is overrunning nearby Little Italy as well as the Lower East Side. Streets here teem with grocery stores, gift shops, and hundreds of Chinese restaurants; even the plainest offer good food. What is left of Little Italy can be found at Mulberry and Grand streets, where old-world flavor abounds.

The market stalls on Canal Street have a wide range of bargains in new and used clothes and fresh produce.

Canal Street subway (lines R, N, Q, 6)

The Eastern States Buddhist Temple at 64b Mott Street contains over 100 golden Buddhas.

❺ ★ Chinatown
Home to a thriving – and still expanding – community of Chinese immigrants, this area is famous for its restaurants and hectic street life. The area truly comes alive around the Chinese New Year in January or February.

❼ Columbus Park
Once a slum, this park now fills with residents playing mahjong.

Bloody Angle, where Doyers Street turns sharply, was the gruesome site of many gangland ambushes during the 1920s.

Chatham Square has a memorial dedicated to the Chinese-American war dead, and to Lin Zexu, a Qing dynasty official, revered for his crackdown on the opium trade.

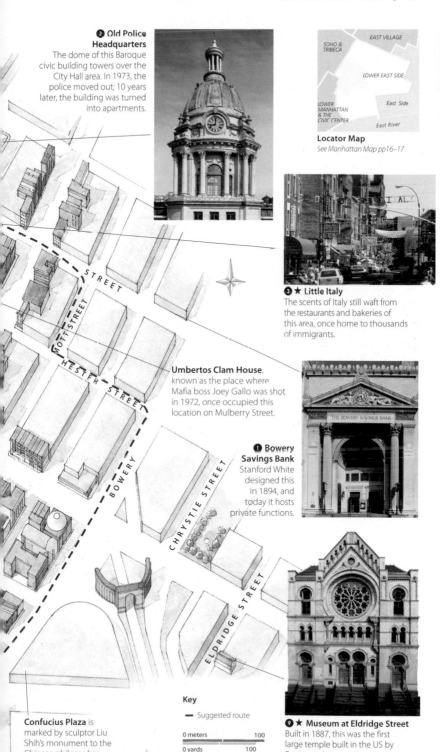

❷ Old Police Headquarters
The dome of this Baroque civic building towers over the City Hall area. In 1973, the police moved out; 10 years later, the building was turned into apartments.

Locator Map
See Manhattan Map pp16–17

SOHO & TRIBECA
EAST VILLAGE
LOWER EAST SIDE
LOWER MANHATTAN & THE CIVIC CENTER
East Side
East River

❸ ★ Little Italy
The scents of Italy still waft from the restaurants and bakeries of this area, once home to thousands of immigrants.

Umbertos Clam House, known as the place where Mafia boss Joey Gallo was shot in 1972, once occupied this location on Mulberry Street.

❶ Bowery Savings Bank
Stanford White designed this in 1894, and today it hosts private functions.

Confucius Plaza is marked by sculptor Liu Shih's monument to the Chinese philosopher.

Key

— Suggested route

0 meters 100
0 yards 100

❾ ★ Museum at Eldridge Street
Built in 1887, this was the first large temple built in the US by European Jews.

❶ Bowery Savings Bank

130 Bowery. **Map** 4 F4.
Ⓜ Grand St, Bowery.

Imposing inside and out, this Classical Revival building was built for the Bowery Savings Bank in 1894. Architect Stanford White designed the ornamented lime-stone facade to wrap around the rival Butchers' and Drovers' Bank, which refused to sell the corner plot. The interior is decorated with marble pillars and a ceiling scattered with gilded rosettes.

By the mid-20th century, the bank was a contrast to the Bowery with its vagrants and flophouses. It is now the site of opulent Capitale, and open only for private functions.

❷ Old Police Headquarters

240 Centre St. **Map** 4 F4. Ⓜ Canal St.
Closed to the public.

Completed in 1909, this was a fitting home for the city's new professional police force. The main portico and end pavilions have Corinthian columns, and the dome dominates the sky-line. However, lack of space meant the headquarters had to fit into a wedge-shaped site in the midst of Little Italy.

For nearly three-quarters of a century, this was where

Decorative detail from Bowery Savings Bank

"New York's finest" came to work. During Prohibition, Grand Street from here to the Bowery was known as "Bootleggers' Row," and alcohol was easily obtained, except when a police raid was due. The liquor merchants paid handsomely for a tip-off from inside police headquarters.

The police moved to different head-quarters in 1973, and in 1987 the building was converted into a luxury cooperative apartment project.

A street scene in Little Italy

❸ Little Italy and Nolita

Streets around Mulberry St. **Map** 4 F4.
Ⓜ Canal St. Ⓦ littleitalynyc.com
Italian-American Museum: 155 Mulberry St. **Map** 4 F4. **Tel** (212) 965-9000. Ⓜ Canal St, Grand St.
Open noon–6pm Fri–Sun.
Ⓦ italianamericanmuseum.org

Originally inhabited by the Irish, Little Italy and Nolita (or NoLita, shortened from "north of Little Italy") saw an influx of Italian immigrants in the 1800s. Natives from Campania and Naples settled on Mulberry

Street, while the Sicilians stayed on Elizabeth Street. Mott Street was divided between people from Calabria and Puglia. However, after World War II, many Italians relocated to the suburbs and today, the district is much smaller – Mulberry Street is the only remaining Italian territory.

The most exciting time to visit is during the eleven-day Festa di San Gennaro (Feast of San Gennaro) around September 19 (see p54). Italians from around the city meet at Mulberry Street for a wild celebration of the patron saint of Naples. The street is full of stalls and Italian snack vendors, and there is much music and dancing.

Many of Little Italy's restaurants offer simple, rustic food served in friendly surroundings at reasonable prices. Some original cafés and *salumerias* (specialty food stores) still survive, such as Ferrara's at 195 Grand Street. For more information about the history of the area, the **Italian-American Museum**, located in the former Banca Stabile, is a great place to visit.

❹ Museum of Chinese in America

215 Centre St. **Map** 4 F4. **Tel** (212) 619-4785. Ⓜ Canal St. **Open** 11am–6pm Tue, Wed, & Fri–Sun, 11am–9pm Thu.
Ⓦ mocanyc.org

Visitors can learn about the Chinese-American experience from the 18th century to the present day, at this artful museum. The compelling mix of artifacts, interviews, and multimedia displays, provides an excellent overview of the past. The issues explored are historically significant – among others, the Chinese Exclusion Act of 1882, which forbade Chinese workers entry for ten years; and the immigration quotas imposed in the early 20th century, such as the 1924 National Origins Provision (NOP), which restricted entry further.

Stonework figures adorning the Old Police Headquarters building

A Chinese grocer tending his shop on Canal Street

The exhibits flag various historical and cultural phases in the Chinese-American narrative – from the emergence of "Chop-Suey" restaurants and so-called "Yellowface" movies in the 1930s, to the evolution of identity after the 1960s for second-generation Chinese-Americans. In 1965, the Immigration Act did away with the NOP, and almost twenty thousand Chinese immigrants arrived in Chinatown.

The museum was designed by Maya Lin, best known for her creation of the Vietnam Memorial in Washington, D. C. Galleries are arranged around a sunlit courtyard, reminiscent of a traditional Chinese house.

Bright street signs along the roads in Chinatown

❺ Chinatown

Streets around Mott St. **Map** 4 F5. Ⓜ Canal St. Eastern States Buddhist Temple: 64b Mott St. **Open** 9am–6pm daily. Ⓦ **explorechinatown.com**

Since the 1850s, Chinese immigrants have been settling in this part of New York, making Chinatown one of the biggest and oldest Chinese districts in the West. The neighborhood is divided by the east–west thoroughfare of Canal Street, with Mott Street cutting north–south. The streets around, which include Pell, Bayard, Doyers, and the Bowery, are lined with fresh fish and fruit stalls, dim sum restaurants, souvenir and antiques stores, and tea-and-rice shops.

On the corner of Pell Street and the Bowery lies Huang Daxian Temple, one of the few remaining Taoist temples, with a converted shop front. Further along Pell Street, No. 16 is the headquarters of the Hip Sing Tong, once a secret society. During an attack in 1924, 70 people were killed when On Leong Tong, part of a criminal fraternity, attacked the building. Halfway along Pell is tiny, crooked Doyers Street, once known as the "Bloody Angle" for its role as battleground during the Tong Wars in the early 1900s.

Today more than 100,000 Chinese-Americans live here. Many visit the neighborhood to sample the cuisine, but there is more to do here than eat. There are galleries, curio shops, and Asian festivals (see p55). To glimpse another side of

Chinatown, step into the incense-scented Eastern States Buddhist Temple at 64 Mott Street, where offerings are piled up before tiny golden Buddhas.

❻ Ten Ren Tea

75 Mott St. **Map** 4 F5. **Tel** (212) 349-2286. Ⓜ Canal St. **Open** 10am–8pm daily. Ⓦ **tenrenusa.com**

This revered Taiwanese tea shop was established in the 1950s, and has remained a tea-lover's paradise. From costly oolong teas to cheap green teas, there is much to explore. The "Oriental Beauty," a heavily fermented oolong with a delicious touch of honey, is one of the best available – some say it was Queen Victoria who gave the tea its name. You can sample teas while you shop, and for a more contemporary tea experience – think bubble tea – visit Ten Ren's Tea Time at 73 Mott Street.

Serene Columbus Park, located in bustling Chinatown

❼ Columbus Park

Map 4 F5. Ⓜ Canal St.

The tranquillity of Columbus Park today could not be further removed from the scene near this site in the early 1800s. The area, known as Mulberry Bend, was a red-light district, part of the infamous Five Points slum. Gangs with names such as the Dead Rabbits and the Plug Uglies roamed the streets. A murder a day was commonplace; even the police were afraid to pass through. Partly as a result of the writings of reformer Jacob Riis, the slum was taken down in 1892. The park is now the only open space in Chinatown.

Gold idol of Buddha on the main altar at the Mahayana Buddhist Temple

8 Mahayana Buddhist Temple

133 Canal St. **Map** 5 A5. **Tel** (212) 925-8787. Ⓜ Canal St. **Open** 8:30am–6pm daily. Ⓦ mahayana.us

Larger than its counterpart on Mott Street, this opulent Buddhist temple was built by the Ying family, who were from Ningbo, China. Constructed in 1997, the temple boasts classic Chinese designs, and the main altar contains a massive gold idol of the Buddha, bathed in blue neon lighting and surrounded by candles.
The 32 plaques along the walls tell the story of Buddha's life. A small shrine to Guanyin, the Chinese Goddess of Mercy, stands in the entrance hall. There is a small shop upstairs that sells statues, books, and other knick-knacks.

On the other side of the Bowery, the former Citizens Savings Bank is a local landmark, its Neo-Byzantine bronze dome completed in 1924. The building now functions as a branch of HSBC.

9 Museum at Eldridge Street

12 Eldridge St. **Map** 5 A5. **Tel** (212) 219-0888. Ⓜ East Broadway. **Open** 10am–5pm Sun–Thu, 10am–3pm Fri. 🅿 ♿ 🎥 Every half-hour from 10am until 3pm. 📷 Ⓦ eldridgestreet.org

Constructed in 1887, this was the first synagogue to be built by the Eastern European Orthodox Jews in the US. In 2007, the site opened as a museum, after an overhawling restoration. The facade is a grand hybrid of Romanesque, Moorish, and Gothic influences in terracotta and brick, but the real attraction is the sanctuary upstairs. Visitors can view the stained-glass windows, stunning chandelier, rich woodwork, and painted ceiling within. The women's balcony offers a closer view of the detailed artwork. The rose window, an incredible Star of David roundel, looks stunning on the western wall. There are also displays that show the synagogue's state of

dilapidation in the early 1970s. Although the building is a functioning house of worship, its interiors can be explored with the help of guided tours. These begin on the lower level, where the Bes Medrash (House of Study) also serves as a synagogue.

🔟 Lower East Side Tenement Museum

97 Orchard St. **Map** 5 A4. **Tel** (212) 431-0233. Ⓜ Canal, Delancey, Essex, Grand St. **Open** for tours only. 🕐 every 15–30 mins; 11:45am–5pm Mon–Wed & Fri (until 6:30pm Thu), 10:30am–5pm Sat & Sun. 🅿 ♿ Lectures, films, videos. 📷 (daily). Ⓦ tenement.org

This building, dating from 1863, provides a rare opportunity to experience a claustrophobic and crumbling interior of a historic tenement. Apartments have been re-created to reflect the lives of their former tenants. There were no indoor toilets – two external toilets would have instead been shared among four families. Tenements also lacked any electricity, plumbing, or heating. The rooms give a real sense of the cramped and deplorable conditions in which so many lived.

Brick and terracotta facade of the Museum at Eldrige Street

Explore the building's past with the help of the themed guided tours. There are two-hour walking tours of the neighborhood as well. Tickets are available at the nearby visitor center, where an introductory video offers insight into the tours. There is also a great bookshop here.

⑪ Orchard Street

Map 5 A3. Ⓜ Delancey, Grand St.
See Shopping p314.
Ⓦ **lowereastsideny.com**

Jewish immigrants founded the New York garment industry on this street, named for the orchards that once stood here on James De Lancey's Colonial estate. For years the street was filled with pushcarts loaded with goods for sale. The pushcarts are long gone, and few of the shopkeepers are Jewish, but the flavor remains. On Sunday there is an outdoor market, and shoppers fill the street from Houston to Canal, looking for clothing bargains.

Orchard Street is also at the heart of the Lower East Side's gentrification. Boutiques and vintage stores nestle alongside bars, clubs, restaurants, and the boutique Blue Moon Hotel, formerly a tenement.

⑫ The Pickle Guys

49 Essex St. **Map** 5 B4. **Tel** (212) 656-9739. Ⓜ Grand St. **Open** 9am–6pm Sun–Thu, 9am–4pm Fri.
Ⓦ **pickleguys.com**

The scent of pickles permeates this little section of Essex Street, just as it did in the early 1900s, when Jewish pickle shops filled the area. True to the old Eastern European recipe, The Pickle Guys store their pickles in barrels filled with brine, garlic, and spices; this mixture preserves the pickles for months on end. Pickle varieties include full sour, three-quarters sour, half sour, new, and hot.

Barrels and cans of various pickles at The Pickle Guys

No chemicals or preservatives are added, and the shop operates to strict Kosher rules.

The store also carries pickled tomatoes, pickled celery, olives, mushrooms, hot peppers, sun-dried tomatoes, sweet kraut, sauerkraut, and herring. It is run like a family business, with a friendly, chatty atmosphere, which perpetuates the neighborhood's traditions

⑬ Bialystoker Synagogue

7–11 Willett St **Map** 5 C4.
Tel (212) 475-0165. Ⓜ Essex St.
✡ frequent services.
🕐 7–10am Mon–Thu (call in advance). Ⓦ **bialystoker.org**

This 1826 Federal-style building was originally the Willett Street Methodist Church. It was bought in 1905 by Jewish immigrants from the Bialystok province of Poland, who converted it into a synagogue.

The synagogue has a beautiful interior, with lovely stained-glass windows, a three-story carved wooden ark, and murals representing views of the Holy Land and the signs of the zodiac, including an interesting oddity: a lobster meant to represent Cancer, the crab. There is also a memorial plaque to the infamous mobster Benjamin "Bugsy" Siegel, who prayed here as a child.

Mural representing the zodiac sign Cancer in Bialystoker Synagogue

⑭ East Houston Street

East Houston St. **Map** 4 F3, 5A3.
Ⓜ Second Ave.

The dividing line between
the Lower East Side and the
East Village, East Houston
between Forsyth and Ludlow
streets clearly demonstrates the
changing mix of old and new
in the area. Between Forsyth
and Eldridge streets is the
Yonah Schimmel Knish Bakery,
a fixture since 1890, still with
its original showcases. Further
down the block is the Sunshine
Theater, constructed as a
Dutch Church in the 1840s
and later used as a boxing
arena and a Yiddish vaudeville
theater. Today it shows art films.
    While much of the Jewish
flavor of the Lower East Side
has disappeared, there are
two survivors farther along
East Houston. Russ and
Daughters is a culinary
landmark, a third-generation
family business that began on
a pushcart, around 1907. At this
location since 1920, the store
has seen its fortunes change
with the neighborhood. It is
famed for traditional smoked
fish and herring, and has an
impressive stock of caviar.
    At the corner of Ludlow
Street is perhaps the best-
known and much-loved
survivor, the bustling Katz's
Delicatessen *(see p294)*,
established in 1888 and still
packing people in for pastrami
and corned beef sandwiches.

Beautiful interiors of the Basilica of
St. Patrick's Old Cathedral

⑮ Basilica of St. Patrick's Old Cathedral

263 Mulberry St. **Map** 4 F3.
Tel (212) 226-8075. Ⓜ Prince St.
Open 8am–12:30pm & 3:30–6pm
Thu–Tue. ✝ 9am & noon Mon–Fri;
5:30pm Sat; 9:15am & 12:45pm Sun;
Spanish: 11:30am Sun.
Ⓦ **oldcathedral.org**

The first St. Patrick's was
consecrated in 1815, making
this one of the oldest churches
in the city. When fire destroyed
the original in the 1860s, it was
rebuilt much as it is today. When
the archdiocese transferred the
see to the new St. Patrick's
Cathedral uptown *(see pp174–5)*,
Old St. Patrick's became the
local parish church, and it has
flourished despite a constantly
changing ethnic congregation.
    Below the church are vaults
the remains of, among others,
one of New York's most famous
families of restaurateurs, the
Delmonicos. Pierre Toussaint
was also buried here, but in
1990 his remains were moved
from the old graveyard beside
the church to a more prestigious
burial place in a crypt in the
new St. Patrick's Cathedral. Born
a slave in Haiti in 1766, Toussaint
was brought to New York, where
he lived as a free man and
became a prosperous wig-maker.
He later devoted himself to
caring for the poor, also tending
cholera victims and using his
money to build an orphanage.

⑯ New Museum of Contemporary Art

235 Bowery St. **Map** 4 E3. **Tel** (212)
219-1222. Ⓜ Spring St, Bowery.
Open 11am–6pm Wed–Sun (to 9pm
Thu). 🎨 free 7–9pm Thu. 🚻 ♿ 📷
Lectures, readings, music. 📷
Ⓦ **newmuseum.org**

Marcia Tucker left her post as the
Whitney Museum's Curator of
Painting and Sculpture in 1977 to
found this museum. Her aim was
to exhibit the kind of work she
felt was missing from more
traditional museums. She created
one of New York's most cutting-
edge exhibition spaces, which

Stunning architecture of the New Museum
of Contemporary Art

includes an innovative Media
Lounge for digital art, video
installations, and sound works.
    The rotating collection features
a wide range of art, from large-
scale photographs of 1960s
America to geometric abstracts.
The museum takes an inclusive
approach, showcasing both
emerging and established
artists, including Mark Rothko
and Roy Lichtenstein.
    The striking seven-story
building, designed by Tokyo-
based architects Sejima &
Nishizawa, is a notable addition
to this part of Manhattan. It rises
like a sculptural stack of glowing
cubes and is the first art
museum to be built in downtown Manhattan in over a century.
It has 60,000 sq ft (5,574 sq m) of
exhibition space, a theater, store,
café, and a rooftop terrace offering stunning views of the city.

⑰ FusionArts Museum

57 Stanton St. **Map** 5 A3. **Tel** (212)
995-5290. Ⓜ Second Ave-Houston St.
Open noon–6pm Tue–Fri & Sun. ♿
📷 Ⓦ **fusionartsmuseum.org**

With psychedelic metal sculptures
that give a foretaste of the pieces
displayed inside, the entrance to
this museum is hard to miss. It is
dedicated to showing "fusion art,"
defined as art in which various
artistic disciplines, such as
painting, sculpture, photography,
and video, meld to form a
distinct genre in themselves.

The museum's location gives it access to an underground art scene that uptown contemporary art museums often neglect, and it also offers lesser-known artists the opportunity to exhibit their work in a reputable gallery.

Many New York City artists who have been creating fusion art on the Lower East Side for several decades have already shown their work in group exhibitions here.

⑱ Economy Candy

108 Rivington St. **Map** 5 B3. **Tel** 1-800 352-4544. **M** Second Ave–Houston St. **Open** 10am–6pm Mon & Sat, 9am–6pm Tue–Fri & Sun. **W** economycandy.com

A Lower East Side landmark since 1937, this family-owned candy store stocks hundreds of varieties of candy, nuts, and dried fruit. Lined with floor-to-ceiling shelves packed with old-fashioned dispensers, the store is one of the few businesses on Lower East Side that has remained almost unchanged in name and specialty throughout the neighborhood's fluctuating fortunes over 50 or so years.

This is due in no small part to Jerry Cohen's enterprise in transforming his father's "Nosher's Paradise" from a penny candy store to a national company. The shop carries treats from all over the world, as well as numerous food items dipped in chocolate and 21 colors of candy-covered chocolate buttons.

⑲ Angel Orensanz Center

172 Norfolk St. **Map** 5 B3. **Tel** (212) 529-7194. **M** Essex St, Delancey St. **Open** 10am–5pm Mon–Fri and by appt. **&** **W** orensanz.org

Built in 1849, this cherry-red Neo-Gothic structure was once the oldest synagogue in New York. With ceilings 54 ft (16 m) high and seating for 1,500, it was also the largest in the United States at the time. It was designed by the Berlin architect Alexander Saelzer in the tradition of the German

Interior of the Angel Orensanz Center, once a large synagogue

Reform Movement, and resembles Cologne Cathedral and the Friedrichswerdersche Kirche in the Mitte district in Berlin.

After World War II and the decline of Lower East Side's Yiddish population, the synagogue was one of many to close. In 1986, the building was acquired by Spanish sculptor Angel Orensanz, who turned it into an art studio. It now serves as a spiritual and cultural center with a program of events.

⑳ Essex Street Market

120 Essex St. **Map** 5 B3. **Tel** (212) 312-3603/388-0449. **M** Essex St, Delancey St. **Open** 8am–7pm Mon–Sat, 10am–6pm Sun. **W** essexstreetmarket.com

This indoor market was created in 1939 by Mayor Fiorello H. La Guardia to bring pushcart

vendors together and out of the way of traffic, especially police cars and fire trucks that used the narrow streets.

Two dozen meat, cheese, produce, and spice stalls fill the market. Shopsin's, an iconic diner from Greenwich Village, is among the stalls here. Also here are the Essex Restaurant, which serves Latin/Jewish fare, and Cuchifritos, an art gallery showing the work of the neighborhood's artists.

㉑ International Center of Photography

250 Bowery. **Map** 4 F3. **Tel** (212) 857-0000. **M** 2nd Ave. **Open** 10am–6pm Tue, Wed, Sat & Sun; 10am–8pm Thu & Fri. **Closed** major hols. **& & ** 10am–5pm Tue–Sun. **W** icp.org

This museum was founded by Cornell Capa in 1974 to conserve the work of such photojournalists as his brother Robert, who was killed on assignment in 1954. The collection of 12,500 original prints includes work by top photographers including Ansel Adams, Henri Cartier-Bresson, and W. Eugene Smith.

Special, temporary exhibitions are organized from the Center's archive as well as from outside sources. The museum moved into its current premises in 2016.

Items on display at the indoor Essex Street Market

SOHO AND TRIBECA

Shops, eateries, and architecture are the lures that have transformed these formerly industrial districts. SoHo (south of Houston) was threatened with demolition in the 1960s until preservationists drew attention to its rare historic cast-iron architecture. The district was saved, and by the 1980s SoHo offered a vibrant art scene in New York. Today,

the area serves as an enormous outdoor shopping mall, scattered with bars and bistros. TriBeCa (Triangle Below Canal), once a wholesale food district, contains the spacious loft apartments of famous celebrities and Robert De Niro helped found both the Tribeca Film Center and the Tribeca Film Festival in 2002.

Sights at a Glance

Historic Streets and Buildings
1 Haughwout Building
2 St. Nicholas Hotel
3 Greene Street
4 Singer Building
8 Harrison Street

Museums and Galleries
5 Children's Museum of the Arts
6 New York Earth Room
7 New York City Fire Museum

Parks and Squares
9 Hudson River Park

Restaurants see pp294–9
1 Aquagrill
2 Balthazar
3 Boqueria
4 Bouley
5 Bubby's
6 Dos Caminos
7 The Dutch
8 L'Ecole
9 Hundred Acres
10 Locanda Verde
11 Mission Chinese Food
12 Megu
13 Nobu
14 Odeon
15 Spring Street Natural
16 Veselka

| 0 meters | | 500 |
| 0 yards | | 500 |

◀ Cast-iron facades in TriBeCa with Art Deco tower in the background

See also Street Finder map 3, 4

For keys to symbols see back flap

Street by Street: SoHo Cast-Iron Historic District

The largest concentration of cast-iron architecture in the world *(see p44)* survives in the area between West Houston and Canal streets. The heart of the district is Greene Street, where 50 buildings erected between 1869 and 1895 are found on five cobblestoned blocks. Most of their intricately designed cast-iron facades are in the Neo-Classical Revival style, with Corinthian columns and pediments. Mass-produced in a foundry, they were relatively inexpensive, and easy to erect and maintain. Now they are rare works of industrial art, well suited to the present character of this district.

West Broadway, as it passes through SoHo, combines striking architecture with a string of art galleries, shoe shops, designer boutiques, and small restaurants.

The Broken Kilometer, at 393 West Broadway, is an installation by Walter De Maria *(see p101)*. Its 500 brass rods are arranged to play tricks with perspective. Laid end to end, the rods would measure 3,280 ft (1,000 m).

72–76 Greene Street, the "King of Greene Street," is a splendid Corinthian-columned building. It was the creation of Isaac F. Duckworth, one of the masters of cast-iron design.

Performing Garage is a tiny experimental theater that pioneers the work of avant-garde artists.

WEST BROADWAY
WOOSTER STREET
BROOME STREET
GREENE STREET
GRAND STREET

Canal Street-Broadway subway (2 blocks)

❸ ★ Greene Street
Of all Greene Street's fine cast-iron buildings, one of the best is 28–30, the "Queen," which was erected by Duckworth in 1872 and has a tall mansard roof.

10–14 Greene Street dates from 1869. Note the glass circles in the risers of the iron stoop – these allowed daylight to reach the basement.

15–17 Greene Street is a late addition, dating from 1895, in a simple Corinthian style.

❹ ★ Singer Building
This terracotta beauty was built in 1904 for the famous sewing machine company.

Richard Haas, the prolific muralist, has transformed a blank wall into a convincing cast-iron frontage.

Locator Map
See Manhattan Map pp16–17

Key

— Suggested route

Prince Street subway station (lines N, R)

Dean & DeLuca is one of the best gourmet food stores in New York. Its range includes a global choice of coffee beans (see p330).

101 Spring Street, with its simple, geometric facade and large windows, is a fine example of the style that led to the skyscraper.

Spring Street subway station

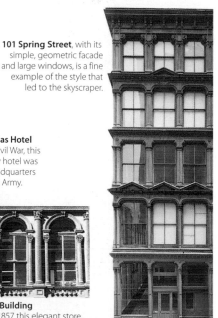

❷ St. Nicholas Hotel
During the Civil War, this former luxury hotel was used as a headquarters for the Union Army.

0 meters 100
0 yards 100

❶ Haughwout Building
Dating back to, 1857 this elegant store, featured the first Otis safety elevator.

Haughwout Building facade

❶ Haughwout Building

488–492 Broadway. **Map** 4 E4.
Ⓜ Canal St, Spring St.

This cast-iron building was erected in 1857 for the E.V. Haughwout china and glassware company, which once supplied the White House. The design is superb: rows of windows are framed by arches set on columns flanked by taller columns. Mass-produced sections repeat the pattern over and over. The building was the first to use a steam-driven Otis safety elevator, an innovation that made the skyscraper a possibility.

❷ St. Nicholas Hotel

521–523 Broadway. **Map** 4 E4.
Ⓜ Prince St, Spring St.

English parliamentarian W. E. Baxter, visiting New York in 1854, reported of the recently opened St. Nicholas Hotel: "Every carpet is of velvet pile; chair covers and curtains are made of silk or satin damask... and the embroidery on the mosquito nettings itself might be exhibited to royalty."

St. Nicholas Hotel in its heyday in the mid-19th century

It is small wonder, then, that it cost over $1 million to build – and with profits of over $50,000 for that year it must have seemed money well spent. Its glory was short-lived, however. In the Civil War it served as a Union Army headquarters. Afterward, the better hotels followed the entertainment district uptown, and by the mid-1870s the St. Nicholas had closed. There is little left on the ground floor to attest to its former opulence, but look up to the remains of its once-stunning marble facade.

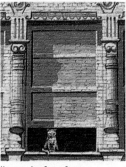

Haas mural on Greene Street

❸ Greene Street

Map 4 E4. Ⓜ Canal St.

This is the heart of SoHo's Cast-Iron District. Along five cobblestoned blocks are 50 cast-iron buildings dating from 1869 to 1895. The block between Broome and Spring streets has 13 full cast-iron facades, and from 8–34 is the longest row of cast-iron buildings in the world. Those at 72–76 are known as the "King of Greene Street," but 28–30, the "Queen," is considered to be the finest. The architecture is best appreciated as a streetscape, with row upon row of columned facades. Walk into any of the

stores housed within to see the spacious interior lofts. At the corner of Greene and Prince streets, the illusionistic muralist Richard Haas has created an eye-catching work, disguising a plain brick sidewall as a cast-iron frontage. Look for the detail of the little gray cat, which sits primly in an "open window."

❹ Singer Building

561–563 Broadway. **Map** 4 E3.
Ⓜ Prince St.

The "little" Singer Building built by Ernest Flagg in 1904 is the second and smaller Flagg structure by this name, and many critics think it superior to the 41-story tower on lower Broadway that was torn down in 1967. The charmingly ornate building is adorned with wrought-iron balconies and graceful arches painted in striking dark green. The 12-story facade of terra-cotta, glass, and steel was advanced for its day, a forerunner of the metal and glass walls to come in the 1940s and 1950s. The building was an office and warehouse for the Singer sewing machine company, and the original Singer name can be seen cast in iron above the entrance to the Mango store on Prince Street.

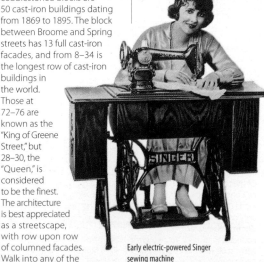

Early electric-powered Singer sewing machine

❺ Children's Museum of the Arts

103 Charlton St. **Map** 3 C4. **Tel** (212) 274-0986. **M** Houston St. 🚌 M20, M21. **Open** noon–5pm Mon, noon–6pm Thu & Fri, 10am–5pm Sat & Sun. 🗺️ ♿ **W** cmany.org

Founded in 1988, this innovative museum aims to make the most of children's artistic potential by providing plenty of hands-on activities, sing-alongs, workshops, and performances. Children aged 1–12 can busy themselves with paint, glue, paper, and other messy materials to create their own drawings and sculptures. For inspiration, displays of work by local artists are exhibited alongside examples of children's art from around the world. Kids can play around in the dressing-up room and the ball pond, and the museum also hosts a varied program of events appealing to children and families.

Brightly colored exhibition space at the Children's Museum of the Arts

❻ New York Earth Room

141 Wooster St. **Map** 4 E3. **Tel** (212) 989-5566. **M** Prince St. **Open** noon–3pm & 3:30–6pm Wed–Sun. **Closed** mid-Jun–mid-Sep. ♿ ✉️ **W** diaart.org/sites/main/earthroom

Of the three Earth Rooms created by conceptual artist Walter De Maria (1935–2013), this is the only one still in existence. Commissioned by the Dia Art Foundation in 1977, the interior earth sculpture consists of 280,000 lb (127,000 kg) of dirt

piled 22 inches (56 cm) deep in a 3,600-sq-ft (334-sq-m) room. *The Broken Kilometer*, another sculpture by De Maria, can be seen at 393 West Broadway. It is composed of 500 solid brass rods arranged in five parallel rows.

A 1901 La France horse drawn steam pumper in the City Fire Museum.

❼ New York City Fire Museum

278 Spring St. **Map** 4 D4. **Tel** (212) 691-1303. **M** Spring St. **Open** 10am–5pm daily. **Closed** public hols. 🗺️ ♿ 📷 **W** nycfiremuseum.org

This museum is housed in a Beaux Arts–style 1904 firehouse. New York City's unsurpassed collection of firefighting equipment and memorabilia from the 18th century to 1917 includes scale models, bells, and hydrants. Upstairs, fire engines are neatly lined up for an 1890 parade. An interactive fire simulation, available for groups, gives an insight into firefighting. The museum's first floor features an exhibition on 9/11, filled with tributes.

❽ Harrison Street

Map 4 D5. **M** Chambers St.

Surrounded by modern high-rise blocks, this rare row of eight beautifully restored Federal town houses, with their pitched roofs and distinctive dormer windows, almost seems like a stage set. The houses were constructed in the late 1700s and early 1800s. Two of the buildings were designed by John McComb, Jr., New York's first major native-born architect,

and were moved from Washington Street, their original site, for preservation purposes. The houses had previously been used as warehouses and were about to be razed to the ground, when, in 1969, the Landmarks Preservation Commission intervened to secure the necessary funding to enable them to be restored. They are now privately owned.

On the other side of the high-rise complex is Washington Market Park. This area was formerly the site of New York City's wholesale produce center. The market relocated to the Bronx in the 1970s.

❾ Hudson River Park

Map 4 E5. **Tel** (212) 627-2020. **M** Canal St, Franklin St, Houston St. **W** hudsonriverpark.org

Immediately beyond West Side Highway is the Hudson River Park, a landscaped promenade that stretches north towards Chelsea and Midtown. Visitors can walk to the tip of the island along the shady Battery Park City Esplanade all the way to Battery Park. The once-decaying piers and wharves have been transformed, with fountains, gardens, dog parks, and tennis courts. Pier 25 features Grand Banks, an oyster bar on an old sailing ship, mini-golf and beach volley-ball, plus a host of snack stalls.

View of the city skyline from Hudson River Park

GREENWICH VILLAGE

Since the 1920s, Greenwich Village has been the bohemian heart of New York. Popularly known as the West Village, or just "the Village," the area became a sanctuary for city dwellers during the yellow fever epidemic in 1822. The 1950s saw the emerging Beat Movement, while the 1960s witnessed folk singers, such as Bob Dylan, beginning their careers here. The Stonewall Riots of 1969, which initiated the gay rights movement, began at the Stonewall Inn.

With its quaint streets and charming brownstones, Greenwich Village is one of the city's more artistic, liberal neighborhoods. It has steadily become an expensive part of Manhattan, with large expanses owned by New York University.

Sights at a Glance

Historic Streets and Buildings
1 St. Luke's Place
2 75½ Bedford Street
3 Grove Court
4 Isaacs-Hendricks House
6 Meatpacking District
8 Jefferson Market Courthouse
9 Patchin Place
11 Salmagundi Club
14 Washington Mews
15 New York University

Museums and Galleries
5 *Whitney Museum of Art pp 108–9*
10 Grey Art Gallery

Churches
12 First Presbyterian Church
13 Church of the Ascension
16 Judson Memorial Church

Parks and Squares
7 Sheridan Square
17 Washington Square

See also Street Finder maps 3, 4

☐ **Restaurants** *see pp294–9*
1 Babbo
2 Blue Hill
3 Blue Ribbon Bakery
4 Corner Bistro
5 Da Silvano
6 Fatty Crab
7 Gotham Bar & Grill
8 Jane
9 Kesté
10 The Little Owl
11 Lupa
12 Minetta Tavern
13 Moustache
14 One if by Land, Two if by Sea
15 Otto
16 Pearl Oyster Bar
17 Spice Market
18 The Spotted Pig
19 The Standard Grill
20 Strip House
21 Tertulia
22 The Waverly Inn and Garden
23 Westville

0 meters 500
0 yards 300

◀ Entrance to a charming, old-fashioned house in Greenwich Village

For keys to symbols *see back flap*

Street by Street: Greenwich Village

A stroll through historic Greenwich Village is a feast of unexpected small pleasures – charming row houses, hidden alleys, and leafy courtyards. The often quirky architecture suits the bohemian air of the Village. Many famous people, particularly artists and writers, such as playwright Eugene O'Neill and actor Dustin Hoffman, have made their homes in the houses and apartments that line these old-fashioned narrow streets. By night, the Village really comes alive. Late-night coffeehouses and cafés, experimental theaters, and music clubs, including some of the city's best jazz venues, beckon you at every turn.

The Lucille Lortel Theater is at No. 121 Christopher Street; it opened in 1955 with *The Threepenny Opera*.

Christopher Street, popular with New York's gay community, is lined with all kinds of shops, bookstores, and bars.

Twin Peaks at No. 102 Bedford Street began life in 1830 as an ordinary house. It was rebuilt in 1926 by architect Clifford Daily to house artists, writers, and actors. Daily believed that the quirky house would help their creativity flourish.

❸ **Grove Court**
Six houses dating from 1853–4 are set at the back of a quiet leafy courtyard.

The building at 90 Bedford Street was used as the exterior of Monica's apartment block in the TV sitcom *Friends*.

❶ ★ **St. Luke's Place**
This beautiful row of Italianate houses was built in the 1850s.

Christopher St subway

❷ **No. 75½ Bedford Street**
Built in 1873 in an alley, this is the city's narrowest house. The poet Edna St. Vincent Millay lived here in the 1920s.

To Houston Street subway (2 blocks)

The Cherry Lane Theatre was founded in 1924. Originally a brewery, it was one of the first of the Off-Broadway theaters.

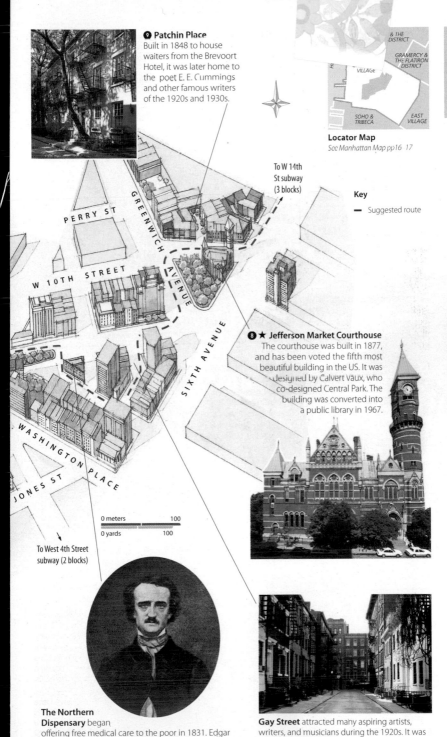

❾ Patchin Place
Built in 1848 to house waiters from the Brevoort Hotel, it was later home to the poet E. E. Cummings and other famous writers of the 1920s and 1930s.

Locator Map
See Manhattan Map pp16–17

Key
— Suggested route

To W 14th St subway (3 blocks)

PERRY ST
GREENWICH AVENUE
W 10TH STREET
SIXTH AVENUE
WASHINGTON PLACE
JONES ST

❽ ★ Jefferson Market Courthouse
The courthouse was built in 1877, and has been voted the fifth most beautiful building in the US. It was designed by Calvert Vaux, who co-designed Central Park. The building was converted into a public library in 1967.

0 meters 100
0 yards 100

To West 4th Street subway (2 blocks)

The Northern Dispensary began offering free medical care to the poor in 1831. Edgar Allan Poe (1809–49) was treated here for a cold in 1837. Since 1998, the building has been unoccupied.

Gay Street attracted many aspiring artists, writers, and musicians during the 1920s. It was the setting for Ruth McKenney's novel *My Sister Eileen* and the film *Carlito's Way* (1993).

Row houses on St. Luke's Place, a street with literary associations

❶ St. Luke's Place

Map 3 C3. Ⓜ Houston St.

Fifteen attractive row houses, dating from the 1850s, line the north side of this street. The park opposite is named for a previous resident of St. Luke's Place, Mayor Jimmy Walker, the popular dandy who ran the city from 1926 until he was forced to resign after a financial scandal in 1932. In front of the house at No. 6 are the tall lamps that always identify a mayor's home in New York. The most recognizable house on the block is probably No. 10, used as the exterior of the Huxtable family home in *The Cosby Show* (although the series places it in Brooklyn). This is also the block where *Wait Until Dark* was filmed, starring Audrey Hepburn as a blind woman living at No. 4. Theodore Dreiser and the poet Marianne Moore are just two of the several writers who have lived here. Dreiser wrote *An American Tragedy* while living at No. 16. One block north, the corner of Hudson and Morton streets marked the edge of the Hudson River in the 18th century.

Mayor's lamp at No. 6

❷ 75½ Bedford Street

Map 3 C2. Ⓜ Houston St. **Closed** to the public. Ⓦ **cherrylanetheatre.org**

New York's narrowest home, just 9½ ft (2.9 m) wide, was built in 1893 in a former passageway. The poet Edna St. Vincent Millay lived here briefly, followed by the actor John Barrymore, and later Cary Grant. The three-story building, now renovated, is marked by a plaque.

Just around the corner, at 38 Commerce Street, Miss Millay founded the Cherry Lane Theater in 1924 as a site for avant-garde drama. It still premieres new works. Its biggest hit was the 1960s musical *Godspell*.

❸ Grove Court

Map 3 C2. Ⓜ Christopher St/ Sheridan Sq.

An enterprising grocer named Samuel Cocks built the six town houses here, in an area formed by a bend in the street. (The bends in this part of the Village originally marked divisions between colonial properties.) Cocks reckoned that having residents in the empty passage between 10 and 12 Grove Street would help his business at No. 18.

But residential courts, now highly prized, were not considered respectable in 1854, and the lowbrow residents attracted to the area earned it the nickname "Mixed Ale Alley." O. Henry later chose this block as the setting for his 1902 work *The Last Leaf*.

Isaacs-Hendricks House

❹ Isaacs-Hendricks House

77 Bedford St. **Map** 3 C2. Ⓜ Houston St. **Closed** to the public.

This is the oldest surviving home in the Village, built in 1799. The old clapboard walls are visible on the sides and rear; the brickwork and third floor came later. The first owner, John Isaacs, bought the land for $295 in 1794. Next came Harmon Hendricks, a copper dealer and associate of revolutionary Paul Revere. Robert Fulton, who used copper for the boilers in his steamboat, was one of Hendricks's customers.

❺ Whitney Museum of Art

See pp108–109.

❻ Meatpacking District

Map 3 B1 Ⓜ 14th St (on lines A, C, E); 8th Ave L.

Once the domain of butchers in blood-stained aprons hacking at sides of beef, these days (and particularly nights) the Meatpacking District is very different. Squeezed into an area

The mid-19th-century town houses at Grove Court

south of 14th Street and west of 9th Avenue, the neighborhood is now dotted with trendy clubs, lounges, and boutique hotels that swell with New Yorkers out for a good time. The neighborhood's hipness factor rose when Soho House, the New York branch of the London private members' club, moved in, followed by the classy Hotel Gansevoort, with its rooftop swimming pool. Fashionable clothiers, including Stella McCartney and Marc Jacobs, have outlets here; upscale restaurants have opened; and new nightclubs and bars pop up every month.

The great allures of the Meatpacking District are the Whitney Museum of American Art (see pp108–9), and the High Line (see p134), which begins on Gansevoort Street. The face of the neighborhood may be forever changed, but club-hoppers might still catch the occasional whiff of the meat-processing business that gave the area its name.

❼ Sheridan Square

Map 3 C2. Ⓜ Christopher St-Sheridan Sq.

This square, where seven streets converge, is the heart of the Village. It was named for the Civil War General Philip Sheridan, who became commander in chief of the US Army in 1883. His statue stands in nearby Christopher Park.

The Draft Riots of 1863 took place here. Over a century later, another famous disturbance rocked the square. The Stonewall Inn on Christopher Street was a gay bar, at a time when it was illegal for gays to gather in bars, that had stayed in business by paying off the police. However, on June 28, 1969, the patrons rebelled, and in the pitched battle that ensued police officers were barricaded inside the bar. It was a landmark moral victory for the budding gay rights movement. The inn that stands today is not the original. The Village remains a focus for the city's gay community.

"Old Jeff," the pointed tower of Jefferson Market Courthouse

❽ Jefferson Market Courthouse

425 Ave of the Americas. **Map** 4 D1. **Tel** (212) 243-4334. Ⓜ W 4th St-Washington Sq. **Open** 10am–8pm Mon & Wed, 11am–6pm Tue & Thu, 10am–5pm Fri & Sat. **Closed** public hols. Ⓐ Ⓦ nypl.org

This treasured Village landmark was saved from the wrecking ball and converted into a branch of the New York Public Library through a spirited preservation campaign that began at a Christmas party in the late 1950s.

In 1833 the site became a market named after former president Thomas Jefferson. Its fire lookout tower had a giant bell that was rung to alert the neighborhood's volunteer firefighters. In 1865, the founding of the municipal fire department made the bell obsolete, and the Third Judicial District, or Jefferson Market, Courthouse was built. With its Venetian Gothic-style spires and turrets, it was named one of the ten most beautiful buildings in the country when it opened in 1877. The old fire bell was installed in the tower. Here, in 1906, Harry Thaw was tried for Stanford White's murder (see p122). By 1945,

Statue of General Sheridan in Christopher Park

the market had moved, court sessions had been discontinued, the four-sided clock had stopped, and the building was threatened with demolition. In the 1950s, preservationists campaigned first to restore the clock and then the whole building. Its renovation was undertaken by architect Giorgio Cavaglieri, who preserved many of the original details, including the stained glass and a spiral staircase that now leads to the library's dungeonlike reference room.

A busy street in the trendy Meatpacking District

❾ Patchin Place

W 10th St. **Map** 4 D1. Ⓜ W 4th St-Washington Sq.

One of many delightful and unexpected pockets in the Village is this tiny block of small residences. It is lined with ailanthus trees that were planted in order to "absorb the bad air." The houses were built in the mid-19th century for Basque waiters working at the Brevoort Hotel on Fifth Avenue.

Later, the houses became fashionable addresses, with many writers living here. The poet E. E. Cummings lived at No. 4 from 1923 until his death in 1962. The English poet laureate John Masefield also lived on the block, as did the playwright Eugene O'Neill and John Reed, whose eyewitness account of the Russian Revolution, *Ten Days That Shook The World* was made into a film, *Reds* (1981), directed by Warren Beatty.

❺ Whitney Museum of American Art

The Whitney Museum is the foremost show-case for American art of the 20th and 21st centuries. It was founded in 1930 by sculptor Gertrude Vanderbilt Whitney after the Metropolitan Museum of Art turned down her collection of works by artists such as Bellows and Hopper. From 1966, the Whitney was located on the Upper East Side. It moved to the present building designed, by Renzo Piano, in 2015. The Whitney Biennial, held in even years, is the most significant exhibition of new trends in American art.

The angular exterior of the Whitney Museum

Floor 8

Three Flags (1958)
Jasper Johns's use of familiar objects in an abstract form was influential in the development of Pop Art.

Library

Floor 7

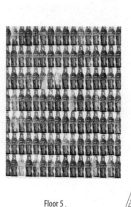

Green Coca-Cola Bottles
Andy Warhol's 1962 work is a commentary on mass production and monopoly.

Floor 5

Little Big Painting
The 1965 work by Roy Lichtenstein is a comic critique of Abstract Expressionist painting.

Theater

Early Sunday Morning (1930)
Edward Hopper's paintings often convey the emptiness of American city life.

Museum Guide

The sixth and seventh floors showcase pieces from the museum's collection – there is not a permanent display, rather a constant rotation of works. Special, temporary exhibitions occupy the first, fifth and eighth floors.

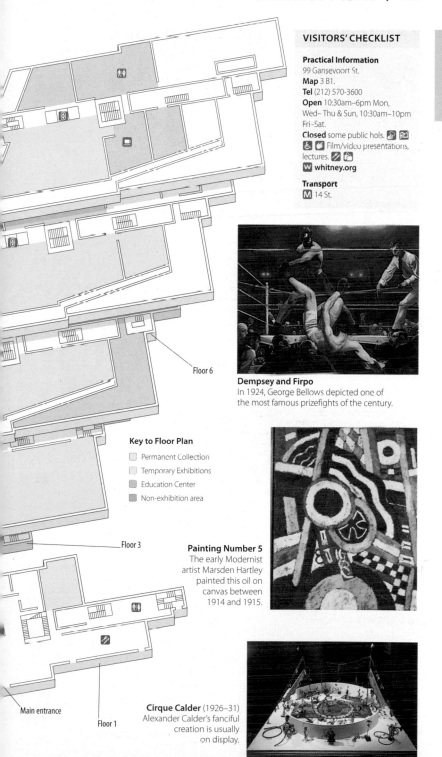

VISITORS' CHECKLIST

Practical Information
99 Gansevoort St.
Map 3 B1.
Tel (212) 570-3600
Open 10:30am–6pm Mon,
Wed– Thu & Sun, 10:30am–10pm
Fri–Sat.
Closed some public hols. 🎨 🎨
♿ 📷 Film/video presentations,
lectures. 🎨 📷
W whitney.org

Transport
Ⓜ 14 St.

Dempsey and Firpo
In 1924, George Bellows depicted one of
the most famous prizefights of the century.

Key to Floor Plan
- ☐ Permanent Collection
- ☐ Temporary Exhibitions
- ☐ Education Center
- ☐ Non-exhibition area

Floor 6

Floor 3

Painting Number 5
The early Modernist
artist Marsden Hartley
painted this oil on
canvas between
1914 and 1915.

Main entrance

Floor 1

Cirque Calder (1926–31)
Alexander Calder's fanciful
creation is usually
on display.

Washington Mews, a hidden quarter that once housed stables

⑩ Grey Art Gallery

100 Washington Sq E. **Map** 4 E2.
Tel (212) 998-6780. Ⓜ W 4th St, 8th St.
Open 11am–6pm Tue, Thu & Fri,
11am–8pm Wed, 11am–5pm Sat.
Ⓦ nyu.edu/greyart

This fine arts museum belongs
to New York University, and
features exemplary traveling
exhibitions in a wide range of
media, such as photography,
experimental video art,
paintings, and scupture. The
exhibitions are displayed on
rotation every three months.
There are temporary exhibits
from the university's permanent
collection – American paintings,
between the 1940s to now, are
particularly well represented.
The gallery is located in the
Silver Center, which was the
site of the original University
Building, demolished in 1892.
Henry James based much of his
novel *Washington Square* on his
grandmother's house, located
at nearby Washington Square
North 19.

⑪ Salmagundi Club

47 5th Ave **Map** 4 E1. **Tel** (212)
255-7740. Ⓜ 14th St-Union Sq.
Open 1–6pm Mon–Fri, 1–5pm Sat
& Sun. ✉ Ⓦ salmagundi.org

America's oldest artists' club
resides in the last remaining
mansion on lower Fifth Avenue.
Built in 1852 for industrialist
Irad Hawley, it now houses
the American Artists'
Professional League and the

American Watercolor Society.
Washington Irving's satiric
periodical, *The Salmagundi
Papers*, gave the club its name.
   Founded in 1871, the
club moved here in 1917.
Periodic art exhibits open the
late 19th-century interior to
the public.

Exterior of the Salmagundi Club

⑫ First Presbyterian Church

12 W 12th St. **Map** 4 D1. **Tel** (212)
675-6150. Ⓜ 14th St-Union Sq.
Open 11:45am–12:30pm Mon, Wed,
Fri, 11am–12:30pm Sun. ✟ 6pm Wed
in chapel. Ⓦ fpcnyc.org

Designed by Joseph C. Wells
in 1845, this Gothic church
was modeled on the Church
of St Saviour in Bath, England.
The church is noteworthy for
its brownstone tower. The
carved wooden plaques on
the altar list every pastor since
1716. The south transept by
McKim, Mead & White was
added in 1893. The fence of
iron and wood was built in
1844 and restored in 1981.

⑬ Church of the Ascension

36–38 5th Ave. **Map** 4 E1.
Tel (212) 254-8620. Ⓜ 14th St-Union
Sq. **Open** noon–2pm & 5–7pm daily.
✟ 6pm Mon–Fri, 9am & 11am Sun
(except during services).
Ⓦ ascensionnyc.org

This English Gothic Revival
church was designed in
1840–41 by Richard Upjohn,
architect of the Trinity Church.
The interior was re-done in
1888 by Stanford White, with
an altar relief by Augustus Saint-
Gaudens. Above the altar hangs
The Ascension, a mural by John
La Farge, who also designed
some of the stained glass.
The belfry tower is lit at
night to show off the colors.
In 1844, President John Tyler
married Julia Gardiner here;
she lived in nearby Colonnade
Row *(see p116)*.

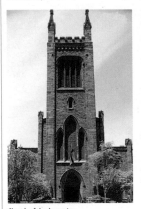
Church of the Ascension

⑭ Washington Mews

Between Washington Sq N and E 8th
St. **Map** 4 E2. Ⓜ W 4th St.

Built originally as stables, this
hidden enclave was turned
into carriage houses around
1916. The south side was
added in 1939. Gertrude
Vanderbilt Whitney, founder
of the Whitney Museum *(see
pp108–109)*, once lived here.
   At No. 16 is NYU's French
House, remodeled in the French
style. Movies, lectures, and
classes in French are held here.

Bust of Sylvette by Picasso, between Bleecker and West Houston streets

⓯ New York University

Washington Sq. **Map** 4 L2. **Tel** (212) 998-1212, (212) 998-4636. Ⓜ W 4th St. Ⓦ nyu.edu

Originally called the University of the City of New York, NYU was founded in 1831 as an alternative to Episcopalian Columbia University. It is now the largest private university in the US and extends for blocks around Washington Square. The visitor center is on West 4th St.

Construction of the school's first building on Waverly Place sparked the Stonecutters' Guild Riot of 1833: contractors protested the use of inmates from a state prison to cut stone. The National Guard restored order. The original building no longer exists, but a memorial with a piece of the original tower is on a pedestal set into the pavement on Washington Square South. Samuel Morse's telegraph, John W. Draper's first ever photographic portrait, and Samuel Colt's six-shooter were invented here.

The Brown Building, on Washington Place near Greene Street, was the site of the Triangle Shirtwaist Company. In 1911, 146 factory workers died in a fire here, leading to new fire safety and labor laws.

A 36-ft (11-m) enlargement of Picasso's *Bust of Sylvette* is in University Village.

⓰ Judson Memorial Church

55 Washington Sq S. **Map** 4 D2. **Tel** (212) 477-0351. Ⓜ W 4th St. **Open** 10am–1pm & 2–6pm Mon–Fri. ✝ 11am Sun. Ⓦ judson.org

Built in 1892, this McKim, Mead & White church is an impressive Italianate building with stained glass by John La Farge. Designed by Stanford White, it is named after the first American missionary sent to foreign soil, Adoniram Judson, who served in Burma in 1811. A copy of his Burmese translation of the Bible was put in the cornerstone when the building was dedicated.

It is the unique spirit of this church, not the architecture, that makes it stand out. Judson Memorial has played an active role in local and world concerns and has been the site of activism on issues ranging from AIDS to the arms race. It is also home to avant-garde art exhibitions and Off-Off-Broadway plays.

Arch on the north side of Washington Square

⓱ Washington Square

Map 4 D2. Ⓜ W 4th St.

This vibrant open space was once marshland through which the quiet Minetta Brook flowed. By the late 1700s, the area had been turned into a public cemetery – when excavation began for the park, some 10,000 skeletal remains were exhumed.

The square was used as a dueling ground for a time, then as a site for public hangings until 1819. The "hanging elm" in the northwest corner remains. In 1826 the marsh was filled in and the brook diverted underground, where it still flows; a small sign on a fountain at the entrance to Two Fifth Avenue marks its course.

The magnificent marble arch by Stanford White was completed in 1892 and replaced an earlier wooden arch that spanned lower Fifth Avenue to mark the centenary of George Washington's inauguration. A stairway is hidden in the right side of the arch. In 1916, a group of artists led by Marcel Duchamp and John Sloan broke in, climbed atop the arch, and declared the "free and independent republic of Washington Square, the state of New Bohemia."

Across the street is "the Row." Now part of NYU, this block was once home to New York's most prominent families. The Delano family, writers Edith Wharton, Henry James, and John Dos Passos, and artist Edward Hopper all lived here. No. 8 was once the mayor's official home.

Today, street entertainers, students, families, and free spirits mingle and enjoy the park side by side.

Window on the corner of West 4th Street and Washington Square

EAST VILLAGE

In the 17th century, Peter Stuyvesant had a country estate in the area now occupied by the East Village, but the neighborhood really took shape in the early 1900s. The Irish, Germans, Jews, Poles, Ukrainians, and Puerto Ricans all left their mark on the area, not least in the form of Manhattan's most varied and least expensive ethnic restaurants. In the 1950s, low rents attracted the "Beat Generation," and, ever since, music clubs and theaters abound in the area. From the 1990s, the culinary and bar scene here blossomed, making this one of the city's most fashionable districts. To the west lies NoHo (north of Houston), while to the east, avenues lettered A–D make "Alphabet City," a trendy district of restaurants and gardens.

Sights at a Glance

Historic Streets and Buildings
1 Cooper Union
3 Colonnade Row
8 Bayard-Condict Building

Museums and Galleries
4 Merchant's House Museum

Churches
5 St. Mark's-in-the-Bowery Church
6 Grace Church

Parks and Squares
7 Tompkins Square

Famous Theaters
2 The Public Theater

Restaurants see pp294–9
1 Angelica Kitchen
2 Il Bagatto
3 Caracas Arepa Bar
4 Dirt Candy
5 Dumpling Man
6 Edi & the Wolf
7 Empellón Cocina
8 Great Jones Cafe
9 Hearth
10 Jewel Bako
11 Lil' Frankies
12 The Mermaid Inn
13 Momofuku Noodle Bar
14 La Palapa
15 Pardon My French
16 Prune
17 Zum Schneider

Gothic bas-relief on the facade of Grace Church

0 meters   400
0 yards   400

See also Street Finder maps 4, 5

◀ People relaxing in Tompkins Square Park

For keys to symbols see back flap

Street by Street: East Village

At the spot where 10th and Stuyvesant streets now intersect, Governor Peter Stuyvesant's country house once stood. His grandson, also named Peter, inherited most of the property and had it divided into streets in 1787. Among the prize sites of the St. Mark's Historic District are the St. Mark's-in-the-Bowery Church, the Stuyvesant-Fish house and the 1795 home of Nicholas Stuyvesant, both on Stuyvesant Street. Many other homes in the district were built between 1871 and 1890 and still have their original stoops, lintels, and other architectural details.

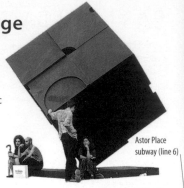

Astor Place
subway (line 6)

Alamo is the title of the 15-ft (4.6-m) black steel cube in Astor Place designed by Bernard Rosenthal. It revolves when pushed.

Astor Place saw rioting in 1849. English actor William Macready, playing Hamlet at the Astor Place Opera House, criticized American actor Edwin Forrest. Forrest's fans revolted, and there were 34 deaths.

E 8TH ST

ASTOR PLACE

LAFAYETTE STREET

STABLE COURT

FOURTH AVENUE

BOWERY

❸ **Colonnade Row**
Built in the Greek Revival style in the 1830s, these buildings were once expensive town houses. The houses, of which only four are left, are unified by one facade in the European style. The Astor Place Theatre, which is located here, has been home to the Blue Man Group since 1991.

❷ **The Public Theater**
In 1965 the late Joseph Papp convinced the city to buy the Astor Library (1849) as a home for the theater. Now restored, it sees the opening of many famous plays.

❹ ★ **Merchant's House Museum**
This museum displays Federal, American Empire, and Victorian furniture.

❶ ★ Cooper Union
This institution, known for its art and engineering programs, provided free education to its students until 2014.

The Stuyvesant-Fish House
(1803–4) was constructed out of brick. It is a classic example of a Federal-style house.

Renwick Triangle is a group of 16 houses built in the Italianate style in 1861.

❺ St. Mark's Church-in-the-Bowery
The church was built in 1799, and the steeple added in 1828.

Locator Map
See Manhattan Map pp16–17

Key
— Suggested route

Stuyvesant Polyclinic was built in 1884 as the German Dispensary and was used as a clinic until 2007. The facade is decorated with the busts of many famous physicians and scientists. It now houses a consulting firm.

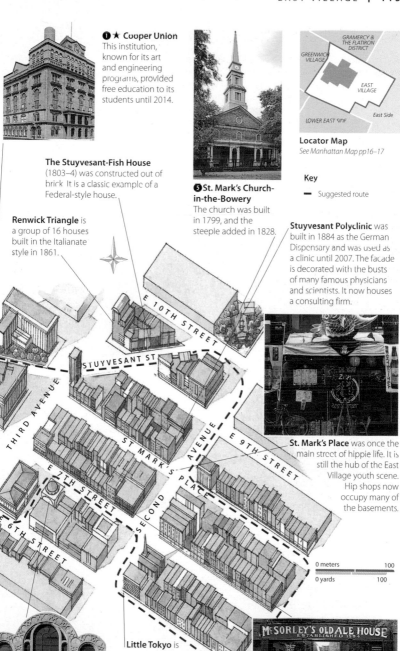

St. Mark's Place was once the main street of hippie life. It is still the hub of the East Village youth scene. Hip shops now occupy many of the basements.

E 10TH STREET

STUYVESANT ST

THIRD AVENUE

ST MARK'S PLACE

SECOND AVENUE

E 9TH STREET

E 7TH STREET

E 6TH STREET

0 meters 100
0 yards 100

Little Tokyo is a belt of noodle shops, sushi bars, and Japanese businesses, located on and around East 9th Street.

Little Ukraine is home to around 25,000 Ukrainians. The hub is St. George's Ukrainian Catholic Church.

McSorley's Old Ale House still brews its own ale and serves it in surroundings virtually unchanged since it opened in 1854 (see p311).

Great Hall at Cooper Union, where Abraham Lincoln spoke

❶ Cooper Union

7 East 7th St. **Map** 4 F2. **Tel** (212) 353-4000. Ⓜ Astor Pl. **Open** 11am–7pm Mon–Fri, 11am–5pm Sat, and for lectures and concerts in the Great Hall. **Closed** Jun–Aug, public hols. ♿ ⓦ **cooper.edu**

Peter Cooper, the wealthy industrialist who built the first US steam locomotive, made the first steel rails, and was a partner in the first transatlantic cable venture, had no formal schooling. In 1859 he founded New York's first free, non-sectarian coeducational college specializing in design, engineering, and architecture. Though no longer free, the school still inspires intense competition for places. The six-story building, renovated in 1973–4, was the first with a steel frame, made of Cooper's own rails. The Great Hall was inaugurated in 1859 by Mark Twain, and Lincoln delivered his "Right Makes Might" speech there in 1860.

❷ The Public Theater

425 Lafayette St. **Map** 4 F2. **Tel** (212) 967-7555 (tickets). Admin (212) 539-8500. Ⓜ Astor Pl. *See also Entertainment p336.* ⓦ **publictheater.org**

This large red-brick and brown-stone building began its life in 1854 as the Astor Library,

The Public Theater on Lafayette Street

the city's first free library, thanks to a bequest from millionaire John Jacob Astor. It is a prime American example of German Romanesque Revival style.

When the building was threatened with demolition in 1965, Joseph Papp, founder of the New York Shakespeare Festival, which became The Public Theater, persuaded New York City to buy it as a home for the company. Renovation began in 1967, and much of the handsome interior was preserved during conversion into six theaters. Although much of the work shown is experimental, The Public Theater was the original home of hit musicals *Hair* and *A Chorus Line* and hosts the popular Shakespeare in the Park (in Central Park) every summer.

❸ Colonnade Row

428–434 Lafayette St. **Map** 4 F2. **Tel** (800) 258-3626. Ⓜ Astor Pl. ⓦ **blueman.com**

The Corinthian columns across these four buildings are all that remain of a once-magnificent row of nine Greek Revival town houses. They were completed in 1833 by developer Seth Geer and were known as "Geer's Folly" by skeptics, who thought no one would live so far east. They were proved wrong when the houses were taken by such

eminent citizens as John Jacob Astor and Cornelius Vanderbilt. Washington Irving, author of *Rip Van Winkle* (1819)and other classic American tales, lived here for a time, as did two English novelists, William Makepeace Thackeray and Charles Dickens. Five of the houses were lost when the John Wanamaker Department Store razed them in the early 20th century to make room for a garage. The remaining buildings are being restored, with the Blue Man Group occupying the Astor Place Theatre (No. 434).

The original 19th-century iron stove in the kitchen of the Merchant's House Museum

❹ Merchant's House Museum

29 E 4th St. **Map** 4 F2. **Tel** (212) 777-1089. Ⓜ Astor Pl., Bleecker St. **Open** noon–5pm Mon, Fri–Sun, noon–8pm Thu. ♿ ⓦ **merchantshouse.com**

This remarkable Federal-style brick town house, improbably tucked away on an East Village block, is a time capsule of a vanished way of life. It still has both its original fixtures and its kitchen, and is filled with the actual furniture, ornaments, and utensils of the family who lived here for almost 100 years. Built in 1832, it was bought in 1835 by Seabury Tredwell, a wealthy merchant, and stayed in the family until Gertrude Tredwell, the last member, died in 1933. She had maintained her father's home just as he would have liked it, and a relative opened the house as a museum in 1936. The first-floor parlors are very grand, a sign of how well New York's merchant class lived in the 1800s.

❺ St. Mark's-in-the-Bowery Church

131 E 10th St. **Map** 4 F1. **Tel** (212) 674-6377. Ⓜ Astor Pl. **Open** 10am–4pm Mon–Fri (hours may vary). ✝ 6:30pm Wed, 11am Sun; in Spanish 5:30pm Sat. ⓦ stmarksbowery.org

One of New York's oldest churches, this 1799 building replaced a 1660 church on the *bouwerie* (farm) of Governor Peter Stuyvesant. He is buried here, along with seven generations of his descendants and many other prominent early New Yorkers. Poet W. H. Auden was a parishioner and is also commemorated here.

In 1878, a grisly kidnapping took place when the remains of department store magnate A. T. Stewart were removed from the site and held for $20,000 ransom.

The church rectory at 232 East 11th Street dates from 1900 and is by Ernest Flagg, who achieved renown for his Singer Building (see p100).

❻ Grace Church

802 Broadway. **Map** 4 F1. **Tel** (212) 254-2000. Ⓜ Astor Pl, Union Sq. 🚌 M1–3, M8, M101–3. ✝ Jul & Aug: 10am, 6pm Sun; Sep–Jun. 9am, 11am, 6pm Sun. ♿ 🔊 **Concerts.** ⓦ gracechurchnyc.org

James Renwick, Jr., the architect of St. Patrick's Cathedral, was only 23 when he designed this church, yet many consider it his finest achievement. Its delicate early Gothic lines have a grace befitting the church's name. The interior is just as beautiful, with Pre-Raphaelite stained glass and a handsome mosaic floor.

The church's peace and serenity were briefly shattered in 1863, when Phineas T. Barnum staged the wedding

Tom Thumb and his bride at Grace Church

of midget General Tom Thumb here; the crowds turned the event into complete chaos.

The marble spire replaced a wooden steeple in 1888 amid fears that it might prove too heavy for the church – and it has since developed a distinct lean. The church is visible from afar because it is on a bend on Broadway. Henry Brevoort forced the city to bend Broadway to divert it around his apple orchard.

Grace Church altar and window

❼ Tompkins Square

Map 5 B1. Ⓜ 2nd Ave, 1st Ave. 🚌 M8, M9, M14A.

This English-style park has the makings of a peaceful spot, but its past has more often been dominated by strife. It was the site of America's first organized labor demonstration in 1874, the main gathering place during the neighborhood's hippie era of the 1960s, and, in 1988, an arena for violent riots when the police tried to evict homeless people who had taken over the grounds. The square also contains a poignant monument to the

neighborhood's greatest tragedy. A small statue of a boy and a girl looking at a steamboat commemorates the deaths of over 1,000 local residents in the *General Slocum* steamer disaster. On June 15, 1904, the boat caught fire during a pleasure cruise on the East River. The boat was crowded with women and children from this then-German neighborhood. Many local men lost their entire families and moved away, leaving the area and its memories behind.

❽ Bayard-Condict Building

65 Bleecker St. **Map** 4 F3. Ⓜ Bleecker St.

The graceful columns, elegant filigreed terra-cotta facade, and magnificent cornice on this 1898 building mark the only New York work by Louis Sullivan, the great Chicago architect who taught Frank Lloyd Wright. He died in poverty and obscurity in Chicago in 1924.

Sullivan is said to have objected vigorously to the sentimental angels supporting the Bayard-Condict Building's cornice, but he eventually gave in to the wishes of Silas Alden Condict, the owner.

Because this building is squeezed into a commercial block, it is better appreciated from a distance. Cross the street and walk a little way down Crosby Street for the best view.

The Bayard-Condict Building

PETE'S TAVERN

O HENRY'S WAY

E 18 ST

ONE WAY

PETE'S TAVER

70 Irving Place

GRAMERCY AND THE FLATIRON DISTRICT

Four squares were laid out in this area by real-estate developers in the 1830s and 1840s to emulate the quiet, private residential areas in many European cities. Chief among them is Union Square, a bustling space that hosts New York's best farmers' market. To the northeast lies Gramercy, with its private clubs and posh town houses, designed by Calvert Vaux and Stanford White. Gertrude Vanderbilt Whitney's bronze statue of Peter Stuyvesant, overlooked by the stately St. George Episcopal Church, stands in tranquil Stuyvesant Square. Finally, at the north end of the Flatiron District is Madison Square Park.

Sights at a Glance

Historic Streets and Buildings

- ❷ New York Life Insurance Company
- ❸ Appellate Division of the Supreme Court of the State of New York
- ❹ Metropolitan Life Insurance Company
- ❺ Flatiron Building
- ❻ Ladies' Mile
- ❽ National Arts Club
- ❾ The Players
- ⓫ Block Beautiful
- ⓮ Con Edison Building

Museums and Galleries

- ❼ Theodore Roosevelt Birthplace

Churches

- ⓰ The Little Church Around the Corner

Parks and Squares

- ❶ Madison Square
- ❿ Gramercy Park
- ⓭ Stuyvesant Square
- ⓯ Union Square

Markets

- ⓬ Eataly

Restaurants *see pp294–9*

1. Aldea
2. Artisinal
3. Blue Smoke
4. Craft
5. Dirty French
6. Eleven Madison Park
7. Gramercy Tavern
8. Ippudo
9. Ivan Ramen
10. Mighty Quinn's Barbeque
11. Red Farm
12. Saravanaa Bhavan
13. Shake Shack
14. Tamarind
15. Tocqueville
16. I Trulli

◀ Pete's Tavern, a popular neighborhood bar in Gramercy Park District

For keys to symbols *see back flap*

Street by Street: Gramercy Park

Gramercy Park and nearby Madison Square tell a tale of two cities. Madison Square is ringed by offices and traffic and is used mainly by those who work nearby, but the fine surrounding commercial architecture and statues make it well worth visiting. It was once the home of Stanford White's famous pleasure palace, the old Madison Square Garden, a place where revelers always thronged. Gramercy Park, however, retains the air of dignified tranquility it has long been known for. Here, the residences and clubs remain, set around New York's last private park, for which only those who live on the square have keys.

❶ ★ Madison Square
The Knickerbocker Club played baseball here in the 1840s and was the first to codify the game's rules. Today, office workers enjoy the park's many statues of 19th-century figures, among them Civil War hero Admiral David Farragut.

Statue of Diana atop the old Madison Square Garden

23rd Street subway (lines N, R)

❺ ★ Flatiron Building
The triangle made by Fifth Avenue, Broadway, and 22nd Street is the site of one of New York's most famous early skyscrapers. When it was built in 1903, the flatiron was the world's tallest building.

A sidewalk clock found in front of 200 Fifth Avenue marks the very end of the once-fashionable shopping area, known as Ladies' Mile.

BROADWAY (LADIES' MILE)

E 21ST STREET

❻ Ladies' Mile
Broadway from Union Square to Madison Square was once New York's finest shopping area.

E 19TH STREET

❼ Theodore Roosevelt Birthplace
The house is a replica of the one in which the 26th American president was born.

E 17TH STREET

❽ National Arts Club
This is a private club for the arts, on the south side of the park.

0 meters	100
0 yards	100

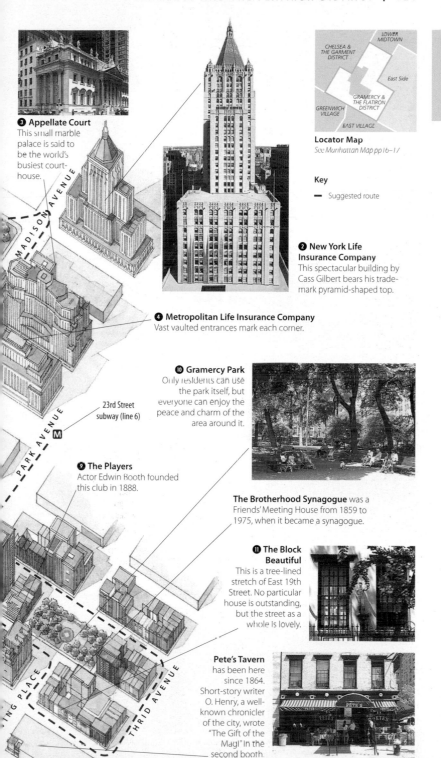

❸ Appellate Court
This small marble palace is said to be the world's busiest court-house.

Locator Map
See Manhattan Map pp16–17

Key

— Suggested route

❷ New York Life Insurance Company
This spectacular building by Cass Gilbert bears his trade-mark pyramid-shaped top.

❹ Metropolitan Life Insurance Company
Vast vaulted entrances mark each corner.

❿ Gramercy Park
Only residents can use the park itself, but everyone can enjoy the peace and charm of the area around it.

23rd Street subway (line 6)

❾ The Players
Actor Edwin Booth founded this club in 1888.

The Brotherhood Synagogue was a Friends' Meeting House from 1859 to 1975, when it became a synagogue.

⓫ The Block Beautiful
This is a tree-lined stretch of East 19th Street. No particular house is outstanding, but the street as a whole is lovely.

Pete's Tavern
has been here since 1864. Short-story writer O. Henry, a well-known chronicler of the city, wrote "The Gift of the Magi" in the second booth.

MADISON AVENUE

PARK AVENUE

THIRD AVENUE

Farragut statue, Madison Square

❶ Madison Square

Map 8 F4. Ⓜ 23rd St.

Planned as the center of a fashionable residential district, this square became a popular entertainment center after the Civil War. It was bordered by the elegant Fifth Avenue Hotel, the Madison Square Theater, and Stanford White's Madison Square Garden. The torch-bearing arm of the Statue of Liberty was exhibited here in 1884.

The Shake Shack is a top lunchtime spot for neighborhood office workers, while the surrounding park makes for a leisurely stroll to admire the sculptures. The 1880 statue of Admiral David Farragut is by Augustus Saint-Gaudens, with a pedestal by Stanford White. Farragut was the hero of a Civil War sea battle; figures representing Courage and Loyalty are carved on the base. The statue of Roscoe Conkling commemorates a US senator who died during the great blizzard of 1888. The Eternal Light flagpole, by Carrère and Hastings, honors the soldiers who fell during World War I.

❷ New York Life Insurance Company

51 Madison Ave. **Map** 9 A3. Ⓜ 28th St. **Open** office hours.

This imposing building was designed in 1928 by Cass Gilbert of Woolworth Building fame. The interior is a masterpiece, adorned with enormous hanging lamps, bronze doors and paneling, and a grand staircase leading, of all places, to the subway station.

Other famous buildings have stood on this site. Barnum's

Hippodrome was here in 1874, then the first Madison Square Garden opened in 1879. A wide range of entertainments were put on, including the prizefights of heavyweight boxing hero John L. Sullivan in the 1880s. The next Madison Square Garden – Stanford White's legendary pleasure palace – opened on the same site in 1890. Lavish musical shows and social events were attended by New York's elite, who paid over $500 for a box at the prestigious annual horse show.

The building had street-level arcades and a tower modeled on the Giralda in Seville. A gold statue of the goddess Diana stood atop the tower. Her nudity was shocking, but far more scandalous was the decadent life and death of White himself. In 1906, while watching a revue in the roof garden, he was shot dead by millionaire Harry K. Thaw, the husband of White's former mistress, showgirl Evelyn Nesbit. The headline in the journal *Vanity Fair* summed up popular feeling: "Stanford White, Voluptuary and Pervert, Dies the Death of a Dog." The ensuing trial's revelations about decadent Broadway high society leave modern soap operas far behind.

New York Life Insurance Company's golden pyramid roof

Statues of *Justice* and *Study* above the Appellate Court

❸ Appellate Division of the Supreme Court of the State of New York

E. 25th St at Madison Ave. **Map** 9 A4 Ⓜ 23rd St. **Open** 9am–5pm Mon–Fri (court in session from 2pm Tue–Thu, from 10am Fri). **Closed** public hols. ✉

Appeals relating to civil and criminal cases for New York and the Bronx are heard here, in what is widely considered to be the busiest court of its kind in the world. James Brown Lord designed the small yet noble Palladian Revival building in 1900. It is decorated with more than a dozen handsome sculptures, including Daniel Chester French's *Justice* flanked by *Power* and *Study*. During the week, the public is invited to step inside to admire the fine interior, designed by the Herter brothers, including the courtroom, when the court is not in session. Among the elegant details worth looking for are the fine stained-glass windows and dome, the murals, and the striking cabinetwork.

Displays in the lobby often feature some of the more famous – and infamous – cases that have been heard in this court. Among the celebrity names that have been involved in appeals settled here are Babe Ruth, Charlie Chaplin, Fred Astaire, Harry Houdini, Theodore Dreiser, and Edgar Allan Poe.

Clock tower of the Metropolitan Life Insurance Company building

❹ Metropolitan Life Insurance Company

1 Madison Ave. **Map** 9 A4. Ⓜ 23rd St.
Open office hours. ✉

In 1909, the addition of a 700-ft (213-m) tower to the "MetLife" Building ousted the Flatiron as the tallest in the world. The huge four-sided clock has minute hands said to weigh 1000 lb (454 kg) each. The tower is lit up at night and is a familiar part of the evening skyline. It served as the company symbol "the light that never fails." A series of historical murals by N. C. Wyeth, the famed illustrator of such classics as *Robin Hood, Treasure Island,* and *Robinson Crusoe* (and the father of painter Andrew Wyeth), once graced the walls of the cafeteria. The North building, built in 1933, now houses Credit Suisse.

❺ Flatiron Building

175 5th Ave. **Map** 8 F4. Ⓜ 23rd St.
Open office hours.

Originally named the Fuller Building after the construction company that owned it, this building by Chicago architect Daniel Burnham was the tallest in the world when it was completed in 1902. One of the first buildings to use a steel frame, it heralded the era of the skyscrapers.

It soon became known as the Flatiron for its unusual triangular shape, but some called it "Burnham's folly," predicting that the winds created by the building's shape would knock it down. It has withstood the test of time, but the winds along 23rd Street did have one notable effect. In the building's early days, they drew crowds of males hoping to get a peek at women's ankles as their long skirts got blown about. Police officers had to keep people moving along, and their call, "23-skidoo," became slang for "scram."

The stretch of Fifth Avenue to the south of the building, formerly rather run-down, has come to life with chic shops such as Michael Kors and Paul Smith, giving the area new cachet and a new name, "the Flatiron District."

Arnold Constable store

❻ Ladies' Mile

Broadway (Union Sq to Madison Sq).
Map 8 F4–5, 9 A5. Ⓜ 14th St, 23rd St.

In the 19th century, the "carriage trade" came here in shiny traps from their town houses nearby to shop at stores such as Arnold Constable (Nos. 881–887) and Lord & Taylor (No. 901). The ground-floor exteriors have changed beyond recognition; look up to see the remains of once-grand facades.

President Teddy Roosevelt

❼ Theodore Roosevelt Birthplace

28 E. 20th St. **Map** 9 A5. **Tel** (212) 260-1616. Ⓜ 14th St-Union Sq-23rd St.
Open 9am–5pm Tue–Sat (last adm: 4pm). **Closed** pub hols. ♿ 🎧 hourly. Lectures, concerts, films, videos. 📷
🅦 nps.gov/thrb

The reconstructed boyhood home of the colorful 26th president displays everything from the toys with which the young Teddy played to campaign buttons and emblems of the trademark "Rough Rider" hat that Roosevelt wore in the Spanish-American War. One exhibit features his explorations and interests; the other covers his political career.

The Flatiron Building during its construction

Bas-relief faces of great writers at the National Arts Club

⑧ National Arts Club

15 Gramercy Pk S. **Map** 9 A5. **Tel** (212) 475-3424. Ⓜ 23rd St. **Open** noon–5pm Mon–Fri during exhibitions.
ⓦ nationalartsclub.org

This brownstone was the residence of New York governor Samuel Tilden, who condemned "Boss" Tweed and established a free public library. He had the facade redesigned by Calvert Vaux in 1881–4. In 1906 the National Arts Club bought the home and kept the original high ceilings and stained glass by John La Farge. Members have included most leading American artists of the late 19th and early 20th century, who were asked to donate a painting or sculpture in return for life membership; these gifts form the permanent collection. The club is open to the public for exhibitions only.

⑨ The Players

18 Gramercy Pk S.
Map 9 A5. **Tel** (212) 228-7610.
Ⓜ 23rd St. **Closed** except for prebooked group tours.
ⓦ theplayersnyc.org

This two-story brownstone was the home of actor Edwin Booth, brother of John Wilkes Booth, President Lincoln's assassin. Architect Stanford White remodeled the building as a club in 1888. Although intended primarily for actors,

members have included White himself, author Mark Twain, publisher Thomas Nast, and Winston Churchill, whose mother, Jennie Jerome, was born nearby. A statue of Booth playing Hamlet is across the street in Gramercy Park.

Decorative grille at The Players club

⑩ Gramercy Park

Map 9 A4. Ⓜ 23rd St, 14th St-Union Sq.

Gramercy Park is one of four squares (with Union, Stuyvesant, and Madison) laid out in the 1830s and 1840s to attract society residences. It is the city's only private park, and residents in the surrounding buildings have keys to the park gate, as the original owners once did. Look through the railings at the southeast corner to see Greg Wyatt's fountain, with giraffes leaping around a smiling sun.

The buildings around the square were designed by some of the city's most famous architects, including Stanford White, whose house was

located on the site of today's Gramercy Park Hotel. Particularly fine are Nos. 3 and 4, with graceful cast-iron gates and porches. The lanterns in front of No. 4 serve as symbols marking the house of a former mayor of the city, James Harper. No. 34 (1883) has been the home of the sculptor Daniel Chester French, the actor James Cagney, and circus impresario John Ringling (who had a massive pipe organ installed in his apartment).

House facade on the Block Beautiful on East 19th Street

⑪ Block Beautiful

E 19th St. **Map** 9 A5. Ⓜ 14th St-Union Sq, 23rd St.

This is a serene, tree-lined block of 1920s residences, beautifully restored. None of them is exceptional on its own, but together they create a wonderfully harmonious whole. No. 132 had two famous theatrical tenants: Theda Bara, silent movie star and Hollywood's first sex symbol, and the fine Shakespearean actress Mrs. Patrick Campbell, who originated the role of Eliza Doolittle in George Bernard Shaw's *Pygmalion* in 1914.

The hitching posts outside No. 141 and the ceramic relief of giraffes outside 147–149 are two of the many details to look for as you walk along the block.

Fountain with sun and giraffes by Greg Wyatt in Gramercy Park

⓬ Eataly

200 Fifth Ave. **Map** 8 F4. **Tel** (212) 229-2560. Ⓜ Astor Place, 8th St. **Open** 10am–11pm daily. Ⓦ eataly.com

Celebrity chef Mario Batali began this Italian restaurant and food market in 2010, and it has remained an incredibly popular venture. The market offers a great range of wine, cheese, bread, seafood, and meat, sourced locally or flown in from Italy. Highlights include a fresh gelato counter, a Nutella Bar, and the Caffè Vergnano espresso bar. La Piazza is an *enoteca* (wine shop) that serves wine and antipasti (standing only).

The rooftop has a lovely beer garden, La Birreria, that offers home-made sausages and hand-crafted ales from Bologna under a retractable roof, which opens on sunny days. Batali now operates restaurants and food markets all over the world, although he still lives in Greenwich Village.

⓭ Stuyvesant Square

Map 9 B5. Ⓜ 3rd Ave, 1st Ave.

This oasis, in the form of a pair of parks divided by Second Avenue, was part of Peter Stuyvesant's original farm in the 1600s. It was still in the Stuyvesant family when the park was designed in 1836; Peter G. Stuyvesant sold the land to the city for the nominal sum of $5 (much to the delight of those living nearby, who saw real estate values jump). A statue of Stuyvesant by Gertrude Vanderbilt Whitney stands in the park, along with a sculpture of Czech composer Antonín Dvořák, who lived nearby in the 1890s.

⓮ Con Edison Building

145 E 14th St. **Map** 9 A5. Ⓜ 3rd Ave, 14th St-Union Sq. **Closed** to the public.

The clock tower of this building, which dates from 1929, is a local landmark. The building was

The towers of the Empire State, Metropolitan Life and Con Edison

conceived by Henry Hardenbergh in 1910, the architect best known for such buildings as the Dakota *(see p212)* and the Plaza *(see p177)*. The 26-story tower was built by Warren & Wetmore, the same firm that designed Grand Central Terminal. Near the top of the tower, a 38-ft (11.6-m) bronze lantern was built as a memorial to Con Ed's employees who died in World War I. The tower itself is not as tall as nearby the Empire State Building, but when it is lit up at night, it makes an attractive showpiece, in addition to a potent symbol of the company that keeps Manhattan and the other four boroughs shining.

Greenmarket day at Union Square

⓯ Union Square

Map 9 A5. Ⓜ 14th St-Union Sq. Farmers' Market. **Open** 8am–6pm Mon, Wed, Fri & Sat.

Created in the 1830s, this park joined Bloomingdale Road (now Broadway) with the Bowery Road (Fourth Avenue or Park), and hence its name. Today, it is an inviting public space, best known for its

enormous greenmarket, which sells all sorts of seasonal produce. Statues in the square include that of George Washington and a Lafayette by Bartholdi. The square is flanked by restaurants, gourmet supermarkets, and department stores. Nearby stands the Decker Building, where Andy Warhol moved his studio in 1968. The Union Square Theatre, once the headquarters of the Democratic Party, is another landmark.

⓰ The Little Church Around the Corner

1 E 29th St. **Map** 8 F3. **Tel** (212) 684-6770. Ⓜ 28th St. **Open** 8:30am–6pm daily. 🕇 12:10pm Mon–Fri; 8:30am & 11am Sun. For lectures & concerts, see website. ♿ 🎧 Sun, after 11am service. Ⓦ littlechurch.org

Built from 1849 to 1856, the Episcopal Church of the Transfiguration is a tranquil retreat. It has been known by its nickname since 1870, when Joseph Jefferson tried to arrange the funeral of fellow actor George Holland. The pastor at a nearby church refused to bury a person of so lowly a profession. Instead, he suggested "the little church around the corner." The name stuck and the church has had special ties with the theater ever since.

The south transept window, by John La Farge, shows Edwin Booth playing Hamlet. Jefferson's cry of "God bless the little church around the corner" is commemorated in a window in the south aisle.

CHELSEA AND THE GARMENT DISTRICT

Developed on former farmland, this area really began to take shape in 1830. This was largely thanks to Clement Clarke Moore, who wrote 'Twas the Night Before Christmas – his estate comprised most of what is now Chelsea.

After a long period as a rather gritty area, a new and fashionable Chelsea emerged. When Macy's arrived at Herald Square, garment and retail districts sprouted around it. Some of New York's best art galleries flourished in the early 1990s, and more recently, the transformation of the High Line has triggered the development of major condo conversions, affluent town houses, and shops of every variety here.

Sights at a Glance

Historic Streets and Buildings
2 Empire State Building pp132–3
7 James A. Farley Post Office Building
11 Chelsea Art Galleries
12 General Theological Seminary
13 Chelsea Historic District
15 Hugh O'Neill Dry Goods Store

Museums and Galleries
8 Rubin Museum of Art

Churches
1 Marble Collegiate Reformed Church
5 St. John the Baptist Church

Modern Architecture
6 Madison Square Garden
10 Chelsea Piers Complex

Parks and Squares
3 Herald Square
9 High Line

Markets
14 Chelsea Market

Landmark Stores
4 Macy's

☐ **Restaurants** see pp299–302
1 Bottino
2 Buddakan
3 Hill Country
4 Morimoto
5 The Red Cat
6 Russian Tea Room
7 Tia Pol
8 Trestle on Tenth

See also Street Finder maps 7, 8

◀ The Empire State Building, an enduring symbol of New York

For keys to symbols see back flap

Street by Street: Herald Square

Herald Square is named for the *New York Herald*, which had
its office here from 1894 to 1921. Today full of shoppers, the
area was once one of the raunchiest parts of New York. During
the late 19th century, it was known as the Tenderloin District
and was filled with dance halls and bordellos. When Macy's
opened in 1902, the focus moved from flesh to fashion.
New York's Garment District now fills the streets near Macy's
around Seventh Avenue, also known as Fashion Avenue.
To the east on Fifth Avenue is the Empire State Building, with
some of the city's best views from the observation deck.

Manhattan Mall is on
the former site of Gimbel's,
once Macy's arch-rival.
It holds dozens of
stores, including a
massive J. C. Penney.

Fashion Avenue is another name for the
stretch of Seventh Avenue around 34th
Street. This area is the heart of New York's
garment industry. The streets are still full of
men pushing racks of clothes.

The Hotel Pennsylvania
was a center for the 1930s
big bands – Glenn Miller's
song "Pennsylvania 6-5000"
made its telephone
number famous.

34th Street subway
(1, 2, 3)

❺ **St. John the
Baptist Church**
A beautiful set of carved
Stations of the Cross is
hung on the walls of
the white marble
interior of this church.

The SJM Building is at 130 West
30th Street. Mesopotamian-style
friezes adorn the outside of
the building.

The Fur District is at the southern end of
the Garment District. Furriers ply their trade
between West 27th and 30th streets.

SEVENTH AVENUE

W 31ST STREET

W 28TH STREET

SIXTH AVENUE

The Flower District,
around Sixth Avenue and
West 28th Street, hums
with activity in the early
part of the day, as florists
pack their vans with their
highly scented, brightly
colored wares.

28th Street subway
(lines N, R)

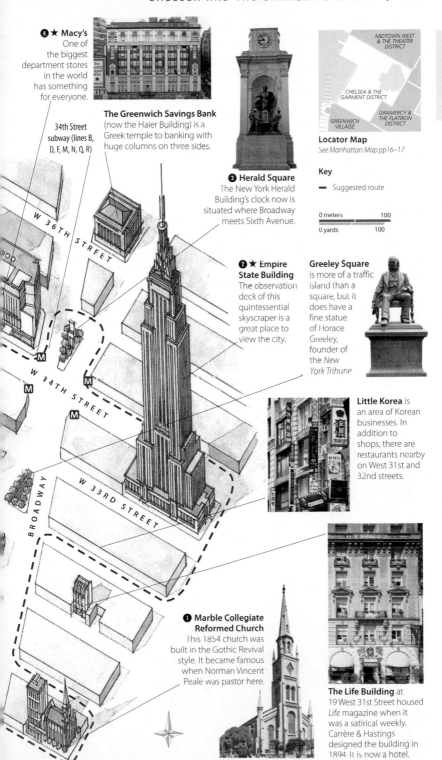

❹ ★ Macy's One of the biggest department stores in the world has something for everyone.

34th Street subway (lines B, D, F, M, N, Q, R)

The Greenwich Savings Bank (now the Haier Building) is a Greek temple to banking with huge columns on three sides.

❸ Herald Square The New York Herald Building's clock now is situated where Broadway meets Sixth Avenue.

MIDTOWN WEST & THE THEATER DISTRICT

CHELSEA & THE GARMENT DISTRICT

GRAMERCY & THE FLATIRON DISTRICT

GREENWICH VILLAGE

Locator Map See Manhattan Map pp16–17

Key
— Suggested route

0 meters 100
0 yards 100

❷ ★ Empire State Building The observation deck of this quintessential skyscraper is a great place to view the city.

Greeley Square is more of a traffic island than a square, but it does have a fine statue of Horace Greeley, founder of the New York Tribune

Little Korea is an area of Korean businesses. In addition to shops, there are restaurants nearby on West 31st and 32nd streets.

❶ Marble Collegiate Reformed Church This 1854 church was built in the Gothic Revival style. It became famous when Norman Vincent Peale was pastor here.

The Life Building at 19 West 31st Street housed Life magazine when it was a satirical weekly. Carrère & Hastings designed the building in 1894. It is now a hotel.

Marble Collegiate's Tiffany stained-glass windows

❶ Marble Collegiate Reformed Church

1 W 29th St. **Map** 8 F3. **Tel** (212) 686-2770. Ⓜ 28th St. **Open** 8:30am–8:30pm Mon–Fri, 9am–4pm Sat, 8am–3pm Sun. **Closed** public hols. 🕋 11:15am Sun. 🎦 during services. ♿ Sanctuary 3 W 29th St. **Open** 10am–noon & 2–4pm Mon–Fri. 🌐 **marblechurch.org**

This church is best known for its former pastor Norman Vincent Peale, who wrote *The Power of Positive Thinking*. Another positive thinker, future US president Richard M. Nixon, attended services here when he was a lawyer in his pre-White House days.

The church was built in 1854 using the marble blocks that give it its name. Fifth Avenue was then no more than a dusty country road, and the cast-iron fence was there to keep livestock out.

The original white and gold interior walls were replaced with a stenciled gold fleur-de-lis design on a soft rust background. Two stained-glass Tiffany windows, depicting Old Testament scenes, were placed in the south wall in 1900 and 1901.

❷ Empire State Building

See pp132–3.

❸ Herald Square

6th Ave. **Map** 8 E2. Ⓜ 34th St-Penn Station. *See Shopping p314.*

Named after the *New York Herald*, which occupied a fine arcaded, Italianate Stanford White building here from 1893 to 1921, the square was the hub of the rowdy Tenderloin district in the 1870s and 1880s. Theaters such as the Manhattan Opera House, dance halls, hotels, and restaurants kept the area humming with life until reformers clamped down on sleaze in the 1890s. The ornamental Bennett clock, named for James Gordon Bennett Jr., publisher of the *Herald*, is now all that is left of the Herald Building.

The Opera House was razed in 1901 to make way for Macy's and, soon after, other department stores followed, making Herald Square a mecca for shoppers. One such store was the now-defunct Gimbel Brothers Department Store, once arch-rival to Macy's. (The rivalry was affectionately portrayed in the New York Christmas movie *A Miracle on 34th Street*.) In 1988, the store was converted into a vertical mall with a glittery neon front. Most of the old names have gone, but Herald Square is still a key shopping district packed with chain stores. It also features a pedestrian plaza.

❹ Macy's

151 W. 34th St. **Map** 8 E2. **Tel** (212) 695-4400. Ⓜ 34th St- Penn Station. **Open** 9:30am–10pm Mon–Fri, 10am–10pm Sat, 11am–9pm Sun. *See Shopping p313.* 🌐 **macys.com**

The "world's largest store" covers a square block, and the merchandise inside includes any item you could imagine in every price range.

Macy's was founded by a former whaler named Rowland Hussey Macy, who opened a small store on West 14th Street in 1858. The store's red star logo came from Macy's tattoo, a souvenir of his sailing days.

By the time Macy died in 1877, his little store had grown to a row of 11 buildings. By the turn of the century, Macy's had outgrown its 14th Street premises, and the firm acquired its present site, which covers about 2 million sq ft (186,000 sq m) and opened in 1902.

Macy's 34th Street facade

The nave of St. John the Baptist Church

The eastern facade has a modern entrance but still bears the bay windows and Corinthian pillars of the 1902 design. The 34th Street facade even has its original caryatids guarding the entrance, along with the clock, canopy, and lettering. Inside, many of the early wooden escalators are still in good working order. Unsurprisingly, Macy's is a designated National Historic Landmark.

Macy's sponsors New York's renowned Thanksgiving Day parade (see p54) and the Fourth of July fireworks (see p53). The store's popular Spring Flower Show draws thousands of visitors.

❺ St. John the Baptist Church

210 W 31st St. **Map** 8 E3. **Tel** (212) 564-9070. **M** 34th St–Penn Station. **Open** 6:15am–6pm daily. 8:45am, 10:30am & 5:15pm daily.

Founded in 1840 to serve a congregation of newly arrived immigrants, today this small Roman Catholic church is almost lost in the heart of the Fur District. The exterior

has a single spire. Although the brownstone facade on 30th Street is dark with city soot, many treasures lie within this dull exterior. The entrance is through the modern Friary on 31st Street.

The sanctuary by Napoleon Le Brun is a marvel of Gothic arches in glowing white marble surmounted by gilded capitals. Painted reliefs of religious scenes line the walls; sunlight streams through the stained-glass windows. Also off the Friary is the Prayer Garden, a small, green, and peaceful oasis with religious statuary, a fountain, and stone benches.

❻ Madison Square Garden

4 Pennsylvania Plaza. **Map** 8 D2. **Tel** (212) 465-6741. **M** 34th St–Penn Station. **Open** Mon–Sun, times vary according to shows. See Entertainment p346. daily except during shows. **w** thegarden.com

There's only one good thing to be said for the razing of the extraordinarily lovely McKim, Mead & White Pennsylvania Station building in favor of this undistinguished 1968 complex: it so enraged city preservationists that they formed an alliance to ensure that such a thing would never be allowed to happen again.

Madison Square Garden itself, which sits atop underground Pennsylvania Station, is a cylinder of precast concrete, functional enough as a 20,000-seat, centrally located home for the NBA's famous New York

Knicks (basketball), Liberty (women's basketball), and New York Rangers (hockey) teams. It offers a packed calendar of other events: rock concerts, championship tennis and boxing, outrageously staged wrestling, the Westminster Kennel Club Dog Show, and more. There is also a 5,600-seat theater. Tours are available daily.

Despite extensive renovations, Madison Square Garden lacks the panache of its earlier location, which combined a stunning Stanford White building with extravagant entertainment (see p122).

The massive interior of Madison Square Garden

❼ James A. Farley Post Office Building

421 8th Ave. **Map** 8 D2. **Tel** (800) ASK-USPS. **M** 34th St–Penn Station. **Open** 7am–10pm Mon–Fri, 9am–9pm Sat, 11am–7pm Sun. See Practical Information p371.

Designed by McKim, Mead & White in 1913, in a style to complement their 1910 Pennsylvania Station across the street, the James A. Farley Post Office Building is a perfect example of a public building of the Beaux Arts period. The imposing, two-block-long structure has a broad staircase leading to a facade with 20 Corinthian columns and a pavilion at each end. The 280-ft (85-m) inscription across it is based on a description of the Persian Empire's postal service, from around 520 BC: "Neither snow nor rain nor heat nor gloom of night stays these couriers from the swift completion of their appointed rounds."

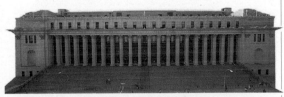

The Corinthian colonnade of the James A. Farley Post Office Building

❷ Empire State Building

The Empire State Building is one of the tallest skyscrapers in the United States. Named after the state's nickname, it has become an enduring symbol of the city. Construction began in March 1930, not long after the Wall Street Crash, and by the time the skyscraper opened in 1931 space was so difficult to rent that it was nicknamed "the Empty State Building." Only the immediate popularity of the observatories saved the building from bankruptcy – they still attract more than 3.5 million visitors a year.

Symbols of the modern age are depicted on these bronze Art Deco medallions placed throughout the lobby.

Empire State Building

Construction

The building was designed for ease and speed of construction. Everything possible was prefabricated and slotted into place at a rate of about four stories per week.

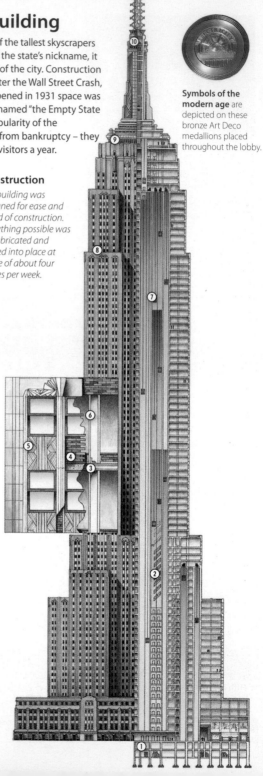

KEY

① **Over 200 steel and concrete piles** support the 365,000-ton building.

② **Nine minutes 33 seconds** is the record, set in 2003, for racing up the 1,576 steps from the lobby to the 86th-floor observatory, in the annual Empire State Run-Up.

③ **Sandwich space** between the floors houses the wiring, pipes, and cables.

④ **Ten million bricks** were used to line the whole building.

⑤ **Aluminum panels** were used instead of stone around the 6,514 windows. The steel trim masks rough edges on the facing.

⑥ **The framework** is made from 60,000 tons of steel and was built in 23 weeks.

⑦ **High-speed** elevators travel at up to 1,000 ft (305 m) a minute.

⑧ **Colored floodlighting** of the top 30 floors marks special events.

⑨ **The Empire State** was planned to be just 86 stories high, but a then 150-ft (46-m) mooring mast for zeppelins was added. The mast, now 204 ft (62 m), transmits TV and radio to the city and four states.

⑩ **102nd-floor observatory**

★ **Views from the Observatories**
The 86th-floor observatory offers superb views, both from its indoor galleries and its 360-degree outdoor deck. The 102nd-floor observatory, 1,250 ft (381 m) high, requires an extra fee, payable at the second-floor Visitors' Center or online.

VISITORS' CHECKLIST

Practical Information
350 5th Ave.
Map 8 F2.
Tel (212) 736-3100. Observatories:
Open 8am–2am (last adm:
1:15am); opening hours may be
shorter on Jan 1 & Dec 24 and 31.
🖼 📷 ♿ ✏️ 🗤 esbnyc.com

Transport
Ⓜ A, B, C, D, E, F, N, Q, R, 1, 2, 3 to
34th St. 🚌 M1–5, M16, M34, Q32.

A Head for Heights
As the building took shape, construction workers often showed great bravery. Here, a worker clings to a crane hook. The Chrysler Building and other skyscrapers in the background appear surprisingly small.

Lightning Strikes
The Empire State Building is a natural lightning conductor, struck up to 100 times a year. The observation deck is open even during unfavorable weather.

Pecking Order
New Yorkers are justly proud of their city's symbol, which towers above the icons of other countries.

Big Ben 315 ft (96 m)

Great Pyramid 449 ft (137 m)

Eiffel Tower 1,063 ft (324 m)

Empire State 1,454 ft (443 m) with mast

★ **Fifth Avenue Entrance Lobby**
A relief image of the skyscraper is superimposed on a map of New York State in the marble-lined lobby.

Encounters in the Sky

The Empire State Building has been seen in many films and the finale from the 1933 classic *King Kong* is easily its most famous guest appearance, as the giant ape straddles the spire to do battle with army aircraft. In 1945 a B-25 bomber flew too low over Manhattan in fog and struck the building just above the 78th floor. The luckiest escape was that of a young elevator operator whose cabin plunged 79 floors. The emergency brakes saved her life.

8 Rubin Museum of Art

150 W. 17th St. **Map** 8 E5. **Tel** (212) 620-5000. Ⓜ 14th St, 18th St. **Open** 11am–5pm Mon & Thu, 11am–9pm Wed, 11am–10pm Fri, 11am–6pm Sat & Sun. Ⓦ **rubinmuseum.org**

This museum is a lesser-known treasure, with a collection of 2,000 paintings, sculptures, and textiles from the Himalayas, Tibet, India, and the neighboring regions. The Tibetan Buddhist Shrine Room recreates an authentic shrine with flickering lamps, and an exhibit that rotates every two years to display the four Tibetan religious traditions.

The museum also hosts captivating travel exhibitions and programs, with concerts, debates, and films. Café Serai, on the ground floor, serves Himalayan food.

9 High Line

Access at Gansevoort St, 14th St, 16th St, 18th St, and every two or three blocks to 34th St. **Map** 3 B1. **Tel** (212) 500-6035. Ⓜ 23rd St; 14th St (on lines A, C, E); 8th Ave L; Christopher St/Sheridan Sq. **Open** 7am–11pm daily (to 7pm in winter). Ⓦ **thehighline.org**

An ambitious urban renewal project that links Midtown, Chelsea, and the Meatpacking District, the High Line is a fantastic transformation of a disused, elevated railway. While the line was originally built between 1929 and 1934, it lay abandoned for years. In 1999, two local residents created

The High Line links Chelsea, Midtown, and the Meatpacking District

the organization Friends of the High Line to save the structure from demolition.

Extending from Gansevoort Street to 34th Street, the park has played an important role in the gentrification of the neighborhood. The sensational elevated promenade-cum-public-park stands 30-ft (9-m) high, with views and gardens en route. At intervals, there are art installations and food vendors. Highlights include a subtle water feature between 14th and 15th streets, and an amphitheater that offers an incredible view of 10th Avenue.

10 Chelsea Piers Complex

11th Ave (17th to 23rd Sts) **Map** 7 B5. **Tel** (212) 336-6666. Ⓜ 14th St, 18th St, 23rd St. 🚌 M14, M23. **Open** daily. 🅿 Ⓦ **chelseapiers.com**

For this mammoth complex, four neglected piers were converted

into a center with a vast range of sports and leisure activities. The facilities include skating rinks, running tracks, a rock-climbing wall, a golf driving range, a marina, and TV and film production sound stages.

11 Chelsea Art Galleries

Between W 19th St and W 27th St, around 10th and 11th Aves. **Map** 7 C4. Ⓜ 23rd St. **Open** usually 10am–6pm Tue–Sat. Ⓦ **nygallerytours.com**

Attracted by cheap rents, the many galleries that set up shop in Chelsea during the 1990s were a driving force in this area's resurgence. Between 150 and 200 venues are here, exhibiting work from up-and-coming artists in all manner of media. Check out P.P.O.W. or David Zwirner, which have a reputation for intriguing or provocative work. Try to avoid Saturdays, when art-crawler traffic is at its heaviest.

12 General Theological Seminary

440 W 21st St. **Map** 7 C4. **Tel** (212) 243-5150. Ⓜ 23rd St. **Open** 10am–3pm Mon–Fri. ✝ 11:45am Mon & Wed–Fri, 6pm Tue & Sun. ✉ ♿ Ⓦ **gts.edu**

Founded in 1817, this block-square campus accepts 150 students at a time to train for the Episcopal priesthood. Clement Clarke Moore, a professor of

Aerial view of the Chelsea Piers Complex

A 15th-century music manuscript in the General Theological Seminary

Oriental Languages at what is today Columbia University (see p218), donated the site, officially known as Chelsea Square. The earliest remaining building dates from 1836; the most modern, St. Mark's Library, was built in 1960 and holds the largest collection of Latin Bibles in the world.

Inside, the garden is laid out in two quadrangles, like an English cathedral close; it is especially lovely in the spring.

Exterior of a red-brick house on Cushman Row

⓭ Chelsea Historic District

W 20th St from 9th to 10th Aves. **Map** 8 D5. Ⓜ 18th St. 🚌 M11.

Although he is better known as the author of the poem "A Visit from St. Nicholas" than as an urban planner, Clement Clarke Moore owned an estate here and divided it into lots in the 1830s, creating handsome rows of town houses. Restoration has since rescued many of the original buildings here.

Of these, the finest are seven houses known as Cushman Row, running from 406–418 West 20th Street, and built from 1839–40 for Don Alonzo Cushman, a merchant who also founded the Greenwich Savings Bank. Cushman joined Moore and James N. Wells in the development of Chelsea. Rich in detail and intricate ironwork, Cushman Row is ranked with Washington Square North as a supreme example of Greek Revival architecture. Look for cast-iron wreaths around attic windows and the pineapples on the newel posts of two of the houses – old symbols of hospitality.

Farther along West 20th Street, from 446–450, there are fine examples of the Italianate style for which Chelsea is also renowned. The detailed brickwork arches of windows and fanlights subtly implied the wealth of the owner, being able to afford this expensive effect.

⓮ Chelsea Market

75 9th Ave (between 15th and 16th sts). **Map** 7 C5. Ⓜ 14th St. **Open** 7am–9pm Mon–Sat, 8am–8pm Sun. 🅦 chelseamarket.com

This enclosed food court and shopping mall is one of New York's unmissable destinations for foodies. Visitors can pick up a range of gourmet ingredients, exotic foodstuffs, and charming gifts here. The retail options include Lucy's Whey, for artisanal US cheeses; Chelsea Wine Vault, for a global selection of wines; and Bowery Kitchen Supply, for professional-quality equipment. Several high-end purveyors maintain bakeries and kitchens, ensuring only the

Enjoying a snack in the inviting Chelsea Market

freshest, highest-quality snacks and meals. Chelsea Market also houses the TV production facilities for the Food Network.

⓯ Hugh O'Neill Dry Goods Store

655–671 6th Ave. **Map** 8 E4. Ⓜ 23rd St.

Though the store is long gone, the 1890 cast-iron columned and pilastered façade clearly shows the scale and grandeur of the emporiums that once lined Sixth Avenue from 18th to 23rd streets – the area known as Fashion Row. O'Neill, whose sign can still be seen on the façade, was a showman and super-salesman whose trademark was a fleet of shiny delivery wagons. His customers came in droves via the conveniently close Sixth Avenue Elevated Railway. They were not the "carriage trade" enjoyed by Ladies' Mile (see p123), but their numbers allowed the Row to flourish until around 1915, when the retailing district continued its move uptown. Now mostly restored, the buildings have turned into stores and high-end condos.

Hugh O'Neill Dry Goods Store

MIDTOWN WEST AND THE THEATER DISTRICT

At the heart of Midtown lies Times Square, where huge neon displays flash and crowds bustle. The Theater District lies north of 42nd Street, and offers a fabulous concentration of live theater. It was the move of the Metropolitan Opera House to Broadway at 40th Street in 1883 that first drew theaters and restaurants here. In the 1920s, movie palaces added the glamour of neon to Broadway, the signs getting bigger and brighter, until eventually the street came to be known as the "Great White Way." After World War II, the draw of the films waned, and the glitter was replaced by grime. Fortunately, since the 1990s, redevelopment has brought the public and bright lights of Broadway back.

Sights at a Glance

Historic Streets and Buildings
- **5** New York Discovery Times Square Exposition
- **8** New York Public Library
- **11** McGraw Hill Building
- **12** Paramount Building
- **13** Shubert Alley
- **17** Alwyn Court Apartments
- **20** Hell's Kitchen

Museums and Galleries
- **18** Intrepid Sea, Air & Space Museum
- **19** Museum of Arts and Design

Modern Architecture
- **1** Rockefeller Center
- **14** 1740 Broadway

Parks and Squares
- **6** Bryant Park
- **9** Times Square

Famous Theaters
- **3** Lyceum Theatre
- **10** New Amsterdam Theatre
- **15** New York City Center
- **16** Carnegie Hall

Landmark Hotels and Restaurants
- **4** Algonquin Hotel
- **7** Bryant Park Hotel

Landmark Stores
- **2** Diamond District

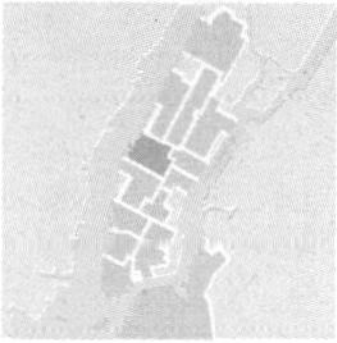

See also Street Finder maps 7, 8, 11, 12

Restaurants see pp299–302

1 Aureole	10 Marseille
2 Becco	11 Molyvos
3 Le Bernardin	12 Norma's
4 Burger Joint at Le Parker Meridien	13 Osteria al Doge
5 Carnegie Deli	14 Quality Meats
6 DB Bistro Moderne	15 The Sea Grill
7 Esca	16 Taboon
8 Estiatorio Milos	17 Virgil's Real Barbecue
9 Marea	

0 meters 500
0 yards 500

◀ Grand chandelier hanging from the ceiling of the New York Public Library

For keys to symbols see back flap

Street by Street: Times Square

Named for the 25-story New York Times Tower, which opened in 1906, Times Square has been at the heart of the city's theater district since 1899, when Oscar Hammerstein built the Victoria and Republic theaters. Since the 1920s, the glowing neon of theater billboards has combined with the *Times'* illuminated newswire and other advertising to create a spectacular lightshow. After a period of decline starting in the 1930s, which saw sex shows taking over many of the grand theaters, rejuvenation of the district began during the 1990s. Old-style Broadway glamor again rubs shoulders with modern entertainment in this part of the city.

Paramount Hotel
Designed by Philippe Starck, this hotel is the hip haunt of the theater crowd who drink in the late-night Paramount Bar *(see p310)*.

Sardi's was established in Times Square in 1921, and has walls lined with caricatures of Broadway stars of yesterday and today.

Westin Hotel is a striking 45-story building that consists of a prism split by a curving beam of light. Stunning views over the city.

E-Walk entertainment and retail complex has a multiplex cinema, restaurants, a hotel, and the B. B. King Blues Club.

W 48TH

W 47TH ST

W 45TH ST

W 43RD ST

Ⓜ

42nd St-Port Auth Bus Terminal subway (Lines A, C & E)

W 41ST ST

SEVENTH AV

Ⓜ

Times Sq-42nd St subway (lines N, Q, R, S, 1, 2, 3, 7)

❾ ★ **One Times Square**
Every New Year's Eve at midnight, the famed crystal ball drops from the top of One Times Square. There are great views from the front of this New York landmark.

★ **New Victory Theater**
This classic Broadway theater is used as a young people's performance space.

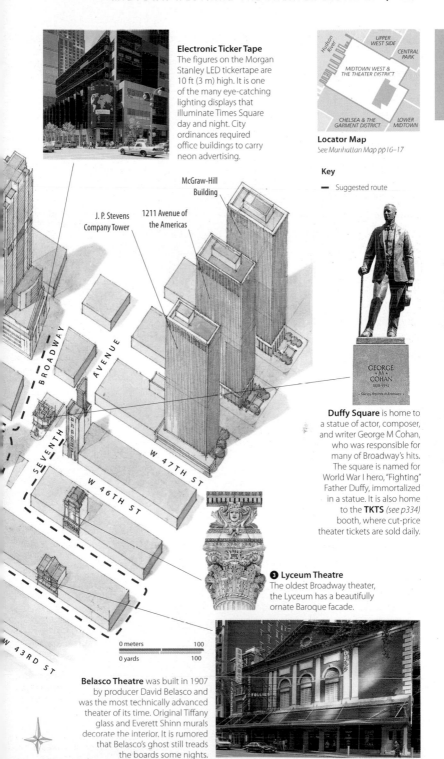

Electronic Ticker Tape
The figures on the Morgan Stanley LED tickertape are 10 ft (3 m) high. It is one of the many eye-catching lighting displays that illuminate Times Square day and night. City ordinances required office buildings to carry neon advertising.

Locator Map
See Manhattan Map pp16–17

Key
— Suggested route

McGraw-Hill Building

J. P. Stevens Company Tower

1211 Avenue of the Americas

BROADWAY

AVENUE

SEVENTH

W 47TH ST

W 46TH ST

W 43RD ST

0 meters 100
0 yards 100

Duffy Square is home to a statue of actor, composer, and writer George M Cohan, who was responsible for many of Broadway's hits. The square is named for World War I hero, "Fighting" Father Duffy, immortalized in a statue. It is also home to the **TKTS** (see p334) booth, where cut-price theater tickets are sold daily.

❸ **Lyceum Theatre**
The oldest Broadway theater, the Lyceum has a beautifully ornate Baroque facade.

Belasco Theatre was built in 1907 by producer David Belasco and was the most technically advanced theater of its time. Original Tiffany glass and Everett Shinn murals decorate the interior. It is rumored that Belasco's ghost still treads the boards some nights.

A Christmas tree stands above the Rockefeller Plaza skating rink for the holiday season.

❶ Rockefeller Center

Map 12 F5. Ⓜ 47th–50th Sts. **Tel** (212) 332-6868 (information). ♿🚫📧☕ NBC, Rockefeller Center, daily. **Tel** (212) 664-7174 (reservations advised). Radio City Music Hall, daily. **Tel** (212) 247-4777. Top of the Rock, daily. **Tel** (212) 698-2000. 🆆 rockefellercenter.com 🆆 nbc.com 🆆 radiocity.com 🆆 topoftherocknyc.com

When the New York City Landmarks Preservation Commission unanimously voted to declare Rockefeller Center a landmark in 1985, they rightly called it "the heart of New York ... a great unifying presence in the chaotic core of midtown Manhattan."

It is the largest privately owned complex of its kind. The Art Deco design was by a team of top architects headed by Raymond Hood. Works by 30 artists can be found in foyers, on facades, and in the gardens. The site, once a botanic garden owned by Columbia University, was leased in 1928 by

John D. Rockefeller, Jr., as an ideal central home for an opera house. When the 1929 Depression scuttled these plans, Rockefeller, stuck with a long lease, went ahead with his own development. The 14 buildings erected between 1931 and 1940 provided jobs for up to 225,000 people during the Depression; by 1973, there were 19 buildings.

In December 1932, Radio City Music Hall opened within the complex. It still hosts its famous Christmas and Easter shows here.

Wisdom by Lee Lawrie, Rockefeller Center

Later, NBC opened its TV studios here. Rockefeller Plaza is home to a well-known ice-skating rink in winter; it is also the site of a famous Christmas tree.

The Top of the Rock, an observatory on the 67th, 69th and 70th floors of the center, offers a dizzying 360-degree panoramic view of the city. On the 67th and 69th floors, the outdoor terraces feature transparent safety glass for stunning views downwards.

❷ Diamond District

47th St, between 5th and 6th Aves. **Map** 12 F5. Ⓜ 47th–50th Sts. *See Shopping p322.* 🆆 diamond district.org

Most shop windows on 47th Street glitter with gold and diamonds. The buildings are filled with booths and work-shops where jewelers vie for customers, while, upstairs, vast sums of money change hands. The Diamond District was born in the 1930s, when the Jewish diamond cutters of Antwerp and Amsterdam fled to the US to escape Nazism. Today, Jewish dealers still predominate. Although mainly a wholesale district, individual customers are welcome. Bring cash, compare prices, haggle, and stay away if you know nothing about the value of diamonds.

❸ Lyceum Theatre

149 W 45th St. **Map** 12 E5. **Tel** Tele-charge (212) 239-6200. Ⓜ 42nd St, 47th St, 49th St. *See Entertainment p339.* 🆆 lyceum-theatre.com

The oldest active New York theater is a frilly, Baroque-style bandbox. This 1903 triumph was the first theater by Herts and Tallant, later renowned for their extravagant style. The Lyceum made history with a record run of 1,600 performances of the comedy *Born Yesterday*. It was the first theater to be designated a historic landmark, and, though the Theater District has shifted westward, there are still many shows here.

❹ Algonquin Hotel

59 W 44th St. **Map** 12 F5. **Tel** (212) 840-6800. Ⓜ 42nd St. *See Where to Stay p289.* ⓦ **algonquinhotel.com**

No other hotel captures the city's formidable literary history quite like the Algonquin Hotel. For more than a century it has played host to home-grown talent and international luminaries. In the 1920s, the Rose Room was home to America's best-known luncheon club, the Round Table, with literary lights such as Alexander Woollcott, Franklin P. Adams, Dorothy Parker, Robert Benchley, and Harold Ross. All were associated with *The New Yorker* (Ross was the founding editor), whose 25 West 43rd Street headquarters had a back door opening into the hotel.

Renovations have preserved the old-fashioned, civilized feel of the cozy, paneled lobby, where publishing types and theatergoers still like to gather for drinks, settling into comfortable armchairs and ringing a brass bell to summon the waiters.

Elegant interior of the Lobby in the Algonquin Hotel

❺ New York Discovery Times Square Exposition

224 W 44th St. **Map** 12 E5. **Tel** (646) 368-6759. Ⓜ Times Sq–42nd St. **Open** 10am–8pm Mon–Thu & Sun, 10am–9pm Fri & Sat. ⓦ **discoverytsx.com**

Explore a host of specialized, large-scale exhibitions at this

Entrance to the New York Discovery Times Square Exposition

exposition space. Partially sponsored by the US Discovery Channel, the shows here are informative, interactive, and educational. A range of subjects are showcased – from ancient history, with major installations on King Tut, the Dead Sea Scrolls, and Pompeii, to Hollywood blockbusters, such as *The Hunger Games* and *The Avengers*. The ongoing permanent exhibition "Body Worlds: Pulse" comprises a series of real cadavers, preserved by plastination, and displayed to reveal various body parts.

❻ Bryant Park

Map 8 F1. Ⓜ 42nd St. ⓦ **bryantpark.org**

In 1853, with the New York Public Library site still occupied by Croton Reservoir, Bryant Park (then Reservoir Park) housed a dazzling Crystal Palace, built for the World's Fair of that year *(see p27).*

In the 1960s the park was a hangout for drug dealers and other undesirables. In 1989 the city renovated the park, reclaiming it for workers and visitors to relax in. In winter there is a free ice-skating rink here; in the summer, classic movies are screened.

Over seven million books lie in storage stacks beneath the park.

❼ Bryant Park Hotel

40 W 40th St. **Map** 8 F1. **Tel** (212) 869-0100. Ⓜ 42nd St. ⓦ **bryantparkhotel.com**

The American Radiator building (now the Bryant Park Hotel) was the first major New York work by Raymond Hood and John Howells, who went on to design the Daily News Building *(see p151),* the McGraw-Hill building, and Rockefeller Center. The 1924 structure is reminiscent of one of Hood's best-known Gothic buildings, Chicago's Tribune Tower. Here, the design is sleeker, giving the building the illusion of being taller than its actual 23 stories. The black brick facade is set off by gold terra-cotta trim, evoking images of flaming coals – a comparison that would have suited its original owners well, since they made heating equipment. The building is now a luxury hotel *(see p285)* across the street from Bryant Park and boasts the New York outpost of trendy LA eatery Koi.

Statue of poet William Cullen Bryant in Bryant Park

The Bryant Park Hotel, formerly the American Radiator Building

Doorway leading to New York Public
Library's Main Reading Room

❽ New York Public Library

5th Ave & 42nd St. **Map** 8 F1. **Tel** (212)
930-0830. Ⓜ 42nd St-Grand Central,
42nd St-5th Ave. **Open** 10am–6pm
Mon & Thu–Sat (till 8pm Tue & Wed),
1–5pm Sun. **Closed** public hols. ♿
📷 11am & 2pm Tue–Thu. Lectures.
📷 🆆 nypl.org

Barrel vaults of carved white marble over the stairs in the Astor Hall

In 1897 the coveted job of
designing New York's main
public library was awarded to
architects Carrère & Hastings.
The library's first director
envisaged a light, quiet, airy
place for study, where millions
of books could be stored and
yet be available to readers as
promptly as possible. In the
hands of Carrère & Hastings,

his vision came true, in what
is considered the epitome of
New York's Beaux Arts period.
Built on the site of the former
Croton Reservoir (see p26), it
opened in 1911 to immediate
acclaim, despite having cost the
city $9 million. The vast, paneled
Main Reading Room stretches
two full blocks and is suffused
with daylight from the
two interior court-
yards. Below it are
88 miles (142 km) of
shelves, holding over
seven million volumes.
A staff of over 100
and a computerized
dumb-waiter can
supply any book
within 10 minutes.
The Periodicals
Room holds 10,000
current periodicals
from 128 countries.
On its walls are murals
by Richard Haas,
honoring New York's
great publishing
houses. The original
library combined the
collections of John
Jacob Astor and

James Lenox. Its collections today
range from Thomas Jefferson's
handwritten copy of the
Declaration of Independence
to T. S. Eliot's typed copy of "The
Waste Land." More than 1,000
queries are answered daily, using
the vast database of the CATNYP
and LEO computer catalogs.
This library is the hub of a
network of 82 branches, with
nearly seven million users.
Some branches are very well-
known, such as the New York
Public Library for the Performing
Arts at the Lincoln Center
(see p206) and the Schomburg
Center in Harlem (see p223).

❾ Times Square

Map 8 E1. Ⓜ 42nd St-Times Sq.
ℹ️ NYC Information Center, Seventh Ave
at 44th St, 9am–6pm daily. 📷 (212)
484-1222. 🆆 timessquarenyc.org

The 1990s saw a transformation
in Times Square, reversing a
decline that began during the
Depression. The Square is now
a safe and vibrant place where
Broadway traditions comfortably
coexist with modern innovations.

The Main Reading Room, with its original
bronze reading lamps

W. C. Fields (far left) and Eddie Cantor (holding top hat, right) in the 1918 *Ziegfeld Follies* at the New Amsterdam Theatre

Although *The New York Times* has moved on from its original headquarters at the south end of the Square, the glistening ball (now of Waterford crystal) still drops at midnight on New Year's Eve, as it has since the building opened with fanfare and fireworks in 1906. New buildings, such as the Bertelsmann and the fashionably minimalist Condé Nast offices, sit comfortably alongside the classic Broadway theaters.

Broadway's fortunes have also revived. Many theaters have been renovated and are again housing new, more contemporary productions; theater-goers throng the area's bars and restaurants each evening.

One of the area's landmarks is the 57-story skyscraper designed by Miami architects Arquitectonica, that tops the E-Walk entertainment and retail complex at 42nd Street and Eighth Avenue (see p138). Other attractions include an outpost of Madame Tussauds wax museum at 42nd Street, between Seventh and Eighth Avenues; a massive Disney Store; Bowlmor Lanes bowling alley; a pedestrian plaza; and Toys "R"Us at 1514 Broadway.

⑩ New Amsterdam Theatre

214 W 42nd St. **Map** 8 E1. **Tel** (212) 282-2900. Ⓜ 42nd St-Times Sq. 🕙 10am–3pm Mon–Tue, 10am–11am Thu–Sat, 10am Sun; (212) 282-2907.

This was the most opulent theater in the United States when it opened in 1903, and the first to have an Art Nouveau interior. It was owned for a time by Florenz Ziegfeld, who produced his famous *Follies*

revue here between 1914 and 1918 – with Broadway's first $5 ticket price. He remodeled the roof garden into another theater, the Aerial Gardens. This is one of the fine early theaters on 42nd Street that fell on hard times. With the rehabilitation of Times Square, its fortunes rose again and it is once more in Show Business.

⑪ McGraw-Hill Building

330 W 42nd St. **Map** 8 D1. Ⓜ 42nd St-8th Ave. **Open** office hours.

This 1931 design by Raymond Hood was the only New York building selected for the influential International Style architectural survey of 1932 (see p45). Its unusual design gives it a stepped profile seen from east and west, but a slab effect viewed from the north or south. The exterior's horizontal bands of bluish green terra-cotta have earned it the nickname "jolly green giant." Step inside to see the classic Art Deco lobby of opaque glass and stainless steel.

One block west is Theater Row, a pleasant group of Off-Broadway theaters and cafés.

⑫ Paramount Building

1501 Broadway. **Map** 8 E1. Ⓜ 34th St.

The fabulous ground-floor movie theater, where bobby-soxers stood in line in the 1940s to hear Frank Sinatra perform, is gone, but there's still a theatrical feel to the

Art Deco top of the Paramount Building

massive building designed by Rapp & Rapp in 1927. On each side, 14 symmetrical setbacks rise to an Art Deco crown – a tower, clock, and globe. In the heyday of the "Great White Way," the tower was lit, with an observation deck at the top. The Hard Rock Cafe is now here, along with a retail store and a concert area.

⑬ Shubert Alley

Between W 44th and W 45th St. **Map** 12 E5. Ⓜ 42nd St-Times Sq. See Entertainment p336.

The playhouses on the streets west of Broadway are rich in theater lore – and in notable architecture. Two classic theaters built in 1913 are the Booth (222 West 45th Street), named after actor Edwin Booth, and the Shubert (225 West 44th), after theater baron Sam S. Shubert. They form the west wall of Shubert Alley, where aspiring actors once lined up, hoping for a casting in a Shubert play.

A Chorus Line ran at the Shubert until 1990, for a record 6,137 performances; Katharine Hepburn starred earlier in *The Philadelphia Story*. Across from the 44th Street end of the alley is the St. James, where Rodgers and Hammerstein made their debut with *Oklahoma!* in 1941, followed by *The King and I*. Nearby is Sardi's, the restaurant where actors waited for opening-night reviews. Irving Berlin staged *The Music Box Revue* opposite the other end of the alley in 1921. His Music Box Theatre has since housed many famous productions.

⑭ 1740 Broadway

1740 Broadway. **Map** 12 E4. Ⓜ 57th St-Seventh Ave. **Closed** to the public.

Built in 1950, the former head office of the Mutual of New York insurance company (acquired by AXA in 2004) has a weather vane that once told you everything except the wind direction. The mast turned green for fair, orange for cloudy, flashing orange for rain, and white for snow. Lights moving up the mast meant warmer weather; lights going down meant get out your overcoat! The lights remain, but are now for display only. The temperature and time are still shown.

⑮ New York City Center

131 W 55th St. **Map** 12 E4. **Tel** (212) 581-1212. Ⓜ 57th St-Seventh Ave. ✉ ♿ *See Entertainment p340.* Ⓦ **nycitycenter.org**

This highly ornate Moorish structure with its dome of Spanish tiles was designed in 1924 as a Masonic Shriners' Temple. It was saved from the developers by Mayor LaGuardia, becoming home to the New York City Opera (1944–1964) and Ballet (1948–1966). When the troupes moved to Lincoln Center, City Center lived on as

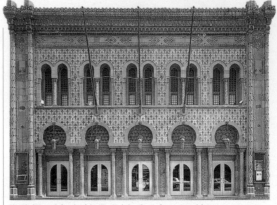

The tiled Moorish facade of the New York City Center for music and dance

a key venue for dance. Today the Alvin Ailey American Dance Theater, and the Manhattan Theatre Club are based here.

⑯ Carnegie Hall

154 W 57th Street. **Map** 12 E3. **Tel** (212) 247-7800. Ⓜ 57th St-Seventh Ave. Museum: **Open** 11am–4:30pm daily & during concert intermissions. **Closed** Wed. ✉ ♿ 🎧 11:30am, 12:30pm, 2pm & 3pm Mon–Fri; 11:30am & 12:30pm Sat; 12:30pm Sun. 📷 *See Entertainment p344.* Ⓦ **carnegiehall.org**

Financed by millionaire philanthropist Andrew Carnegie, New York's first great concert hall opened in 1891. The terracotta and brick Renaissance-style building has among the best acoustics in the world. On opening night, Tchaikovsky was a guest conductor, and New York's finest families attended. For many years it was home to the New York Philharmonic, under conductors such as Arturo Toscanini, Bruno Walter, and Leonard Bernstein. Playing Carnegie Hall quickly became an international symbol of success for musicians.

In the 1950s, a campaign by violinist Isaac Stern saved the site from redevelopment, and in 1964 it was made a national landmark. Renovation in 1986 brought the bronze balconies and the ornamental plaster back to their original splendor. In 1991, the Rose Museum opened next to the first-tier level, telling the story of the first 100 years of "The House that Music Built." In 2003, the Judy and Arthur Zankel Hall reestablished the lower level as a performance venue.

Top orchestras and performers from around the world still fill Carnegie Hall, and the corridors are lined with memorabilia of artists who have performed here.

⑰ Alwyn Court Apartments

180 W 58th St. **Map** 12 E3. Ⓜ 57th St-Seventh Ave. **Closed** to the public.

You can't miss it – not with the fanciful crowns, dragons, and

Carnegie Hall, offering some of the best acoustics in the world

other French Renaissance-style terra-cotta carvings covering the exterior of this 1909 Harde and Short apartment building. The ground floor has lost its cornice, but the rest of the building remains intact, and it's one of a kind in New York City.

The intricate façade follows the style of French King Francis I, whose symbol, a crowned salamander, can be seen above the entrance to the building.

The interior courtyard features a dazzling display of the illusionistic skills of artist Richard Haas, in which plain walls are transformed into "carved" stonework.

The crowned salamander, symbol of Francis I, on Alwyn Court

⑱ Intrepid Sea, Air & Space Museum

Pier 86, W 46th St. **Map** 11 A5. **Tel** (877) 957-SHIP. 🚌 M42, M50. **Open** Apr–Oct: 10am–5pm Mon–Fri; 10am–6pm Sat, Sun and hols; Nov–Mar: 10am–5pm daily. 🚇 📷 🅦 **intrepidmuseum.org**

Exhibits on board this World War II aircraft carrier include fighter planes from the 1940s, the A-12 Blackbird, the world's fastest spy plane, and the USS *Growler*, a guided-missile submarine launched in 1958 at the height of the Cold War.

The museum's family-friendly Exploreum Hall contains two G-Force flight simulators, a 4D motion ride theater, a Bell 47 helicopter, and an interactive submarine. In 2012, the museum introduced the Space Shuttle Pavilion, which houses the historic space shuttle *Enterprise*.

The flight deck of the *Intrepid*, with fighter jets and spy planes on display

The *Intrepid* itself was built in 1943, and survived both World War II and the Vietnam War. An exhibit chronicles the history of the aircraft carrier.

⑲ Museum of Arts and Design

2 Columbus Circle. **Map** 12 D3. **Tel** (212) 299-7777. 🚇 59th St- Columbus Circle. **Open** 10am–6pm Tue–Sun (to 9pm Thu & Fri). **Closed** public hols. 🚻 ✉ ♿ 🚇 Lectures, films. 📷 🅦 **madmuseum.org**

The leading American cultural institution of its kind, this museum, housed in a modern, and eye-catching building is dedicated to contemporary objects in an array of media, from clay and wood to metal and fiber. The permanent collection has over 2,000 artifacts by international craftsmen and designers.

Its four exhibition floors host special exhibitions and include the Tiffany & Co. Foundation Jewelry Gallery, which focuses on studio jewelry. Items by top-class American craftsmen are on sale in The Store at MAD.

⑳ Hell's Kitchen

Map 11 B5–C5. 🚇 50th St:

West of Times Square, roughly between 30th and 59th streets, lies Clinton, more commonly known as Hell's Kitchen. Today the area has a culinary reputation, but in the late 1800s it was a poor Irish enclave, reputed to be one of New York's most violent neighborhoods, as Greeks, Puerto Ricans, and African Americans moved in and tensions rapidly developed. Such rivalries were popularized in the musical *West Side Story* (1957). The area has been cleaned up, with rents sky-rocketing and Ninth Avenue especially crammed with restaurants, bars, and delis. There's also a strong gay community, with as many gay bars as in Chelsea or the East Village.

Restaurants and bars in Hell's Kitchen

LOWER MIDTOWN

From Beaux Arts to Art Deco, this section of Midtown boasts some fine architecture, chic boutiques, and towering skyscrapers, primarily scattered along Fifth, Madison, and Park avenues. Quiet, residential Murray Hill, between East 34th and East 40th streets, was named for a country estate that once occupied the site. By the turn of the 20th century, it was home to many of New York's first families, including the financier J. P. Morgan, whose library, now a museum, reveals the grandeur of the age. The commercial pace quickens at 42nd Street, near Grand Central Terminal, where tall office buildings line the streets. However, few of the newer buildings have equaled the Beaux Arts Terminal itself or such Art Deco beauties as the Chrysler Building, while the Modernist United Nations complex overlooks the East River.

Sights at a Glance

Historic Streets and Buildings
2 Grand Central Terminal pp152–3
3 Bowery Savings Bank Building
4 Chanin Building
5 Chrysler Building
6 Daily News Building
7 Ford Foundation Building
8 Helmsley Building
12 Fred F. French Building
15 Sniffen Court

Museums and Galleries
11 Japan Society
14 The Morgan Library & Museum pp160–61

Modern Architecture
1 MetLife Building
9 1 and 2 United Nations Plaza
10 United Nations pp156–9

Churches
13 Church of the Incarnation

See also Street Finder
maps 8, 9, 12, 13

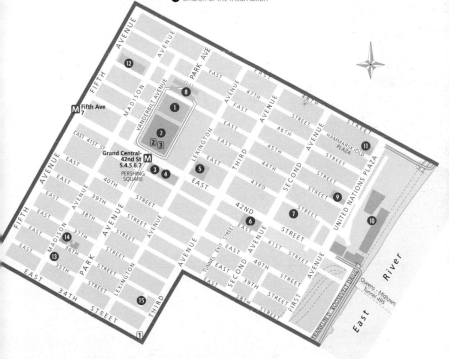

0 meters 400
0 yards 400

◀ Terraced arches with triangular windows on the spire of the Chrysler Building   **For keys to symbols** see back flap

Street by Street: Lower Midtown

A walk in the neighborhood allows you to see an eclectic mix of New York's architectural styles. Step back to appreciate the contours of the tallest skyscrapers, and step inside to experience the many fine interiors, from modern atriums such as those in the Philip Morris and Ford Foundation buildings, to the ornate details of the Bowery Savings Bank Building and the soaring spaces of Grand Central Terminal.

❶ MetLife Building
This skyscraper, built by Pan Am in 1963, towers above Park Avenue.

❷ ★ Grand Central Terminal
The vast, vaulted interior is a splendid reminder of the heyday of train travel. This historic building also features specialty shops and gourmet restaurants.

Grand Central-42nd St subway (lines S, 4, 5, 6, 7)

PARK AVENUE

E 41ST ST

LEXINGTON AVENUE

❹ Chanin Building
Built for self-made real estate mogul Irwin S. Chanin in the 1920s, this building has a fine Art Deco lobby.

❸ ★ Bowery Savings Bank Building
Formerly the headquarters of the Bowery Savings Bank, this is one of the finest bank buildings in New York. Architects York & Sawyer designed it to resemble a Romanesque palace.

The Mobil Building has a self-cleaning stainless steel facade that is embossed in geometric patterns to prevent it from warping. It was built in 1955.

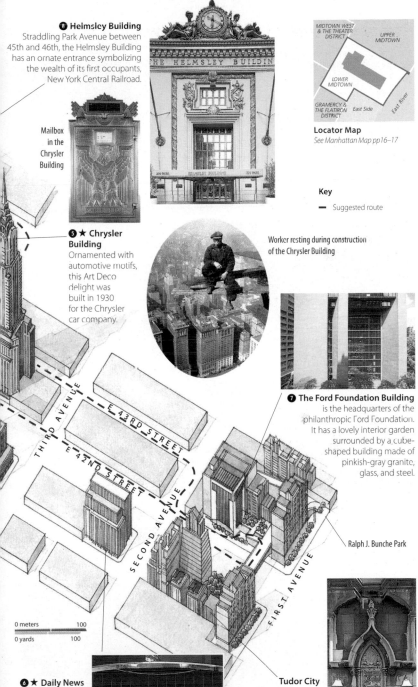

8 Helmsley Building
Straddling Park Avenue between 45th and 46th, the Helmsley Building has an ornate entrance symbolizing the wealth of its first occupants, New York Central Railroad.

Mailbox in the Chrysler Building

Locator Map
See Manhattan Map pp16–17

MIDTOWN WEST & THE THEATER DISTRICT

UPPER MIDTOWN

LOWER MIDTOWN

GRAMERCY & THE FLATIRON DISTRICT East Side

East River

Key
— Suggested route

5 ★ Chrysler Building
Ornamented with automotive motifs, this Art Deco delight was built in 1930 for the Chrysler car company.

Worker resting during construction of the Chrysler Building

7 The Ford Foundation Building
is the headquarters of the philanthropic Ford Foundation. It has a lovely interior garden surrounded by a cube-shaped building made of pinkish-gray granite, glass, and steel.

THIRD AVENUE

E 43RD STREET

E 42ND STREET

SECOND AVENUE

FIRST AVENUE

Ralph J. Bunche Park

0 meters 100
0 yards 100

6 ★ Daily News Building
The Art Deco former home of the eponymous newspaper has a revolving globe in the lobby.

Tudor City
This 1928 private residential complex has 3,000 apartments. Built in the Tudor style, it features fine stonework details.

Lobby of the MetLife Building

❶ MetLife Building

200 Park Ave. **Map** 13 A5. Ⓜ 42nd St-
Grand Central. **Open** office hours.
🚹 ⬇

Once, the sculptures atop the
Grand Central Terminal stood
out against the sky. Then this
colossus, formerly called the Pan
Am Building and designed in
the Modernist style by Walter
Gropius, Emery Roth and Sons,
and Pietro Belluschi, rose up in
1963 to block the Park Avenue
view. It dwarfed the terminal
and aroused universal dislike.
At the time it was the largest
commercial building in the
world, and the dismay over its
scale helped thwart a later plan
to build a tower over the
terminal itself.

It is ironic that the New York
skies were blocked by Pan Am,
a company that had opened
up the skies as a means of
travel for millions of people.
When the company began
in 1927, Charles Lindbergh,
fresh from his solo transatlantic flight, was one of
their pilots and an adviser on
new routes. By 1936, Pan Am
managed to introduce the first
trans-Pacific passenger route,
and in 1947 they introduced the
first round-the-world route.

The building's rooftop heliport
was abandoned in 1977 after a
freak accident showered debris
onto the surrounding streets.
In 1981 the building was sold to
the Metropolitan Life organization, and then on to Tishman
Speyer Properties.

❷ Grand Central Terminal

See pp152–3.

❸ Bowery Savings Bank Building

110 E 42nd St. **Map** 9 A1. Ⓜ 42nd St-
Grand Central. **Open** by appt only.
Cipriani **Tel** (646) 723-0826.

Many consider this 1923 building
the best work of bank
architects York &
Sawyer, who chose the
style of a Romanesque
basilica for the offices of
the venerable Bowery
Savings Bank (now part
of Capital One Bank).
An arched entry leads
into the vast banking
room, with a high-
beamed ceiling, marble
mosaic floors, and marble
columns that support the stone
arches that soar overhead.

Facade of the Bowery
Savings Bank Building

Between the columns are
unpolished mosaic panels of
marble from France and Italy.
The building is also home to
Cipriani restaurant, whose
opulent decor lures high
rollers for celebratory dinners.

Stonework detail on the Chanin Building

❹ Chanin Building

122 E 42nd St. **Map** 9 A1. Ⓜ 42nd St-
Grand Central. **Open** office hours.

Once the headquarters of
Irwin S. Chanin, one of New
York's leading real estate
developers, the 56-story tower
was the first skyscraper in the
Grand Central area, a harbinger
of things to come.
It was designed by
Sloan & Robertson
in 1929 and is one of
the best examples of
the Art Deco period.
A wide bronze band,
patterned with birds
and fish, runs the full
length of the facade;
the terra-cotta base
is decorated with a
luxuriant tangle of stylized
leaves and flowers. Inside,
Radio City's sculptor René
Chambellan worked on the
reliefs and the bronze grilles,
elevator doors, mailboxes,
clocks, and pattern of waves
in the floor. The vestibule reliefs
chart the career of Chanin, who
was a self-made man.

Carved detail in the former banking hall of the Bowery Savings Bank

Stainless-steel gargoyle on the Chrysler Building

❺ Chrysler Building

405 Lexington Ave. **Map** 9 A1.
Tel (212) 682-3070. Ⓜ 42nd St-Grand
Central. **Open** office hours
(7am–6pm), lobby only. ♿

Walter P. Chrysler began his career in a Union Pacific Railroad machine shop, but his passion for the motor car helped him rise swiftly to the top of this industry, to found, in 1925, the corporation bearing his name. His wish for a headquarters in New York that symbolized his company led to a building that will always be linked with the golden age of motoring. Following Chrysler's wishes, the stainless-steel Art Deco spire resembles a car radiator grille; the building's series of stepped setbacks are emblazoned with winged radiator caps, wheels, and stylized automobiles; and there are gargoyles modeled on hood ornaments from the 1929 Chrysler Plymouth.

It stands at 1,046ft (320 m), but it lost the title of tallest building in the world to the Empire State Building a few months after its completion in 1930. William Van Alen's 77-story Chrysler Building and its shining crown are still, however, among the city's best-known and most-loved landmarks.

The crowning spire was kept a secret until the last moment, when, having been built in the fire shaft, it was raised into position through the roof, ensuring that the building would be higher than the Bank of Manhattan, then just completed downtown by Van Alen's great rival, H. Craig Severance.

Van Alen was poorly rewarded for his labors. Chrysler accused him of accepting bribes from contractors and refused to pay him. Van Alen's career never recovered from the slur.

The stunning lobby, once used as a showroom for Chrysler cars, was perfectly restored in 1978. It is lavishly decorated with patterned marbles and granite from around the world and has a chromed steel trim. A vast painted ceiling by Edward Trumball shows transportation scenes of the late 1920s.

Although the Chrysler Corporation never occupied the building as their headquarters, their name remains, as firm a fixture as the gargoyles.

Elevator door at the Chrysler Building

Entrance to the Daily News Building

❻ Daily News Building

220 E 42nd St. **Map** 9 B1.
Ⓜ 42nd St-Grand Central.
Open 8am–6pm Mon–Fri.

The *Daily News* was founded in 1919, and by 1925 it was a million-seller. It was known, rather scathingly, as "the servant girl's bible," for its concentration on scandals, celebrities, and murders, its readable style, and heavy use of illustration. Over the years it has stuck to what it does best, and the formula paid off handsomely. It revealed stories such as the romance of Edward VIII and Mrs. Simpson, and has become renowned for its punchy headlines. Its circulation figures are still among the highest in the United States.

Its headquarters, designed by Raymond Hood in 1930, have rows of brown and black brick alternating with windows to create a vertical striped effect. Hood's lobby is familiar to many as that of the *Daily Planet* in the 1980s *Superman* movies. It includes the world's largest interior globe, and bronze lines on the floor indicate the direction of world cities and the position of the planets. At night, the intricate detail over the front entrance of the building is lit from within by neon. The newspaper's offices are now at 4 New York Plaza, but this building has been designated as a national historic landmark.

❷ Grand Central Terminal

In 1871 Cornelius Vanderbilt (1794–1877) opened a railway station on 42nd Street. Although often revamped, it was never large enough and was finally demolished. The present station opened in 1913. This Beaux Arts gem has been a gateway to and symbol of the city ever since. Its glory is the soaring main concourse and the way it separates pedestrian and train traffic. The building has a steel frame covered with plaster and marble. Reed & Stern were in charge of the logistical planning; Warren & Wetmore, the overall design. The restoration by architects Beyer Blinder Belle is outstanding.

42nd Street colonnaded facade

Statuary on the 42nd Street Facade
Jules-Alexis Coutan's sculptures of Mercury, Hercules, and Minerva, in his work *Glory of Commerce*, crown the main entrance.

Cornelius Vanderbilt
The railroad magnate was known as the "Commodore."

KEY

① **Subway**

② **Circumferential Road**

③ **As many as 750,000 people** pass through the terminal each day. An escalator leads up into the MetLife Building, where there are specialty shops and restaurants.

④ **Main Concourse Level**

⑤ **Vanderbilt Hall**, adjacent to the Main Concourse, is a fine example of Beaux Arts architecture. It is decorated with gold chandeliers and pink marble.

⑥ **The Lower Level** is linked to the other levels by stairways, ramps, and escalators.

Grand Central Oyster Bar
This popular spot *(see p302)*, with its yellow Guastavino tiles, is one of the many eateries in the station. The dining concourse, on the lower level, is enormous, with food, snacks, and drinks to suit all tastes.

★ **Main Concourse**
This vast area with its vaulted ceiling is dominated by three great arched windows on each side.

Vaulted Ceiling
A medieval manuscript provided the basis for French artist Paul Helleu's zodiac design containing over 2,500 stars. Lights pinpoint the major constellations.

Grand Staircase
There are now two of these double flights of marble steps, styled after the staircase in Paris's opera house, and a vivid reminder of the glamorous days of early rail travel.

★ **Central Information**
This four-faced clock tops the travel information booth on the Main Concourse.

❼ Ford Foundation Building

320 E 43rd St. **Map** 9 B1. Ⓜ 42nd St–Grand Central.

Built in 1968, this building was designed by architect Kevin Roche, and featured the first of the atria, now common across Manhattan. The structure stands as one of the most unique spaces in New York, embodied by pink-and-brown granite, and weathered steel. The atrium resembles an enormous greenhouse, supported by towering columns of granite. A subtropical garden of its own, the atrium transforms with the seasons – it was one of the first attempts at a natural environment within a building. It is fringed by two walls of offices that are visible through glass windows, and yet the enclave is incredibly tranquil. The din of 42nd Street disappears, and all that remains is the echo of voices, the murmur of fountains, and the sound of shoes on brick walkways.

Stairway to the captivating Ford Foundation Building

❽ Helmsley Building

230 Park Ave. **Map** 13 A5. Ⓜ 42nd St-Grand Central. **Open** office hours.

One of the great New York views looks south down Park Avenue to the Helmsley

Performance at the Japan Society

Building straddling the busy traffic flow beneath. There is just one flaw – the monolithic MetLife Building (which was built by Pan Am as its corporate headquarters in 1963) that towers behind it, replacing the building's former backdrop, the sky.

Built by Warren & Wetmore in 1929, the Helmsley Building was originally the headquarters of the New York Central Railroad Company. Its namesake, the late Harry Helmsley, was a billionaire who began his career as a New York office boy for $12 per week. His wife Leona, who passed away in 2007, was a prominent feature in all the advertisements for their hotel chain – until her imprisonment in 1989 for tax evasion on a grand scale. Many observers believe that the extravagant glitter of the building's face-lift is due to Leona's overblown taste in decor.

❾ 1 and 2 United Nations Plaza

Map 13 B5. Ⓜ 42nd St–Grand Central. 🚌 M15, M42, M50.

These two great columns of blue-green mirrored glass are set at an angle to each other; the play of light and reflections on their gleaming sides and sloping setbacks make them seem a giant, ever-changing work of modern art. The marble and mirrored interiors are also stunning. They house streamlined modern offices and, in No. 1, the ONE UN New York Hotel. Here, the guest list frequently includes many UN delegates from all over the world as well as a number of visiting heads of state. Even the stresses of international diplomacy must ease when one is floating lazily in the glassed-in swimming pool, enjoying the bird's-eye views of the city and the United Nations itself.

❿ United Nations

See pp156–9.

⓫ Japan Society

333 E 47th St. **Map** 13 B5. **Tel** (212) 832-1155. Ⓜ 42nd St-Grand Central. 🚌 M15, M50. Gallery: **Open** 11am–6pm Tue–Thu, 11am–9pm Fri, 11am–5pm Sat & Sun. ✉ ♿ 🎦 Ⓦ japansociety.org

The headquarters of the Japan Society, founded in 1907 to foster understanding and cultural exchange between Japan and the US, was built with

Roman gods reclining against the Helmsley Building clock

the help of John D. Rockefeller III, who underwrote costs of some $4.3 million. The striking black building with its delicate sun grilles was designed by Tokyo architects Junzo Yoshimura and George Shimamoto in 1971. It includes an auditorium, a language center, a research library, a museum gallery, and traditional Oriental gardens.

Changing exhibits include a variety of Japanese arts, from swords to kimonos to scrolls. The society offers programs of Japanese performing arts, lectures, language classes, and many business workshops for American and Japanese executives and managers.

⑫ Fred F. French Building

521 5th Ave. **Map** 12 F5. Ⓜ 42nd St–Grand Central. **Open** office hours.

Built in 1927 to house the best-known real estate firm of the day, this edifice is a fabulously opulent creation.

It was designed by French's chief architect, H. Douglas Ives, in collaboration with Sloan & Robertson, whose other work

Tiffany stained-glass window in the Church of the Incarnation

included the Chanin Building (see p150). They handsomely blended Near Eastern, ancient Egyptian, and Greek styles with early Art Deco forms.

Multicolored faience ornaments decorate the upper facade, and the water tower is hidden in a false top level of the building. Its disguise is an elaborate one, with reliefs showing a rising sun flanked by griffins and bees and symbols of virtues such as integrity and industry. Winged Assyrian beasts ride on a bronze frieze over the entrance. These exotic themes continue into the vaulted lobby, with its elaborate polychrome ceiling decoration and 25 gilt-bronze doors. This was the first building project to employ members of the Native Canadian Caughnawaga tribe as construction workers. They did not fear heights and soon became highly sought after as scaffolders for many of the city's most famous skyscrapers.

⑬ Church of the Incarnation

209 Madison Ave. **Map** 9 A2. **Tel** (212) 689-6350. Ⓜ 42nd St-Grand Central, 33rd St. **Open** 11:30am–2pm Mon–Fri (also 4–7pm Tue, 5–7pm Wed), 1–4pm Sat, 8:15am–12:30pm Sun. ✝ 12:15pm & 6:30pm Wed, 12:45pm Fri, 8:30am & 11am Sun. ♿ ⓖ by appointment. ⓦ **churchoftheincarnation.org**

This Episcopal church dates from 1864, when Madison Avenue was home to the elite. Its patterned sandstone and brownstone exterior is typical of the period. The interior has an oak communion rail by Daniel Chester French; a chancel mural by John La Farge; and stained-glass windows by La Farge, Tiffany, William Morris, and Edward Burne-Jones.

⑭ The Morgan Library & Museum

See pp160–61.

⑮ Sniffen Court

150–158 E 36th St. **Map** 9 A2. Ⓜ 33rd St.

Here is a delightful, intimate courtyard of 10 brick Romanesque Revival carriage houses, built by John Sniffen in the 1850s. They are perfectly and improbably preserved off a busy block in modern New York. The house at the south end was used as a studio by the American sculptor Malvina Hoffman, whose plaques of Greek horsemen decorate the exterior wall.

Malvina Hoffman's studio

Lobby of the Fred F. French Building

⑩ United Nations

Founded in 1945 with 51 members, the United Nations now numbers 193 nations. Its aims are to preserve world peace, to promote self-determination, and to aid economic and social well-being around the globe. New York was chosen as the UN headquarters, and John D. Rockefeller, Jr. donated $8.5 million for the purchase of the site. The chief architect was American Wallace Harrison, who worked with an international Board of Design Consultants, and completed the core complex of the site between 1948 and 1952. The 18-acre (7-ha) site is an international zone, with its own stamps and post office. In 2006, the UN's General Assembly approved a $1.9-billion renovation of the complex, and this was completed in 2015.

United Nations headquarters

★ **Security Council**
Delegates and their assistants confer around the horseshoe-shaped table, while verbatim reporters and other UN staff members sit at the long table in the center.

KEY

① **Economic and Social Council**

② **Trusteeship Council**

③ **The Conference Building** houses meeting rooms for the Security Council, the Trusteeship Council, and the Economic and Social Council.

④ **Secretariat building**

⑤ **The statue of peace** was a gift from the former Yugoslavia.

★ **Peace Bell**
Cast from the coins of 60 nations, this gift from Japan hangs on a cypress pagoda shaped like a Shinto shrine.

Rose Garden
Twenty-five varieties of roses adorn the manicured gardens on the East River.

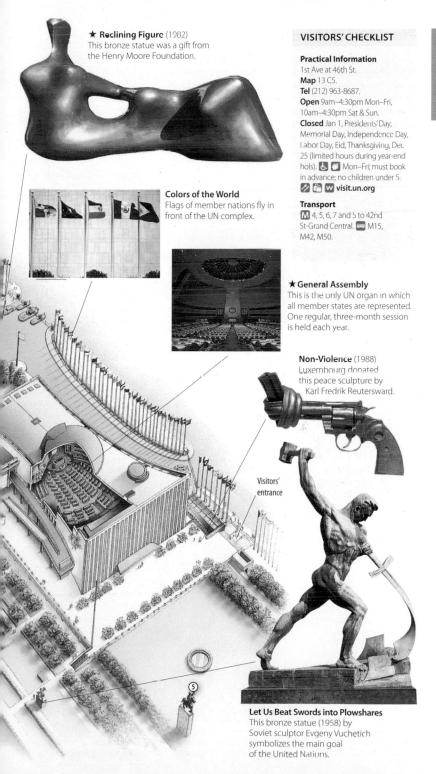

★ **Reclining Figure** (1982)
This bronze statue was a gift from the Henry Moore Foundation.

Colors of the World
Flags of member nations fly in front of the UN complex.

★ **General Assembly**
This is the only UN organ in which all member states are represented. One regular, three-month session is held each year.

Non-Violence (1988)
Luxembourg donated this peace sculpture by Karl Fredrik Reutersward.

Visitors' entrance

Let Us Beat Swords into Plowshares
This bronze statue (1958) by Soviet sculptor Evgeny Vuchetich symbolizes the main goal of the United Nations.

The Work of the United Nations

The goals of the United Nations are pursued by three UN councils and a General Assembly comprising all of its member nations. The Secretariat carries out the administrative work of the organization. Guided tours allow visitors to see the Security Council Chamber. Often there is a chance to briefly observe a meeting.

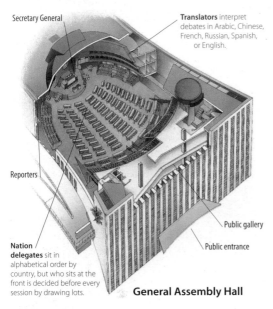

Secretary General

Translators interpret debates in Arabic, Chinese, French, Russian, Spanish, or English.

Reporters

Public gallery

Public entrance

Nation delegates sit in alphabetical order by country, but who sits at the front is decided before every session by drawing lots.

General Assembly Hall

General Assembly

The General Assembly is the governing body of the UN and has regular sessions each year from mid-September to mid-December. Special sessions are also held when the Security Council or a majority of members request one. All of the member states are represented with an equal vote, regardless of size. The General Assembly may discuss any international problem raised by the members or by other UN bodies. Although it cannot enact laws, its recommendations strongly influence world opinion; these require a two-thirds majority vote.

Lots are drawn before each session to determine the seating in the chamber for the delegations. All 1,898 seats in the chamber are equipped with earphones that offer simultaneous translations in several languages. The General

Assembly also appoints the Secretary General (on the recommendation of the Security Council), approves the UN budgets, and elects the non-permanent members of the Councils. Together with the

Foucault's Pendulum (Holland); its slowly rotating swing is proof of the earth's rotation on its axis

Security Council, it also appoints the judges of the International Court of Justice, based in the Netherlands.

Mural symbolizing peace and freedom by Per Krohg (Norway)

Security Council

The most powerful part of the UN is the Security Council. It strives to achieve international peace and security and intervenes in crises such as the fighting in Iraq and Afghanistan. It is the only body whose decisions member states are obliged to obey, as well as the only one in continuous session.

Five of its members – China, France, the Russian Federation, the United Kingdom, and the United States – are permanent. The other nations are elected by the General Assembly to serve two-year terms.

When international conflicts arise, the Council first tries to seek agreement by mediation. If fighting breaks out, it may issue cease-fire orders and impose military or economic sanctions. It could also decide to send UN peacekeeping missions into troubled areas to separate opposing factions until issues can be resolved through diplomatic channels.

Military intervention is the Council's last resort. UN forces may be deployed, and peace-keeping forces are resident in such places as Cyprus and the Middle East.

Trusteeship Council

The smallest of the councils, this is the only UN body whose workload is decreasing. The council was established in 1945 with the goal of fostering peaceful independence for non-self-governing territories or colonies. Since then, more than 80 colonies have gained self-rule, and the number of people living in dependent territories has been reduced from 750 million to about 3 million. The Trusteeship Council consists of the five permanent members of the Security Council.

Trusteeship Council Chamber

Economic and Social Council

The 54 members of this Council work to improve the standard of living and social welfare around the world, goals that consume 80 per cent of the UN's resources. It makes recommendations to the General Assembly, to each member nation, and to the UN's specialized agencies. The Council is assisted by commissions dealing with regional economic problems, human rights abuses, population, narcotics, and women's rights. It also works with the International Labor Organization, the World Health Organization, UNICEF, and other global welfare organizations.

Secretariat

An international staff of 16,000 works for the Secretariat to carry out the day-to-day work of the United Nations. The Secretariat is headed by the Secretary General, who plays a key role as a spokesperson in the organization's peace-keeping efforts. The Secretary General is appointed by the General Assembly for a five-year term. On January 1, 2012, Ban Ki-moon of South Korea was elected for a second term as Secretary General.

Zanetti mural (Dominican Republic), in the Conference Building, depicting the struggle for peace

Important Events in UN History

The UN depends on voluntary compliance and military support from its members to keep the peace in the event of disputes. In 1948, the UN declared South Korea the legitimate government of Korea; two years later, it played a major role in defending South Korea against North Korea. In 1949, the UN helped negotiate a cease-fire between Indonesia and the Netherlands and set up a conference that led to the Dutch granting independence to Indonesia.

In 1964 a UN military force was sent to Cyprus to keep peace between the Greeks and Turks, and it still remains. Persistent issues in the Middle East have kept UN forces in the area since 1974, the year that China – long refused membership

in favor of Taiwan – gained UN membership. In the 1990s, the UN was involved in the break-up of Yugoslavia, and more recently in the conflicts in Afghanistan, Libya and Syria. A 2004 UN mission to Congo was plagued by accusations of sexual abuse by UN peacekeepers. In 2006–7 there were arrests over kick-backs in the UN oil-for-food program to Iraq.

At any given time at least half a dozen missions are active somewhere in the world. The UN was awarded the Nobel Peace Prize in 1988 and 2001.

Soviet premier Khrushchev speaking to the General Assembly in 1960

Works of Art at the UN

The UN Building has acquired numerous works of art and reproductions by major artists; many have been gifts from member nations. Most of them have either a peace or international friendship theme. The legend on Norman Rockwell's *The Golden Rule* reads "Do unto others as you would have them do unto you." Marc Chagall designed a large stained-glass window as a memorial to former Secretary General Dag Hammarskjöld, who was accidentally killed while on a peace mission in 1961. There is a Henry Moore sculpture in the grounds (limited access) and many other sculptures and paintings by the artists of many nations.

The Golden Rule (1985), a large mosaic by Norman Rockwell

⓮ The Morgan Library & Museum

The Morgan Library's collection, accumulated by banker Pierpont Morgan, is housed in a magnificent palazzo-style 1906 building by architects McKim, Mead & White. Morgan's son, J. P. Morgan, Jr., made it a public institution in 1924. One of the world's finest collections of rare manuscripts, drawings, prints, books, and bindings is on display in a complex that includes the original library, completed in 1928, and the brownstone home of J. P. Morgan, Jr.

Exterior of the original library building

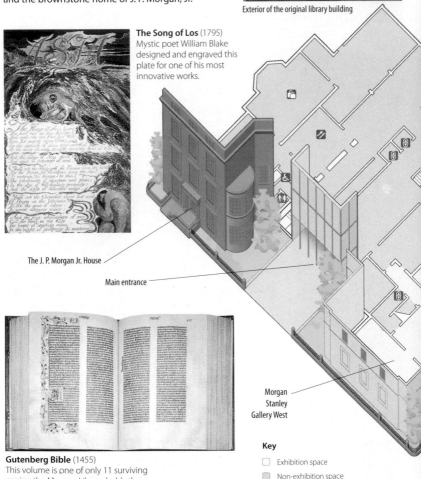

The Song of Los (1795)
Mystic poet William Blake designed and engraved this plate for one of his most innovative works.

The J. P. Morgan Jr. House

Main entrance

Morgan Stanley Gallery West

Key
☐ Exhibition space
▨ Non-exhibition space

Gutenberg Bible (1455)
This volume is one of only 11 surviving copies; the Morgan Library holds three in total.

Mozart's Horn Concerto in E-flat Major
The six surviving leaves of this score are written in different-colored inks.

Library Guide

Mr. Morgan's Study and the original library contain some of his favorite paintings, objets d'art and rare acquisitions. Changing exhibitions feature a wide variety of impressive cultural artifacts.

★ **Mr. Morgan's Study**
Renaissance art and an antique, Florentine wooden ceiling adorn this room.

First floor

★ **Mr. Morgan's Library**
The walls are lined from floor to ceiling with triple tiers of bookcases. Murals show historical figures and their muses, and signs of the zodiac.

★ **The Rotunda**
The entrance foyer of The Morgan Library has marble columns and pilasters; the marble floor is modeled on the floor in Villa Pia in the Vatican gardens.

Clare Eddy
Thaw Gallery

Morgan Stanley
Gallery East

The Nursery Alice
Lewis Carroll's characters are immortalized in Sir John Tenniel's classic illustrations (c.1865).

Pierpont Morgan

Pierpont Morgan (1837–1913) was not only a leading financier but also one of the great collectors of his time. Rare books and original manuscripts were his passion, and inclusion in his collection was an honor. In 1909, when Morgan requested the donation of the manuscript of *Pudd'nhead Wilson*, Mark Twain responded, "One of my high ambitions is gratified."

UPPER MIDTOWN

Upscale New York in all its diversity is here, in this district of churches and synagogues, clubs and museums, grand hotels and famous stores, as well as trendsetting skyscrapers. Upper Midtown was once home to society names, such as Astor and Vanderbilt. The Waldorf Astoria Hotel, completed in 1931, is where the Waldorf salad originated and, in 1934, the Bloody Mary was first served at the King Cole Bar in the St. Regis Hotel. In the 1950s, architectural history was made when the Lever and Seagram buildings were erected. Today, the Museum of Modern Art (MoMA), one of the greatest art galleries in the world, stands here.

Sights at a Glance

Historic Streets and Buildings
1 Fifth Avenue
8 Villard Houses
10 General Electric Building
16 Sutton Place
17 Roosevelt Island
20 Fuller Building

Modern Architecture
3 IBM Building
12 Lever House
13 Seagram Building
14 Citigroup Center

Museums and Galleries
5 Museum of Modern Art (MoMA) pp168–71
6 Paley Center for Media

Churches and Synagogues
4 St. Thomas Church
7 St. Patrick's Cathedral pp174–5
9 St. Bartholomew's Church
15 Central Synagogue

Landmark Hotels
11 Waldorf-Astoria
21 Plaza Hotel

Landmark Stores
2 Tiffany & Co.
19 Bloomingdale's

Parks and Squares
18 Franklin D. Roosevelt Four Freedoms Park

Restaurants see pp299–302
1 Aquavit
2 BLT Steak
3 Dawat
4 Felidia
5 Four Seasons
6 La Grenouille
7 Pampano
8 Rue 57
9 Shun Lee Palace
10 Smith & Wollensky

See also Street Finder maps 12, 13, 14

◄ Beautiful stained-glass windows inside St. Patrick's Cathedral

For keys to symbols see back flap

Street by Street: Upper Midtown

The luxury stores that are synonymous with Fifth Avenue first blossomed as society moved on uptown. In 1917, Cartier acquired the mansion of banker Morton F. Plant, supposedly in exchange for a string of pearls, setting the style for other retailers to follow. But this stretch of Midtown is not simply for shoppers. There are some distinctive museums and a diverse assembly of archi-tectural styles to enjoy, too.

❶ Fifth Avenue
Carriage rides have been replaced with rickshaws and iconic yellow taxis, offering tourists more leisurely ways to view some of the main sights.

The University Club
was built in 1899 as an elite club for gentlemen.

❹ St. Thomas Church
Much of the interior carving was designed by sculptor Lee Lawrie.

❺ ★ Museum of Modern Art
One of the world's finest collections of modern art.

❻ Paley Center for Media
Exhibitions, seasons of special screenings, live events, and a vast library of historic broadcasts are offered at this media museum.

Fifth Avenue subway (lines E, V)

Saks Fifth Avenue
has offered goods in impeccable taste to generations of New Yorkers (see p313).

❼ ★ St. Patrick's Cathedral
This, one of the largest Catholic cathedrals in the United States, is a magnificent Gothic Revival building.

Olympic Tower
combines offices, apartments and a skylit atrium within its sleek walls.

❽ Villard Houses
Five handsome brownstone houses now form part of the Lotte New York Palace Hotel.

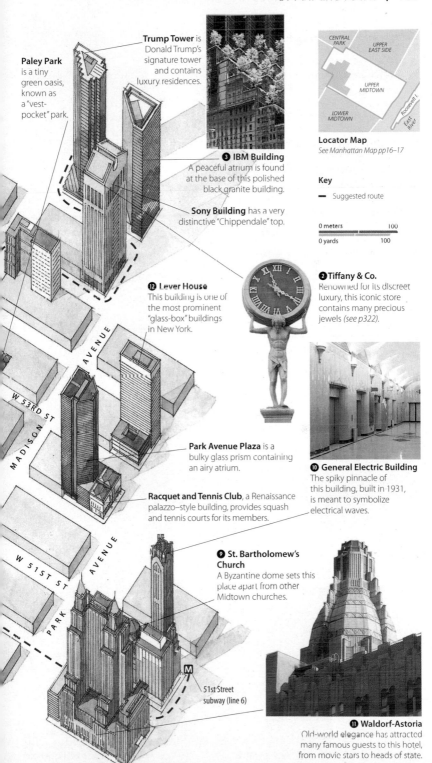

Paley Park is a tiny green oasis, known as a "vest-pocket" park.

Trump Tower is Donald Trump's signature tower and contains luxury residences.

❸ IBM Building
A peaceful atrium is found at the base of this polished black granite building.

Sony Building has a very distinctive "Chippendale" top.

⓬ Lever House
This building is one of the most prominent "glass-box" buildings in New York.

Park Avenue Plaza is a bulky glass prism containing an airy atrium.

Racquet and Tennis Club, a Renaissance palazzo–style building, provides squash and tennis courts for its members.

❾ St. Bartholomew's Church
A Byzantine dome sets this place apart from other Midtown churches.

M 51st Street subway (line 6)

Locator Map
See Manhattan Map pp16–17

Key

— Suggested route

| 0 meters | 100 |
| 0 yards | 100 |

❷ Tiffany & Co.
Renowned for its discreet luxury, this iconic store contains many precious jewels (see p322).

❿ General Electric Building
The spiky pinnacle of this building, built in 1931, is meant to symbolize electrical waves.

⓫ Waldorf-Astoria
Old-world elegance has attracted many famous guests to this hotel, from movie stars to heads of state.

A bright window display at Bergdorf Goodman

❶ Fifth Avenue

Map 12 F3–F4. Ⓜ 5th Ave–53rd St, 5th Ave–59th St.

In 1883, when William Henry Vanderbilt built his mansion at Fifth Avenue and 51st Street, he started a trend that resulted in palatial residences stretching as far as Central Park, built for wealthy families such as the Astors, Belmonts, and Goulds. Only a few remain to attest to the grandeur of the era.

One of these is the Cartier store at 651 Fifth Avenue, once the home of Morton F. Plant, millionaire and commodore of the New York Yacht Club. As retailers swept north up the avenue – a trend that began in 1906 – society gradually moved uptown. In 1917, Plant moved to a mansion at 86th Street, and legend has it that he traded his old home to Pierre Cartier for a perfectly matched string of pearls.

Fifth Avenue has been synonymous with luxury goods ever since. From Cartier at 52nd Street to Henri Bendel at 56th and Tiffany and Bergdorf Goodman at 57–58th, you will find many brands symbolizing wealth and social standing today, just as Astor and Vanderbilt did over a century ago.

❷ Tiffany & Co.

Tiffany's: 727 5th Ave. **Map** 12 F3. **Tel** (212) 755-8000. Ⓜ 5th Ave-53rd St, 5th Ave-59th St. **Open** 10am–7pm Mon–Sat, noon–6pm Sun. Ⓦ **tiffany.com**.

Immortalized by Truman Capote in his famous 1958 novel *Breakfast at Tiffany's*, this prestigious jewelery store was founded in 1837 and remains a must-see for both fans of the book and film buffs. With weathered wood and green marble interiors, the Art Deco store is still best described by Capote's fictional Holly Golightly: "It calms me down right away . . . nothing very bad could happen to you there." A bronze figure of Atlas holds a clock on his shoulders above the doorway.

Next door stands the Trump Tower, a glittering, expensive apartment and office tower rising above a gaudy six-story atrium. Built in 1983, there is an impressive 80-ft- (24-m-) high indoor waterfall inside, while the exterior is lined with hanging gardens. The tower is a flamboyant monument to affluence by the business magnate and 2016 presidential candidate Donald Trump.

Entrance to Tiffany & Co., the exclusive jewelry emporium

❸ IBM Building

590 Madison Ave. **Map** 12 F3. Ⓜ 5th Ave. Garden Plaza **Open** 8am–10pm daily. ♿

Completed in 1983, this 43-story tower was designed by Edward Larrabee Barnes. It is a sleek, five-sided prism of gray-green polished granite, with a cantilevered corner at 57th Street. The Garden Plaza, with its bamboo trees, is open to the public and has been redubbed "The Sculpture Garden." Eight new works, which change four times a year, are on view at any one time. Near the atrium is a work by American sculptor Michael Heizer, entitled *Levitated Mass*. Inside a low, stainless-steel tank is a huge slab of granite that seems to float on air.

On the corner of 57th Street and Madison Avenue is *Saurien*, a bright-orange abstract sculpture by Alexander Calder.

Interior of the Trump Tower atrium

❹ St. Thomas Church

1 W 53rd St. **Map** 12 F4. **Tel** (212) 757-7013. Ⓜ 5th Ave–53rd St. **Open** /am–6pm daily. 🚹 frequent. 📧 ♿ ✔ after 11am service & concerts.
Ⓦ saintthomaschurch.org

This is the fourth home for this parish and the second on this site. Today's church was built between 1909 and 1914 to replace an earlier structure destroyed in a fire in 1905. The previous building had provided the setting for many high-society weddings of the late 19th century. The most lavish of these was in 1895, when heiress Consuelo Vanderbilt married the English Duke of Marlborough.

The limestone building, in French-Gothic style, has a single asymmetrical tower and an off-center nave, novel solutions to the architectural problems posed by its corner position. The richly carved, shimmering white screens behind the altar were designed by architect Bertram Goodhue and sculptor Lee Lawrie. Carvings in the choir stalls, dating from the 1920s, include modern inventions such as the telephone, plus presidents Roosevelt and Wilson, and Lee Lawrie himself.

❺ Museum of Modern Art

See pp168–71.

❻ Paley Center for Media

25 W 52nd St. **Map** 12 F4. **Tel** (212) 621-6600. Ⓜ 5th Ave–53rd St. **Open** noon–6pm Wed–Sun (to 8pm Thu). **Closed** public hols. 📷 📧 ♿ 🎬 📹 Ⓦ paleycenter.org

In this one-of-a-kind repository museum, visitors can watch and listen to a collection of entertainment and sports documentaries from radio and television's earliest days to the present. Pop fans can see the early Beatles or a young Elvis Presley making his television debut. Sports enthusiasts can

The Beatles' Paul, Ringo, and John on *The Ed Sullivan Show* in 1964

relive classic Olympic moments. World War II footage might be chosen by students of history. Six choices at any one time can be selected from a computer catalog that covers a library of over 50,000 programs. The selections are then played in small private areas. There are larger screening sections and a theater for 200, where retrospectives of artists and directors are shown. There are also photo exhibits and memorabilia.

The museum was the brainchild of William S. Paley, a former head of the CBS TV network. It opened in 1975 as the Museum of Broadcasting on East 53rd Street. It was so popular that, in 1991, it moved to this hi-tech $50 million home.

❺ St. Patrick's Cathedral

See pp174–5.

Watch 1960s television star Lucille Ball at the Paley Center for Media

❺ Museum of Modern Art (MoMA)

MoMA contains one of the world's most comprehensive collections of modern art. Founded in 1929, it set the standard for museums of its kind. Following an expansion program, MoMA in Midtown reopened in 2004. The building provides gallery space over six floors. Stretches of glass allow abundant natural light both to penetrate inside the building and to bathe the sculpture garden. A major expansion project unveiled in 2014 should be complete by 2019.

Museum facade on 54th Street

Christina's World (1948)
Andrew Wyeth contrasts an overwhelming horizon with the minutely studied surroundings of his disabled neighbor.

Gallery Guide

The sculpture garden is on the first floor and contemporary art, print, and media galleries are on the second floor. Painting and sculpture are exhibited on the second, fourth, and fifth floors while architecture and design, photography, and drawings are all on the third floor. Changing exhibitions are displayed on the third and sixth floors. Films are shown on the lower level.

Sculpture Garden
The Abby A. Rockefeller Sculpture Garden has a peaceful atmosphere.

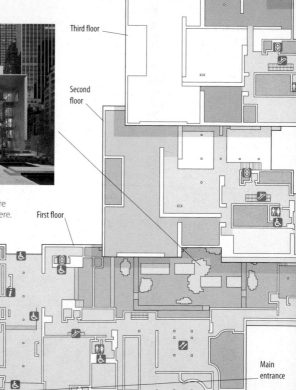

Third floor

Second floor

First floor

Main entrance

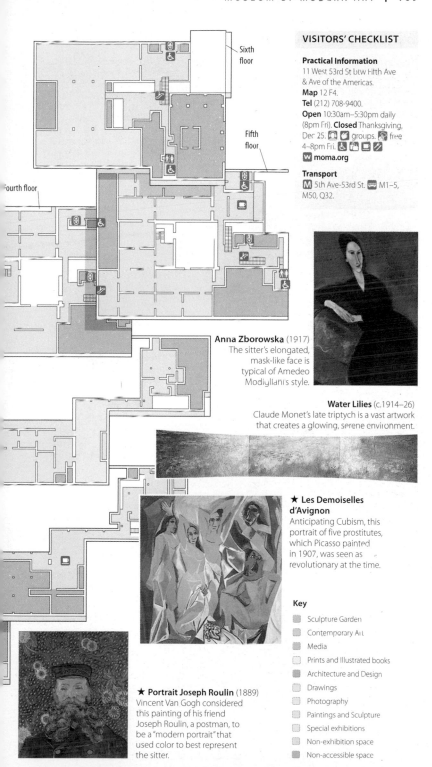

Sixth floor

Fifth floor

Fourth floor

VISITORS' CHECKLIST

Practical Information
11 West 53rd St btw Fifth Ave
& Ave of the Americas.
Map 12 F4.
Tel (212) 708-9400.
Open 10:30am–5:30pm daily
(8pm Fri). **Closed** Thanksgiving,
Dec 25. 🄍 🛍 groups. 🖼 free
4–8pm Fri. 🛬 🛗 🖼 🖋
Ⓦ moma.org

Transport
Ⓜ 5th Ave-53rd St. 🚌 M1–5,
M50, Q32.

Anna Zborowska (1917)
The sitter's elongated,
mask-like face is
typical of Amedeo
Modigliani's style.

Water Lilies (c.1914–26)
Claude Monet's late triptych is a vast artwork
that creates a glowing, serene environment.

★ **Les Demoiselles
d'Avignon**
Anticipating Cubism, this
portrait of five prostitutes,
which Picasso painted
in 1907, was seen as
revolutionary at the time.

Key

- Sculpture Garden
- Contemporary Art
- Media
- Prints and Illustrated books
- Architecture and Design
- Drawings
- Photography
- Paintings and Sculpture
- Special exhibitions
- Non-exhibition space
- Non-accessible space

★ **Portrait Joseph Roulin** (1889)
Vincent Van Gogh considered
this painting of his friend
Joseph Roulin, a postman, to
be a "modern portrait" that
used color to best represent
the sitter.

Exploring the Collection

The Museum of Modern Art has almost 200,000 works of art by more than 10,000 artists, ranging from Post-Impressionist classics to an unrivaled collection of modern and contemporary art, as well as fine examples of design and early masterpieces of photography and film.

The Persistence of Memory by the Surrealist Salvador Dalí (1931)

1880s to 1940s Painting and Sculpture

Paul Cézanne's monumental *The Bather* and Vincent van Gogh's *Portrait of Joseph Roulin* are two of the seminal works in the museum's collection of late 19th-century painting. Both Fauvism and Expressionism are well represented with works by Matisse, Derain, Kirchner, and others, while Pablo Picasso's *Les Demoiselles d'Avignon* marks a transition to the Cubist style of painting.

The collection also has an unparalleled number of Cubist paintings, providing an overview of a movement that radically challenged our perception of the world. Among the vast range are Picasso's *Girl with a Mandolin*, Georges Braque's *Man with a Guitar* and *Soda*, and *Guitar and Glasses* by Juan Gris. Works by the Futurists, who brought color and movement to Cubism to depict the dynamic modern world, include *Dynamism of a Soccer Player* by Umberto Boccioni, plus works by Balla, Carrà, and Jacques Villon. The geometric abstract art of the Constructivists is included in a strong representation of El Lissitzky, Malevich, and Rodchenko: De Stijl's influence is seen in paintings by Piet Mondrian, such as *Broadway Boogie Woogie*. There is a large body of work by Matisse, such as *Dance (I)* and *Red Studio*. Dalí, Miró, and Ernst feature among the bizarre, strangely beautiful Surrealist works.

Postwar Painting and Sculpture

The extensive collection of postwar art includes works by Bacon and Dubuffet, and has a particularly strong representation of American artists. The collection of Abstract Expressionist art, for example, includes Jackson Pollock's *One [Number 31, 1950]*, Willem de Kooning's *Women, I*, Arshile Gorky's *Agony*, and *Red, Brown, and Black* by Mark Rothko.

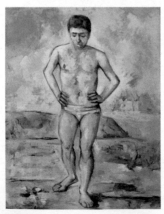

The Bather, an oil painting by French Impressionist Paul Cézanne

Other notable works include Jasper Johns' *Flag*, Robert Rauschenberg's *First Landing Jump*, composed of urban refuse, and *Bed*, which consists of bed linen. The Pop Art collection includes Roy Lichtenstein's *Girl with Ball* and *Drowning Girl*, Andy Warhol's famous *Gold Marilyn Monroe*, and Claes Oldenburg's *Giant Soft Fan*.

Works after about 1965 include pieces by Judd, Flavin, Serra, and Beuys, among many others.

Man with a Hat by Pablo Picasso (1912), a collage with charcoal

Drawings and Other Works on Paper

More than 7,000 artworks ranging in size from tiny preparatory pieces to large mural-sized works are among MoMA's holdings. Many drawings use conventional materials, such as pencil, charcoal, pen and ink, pastel, and watercolor. However, there are also collages and mixed-media works composed of paper ephemera, natural products, and man-made goods.

The collection provides an overview of Modernism, from the late 19th century to the present day, including movements such as Cubism, Dadaism, and Surrealism. Drawings by famous and well-established artists, such as Picasso, Miró, and Johns, are exhibited alongside a growing number of works by talented emerging artists.

American Indian Theme II by Roy Lichtenstein (1980)

Prints and Illustrated Books

All significant art movements from the 1880s onward are represented in this extensive collection, which provides a fascinating overview of printed art. With more than 50,000 items in the department's holdings, there are wide-ranging examples of historical and contemporary printmaking. Works created using traditional media such as etchings, lithographic prints, screenprints, and woodcuts are displayed alongside pieces created by more experimental techniques.

There are some particularly fine examples of works by Andy Warhol, who is widely considered to be the most important printmaker of the 20th century. There are also many illustrations and prints by other artists including Redon, Munch, Matisse, Dubuffet, Johns, Lichtenstein, Freud, and Picasso.

Photography

The photography collection begins with the invention of the medium around 1840. It includes pictures by fine artists, journalists, scientists, and entrepreneurs, as well as amateur photographers.

Among the highlights of the collection are some of the best-known works by American and European photographers including Atget, Stieglitz, Lange, Arbus, Steichen, Cartier-Bresson, and Kertesz. There is also a range of contemporary

Film Department

With a collection of over 22,000 films and four million stills, the collection offers a wide range of programs, including retrospectives of individual directors and actors, films in specific genres, and experimental work, as well as a broad range of other exhibitions. Film conservation is a key part of the department's work. Many of today's top directors have donated copies of their films to help fund this expensive but vital work.

Film still of Charlie Chaplin and Jackie Coogan in *The Kid* (1921)

Sunday on the Banks of the Marne, photographed by Henri Cartier-Bresson in 1939

practitioners, most notably Friedlander, Cindy Sherman, and Nicholas Nixon.

The photographers have covered an extensive variety of subject matter in both colour and black and white: delicate landscapes, scenes of urban desolation, abstract imagery, and stylish portraiture, including some beautiful silver-gelatin print nudes by the French Surrealist Man Ray. Together, they form a complete history of photographic art and represent one of the finest collections in existence.

Architecture and Design

The Museum of Modern Art was the first art museum to include utilitarian objects in its collection. These range from such household appliances as stereo equipment, furniture, lighting, textiles, and glassware to industrial ball bearings and silicon chips. Architecture is represented in the collection through photographs, scale models, and drawings of buildings that have been or might have been built.

Graphic design is shown in typography and posters. Larger exhibits that look as if they belong in a museum of transportation include a Willys-Overland Jeep and the Bell helicopter, which dates from 1945.

Reclining rocking chair of steam-bent beech and cane by Gebrüder Thonet (c.1880)

❽ Villard Houses

457 Madison Ave (Lotte New York Palace). **Map** 13 A4. **Tel** (800) NY PALACE. Ⓜ 51st St.
Ⓦ **lottenypalace.com**

Henry Villard was a Bavarian immigrant who became publisher of the *New York Evening Post*, and was one of the first presidents of the Northern Pacific Railroad. In 1881, he bought the land opposite St. Patrick's Cathedral and hired McKim, Mead & White to design town houses on the site. The inspired result, completed in 1884, has six four-story houses set round a central court opening to the street and the church. The interiors were designed by the sculptor Augustus Saint-Gaudens. Soon after completion, financial difficulties forced Villard to sell, and ownership passed to the Roman Catholic archdiocese.

When the church outgrew its space in the 1970s, the houses were saved by the Helmsley chain, who purchased air rights for the 51-story Helmsley (now Lotte New York) Palace Hotel. The hotel was built in 1980 to a design by Emery Roth & Sons, and the building was later restored in 2003. After a stint of ownership by the Sultan of Brunei, the property was bought out by South Korea's Lotte Hotels & Resorts, at $805 million, in 2015.

The upper section of the lobby has a red Verona marble fireplace, with carvings that represent hospitality, joy, and moderation. Dolphins sit on either side as fountains. Saint-Gaudens also designed a zodiac clock, which can be viewed by the ornate marble staircase.

Villard Houses, now the entrance to the Lotte New York Palace

St. Bartholomew's Church

❾ St. Bartholomew's Church

109 E 50th St. **Map** 13 A4. **Tel** (212) 378-0222. Ⓜ 51st St. **Open** 8am–6pm daily (to 7:30pm Thu & 8:30pm Sun). ✝ frequent. ♿ lectures, concerts. 🏛 🎵 after 11am Sunday services. 🎵 (212) 888-2664.
Ⓦ **stbarts.org**

Known fondly to New Yorkers as "St. Bart's," this Byzantine structure with its ornate detail, pinkish brick, open terrace, and a polychromed gold dome brought color and variety to Park Avenue in 1919.

Architect Bertram Goodhue incorporated into the design the Romanesque entrance portico created by Stanford White for the original 1903 St. Bartholomew's on Madison Avenue, and marble columns from the earlier church were used in the chapel.

St. Bartholomew's program of concerts is well known, as is its theater group, which mounts three productions in the church each year.

❿ General Electric Building

570 Lexington Ave. **Map** 13 A4. Ⓜ Lexington Ave. **Closed** to the public.

In 1931 architects Cross & Cross were commissioned to design a skyscraper that would be in keeping with its neighbor, St. Bartholomew's Church. Not an easy task, but the result won acclaim. The colors were chosen to blend and contrast, and the design of the tower complemented the church's polychrome dome.

The General Electric Building on Lexington Avenue

View the pair from the corner of Park and 50th to see how well it works. However, the General Electric is no mere backdrop but a work of art in its own right and a favorite part of the city skyline. It is an Art Deco gem from its chrome and marble lobby to its spiky "radio waves" crown.

Walk one block north on Lexington Avenue to find a place much cherished by movie fans. It is right at this spot that Marilyn Monroe, in a billowing white frock, stood so memorably in the breeze from the Lexington Avenue subway grating in the movie *The Seven-Year Itch*.

⓫ Waldorf-Astoria

301 Park Ave. **Map** 13 A5. **Tel** (212)
355-3000. Ⓜ Lexington Ave, 53rd St.
See Where to Stay p289.
ⓦ waldorfnewyork.com

This Art Deco classic, which
covers an entire city block, was
designed by Schultze & Weaver
in 1931. The original Hotel at
34th Street was demolished to
make way for the Empire State
Building. Still deservedly one
of New York's most prestigious
hotels, the Waldorf-Astoria
serves, too, as a reminder of
a more glamorous era in the
city's history. The 625-ft (190-m)
twin towers, where General
MacArthur, Cole Porter, Frank
Sinatra, and Marilyn Monroe
lived, have hosted numerous
celebrities, including every
US president since 1931. The
giant lobby clock, executed
for the Chicago World's Fair
of 1893, is from the original
hotel, and the piano in the
Peacock Alley cocktail lounge
belonged to Cole Porter when
he was a resident.

Winston Churchill and New York
philanthropist Grover Whalen at the
Waldorf-Astoria in 1946

⓬ Lever House

390 Park Ave. **Map** 13 A4.
Ⓜ 5th Ave-53rd St. Lobby and
building: **Closed** to the public. ♿

Imagine a Park Avenue lined
with sturdy, residential buildings
– and then imagine the sensation
when they were suddenly
reflected here in the first of the
city's glass-walled skyscrapers,
one of the most influential
buildings of the modern era. The
design, by Skidmore, Owings &
Merrill, is simply two rectangular
slabs of stainless steel and glass,
one laid horizontally, the other

Lever House on Park Avenue

stacked to stand tall above it,
to allow light in from every side.
The crisp, bright design was
intended to symbolize the
Lever Brothers' products –
they were known for soap
production and, in 1930, Lever
merged to form Unilever.
    Revolutionary though it was
in 1952, Lever House is now
dwarfed by its many imitators,
but its importance as an
architectural pacesetter remains
undiminished. The Casa Lever
restaurant is a VIP scene.

⓭ Seagram Building

375 Park Ave. **Map** 13 A4.
Ⓜ 5th Ave-53rd St.
Open 9am–5pm Mon–Fri. .

Samuel Bronfman, the late
head of Seagram distillers, was
prepared to put up an ordinary
commercial building until his
architect daughter, Phyllis
Lambert, intervened and
persuaded him to go to the
best – Mies van der Rohe.
The result, which is widely
considered the finest of the

The pool at the Four Seasons
in the Seagram Building

many Modernist buildings
of the 1950s, consists of two
rectangles of bronze and glass
that let the light pour in.
    Within is the exclusive Four
Seasons Restaurant *(see p302)*,
a landmark in its own right.
Designer Philip Johnson has
created a remarkable space,
with the centerpiece of one
room a pool, and another a bar
topped by a quivering Richard
Lippold sculpture.

Office workers at lunch in the spacious
Citigroup Center atrium

⓮ Citigroup Center

153 E 53rd St. **Map** 13 A4. Ⓜ 53rd St-
Lexington Ave. **Open** 7am–11pm
daily. ♿ 🏛 St. Peter's Lutheran
Church 619 Lexington Ave. **Tel** (212)
935-2200. **Open** 9am–9pm daily.
✝ 12:15pm Mon–Fri, 6pm Wed,
8:45am & 11am Sun. Jazz vespers 5pm
Sun. Concerts noon Wed. York Theater
at St. Peter's; **Tel** (212) 935-5820.
ⓦ saintpeters.org

An aluminum-clad spire built on
10-story stilts with a sliced-off
roof, Citigroup Center is unique; it
caused a sensation when it was
completed in 1978. The unusual
base design had to incorporate
St. Peter's Lutheran Church. The
church is separate both in space
and design, a granite sculpture
below a corner of the tower.
Step inside to see the striking
interior and the Erol Beker
Chapel by sculptor Louise
Nevelson. The church is well-
known for its organ concerts,
jazz vespers, and theater
presentations. Citigroup's
slanting top never functioned
as a solar panel as intended, but
it is an unmistakable landmark
on the skyline.

⑦ St. Patrick's Cathedral

The Roman Catholic Church originally intended this site for use as a cemetery, but in 1850 Archbishop John Hughes decided to build a cathedral instead. Many thought that it was foolish to build so far beyond the (then) city limits, but Hughes went ahead anyway. Architect James Renwick built New York's finest Gothic Revival building, one of the largest Catholic cathedrals in the US. The cathedral, which seats 2,500 people, was completed in 1878, though the spires were added between 1885 and 1888.

★ **Lady Chapel**
This chapel honors the Blessed Virgin. The stained-glass windows portray the mysteries of the rosary.

Pietà
American sculptor William O. Partridge created this *Pietà* in 1906. The statue stands at the side of the Lady Chapel.

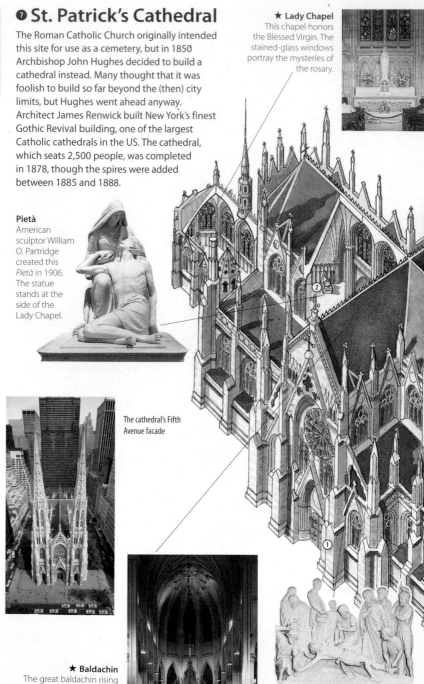

The cathedral's Fifth Avenue facade

★ **Baldachin**
The great baldachin rising over the high altar is made entirely of bronze. Statues of the saints and prophets adorn the four piers supporting the canopy.

Stations of the Cross
Carved of Caen stone in Holland, these reliefs won first prize in the field of religious art at the Chicago World's Fair in 1893.

Saint Elizabeth Ann Seton Shrine

The bronze statue and screen depict the life of the first American to be canonized a saint. She founded the Sisters of Charity (see p77).

★ Great Organ and Rose Window

Measuring 26 ft (8 m) in diameter, the rose window shines above the great organ, which has more than 7,000 pipes.

③

★ Great Bronze Doors

The massive doors weigh 20,000 lb (9,000 kg) and are adorned with important religious figures.

Main entrance

KEY

① **The cathedral façade's** exterior wall is built of white marble. The spires rise 330 ft (101 m) above the pavement.

② **Crypt**

③ **Lady of Guadalupe**

⓯ Central Synagogue

652 Lexington Ave. **Map** 13 A4.
Tel (212) 838–5122. Ⓜ Lexington
Ave-53rd St. **Open** noon–2pm
Tue & Wed. 🔲 12:45pm Wed. ♿
✡ 6pm Fri, also 10am Sat (Jul &
Aug), 10.30am Sat (Sep–Jun).
🅆 centralsynagogue.org

This is New York's
oldest building in
continuous use as a
synagogue. It was
designed in 1870 by
Silesian-born Henry
Fernbach, America's
first prominent Jewish
architect. He also
designed some of
SoHo's finest cast-iron
buildings. Restored
after a 1999 fire, the
Synagogue is
considered the city's
best example of
Moorish-Islamic Revival
architecture. The congregation was founded in 1846 as
Ahawath Chesed (Love of Mercy)
by 18 immigrants, most
of them from Bohemia,
on Ludlow Street on
the Lower East Side.

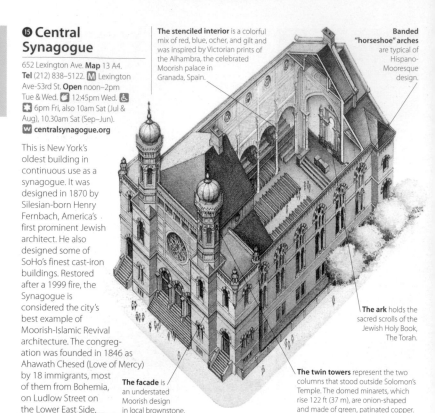

The stenciled interior is a colorful mix of red, blue, ocher, and gilt and was inspired by Victorian prints of the Alhambra, the celebrated Moorish palace in Granada, Spain.

Banded "horseshoe" arches are typical of Hispano-Mooresque design.

The ark holds the sacred scrolls of the Jewish Holy Book, The Torah.

The twin towers represent the two columns that stood outside Solomon's Temple. The domed minarets, which rise 122 ft (37 m), are onion-shaped and made of green, patinated copper.

The facade is an understated Moorish design in local brownstone.

⓰ Sutton Place

Map 13 C3. Ⓜ 59th St, 51st St.
🚌 M15, M31, M57.

Sutton Place is a posh, pleasant neighborhood devoid of busy traffic, and made up of elegant low-rise apartment houses and town houses designed by noted architects. The arrival of New York society in the 1920s transformed an area that had once been the province of factories and tenements. Three Sutton Square is the residence of the secretary-general of the United Nations. Look beyond Sutton Square and 59th Street for a glimpse of Riverview Terrace, a private street of five ivy-covered brownstones fronting on the river. The tiny parks at the end of 55th Street and jutting out at 57th Street offer views of the river and the Queensboro Bridge.

The Ed Koch Queensboro Bridge, to give it its official title, was named after the late mayor. It was completed in 1909, and connected Queens with Manhattan via Roosevelt Island. A popular icon today, it has featured in movies such as *Woody Allen's Manhattan*.

Park at Sutton Place, looking toward Queensboro Bridge and Roosevelt Island

⓱ Roosevelt Island

Map 14 D2. Ⓜ 59th St. Tram,
Roosevelt Island station (F).
🅆 rioc.com

An often overlooked corner of New York, Roosevelt Island sits in the middle of the East River, and has around 13,000 inhabitants. It was known as Minnahannock by the local Native Americans, until ownership passed on to the English farmer, Robert Blackwell, in 1686.

Although it became known as Welfare Island in 1921, much of the island was deserted and forgotten by the 1950s. It was redeveloped in the 1970s, and eventually became a popular residential neighborhood. Today, it boasts a breezy promenade with fabulous views of Midtown. Since 1976, a Swiss cable car departing from Second Avenue at 60th Street, has offered a quick, thrilling ride across the river, with the F subway line servicing the island.

⓲ Franklin D. Roosevelt Four Freedoms Park

1 FDR Four Freedoms Park, Roosevelt Island. **Map** 14 D5. **Tel** (212) 204-8831. Ⓜ Roosevelt Island. **Open** Apr–Sep: 9am–7pm Mon & Wed–Sun (until 5pm Oct–Mar: 9am–5pm Mon & Wed–Sun. Ⓦ **fdrfourfreedomspark.org**

At the southern end of Roosevelt Island is the Franklin D. Roosevelt Four Freedoms Park, designed by architect Louis Kahn in the 1970s. With 120 linden trees lining the park, the triangular expanse ends with a bronze portrait of the 32nd president. Nearby, there is an engraving of his "four freedoms" on slabs of granite. In a speech from 1941, these four tenets were described as the freedom of speech, freedom of worship, freedom from want, and freedom from fear.

The clock statues above the Fuller Building entrance

Bloomingdale's store sign

⓳ Bloomingdale's

1000 3rd Ave. **Map** 13 A3. **Tel** (212) 705-2000. Ⓜ 59th St. **Open** 10am–8:30pm Mon–Sat, 11am–7pm Sun. See Shopping p313. Ⓦ **bloomingdales.com**

For a while in the booming 1980s, "Bloomies" was synonymous with the good life. Founded by Joseph and Lyman Bloomingdale in 1872, this famous department store had a bargain-basement image until the 3rd Avenue El (elevated railway) was taken down in the 1960s. Then came the store's transformation to the epitome of trendy, sophisticated shopping. But the late 1980s brought new ownership and eventual bankruptcy. While not as flashy as in the past, Bloomingdale's is open every day and remains one of the city's best-stocked stores. Downtown shoppers can head to the SoHo location, at 504 Broadway.

⓴ Fuller Building

41 E 57th St. **Map** 13 A3. James Goodman Gallery. **Tel** (212) 593-3737. **Open** 10am–5:30pm Mon–Fri. Ⓜ 59th St.

This slim-towered black, gray, and white 1929 beauty by Walker & Gillette is a prime example of geometric Art Deco design. The striking statues on either side of the clock above the entrance are by Elie Nadelman. Step inside to admire the intricate mosaic tile floors; one panel shows the Fuller Company's former home in the famous Flatiron Building on

Fifth Avenue *(see p123)*. The Fuller Building is a hive of exclusive art galleries, most of which are open to the public on weekdays.

French Renaissance-style façade of the Plaza Hotel

㉑ Plaza Hotel

5th Ave & Central Park South. **Map** 12 F3. Ⓜ Fifth Ave-59th St. Ⓦ **theplazany.com**

The city's grande dame of hotels was designed by Henry J. Hardenbergh, known for the Dakota *(see p212)* and the original Waldorf-Astoria. Completed in 1907 at the exorbitant cost of $12.5 million, the Plaza was proclaimed "the best hotel in the world," with 800 rooms, 500 baths, a two-story ballroom, five marble staircases, and 14- to 17-room apartments for such families as the Vanderbilts and the Goulds *(see p51)*.

The 18-story cast-iron structure resembles a French Renaissance château. Much of the interior decoration came from Europe. The Palm Court still has mirrored walls and Italian carvings of the four seasons, and is a lovely place for afternoon tea.

Already lavishly restored by its former owner Donald Trump, the building underwent a $400-million conversion in 2005, and is now a mix of apartments, hotel condominiums, and a 282-room hotel. There are also six floors of luxury retail and upscale dining, including a gourmet food hall.

UPPER EAST SIDE

An enclave of New York's upper class since the 1890s, the area was once home to dynasties such as the Astors, Rockefellers, and Whitneys. Many of their Beaux Arts mansions are now museums and embassies, such as the Met and the buildings on Museum Mile, but the well-to-do still occupy apartment buildings on Fifth and Park avenues. Chic shops and galleries line Madison Avenue. Farther east lies what is left of German and Hungarian Yorkville in the East 80s, and little Bohemia, with its Czech population, below 78th Street. Although many of these ethnic groups no longer occupy the area, their churches, restaurants, and shops still remain.

Sights at a Glance

Historic Streets and Buildings
⑨ Park Avenue Armory
⑮ Gracie Mansion

Museums and Galleries
① Neue Galerie
② Jewish Museum
③ Cooper Hewitt, Smithsonian Design Museum
④ National Academy Museum
⑤ Solomon R. Guggenheim Museum pp184–5
⑥ The Metropolitan Museum of Art pp186–93
⑦ The Frick Collection pp196–7
⑧ Asia Society
⑪ Society of Illustrators
⑫ Mount Vernon Hotel Museum and Garden
⑭ The Met Breuer
⑱ Museum of the City of New York

Churches and Synagogues
⑩ Temple Emanu-El
⑬ Christ Church United Methodist
⑯ Church of the Holy Trinity
⑰ St. Nicholas Russian Orthodox Cathedral

Restaurants see pp302–304
1 Beyoglu
2 Brother Jimmy's BBQ
3 Café Boulud
4 Café d'Alsace
5 Café Sabarsky
6 Daniel
7 Flex Mussels
8 Maya
9 Penrose
10 Sasabune
11 Sfoglia
12 Shanghai Pavilion

See also Street Finder maps 12, 13, 16–18, 21

◀ Brightly lit facade of the Solomon R. Guggenheim Museum

For keys to symbols see back flap

Street by Street: Museum Mile

Many of New York's museums are clustered on the Upper East Side, in homes ranging from the former Frick and Carnegie mansions to the modernistic Guggenheim, designed by Frank Lloyd Wright. The displays are as varied as the architecture, running the gamut from Old Masters to photographs to decorative arts. Presiding over the scene is the vast Metropolitan Museum of Art, New York's answer to Paris's Louvre. Some of the museums stay open late one day a week.

② Jewish Museum
The most extensive collection of Judaica in the world is housed here. It includes coins, archaeological objects, and ceremonial and religious artifacts.

③ ★ Cooper Hewitt, Smithsonian Design Museum
Ceramics, glass, furniture, and textiles are well represented here.

The Church of the Heavenly Rest was built in 1929 in the Gothic style. The madonna in the pulpit is by sculptor Malvina Hoffman.

④ National Academy Museum
The Academy, founded in 1825, moved here in 1940. Its fine collection includes paintings and sculptures by its members.

Graham House is an apartment building with a splendid Beaux Arts entrance. It was built in 1892.

⑤ ★ Solomon R. Guggenheim Museum
Architect Frank Lloyd Wright's building, which is in the form of a spiral, is floodlit at dusk. The best way to see one of the world's premier collections of modern and contemporary art is to take the elevator to the top and walk down.

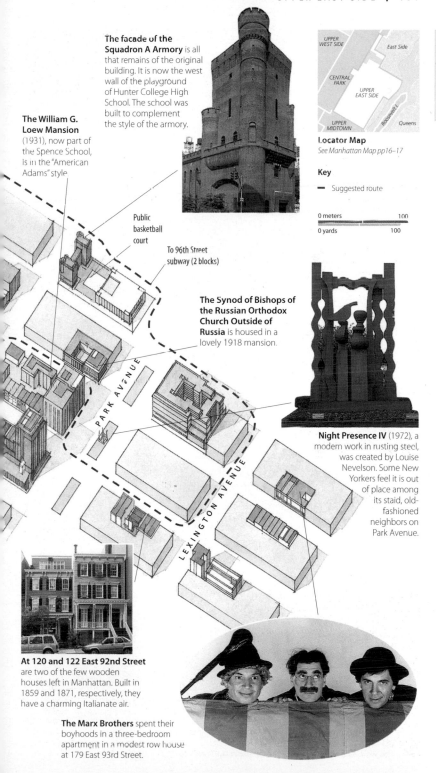

The facade of the Squadron A Armory is all that remains of the original building. It is now the west wall of the playground of Hunter College High School. The school was built to complement the style of the armory.

The William G. Loew Mansion (1931), now part of the Spence School, is in the "American Adams" style

Locator Map
See Manhattan Map pp16–17

Key

— Suggested route

| 0 meters | 100 |
| 0 yards | 100 |

Public basketball court

To 96th Street subway (2 blocks)

The Synod of Bishops of the Russian Orthodox Church Outside of Russia is housed in a lovely 1918 mansion.

PARK AVENUE

LEXINGTON AVENUE

Night Presence IV (1972), a modern work in rusting steel, was created by Louise Nevelson. Some New Yorkers feel it is out of place among its staid, old-fashioned neighbors on Park Avenue.

At 120 and 122 East 92nd Street are two of the few wooden houses left in Manhattan. Built in 1859 and 1871, respectively, they have a charming Italianate air.

The Marx Brothers spent their boyhoods in a three-bedroom apartment in a modest row house at 179 East 93rd Street.

❶ Neue Galerie New York

1048 5th Ave at E 86th St. **Map** 16 F3.
Tel (212) 628-6200. **M** 86th St. ▦
M1–4. **Open** 11am–6pm Thu–Mon.
Closed public hols. 🅿 🄰 ⊠ ✐
Café 9am–6pm daily (to 9pm Thu–
Sun). 🄰 🅱 **w** neuegalerie.org

This museum was founded by
art dealer Serge Sabarsky and
philanthropist Ronald Lauder. Its
objective is to collect, research,
and exhibit the fine and decorative
arts of Germany and Austria
from the early 20th century.

The Louis XIII-style Beaux Arts
structure was completed in
1914 by Carrère & Hastings,
who also designed the New
York Public Library (see p142).
Once occupied by Mrs. Cornelius
Vanderbilt III, the mansion was
purchased by Lauder and
Sabarsky in 1994. The ground
floor houses the
entrance, a book-
shop, and the Café
Sabarsky (see p303).
The second floor is devoted
to the works of Klimt,
Schiele, and Wiener
Werkstätte objects. The upper
floors feature works from Der
Blaue Reiter (artists such as
Klee, Kandinsky), the Bauhaus
(Feininger, Schlemmer), and Die
Brücke (Mies van der Rohe, Breuer).
Klimt's *Portrait of Adele Bloch-
Bauer I* (1907) is the star of the
museum. A resplendent piece
from his "Golden Period", the
portrait depicts Adele Bloch-
Bauer, a member of one of
Vienna's richest Jewish families.
The painting was later stolen by
the Nazis in 1938.

❷ Jewish Museum

1109 5th Ave. **Map** 16 F2. **Tel** (212) 423-
3200. **M** 86th St, 96th St. ▦ M1–4.
Open 11am–5:45pm Thu–Tue
(to 8pm Thu, to 5:45pm Fri Mar–Nov).
Closed public & Jewish hols.
🅿 ⊠ 🅱 ✐ ▱ 🄰
w thejewishmuseum.org

The exquisite château-like
residence of Felix M. Warburg,
financier and leader of the
Jewish community, was
designed by C. P. H. Gilbert in
1908. It now houses one of the
world's largest collections of
Jewish fine and ceremonial
art, and historical Judaica. The
stonework in an extension is
by the stonemasons of St. John
the Divine (see pp220–21).

Objects have been brought
here from all over the world,
some at great risk of persecution
to the donors. Covering 4,000
years, artifacts include Torah
crowns, candelabras, kiddush
cups, plates, scrolls, and silver
ceremonial objects.

There is a Torah ark from the
Benguiat Collection, the exquisite
faience entrance wall of a
16th-century Persian synagogue,
and the powerful *Holocaust* by
sculptor George Segal. Changing
exhibitions reflect Jewish life and
experience around
the world.

A 19th-century ewer and basin from
Istanbul at the Jewish Museum

❸ Cooper Hewitt, Smithsonian Design Museum

2 E 91st St. **Map** 16 F2. **Tel** (212) 849-
8400. **M** 86th St, 96th St. ▦ M1–4.
Open 10am–6pm Sun–Fri (to 9pm
Sat). **Closed** Jan 1, Thanksgiving,
Dec 25. 🅿 🅱 ✐ 🄰 ▱
w cooperhewitt.org

Housed in the former mansion
of industrialist Andrew Carnegie,
this museum underwent a
massive redevelopment project,
which culminated in 2014.
The modern galleries are now
scattered around the original
staircase, with the mansion's
wooden interiors and parquet
floors still intact. On the second
story is the Carnegie Library,
with its intricate teak carvings.

The museum offers a variety
of displays, from digitally
printed fruit to steel necklaces,
rubber chairs, and porcelain

Cooper Hewitt, Smithsonian Design
Museum entrance

chess sets. It also has the largest
ensemble of paintings by the
American artists, Frederic Edwin
Church and Winslow Homer.
Apart from the permanent
collection, there are several
temporary exhibits as well.

❹ National Academy Museum

1083 5th Ave. **Map** 16 F3. **Tel** (212)
369-4880. **M** 86th St. ▦ M1–4.
Open 11am–6pm Wed–Sun.
Closed public hols. 🅿 ⊠ 🅱 🄰
w nationalacademy.org

Over 6,000 paintings, drawings,
and sculptures, including works
by Thomas Eakins, Winslow
Homer, and Frank Lloyd Wright,
comprise the collection of the
National Academy Museum,
founded in 1825 by a group of
artists. The group's mission was
(and is) to train artists and
exhibit their work.

In 1940, Archer Huntington,
an art patron and philan-
thropist, donated his house,
an attractive building with
patterned marble floors. The
grand entrance foyer has a
statue of Diana by sculptor
Anna Hyatt Huntington.

Statue of Diana in the National Academy
Museum entrance foyer

❺ Solomon R. Guggenheim Museum

See pp184–5.

❻ The Metropolitan Museum of Art

See pp186–93.

❼ The Frick Collection

See pp196–7.

❽ Asia Society

725 Park Ave. **Map** 13 A1. **Tel** (212) 288-6400. Events: (212) 517-ASIA. Ⓜ 68th St. **Open** 11am–6pm Tue–Sun (to 9pm Fri). **Closed** public hols. 🏛 🎫 2pm Tue–Sat, 6:30pm Fri. 📷 ♿ 🏠 💻 ⓦ asiasociety.org

Founded by John D. Rockefeller III in 1956 to increase under-standing of Asian culture, the society is a forum for 30 countries in the Asia-Pacific region from Japan to Iran, Central Asia to Australia.

The 1981 eight-story building was designed by Edward Larrabee Barnes and is made of red granite. After a renovation in 2001, the museum has increased gallery space. One

South Asian sculpture at the Asia Society

gallery is permanently devoted to Rockefeller's own collection of Asian sculptures, amassed by him and his wife on frequent trips to the East. It includes Chinese ceramics from the Song and Ming periods, and a copper Bodhisattva statue, inlaid with precious stones, from Nepal.

Changing exhibits show a wide variety of Asian arts, and the society has a full program of films, dance, concerts, and lectures and a well-stocked bookstore.

Entrance hall of the Park Avenue Armory

❾ Park Avenue Armory

643 Park Ave. **Map** 13 A2. **Tel** (212) 616-3930. Ⓜ 68th St. 🎫 10am Tue & Thu (excluding holidays). 📷 ♿ ⓦ armoryonpark.org

From the War of 1812 through two world wars, the Seventh Regiment, an elite corps of "gentlemen soldiers" from prominent families, has played a vital role. Within the fortresslike exterior of their armory are extraordinary rooms filled with lavish Victorian furnishings, objets d'art, and regimental memorabilia.

The design by Charles W. Clinton, a veteran of the regiment, had offices facing Park Avenue, with a vast drill hall stretching behind to Lexington Avenue. The reception rooms include the Veterans' Room and the Library by Louis Comfort Tiffany. The drill hall is now the site of the Winter Antiques Show *(see p55)* and a favorite venue for charity balls. The Armory hosts a large number of cultural performances, from modern dance to concerts by the New York Philhar-monic Orchestra.

❿ Temple Emanu-El

1 E 65th St. **Map** 12 F2. **Tel** (212) 744-1400. Ⓜ 68th St, 63rd St. **Open** 10am–4:30pm Sun–Thu. **Closed** Jewish hols. ✡ 5:30pm Sun–Thu, 5:15pm Fri, 10:30am Sat. ♿ 🎫 🏠 ⓦ emanuelnyc.org

This impressive limestone edifice of 1929 is one of the largest synagogues in the world, with seating for 2,500 in the main sanctuary alone. It is home to the oldest Reform congregation in New York, and the wealthiest members of Jewish society worship here.

Among the synagogue's many fine details are the Ark's bronze doors, which represent an open Torah scroll. The Ark also has stained glass depicting biblical scenes and showing the tribal signs of the houses of Israel. These signs also appear on a great recessed arch that frames a magnificent wheel window, the dominant feature of the Fifth Avenue façade.

The synagogue stands on the site of the palatial home of Mrs. William Astor, the famed society hostess. Lady Astor moved to the Upper East Side after a feud with her nephew, who previously lived next door to her. Her wine cellar and three marble fireplaces still remain at the synagogue.

The Ark at Temple Emanu-El

❺ Solomon R. Guggenheim Museum

Home to one of the world's finest collections of modern and contemporary art, the building itself, designed by Frank Lloyd Wright, is perhaps the Guggenheim's greatest masterpiece. The exterior of the museum was beautifully restored in celebration of the 50th anniversary of the building in 2009. The shell-like facade is a veritable New York landmark. Inside, the spiral ramp curves down and inward from the dome, passing works by major 19th-, 20th-, and 21st-century artists along the way.

Paris Through the Window
The vibrant colors of Marc Chagall's 1913 masterpiece illuminate the canvas, conjuring up images of a magical and mysterious city where nothing is quite what it appears to be.

Main entrance

Woman Ironing (1904)
A work from Pablo Picasso's Blue Period, this painting is his quintessential image of hard work and fatigue.

KEY

① Sackler Center for Arts Education
② Small Rotunda
③ Tower
④ Great Rotunda
⑤ Café

Yellow Cow (1911)
Franz Marc's late work focused on nature and color.

Nude (1917)
This sleeping figure is typical of Amedeo Modigliani's stylized work.

Museum Guide

The Great Rotunda features special exhibitions. The Small Rotunda shows some of the museum's Impressionist and Post-Impressionist holdings. The Tower galleries (also known as The Annex) hold exhibitions of work from the permanent collection, as well as contemporary pieces. The permanent collection is shown on a rotating basis, and only parts of it are on display at any one time.

Before the Mirror (1876)
In trying to capture the flavor of 19th-century society, Edouard Manet often used the image of the courtesan.

Woman Holding a Vase
Fernand Léger incorporated elements of Cubism into this work from 1927.

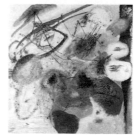

Black Lines (1913)
This is one of Vasily Kandinsky's earliest examples of his work in "non-objective" art.

Woman with Yellow Hair (1931)
The gentle, voluptuous figure of Picasso's mistress often appears in his work.

Frank Lloyd Wright

During his lifetime, Wright was considered the great innovator of American architecture. Characteristic of his work are Prairie-style homes and office buildings of concrete slabs, glass bricks, and tubing. Wright received the Guggenheim commission, his only New York building, in 1942 and it was completed after his death in 1959.

Interior of the Guggenheim's Great Rotunda

⑥ The Metropolitan Museum of Art

Founded in 1870 by a group of artists and philanthropists who dreamed of an American art institution to rival those of Europe, this collection is thought to be the most comprehensive in the Western world. Works date from prehistoric times to the present. The museum opened here in 1880 and houses collections from all continents. The Greek and Roman galleries on the first floor are especially popular.

The entrance of the Metropolitan Museum of Art

Ground floor

★ **Jeanne Hébuterne** (1919) Amedeo Modigliani's mistress, Hébuterne, appears in over 20 of his works. She killed herself the day after he died in 1920.

Mezzanine floor

Pendant Mask
The kingdom of Benin (now part of Nigeria) was renowned for its art. This mask was made in the 16th century.

Gallery Guide

Most of the collections are housed on the two main floors. Works from 19 curatorial areas are in the permanent galleries, with designated sections for temporary exhibitions. Central on the first and second floors are European painting, sculpture, and decorative arts. The Costume Institute is situated on the ground level, directly below the Egyptian galleries on the first floor.

Seated Man with Harp
This statuette was made in the Cyclades c.2800 BC.

Key

- ▢ The American wing
- ▢ Art of Africa, Oceania, and the Americas
- ▢ Arms and armor
- ▢ Egyptian art
- ▢ European sculpture and decorative arts
- ▢ Greek and Roman art
- ▢ Medieval art
- ▢ Modern and Contemporary art
- ▢ Robert Lehman Collection
- ▢ Special exhibitions
- ▢ Non-exhibition space

★ **Portrait of the Princesse de Broglie**
This portrait, painted in 1851–3, was J. A. D. Ingres' last.

VISITORS' CHECKLIST

Practical Information
1000 Fifth Ave. **Map** 16 F4.
Tel (212) 535-7710. **Open** 10am–
5:30pm Mon–Thu & Sun, 10am–
9pm Fri & Sat. **Closed** Jan 1,
Thanksgiving, Dec 25.
Concerts, lectures, classes, seminars, film & video presentations.
W metmuseum.org

Transport
M 4, 5, 6 to 86th St. M1–4.

First floor

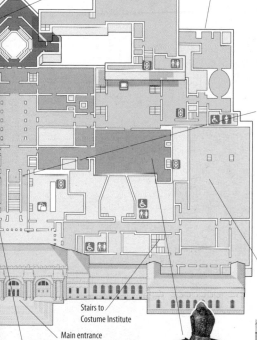

★ **Byzantine Galleries**
This marble panel with a griffin is from Greece or the Balkans (c.1250). It is just one of the pieces on display in the Byzantine Galleries.

Stairs to Costume Institute

Main entrance

The Marriage Feast at Cana
This rare 16th-century panel painting by Juan de Flandes is part of the Linsky Collection.

English Armor
This was made for Sir George Clifford around 1580.

★ **The Temple of Dendur (10 BC)**
The Roman emperor Augustus built this three-room temple, which is located in the Egyptian Art section.

Metropolitan Museum of Art: Upper Levels

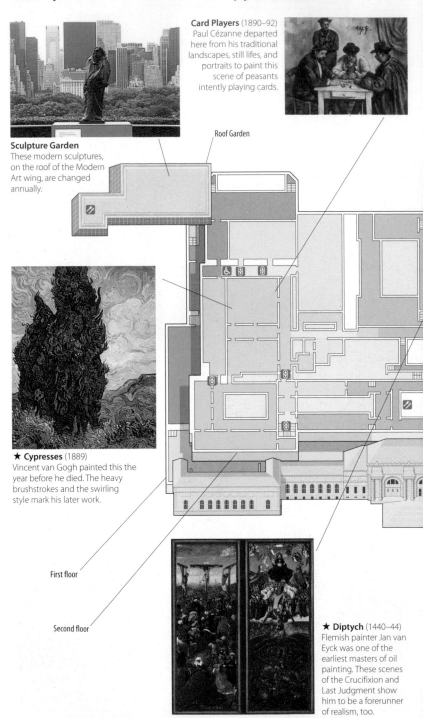

Card Players (1890–92)
Paul Cézanne departed here from his traditional landscapes, still lifes, and portraits to paint this scene of peasants intently playing cards.

Sculpture Garden
These modern sculptures, on the roof of the Modern Art wing, are changed annually.

Roof Garden

★ **Cypresses** (1889)
Vincent van Gogh painted this the year before he died. The heavy brushstrokes and the swirling style mark his later work.

First floor

Second floor

★ **Diptych** (1440–44)
Flemish painter Jan van Eyck was one of the earliest masters of oil painting. These scenes of the Crucifixion and Last Judgment show him to be a forerunner of realism, too.

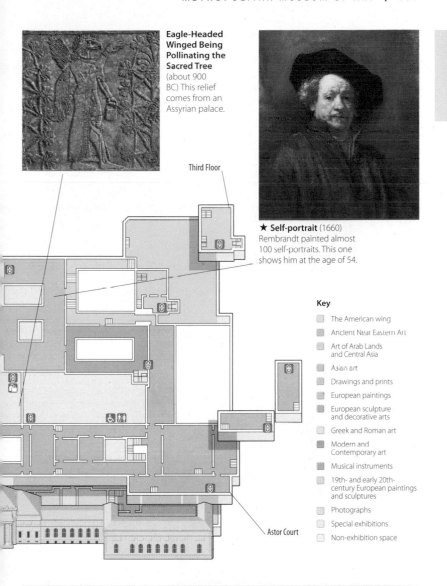

Eagle-Headed Winged Being Pollinating the Sacred Tree (about 900 BC) This relief comes from an Assyrian palace.

Third Floor

★ **Self-portrait** (1660)
Rembrandt painted almost 100 self-portraits. This one shows him at the age of 54.

Key

- The American wing
- Ancient Near Eastern Art
- Art of Arab Lands and Central Asia
- Asian art
- Drawings and prints
- European paintings
- European sculpture and decorative arts
- Greek and Roman art
- Modern and Contemporary art
- Musical instruments
- 19th- and early 20th-century European paintings and sculptures
- Photographs
- Special exhibitions
- Non-exhibition space

Astor Court

The Astor Court

In 1979, 27 craftspeople from China, responsible for the care of Suzhou's historic gardens, came to New York to replicate a Ming-style scholar's garden in the Metropolitan Museum. They used centuries-old techniques and handmade tools that had been passed down for generations. It was the first cultural exchange between the United States and the People's Republic of China. The result is a quiet garden for meditation, a Western parallel to Suzhou's Garden of the Master of the Fishing Nets.

Exploring the Metropolitan

The treasures of the "Met" include a vast collection of American art and more than 2,500 European paintings, including masterpieces by Rembrandt and Vermeer. There are also many Islamic exhibits, plus the greatest collection of Egyptian art outside Cairo.

A painted gold funerary mask (10th–11th century) from the necropolis of Batán Grande, Peru

Mysterious in identity and origin, the rare copper *Head of a Ruler* (c. 2300–200 BC) from the Near East

Art of Africa, Oceania, and the Americas

Nelson Rockefeller built the Michael C. Rockefeller Wing in 1982 in memory of his son, who lost his life on an art-finding expedition in New Guinea. The wing showcases a superb collection of over 1,600 objects from Africa, the islands of the Pacific, and the Americas.

Among the African works, the ivory and bronze sculptures from the royal kingdom of Benin (Nigeria) are outstanding, as is the wooden sculpture by the Dogon, Bamana, and Senufo peoples of Mali. From the Pacific come carvings by the Asmat people of New Guinea and decorations and masks from the Melanesian and Polynesian islands. From Mexico and Central and South America come pre-Columbian gold, ceramics, and stonework. The wing also contains fine Native American artifacts by the Inuit and other groups.

The American Wing

Gilbert Stuart's portrait of George Washington, George Caleb Bingham's *Fur Traders Descending the Missouri*, John Singer Sargent's notorious portrait of *Madame X*, and the monumental *Washington Crossing the Delaware* by Emanuel Leutze are among the icons in the American Wing.

It holds not only one of the world's finest collections of American painting and sculpture but also of decorative arts from Colonial times to the beginning of the 20th century. Highlights range from elegant Neo-Classical silver vessels made by Paul Revere to innovative glassware by Tiffany & Co. In the furniture section are settees, dining chairs, tables, bookcases, and desks from major centers of American cabinetmaking such as Boston, Newport, and Philadelphia.

Period rooms, with their original decorative woodwork and furnishings, range from the saloon hall in which George Washington celebrated his last birthday to the elegant prairie-style living room from the house that Frank Lloyd Wright designed for Francis W. Little in Wayzata, Minnesota, in 1912.

The Charles Engelhard Court is an indoor sculpture garden with large-scale architectural elements, including the lovely stained-glass and mosaic loggia from Louis Comfort Tiffany's Long Island estate and the facade of an 1824 United States Branch Bank that once stood on Wall Street.

Ancient Near Eastern and Islamic Art

Massive stone sculptures of winged, human-headed animals, once the guardians of the 9th-century BC Assyrian palace of Ashurnasirpal II, stand at the entrance to the Ancient Near Eastern galleries. Inside is a collection spanning 8,000 years, rich in Iranian bronzes, Anatolian ivories and Sumerian sculptures, and Achaemenian and Sassanian silver and gold. The adjacent Arts of Arab Lands section contains Islamic art of the 7th to the 19th centuries; glass and metalwork from Egypt, Syria, and Meso-potamia; royal miniatures from Persia and Mughal India; 16th- and 17th-century rugs; and an 18th-century room from Syria.

Arms and Armor

Mounted knights in full armor charge at each other across the equestrian court here. These galleries are a favorite with children and anyone moved by medieval romance or thrilled by power.

There are suits of armor, rapiers and sabers with hilts of precious stones and gold, firearms inlaid with ivory and mother-of-pearl, plus colorful

The pistol of Holy Roman Emperor Charles V (16th century)

heraldic banners and shields. Highlights include the armor of gentleman-pirate Sir George Clifford, a favorite of Queen Elizabeth I. The rainbow-colored armor of a 14th-century Japanese Shogun and a collection of Wild West revolvers that once belonged to gunmaker Samuel Colt are also exhibited here.

The Old Plum, a Japanese paper screen from the early Edo period (about 1650)

Asian Art

Many outstanding galleries contain masterpieces of Chinese, Japanese, Korean, Indian, and Southeast Asian art, dating from the second millennium BC to the 20th century. A full-scale Ming-style Chinese scholar's garden was built by craftspeople from Suzhou as part of the first cultural exchange between the United States and the People's Republic of China. The museum also has one of the finest collections of Song and Yuan dynasty paintings in the world, Chinese Buddhist monumental sculptures, fine Chinese ceramics and jade, and an important display of the arts of ancient China.

The full range of Japanese arts is represented in a breathtaking suite of eleven galleries featuring chronological and thematic displays of Japanese lacquer, ceramics, painting, sculpture, textiles, and screens. Indian, Southeast Asian, and Korean galleries display superb sculptures and other arts from these regions.

Costume Institute

The 31,000-piece collection of costumes and accessories has expanded by over 23,000 items under an agreement with the Brooklyn Museum (see pp238–41). There is no permanent display due to the fragility of the objects, but there are two special exhibitions a year.

The collection spans five centuries from the 17th century to the present and is a definitive compendium of fashionable dress, from the elaborately embroidered dresses of the late 1600s to gowns from the Napoleonic era. The designs of Elsa Schiaparelli, Worth, and Balenciaga are also included, along with Ballets Russes costumes and even David Bowie's sequined jockstrap.

The Art of Dress audio tour, narrated by actress Sarah Jessica Parker, focuses on how artists have used clothing to express identity and power.

The Institute is sophisticated in its understanding of conservation techniques, with a state-of-the-art laboratory.

A 17th-century European silk-and-satin doublet

Drawings and Prints

These eclectic galleries began as a gift of 670 pieces from Museum trustee Cornelius Vanderbilt, in 1880. Today the Museum holds over 17,000 drawings, some 12,000 illustrated books from both Western Europe and America,

Michelangelo's studies of a Libyan Sibyl for the ceiling of the Sistine Chapel (1508)

and an incredible 1.2 million prints. The drawings collection is especially rich in Italian and French art from the 15th to the 19th century. Specific exhibits of the drawings in this collection are shown on a rotating basis because of the light-sensitive nature of works on paper.

Highlights among the 17,000 drawings include works by Michelangelo, Leonardo da Vinci, Raphael, Ingres, Goya, Rubens, Rembrandt, Tiepolo, and Seurat.

The encyclopedic print collection includes major works by virtually every master printmaker, from an early German woodcut entitled Virgin and Child to some of Dürer's most accomplished works and Goya's The Giant. Influential gallery-owner Alfred Stieglitz's donation of his own extensive collection of photographs brought here such gems as Edward Steichen's The Flatiron. It formed the core of a photography collection that is now also particularly strong in Modernist works dating from between the world wars.

Ephemera such as posters and advertisements form another part of this collection.

Egyptian Art

One of the museum's best-loved areas is the ancient Egyptian wing, which displays every one of its thousands of holdings – from the prehistoric period to the 8th century AD. Objects range from the fragmented jasper lips of a 15th-century BC queen to the massive Temple of Dendur. Other amazing archaeological finds, most of them originating from museum-sponsored expeditions undertaken early in the 20th century, include sculptures of the notorious Queen Hatshepsut, who seized the Theban throne in the 16th century BC; 100 carved reliefs of Amenhotep IV's reign; and tomb figures such as the blue faïence hippo that has become the museum's mascot.

Fragment of the head of a pharoah's queen

European Paintings

The heart of the museum is its awe-inspiring collection of over 3,000 European paintings. The Italian works include Botticelli's *Last Communion of St. Jerome* and Bronzino's *Portrait of a Young Man*. The Dutch and Flemish canvases are among the world's finest, with

Young Woman with a Water Pitcher (c. 1662) by Johannes Vermeer

Brueghel's *The Harvesters*, several works by Rubens, Van Dyck, and Rembrandt, and more Vermeers than any other museum. The collection also has masterpieces by Spanish artists El Greco, Velázquez, and Goya, and by French artists Poussin and Watteau. Some of the finest Impressionist and Post-Impressionist canvases reside here: 34 Monets, including *Garden at Sainte-Adresse;* 18 Cézannes; and several van Goghs, including *Cypresses.*

European Sculpture and Decorative Arts

In the Kravis wing and adjacent galleries are works from the impressive 60,000-object collection of European sculpture and decorative arts. The galleries include exquisite pieces such as Tullio Lombardo's marble statue of Adam; a bronze statuette of a rearing horse, after a model by Leonardo; and dozens of works by Degas and Rodin. Period settings include the patio from a 16th-century Spanish castle and a series of ornate

18th-century French domestic interiors known as the Wrightsman Rooms. The Petrie European Sculpture Court features French and Italian sculpture in a beautiful garden setting reminiscent of Versailles in France.

Greek and Roman Art

A Roman sarcophagus from Tarsus, donated in 1870, was the first work of art in the Met's collections. It can still be seen in the museum's Greek and Roman galleries, along with breath-taking wall panels from a villa that was buried under the lava of Vesuvius in AD 79, Etruscan mirrors, Roman portrait busts, exquisite objects in glass and silver, and Greek vases. A monumental 7th- century BC statue of a youth shows the movement toward naturalism in sculpture, and the Hellenistic *Marble Statue of an Old Market Woman* demonstrates how the Greeks had mastered realism by the 2nd century BC.

An amphora by Exekias, showing a wedding (540 BC)

Egyptian Tomb Models

In 1920, a Met researcher's light illuminated a room, which had been closed for 2,000 years, in the tomb of the nobleman Meketre. Within were 24 tiny, perfect replicas of his daily life: his house and garden, fleet of ships, and herd of cattle. Meketre is there, too, on his boat, inhaling a lotus's scent and enjoying the music of his singer and harpist. The museum has 13 of these delightful replicas.

Lehman Collection

What had been one of the the finest private art collections in the world, that of investment banker Robert Lehman, came to the museum in 1969. The Lehman Wing is a dramatic glass pyramid housing an extraordinarily varied collection rich in Old Masters and 19th-century French paintings, drawings, bronzes, Renaissance

A panel from the stained-glass *Death of the Virgin* window, from the 12th-century cathedral of St. Pierre in Troyes, France

majolica, Venetian glass, furniture, and enamels. Among the canvases are works by North European masters, Dutch and Spanish paintings, French masterpieces, Post-Impressionists and Fauves.

Medieval Art

The Metropolitan's medieval collection includes works dating from the 4th to the 16th century, roughly from the fall of Rome to the beginning of the Renaissance. The collection is split between the main museum and its uptown branch, the Cloisters (*see pp246–9*). In the main building are a chalice once thought to be the Holy Grail, six silver Byzantine plates showing scenes from the life of David, a 1301 pulpit by Giovanni Pisano in the shape of an eagle, and several monumental sculptures of the Virgin and Child. Other exhibits include Migration jewelry, liturgical vessels, stained glass, ivories, and 14th- and 15th-century tapestries.

Musical Instruments

The world's oldest piano, Andrés Segovia's guitars, and a sitar shaped like a peacock are some of the features of a broad and sometimes quirky collection of musical instruments that spans six continents and dates from prehistory to the present. The instruments illustrate the history of music and performance, and most of them are conserved to remain in playable condition.

Worth particular mention are instruments from the European courts of the Middle Ages and the Renaissance; rare violins; harpsichords; instruments inlaid with precious materials; and a fully equipped traditional violin-maker's workshop; there are also African drums, Asian *pi-pas*, or lutes; and Native American flutes. Visitors can use audio equipment to hear many of the instruments playing the music of their day.

Stradivari violin from Cremona, Italy (1691)

Modern and Contemporary Art

Since its foundation in 1870, the museum has been acquiring contemporary art, but it was not until 1987 that a permanent home for 20th-century art was built – the Lila Acheson Wallace Wing. Other museums in New York have larger collections of modern art, but this display space is considered among the finest. European and American works from 1900 onward are featured on three levels, starting with Europeans such as Picasso, Kandinsky, Braque, and Bonnard. The collection's greatest strength lies in its collection of modern American art, with works by New York school "The Eight," including John Sloan; such Modernists as Charles Demuth and Georgia O'Keeffe; American Regionalist Grant Wood; Abstract Expressionists, including Willem de Kooning and Jackson Pollock; and such Color Field painters as Clyfford Still. Special areas of the wing house Art Nouveau and Art Deco furniture and metalwork; a large collection of works on paper by Paul Klee; and the Sculpture Gallery, with its large-scale sculptures and canvases.

Gems of the collection include Picasso's portrait of Gertrude Stein, Matisse's *Nasturtiums* with the painting *Dance (1)* Demuth's *I Saw the Figure 5 in Gold*, and Andy Warhol's last self-portrait.

Each year the Cantor Roof Garden at the top of the wing features a new installation of contemporary sculpture, especially dramatic against the backdrop of the New York skyline and Central Park.

Grant Wood's *The Midnight Ride of Paul Revere* (1931)

Book cover (1916) by illustrator N. C. Wyeth

⓫ Society of Illustrators

128 E 63rd St. **Map** 13 A2. **Tel** (212) 838-2560. Ⓜ Lexington Ave. **Open** 10am–8pm Tue, 10am–5pm Wed–Fri, noon–4pm Sat. **Closed** public hols. ♿ restricted. Ⓒ Ⓒ Ⓦ societyillustrators.org

Established in 1901, this society was formed to promote the illustrator's art. Its notable roster included Charles Dana Gibson, N. C. Wyeth, and Howard Pyle. It was at first concerned with education and public service, and still holds monthly lectures. In 1981, the Museum of American Illustration opened in two galleries. Changing thematic exhibitions show the history of book and magazine illustration, with an annual exhibition of the year's finest American illustrations.

⓬ Mount Vernon Hotel Museum

421 E 61st St. **Map** 13 C3. **Tel** (212) 838-6878. Ⓜ Lexington Ave, 59th St. **Open** 11am–4pm Tue–Sun. **Closed** Aug, public hols. Ⓒ Ⓒ Ⓒ Ⓒ Ⓦ mvhm.org

Built in 1799, the Mount Vernon Hotel Museum and Garden was once a country day hotel for New Yorkers who needed to escape from the crowded city,

then only at the south end of the island. The stone building sits on land once owned by Abigail Adams Smith, daughter of President John Adams.

It was acquired by the Colonial Dames of America, a women's patriotic society, in 1924 and turned into a charming re-creation of a Federal home. Costumed guides show visitors through eight rooms, which exhibit Chinese porcelain, Sheraton chests, and a Duncan Phyfe sofa. One bedroom even contains a baby's cradle and children's toys. An 18th-century-style garden has been planted around the house.

Stunning mosaics on the dome of the Christ Church United Methodist

⓭ Christ Church United Methodist

524 Park Ave. **Map** 13 A3. **Tel** (212) 838-3036. Ⓜ Fifth Ave, 59th St. **Open** 7am–6pm Mon–Fri, 9am & 11am Sun for services. Ⓦ christchurchnyc.org

With deceptively simple exteriors, this dazzling Romanesque structure was designed in 1931, by architect Ralph Adams Cram. Gold-leaf mosaics fill the vaulted ceiling and apse, while parts of the choir screen date from 1660, and were once owned by Tsar Nicholas II of Russia. The altar is carved from Spanish marble, the nave columns and from veined, purple Levanto marble.

Exterior of the elegant Mount Vernon Hotel Museum

⓮ The Met Breuer

945 Madison Ave. **Map** 17 A5. Ⓜ 77th St. **Open** visit website for full opening times. Ⓦ metmuseum.org

An extension of The Metropolitan Museum of Art, The Met Breuer opened in March 2016 in the old premises of the Whitney Museum of American Art. Created by architect Marcel Breuer, the building's Brutalist design was a controversial addition to the town houses of the Upper East Side in 1966. The Met Breuer provides further exhibition space for 20th and 21st century art, along with residencies, educational programs, and unique performances.

⓯ Gracie Mansion

East End Ave at 88th St. **Map** 18 D3. **Tel** (212) 639-9675. Ⓜ 86th St. 🚌 M31, M79, M86. **Open** 10am, 11am, 1pm, 2pm most Weds for prebooked guided tours only. Ⓒ Ⓒ ♿ Ⓒ Ⓦ nyc.gov/gracie

This gracious, balconied wooden 1799 country home is the official mayor's residence. Built by wealthy merchant Archibald Gracie, it is one of the best Federal houses left in New York.

Acquired by the city in 1896, it was the first home of the Museum of the City of New York. In 1942 it became the

Front view of Gracie Mansion

official Mayoral Residence. When Fiorello La Guardia moved in after nine years in office, preferring it to a 75-room palace on Riverside Drive, he said that even the modest Gracie Mansion was too fancy for him. "The Little Flower" (from Fiorello) had fought corruption in the city.

Arched doorway of the Church of the Holy Trinity

⑯ Church of the Holy Trinity

316 E 88th St. **Map** 17 B3. **Tel** (212) 289-4100. **M** 86th St. **Open** 9am–5pm Mon–Fri, 7:30am–2pm Sun. 🕇 8:45am Tue & Thu, 8am, 10:30am & 6pm Sun. **W** holytrinity-nyc.org

Delightfully placed in a serene garden setting, this church was constructed in 1889 of glowing golden brick and terra-cotta in the French Renaissance style. It boasts one of New York's best bell towers, which holds a handsome wrought-iron clock with brass hands. The arched doorway is richly decorated with carved images of the saints and prophets.

The complex was donated by Serena Rhinelander in memory of her father and grandfather. The land was part of the Rhinelander farm, which the family had owned for 100 years.

Farther down at 350 E. 88th Street is the Rhinelander Children's Center, also a gift, and the headquarters of the Children's Aid Society.

⑰ St. Nicholas Russian Orthodox Cathedral

15 E 97th St. **Map** 16 F1. **Tel** (212) 876-2190. **M** 96 St. **Open** by appt. 🕇 throughout the week, including 10am & 6pm Wed & Sun.

Built in Muscovite Baroque style in 1902, this church has five onion domes crowned with crosses, and blue and yellow tiles on a red brick and white stone facade. Among the early worshipers were White Russians who had fled, mostly intellectuals and aristocrats who soon became a part of New York society. Later, there were further waves of refugees, dissidents, and defectors.

The cathedral now serves a scattered community, and the congregation is small. Mass is celebrated in Russian with great pomp and dignity.

The cathedral is filled with the scent of incense. The high central sanctuary has marble columns with blue and white trim above. Ornate wooden screens trimmed with gold enclose the altar. It is unique, an unexpected find on a side street in this staid part of Manhattan.

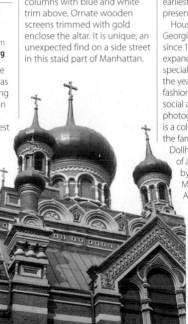

Facade and domes of St. Nicholas Russian Cathedral

Facade of the Museum of the City of New York

⑱ Museum of the City of New York

1220 5th Ave at 103rd St. **Map** 21 C5. **Tel** (212) 534 1672. **M** 103rd St. **Open** 10am–6pm daily (to 8:30pm Sat). **Closed** Jan 1, Thanksgiving, Dec 25. 🐾 🕭 📷 🖥 🏠 **W** mcny.org

Founded in 1923 and at first housed in Gracie Mansion, this museum is dedicated to New York's development from its earliest beginnings up to the present and on to the future.

Housed in a handsome Georgian Colonial building since 1932, the museum has expanded its public space, with special exhibitions throughout the year on subjects such as fashion, architecture, theater, social and political history, and photography. In addition there is a collection of toys, including the famed Stettheimer Dollhouse, with original works of art in miniature, painted by such luminaries as Marcel Duchamp and Albert Gleizes.

A core exhibition of the museum is the film *Timescapes: A Multimedia Portrait of New York* (every 30 mins, 10:15am–4:45pm). It uses images from the museum's collection and historic maps to chart the growth of New York, from its early days as a tiny settlement to its current status as one of the largest cities in the world.

❼ The Frick Collection

The art collection of steel magnate Henry Clay Frick (1849–1919) is exhibited in a residential setting amid the furnishings of his opulent mansion, which provides a rare glimpse of how the extremely wealthy lived in New York's gilded age. Henry Frick intended the collection to be a memorial to himself, and on his death he bequeathed the entire house to the nation. The collection includes important Old Master paintings, major works of sculpture, French furniture, rare Limoges enamels, and beautiful Oriental rugs.

The Harbor of Dieppe (1826)
J. M. W. Turner was criticized by some skeptical contemporaries for depicting this northern European port suffused with light.

The Polish Rider
The identity of the rider in this equestrian portrait, painted by Rembrandt in c. 1655, is unknown. The somber, rocky landscape creates an eerie atmosphere of unknown danger.

Oval Room

Garden Court

Library

West Gallery

Living Hall

★ **Sir Thomas More** (1527)
Holbein's portrait of Henry VIII's Lord Chancellor was painted eight years before More's execution for treason.

Gallery Guide

Of special interest are the West Gallery, with oils by Vermeer, Hals, and Rembrandt; the East Gallery, featuring Van Dyck and Whistler; the Oval Room, featuring Gainsborough; the Library and Dining Room, with English works; and the Living Hall, with works by Titian and Holbein.

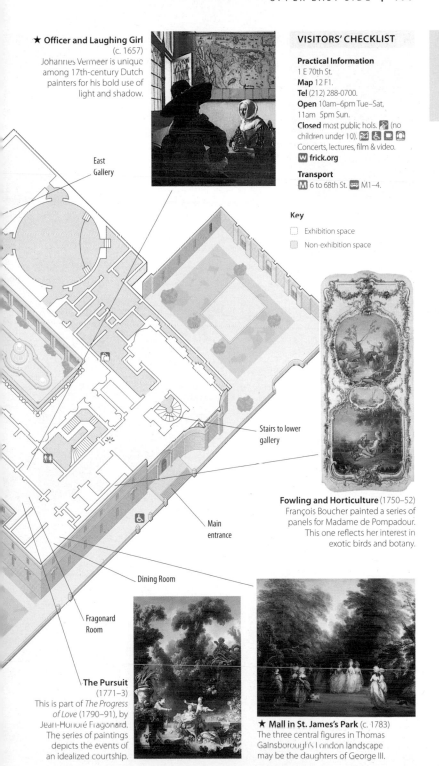

★ **Officer and Laughing Girl** (c. 1657)
Johannes Vermeer is unique among 17th-century Dutch painters for his bold use of light and shadow.

East Gallery

VISITORS' CHECKLIST

Practical Information
1 E 70th St.
Map 12 F1.
Tel (212) 288-0700.
Open 10am–6pm Tue–Sat,
11am 5pm Sun.
Closed most public hols. (no children under 10). Concerts, lectures, film & video.
W frick.org

Transport
M 6 to 68th St. M1–4.

Key
☐ Exhibition space
☐ Non-exhibition space

Stairs to lower gallery

Fowling and Horticulture (1750–52)
François Boucher painted a series of panels for Madame de Pompadour. This one reflects her interest in exotic birds and botany.

Main entrance

Dining Room

Fragonard Room

The Pursuit
(1771–3)
This is part of *The Progress of Love* (1790–91), by Jean-Honoré Fragonard. The series of paintings depicts the events of an idealized courtship.

★ **Mall in St. James's Park** (c. 1783)
The three central figures in Thomas Gainsborough's London landscape may be the daughters of George III.

CENTRAL PARK

The city's "backyard" was designed by
Frederick Law Olmsted and Calvert Vaux on
an unpromising site of quarries, pig farms,
swampland, and shacks. Sixteen years of
construction, and five million cubic yards of
stone, earth, and top-soil, turned it into the
lush 843-acre (340-ha) park of today, with its
official opening in 1876. There are hills, lakes,
and lush meadows dotted throughout, and
more than 500,000 trees and shrubs. Over
the years the park has blossomed, with playgrounds, skating rinks, ball fields, and spaces
for every other activity, from chess and
croquet to concerts and events. Cars are
not allowed on weekends, giving bicyclists,
in-line skaters, and joggers the right of way.

Sights at a Glance

Historic Buildings
1 The Dairy
3 Belvedere Castle

Monuments and Statues
2 Strawberry Fields
4 Bow Bridge
5 Bethesda Fountain and Terrace

Lakes and Gardens
6 Conservatory Water
7 Central Park Zoo
8 Conservatory Garden

☐ **Restaurants** *see pp302–304*
1 Loeb Boathouse Restaurant
2 Tavern on the Green

See also Street Finder maps 12, 16, 21

◀ New York's most treasured green space, Central Park

For keys to symbols *see back flap*

A Tour of Central Park

On a short visit, a walking tour from 59th to 79th streets takes in some of Central Park's loveliest features, from the dense, wooded Ramble to the open formal spaces of Bethesda Terrace. Along the way are man-made lakes and more than 30 graceful bridges and arches that link around 68 miles (109 km) of footpaths, bridle paths, and roads in the park. In summer the park is often several degrees cooler than the city streets around it, and thus is a favorite retreat.

❷ ★ **Strawberry Fields**
One of the park's most visited spots, this peaceful area was created in memory of John Lennon, who lived nearby.

❺ ★ **Bethesda Fountain and Terrace**
The richly ornamented formal terrace overlooks the Lake and the wooded shores of the Ramble.

Wollman Rink was restored in the 1980s for future generations of skaters by tycoon Donald Trump.

❼ **Central Park Zoo**
Three climate zones are home to more than 150 species of animals.

SHEEP MEADOW

THE MALL

CENTRAL PARK WEST

CENTRAL PARK SOUTH

TRANSVERSE

65TH ST

FIFTH

❶ ★ **The Dairy**
This Victorian Gothic building houses one of the park's visitor centers. Make it your first stop and pick up a calendar of park events.

❻ ★ **Conservatory Water**
From March to November, this is the scene of model boat races. Many of the tiny craft are stored in the boathouse that adjoins the Lake.

4 Bow Bridge
This cast-iron bridge links the Ramble with Cherry Hill by a graceful arch, 60 ft (18 m) above the Lake.

Locator Map
See Manhattan Map pp16–17

Alice in Wonderland Is immortalized in bronze at the northern end of Conservatory Water, along with her friends the Cheshire Cat, the Mad Hatter, and the Dormouse. Children love to slide down her toadstool seat.

KEY

① **Hans Christian Andersen's** statue Is a favorite Central Park landmark for children. It is on the west side of Conservatory Water and is a popular site for storytelling in the summer.

② **The Frick Collection** (see pp196–7)

③ **Plaza Hotel** (see p177)

④ **The Pond**

⑤ **The Dakota** (see p212)

⑥ **San Remo Apartments** (see p208)

⑦ **American Museum of Natural History** (see pp210–11)

⑧ **Reservoir**

⑨ **Obelisk**

⑩ **The Ramble** is a wooded area of 37 acres (15 ha), crisscrossed by paths and streams. It is a paradise for birdwatchers. More than 275 species of birds have been spotted in the park, which is on the Atlantic migration flyway.

⑪ **Metropolitan Museum** (see pp186–93)

⑫ **Guggenheim Museum** (see pp184–5)

6 ★ Belvedere Castle
From the terraces, there are unequaled views of the city and surrounding park. Within the stone walls is a visitor center.

The Carousel, part of the park's Children's District

● The Dairy

Map 12 F2. **Tel** (212) 794-6564.
Ⓜ Fifth Ave. **Open** 10am–5pm daily.
Slide show. 🅿
Ⓦ centralparknyc.org

Now used as Central Park's Visitor Center, this charming building of natural stone was planned as part of the "Children's District" of the park, which included a playground, the Carousel, a Children's Cottage, and stable. In 1873, there were cows grazing on the meadows in front of the Dairy, a ewe and her lambs feeding nearby, and chickens, guinea fowl, and peacocks roaming the lawn. City children could get fresh milk and other refreshments here. Over the years, the Dairy deteriorated, being used as a shed until restoration in 1979, done according to original photographs and drawings. The Dairy is the place to begin exploring the lush and leafy park; maps and details of events can be obtained here. The less energetic can rent chess and checkers sets for use on the pretty inlaid boards of the *Kinderberg*, the charming little "children's hill" nearby.

● Strawberry Fields

Map 12 E1. Ⓜ 72nd St.

The restoration of this tear-drop-shaped section of the park was Yoko Ono's tribute in memory of her slain husband, John Lennon. They lived in the Dakota apartments overlooking this spot *(see p212)*. Gifts for the garden came from all over the world. A mosaic set in the pathway, inscribed with the word *"Imagine"* (named for Lennon's famous song), was a gift from the city of Naples in Italy.

This broad expanse of the park's landscape was designed by Vaux and Olmsted. Now it is an international peace garden, with 121 species of plants from across the globe, including jetbead, roses, witch hazel, birches – and strawberries.

A tranquil scene in Central Park, overlooked by exclusive apartments

● Belvedere Castle

Map 16 E4. **Tel** (212) 772-0210.
Ⓜ 81st St. **Open** 10am–5pm daily.
Closed Jan 1, Thanksgiving, Dec 25.
♿ to main floor only.

This stone castle atop Vista Rock, complete with tower and turrets, offers one of the best views of the park and the city from its lookout on the rooftop. Inside is the Henry Luce Nature Observatory, with a delightful exhibit telling inquisitive young visitors about the surprising variety of wildlife to be found in the park.

The view to the north from the castle allows you to look down into the **Delacorte Theater**, home to the free productions of Shakespeare in the Park every summer, often featuring big-name stars *(see p341)*. The theater was the gift of George T. Delacorte. Publisher and founder of Dell paperbacks, Delacorte was a delightful philanthropist who was responsible for many of the park's pleasures.

Belvedere Castle with its lookout over the park

● Bow Bridge

Map 16 E5. Ⓜ 72nd St.

This is one of the park's seven original cast-iron bridges and is considered one of the finest. It was designed by Vaux as a bow tying together the two large sections of the Lake. In the 19th century, when the Lake was used for ice skating, a red ball was hoisted from a bell tower on Vista Rock to signal that the ice was safe. The bridge offers expansive views of the park and the buildings bordering it on both the east and west sides.

An 1864 print of Bethesda Fountain and Terrace

❺ Bethesda Fountain and Terrace

Map 12 E1. Ⓜ 72nd St.

Situated between the Lake and the Mall, this is the architectural heart of the park, a formal element in the naturalistic landscape. The fountain was dedicated in 1873. The statue, *Angel of the Waters*, marked the opening of the Croton Aqueduct system in 1842, bringing the city its first supply of pure water; its name refers to a biblical account of a healing angel at the pool of Bethesda in Jerusalem. The Spanish-style detailing, such as the sculptured double staircase, tiles, and friezes, is by Jacob Wrey Mould. The terrace is one of the best spots to relax and take in some people-watching.

❻ Conservatory Water

Map 16 F5. Ⓜ 77th St.

Better known as the Model Boat Pond, this stretch of water is home to model yacht races every weekend. At the north end of the lake, a sculpture of Alice in Wonderland is a delight for children. It was commissioned by George T. Delacorte in honor of his wife. He himself is immortalized in caricature as the Mad Hatter. On the west bank, free story hours are held at the Hans Christian Andersen statue. The author is portrayed reading from his own story, "The Ugly Duckling," while its hero waddles at his feet. Children like to climb on the statue and snuggle in the author's lap. Conservatory Water's literary links continue into adolescence: it is here that J. D. Salinger's Holden Caulfield comes to tell the ducks his troubles in *The Catcher in the Rye*.

Each spring, birdwatchers gather at the pond to see the city's most famous red-tailed hawk, Pale Male, nest on the roof of 927 Fifth Avenue.

❼ Central Park Zoo

Map 12 F2. **Tel** (212) 439-6500. Ⓜ Fifth Ave between 63rd and 66th sts. **Open** 10am–5pm Mon–Fri, 10am–5:30pm Sat, Sun & hols; Nov–Mar: 10am–4:30pm daily. Last adm: 30 mins before closing. 🅰️ ♿ 🖥️ 🎁 Ⓦ centralparkzoo.com

This imaginative zoo has won plaudits for its creative and humane use of small space. More than 150 species of animals are represented in three climate zones: the Tropics, the Polar Circle, and the California coast. An equatorial rainforest is home to monkeys and free-flying birds, while penguins and polar bears populate an Arctic land-scape that allows views both above and under water. At the smaller Tisch Children's Zoo, just across 65th Street, children can get close to goats, sheep, alpacas, cows, and pot-bellied pigs. By its entrance is the Delacorte Clock, which plays nursery rhymes every half-hour, as bronze musical animals (such as a goat playing panpipes) circle around it.

Toward Willowdell Arch is another favorite – the memorial to Balto, leader of a team of huskies that made a heroic journey across Alaska with serum for a diphtheria epidemic.

Statue of Balto, the heroic husky dog, Central Park Wildlife Center

❽ Conservatory Garden

Map 21 B5. Ⓜ Central Pk N, 103rd St. **Tel** (212) 860-1382. **Open** 8am–dusk. ♿

The Vanderbilt Gate on Fifth Avenue is the entry to a 6-acre (2.4-ha) park containing three formal gardens. Each one represents a different national landscape style. The Central Garden, with a large lawn, yew hedges, crab apple trees, and a wisteria pergola recreates an Italian style. The South Garden, spilling over with perennials, represents an English style, with a bronze statue in the reflecting pool of Mary and Dickon, from Frances Hodgson Burnett's *The Secret Garden*. Beyond is a slope with native wild flowers, spreading into the park beyond. The North Garden, in the French style, centers around Samuel Untermyer's bronze fountain of the *Three Dancing Maidens*. It puts on a brief but brilliant display of annuals each summer.

Polar bear in the Central Park Zoo

UPPER WEST SIDE

Once open farmland, this district of New York began to change in 1879, when the Ninth Avenue railroad made commuting to Midtown possible. The streets were leveled and graded, and the city's first luxury apartment house, the Dakota, was built in 1884. Buildings sprang up on Central Park West and Broadway. Today, the area is mainly residential, with a blend of high-rises and old brownstones. The Lincoln Center complex has made it something of a cultural hub, while the American Museum of Natural History is one of the city's most popular family-friendly attractions. Some of the grandest homes in the area can be spotted along Central Park West.

Sights at a Glance

Historic Streets and Buildings
1. Twin Towers of Central Park West
7. Columbus Circle
8. Hotel des Artistes
9. The Dakota
13. Pomander Walk
14. Riverside Drive and Park
16. The Ansonia
17. The Dorilton

Museums and Galleries
10. New York Historical Society
11. American Museum of Natural History pp210–11
12. Rose Center for Earth and Space
15. Children's Museum of Manhattan
18. American Folk Art Museum

Famous Theaters
2. Lincoln Center for the Performing Arts
3. David H. Koch Theater
4. Metropolitan Opera House
5. Lincoln Center Theater
6. Avery Fisher Hall

Restaurants see pp302–304
1. Asiate
2. Bar Boulud
3. Café Fiorello
4. Café Frida
5. Café Luxembourg
6. Calle Ocho
7. Gennaro
8. Jean-Georges
9. Masa
10. Per Se
11. Picholine
12. Pio Pio
13. Rosa Mexicano
14. Telepan

0 meters 500
0 yards 500

See also Street Finder maps 11, 12, 15, 16

◀ The Rose Center for Earth and Space, part of the American Museum of Natural History

For keys to symbols see back flap

Street by Street: Lincoln Center

Lincoln Center was conceived when both the Metropolitan Opera House and the New York Philharmonic required homes, and a large tract on Manhattan's west side was in dire need of revitalization. The notion of a single complex where different performing arts could exist side by side seems natural today, but in the 1950s it was considered both daring and risky. Today Lincoln Center has proved itself by drawing audiences of five million each year. Proximity to its halls prompts both performers and arts lovers to live nearby.

❷ ★ **Lincoln Center for the Performing Arts**
Dance, music, and theater come together in this fine contemporary complex. It is also a great place to sit around the fountain and people-watch.

❺ **Lincoln Center Theater**
The Vivian Beaumont and the Mitzi E. Newhouse theaters are both housed in this building.

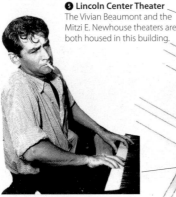

Composer Leonard Bernstein's famous musical *West Side Story*, which was based on Shakespeare's *Romeo and Juliet*, was set in the impoverished neighborhood that was razed to make room for Lincoln Center. Bernstein was later instrumental in setting up the large music complex.

AMSTERDAM AVENUE

COLUMBUS AVENUE

BROADWAY

W 62ND STREET

The Guggenheim Bandshell in Damrosch Park is the site of free concerts.

❸ **David H. Koch Theater**
This is the home of the New York City Ballet, as well as an opera company.

❹ **Metropolitan Opera House**
Lincoln Center's focus is the Opera House. The café at the top of the lobby offers wonderful plaza views.

The College Board Building is an Art Deco delight that now houses condominiums and the administrative offices of the College Board, developers of the college entrance exam.

Early American quilt

⑱ American Folk Art Museum
Quilting, pottery, and furniture are some of the arts displayed here.

James Dean once lived in a one-room apartment on the top floor at 19 West 68th Street.

⑧ ★ Hotel des Artistes
Artists Isadora Duncan, Noël Coward, and Norman Rockwell once lived here.

Locator Map
See Manhattan Map pp16–17

Key
— Suggested route

0 meters 100
0 yards 100

To 72nd Street subway (4 blocks)

An ABC-TV sound stage for soap operas is housed in this castle-like building, formerly an armory.

W 67TH STREET

W 65TH STREET

CENTRAL PARK WEST

55 Central Park West is an Art Deco apartment building, which featured in the film *Ghostbusters*.

The Society for Ethical Culture was one of the city's first Art Nouveau buildings. It also houses a school.

To 59th Street subway (2 blocks)

Central Park West is home to many celebrities, who like the privacy of its highly exclusive apartments.

❶ Twin Towers of Central Park West
One of a group of twin towers, the Century building is visible from Central Park.

The San Remo, a twin-towered apartment house designed by Emery Roth

❶ Twin Towers of Central Park West

Map 12 D1, 12 D2, 16 D3, 16 D5. Ⓜ 59th St-Columbus Circle, 72nd St, 81St, 86th St. **Closed** to the public.

A familiar landmark on the New York skyline, the four twin-towered apartment houses on Central Park West were built between 1929 and 1931, before the Great Depression halted all luxury construction. They are among the most-sought-after residences in New York.

Admired today for their grace and architectural detail, they were designed in response to a city-planning law allowing taller apartments if setbacks and towers were used.

Emery Roth designed the San Remo (145 CPW), whose tenants have included Dustin Hoffman, Paul Simon, and Diane Keaton. Turned down by the residents' committee, Madonna went to live close by at 1 West 64th Street. The towers of the Eldorado (300 CPW), also by Roth, were home to

Groucho Marx, Marilyn Monroe, and Richard Dreyfuss. The Majestic (115 CPW) and the Century (25 CPW) are both sleek classics by Art Deco designer Irwin S. Chanin.

❷ Lincoln Center for the Performing Arts

Map 11 C2. **Tel** (212) 546-2656. Ⓜ 66th St. ♿ 📷 (212) 875-5350. 📷 ⓕ *See Entertainment pp344–5.* 🆆 lincolncenter.org

In May 1959, President Eisenhower traveled to New York to turn a shovelful of earth, Leonard Bernstein lifted his baton, the New York Philharmonic and the Juilliard Choir broke into

Central plaza at Lincoln Center

the Hallelujah Chorus – and the city's major cultural center was born. It soon covered 15 acres (6 ha) on the site of the slums that had been the setting for Bernstein's classic musical *West Side Story.* The plaza fountain is by Philip Johnson, and the sculpture, *Reclining Figure,* is by Henry Moore.

Jazz at the Lincoln Center has developed a state-of-the-art facility dedicated to a wide range of jazz performances. It forms part of a major complex at Columbus Circle.

❸ David H. Koch Theater

Lincoln Center. **Map** 11 D2. **Tel** (212) 870-5570. Ⓜ 66th St. ♿ 📷 📷 ⓕ *See Entertainment pp340–41.* 🆆 nycballet.com

The home base for the highly acclaimed New York City Ballet, and, until 2011, home of the New York City Opera, is a Philip Johnson design. It was inaugurated in 1964.

Gargantuan white marble sculptures by Elie Nadelman dominate the vast four-story foyer. The theater seats 2,800 people. Because of its rhinestone lights and chandeliers both inside and out, some describe the theater as "a little jewel box."

❹ Metropolitan Opera House

Lincoln Center. **Map** 11 D2. **Tel** (212) 362-6000. Ⓜ 66th St. ♿ 📷 📷 📷 *See Entertainment pp344–5.* 🆆 metopera.org 🆆 abt.org

Home to the Metropolitan Opera Company and the American Ballet Theatre, "the Met" is the most spectacular of Lincoln Center's buildings. Five great arched windows offer views of the opulent foyer and two murals by Marc Chagall. (You can't see them in the mornings, when they are protected from the sun.) Inside there are curved white marble stairs, red carpeting, and exquisite starburst crystal chandeliers that are raised to the ceiling just before each performance. All the greats have sung here, including Maria Callas, Jessye Norman, and Luciano Pavarotti. First nights are glittering, star-studded occasions.

The Guggenheim Bandshell, in Damrosch Park next to the Met, is a popular concert site. The high point of the season is the Lincoln Center Out-of-Doors Festival, which takes place over three weeks in August and features global music, dance, and spoken-word performances, all for free.

Concert at Guggenheim Bandshell, Damrosch Park, near the Met

❺ Lincoln Center Theater

Lincoln Center. **Map** 11 C2. **Tel** (212) 362-7600 (Beaumont and Newhouse), (212) 870-1630 (Library). 800-432 7250 (tickets). Ⓜ 66th St. 🚻 📷 🎦 📷 See Entertainment pp344–5. 🆆 lct.org

Three theaters make up this innovative complex, where eclectic and often experimental drama is presented. The theaters are the 1,000-seat Vivian Beaumont, the 280-seat Mitzi E. Newhouse, and the 112-seat Claire Tow. Works by some of New York's best modern playwrights have featured at the Beaumont. Among these was Arthur Miller's After the Fall, the theater's inaugural performance in 1962.

The size of the Newhouse suits workshop-style plays, but it can still make the news with theatrical gems such as Robin Williams and Steve Martin in a

production of Samuel Beckett's Waiting for Godot. The complex also houses the New York Public Library for the Performing Arts, which has exhibits including audio cylinders of early Met performances, and original scores and playbills.

❻ David Geffen Hall

Lincoln Center. **Map** 11 C2. **Tel** (212) 875-5030. Ⓜ 66th St. 🚻 📷 🎦 📷 See Entertainment pp344–5. 🆆 nyphil.org

Located at the northern end of the Lincoln Center Plaza, Avery Fisher Hall is home to America's oldest orchestra, the New York Philharmonic. It also provides a stage for some of the Lincoln Center's own performers, and the Mostly Mozart Festival.

When the venue opened in 1962 as the Philharmonic Hall, critics initially complained about the acoustics. Several structural modifications, however, have rendered the hall an acoustic gem, comparing favorably with other great classical concert halls around the world. For a small fee, the public can attend open rehearsals on some Thursday mornings in the 2,738-seat auditorium.

❼ Columbus Circle

Columbus Circle, New York. **Map** 12 D3. Ⓜ 59th St. Concerts (212) 258-9800. 🆆 jazz.org

Presiding over this urban plaza at the corner of Central Park is a marble statue of explorer Christopher Columbus, perched on top of a tall granite column in the center of a fountain and plantings. The statue is one of the few remaining original features in this circle – it has become one of the largest building projects in all of New York's history.

Multi-use skyscrapers have been erected, attracting national and international businesses. Global

media company Time Warner has its headquarters in an 80-story skyscraper. The 2.8 million sq ft (260,000 sq m) building provides a retail, entertainment, and restaurant facility. Facilities include shops such as Hugo Boss, Williams-Sonoma, and Whole Foods Market, dining at Per Se and Masa; and a Mandarin Oriental hotel.

The Time Warner Center is also home to Jazz at the Lincoln Center. The three venues here – The Appel Room, the Rose Theater, and Dizzy's Club Coca-Cola – together with a jazz hall of fame and education center, comprise the world's first performing-arts facility dedicated to jazz.

Other notable buildings in Columbus Circle include Hearst House, designed by British architect Lord Norman Foster, Trump International Hotel, the Maine Monument, and the eye-catching Museum of Arts and Design, formerly the American Craft Museum.

❽ Hotel des Artistes

1 W 67th St. **Map** 12 D2. **Tel** (212) 877-3500 (café). Ⓜ 72nd St.

Built in 1918 by George Mort Pollard, these two-story apartments were intended to be working artists' studios, but they have attracted a variety of famous tenants, including Alexander Woollcott, Norman Rockwell, Isadora Duncan, Rudolph Valentino, and Noël Coward. The base of the building's facade is decorated with figures of artists.

Decorative figure on the Hotel des Artistes

⑪ American Museum of Natural History

This is one of the world's largest natural history museums. Since the original building opened in 1877, the complex has grown to cover four city blocks, and today holds more than 30 million specimens and artifacts. The most popular areas are the dinosaurs and the Milstein Hall of Ocean Life. The Rose Center for Earth and Space includes the Hayden Planetarium *(see p212)*.

The facade on W. 77th Street

Gallery Guide

The museum houses 46 exhibition halls, research laboratories, and a library, spread over 25 interconnected buildings. Enter at Central Park West onto the second floor to view the Barosaurus exhibit, African, Asian, Central and South American peoples, and animals. First-floor exhibits include ocean life, meteors, minerals and gems, and the Hall of Biodiversity. North American Indians, birds, and reptiles occupy the third floor. Dinosaurs, fossil fishes, and early mammals are on the fourth floor.

★ **Star of India**
This 563-carat gem is the world's largest blue star sapphire. Found in Sri Lanka, it was given to the museum by J. P. Morgan in 1900.

★ **Blue Whale**
The blue whale is the largest animal, living or extinct. Its weight can exceed 100 tons. This replica is based on a female captured off South America in 1925.

★ **Great Canoe**
This 63-ft (19.2-m) seafaring war canoe from the Pacific Northwest was carved out of the trunk of a single cedar. It stands in the Grand Gallery.

Entrance on
W. 77th St

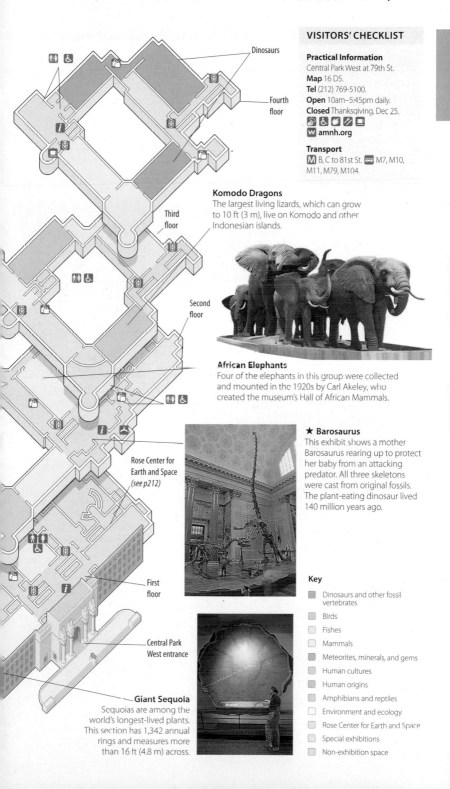

VISITORS' CHECKLIST

Practical Information
Central Park West at 79th St.
Map 16 D5.
Tel (212) 769-5100.
Open 10am–5:45pm daily.
Closed Thanksgiving, Dec 25.
w amnh.org

Transport
M B, C to 81st St. M7, M10, M11, M79, M104.

Komodo Dragons
The largest living lizards, which can grow to 10 ft (3 m), live on Komodo and other Indonesian islands.

African Elephants
Four of the elephants in this group were collected and mounted in the 1920s by Carl Akeley, who created the museum's Hall of African Mammals.

★ Barosaurus
This exhibit shows a mother Barosaurus rearing up to protect her baby from an attacking predator. All three skeletons were cast from original fossils. The plant-eating dinosaur lived 140 million years ago.

Dinosaurs

Fourth floor

Third floor

Second floor

Rose Center for Earth and Space
(see p212)

First floor

Central Park West entrance

Giant Sequoia
Sequoias are among the world's longest-lived plants. This section has 1,342 annual rings and measures more than 16 ft (4.8 m) across.

Key

- Dinosaurs and other fossil vertebrates
- Birds
- Fishes
- Mammals
- Meteorites, minerals, and gems
- Human cultures
- Human origins
- Amphibians and reptiles
- Environment and ecology
- Rose Center for Earth and Space
- Special exhibitions
- Non-exhibition space

❾ The Dakota

1 W 72nd St. **Map** 12 D1. Ⓜ 72nd St. **Closed** to the public.

The name and style reflect the fact that this apartment building was truly "way out West" when Henry J. Hardenbergh, the architect responsible for the Plaza Hotel, designed it in 1880–84. It was New York's first luxury apartment house and was originally surrounded by squatters' shacks and wandering farm animals. Commissioned by Edward S. Clark, heir to the Singer sewing machine fortune, it is one of the city's most prestigious addresses.

The Dakota's 65 luxurious apartments have had many famous owners, including Judy Garland, Lauren Bacall, Leonard Bernstein, and Boris Karloff, whose ghost is said to haunt the place. It was the setting for the film *Rosemary's Baby,* and the site of the tragic murder of former Beatle John Lennon. His widow, Yoko Ono, still lives here.

Carved Indian head over the entrance to the Dakota

❿ New York Historical Society

170 Central Park West. **Map** 16 D5. **Tel** (212) 873-3400. Ⓜ 81st St. Galleries **Open** 10am–6pm Tue–Sat (to 8pm Fri), 11am–5pm Sun. 🖼 Library **Open** 9am–3pm Tue–Fri, 10am–1pm Sat (varies by season). **Closed** public hols. 🖼 🛗 🖼 🖼 🖼 Ⓦ nyhistory.org

Founded in 1804, this society houses a distinguished research library and the city's oldest museum. Its collections include historical material relating to slavery and the Civil War, an outstanding collection of 18th-century newspapers, all 435 watercolors of Audubon's *Birds of America*, and the world's largest collection of Tiffany lamps and glasswork. There are also fine displays of American furniture and silver.

⓫ American Museum of Natural History

See pp210–11.

⓬ Rose Center for Earth and Space

Central Park West at 81st St. **Map** 16 D4. **Tel** (212) 769-5100. Ⓜ 81st St. **Open** 10am–5:45pm daily. IMAX show: every hour on the half-hour 10:30am–4:30pm; Space show: every half-hour 10:30am–4:30pm (from 11am Wed, to 5pm Sat & Sun). Ⓦ amnh.org

On the northern side of the American Museum of Natural History *(see pp210–11)* is the spectacular Rose Center for Earth and Space. Housed within an 87-ft (27-m) sphere, the center contains the technologically advanced Hayden Planetarium; the Cosmic Pathway, a 350-ft (107-m) spiral ramp with a timeline chronicling 13 billion years of evolution; and the Big Bang Theater, where the origins of the universe are explained.

The Hall of Planet Earth, centered around rock samples and using state-of-the-art computer and video displays explaining how the Earth works, explores our geologic history. Exhibits in the Hall of the Universe present the discoveries of modern astrophysics. Four zones have hands-on interactive exhibits. Seen from the street at night, the Rose Center is breathtaking; ≠the exhibits inside prove that, as Carl Sagan said, "We are starstuff."

⓭ Pomander Walk

261–7 W 94th St. **Map** 15 C2. Ⓜ 96th St.

Look through the gate for a delightful surprise – a double row of tiny town houses built in 1921 to look like the London mews setting of a popular play of the same name. It was much favored as a home by movie actors, including Rosalind Russell, Humphrey Bogart, and the Gish sisters.

Facade of a house on Pomander Walk, built to resemble an English neighborhood

⓮ Riverside Drive and Park

Map 15 B1–5, 20 D1–5. Ⓜ 79th St, 86th St, 96th St.

Riverside Drive is one of the city's most attractive streets – broad, with lovely shaded views of the Hudson River. It is lined with the opulent original town houses, as well as more modern apartment buildings. At 40–46, 74–77, 81–89, and 105–107 Riverside Drive are houses designed in the late 19th century by local architect Clarence F. True. The curved gables, bays, and arched windows seem to suit the curves of the road and the flow of the river.

The bizarrely named Cliff Dwellers' Apartments at 243 (between 96th and 97th streets) is a 1914 building with a frieze showing early Arizona cliff dwellers, complete with masks, buffalo skulls, mountain lions, and rattlesnakes.

Soldiers' and Sailors' monument in Riverside Park

Riverside Park was designed by Frederick Law Olmsted in 1880. He also laid out Central Park (see pp198–203).

⓯ Children's Museum of Manhattan

212 W 83rd St. **Map** 15 C4. **Tel** (212) 721-1223. Ⓜ 79th St, 81st St, 86th St. **Open** 10am–5pm daily (to 7pm Sat). **Closed** Jan 1, Thanksgiving, Dec 25. 🅿 ♿ 📷 Ⓦ cmom.org

This particularly imaginative participatory museum was founded in 1973 and is based on the premise that children learn best through play. The exhibit called "Eat, Sleep, Play" links food, the digestive system, and healthy living, while in "Block Party" children can build castles, towns, and bridges out of wooden blocks. Kids also delight in the exhibits on cartoon

Entrance to the Children's Museum of Manhattan

favorites Curious George and Dora the Explorer and her adventurous cousin Diego, where they learn about travel and cultures around the world.

On weekends and holidays there are guest performers, from puppeteers to storytellers, in the 150-seat theater. There is also a gallery for free events, like "Pajama Day," as well as lively, theme-based tours of the museum.

⓰ The Ansonia

2109 Broadway. **Map** 15 C5. Ⓜ 72nd St. **Closed** to the public.

This Beaux Arts gem was built in 1899 by William Earl Dodge Stokes, heir to the Phelps Dodge Company fortune, who brought French architect Paul E. M. Duboy to design a building to rival the Dakota. The hotel was converted to a condominium in 1992. The most prominent features are the round corner tower and the two-story Mansard roof adorned with single and double dormers. The building had a roof garden (complete with Dodge's menagerie: ducks, chickens, and a tame bear) and two swimming pools.

The hotel's thick, sound-muffling walls soon made it a favorite with the musical stars of yesteryear. Florenz Ziegfeld, Arturo Toscanini, Enrico Caruso, Igor Stravinsky, and Lily Pons were once regular guests there.

⓱ The Dorilton

171 W 71st St. **Map** 11 C1. Ⓜ 72nd St. **Closed** to the public.

Opulent detail and an impressive high mansard roof adorn this apartment house. On the West 71st Street side of the building is a nine-story-high gateway. To the modern eye, the Dorilton is gloriously elaborate, but when it was first built in 1902 it provoked this reaction, reported by the *Architectural Record*: "The sight of it makes strong

men swear and weak women shrink affrighted."

What would the critics have made of the Alexandria Condominium, at 135 West 70th Street, just a block away? Built in 1927 as the Pythian Temple, its current name stems from the lavish Egyptian-style motifs that adorned this former Masonic lodge. Many were stripped away when the building was converted to a condominium, but you can still see what the polychrome designs were like. There are lotus leaves, hieroglyphics, ornately carved columns, mythical beasts, and, in majestic splendor on the roof, two seated pharaohs.

Balcony on the Dorilton, supported by groaning figures

⓲ American Folk Art Museum

2 Lincoln Sq. **Map** 11 D2. **Tel** (212) 595-9533. Ⓜ 5th Ave-53rd St. **Open** 11:30am–7pm Tue–Thu & Sat, noon–7:30pm Fri, noon–6pm Sun. 🅿 ♿ 📷 💻 📷 Ⓦ folkartmuseum.org

The permanent home for the appreciation and study of American folk art is conveniently located opposite the Lincoln Center complex. Founded in 1961, the museum comprises 7,000 artworks dating from the 18th century to the present day

With colorful quilts, impressive portraits, and major works by self-taught, contemporary artists, the selection is remarkable. Especially worth seeking out are Henry Darger's water-colors, and Ralph Fasinella's incredible urban commentaries. Exhibitions usually revolve, but the permanent collection is always on display.

MORNINGSIDE HEIGHTS AND HARLEM

Harlem has been at the heart of African-American culture since the 1920s, when poets, activists, and Jazz musicians came together during the Harlem Renaissance. Today, the neighborhood is home to fabulous West African eateries, Sunday gospel choirs, a vibrant local jazz scene, and some of the prettiest blocks in the city. Morningside Heights, near the Hudson River, is home to Columbia University and two of the city's finest churches. Hamilton Heights is further uptown – primarily a residential area, it also contains a Federal-style historic mansion and the City College of New York.

Sights at a Glance

Historic Streets and Buildings
1. Columbia University
2. St. Paul's Chapel
3. Low Library
6. Grant's Tomb
7. City College of the City University of New York
8. Hamilton Grange National Memorial
9. Hamilton Heights Historic District
10. St. Nicholas Historic District

Museums and Galleries
12. Schomburg Center for Research into Black Culture
16. Studio Museum in Harlem
17. Mount Morris Historic District
19. Museo del Barrio

Famous Theaters
13. Harlem YMCA
15. Apollo Theater

Churches
4. Cathedral of St. John the Divine pp220–21
5. Riverside Church
11. Abyssinian Baptist Church

Parks and Squares
18. Marcus Garvey Park

Landmark Restaurants
14. Sylvia's

0 meters 500
0 yards 500

See also Street Finder maps 19–21

◀ Harlem's most famous landmark, the Apollo Theater

Street by Street: Columbia University

This university campus should not be underestimated as a place of interest. After admiring the architecture, linger awhile on Columbia's central quadrangle in front of the Low Library, where you will see the future leaders of America meeting and mingling between classes. Across from the campus on both Broadway and Amsterdam Avenue are the coffee-houses and cafés where students engage in lengthy philosophical arguments, debate the topics of the day, or simply unwind.

Alma Mater was sculpted by Daniel Chester French in 1903 and survived a bomb blast in the 1968 student demonstrations.

116th St/ Columbia University subway (line 1)

The School of Journalism is one of Columbia's many McKim, Mead & White buildings. Founded in 1912 by publisher Joseph Pulitzer, it is the home of the Pulitzer Prize, awarded for the best in letters and music.

Butler Library is Columbia's main library.

❸ **Low Library**
With its imposing facade and high dome, the library dominates the main quadrangle. McKim, Mead & White designed it in 1895–7.

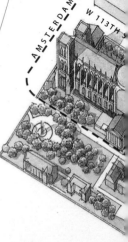

❶ ★ **Columbia University**
Columbia's first buildings were designed by McKim, Mead & White and built around a central quadrangle. This view looks across the quad toward Butler Library.

❷ St. Paul's Chapel
Designed by the architects Howells & Stokes in 1907, this church is known for its fine woodwork and magnificent vaulted interior. It is full of light and has fine acoustics.

The Sherman Fairchild Center was built in 1977 to house the university's life sciences departments.

Locator Map
See Manhattan Map pp16–17

Key

— Suggested route

0 meters	500
0 yards	500

Student demonstrations put Columbia University in the news in 1968. The demonstrations were sparked by the university's plan to build a gymnasium in nearby Morningside Park. The protests forced the university to build elsewhere.

W 116TH ST

MORNINGSIDE DRIVE

Carved stonework decorates the facade of the Cathedral.

The Église de Notre Dame was built for a French-speaking congregation. Behind the altar is a replica of the grotto at Lourdes, France – the gift of a woman who believed her son was healed there.

❹ ★ Cathedral of St. John the Divine
If this Neo-Gothic cathedral is ever finished, it will be the largest in the world. Although one-third of the structure has not yet been built, it can hold 10,000 parishioners.

Alma Mater statue at the Low Library, Columbia University

❶ Columbia University

Main entrance at W 116th St and Broadway. **Map** 20 E3. **Tel** (212) 854-1754. **M** 116th St-Columbia University. Visitors' Center: **Open** 9am–5pm Mon–Fri. 1pm Mon–Fri. **W** columbia.edu

This is the third location of one of America's oldest universities. Founded in 1754 as King's College, it was first situated close to where the World Trade Center stood.

In 1814, when a move uptown was proposed, the university approached the authorities for funding but was instead given a plot of land valued at $75,000 on which to build a new home. The university never built on the land itself, but leased it out and spent the years from 1857 to 1897 in buildings nearby. It finally sold the plot in 1985 to the leaseholders, Rockefeller Center Inc., for $400 million.

The present campus was begun in 1897 on the site of the Bloomingdale Insane Asylum.

Charles McKim, the architect, placed the university on a terrace, serenely above street level. Its spacious lawns and plazas still create a sense of contrast in the busy city.

Columbia is noted for its law, medicine, and journalism schools. Its distinguished faculty and alumni, past and present, include over 50 Nobel laureates. Famous alumni include Isaac Asimov, J. D. Salinger, James Cagney, and Joan Rivers. Across the street is the affiliated Barnard College, a highly selective liberal arts college for women.

Interior brick vaulting of St. Paul's Chapel dome

❷ St. Paul's Chapel

Columbia University. **Map** 20 E3. **Tel** (212) 854-1487, for concert info. **M** 116th St-Columbia Univ. **Open** 10am–11pm Mon–Sat (term time), 10am–4pm (breaks). Sun.

Columbia's most outstanding building, built in 1904, is a mix of Italian Renaissance, Byzantine, and Gothic. The interior Guastavino vaulting is of intricate patterns of aged red brick; the whole chapel is bathed in light from above.

The free organ concerts offer an exceptionally fine way to appreciate the beauty and acoustics of this church. The Aeolian-Skinner pipe organ is renowned for its fine tone.

Facade of St. Paul's Chapel

❸ Low Library

Columbia University. **Map** 20 E3. **M** 116th St-Columbia University.

A Classical columned building atop three flights of stone stairs, the library was donated by Seth Low, a former mayor and college president. The statue in front of it, *Alma Mater* by Daniel Chester French, became familiar as the backdrop to the many 1968 anti-Vietnam War student demonstrations. The building is now used as offices, and its rotunda for a variety of academic and ceremonial purposes. The books were moved in 1934 to the Butler Library, across the quadrangle. The university's library collections total more than six million volumes.

❹ Cathedral of St. John the Divine

See pp220–21.

❺ Riverside Church

490 Riverside Dr at 122nd St. **Map** 20 D2. **Tel** (212) 870-6700. **M** 116th St-Columbia Univ. **Open** 7am–10pm daily. 10:45am Sun. Carillon bell concerts; (212) 870-6784; 10:30am, 12:30pm & 3pm Sun. Theater; (212) 870-6784. **W** theriversidechurchny.org

A 21-story steel frame with a Gothic exterior, the church design was inspired by the cathedral at Chartres, France. It was lavishly funded by John D. Rockefeller, Jr., in 1930. The Laura Spelman Rockefeller

Columbia University's main courtyard and the Low Library

Memorial Carillon (in honor of Rockefeller's mother) is the largest in the world, with 74 bells. The 20-ton Bourdon, or hour bell, is the largest and heaviest tuned carillon bell ever cast. The organ, with its 22,000 pipes, is among the largest in the world.

At the rear of the second gallery is a figure by Jacob Epstein, *Christ in Majesty*, cast in plaster and covered in gold leaf. Another Epstein statue, *Madonna and Child*, stands in the court next to the cloister. The panels of the chancel screen honor eight men and women whose lives have exemplified the teachings of Christ. They range from Socrates and Michelangelo to Florence Nightingale and Booker T. Washington.

For quiet reflection, enter the small, secluded Christ Chapel, patterned after an 11th-century Romanesque church in France.

The church is particularly welcoming during the holiday season, as the public is invited to a host of festive activities such as caroling by candlelight.

Mosaic mural in Grant's Tomb showing Grant (right) and Robert E. Lee

❻ Grant's Tomb

W 122nd St and Riverside Dr. **Map** 20 D2. **Tel** (212) 666-1640. 🚇 116th St-Columbia Univ. 🚌 M5. **Open** 9am–5pm Wed–Sun. **Closed** in bad weather (call ahead), Jan 1, Thanksgiving, Dec 25. 🅆 nps.gov/gegr

This grandiose monument honors America's 18th president, Ulysses S. Grant, the commanding general of the Union forces in the Civil War. The mausoleum contains the coffins of General Grant and his wife, in accordance with the president's last wish that they be buried together. After Grant's death in 1885, more than 90,000 Americans contributed $600,000 to build the sepulcher, which was inspired by Mausoleus's tomb at Halicarnassus, one of the Seven Wonders of the Ancient World.

General Grant on a Civil War campaign

The tomb was dedicated on what would have been Grant's 75th birthday, April 27, 1897. The parade of 50,000 people, along with a flotilla of ten American and five European warships, took more than seven hours to pass in review.

The interior was inspired by Napoleon's tomb at Les Invalides in Paris. Each sarcophagus weighs 8.5 tons. Two exhibit rooms feature displays on Grant's personal life and his presidential and military career. Surrounding the north and east sides of the building are 17 sinuously curved mosaic benches that seem totally out of keeping with the formal architecture of the tomb. They were designed in the early 1970s by the Chilean-born Brooklyn artist Pedro Silva and were built by 1,200 local volunteers, who worked under his supervision. The benches were inspired by the work of Spanish architect Antoni Gaudí in Barcelona. The mosaics depict subjects ranging from the Inuit to New York taxis to Donald Duck.

A short walk north of Grant's Tomb is another monument. An unadorned urn on a pedestal marks the resting place of a young child who fell from the riverbank and drowned. His grieving father placed a marker that simply reads: "Erected to the memory of an amiable child, St. Claire Pollock, died 15 July 1797 in his fifth year of his age."

The 21-story Riverside Church, from the north

❹ Cathedral of St. John the Divine

Started in 1892 and still only two-thirds finished, this will be the largest cathedral in the world. The interior is over 600 ft (183 m) long and 146 ft (45 m) wide. It was originally designed in Romanesque style by Heins & LaFarge; Ralph Adams Cram took over the project in 1911, devising a Gothic nave and west front. Medieval construction methods, such as stone-on-stone supporting buttresses, continue to be used to complete the cathedral, which also serves as a venue for theater, music, and avant-garde art.

★ Peace Fountain
The sculpture is the creation of Greg Wyatt and represents nature in its many forms. It stands within a granite basin on the Great Lawn, south of the cathedral.

Nave
Rising to a height of over 100 ft (30 m), the piers of the nave are topped by graceful stone arches.

★ West Front Entrance
The portals of the cathedral's west front are adorned with many fine stone carvings. Some are recreations of medieval religious sculpture, but others have modern themes. This apocalyptic vision of New York's skyline, by local stonemason Joe Kincannon, seems almost to predict the events of September 11, 2001 *(see p56)*.

KEY

① Pulpit

② **The Bishop's Chair** is a copy from the Henry VII chapel in Westminster Abbey, in London.

★ Rose Window
Completed in 1933, the stylized motif of the Great Rose is symbolic of the many facets of the Christian Church.

Baptistery
The Gothic Baptistery has Italian, French, and Spanish influences.

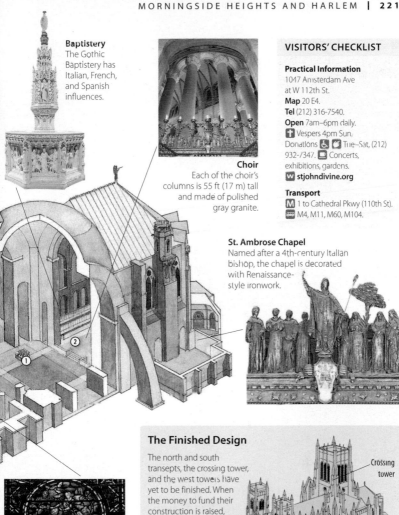

Choir
Each of the choir's columns is 55 ft (17 m) tall and made of polished gray granite.

VISITORS' CHECKLIST

Practical Information
1047 Amsterdam Ave at W 112th St.
Map 20 E4.
Tel (212) 316-7540.
Open 7am–6pm daily.
🕇 Vespers 4pm Sun.
Donations ♿ 🅿 Tue–Sat, (212) 932-7347. 🖵 Concerts, exhibitions, gardens.
🅦 stjohndivine.org

Transport
Ⓜ 1 to Cathedral Pkwy (110th St).
🚌 M4, M11, M60, M104.

St. Ambrose Chapel
Named after a 4th-century Italian bishop, the chapel is decorated with Renaissance-style ironwork.

The Finished Design
The north and south transepts, the crossing tower, and the west towers have yet to be finished. When the money to fund their construction is raised, the proposed design will still take at least another 50 years to complete.

Crossing tower

West towers

South transept

★ Bay Altars
The bay altar windows are devoted to human endeavor. The sports window shows feats of skill and strength.

1823 Cathedral planned for Washington Square

1891 Site chosen and designated Cathedral Parkway

1909 Pulpit designed by Henry Vaughan

1911 Cram design replaces earlier ones

2001 Major fire destroys interior and roof of north transept

2008 Cathedral reopens after seven-year closure for renovations

1800	1850	1900	1950	2000	2050

1873 Charter granted

1888 Competition to design cathedral won by Heins & LaFarge

1892 December 27 (St. John's Day), cornerstone laid

1916 Ground broken for nave

1941 Work is halted by World War II and does not resume until 1978

1978–89 Third phase of building. Stonemasons' Yard opened, and south tower heightened

❼ City College of the City University of New York

Main entrance at W 138th St and Convent Ave. **Map** 19 A2. **Tel** (212) 650-7000. Ⓜ 137th St-City College. 🌐 ccny.cuny.edu

Set high on a hill adjoining Hamilton Heights, the original Gothic quadrangle of this college, built between 1903 and 1907, is very impressive. The material used for the buildings is Manhattan schist, a stone that had been excavated in building the IRT subway. Later, contemporary buildings were added to the school, which enrolls nearly 15,000 students.

Once free to all residents of New York, City College still offers an education at low tuition rates. Three-quarters of the students are from minority groups, and a large number of them are the first in their families to attend college.

Shepard Archway at City College of the City University of New York

❽ Hamilton Grange National Memorial

St. Nicholas Park, 414 W 141st St. **Map** 19 A1. **Tel** (212) 283-5154. Ⓜ 137th St-City College. **Open** 9am–5pm Wed–Sun. **Closed** Thanksgiving & Dec 25. 📷 hourly. 🌐 nps.gov/hagr

Completed in 1802, this was the country home of Alexander Hamilton. He was one of the architects of the federal government system, First Secretary of the treasury and founder of the National

Statue of Alexander Hamilton on Convent Avenue

Bank. His face is on the $10 bill. Hamilton lived in The Grange for the last two years of his life. He was killed in a duel with political rival Aaron Burr in 1804.

In 1889, St. Luke's Episcopal Church acquired the site, and the building was moved four blocks west. A second relocation in 2008 moved the building to its current site in St. Nicholas Park.

❾ Hamilton Heights Historic District

W 141st–W 145th St and Convent Ave. **Map** 19 A1. Ⓜ 137th St- City College.

Originally this was a setting for the impressive country estates of the wealthy. Also known as Harlem Heights, it was developed during the 1880s following the extension of the El line (Elevated Railway) into the neighborhood. The privacy of the enclave, on a high hill above Harlem, made it a very desirable location.

The section of Hamilton Heights known as Sugar Hill was highly favored by Harlem's elite – US Supreme Court Justice Thurgood Marshall, notable jazz musicians Count Basie, Duke Ellington, wand

Cab Calloway, and world champion boxer Sugar Ray Robinson have all lived there.

The handsome three- and four-story stone row houses were built between 1886 and 1906 mixing Flemish, Roman-esque, and Tudor influences. In fine condition, many are used as residences by the faculty of City College.

Row houses in Hamilton Heights

❿ St. Nicholas Historic District

202–250 W 138th & W 139th St. **Map** 19 B2. Ⓜ 135th St (B, C).

A startling contrast to the surrounding streets, the two blocks here, known as the King Model Houses, were built in 1891, when Harlem was considered a neighborhood for New York's gentry. They are still among the city's most distinctive examples of row town houses.

The developer, David King, chose three leading architects, who succeeded in blending their different styles to create a harmonious whole. The most famous of these was the firm

Houses in St. Nicholas district

Adam Clayton Powell, Jr. addressing a civil rights campaign

of McKim, Mead & White, designers of The Morgan Library *(see pp160–61)* and Villard Houses *(see p172)*, who were responsible for the northernmost row of solid brick Renaissance palaces. Their homes featured ground-floor entrances rather than the typical New York brownstone stoops. Also, the elaborate parlor floors have ornate wrought-iron balconies below, as well as carved decorative medallions above their windows.

The Georgian buildings designed by Price and Luce are built of buff brick with white stone trim. James Brown Lord's section of buildings, also Georgian in architectural style, feels much closer to Victorian, with outstanding red-brick facades and bases constructed of brownstone.

Successful blacks were attracted here in the 1920s and 1930s, giving it the nickname Strivers' Row. Among them were celebrated musicians W. C. Handy and Eubie Blake.

⓫ Abyssinian Baptist Church

132 W 138th St. **Map** 19 C2. **Tel** (212) 862-7474. ⓜ 135th St (B, C, 2, 3). ✝ 11am Sun. Groups of 10 or more need reservations.
ⓦ abyssinian.org

Founded in 1808, New York's oldest black church became famous through its charismatic pastor Adam Clayton Powell, Jr. (1908–72), a congressman

and civil-rights leader. Under his leadership it became the most powerful black church in America. A room in the church houses memorabilia from his life.

The church, a fine 1923 Gothic building, welcomes properly dressed visitors to Sunday services and to hear its superb gospel choir.

⓬ Schomburg Center for Research into Black Culture

515 Malcolm X Blvd. **Map** 19 C2. ⓜ 135th St (2, 3). **Tel** (212) 491-2200. **Open** noon–8pm Tue–Thu, 10am–6pm Fri & Sat. **Closed** public hols. 🎞 (212) 491-2207. ♿ 📷
ⓦ **nypl.org/locations/schomburg**

Housed in a sleek contemporary complex opened in 1991, this is the largest research center of black and African culture in the United States. The immense collection was assembled by the late Arthur Schomburg, a black man of Puerto Rican descent, who was told by a teacher that there was no such thing as "black history." The Carnegie Corporation bought the collection in 1926

Kurt Weill, Elmer Rice, and Langston Hughes at the Schomburg Center

and gave it to the New York Public Library; Schomburg was made curator in 1932.

The library was the unofficial meeting place for writers involved in what later became known as the Harlem Renaissance of the 1920s, including Langston Hughes, W. E. B. Du Bois, and Zora Neale Hurston. It also hosted many poetry readings and literary gatherings.

The Schomburg Library has excellent facilities for conserving and making available the archive's treasures, which include rare books, photographs, movies, art, and recordings. The library was planned and designed to double as a cultural center and includes a theater and two art galleries, which feature changing shows of art and photography. The center is also the resting place of Langston Hughes' ashes.

Sociologist W. E. B. Du Bois

⓭ Harlem YMCA

180 W 135th St. **Map** 19 C3. **Tel** (212) 281-4100. ⓜ 135th St (2, 3).

Paul Robeson and many others made their first stage appearances here in the early 1920s. The Krigwa Players, organized by W.E.B. Du Bois in the basement in 1928, was founded to counter the derogatory images of blacks often presented in Broadway reviews of the time. The "Y" also provided temporary lodgings for some notable new arrivals in Harlem, including writer Ralph Ellison.

Gospel singers performing at Sylvia's during Sunday brunch

🄐 Sylvia's

328 Malcolm X Blvd. **Map** 21 B1.
Tel (212) 996-0660. Ⓜ 125th St (2, 3).
🆆 sylviasrestaurant.com

Harlem's best-known soul food restaurant since 1962, serves up Southern-fried or smothered chicken, spicy ribs, black-eyed peas, collard greens, candied yams, sweet potato pie, and other comforting Southern delicacies. Sunday brunch here is served to the accompaniment of Gospel singers.

Harlem's culinary scene has blossomed over the years, with eateries such as Marcus Samuelsson's Red Rooster *(see p304)*, simply a block down from Sylvia's. Founder Sylvia Woods, or the "Queen of Soulfood" as she was once known, passed away in 2012.

🄑 Apollo Theater

253 W 125th St. **Map** 21 A1.
Tel (212) 531-5300. Ⓜ 125th St.
Open at showtimes. 🄖 Groups only.
🛆 🄙 *See Entertainment p347.*
🆆 apollotheater.com

The Apollo opened in 1913 as a whites-only opera house. Its great fame came when Frank Schiffman, a white entrepreneur, took over in 1934. He then opened the

Apollo
Theater

theater to everyone and turned it into Harlem's best-known showcase, with great artists such as Bessie Smith, Billie Holiday, Duke Ellington, and Dinah Washington.

Wednesday Amateur Nights, (begun in 1935) with winners determined by audience applause, were famous, and there was a long waiting list for performers. These amateur nights helped launch the careers of Sarah Vaughan, Pearl Bailey, James Brown, and Gladys Knight, among others, and they still attract hopefuls.

The Apollo was *the* place during the swing band era; following World War II, a new generation of musicians, such

as Charlie "Bird" Parker, Dizzy Gillespie, Thelonious Monk, and Aretha Franklin, continued the tradition.

Rescued from decline and refurbished in the 1980s, the Apollo once again features top black entertainers and hosts Amateur Nights.

🄬 Studio Museum in Harlem

144 W 125th St. **Map** 21 B2.
Tel (212) 864-4500. Ⓜ 125th St (2, 3). **Open** noon–9pm Thu & Fri, 10am–6pm Sat, noon–6pm Sun.
Closed public hols. 🄖 donations; free Sun. 🄘 🛆 🄖 Lectures, films, children's programs, video presentations. 🄙 🄚
🆆 studiomuseum.org

The museum was founded in 1967 in a loft on upper Fifth Avenue with the mission of becoming the world's premier center for the collection and exhibition of the art and artifacts of African Americans.

The present premises, a five-story building on Harlem's main commercial street, was donated to the museum by the New York Bank for Savings in 1979. There are galleries on two levels for changing exhibitions featuring artists and cultural themes, and three galleries are devoted to the permanent collection of works by major black artists.

The photographic archives comprise one of the most complete records in existence of Harlem in its heyday. A side door opens onto a small sculpture garden.

Exhibition space at the Studio Museum in Harlem

In addition to its excellent exhibitions, the Studio Museum also maintains a national artist-in-residence program, and offers regular lectures, seminars, children's programs, and film festivals. An excellent shop sells a range of books, unique prints, and various African crafts.

⓱ Mount Morris Historical District

W 119th–W 124th Sts. **Map** 21 B2.
Ⓜ 125th St (2, 3).

Despite many of the buildings here being in need of renovation, it is still clear that the late 19th-century Victorian-style town houses near Marcus Garvey Park were once grand. This was a favorite neighborhood of German Jews moving up in the world from the Lower East Side. After a long period of neglect, the area is undergoing redevelopment.

A few impressive churches, such as St. Martin's Episcopal Church, remain. There are some interesting juxtapositions of faiths to be seen: the columned Mount Olivet Baptist Church, at 201 Malcolm X Boulevard, was once Temple Israel, one of the most imposing synagogues in the city; and at the Ethiopian Hebrew Congregation, 1 West 123rd Street, housed in a former mansion, the choir sings in Hebrew on Saturdays.

St. Martin's Episcopal Church on Malcolm X Boulevard

The flamboyant black nationalist leader Marcus Garvey

⓲ Marcus Garvey Park

120th–124th Sts. **Map** 21 B2. Ⓜ 125th St (2, 3). Ⓦ nycgovparks.org

This hilly, rocky, two-block square of green is the site of New York's last fire watchtower, an open cast-iron structure built in 1857, with spiral stairs leading to the 47 ft (14-m) high observation deck. The bell below the deck sounded the alarm. The tower was temporarily dismantled in 2015 for a reconstruction, and should be restored by 2017.

Previously known as Mount Morris Park, it was renamed in 1973 in honor of Marcus Garvey. He came to Harlem from Jamaica in 1916 and founded the Universal Negro Improvement Association, which promoted self-help, racial pride, and a back-to-Africa movement.

⓳ Museo del Barrio

1230 5th Ave. **Map** 21 C5. **Tel** (212) 831-7272. Ⓜ 103rd St, 110th St. **Open** 11am–6pm Wed–Sat. **Closed** Jan 1, Jul 4, Thanksgiving, Dec 25. 🅿️ 🎫 ♿ 🏛️
Ⓦ elmuseo.org

Founded in 1969, this was North America's first museum devoted to Latin American art. It specializes in the culture of Puerto Rico. Exhibitions feature contemporary painting and sculpture, folk art, and historical artifacts. The stars of the collection are about 240 wooden Santos (carved figures of saints) and a reconstructed *bodega*, or Latino corner grocery. The exhibits change usually, but some of the Santos are often on display. The Pre-Columbian collection contains rare artifacts from the Caribbean. Situated at the far end of Museum Mile (see pp180–81), this venue attempts to bridge the gap between the lofty Upper East Side and Spanish Harlem. A store sells eye-catching objects by artists from all over Latin America.

Folk art at the Museo del Barrio: one of the Three Wise Men (left) and the "Omnipotent Hand"

BROOKLYN

Brooklyn became a New York borough in 1898, and for decades after served primarily as a residential and industrial neighborhood. It has drastically changed since the start of the 21st century. Districts such as Fort Greene, Williamsburg, Bushwick, and Cobble Hill are now among the most fashionable in the city, popular for their bars, flea markets, and hipster culture. Brooklyn offers a multitude of experiences. Its brownstone town houses and tree-lined streets give way to museums, inventive restaurants, and performance spaces such as BAM and the Barclays Center.

Sights at a Glance

Historic Sights and Buildings
1 Brooklyn Bridge pp232–5
2 Fulton Ferry District
3 Dumbo
5 Red Hook
6 Fort Green & BAM
7 Williamsburg & Greenpoint
10 Park Slope Historic District
14 Green-Wood Cemetery

Museums and Galleries
4 New York Transit Museum
8 Brooklyn Children's Museum
12 Brooklyn Museum pp238–41

Parks and Squares
9 Grand Army Plaza
11 Prospect Park
13 Brooklyn Botanic Garden

Restaurants p305
1 al di la trattoria
2 Fette Sau
3 Frankie's 457 Spuntino
4 Grimaldi's
5 Marlow & Sons
6 Peter Luger Steak House
7 Pies 'n' Thighs
8 Pok Pok NY
9 Prime Meats
10 Red Hook Lobster Pound
11 Rye Restaurant

See also Street Finder map 23

◀ The spectacular Brooklyn Bridge

0 kilometers 1
0 miles 1

For map symbols see back flap

Street by Street: Brooklyn Heights

Facing Lower Manhattan, across the East River, Brooklyn Heights is one of New York's most elegant and historic neighborhoods. The city's wealthy elites built brownstone town houses here in the 1820s, when the Heights became the city's first commuter suburb. The completion of the Brooklyn Bridge in 1883, and the opening of the subway in 1908, led to intensified development. Today, Brooklyn Heights is an extremely affluent neighborhood.

Locator Map
See Manhattan Map pp16–17

Brooklyn Bridge Park/
Dumbo Ferry Terminal

Bargemusic, moored just under the Brooklyn Bridge, is a renovated coffee barge dating from the late 19th century, and holds nightly chamber music performances.

Brooklyn Ice Cream Factory is based in an early 20th-century fireboat house on the Fulton Ferry Pier, and serves just eight flavors of ice cream.

70 Willow Street is said to be where Truman Capote wrote *Breakfast at Tiffany's*.

★ **Brooklyn Heights Promenade**
This pedestrian path offers sensational views of the Statue of Liberty, Lower Manhattan's skyscrapers, and the Brooklyn Bridge.

★ **Juliana's Pizza**
is the original location
of Patsy Grimaldi's famous
coal-oven pizzas, not to be
confused with the newer
Grimaldi's next door.

| 0 meters | 500 |
| 0 yards | 500 |

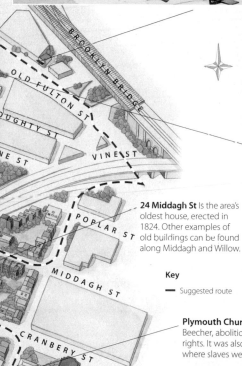

24 Middagh St Is the area's
oldest house, erected in
1824. Other examples of
old buildings can be found
along Middagh and Willow.

Key

— Suggested route

❷ ★ **Fulton Ferry District**
Just below the Brooklyn Bridge, this historic
wharf area is named after Robert Fulton, the
steamboat king. It features iconic landmarks such as the Eagle Warehouse
with its large, glass clock-window.

Plymouth Church was the base of pastor Henry Ward
Beecher, abolitionist and campaigner for women's
rights. It was also a stop on the Underground Railroad,
where slaves were hidden on their way to freedom.

★ **Brooklyn Historical Society**
This Museum and educational center hosts changing
exhibits on the diverse history of the district.

Ⓜ Clark St subway
(Lines A,C)
🚶 Brooklyn Historical Society

Eagle Warehouse, an industrial structure that now contains apartments

❶ Brooklyn Bridge

See pp232–5.

❷ Fulton Ferry District

Map 23 A3. Ⓜ High Street Subway.

This small historic district at the foot of the Brooklyn Bridge was once the busiest section of the East River, thanks to Robert Fulton's steamboat ferries. Among the landmarked 19th-century buildings is the Eagle Warehouse, built in Romanesque Revival style for the Brooklyn Eagle newspaper in 1893. Today, it is occupied by expensive apartments.

The old pier area still hosts New York Water Taxis from Manhattan, as well as popular concerts at Bargemusic. The original Grimaldi's pizza recipe can be enjoyed at Juliana's Pizza, while Brooklyn Ice Cream Factory *(see pp228–9)* offers freshly-made ice creams in just eight perfect flavours.

❸ Dumbo

Map 23 A3. Ⓜ York Street, High Street.

Short for "Down Under the Manhattan Bridge Overpass," Dumbo is a ritzy area of converted brick factories, located between the Manhattan and Brooklyn bridges. Primarily industrial in the 19th century, the district's spacious lofts were colonized by artists in the 1970s. Since the 1990s, the neighborhood has been transformed by art galleries, hip restaurants, luxury condominiums, and bars. The redeveloped waterfront of gardens and playgrounds offers an unmissable view of Manhattan from the Brooklyn Bridge Park. St. Ann's Warehouse, a revered arts institution, occupies an old Tobacco Warehouse on the park's edge.

❹ New York Transit Museum

Boerum Pl and Schermerhorn St, Brooklyn Heights. **Map** 23 A3. **Tel** (718) 694-1600. Ⓜ Borough Hall, Jay St–MetroTech. **Open** 10am–4pm Tue–Fri, noon–5pm Sat & Sun. ♿🐾🛍 📷 **W** mta.info/mta/museum

Charting the evolution of the city's public transit system, this museum is housed underground in the refurbished Court Street shuttle station, which was originally built in 1936.

Model of "City Car" Number 100 at the New York Transit Museum

Brooklyn Bridge, as seen in Dumbo neighborhood

The station closed in 1946, but the museum opened here 30 years later.

The museum exhibits include photographs, models, and maps, as well as aged turnstiles and a few interactive displays of fuel technologies. Visitors can jump on and off the various models of the restored subway and tram carts on the old station platforms.

❺ Red Hook

Map 23 A5. Ⓜ Smith St–9th St.

First settled in by the Dutch in 1636, Red Hook ("Roode Hoek" in Dutch) got its name from the color of the soil and the shape of the land, which forms a *hoek* (corner), where the New York Bay meets the Gowanus Bay. It later became one of the busiest and toughest docklands in the US, inspiring the 1954 film *On the Waterfront*, and Arthur Miller's play *A View from the Bridge* (1955).

Today, Red Hook's waterfront is a surprising blend of red-brick warehouses, cycle paths, cobblestoned blocks, and stores. Its laid-back vibe makes it unlike any other part of the city. A handful of independent stores, restaurants, and cafés dot Van Brunt Street, the area's busiest strip. The Red Hook Ball Fields host local soccer tournaments, and Latino food stalls on summer weekends.

❻ Fort Greene & BAM

Map 23 B3. Brooklyn Academy of Music, 30 Lafayette Ave. **Tel** (718) 636-4100. Ⓜ Atlantic Ave, Fulton St, Pacific St. Ⓦ **bam.org**

Home to Saturday's Brooklyn Flea, Fort Greene is historically an African-American neighborhood, full of beautiful Italianate and Eastlake town houses built in the mid-19th century. At its heart lies Fort Greene Park, designed by Frederick Law Olmsted and Calvert Vaux in 1867. The park is crowned by the Prison Ship Martyrs'

Prison Ship Martyrs' Monument at Fort Greene

Monument (1908), a 149-ft (45 m) column that commemorates the estimated 11,500 Americans who died in the floating prison camps, maintained by the British during the Revolutionary War.

The **Brooklyn Academy of Music (BAM)** is the borough's leading cultural venue, founded in 1858. It offers outstanding performances, often leaning towards the avant-garde. BAM's main building is the 1908 Howard Gilman Opera House, a Beaux Arts gem, designed by Herts & Tallant. The nearby 1904 Harvey Theater stages most of BAM's plays.

❼ Williamsburg & Greenpoint

Map 23 B2 & 23 A1. Ⓜ Bedford Ave.

One of the city's trendiest neighborhoods, Williamsburg occupies much of northeast Brooklyn. Established in 1827, the area was a mix of industrial lots, cheap clapboard homes, and tenements until recent regeneration. The main strip at Bedford Avenue is now crowded with boutiques, record stores, bars, coffee shops, and restaurants. Big on nightlife, this area is especially popular as an indie rock venue.

Williamsburg's culinary attractions include the Brooklyn Brewery, which opened in 1996, and Smorgasburg, a food market that runs from mid-May to mid-November. The Brooklyn

Flea operates at the same location on Sundays.

To the north, **Greenpoint** is a traditional Polish stronghold, flooded by an artsy crowd from Williamsburg. The Russian Orthodox Cathedral of the Transfiguration sits at North 12th Street on Driggs Avenue. A Byzantine Revival landmark from 1922, the church has five patinated copper onion domes that loom above the trees of McCarren Park. The park itself dates back to 1903 and forms an unofficial boundary between Greenpoint and Williamsburg. In addition to playgrounds, tennis courts, and dog runs available to the public, there is a historic swimming pool (1936) and the renowned McCarren Hotel.

Enjoying views from the waterfront at Williamsburg

❶ Brooklyn Bridge

Completed in 1883, the Brooklyn Bridge was the largest suspension bridge in the world and the first to be made of steel. Engineer John A. Roebling conceived of a bridge spanning over the East River while ice-bound on a ferry to Brooklyn. The bridge took 16 years to build, required 600 workers, and claimed over 20 lives, including Roebling's. Most died of caisson disease (known as "the bends") after coming up from the underwater excavation chambers. When finished, the bridge linked Manhattan and Brooklyn, then two separate cities.

Souvenir medal cast for the opening of the bridge

Brooklyn Bridge
From making the wire to sinking the supports, the bridge was built using new techniques.

Anchorage
The ends of the bridge's four steel cables are fastened to a series of anchor bars held in place by anchor plates. These are held down by giant granite vaults up to three stories high. Their vast interiors, once used for storage, are now used for summer art displays.

Caissons
The towers rose up above caissons, each the size of four tennis courts, which provided a dry area for underwater excavation. As work went on, they sank deeper beneath the river.

Shaft

Anchor Plates
Each of the four cast-iron anchor plates holds one cable. The masonry was built up around them after they were placed in position.

Granite vault

Cable to tower

Anchor bar

Anchor plates

Anchor plate

Vault

Central span is 1,595 ft (486 m) long

Vault

Roadway from anchorage to anchorage is 3,579 ft (1,091 m)

First Crossing
Master mechanic E. F. Farrington in 1876 was the first to cross the river on the bridge-in-progress, using a steam-driven traveler rope. His journey took 22 minutes.

Steel Cable Wire
Each cable contains 3,515 miles (5,657 km) of wire, galvanized with zinc for protection from the wind, rain, and snow.

Brooklyn Tower (1875)
Two Gothic double arches, each 271 ft (83 m) high, one in Brooklyn, the other in Manhattan, were meant to be the portals of the cities.

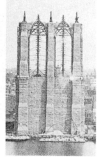

Inside the Caisson
Immigrant workers broke up rocks in the riverbed.

John A. Roebling
The German-born Roebling designed the bridge. In 1869, just before construction started, his foot was crushed between an incoming ferry and the ferry slip. He died three weeks later. His son, Washington Roebling, finished the bridge, but in 1872 he was taken from a caisson suffering from the bends and became partly paralyzed. His wife, under his tutelage, then took over.

Making the Cables

Thickness of steel wire (actual size)

End of wire

How the Cables Were Made
Each of the four main cables has 19 strands, each made of 278 steel wires. The wires were not twisted, but laid parallel.

The 19 strands of a main cable

The strands were laid in order: after the bottom 12 strands were laid, the center strands were bound together.

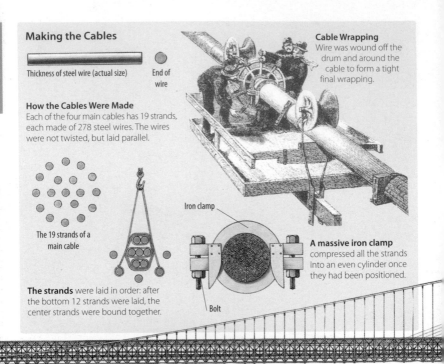

Cable Wrapping
Wire was wound off the drum and around the cable to form a tight final wrapping.

Iron clamp

A massive iron clamp compressed all the strands into an even cylinder once they had been positioned.

Bolt

The 1983 Centennial Fireworks over the Brooklyn Bridge
Celebrating the bridge's 100th year, this display was spectacular.

Bustling Bridge
This 1883 view from the Manhattan side shows the original two outer lanes for horse-drawn carriages, two middle lanes for cable cars, and the elevated center walkway.

Panic on Memorial Day, 1883
After a woman tripped on the bridge, panic broke out. Of the estimated 20,000 people on the bridge, 12 were crushed to death.

Holding the Cables
Saddle plates anchor the cables at the top of each of the two towers.

Cable

Diagonal stays

Suspender wires

Nearing Completion (1883)
Vertical suspender wires lashed to diagonal stays hold the floor beams in place.

Floor Beams
The steel floor beams weigh 4 tons each.

Odlum's Jump
Robert Odlum was the first to jump off the bridge, on a bet, in May 1885. He later died from internal bleeding.

Elevated Walkway
Poet Walt Whitman said that the view from the walkway – 18 ft (5.5 m) above the road – was "the best, most effective medicine my soul has yet partaken."

Totally Tots exhibition at the Brooklyn Children's Museum

⑧ Brooklyn Children's Museum

145 Brooklyn. **Map** 23 C4. **Tel** (718) 735-4400. Ⓜ Kingston Ave (3), Kingston–Throop Ave (C). **Open** 10am–5pm Tue–Sun. **Closed** public hols. 🅿 ♿ 📷 🖥 🌐 **brooklynkids.org**

Founded in 1899, the Brooklyn Children's Museum was the first to be designed especially for children. Since then, it has been a model, inspiration, and consultant for the development of more than 250 museums for children across the country and all over the world. Housed in a hi-tech, specially designed underground building dating from 1976, it is one of the most imaginative children's museums anywhere. In 2008, a "green" renovation was carried out by the Uruguayan architect Rafael Viñoly – he added solar panels and other energy-saving devices, and and also expanded the museum space.

Galleries contain hands-on exhibitions that focus on the environment, science, and local neighborhood life – which highlights various ethnic districts around Brooklyn. The "Totally Tots" Area is dedicated to children under the age of five, with a "Water Wonders" play quarter. The live animals on display downstairs will especially thrill the little ones. There are also play stores and restaurants where children can buy, sell, and even make (fake) pizza. Special events and classes, such as Zumba for kids, touch tank workshops, and art projects, take place daily.

⑨ Grand Army Plaza

Plaza St at Flatbush Ave. **Map** 23 C4. Ⓜ Grand Army Plaza (2, 3). Arch: **Open** for occasional exhibitions.

Frederick Law Olmsted and Calvert Vaux laid out this grand oval in 1870 as a gateway to Prospect Park. The Soldiers' and Sailors' Arch and its sculptures were added in 1892 as a tribute to the Union Army. Designed by John H. Duncan, the arch has a sense of Imperial Roman monuments, with its intricate carving and detail. Stanford White modified the arch between 1894–1901 to accommodate the bronze sculptures by Philip Martiny and Frederick MacMonnies. The bust of John F. Kennedy here is the only official New York monument to the 35th president of the United States.

⑩ Park Slope Historic District

Map 23 B4. Streets from Prospect Park W below Flatbush Ave, to 8th/7th/5th Aves. Ⓜ Grand Army Plaza (2, 3), 7th Ave (F).

This wonderful enclave of beautiful Victorian town houses was developed on the edge of Prospect Park in the 1880s. It served the upper-middle-class professionals who were able to commute into Manhattan after the Brooklyn Bridge was opened in 1883. The shady streets are lined with two- to five-story houses in every architectural style popular in the late 19th century, some with the towers, turrets, and curlicues so representative of the era. Particularly fine examples are in the Romanesque Revival style, with rounded entry arches.

The Montauk Club at 25 Eighth Avenue combines the style of Venice's Ca' d'Oro palazzo with the friezes and gargoyles of the Montauk Indians, for whom this popular 19th-century gathering place was named.

⑪ Prospect Park

Map 23 C5. Ⓜ Grand Army Plaza, Prospect Park (B, Q). 🎨 & information (718) 287-3400. 🖥 📷 🌐 **prospectpark.org**

Olmsted and Vaux considered this park, which opened in 1867, better than their earlier

The Soldiers' and Sailors' Arch at Grand Army Plaza

Carousel horse in Prospect Park

Central Park *(see pp198–203)*. The Long Meadow, a sweep of broad lawns and grand vistas, is the longest unbroken swath of green space in New York.

Olmsted's belief was that "a feeling of relief is experienced by entering them [the parks] on escaping from the cramped, confining and controlling circumstances of the streets of the town." That vision is still as true today as it was a century and a half ago.

Among the many notable features are Stanford White's colonnaded Croquet Shelter, and the pools and weeping willows of the Vale of Cashmere. The Music Grove bandstand shows Japanese influences and hosts both jazz and classical music concerts throughout the summer.

A favorite feature of the park is the Camperdown Elm, an ancient and twisted tree that was planted in 1872. The Friends of Prospect Park continue to raise money to keep it and all the other park trees healthy. This old elm has inspired many poems and paintings. Prospect Park has a wide variety of landscapes, from classical gardens dotted with statues to rocky glens with running brooks. A guided tour with a ranger is the best way to see the park.

⓬ Brooklyn Museum

See pp238–41.

⓭ Brooklyn Botanic Garden

900 Washington Ave. **Map** 23 C4 **Tel** (718) 623-7200. Ⓜ Prospect Pk (B, Q), Eastern Pkwy (2, 3). Grounds **Open** Mar–Oct: 8am–6pm Tue–Fri (10am Sat, Sun, & public hols); Nov–Feb: 8am–4:30pm (10am Sat, Sun, & public hols). **Closed** Jan 1, Labor Day, Thanksgiving, Dec 25. 🏛 Mar–mid-Nov: free Tue & 10am–noon Sat; mid-Nov–late Feb: free for under-16s Mon–Fri. ♿ 📷 🌐 **bbg.org**

Though this 50-acre (20-ha) garden is not vast, you will find that it holds many delights. The area was designed by the Olmsted Brothers in 1910 and features an Elizabethan-style "knot" herb garden and one of North America's largest collections of roses.

The central showpiece is a Japanese hill-and-pond garden, complete with a teahouse and Shinto shrine. In late April and early May the park promenade is aglow with delicate Japanese cherry blossoms, which have prompted an annual festival featuring typical Japanese culture, food, and music. April is also the time for tourists to appreciate Magnolia Plaza, where some 80 trees display their beautiful, creamy blossoms against a backdrop of daffodils on Boulder Hill.

The Fragrance Garden is planted in raised beds, where the heavily scented, textured and flavored plants are all labeled in Braille, giving blind visitors an opportunity to identify them as well.

The conservatory houses one of America's largest bonsai collections and some rare rain forest trees, whose extracts allow scientists to produce life-saving drugs.

Lily pond at the beautiful Brooklyn Botanic Garden

⓮ Green-Wood Cemetery

Map 23 B5. 500 25th St at Fifth Ave. **Tel** (718) 210-3080. Ⓜ 25th St (R). **Open** Mar–Apr & Sep–Oct: 7:45am–6pm daily; May–Aug: 7am–7pm daily; Nov–Feb: 8am–5pm daily. 🌐 **green-wood.com**

This 478-acre (193-ha) cemetery was founded in 1838 and today it is almost a city park, being both sprawling and beautiful. Several famous citizens are interred here, including the street artist Jean-Michel Basquiat (1960–88), abolitionist Henry Ward Beecher (1813–87), composer Leonard Bernstein (1918–90), and glass artist Louis Comfort Tiffany (1848–1933). The whole Steinway family *(see p257)* of the piano dynasty also lie at rest in a 119-room mausoleum.

The façade of the Brooklyn Public Library on Grand Army Plaza

⑫ Brooklyn Museum

When it opened in 1897, the Brooklyn Museum building, designed to be the largest cultural edifice in the world, was the greatest achievement of New York architects McKim, Mead & White. Though only one-sixth of the building completed, the museum is today one of the most impressive cultural institutions in the United States, with a permanent encyclopedic collection of some one million objects, housed in a grand structure covering 560,000 sq ft (50,025 sq m).

North facade of the museum, designed by McKim, Mead & White

★ Female Figurine
This 5,000-year-old rare statuette is a highlight of the museum's impressive Egyptian collection.

Key

- Arts of Africa and the Americas
- Arts of Asia and the Islamic World
- Williamsburg Murals
- Egyptian and Classical art
- Decorative arts
- Painting and sculpture
- Connecting Cultures
- Special exhibitions
- Nonexhibition space

Chinese Jar
Cobalt blue fish and water plants adorn this 14th-century Yuan dynasty blue-and-white porcelain wine jar.

Iris and B. Cantor Auditorium

★ Beaded Crown
This 19th-century crown from Nigeria is the ultimate symbol of Yoruba kingship.

Con Edison Education Gallery

Great Hall

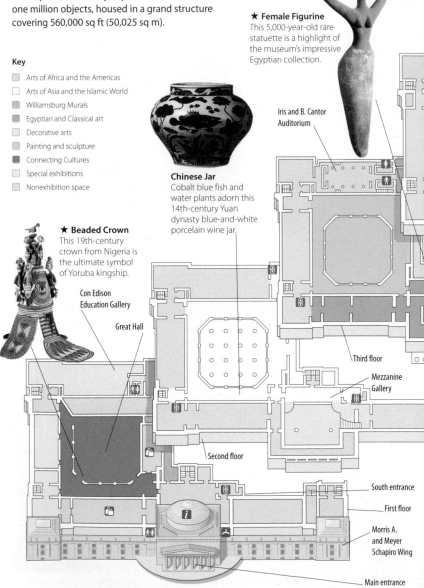

Third floor

Mezzanine Gallery

Second floor

South entrance

First floor

Morris A. and Meyer Schapiro Wing

Main entrance

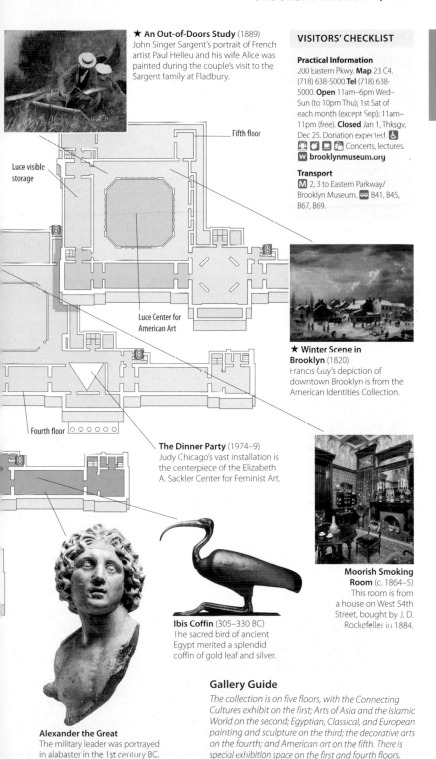

★ **An Out-of-Doors Study** (1889)
John Singer Sargent's portrait of French artist Paul Helleu and his wife Alice was painted during the couple's visit to the Sargent family at Fladbury.

Fifth floor

Luce visible storage

Luce Center for American Art

★ **Winter Scene in Brooklyn** (1820)
Francis Guy's depiction of downtown Brooklyn is from the American Identities Collection.

Fourth floor

The Dinner Party (1974–9)
Judy Chicago's vast installation is the centerpiece of the Elizabeth A. Sackler Center for Feminist Art.

Moorish Smoking Room (c. 1864–5)
This room is from a house on West 54th Street, bought by J. D. Rockefeller in 1884.

Ibis Coffin (305–330 BC)
The sacred bird of ancient Egypt merited a splendid coffin of gold leaf and silver.

Alexander the Great
The military leader was portrayed in alabaster in the 1st century BC.

Gallery Guide
The collection is on five floors, with the Connecting Cultures exhibit on the first; Arts of Asia and the Islamic World on the second; Egyptian, Classical, and European painting and sculpture on the third; the decorative arts on the fourth; and American art on the fifth. There is special exhibition space on the first and fourth floors.

Exploring the Collection

The Brooklyn Museum houses one of the finest art collections in the United States. Its strengths include an outstanding collection of Native American art from the Southwest; American period rooms; exquisite pieces of ancient Egyptian and Islamic art; and important American and European paintings.

Arts of Africa, the Pacific, and the Americas

The Brooklyn Museum set a precedent in the United States in 1923 by exhibiting African objects as works of art rather than artifacts. Since then, the African art collection has grown steadily in both importance and size.

Exhibits include a rare intricately carved ivory gong from the Benin kingdom of 16th-century Nigeria, one of only five in existence.

The Brooklyn Museum also has a notable collection of Native American items, including totem poles, textiles, and pottery. One article, a 19th-century deerskin shirt, once worn and owned by a chief of the Blackfoot tribe, depicts its owner's brave and daring exploits in battle.

Ancient American artistic traditions are represented by Peruvian textiles, Central American gold, and Mexican sculpture. A beautifully preserved tunic from Peru, dating from AD 600, is so tightly woven that its vibrant symbolic designs appear to have been painted onto the cloth rather than woven in the traditional manner.

The Oceanic collection includes sculpture from the Solomon Islands, Papua New Guinea, and New Zealand.

Asian Art

Changing exhibitions from the museum's permanent collection of Chinese, Japanese, Korean, Indian, Southeast Asian, and Islamic art are always on display. Japanese and Chinese paintings, Indian miniatures, and Islamic calligraphy complement the Asian sculpture, textiles, and ceramics. The collections of Japanese folk art, Chinese cloisonné (enamel work), and Oriental carpets are of particular note. Good examples of Buddhist art range from a variety of Chinese, Indian, and Southeast Asian Buddhas to a mandala-patterned temple banner from 14th-century Tibet, painted in rich, luminous watercolors.

Seated Buddha torso in limestone, from India (late 3rd century AD)

Decorative Arts

The decorative arts collection reflects changes in domestic life and design from the 17th century to the present.

The Moorish Smoking Room, from John D. Rockefeller's brownstone house, embodies elegant New York living in the 1860s. There is also a 1928–30 Art Deco study from a Park Avenue apartment, including a walk-in bar that was hidden behind paneling during the Prohibition era *(see pp30–31)*.

More than 350 items from the museum's collection of silver, furniture, ceramics, and textiles are featured in the Luce Center for American Art. Although centered mostly on American art, the selection also includes pieces of Native American and Spanish colonial art.

Blackfoot tribe deerskin shirt, decorated with porcupine quills and glass beads (19th century)

Ocean-liner inspired *Normandie* chrome pitcher, by Peter Müller-Munk (1935)

The Luce galleries are arranged thematically and explore crucial moments and ideas in American visual culture over the past 300 years. Among the collection are pieces by John Singer Sargent, Frank Lloyd Wright, and Georgia O'Keeffe.

Egyptian, Classical, and Ancient Near Eastern Art

Recognized as among the world's finest, the Egyptian collection holds many master-pieces. It begins with an early female figure dating from 3,500 BC, and encompasses sculptures, statues, tomb paintings, and reliefs as well as funerary para-phernalia. Of the latter, the most unusual is the coffin of an ibis, probably recovered from the vast animal cemetery of Tuna el-Gebel in Middle Egypt. The ibis was a sacred bird representing the god Thoth, and this coffin is made of solid silver and wood overlaid with gold leaf, with rock crystal for the bird's eyes. These galleries have been renovated into a state-of-the-art, hi-tech installation.

Among the artifacts from the Greek and Roman civilizations are statuary, pottery, bronzes, jewelry, and mosaics.

Among the Ancient Near and Middle Eastern exhibits are an extensive collection of pottery and 12 alabaster reliefs from the Assyrian palace of King Ashurnasirpal II. These date from around 883–859 BC and depict the king fighting, overseeing his crops, and purifying the "sacred tree," a major icon in Assyrian religion.

Pierre de Wiessant (1887) by Auguste Rodin, from his *Burghers of Calais* group

Painting and Sculpture

This collection contains works from the 14th century to the present, including a well-known and outstanding 19th-century French art collection with works by Degas, Rodin, Monet, Cézanne, Matisse, and Pissarro. It also boasts one of the largest holdings of Spanish Colonial paintings and one of the best collections of North American paintings to be found in the United States. The museum's 20th-century American collection includes,

appropriately, *Brooklyn Bridge* by Georgia O'Keeffe.

The Sculpture Garden holds architectural ornamentation taken from demolished New York buildings, including statues rescued from the original Penn Station, and a replica of the Statue of Liberty.

Rotherhithe, an etching by James McNeill Whistler (1860)

Prints, Drawings, and Photographs

The museum has an important collection of prints, drawings, and photographs that are constantly rotated for conser-vation purposes, and so this isn't on the floorplan (*see pp238–9*). The range includes a rare wood-cut print by Dürer entitled *The Great Triumphal Chariot* and works by Piranesi. The Impressionist and Post-Impressionist collection includes works by Toulouse-Lautrec and Mary Cassatt, the only American woman associated with the Impressionist move-ment. There are lithographs by James McNeill Whistler, Winslow Homer engravings, and a superb selection of drawings by Fragonard, Paul Klee, van Gogh, Picasso, and Arshile Gorky, among others.

The photography collection consists mainly of works by major 20th-century American photographers, including a 1924 portrait of silent-film actress Mary Pickford by Edward Steichen and work by Margaret Bourke-White, Berenice Abbott, and Robert Mapplethorpe.

Sandstone reliefs from Thebes in Egypt (c.760–656 BC), depicting the great god Amun-Re and his consort Mut

FARTHER AFIELD

Though officially part of New York City, Upper Manhattan and the outer boroughs (the Bronx, Queens and Staten Island) are quite different in feel. They are mostly residential and don't have the famous skyscrapers and world-famous sights that are typically associated with New York. However, these outlying areas boast many attractions, including the city's biggest zoo, botanical gardens, museums, beaches, and sports arenas, and restaurants representing almost every ethnicity.

Sights at a Glance

Historic Streets and Buildings

- ❷ Morris-Jumel Mansion
- ❸ George Washington Bridge
- ❺ Poe Cottage
- ❾ Belmont and
     Arthur Avenues
- ❿ Yankee Stadium
- ⓯ Steinway & Sons
- ⓰ Noguchi Museum & Socrates
     Sculpture Park
- ⓳ Historic Richmond Town
- ⓴ Alice Austen House

Museums and Galleries

- ❶ Audubon Terrace
- ❹ *The Cloisters Museum pp238–41*

- ⓫ The Bronx Museum
     of the Arts
- ⓭ Queens Museum
- ⓮ Louis Armstrong House Museum
- ⓱ Museum of the Moving Image
     and Kaufman Astoria Studio
- ⓲ MoMA PS1, Queens
- ⓴ Jacques Marchais Museum of
     Tibetan Art
- ㉑ The Snug Harbor Cultural Center &
     Botanical Garden

Parks and Gardens

- ❼ *New York
     Botanical Garden pp244–5*
- ❽ *Bronx Zoo pp246–7*
- ⓬ Flushing Meadow-Corona Park

Cemeteries

- ❻ Woodlawn Cemetery

Beaches

- ㉓ Coney Island

Key

- ━━ Freeway
- ━━ Major road
- ═══ Other road
- ▮ Main sightseeing areas

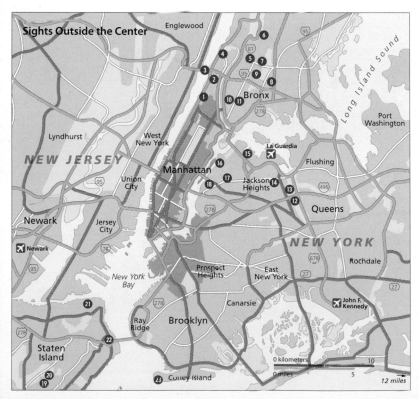

Sights Outside the Center

◀ Orchids in bloom at the New York Botanical Garden

For keys to symbols *see back flap*

Upper Manhattan

It was in Upper Manhattan that the 18th-century Dutch settlers established their farms. Now a suburban area with little of the bustle of downtown Manhattan, it is a good place to escape the inner city for some relaxed museum and landmark sightseeing. The Cloisters *(see pp246–9)* displays a magnificent collection of medieval art, housed within original European buildings of the period. A piece of New York history is found at the Morris-Jumel Mansion in north Harlem: from his headquarters here, George Washington mounted the defense of Manhattan in 1776.

The American Academy of Arts and Letters

❶ Audubon Terrace

Broadway at 155th St. Ⓜ 157th St. American Academy of Arts and Letters: (212) 368-5900. **Open** mid-Mar–mid-Apr, mid-May–mid-Jun: 1–4pm Thu–Sun. 🖼 Hispanic Society of America: (212) 926-2234. **Open** 10am–4:30pm Tue–Sat, 1–4pm Sun. **Closed** public hols. Donations. 📷 2pm Sat. 📷 🖥 **hispanicsociety.org**

This 1908 complex of Classical Revival buildings by Charles Pratt Huntington is named for the great naturalist John James Audubon, whose estate once included this land. Audubon is buried in the nearby Trinity Cemetery. His gravestone, a Celtic cross, bears the symbolic images of his adventurous career: the birds he painted, his palette and brushes, and his rifles. The complex was funded by the

architect's cousin, civic bene-factor Archer Milton Huntington, whose dream was that it should be a center of culture and study. A central plaza contains statues by his wife, sculptor Anna Hyatt Huntington.

Audubon Terrace contains two themed museums that are worth seeking out. The **American Academy of Arts and Letters** was set up to honor American writers, artists, and composers, and 75 honorary members from overseas. On this illustrious roll are writers John Steinbeck and Mark Twain, painters Andrew Wyeth and Edward Hopper, and composer Aaron Copland. Exhibitions feature members' work. The library (for scholars, by appointment) has old manuscripts and first editions.

The **Hispanic Society of America** is a public museum and library based upon a personal collection amassed by Archer M. Huntington. There are extensive collections of Spanish sculpture, decorative arts, prints, and photographs, with changing exhibits throughout the year. The main gallery, in Spanish Renaissance style,

Bronze door, American Academy

holds Goya's famous *Duchess of Alba*. The adjacent Bancaja Gallery contains Joaquín Sorolla y Bastida's *Vision of Spain*, commissioned in 1911. It contains 14 large murals that depict people and life in different regions of Spain. Upstairs, there are galleries of painted tiles, ceramics, Roman mosaics, and rare Spanish lusterware. However, the balcony above the main gallery offers some of the best works: classic paintings by El Greco, such as *Holy Family*, and characteristic portraits by Velázquez and Goya.

Statue of El Cid by Anna Hyatt Huntington at Audubon Terrace

❷ Morris-Jumel Mansion

65 Jumel Terrace at W 160th St and Edgecombe Ave. **Tel** (212) 923-8008. Ⓜ 163rd St. **Open** 10am–4pm Tue–Fri (to 5pm Sat & Sun). **Closed** public hols. 🅿 📷 noon Sat by appt. 📷 🆆 **morrisjumel.org**

This is one of New York's few pre-Revolutionary buildings. Now a museum with nine restored period rooms, it was built in 1765 for Roger Morris. His former military colleague George Washington used it as temporary headquarters while defending Manhattan in 1776. In 1810 it was bought and updated by Stephen Jumel, a merchant of French-Caribbean descent, and his wife Eliza.

The pair furnished the house with souvenirs of their many visits to France. Her boudoir has a "dolphin" chair, reputedly bought from Napoleon. Eliza's social climbing and love affairs scandalized New York society. It was rumored that she let her husband bleed to death in 1832 so she could inherit his fortune. She later married Aaron Burr, aged 77, and divorced him three years later on the day he died.

The exterior of the Palladian-style, wood-sided Georgian house with Classical portico and octagonal wing has been restored. The museum exhibits include many original Jumel pieces.

The 3,500-ft (1,065-m) span of the George Washington Bridge

❸ George Washington Bridge

Ⓜ 175th St. 🆆 **panynj.gov**

French architect Le Corbusier called this "the only seat of grace in the disordered city." While not as famous a landmark as its Brooklyn equivalent, this bridge by engineer Othmar Ammann and his architect Cass Gilbert has its own character and history. Plans for a bridge linking Manhattan to New Jersey had been in the pipeline for more than 60 years before the Port of New York Authority raised the $59 million to fund the project. It was Ammann

The Little Red Lighthouse under Washington Bridge

who suggested a road bridge rather than the more expensive rail link. Work began in 1927, and the bridge was opened in 1931: first across were two young roller skaters from the Bronx.

Today it is a vital link for commuter traffic and is in constant use.

Gilbert had plans to clad the two towers with masonry but funds did not permit it, leaving an elegant skeletal structure 600 ft (183 m) high and 3,500 ft (1,067 m) long.

Ammann had also allowed for a second deck in his plan, and this lower deck was added in 1962, increasing the bridge's capacity enormously. Now the eastbound toll collection shows a traffic level of over 53 million cars per year.

Below the eastern tower in Fort Washington Park is a lighthouse that dates from 1889, and was saved from possible demolition in 1951 by public pressure. Many thousands of young New Yorkers and children all around the world have loved the bedtime story *The Little Red Lighthouse and the Great Gray Bridge* (1942), and wrote letters to save the lighthouse. Author Hildegarde Hoyt Swift wove the tale around her two favorite New York landmarks.

The Little Red Lighthouse Festival is held here every September. The event includes a special guest reading of the famous book.

Morris-Jumel Mansion, built in 1765, with its original colossal portico

❹ The Cloisters Museum

This world-famous museum of medieval art resides in a building constructed between 1934 and 1938, incorporating medieval cloisters, chapels, and halls. Sculptor George Grey Barnard founded the museum in 1914; John D. Rockefeller, Jr. funded the Metropolitan Museum of Art's 1925 purchase of the collection and donated the site at Fort Tryon Park and also the land on the New Jersey side of the Hudson River, directly across from The Cloisters.

Tomb Effigy of Jean d'Alluye
This tomb immortalizes the 13th-century French crusader.

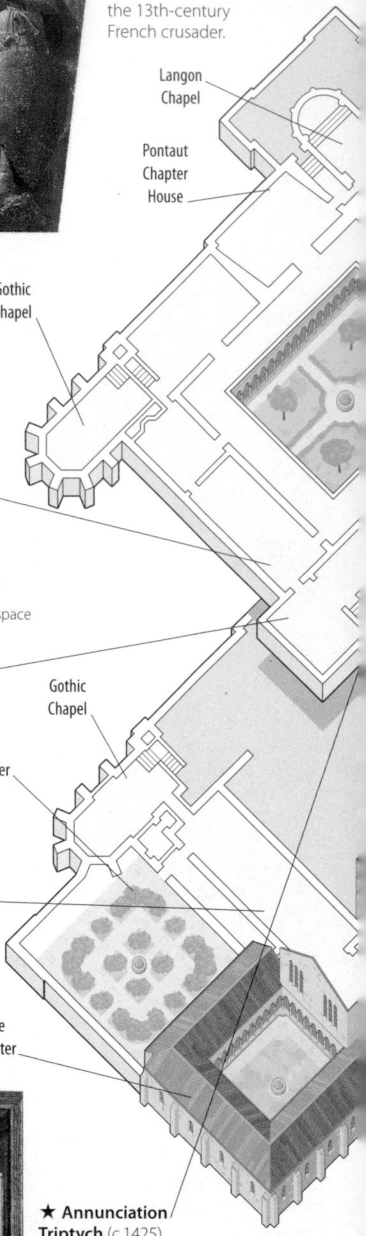

Langon Chapel

Pontaut Chapter House

Gothic Chapel

★ Unicorn Tapestries
The set of beautiful tapestries, woven in the Netherlands around 1500, depicts the quest and capture of the mythical unicorn.

Key

☐ Exhibition space
☐ Non-exhibition space

Gothic Chapel

Bonnefort Cloister

Glass Gallery

Boppard Stained-Glass Lancets (1440–47)
Below the lancet of St. Catherine, angels display the arms of the Coopers' Guild, of which Catherine was patron.

Trie Cloister

★ Annunciation Triptych (c.1425)
The Campin Room is the location of this small Robert Campin of Tournai triptych, a magnificent example of early Netherlandish painting.

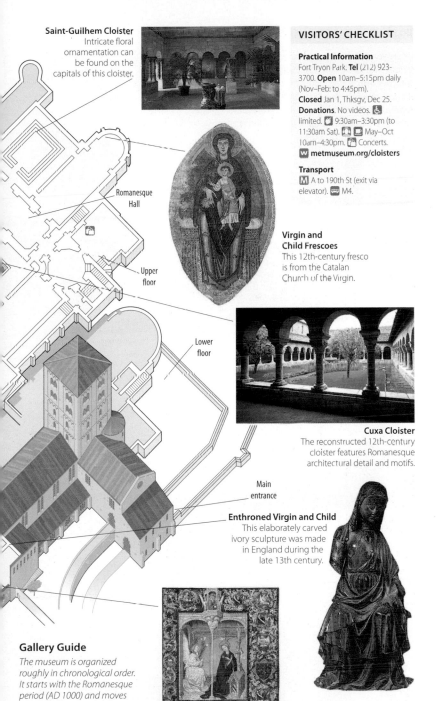

Saint-Guilhem Cloister
Intricate floral ornamentation can be found on the capitals of this cloister.

VISITORS' CHECKLIST

Practical Information
Fort Tryon Park. **Tel** (212) 923-3700. **Open** 10am–5:15pm daily (Nov–Feb: to 4:45pm). **Closed** Jan 1, Thksgv, Dec 25. **Donations**. No videos. limited. 9:30am–3:30pm (to 11:30am Sat). May–Oct 10am–4:30pm. Concerts. W **metmuseum.org/cloisters**

Transport
M A to 190th St (exit via elevator). M4.

Romanesque Hall

Upper floor

Virgin and Child Frescoes
This 12th-century fresco is from the Catalan Church of the Virgin.

Lower floor

Cuxa Cloister
The reconstructed 12th-century cloister features Romanesque architectural detail and motifs.

Main entrance

Enthroned Virgin and Child
This elaborately carved ivory sculpture was made in England during the late 13th century.

Gallery Guide

The museum is organized roughly in chronological order. It starts with the Romanesque period (AD 1000) and moves to the Gothic (1150 to 1520). Sculptures, stained glass, paintings, and the gardens are on the lower floor. The Unicorn Tapestries are on the upper floor.

★ Belles Heures
This book of hours, commissioned by Jean, Duc de Berry, is among a rotating installation of exquisite illuminated books and folios.

Exploring The Cloisters Museum

Known particularly for its Romanesque and Gothic architectural sculpture, The Cloisters' collection also includes illuminated manuscripts, stained glass, metalwork, enamels, ivories, and paintings. Among its tapestries is the renowned *Unicorn* series. The Cloisters' splendid medieval complex is unrivaled in North America.

A 16th-century Flemish boxwood rosary bead from the Treasury

A lifesized 12th-century Spanish crucifix portraying Christ as the King of Heaven

Romanesque Art

Fanciful beasts and people, acanthus blossoms and scrollwork top the columns around The Cloisters. Many are in the Romanesque style that flourished in the 11th and 12th centuries. The museum has numerous masterpieces of Romanesque art and architecture, showing the style's powerful rounded arches and intricate details. Highly embellished capitals and warm, pink marble typify the 12th-century Cuxa Cloister from the Pyrenees in France. A griffin, a dragon, a centaur, and a basilisk are among the creatures parading over the Narbonne Arch nearby.

In a more solemn style, the apse from the church of St. Martín in Fuentidueña, Spain, is a massive rounded vault constructed from 3,300 blocks of limestone. It is decorated with a 12th-century fresco of the Virgin and Child and has a golden-crowned Christ depicted as triumphant over death.

More than 800 years ago, Benedictine and Cistercian monks sat on the cold stone benches in the Pontaut Chapter House. By the 19th century the building had become so neglected that it was used as a stable. Its ribbed vaulting is a foretaste of the Gothic style to come.

Gothic Art

Where Romanesque art was solid, the Gothic style that followed (from 1150 to around 1520) was open, with pointed arches, glowing stained-glass windows, and three-dimensional sculpture. Gothic depictions of the Virgin and Child typically display exquisite craftsmanship.

The Gothic Chapel's brilliantly colored windows show scenes and figures from biblical stories. Lifesized tomb sculptures include the effigy of the Crusader knight Jean d'Alluye. During the 1790s, the statue's original home,

Vaulted ceiling of the Pontaut Chapter House

La Clarté-Dieu Abbey in France, was vandalized, and the statue was used to bridge a stream.

In the Boppard Room, the lives of the saints are told in marvelous late Gothic stained glass from Germany.

Robert Campin's Flemish masterwork, the *Annunciation* altarpiece, is the focus of the Campin Room. This is an intimate space with furnishings that might have belonged to a wealthy 15th-century family.

Medieval Gardens

More than 300 varieties of plants grown in the Middle Ages can be found in the Cloisters' gardens. The Bonnefont Cloister has many species of aromatic, magic, medicinal, and culinary herbs. The Trie Cloister features plants shown in the *Unicorn Tapestries* and reveals the use of flowers in medieval symbolism: roses (for the Virgin Mary), pansies (the Holy Trinity), and daisies (the eye of Christ).

Bonnefont Cloister

The Tapestries

The Cloisters' tapestries are full of rich imagery and symbolism, and are among the museum's most highly prized treasures. The four *Nine Heroes Tapestries* bear the coat of arms of Jean, Duc de Berry, who was a brother of the King of France and one of the greatest art patrons of the Middle Ages. These tapestries are one of only two sets that survived from the late 14th century; the other set belonged to Jean's brother, Louis, Duc d'Anjou.

Nine great heroes of the past – three pagan, three Hebrew, three Christian – are shown with members of the medieval court, from cardinals, knights, and damsels to musicians.

In an adjacent room is the magnificent *Hunt of the Unicorn*, a series of seven tapestries woven in the Netherlands around 1500. It depicts the symbolic hunt of the mythical unicorn and its capture by a maiden.

Although they were misused in the 19th century to protect fruit trees from frost damage,

the tapestries are remarkably well preserved. They are also astonishing in detail, with

Julius Caesar, entertained by court musicians, in a *Nine Heroes* tapestry

literally hundreds of minutely observed plants and animals. Their story can be read as a tale of courtly love, but the series is also an allegory of the Crucifixion and the Resurrection of Christ.

The Treasury

In medieval times, precious objects were stored for safekeeping in sanctuaries. At the Cloisters, they are found in the Treasury.

The collection includes several Gothic illuminated "books of hours." These were used for the private devotions of the nobility, such as the Limbourg brothers' *Belles Heures*, made for Jean, Duc de Berry, in 1410, and the tiny, palm-sized version made by Gothic master Jean Pucelle for the Queen of France around 1325.

Other religious artifacts range from a 13th-century English ivory Virgin to the 14th-century silver gilt-and-enamel reliquary shrine thought to have belonged to Queen Elizabeth of Hungary, along with censers, chalices, candlesticks, and crucifixes.

Curiosities here include the "Monkey Cup," an enameled beaker probably made for the 15th-century Burgundian court, showing mischievous monkeys robbing a sleeping peddler; an intricately carved rosary bead the size of a walnut; a 13th-century boat-shaped, jeweled salt cellar; and a full set of playing cards dating to the 15th century.

Hunting images and symbols depicted on a 15th-century deck of playing cards

The Bronx

This borough was originally a relatively prosperous suburb, its Grand Concourse lined with lavish apartment buildings. Serious poverty emerged only in the 1950s, and when the South Bronx was left to burn in the 1970s, the entire borough became a byword for urban decay. Despite a few signs of gentrification, the South Bronx remains one of the city's poorest areas. The rest of the borough features historic mansions, tranquil parks, an outstanding botanic garden and zoo, and the Yankee Stadium.

A memorial at the beautiful Woodlawn Cemetery

❺ Poe Cottage

2640 Grand Concourse. **Tel** (718) 881-8900. **M** Kingsbridge Rd. **Open** 10am–3pm Thu & Fri, 10am–4pm Sat, 1–5pm Sun. 🅿 🅰 Poe Park Visitor Center: 2650 Grand Concourse. **Open** 8am–5pm Tue–Sat. ♿ 🚾 **bronxhistoricalsociety.org**

Built as a modest laborer's dwelling around 1812, this white-clapboard house, set incongruously today in the midst of working-class Latino housing blocks, was Edgar Allan Poe's rural home from 1846 to 1849. The charming house originally stood on farmland a short distance away on East Kingsbridge Road, but it was moved here (at the northern tip of the specially created Poe Park) in 1913.

Although Poe was already relatively successful as the writer of The Raven, he was dogged by financial problems in the mid-1800s. He moved in with his wife, Virginia, and her mother, Maria in search of fresh rural air. Sadly, soon after they arrived at the cottage, Virginia died of tuberculosis. Heartbroken, Poe managed to write a few revered works while in mourning, including the moving poem Annabel Lee, which was written in memory of his wife. Maria outlived them both, and moved out of the cottage shortly after Poe's mysterious death in Baltimore two years later.

Today, the restored cottage contains several rooms set up to look as they did during Poe's time. There is also a small gallery of artwork from the 1840s within the vicinity.

The elegant Poe Park Visitor Center stands separate from the actual house. Designed by the Japanese architect Toshiko Mori, the educational facility features rotating art exhibitions and, interestingly, its sharply-angled roof vaguely resembles a raven.

❻ Woodlawn Cemetery

Webster Ave and E 233rd St. **Tel** (718) 920-0500. **M** Woodlawn. **Open** 8:30am–4:30pm daily. **Closed** public hols. 🅿 ♿ 🅰 🚾 **thewoodlawncemetery.org**

Established in 1863, Woodlawn Cemetery is the burial place of many a wealthy and distinguished New Yorker. Memorials and tombstones are set in beautiful grounds. F. W. Woolworth and many members of his family are interred in a mausoleum only a little less ornate than the building that carries the family name. The pink marble vault of meat magnate Herman Armour is oddly reminiscent of a ham.

Other New York notables buried here include Mayor Fiorello La Guardia; Rowland Hussey Macy, the founder of the great department store; author Herman Melville; and jazz legend Duke Ellington.

Traditional Italian specialty market at the Bronx

➐ New York Botanical Garden

See pp252–3.

➑ Bronx Zoo

See pp254–5.

➒ Belmont and Arthur Avenue

Ⓜ Fordham Rd (B, D, 4), then take the Eastbound bus.
Ⓦ arthuravenuebronx.com

Within walking distance of the botanical garden and zoo is Belmont, home to one of New York's largest Italian-American communities. A more authentic alternative to Little Italy in Manhattan, its main thoroughfare, Arthur Avenue, is lined with Italian bakeries, pizzerias, and restaurants. The Arthur Avenue Retail Market includes pastry shops, butchers, pasta-makers, pork stores, fish stalls, and coffee shops. Every September, the neighborhood celebrates Ferragosto, a harvest festival, with dancing, food stalls, live performances, and a cheese-carving contest.

➓ Yankee Stadium

E 161st St at River Ave, Highbridge.
Tel (718) 293-6000. Ⓜ 161st St.
🎟 noon–1:40pm daily (except on game afternoons); ticketed tours available. *See Sport p354.*
Ⓦ newyork.yankees.mlb.com

This has been the home of the New York Yankees baseball team since 1923. Among Yankee heroes are two of the greatest players of all time: Babe Ruth and Joe DiMaggio (who was also famous for marrying the actress Marilyn Monroe in 1954). In 1921 left-hander Babe Ruth, wearing the Yankees' distinctive pinstripes, hit the stadium's first home run – against the Boston Red Sox, his former team. The stadium was completed two years later by Jacob Ruppert, the owner of the Yankees, and

became known as "the house that Ruth built".

The Yankee Stadium was given a facelift in the mid-1970s to seat up to 54,000 people. One of the largest annual gatherings has been that of the Jehovah's Witnesses, and in 1950, some 123,707 people attended in a single day. In 1965 Pope Paul VI celebrated mass before a crowd of more than 80,000. It was the first visit to North America by a pope – the second was made in 1979, when John Paul II also visited the stadium.

In 2009, the Yankees moved to a new stadium that was located parallel to the old site. This stadium is one of the most expensive venues ever built, at a cost of around $1.5 billion.

The Yankees remain one of the top teams in the American League. There are multiple Yankee Clubhouse stores in New York, where tickets for tours and games can be purchased.

⓫ The Bronx Museum of the Arts

1040 Grand Concourse. **Tel** (718) 681-6000. Ⓜ 167th St–Grand Concourse. **Open** 11am–6pm Wed, Thu, Sat & Sun, 11–8pm Fri. ♿🔲🎫 for groups
Ⓦ bronxmuseum.org

Founded in 1971, this art museum showcases contemporary works by Asian, Latino, and African-American artists.

Joe DiMaggio in action at the Yankee Stadium

Regular readings, performances, and other such events are also held here.

The museum owns over 1,000 contemporary artworks in a variety of mediums. Among those represented are Romare Bearden (1911–88), a multi-media artist known for his depictions of everyday African-American life; Bronx-born Whitfield Lovell (b. 1959), renowned for his African-American figures in pencil and charcoal; Cuban installation and performance artist Tania Bruguera (b. 1968); lauded photographer Seydou Keïta (1921–2001) from Mali; Brazilian visual artist Hélio Oiticica (1937–80); contemporary African-American artist Kara Walker (b. 1969); and the Chinese artist Xu Bing (b. 1955).

In 1982, the museum moved into a former synagogue donated by the City of New York, and this has since remained its premise. Between 2004 and 2006, the museum was modernized and expanded by the Miami-based firm, Arquitectonica. This can be seen from the jagged steel-and-glass "accordion" facade.

An exhibition at The Bronx Museum of the Arts

❼ New York Botanical Garden

The New York Botanical Garden offers 250 acres (100 ha) of dazzling beauty and hands-on enjoyment. From the nation's most glorious Victorian glasshouse to the 12-acre (5-ha) Everett Children's Adventure Garden, it is alive with things to discover. One of the oldest and largest botanical gardens in the world, it has 50 gardens and plant collections, and 50 acres (20 ha) of uncut forest. The spectacular Enid A. Haupt Conservatory houses a "A World of Plants," with climates ranging from misty tropical rain forests to dramatic deserts.

Entrance to the Enid A. Haupt Conservatory

Seasonal Exhibition Galleries

Deserts of Africa

④ **Rock Garden**
Rock outcroppings, streams, a waterfall, and a flower-rimmed pond create an alpine habitat for plants from around the world.

⑤ **Thain Family Forest**
One of New York City's last surviving natural forest areas includes red oak, white ash, tulip trees, and birch.

Deserts of the Americas

⑧ **Everett Children's Adventure Garden**
Kids can discover the wonders of ecology and plants.

Entrance

⑥
① ② ③ ④ ⑤
⑨
⑧
⑦

Entrance

Locator Map

⑦ **Peggy Rockefeller Rose Garden**
Over 2,700 rose bushes have been planted in the Rose Garden, laid out in 1988 according to the 1916 design.

Palms of the Americas Gallery
A hundred majestic palms soar into a 90-ft (27-m) glass dome. A tranquil reflecting pool is surrounded by tropical plants.

① **The Enid A. Haupt Conservatory** consists of 11 interconnecting glass galleries housing "A World of Plants," including rain forests, deserts, aquatic plants, and seasonal exhibitions.

⑥ **Garden Cafe**
This is a delightful spot to enjoy a meal. You can eat outside on terraces overlooking beautiful gardens.

Conservatory

② **Jane Watson Irwin Perennial Garden**
Flowering perennials are arranged in dramatic patterns according to height, shade, color, and blooming time.

Tropical Lowland Rain Forest Gallery

Courtyard Pool

⑨ **Leon Levy Visitor Center**
This modern pavilion has a shop, a café, and a visitor orientation facility.

Aquatic Plants and Vines Gallery

Tropical Upland Rain Forest Gallery

③ **Tram**
The half-hour tour of the gardens provides information about horticultural, educational, and botanical research programs. Passengers can alight at a number of stops to explore the gardens before reboarding.

❶ Bronx Zoo

Opened in 1899, the Bronx Zoo is the largest urban zoo in the United States. It is home to more than 4,000 animals of 500 species, which live in realistic representations of their natural habitats. The zoo is a leader in the perpetuation of endangered species, such as the Indian rhinoceros and the snow leopard. Its 265 acres (107 ha) of woods, streams, and parklands include, in season, a children's zoo, the Butterfly Garden, the Wild Asia Monorail, and camel rides. Other attractions include daily sea lion feedings, a one-of-a-kind bug carousel, and a 4-D theater experience.

★ **The Congo Gorilla Forest**
This award-winning replica of a central African rain forest is home to the largest population of Western Lowland gorillas in the US, as well as a family of pygmy marmosets, the world's smallest monkeys.

Baboon Reserve
Visitors walk along a dry riverbed to see wildlife in an Ethiopian mountain habitat.

Asia entrance

Camel Rides
Children enjoy such seasonal experiences as camel rides and other attractions.

★ **African Plains**
Wild dogs, zebras, lions, giraffes, and gazelles roam the African Plains. Predators and prey are separated by a moat.

★ **JungleWorld**
A climate-controlled tropical rain forest harbors mammals, birds, and reptiles from South Asia. The animals are kept apart from visitors by ravines, streams, and cliffs.

Monkeys in JungleWorld

Children's Zoo
Kids can crawl through
a prairie dog tunnel, try on a
turtle shell, and pet and feed
the animals.

Great
hornbill

★ World of Birds
Exotic birds soar free in the lush
surroundings of a rain forest. An
artificial waterfall rushes down
a 50-ft (15-m) fiberglass cliff in
this walk-through habitat.

Southern
Boulevard
entrance

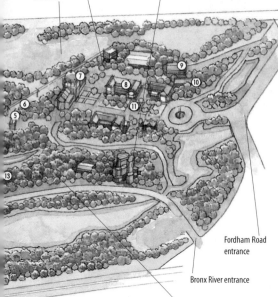

KEY

① 4-D Theater
② Wild Asia Monorail
③ Carter Giraffe Building
④ Dancing Crane Café
⑤ World of Reptiles
⑥ Butterfly Garden
⑦ The Zoo Center
⑧ Madagascar!
⑨ Aquatic Bird House
⑩ Sea Bird Colony
⑪ Sea Lions
⑫ Mouse-House
⑬ **Himalayan Highlands**, a habitat
for endangered species, such as
snow leopards and red pandas.

Fordham Road
entrance

Bronx River entrance

★ Wild Asia Monorail
From May to October, the monorail
journeys through forests and meadows,
where rhinos, tigers, and Mongolian wild
horses roam free.

★ Tiger Mountain
Amur tigers are on view all year. Only 1 inch (2.5 cm) of
glass separates visitors from these magnificent wild cats.

Queens

The city's largest borough, Queens has a diverse variety of attractions and a huge erray of ethnic restaurants. From the thriving Greeks, Egyptians and Bosnians in Astoria, and Woodside's dynamic communities of Thais, Koreans and Filipinos, to the huge Chinatown in Flushing, plus Little India, Little Pakistan, Little Bangladesh and Little Colombia in Jackson Heights – it's a real melting pot of cultures. Long Island City and Astoria also harbor major attractions.

⑫ Flushing Meadow-Corona Park

Ⓜ Willets Point-Shea Stadium.
See Sports pp354–5.

The site of New York's two World's Fairs offers expansive waterside picnic grounds and a multitude of attractions. These include the 41,000-seat Citi Field stadium, home of the New York Mets baseball team, and a popular site for rock concerts. Flushing Meadow is also home to the National Tennis Center *(see p354–5)*, where the prestigious United States Open is played. The courts are open for would-be Nadals, Sharapovas, and Federers for the remainder of the year.

In the 1920s this area was known as the Corona Dump, a nightmarish place of salt marshes and great piles of smoldering trash. In *The Great Gatsby*, author F. Scott Fitzgerald dubbed it the "valley of ashes." It reeked of rotting garbage and glowed red at night. New York's Parks' Commissioner Robert Moses was the driving force behind its transformation. A whole mountain of trash was removed, and the river was totally rechanneled. The

The 1964 World's Fair Unisphere at Flushing Meadow-Corona Park

marsh was drained, and sewage works were built, helping to restore the area. This site was to serve as the location for the 1939 World's Fair, at which a world on the brink of war saluted the elusive notion of world peace.

The Unisphere, symbol of the 1964 fair, still dominates the remains of the fairground. This giant hollow ball of green steel, built by the US Steel Corporation, is 12 stories high and weighs a massive 350 tons.

⑬ Queens Museum

New York City Building, Flushing Meadows-Corona Park. **Tel** (718) 592-9700. Ⓜ 111th St. **Open** noon–6pm Wed–Sun. ♿🚻📷 free: 2pm, 3pm & 4pm Sun (English and Spanish)
🖥 **queensmuseum.org**

Located next to the Unisphere, the museum building is from the 1939 World's Fair, and is the only remaining structure from the event. Originally designed to house the New York City Pavilion, it later served as a recreation center. Today, the galleries house temporary exhibitions, as well as two long-term installations – the Neustadt Collection of Tiffany Glass, by Louis Comfort Tiffany, who established his design studios in the 1890s in Corona; and "From Watersheds to Faucets: The Marvel of the NYC Water Supply System." The star exhibit in the latter is a large wood-and-plaster relief map of New York's water-supply system, created for the 1939 World's Fair and was kept under wraps for decades.

The museum's other major attraction is the Panorama of the City of New York, a product of the 1964 World's Fair. The

9,300-sq-ft (864-sq-m) panorama is the world's largest architectural model. It consists of 895,000 buildings, each one carved out of wood, along with harbors, rivers, bridges, and miniature airplanes gliding in and out of the airports.

Architect Aymar Embury III, who also built Central Park Zoo, designed this grand structure in a Modern-Classical style, with a facade of colonnades supported by limestone pilasters, trimmed in dark, polished granite. The Queens Museum occupied the north side of the structure in 1972, with Rafael Viñoly bringing about the first major renovation in 1994. After another renovation in 2013, the galleries doubled in size. A large glass facade was added, which created a spacious, skylit atrium.

Interior of the Louis Armstrong House Museum

⑭ Louis Armstrong House Museum

34–56 107th St. **Tel** (718) 478-8274. Ⓜ 103rd St–Corona Plaza. **Open** 10am–5pm Tue–Fri. 🎟 hourly (4pm last tour). 🖥 **louisarmstronghouse.org**

Legendary trumpeter Louis Armstrong (1901–71) lived here from 1943 until his death in 1971, when he was buried in the nearby Flushing Cemetery. The jazz artist's relatively humble home has been preserved just as he and his fourth wife, singer Lucille Wilson, left it. Audio recordings made by Armstrong play in the house, revealing everyday goings-on and Louis practicing his trumpet, enjoying a meal, or chatting with friends. Guided tours provide context to the displays and furnishings.

The visitors' center across the street displays more of Armstrong's personal archives, and concerts are sometimes held in the family's garden behind the house. In addition to Dizzy Gillespie and Cannonball Adderley, who lived near Armstrong, luminaries such as Ella Fitzgerald, Count Basie, Lena Horne, Fats Waller, and, briefly, Charles Mingus, called the borough home.

⓯ Steinway & Sons

1 Steinway Place, 19th Ave. **Tel** (718) 721-2600. Ⓜ Ditmars Boulevard. ⏰ 9:30am Tue, not offered Jul & Aug. 🆆 steinway.com

Heinrich Steinweg (1797–1871) emigrated from Germany to America in 1850. After anglicizing his name to Henry Steinway, he founded Steinway & Sons in 1853. The company gained recognition for producing the finest pianos, and rapidly expanded after it began winning prizes at international trade fairs. In the 1870s, Henry's son, William, moved the factory from Manhattan to Astoria. However, it was his great grandson, Henry Z. Steinway, who worked here until his death in 2008. He was the last family member to be president of the company.

About 1,250 Steinway grand pianos are built at the Queens complex every year, selling for anything from $40,000 to well above $100,000. Considered to be among the most complex, handmade objects, the pianos have 12,000 parts that are assembled over the course of a year, using Canadian maple.

⓰ Noguchi Museum & Socrates Sculpture Park

9-01 33rd Rd. **Tel** (718) 204-7088. Ⓜ Broadway, take the Q104 bus. **Open** 10am–5pm Wed–Fri, 11am–6pm Sat & Sun. 🆆 noguchi.org Socrates Sculpture Park: 32-01 Vernon Blvd. **Tel** (718) 956-1819. **Open** 10am–sunset daily. ♿📷🎫 2pm Wed–Sun 🆆 socratessculpturepark.org

Devoted to Japanese-American abstract sculptor Isamu Noguchi (1904–88), this museum and

garden was created to provide an artistic space for visitors to experience Noguchi's creative vision. The garden is adorned with his stone sculptures, and the surrounding galleries display his exhibits. Noguchi is probably best remembered for his work with the Herman Miller company in 1947, when he created the iconic Noguchi table. He also designed the Red Cube installation, which still stands outside the Marine Midland Building in Lower Manhattan.

The Socrates Sculpture Park is a short stroll from the museum. The park was created in 1986, when abstract expressionist sculptor Mark di Suvero converted an old landfill into an outdoor studio. Since then, several artists have used the space to exhibit their work on a massive scale. The museum also hosts events such as free yoga classes, music performances, and a kite festival.

⓱ Museum of the Moving Image and Kaufman Astoria Studio

36-01 35th Ave at 36th St, Astoria. **Tel** (718) 777-6888. Ⓜ 36th St. **Open** 10:30am–5pm Wed–Sun (to 8pm Fri, to 7pm Sat & Sun). Screenings: 7pm Fri, afternoon and eves Sat & Sun. 📷 (free 4–8pm Fri). 🎫 2pm Sat & Sun. **Closed** Memorial Day, Thanksgiving, Dec 25. Studio: **Closed** to public. ♿📷🎬 🆆 movingimage.us

In New York's filmmaking heyday, Rudolph Valentino, W. C. Fields, the Marx Brothers, and Gloria Swanson all made films in the Astoria Studio, which was opened in 1920 by Paramount Pictures. When the movies went west, the army took over, making training films from 1941 to 1971.

The complex stood empty until 1977 when Astoria Motion Picture and Television Foundation was created to preserve it. *The Wiz*, a musical starring Michael Jackson and Diana Ross, was made here, helping to pay for restoration.

Movie poster at the Museum of the Moving Image

Today, the studios house the largest moviemaking facilities on the East Coast.

In 1981 one of the studio buildings was transformed into the Museum of the Moving Image. Today the museum displays various memorabilia, from Ben Hur's chariot through to *Star Trek* costumes. The museum's main gallery draws from the permanent collection of over 85,000 movie artifacts. State-of-the-art facilities include a 254-seat theater, a video-screening ampitheater, and an educational 71-seat screening room.

⓲ MoMA PS1, Queens

22–25 Jackson at 46th Ave, Long Island City. **Tel** (718) 784-2084. Ⓜ E, M to 23rd St-Ely Ave; 7 to 45 Road-Courthouse Square; G to Court Sq or 21 St-Van Alst. 🚌 B61, Q67. **Open** noon–6pm Thu–Mon. **Closed** Jan 1, Dec 25. 📷♿📷 🆆 momaps1.org

Housed in an elementary school, PS1 was founded in 1971 under a scheme to transform abandoned city buildings into exhibition, performance, and studio spaces for artists. The museum is affiliated to the Museum of Modern Art (*see pp168–71*) and is one of the oldest art organizations in the US devoted solely to contemporary art. Temporary exhibitions are hosted alongside permanent works and many pieces are interactive. In summer, music is performed in the courtyard.

Staten Island

Apart from the famous ferry ride, Staten Island and its attractions are not well known to New Yorkers in general. Yet it would be a mistake to dismiss the "forgotten borough" so readily. Visitors who venture beyond the ferry terminal will be pleasantly surprised to find hills, lakes, and greenery, with expanses of open space, amazing harbor views, and well-preserved early New York buildings. One of the biggest surprises here is a cache of Tibetan art that is hidden away in a replica of a Buddhist temple.

The Voorlezer House at Richmond

🄆 Historic Richmond Town

441 Clarke Ave. **Tel** (718) 351-1611. 🚌 S74 from ferry. **Open** 1–5pm Wed–Sun. **Closed** Jan 1, Easter Sun, Thanksgiving, Dec 25. 🅿 🅵 🄫 🄫 🄫 **W** historicrichmondtown.org

There are now 29 buildings, some 14 of which are open to the public, in New York's only restored village and outdoor museum. The village was first named Cocclestown, after the local shellfish, but this was soon corrupted to "Cuckoldstown," much to the annoyance of the residents.

By the end of the Revolutionary War, the alternative name of Richmondtown had been adopted. The community was the county seat until Staten Island was made part of the city

Cologne at the General Store

in 1898, and has been preserved as an example of an early New York settlement.

The Voorlezer's House, built in the Dutch style around 1695, is the oldest elementary school to be found in the country. The Stephens General Store, which opened in 1837, doubled as the local post office – it has been well restored, right down to the contents of the shelves. The complex, set on 100 acres (40 ha), includes wagon sheds, a courthouse built in 1837, houses, several shops, and a tavern. There are also seasonal workshops where traditional rural crafts are demonstrated to visitors. St. Andrew's Church, dating to 1708, and its old graveyard are just across the Mill Pond stream, and the Historical Society Museum is in the County Clerk's and Surrogate's Office. The toy room is a delight.

Sacred sculpture at the Jacques Marchais Museum of Tibetan Art

🄔 Jacques Marchais Museum of Tibetan Art

338 Lighthouse Ave. **Tel** (718) 987-3500. 🚌 S74 from ferry. **Open** 1–5pm Wed–Sun (Dec–: Fri–Sun only). **Closed** public hols. 🅿 🄫 🄫 **W** tibetanmuseum.org

A hilltop provides a tranquil setting for one of the largest collections of privately owned Tibetan art of the 15th to the 20th centuries outside Tibet. The main building is a replica of a mountain monastery with an authentic altar in three tiers, crowded with gold, silver, and bronze figures.

The second building is used as a library. The soothing garden has some stone sculptures, including life-sized Buddhas. The museum was completed in 1947 by Mrs. Jacques Marchais, a dealer in Asian art. The Dalai Lama paid his first visit here in 1991.

An old cottage at The Snug Harbor Cultural Center

🄖 The Snug Harbor Cultural Center & Botanical Garden

1000 Richmond Terrace. **Tel** (718) 448-2500. 🚌 S40 from ferry to Snug Harbor Gate. Grounds: **Open** dawn–dusk daily. Art Gallery: **Open** 10am–5pm Tue–Sun. Children's Museum: **Open** noon–5pm Tue–Sun (summer: 11am–5pm Tue–Sun). **Closed** Jan 1, Thanksgiving, Dec 25. 🅵 limited. **W** snug-harbor.org

Founded in 1801 as an affluent retirement community for "aged, decrepit, and worn-out sailors", this became a complex of museums, galleries, gardens, and art centers in

1975. With an 83-acre (34-ha) leafy campus, the center has 28 remaining buildings, that range from grand Greek Revival-style halls to sophisticated Italianate structures. The oldest is the beautiful, restored Main Hall (Building C), which functions as the Visitor Center. The adjacent Newhouse Center for Contemporary Art showcases local artists.

Other buildings house the award-winning Staten Island Children's Museum, and the Noble Maritime Collection, which features prints and paintings created by the nautical painter John Noble (1913–83); visitors can view his houseboat studio as well. The Staten Island Museum relocated to this complex in 2016 – the museum has a major exhibition on Staten Island history, spanning three centuries.

Most of the Snug Harbor grounds belong to the Staten Island Botanical Garden. Attractions here include an exhibit designed to attract

Clear Comfort, former home of photographer Alice Austen

butterflies and a charming antique rose garden. The tranquil Chinese Scholar's Garden, with its goldfish ponds, pagoda-roofed halls, and bamboo groves, was built in 1999 by artists from Suzhou, China.

㉒ Alice Austen House

2 Hylan Blvd. **Tel** (718) 816-4506. S 51 from ferry to Hylan Blvd. **Open** noon–5pm Thu–Sun; grounds: to dusk. **Closed** Jan, Feb, public hols. Donation limited. **W** aliceausten.org

This small cottage, built around 1690, has the delightful name of Clear Comfort. It was the

home of the photographer Alice Austen, who was born in 1866 and who lived in this house for most of her life. She documented life on the island, in Manhattan, and also on trips to other parts of the country and on her travels to Europe. She lost all her money in the stock market crash of 1929, and her poverty forced her into a public poorhouse at the age of 84.

One year later, her photographic talent was finally recognized by *Life* magazine, which published an article about her, earning her enough money to enter a nursing home. She left 3,500 negatives dating from 1880 to 1930.

Today, the Friends of Alice Austen House mounts exhibitions of her best work.

Even Farther Afield

Entrance to the New York Aquarium, Coney Island

㉓ Coney Island

M Stillwell Ave (D, F, N, Q), W 8th St (F, Q). New York Aquarium Surf Ave. **Tel** (718) 265-FISH. **Open** 10am–5pm daily (to 5:30pm Sat, Sun, & hols). (Jun–Aug: to 6pm Mon–Fri & 7pm Sat, Sun & hols; Nov–Mar: to 4:30pm daily). last adm: 45 mins before closing. **W** nyaquarium.com Coney Island Museum 1208 Surf Ave, near W 12th St. **Tel** (718) 372-5159. **Open** noon–6pm Sat & Sun (May–Aug: noon–7pm Wed–Sat, 2–7pm Sun). **W** coneyisland.com

In the mid 1800s, Brooklyn poet Walt Whitman composed many of his works on Coney Island,

which was at that time purely untamed Atlantic coastline. By the 1920s, Coney Island was billing itself as the "World's Largest Playground," with three huge fairgrounds providing hair-raising rides. The subway arrived in 1920, and the 1921 boardwalk ensured Coney Island's popularity throughout the Depression.

A major attraction is the **New York Aquarium**, with over 350 species. The **Coney Island Museum** has memorabilia, souvenirs, and relics of old rides. Coney Island is in the process of being

modernized, much to the chagrin of local residents, who fear that its character will be lost. However, the boardwalk still yields lovely ocean views, and the Cyclone rollercoaster has been designated an official city landmark. The Mermaid Parade in June is a major annual event.

The iconic Cyclone rollercoaster at the Coney Island amusement park

SEVEN GUIDED WALKS

Walking in New York is an excellent way to discover the human scale of the city. The following 16 pages explore the unique character and charm of New York through seven thematic walks. These range from an exploration of Greenwich Village and SoHo's literary and artistic connections (see pp264–5) to a trip across the Brooklyn Bridge for spectacular views and a glimpse of 19th-century New York (see pp270–71).

In addition, each of the 15 main areas described in the Area by Area section of this book has a short walk on its Street-by-Street map, taking you past many of the interesting sights in that area.

Various organizations run walking tours of the city. These range from serious appraisals of architectural history to a guide to the ghosts of Broadway. Details of tour organizers are listed on page 381. Although New York is generally a safe place to roam, take care of your personal belongings while walking (see p366–7), as in any major city. Plan your route ahead and be extra cautious when exploring after dark.

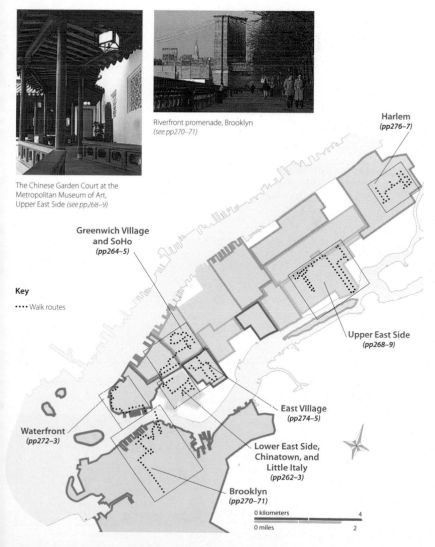

The Chinese Garden Court at the Metropolitan Museum of Art, Upper East Side (see pp268–9)

Riverfront promenade, Brooklyn (see pp270–71)

Harlem (pp276–7)

Greenwich Village and SoHo (pp264–5)

Key

•••• Walk routes

Upper East Side (pp268–9)

East Village (pp274–5)

Waterfront (pp272–3)

Lower East Side, Chinatown, and Little Italy (pp262–3)

Brooklyn (pp270–71)

| 0 kilometers | | 4 |
| 0 miles | | 2 |

◀ Walking across Brooklyn Bridge (see pp232–5)

A 90-Minute Walk in the Lower East Side, Chinatown, and Little Italy

This walk is through old immigrant neighborhoods that have given New York its unique flavor, and illustrates the ever-changing texture of the city as neighborhoods are rediscovered, and one set of newcomers replaces another. Along the way you can experience a variety of cultures and cuisines. Sunday is the most lively day. See more about Lower East Side on pages 86–95.

The Lower East Side

Begin on East Houston Street, the border between the Lower East Side (LES) and the East Village, where some of the best traditional Jewish cuisine can be found at Yonah Schimmel Knish Bakery ① (137). In the same location since 1920, Russ & Daughters, ② (179) is run by the great-grandson of the founder and famed for smoked fish and caviar. Katz's Delicatessen ③ (205) has been a fixture for over 100 years. Continue to Norfolk Street and turn right onto it to see the Angel Orensanz Center ④ (172), housed in New York's oldest synagogue building.

Turn right onto Rivington Street, passing the iconic sweet shop Economy Candy ⑤ built in 1937. Now make a left onto Orchard Street, the traditional center of the Jewish LES.

The LES is now home to cutting-edge boutiques, trendy clubs, and hip restaurants. On Rivington, cool fashion shops share the blocks with the old. The sidewalk stands sell mostly cheap merchandise, but many stores offer discount designer leather and fashion. All are closed on Saturday, so Sunday is the busiest day.

A historical highlight is the Lower East Side Tenement Museum ⑥ (108). An original tenement has been restored to show how three immigrant families lived from 1874 to the 1930s.

Take a short detour to the right down Broome Street for another unique survivor, the Kehila Kedosha Janina Synagogue and Museum ⑦ (280), a small but fascinating congregation with a little upstairs museum.

Return to Orchard Street, continuing along to the right. A left at Grand Street will bring you into New York's former "pickle district" on Essex. At The Pickle Guys store ⑧ (49), you can sample sour, half-sour, and hot pickles. Head back

along Grand Street, taking a left on Eldridge Street, which will take you, just beyond Canal Street, to the grand Eldridge Street Synagogue ⑨ (12). The first Eastern European synagogue in New York, the building also houses the Museum on Eldrige Street, which provides extensive insight into the Jewish community.

Key

··· Walk route

An 1885 iron from the Lower East Side Tenement Museum

Tips for Walkers

Starting point: East Houston St.
Length: 2 miles (3.2 km).
Getting there: Take the subway F or V to Second Avenue; exit East Houston at Eldridge. Other stops: F to Delancey; J, M, Z to Essex. The M15 bus stops on East Houston and on the corner of Delancey and Allen Streets; M14A and M9 run along Essex Street. Returning from Chinatown-Little Italy, Canal Street station is served by the J, N, Q, R, and 6 trains.
Stopping-off points: This walk is designed to take 90 minutes without any stops. Little Italy's cafés are perfect for coffee and cakes. For more substantial fare, Hop Kee at 21 Mott Street is good for Chinese food, or for Italian on Mulberry Street, Il Cortile (125) or Il Palazzo (151). Il Laboratorio del Gelato, at 188 Ludlow Street, is a popular spot in summer, offering dozens of flavors of ice cream and sorbet.

Clothes vendors at Orchard Street market

0 meters

0 yards   500

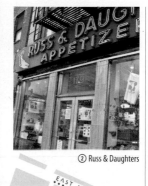

② Russ & Daughters

Chinatown

Turn around and return to Canal Street, pausing to admire the spire of the Chrysler Building and the city skyline in view in the distance from Eldridge. Turn left into Canal and cross the Bowery – as you continue, the shops give way to stalls selling an exotic array of vegetables, and butcher shops with rows of roast ducks in the windows. At 200 Canal Street is New Kam Man. One of the largest Chinese markets in the area, it is a fascinating place to explore. Turn left from Canal on to Mott Street, and you'll know you are right in the

unusual flavors, such as black sesame, taro, and zen butter, as well as more traditional ones. Turn back and walk to Mulberry Street. The curve next to Columbus Park was Mulberry Bend ⑫, once notorious for gang murders and mayhem.

⑬ An Italian deli in Little Italy

Little Italy

Walk up Mulberry Street toward Grand Street, and you are suddenly in Little Italy ⑬. Small in area though it is, and encroached on by Chinatown, this is a colorful few blocks of Old-World restaurants, coffee shops, and stores selling home-made pasta, sausages, breads, and pastries. The Italian population has dwindled over the years, but a staunch group of merchants remains, determined to retain the area's Italian atmosphere. Their stronghold is Mulberry Street, between Broome and Canal streets, with a few shops holding their own on Grand Street near Mulberry. If you continue to walk on Grand, however, you are quickly back into Chinatown.

The big event of the year is the Feast of San Gennaro, named for the patron saint of Naples. For 11 nights in September, Mulberry Street is jammed with locals and visitors enjoying the parades and the Italian food, with rows of sizzling sausage stalls.

Pretzel seller on Orchard Street

heart of Chinatown by all the Chinese neon signs. There are hundreds of restaurants here, from holes-in-the-wall to haute cuisine, all offering a chance to taste authentic Chinese food. For spiritual sustenance, visit the Eastern States Buddhist Temple ⑪ in Mott Street (64b).

At Bayard Street, stop off for an ice cream at the Chinatown Ice Cream Factory (65), which offers decidedly

New Kam Man at 200 Canal Street

A 90-Minute Walk in Greenwich Village and SoHo

A stroll through the patchwork quilt of streets in Greenwich Village takes you to where New York's best-known writers and artists have lived, worked, and played. It ends with a tour of SoHo's impressive cast-iron buildings, galleries, and shops. For more details on sights in Greenwich Village, see pages 102–111, and for SoHo sights, see pages 96–101.

⑬ Facade in Washington Mews

Author Mark Twain, who lived on 10th Street

West 10th Street

The junction of West 8th Street and 6th Avenue ① has many music and clothing stores nearby. Walk up Sixth to West Ninth Street to see (on the left at 425) Jefferson Market Courthouse ②.

Turn right at West 10th Street ③ to the Alexander Onassis Center for Hellenic Studies (58). A passageway at the front once led up to the Tile Club, a gathering place for the artists of the Tenth Street Studio, where Augustus Saint-Gaudens, John LaFarge, and Winslow Homer lived. Mark Twain lived at 24 West 10th Street, and Edward Albee resided at 50 West 10th.

Back across Sixth Avenue is Milligan Place ④, with 19th-century houses, and Patchin Place ⑤, where the poets E. E. Cummings and John Masefield both lived. Farther on is the site of the Ninth Circle bar ⑥, which when it opened in 1898 was known as "Regnaneschi's." It was the subject of John Sloan's painting *Regnaneschi's Saturday Night*. Playwright Edward Albee first saw the question "Who's afraid of Virginia Woolf?" scrawled on a mirror here.

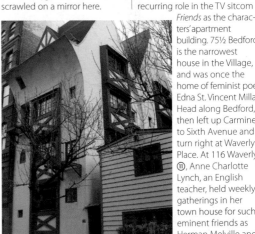

⑨ The unusual exterior of "Twin Peaks"

Greenwich Village

Turn left at Waverly Place past the Three Lives Bookstore (154 West 10th St), a typical literary gathering spot, to Christopher Street and the Northern Dispensary ⑦.

Follow Grove Street along Christopher Park to Sheridan Square, the busy hub of the Village. The Circle Repertory Theater ⑧, which premiered plays by Pulitzer Prizewinner Lanford Wilson, is now closed.

Cross Seventh Avenue and continue on Grove Street. At the corner of Bedford Street, you can't miss "Twin Peaks" ⑨ (102 Bedford), a home for artists in the 1920s. Turn back around to look at the northeast corner of Bedford and Grove streets ⑩ – the exterior of this edifice had a recurring role in the TV sitcom *Friends* as the characters' apartment building. 75½ Bedford is the narrowest house in the Village, and was once the home of feminist poet Edna St. Vincent Millay. Head along Bedford, then left up Carmine to Sixth Avenue and turn right at Waverly Place. At 116 Waverly ⑪, Anne Charlotte Lynch, an English teacher, held weekly gatherings in her town house for such eminent friends as Herman Melville and Edgar Allan Poe, who gave his first reading of *The Raven* here.

A detour left of just half a block will bring you to MacDougal Alley ⑫, a lane of carriage houses in which Gertrude Vanderbilt Whitney had her studio. She opened the first Whitney Museum here in 1932, just behind the studio.

Tips for Walkers

Starting point: 8th St/6th Ave.
Length: 2 miles (3.2 km).
Getting there: Take subway train A, B, C, D, E, or F to West 4th Street-Washington Square station (8th Street exit). Fifth Avenue buses M2 and M3 stop at 8th Street. From here, walk one block west to 6th. The M5 bus loops near Washington Square along 8th Street and up Sixth Avenue.
Stopping-off points: This walk is designed to take 90 minutes without any stops. The Pink Tea Cup, 88 Seventh Ave South, is good for lunch. Fanelli's Café, 94 Prince Street, has been serving customers since 1847 and was once a speakeasy.

Washington Square

From MacDougal, turn left to Washington Square North, to see the finest Greek Revival houses in the United States. Built of red brick, they have marble balustrades and entrances flanked by columns. Writer Henry James set his *Washington Square* in No. 18, his grandmother's home.

Washington Square Park and Arch

SoHo

Walk south on Thompson, a typical Village street lined with bars, cafés, and shops. Turn left at Houston, SoHo's northern limit, and right onto West Broadway, lined with some of the city's most famous galleries along with a large number of chic and arty boutiques.

Turn left at Spring Street for yet more tempting shops, then right at Greene Street ⑮, which is the heart of the Cast-Iron Historic District. Many of these fine buildings now house high-end stores.

Turn left at the end of Greene Street onto Canal Street, the end of SoHo, to see how quickly the atmosphere of New York can change. This noisy street is full of hawkers and discount electronics stores. You can explore bargains for the next two blocks and then turn left up Broadway. Keen shoppers can turn right back onto Spring Street and head for the NoLita district, featuring clothes by trendy, aspiring designers.

Pause at Fifth Avenue to look back at Washington Square Park, with its famous Washington Square Arch. Go across to Two Fifth Avenue; opposite is Washington Mews ⑬, an elegant carriage house complex. John Dos Passos, Edward Hopper, and Rockwell Kent lived in the studio at No. 14a at various times.

Go back up Washington Square North, past some elegant houses. Writer Edith Wharton lived at No. 7. Now walk beneath the arch and across Washington Square Park. On the left, as you leave the park, is the fine Judson Memorial Church and Tower ⑭ by Stanford White and the NYU Loeb Student Center. The Center was built in 1959 on the site of a boarding house, known as the "house of genius," where Theodore Dreiser wrote *An American Tragedy*.

⑮ Cast-iron facade, Greene Street

Key
··· Walk route

0 meters 500
0 yards 500

A Two-Hour Walk in the Upper East Side

A promenade along upper Fifth Avenue and its environs will take you past the best remaining examples of New York's turn-of-the-20th century gilded age. A stroll through the old German district of Yorkville leads to Gracie Mansion, official residence of the city's mayor, dating from 1799. For details on Upper East Side sights, see pages 178–97.

From the Frick to the Met

Begin at the Frick mansion ①, built in 1913–14 for millionaire Henry Clay Frick and home to an exquisite art collection (pp196–7). Many such mansions were built as New York's wealthiest families outdid each other with miniature Versailles châteaux and Venetian palazzos. Most of those still standing have now become either institutions or museums. The apartment building opposite the Frick is typical of those where today's affluent New Yorkers live.

⑯ Church of the Holy Trinity

East on Madison at the corner of 72nd Street, is the big Polo-Ralph Lauren store ②, the 1898 French Renaissance home of Gertrude Rhinelander Waldo. Wander inside to see the elegant restored interior.

Walk back toward Fifth on the north side of 72nd, past two limestone beauties that once housed the Lycée Français de New York ③. Continue along Fifth Avenue to 73rd Street. Turn east to 11, Joseph Pulitzer's former home ④.

A few blocks on, between Lexington and Third, is a fine row of town houses ⑤. Back on Fifth Avenue, walk to 75th Street, to see No. 1, the former residence of

⑨ Ukrainian Institute of America

Edward S. Harkness, son of a founder of Standard Oil. It is now the Commonwealth Fund ⑥. At 1 East 78th, the tobacco millionaire James B. Duke's 18th-century French-style château is now the New York University Institute of Fine Arts ⑦.

At 79th Street and Fifth, the former home of financier Payne Whitney, is the French Embassy ⑧, and 2 East 79th is the Ukrainian Institute of America ⑨. On the southeast corner of 82nd Street is Duke-Semans House ⑩, one of the few grand Fifth Avenue residences that are still privately owned. Save another full day for the Metropolitan Museum of Art ⑪ at 82nd.

86th Street 4.5.6

77th Street 6

0 meters 500
0 yards 500

Carl Schurz Park Promenade

Yorkville

Turn east on 86th
Street for what is left of
German Yorkville –
Bremen House ⑫, cross
Second Avenue,
then stop at

Key

··· Walk route

Heidelberg Café and German
deli Schaller & Weber ⑬ for a
break, or try Papaya King's hot
dogs (179 East 86th Street).

East River and Gracie Mansion
Henderson Place ⑭ at East End
Avenue is a cluster of 24 Queen
Anne town houses. Carl Schurz
Park opposite was named for the
city's most prominent
German immigrant,
editor of *Harper's
Weekly* and the *New
York Post*. The park
promenade atop
East River Drive leads
to a view of Hell Gate,
where the Harlem River,
Long Island Sound, and
New York harbor meet. From
the walkway you can see the
back of Gracie Mansion ⑮, the
mayor's official residence. Walk
northwest on 88th Street past the
Church of the Holy Trinity ⑯. Turn
right onto Lexington Avenue,
then left onto 92nd Street and
west past two of the few wooden
houses left in Manhattan ⑰.

⑲ The Cooper-Hewitt Museum

Carnegie Hill

Back on Fifth Avenue, turn downtown past the Felix Warburg
Mansion of 1908, now the Jewish
Museum ⑱, and continue to
91st Street and the huge Andrew
Carnegie home, now the Cooper
Hewitt, Smithsonian Design
Museum ⑲. Built in 1902 in the
style of an English country manor,
it gave the area the unofficial
name of Carnegie Hill. The James
Burden House ⑳ at 7 East 91st
Street, built for Vanderbilt heiress
Adele Sloan in 1905, has a spiral
staircase under a stained-glass
skylight that was known in society
as "the stairway to heaven." At
1 East 91st, the financier Otto
Kahn's Italian Renaissance-style
residence was a show place with
a drive-through porch and interior
courtyard. Like the Burden
House, it is now the Convent of
the Sacred Heart School.

⑱ Wooden houses on 92nd Street

A Three-Hour Walk in Brooklyn

A trip across New York's most famous crossing leads to Brooklyn Heights, the city's first suburb. This neighborhood has a 19th-century feel, mixed with a hint of Middle Eastern cultures. The riverfront promenade has unrivaled views of Manhattan. For more details on sights in Brooklyn, see pages 226–41.

Fire Station on Old Fulton Street

Fulton Ferry Landing
Brooklyn Bridge yields truly thrilling views of the lower New York skyline and prize photo opportunities. Take a taxi or, if you have time, walk across it to Brooklyn.

On the far side, follow the Tillary Street sign to the right, turn right at the bottom of the stairs, then take the first path through the park and walk down Cadman Plaza West ① under the Brooklyn-Queens Expressway; here Cadman becomes Old Fulton Street. You can see the bridge on the right as you head to the river at Water Street and the Fulton Ferry landing ②. During the Revolutionary War, George Washington's troops fled to

Manhattan from here. In 1814, this was the depot for the ferry connecting Brooklyn and Manhattan Island. This transformed Brooklyn Heights from a predominantly farming area to a residential district. The area is full of character and is still a very popular place to live. To the right is the River Café ③. This restaurant's fine cuisine and spectacular views of the Manhattan skyline make it one of New York's most exceptional dining spots. Double back past the former Eagle Warehouse ④ built in 1893.

Brooklyn Heights
From the landing, turn right to steep Everitt Street up Columbia Heights, on to Middagh Street, and along the streets of Brooklyn Heights. 24 Middagh ⑤ is one of the area's oldest houses, built in 1824.

Next turn right on Willow and left on Cranberry; here the town houses range from wooden clapboards to brick Federal-style to brownstones. Except for cars and a few modern buildings, you could be in the 19th century.

Many famous people have lived here. Truman Capote wrote Breakfast at Tiffany's and In Cold Blood in the basement of 70 Willow, and Arthur Miller once owned 155 Willow. Walt Whitman lived on Cranberry Street when he

④ Eagle Warehouse

was editor of the Brooklyn Eagle. He set the type for his Leaves of Grass at a print shop near the corner of Cranberry and Fulton. The town houses now on the site are called Whitman Close.

Turn right along Hicks. The Hicks family, local farmers, inspired the name "hick" for a yokel. Turn left on Orange Street to the Plymouth Church ⑥, home of Henry Ward Beecher, an antislavery preacher. His sister, Harriet Beecher Stowe, wrote Uncle Tom's Cabin. Meander along Henry

③ Entrance to the River Café

Truman Capote with feathered friend

and Pineapple streets. At Clark Street are marquees of once-luxurious hotels, such as the Towers. Follow Clark Street to 142 Columbia Heights, where Norman Mailer lived ⑦. Washington Roebling, architect of the Brooklyn Bridge, lived at 110.

The Promenade

At Montague, turn onto the riverfront Promenade ⑧. A tablet at the entrance marks the site of Four Chimneys, the house where George Washington lived during the Battle of Long Island. Walk a little farther for a stunning view of Lower Manhattan that will make you catch your breath. Savor this scene, then turn inland again, on Montague. Here, make a quick detour right to 1 Montague Terrace ⑨, where the English poet W. H. Auden lived. Thomas Wolfe finished *Of Time and the River* while he was living at 5 Montague.

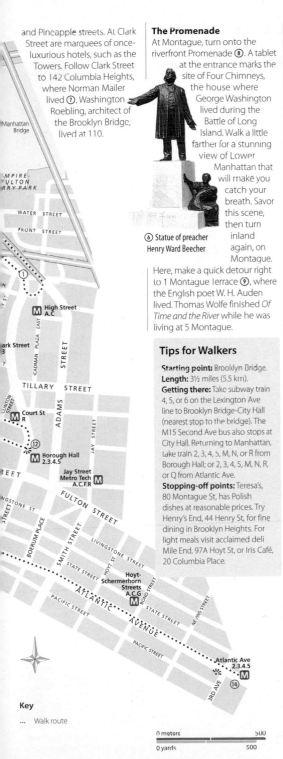

⑥ Statue of preacher Henry Ward Beecher

Tips for Walkers

Starting point: Brooklyn Bridge.
Length: 3½ miles (5.5 km).
Getting there: Take subway train 4, 5, or 6 on the Lexington Ave line to Brooklyn Bridge-City Hall (nearest stop to the bridge). The M15 Second Ave bus also stops at City Hall. Returning to Manhattan, take train 2, 3, 4, 5, M, N, or R from Borough Hall; or 2, 3, 4, 5, M, N, R, or Q from Atlantic Ave.
Stopping-off points: Teresa's, 80 Montague St, has Polish dishes at reasonable prices. Try Henry's End, 44 Henry St, for fine dining in Brooklyn Heights. For light meals visit acclaimed deli Mile End, 97A Hoyt St, or Iris Café, 20 Columbia Place.

The old Montague Street trolley, which led to the river and the ferry

Montague and Clinton Streets

Once back on Montague, walk to the heart of Brooklyn Heights, with its cafés and boutiques. The baseball team, the Brooklyn Dodgers, who relocated to Los Angeles in 1958, got their name from dodging the trolley cars that once ran down the street.

Walk to the intersection of Montague and Clinton to see the stained glass of the 1834 Church of St. Ann and the Holy Trinity ⑩. Walk a block left on Clinton to Pierrepont Street for the Brooklyn Historical Society ⑪. A block farther, at Court Street, is the 1849 Borough Hall ⑫, and the subway back to Manhattan

Brooklyn's Dodgers, who got their name from dodging trolley cars

Atlantic Avenue

Another option is to stay on Clinton Street and walk the five short blocks to Atlantic Avenue. A left turn here leads to a whole string of Middle Eastern emporia, such as Sahadi's ⑬ (at 187 Atlantic Avenue), which stocks a huge selection of foods. The Damascus Bakery at 195 makes the most delicious filo pastries. Various other shops here sell Arabic books, tapes, DVDs, and CDs.

At Flatbush Avenue, look left to the Brooklyn Academy of Music (BAM) ⑭ and the grand front of the Williamsburg Savings Bank. Watch for signs to the subway for your journey back to Manhattan.

Key

... Walk route

0 meters 500
0 yards 500

For keys to symbols *see back flap*

A 90-Minute Waterfront Walk

From the breezy Battery Park City Esplanade with its sweeping river views and upscale condos to the magnificent schooners moored at South Street Seaport, this waterfront route introduces you to New York's formidable maritime legacy. The concrete jungle may lie just a few blocks inland, yet it seems worlds away, as the bleating horns and hiss of the crosstown buses are blessedly muffled. Stroll the green tip of Battery Park for a startling reminder that Manhattan is, in fact, an island. For more details on sights in Lower Manhattan, see pp66–85.

⑤ The many photographs at the Museum of Jewish Heritage

Battery Park City

Begin your walk on the Esplanade ① near Rector Place Park, west of the Rector Street subway stop. Across the Hudson River looms the Jersey City skyline. Stroll toward the South Cove ②, where you'll catch sight, as did more than 100 million immigrants on their arrival, of Lady Liberty herself. Explore Robert F. Wagner, Jr. Park ③, named after a former New York City mayor. The leafy acres of grassy slopes, linden trees, and inviting pavilions are an important link in Lower Manhattan's waterfront

"greenbelt." Climb to the Wagner Park lookout point ④ for vistas of the Hudson River. Here, information panels chronicle New York City's seafaring history, when grand schooners and coastal packets plied these waters.

View of the Statue of Liberty from the waterfront promenade

Battery Place

On Battery Place, visit the Museum of Jewish Heritage ⑤ (see p76) and its outdoor Garden of Stones, a calm, elegant space of dwarf oak saplings growing out of boulders. Since Manhattan is the undisputed king of tall buildings, pay homage at the sleek Skyscraper Museum ⑥, a marvel in stainless steel. Admire skyscraper history and contemporary designs from around the world, as well as the original model, created in 1971, of the former World Trade Center.

⑥ Shiny surfaces and sharp angles at the Skyscraper Museum

⑨ Castle Clinton, an early 19th-century fort built to defend the harbor

Battery Park

On your way to nearby Battery Park, check out Pier A Harbor House ⑦, the wonderfully renovated 1886 grand marine firehouse. Important visitors who arrived by sea were once greeted with festive jets of water pumped into the sky by the fireboats.

The clock on the pier tower used to keep time to the maritime system – eight bells, and all's well. Continue along the waterfront, looking out for the American Merchant Mariners Memorial ⑧, a haunting sculpture of soldiers pulling a desperate comrade out of the waters, based on photographs of a World War II attack on an American ship. Head past Castle Clinton monument ⑨, a fort built during the War of

⑬ Enjoying a well earned rest at a café, South Street Seaport

1812. It later became an opera house, theater, and aquarium, but is now the ticket office for the Statue of Liberty. Stroll through the park, where you can relax on benches in the shade of trees. Continue on to State Street, turn right onto Whitehall, and then left onto South Street, passing the graceful Beaux Arts Battery Maritime Building ⑩.

South Street Seaport

Follow South Street, with the Brooklyn Bridge in the distance. Walk through the Vietnam Veterans Memorial Plaza ⑪, with its glass memorial etched with the poignant words from soldiers to their loved ones. Head north on Water Street, so named because it marks what was once the water's edge, and past Old Slip; all streets named "slip" are where boats used to dock between

piers. Look west up the famed Wall Street ⑫ (see pp68–9) as you cross it, for a view of the spires of the Trinity Church (see p71). Turn right at Maiden Lane, then left onto the quaint and cobblestoned Front Street, which feeds into South Street Seaport ⑬ (see p84), marked by the wooden masts and sails of the tall ships in the harbor. Explore New York's seafaring history at the South Street Seaport Museum, and then wander the shop-lined Fulton Street to Water Street. Take a peek into Bowne & Co Stationers at 211 ⑭, a charming old-fashioned print shop with 19th-century antique hand presses. Amble toward Pier 16 for a further glimpse of tall ships ⑮, including the massive ship, Peking. Continue on to Pier 17 ⑯, which is undergoing extensive renovations, but will soon be bustling with shops and cafés. As you walk the wooden pier, look back for a memorable view of Manhattan – the masts of ancient schooners against the city's towering skyscrapers. Finish up at the inviting Paris Café in the 1873 Meyer's Hotel.

Tips for Walkers

Starting point: The Esplanade near Rector Place.
Length: 2 miles (3.2 km).
Getting there: Take subway train 1 or R to Rector Street. Head west on Rector Street, cross the bridge over West Street to Rector Place, and walk to the Esplanade.
Stopping-off points: Gigino, on Wagner Park at 20 Battery Place, offers savory Italian fare outdoors.

Key

··· Walk route

0 meters   300
0 yards   300

A 90-Minute Walk in the East Village

Originally the farm or *bouwerie* of the Stuyvesant family, this historic area now has a different appeal thanks to its musical and artistic associations, as well as many of the city's buzzing and affordable ethnic bars and restaurants. It also manages to balance a peaceful residential area with business and creativity, which is reflected in the constantly changing trendy record shops, vegan cafés, craft stores, and live music clubs. For more details on sights in the East Village, see pp112–17.

Astor Place

Adjacent to the Astor Place subway stop is a black steel cube called the *Alamo* ① – a meeting point for students and skateboarders. Walk towards Third Avenue through the large buildings that comprise Cooper Union ② *(see p116)*. This scholarship college was founded in 1859 by Peter Cooper, an illiterate but successful business-man and proponent of free education. Across the street is the Continental ③, a live music venue that has hosted acts such as Iggy Pop and Guns N' Roses. In the East Village, 8th Street becomes St. Mark's Place ④, a former jazz, then hippie, then punk hangout. With so many sidewalk cafés and street vendors, this is one of the busiest pedestrian areas of Manhattan. St. Mark's Ale House ⑤ on the right, formerly The Five Spot, was where musicians and poets got together in the 1960s. A few steps down is Trash and Vaudeville ⑥, a punk/goth clothing store that was once the Bridge Theater. The venue was repeatedly shut down due to controversial acts, then reopened. Yoko Ono held

Locals enjoying celebrations on Ukrainian Day

"happenings," and the US flag was burned as an anti-war protest in 1967. At 19–25 St. Mark's Place ⑦, there was a Jewish hangout, then the Italian mafia ruled, until Andy Warhol turned the space into the infamous nightclub Electric Circus from 1967 to 1971. The

Velvet Underground was among the bands who played here.

Little Ukraine

Turn left onto Second Avenue, home to one of the largest and longest-standing Ukrainian populations in the US, with restaurants, bars, and centers such as the Ukrainian National Home ⑧ on the right (140), and the good-value, 24-hour Ukrainian eatery Veselka ⑨ on the corner. Farther up

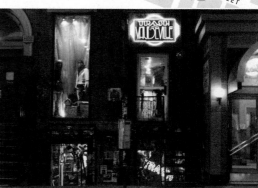
⑥ Trash and Vaudeville store, once a venue known for controversial acts

⑪ The style and elegance of an earlier century at Veniero's

Second Avenue, at East 10th Street, sits the St. Mark's-in-the-Bowery Church ⑩ *(see p117)*. Erected in 1799, this church was Dutch governor Peter Stuyvesant's private chapel, and he is buried here. More recently, the Black Panthers and Young Lords gathered here, and Allen Ginsberg and other writers contributed to The Poetry Project that exists to this day. A right on 11th Street leads to Veniero's ⑪, a stylish Italian bakery that still has many of its original details, such as hand-stamped metal ceilings. Make a right and then a left onto 10th Street, past the three-story Russian and Turkish Baths ⑫, to the northern edge of Tompkins Square ⑬ *(see p117)*.

Tompkins Square

Built in 1834, this square has seen political activism of all kinds. It is also where a sacred elm tree in the middle of the park ⑭ commemorates the first Hare Krishna ceremony on American soil. Jazz great Charlie Parker lived across the street from the park from 1950 to 1955 ⑮. Walk to the southwestern corner on 7th Street, where Miss Lily's ⑯ serves delicious Jamaican food. Down the block, Turntable Lab ⑰ sells DJ equipment and vinyl. If you are thirsty, continue west toward Second Avenue to McSorley's Old Ale House ⑱, one of the oldest bars in the city. Then get back onto Second Avenue and turn right to see where the live venue Fillmore East ⑲ operated between 1968 and 1971 (105). This classic rock scene featured such legends as The Doors, Jimi Hendrix, Janis Joplin, and Pink Floyd. The Who even premiered their rock opera *Tommy* here. Look left at 6th Street – "Indian Restaurant Row" ⑳ – where Bengali curry houses compete for business. Continue southwest down Second Avenue to number 80 ㉑; this was the home of Joe "The Boss" Masseria, head of the Italian mob in the 1920s. Turn right onto 4th Street, where KGB bar ㉒, on the right, is a literary institution. Continue straight along 4th Street to Lafayette Street, and stop off at Other Music ㉓ to check out rare and imported vinyl records. From Lafayette, great Jones Street and a final right onto Bowery lead to the former site (315) of CBGB ㉔, a former punk venue (now a John Varvatos clothing boutique) that gave many rock legends their big break.

⑭ Elm tree, a Hare Krishna memorial, in Tompkins Square Park

Key

··· Walk route

0 meters	200
0 yards	200

⑳ "Indian Restaurant Row," lined with curry houses

For keys to symbols *see back flap*

A 90-Minute Walk in Harlem

Few neighborhoods in New York are as rich in cultural history as Harlem, a haven for African-American heritage. This walk starts in Strivers' Row, one of the few areas that provided affordable housing during the 1920s and 1930s, when the area was bursting with creative and intellectual expression. It takes you past renowned gospel churches, jazz and blues clubs, and ends at the Apollo Theater, Harlem's famous showcase for new artists. For more details on sights in Harlem, see pp214–25.

⑭ Apollo Theater, famous for televised shows and legendary acts

Strivers' Row

The tree-lined area on 138th Street between Seventh and Eighth avenues is the St. Nicholas Historic District, commonly known as Strivers' Row ①. In the 1920s and 1930s wealthy and influential black professionals aiming for better lives moved into homes designed by such great architects as James Brown Lord and McKim, Mead & White. Signs on some of the gates still read "Private road walk your horses."

① An ornate doorway in Strivers' Row

renowned for its truly magnificent Sunday gospel service. Founded in 1921 and named for the East African Americans of its first congregation, this church has hosted such notable pastors as Adam Clayton Powell, Jr.

A stone's throw away on West 137th Street is the Mother Zion church ④, New York's first black church and one of America's oldest. While part of the Underground Railroad (an escape route for slaves), it acquired the nickname "Freedom Church." Continue around to 136th Street, via Malcolm X Boulevard, and the Countee Cullen Library. Next door at No. 108, Madam C. J. Walker (1896–1919) founded the Walker School of Hair ⑤. With her successful cosmetics line and hair-smoothing system, Walker was one of the first self-made female millionaires in the country. An active

A short detour left on Seventh Avenue (Adam Clayton Powell, Jr. Boulevard) and right on 139th Street leads to West 139th Street ②, where in 1932 16-year-old Billie Holiday moved into No. 108 shortly before landing her first singing job at a club in nearby "Jungle Alley."

Abyssinian Baptist Church

Turn right at Malcolm X Boulevard and right back onto 138th Street toward the striking Abyssinian Baptist Church ③ (see p223), which is internationally

philanthropist, she donated to many African-American charities such as the National Association of Colored People (NAACP) and Tuskegee Institute. After her death, her daughter A'Leila turned the salon into an intellectual center for artists, scholars, and activists. It was named "The Dark Tower" after Harlem writer Countee Cullen's protest poem. Back around the corner on Malcolm X Boulevard is

the Schomburg Center for Research into Black Culture ⑥ (see p223), a national research library named for the Puerto Rican-born black scholar who donated his personal collection to the library and served as its curator for six years. Back along West 136th Street at No. 267 is "Niggerati Manor" ⑦, an artist's rooming house, so named by Zora Neale Hurston, who lived here while collaborating with Wallace Thurman, Aaron Douglas, and Bruce

⑩ The famous Sylvia's restaurant, providing authentic soul food

Nugent on *Fire!!*, a magazine devoted to young black artists. Get back on Adam Clayton Powell, Jr. Boulevard and follow it down to West 133rd Street, home to "Jungle Alley" ⑧, the former highlight of Harlem nightlife, which once contained numerous bars, clubs, cabarets, and speakeasies. A detour across 131st Street will bring you to the house ⑨ (235) of Marcus Garvey, a major leader and

⑥ Art displays at the Schomberg Center for Research into Black Culture

② The great jazz singer Billie Holiday

⑧ "Jungle Alley," where Billie Holiday first performed

```
0 meters    200
0 yards     200
```

well as a taste, of modern, trendy Harlem. Continue down to 125th Street, where Malcolm X preached in the 1950s and 1960s – this is also where Bill Clinton established his offices in 2001. In the middle of the next block is The Studio Museum in Harlem ⑬ *(see pp224–5)*, with a variety of contemporary art exhibits, programs, lectures, and performances by artists of African descent. Its store is also worth a browse for its array of posters and books.

Apollo Theater

On West 125th Street is the famous Apollo Theater ⑭ *(see p224)*, where since 1934 "stars are born and legends are made." These performers have ranged in style from Ella Fitzgerald to James Brown. Since 1987, "Amateur Night at the Apollo" has been televised nationwide, and the theater has become one of the most popular tourist destinations in Manhattan.

fierce proponent of black unity, economic independence, and pride. Return to Adam Clayton Powell, Jr Boulevard and make a left on 127th Street until you reach Sylvia's Restaurant ⑩ *(see p224)*, the self-proclaimed "Queen of Soul Food." Family-owned since 1962, Sylvia's serves authentic Southern favorites, such as fried chicken, catfish, and BBQ ribs. Alternatively, stay on Lenox Avenue until 125th Street, where you'll find Red Rooster Harlem ⑪. Stop off here for a glimpse, as

Tips for Walkers

Starting point: Strivers' Row.
Length: 1.75 miles (2.8 km)
Getting there: Take subway train 2 or 3 to 135th St and Lenox Ave, then walk north to 138th St and west to Seventh Ave. Or take M2, M7, or M10 bus to 135th St and walk to Seventh Ave.
Stopping-off Points: Sylvia's on 127th and Lenox is Harlem's most famous soul food restaurant. It is the perfect place to refuel.

Key

··· Walk route

TRAVELERS' NEEDS

WHERE TO STAY

With over 110,000 hotel rooms available, New York offers something for everyone. The city's top hotels are among the most expensive in the US, but there are also many budget and mid-priced hotels. While some of these are basic rather than charming, they offer good value. Other budget options are furnished apartments and studios, and bed and breakfasts, as well as youth hostels and YMCAs. The hotels listed in this guide have been selected for their value, location, and amenities. Entries are separated by theme and price, helping you choose accommodations that best suit your needs. Hotels highlighted as DK Choice offer something special, such as beautiful interiors or remarkable service.

Rooftop terrace at the Peninsula New York (see p289)

Where to Look

The East Side, roughly between 59th and 77th streets, is the traditional location for luxury hotels. The renovation of some landmark Midtown properties by famous hotel chains, however, such as the St. Regis by Starwood, and the former Gotham Hotel, which is now the Peninsula New York, has considerably increased the competition in this price range.

Business travelers tend to favor Midtown, especially the moderately priced hotels lining Lexington Avenue near Grand Central Terminal.

Those seeking relative quiet with access to Midtown should look in the Murray Hill area, while theater-lovers should consider the Times Square area, where there are many hotels within walking distance of the bustling Theater District.

There are a number of good, inexpensive hotels around Herald Square, which is convenient for shopping. Trendy boutique hotels have flourished in SoHo and Lower Manhattan, where there are also plenty of good bars, restaurants, and upscale shops (see pp314–15) as well as fashionable nightclubs.

Harlem has a range of affordable B&Bs, while areas in Brooklyn, such as Williamsburg, boast excellent budget options and plenty of boutique hotels. For more information on specific areas, view the section on Recommended Hotels (see pp282–3).

Hidden Extras

When calculating the cost of hotels in New York, it is not enough simply to take into consideration the quoted room price. Hotel rooms are subject to a total 14.75 per cent tax, plus $3.50 per night per room fee.

Several hotels now include continental breakfast in the room price. This represents a big saving, since standard hotel continental breakfast prices, before tax and tip, start at about $10 and soar to $25 in some of the luxury hotels. To save money, head for the nearest deli or coffee shop and leave the hotel to businesspeople having power breakfasts.

Hotel telephone charges are always high; it is usually much less expensive to use a cell phone, or Wi-Fi (usually free).

Tips are expected. Staff who take your luggage to the room are usually tipped a minimum of $1 per bag – more in a luxury hotel. The concierge need not be tipped for normal services such as arranging transportation or making dinner reservations, but should be rewarded for exceptional services. When you order from room service, a service charge will usually be included in the bill; if not, a 15–20 per cent tip is customary. Solo travelers will find that single room rates are usually at least 80 per cent of the double rate and are sometimes the same as for two people.

Antique furnishings, Inn at Irving Place (see p284)

The Roxy Hotel lobby *(see p285)*

Facilities

Television, radio, and at least one telephone are usually provided in every room, even in modest lodgings, and most hotel bedrooms have private bathrooms. In budget and mid-priced hotels, a shower, rather than a tub, is the norm. Many hotels offer Internet access (often with free Wi-Fi), a business center, and a health club or exercise room. Luxury facilities include minibars in the room, dual phones, private phone-message systems, and electronic checkout.

Although you'd expect hotel rooms in New York City to be noisy, most windows are double- or even triple-glazed to keep out the noise. Air conditioning is a standard feature, so there is no need to open the windows in hot weather. Even so, some rooms are obviously quieter than others, especially if they are at the back of the hotel or overlooking a courtyard – check when reserving. Light sleepers may also want to request a room away from the elevator.

Most of the hotels listed here are within a few minutes' walk of shops and restaurants. Few hotels have their own parking, but valets may park your car in nearby garages. A reduced (but still expensive) daily parking fee is normally offered. If there is no concierge at the hotel, front desk staff will always help to answer any queries.

How to Reserve

It is advisable to make hotel reservations months in advance; otherwise, you may well find that the best rooms and rates have been taken. Most hotels in New York are booked through much of the year, but the busiest periods are at Easter, the New York Marathon week in late October or early November, Thanksgiving, and Christmas.

The easiest way to book a hotel room directly is through the hotel's website. You may be required to pay a deposit or provide a credit card number to secure the booking. Print out a copy of the booking confirmation to give to the hotel when you check in. Reservations through third party websites such as www.expedia.com and www.hotels.com can offer the best value for money.

Most hotels have a toll-free telephone number for use in the United States, but these numbers do not work from Europe and the UK. If the hotel is part of an international chain, an affiliated hotel in your country should be able to reserve a room for you.

Special Rates

Hotels are busiest during the week, when business travelers are in the city, so most of them offer budget weekend packages. It's often possible to move from a standard to a luxury room for the weekend at the same rate.

A lower corporate rate is usually available to employees of large companies. Quite often reservation clerks will grant corporate discounts on request without asking for a company affiliation. It is also worth checking a hotel website for special deals and promotions.

Some reservation agencies offer discount rates. A good travel agent should be able to get the best rates, but compare prices by contacting directly a discount reservation service such as **Quikbook** *(see p283)*, which offers discounts of 20–50 per cent, depending on the time of year. You reserve by credit card and receive a voucher, which you present to the hotel. Sites such as www.kayak.com offer "private sales" of discounted hotel rooms.

Package tours can also provide savings. Their rates may not oblige you to stay with a tour group, only to use their air and hotel arrangements. They may also include airport transfers, an additional saving. Airlines frequently have special deals, particularly during slow travel seasons. A knowledgeable travel agent should be able to tell you the current best deals, but searching online might be an easier and quicker way to find limited offers that can be booked directly. At off-peak times you may net even bigger savings than with the package plans.

Understated elegance at the stylish Kitano *(see p289)*

Travelers with Disabilities

By law, new hotels must provide facilities for disabled visitors. Many older buildings have also been renovated so as to comply with this regulation.

To find out which hotels offer the best facilities, check their websites. These are provided for all the hotels listed on pp284–9. When booking, let the hotel know of any specific needs. Guide dogs are allowed in most hotels, but it is also advisable to check in advance.

The **Mayor's Office for People with Disabilities** produces the "Official Accessibility Guide," with useful information about hotels for disabled travelers.

Traveling with Children

American hotels are generally very welcoming toward children. Cots or cribs as well as lists of reliable babysitters are usually available, and most hotel restaurants cater to young guests.

Traveling with children need not be expensive. Many hotels do not charge for children if they stay in their parents' room, or make only a small charge for an extra bed. There is usually a limit of one or two children per room in these cases, and most hotels stipulate that the children must be under a certain age, most often 12. Parents of older children are expected to pay the full price, although the age limit is occasionally extended to 18. Ask about family rates when you make your reservation.

Budget Accommodations

Though primarily located in the outer boroughs, bed-and-breakfast accommodations in private apartments are also available in Manhattan. While they are often reasonably priced, the higher budget options provide a very personable experience as well. Bed-and-breakfast lodgings can be found through many free booking services. Some agencies have a two-or-more-night minimum stay. Rates for a double room typically start at $130 a night, depending on whether you have a private bathroom.

Sitting area at the Akwaaba Mansion *(see p284)*

Increasingly, one of the most affordable ways to stay in New York is by renting out a private room or property. A number of services facilitate this, including the very popular – and well run – **Airbnb** (www.airbnb.com), which offers a wide range of accommodation in over 35,000 private homes and apartments in New York, from town houses on the Upper East Side to student flats in the East Village and Brooklyn. There are currently regulations that restrict the rental of entire apartments for 30 days or less, as opposed to a room in a shared apartment, so it is best to check the situation with the property host before booking.

Another source for budget lodging is **Couchsurfing** (www.couchsurfing.org), which has many member-hosts in New York. Rates for private apartments vary from about $100 to $300. Be aware that if the address is remote or inconveniently far from bus routes or subway stations, your costs will rise, as you will need frequent cabs. Ask about location and amenities when you reserve.

New York's youth hostel and **YMCA** dormitories offer lodgings for those on a tighter budget. For the longer-term visitor, the **92nd Street Y**, a non-sectarian hostel in the Upper East Side, has good-value rooms, with prices starting from around $1,900 a month. There are no campsites in Manhattan, and, sadly, youth hostels are not as prevalent in New York as they are in large European cities. For those looking for the bare essentials, inexpensive rooms are available in several areas, particularly in Chelsea, the Garment District, and the Upper West Side, and to a lesser extent in such prime neighborhoods as Upper Midtown. Although some of these budget-price rooms are comfortable, with private baths or showers, others may be rather small, perhaps with no air conditioning and shared bathrooms.

Suites

If you'd like extra space – or are planning on an extended stay in NYC – opt for an apartment or all-suite hotel, which feature sizeable kitchenettes. Suites offer extra space plus cooking facilities and a refrigerator. Most suites can accommodate up to four people, which makes them popular with families.

Beyond Manhattan

As Manhattan becomes more expensive, accommodation options are emerging in the outer boroughs for savvy travelers. In addition to Brooklyn and Harlem, cheaper chain hotels can be found in the outer boroughs of Queens, Staten Island, and the Bronx. Across the Hudson, Jersey City offers budget apartment rentals, along with boutique and business hotels. Visitors can find apartments on Airbnb, often rented out at a fraction of the price of similar apartments in Manhattan.

As always, cheaper deals can often be negotiated or found on hotel websites.

Recommended Hotels

Our hotels are divided up into five categories: Bed-and-Breakfast (B&B), Boutique, Budget, Business, and Luxury. B&Bs offer a friendly, personable experience, with cozy rooms and a hearty breakfast. Boutique hotels are generally smaller, chain establishments with high design elements. Budget stays come in a variety of packages, from quaint hostels and rooms with kitchenettes, to superb-value hotels. Business hotels feature sleek and contemporary rooms, and business amenities, from Wi-Fi and business centers to meeting rooms with audio and visual technology. Luxury hotels encompass the finest of New York's upscale hotels, with many luxury amenities, from spas to celebrity-chef restaurants.

Our hotels are further divided into five geographical areas, which encompass the various areas that form this guide: **Downtown** is a richly varied area that spans Lower Manhattan and the Civic Center, the Lower East Side, SoHo and TriBeCa, Greenwich Village, the East Village,

View of the stunning Ritz-Carlton (see p288) in Battery Park

and Gramercy and the Flatiron District. **Midtown** covers both Lower and Upper Midtown, as well as Chelsea and the Garment District, and Midtown West and the Theater District, which is popular with visitors who are in town

to see Broadway shows. **Upper Manhattan** includes the Upper East Side, which features many of New York City's most upscale hotels, plus the Upper West Side, and Morningside Heights and Harlem, which has a broad range of hotels. **Brooklyn**, an up-and-coming location for boutique hotels and B&Bs, has a variety of accommodation, while **Farther Afield** includes notable options in Queens.

Look out for listings labeled as DK Choice. These hotels have been highlighted because they offer a special experience – either for superlative service, beautiful interiors and rooms, top-notch amenities and gadgets, an excellent on-site restaurant or rooftop bar, or a combination of these.

DIRECTORY

Airport Reservations

Accommodations Plus
JFK International Airport.
Tel 800-733-7666.

Meegan Services
JFK International Airport.
Tel (718) 995-9292.

Discount Reservation Services

Booking.com
Tel 888-850-3958.
W booking.com

Expedia
W expedia.co.uk

Hotels.com
Tel 800-246-8357.
W hotels.com

Kayak
W kayak.com

lastminute.com
Tel 0800 083 4000.
W lastminute.com

Quikbook
Tel (212) 779-7666.
W quikbook.com

Trivago
W trivago.com

Disabled Travelers

Mayor's Office for People with Disabilities
100 Gold St, 2nd floor, NY, NY 10038.
Tel (212) 788-2830.
W nyc.gov/mopd

Budget Accommodation

92nd Street Y
1395 Lexington Ave, NY, NY 10128.
Map 17 A2.
Tel (212) 415-5650.
W 92y.org

Affordable New York City
Tel (212) 533-4001.
W affordablenewyorkcity.com

Airbnb
W airbnb.co.uk

At Home in NY
Tel (212) 956-3125.
W athomeny.com

Chelsea Hostel
251 W 20th St, NY, NY 10011.
Map 8 D5.
Tel (212) 647-0010.
W chelseahostel.com

City Lights Bed & Breakfast

Tel (212) 737-7049.
W citylightsnewyork.com

City Sonnet
Tel (212) 614-3034.
W citysonnet.com

Couchsurfing
W couchsurfing.org

Hosteling International, NY
891 Amsterdam Ave at W 103rd St, NY, NY 10025.
Map 20 E5.
Tel (212) 932-2300.
W hinewyork.org

New York's Jazz Hostels
W jazzhostels.com

Vanderbilt YMCA
224 E 47th St, NY, NY 10017.
Map 13 A5.
Tel (212) 912-2500.
W ymcanyc.org

YMCA–West Side
5 W 63rd St, NY, NY 10023.
Map 12 D2.
Tel (917) 441-8800.
W ymcanyc.org

Suite Hotels

Affinia Hotels
Reservations:
Tel (212) 465-3661.
Toll-free: 866-246 2203.
W affinia.com

Beekman Tower
3 Mitchell Pl. Map 13 C5.
Tel 888-754-8044.
W thebeekmanhotel.com

The Benjamin
125 E 50th St.
Map 13 B4.
Tel (212) 715-2500.
W thebenjamin.com

Eastgate Tower
222 E 39th St.
Map 9 B1.

The Phillips Club
155 West 66th St.
Map 12 D2.
Tel 887-644-8900.
W phillipsclub.com

The Surrey
20 E 76th St.
Map 17 A5.
Tel (212) 905-1477.
W thesurrey.com

Where to Stay

Bed-and-Breakfast

Downtown

Inn at Irving Place $$
56 Irving Place, 10003
Tel (212) 533-4600   **Map** 9 A5
W innatirving.com
Exclusive, impeccable
guesthouse in two magnificent
adjoining brownstones.

Upper Manhattan

The Harlem Flophouse $
242 West 123rd St, 10027
Tel (347) 632-1960   **Map** 21 A2
W harlemflophouse.com
Beautiful 1890s brownstone
with four rooms and two shared
bathrooms, that have antique
clawfoot tubs.

Sugar Hill Harlem Inn $$
460 West 141st St, 10031
Tel (212) 234-5432   **Map** 19 A2
W sugarhillharleminn.com
Eco-friendly hotel set in a
charming Victorian town house
from 1906. Serves organic food.

Brooklyn

DK Choice

Akwaaba Mansion $
*347 MacDonough St,
Bedford-Stuyvesant, 11233*
Tel (718) 455-5958
W akwaaba.com
This sophisticated inn offers
themed rooms with Afro-
centric interiors, featuring
Adrinkra fabrics and Daffodil
rag dolls. The inn has a lovely
tearoom and a sunny porch.
Southern-style breakfasts.

Chic interiors and classy lounge area at
Hotel Giraffe, Downtown

Bibi's Garden Bed & Breakfast $
762 Westminster Rd, 11230
Tel (718) 434-3119
W bibisgarden.net
Victorian house with lovely rooms
decorated with antiques. Offers
continental breakfast spread.

The Sofia Inn $
288 Park Place, 11238
Tel (917) 865-7428   **Map** 23 C4
W brooklynbedandbreakfast.net
Historic B&B with traditional
rooms and hardwood floors.
Check out the garden with its
private bath.

Boutique

Downtown

Duane Street Hotel $$
130 Duane St, 10013
Tel (212) 964-4600   **Map** 1 B1
W duanestreethotel.com
Intimate hotel with sleek, loft-
style rooms, smart urban design,
and an inviting restaurant.

Gild Hall $$
15 Gold St, 10038
Tel (212) 232-7700   **Map** 2 D2
W thompsonhotels.com
Elegant hotel with a classy wood-
paneled library and a Champagne
bar. Its proximity to Wall Street
attracts corporate travelers.

DK Choice

Hotel Giraffe $$
365 Park Ave South, 10016
Tel (212) 685-7700   **Map** 9 A4
W hotelgiraffe.com
This hotel is the epitome of
boutique elegance, with a light-
filled lobby and a baby grand
piano. Impeccable rooms with
velveteen chairs and French
doors. There's a rooftop garden
bar. Complimentary breakfast.

Hotel on Rivington $$
107 Rivington St, 10002
Tel (212) 475-2600   **Map** 5 A3
W hotelonrivington.com
Fashionable hotel with spacious
rooms, plush decor, and great
floor-to-ceiling views.

The James $$
27 Grand St, 10013
Tel (212) 465-2000   **Map** 4 E4
W jameshotels.com
Elegant rooms with natural linens,
and rain showers in the
bathrooms. Rooftop bar with
glittering skyline views.

Price Guide

Prices are based on one night's stay in
high season for a standard double room,
inclusive of service charges and taxes.

$	under $200
$$	$200 to $400
$$$	over $400

The Marcel at Gramercy $$
201 East 24th St, 10010
Tel (212) 696-3800   **Map** 9 B4
W themarcelatgramercy.com
Chic rooms with rain showers
in the bathrooms. Beds have
luxurious Italian linens.

Nolitan $$
30 Kenmare St, 10012
Tel (212) 925-2555   **Map** 4 F4
W nolitanhotel.com
Charming and pet-friendly hotel.
Many rooms have private
balconies and rain showers.

The Roger New York $$
131 Madison Ave, 10016
Tel (212) 448-7000   **Map** 9 A3
W therogernewyork.com
Warm, inviting hotel with lots
of amenities. There are terrace
rooms with private balconies.

SIXTY SoHo $$
60 Thompson St, 10012
Tel (877) 431-0400   **Map** 4 D4
W sixtyhotels.com
Very elegant, minimalist rooms
with top-notch gadgets. There's
a fashionable rooftop bar, and a
lovely Italian restaurant.

SoHo Grand Hotel $$
301 West Broadway, 10013
Tel (212) 965-3000   **Map** 4 E4
W sohogrand.com
Sophisticated hotel with tastefully
done-up rooms. The building is
17-stories high with great views
of downtown Manhattan.

**The Standard
East Village** $$
25 Cooper Square, 10003
Tel (212) 475-5700   **Map** 4 F2
W standardhotels.com
Eye-catching hotel designed
by Carlos Zapata. Comfy
rooms with all modern
amenities. Complimentary
continental breakfast.

Wall Street Inn $$
9 South William St, 10004
Tel (212) 747-1500   **Map** 1 C3
W thewallstreetinn.com
This business-friendly hotel
was once owned by the
Lehman Brothers. Comfortable
rooms with period American
interiors and cozy beds.

Washington Square Hotel $$
103 Waverly Place, 10011
Tel (212) 777-9515 **Map** 4 D2
W washingtonsquarehotel.com
A stylish marble lobby gives way to comfy rooms, some with views of lush Washington Square Park.

The Bowery Hotel $$$
335 Bowery, 10003
Tel (212) 505-9100 **Map** 4 F3
W theboweryhotel.com
Luxurious, fashionable hotel with earthy touches such as fireplaces and wood-paneling.

Crosby Street Hotel $$$
79 Crosby St, 10012
Tel (212) 226-6400 **Map** 4 E3
W firmdalehotels.com
A slice of upscale London in the heart of SoHo. Cheerful rooms and afternoon tea.

The Evelyn $$$
7 East 27th St, 10016
Tel (212) 545-8000 **Map** 8 F3
W theevelyn.com
With a modern decor, this hotel has a wide range of accommodation options to suit all budgets.

The Mercer Hotel $$$
147 Mercer St, 10012
Tel (212) 966-6060 **Map** 4 E3
W mercerhotel.com
Intimate hotel with loft-style rooms and an excellent New American restaurant.

Roxy Hotel $$$
2 Sixth Ave, 10013
Tel (212) 519-6600 **Map** 3 F5
W roxyhotelnyc.com
A grand atrium lobby leads to well-appointed rooms. Enjoy top-shelf cocktails at the Church Bar.

Sixty LES $$$
190 Allen St, 10002
Tel (877) 460-8888 **Map** 5 A3
W sixtyhotels.com
Industrial-chic hotel decorated with contemporary art. Unique Andy Warhol filmstrip pool on the roof.

Smyth Tribeca $$$
85 West Broadway, 10007
Tel (212) 587-7000 **Map** 1 B1
W thompsonhotels.com
Modern hotel with classic touches, sleek and sizeable rooms, and marble bathrooms.

Midtown

Roger Smith Hotel $
501 Lexington Ave, 10022
Tel (212) 755-1400 **Map** 13 A5
W rogersmith.com

Colorful outdoor seating with great views at The Standard High Line, Midtown

Charming, arty hotel, set in a 1929 building. The rooms are individually decorated with unique, handpicked furnishings.

70 Park Avenue Hotel $$
70 Park Ave, 10016
Tel (212) 973-2400 **Map** 9 A1
W 70parkave.com
Pet-friendly, inviting hotel with elegant rooms and a nightly hosted wine hour. Offers eco-friendly, in-room spa service.

The Benjamin $$
125 East 50th St, 10022
Tel (212) 715-2500 **Map** 13 A4
W thebenjamin.com
Classic hotel with a focus on comfortable beds, including a plush pillow menu.

Bryant Park $$
40 West 40th St, 10018
Tel (212) 869-0100 **Map** 8 F1
W bryantparkhotel.com
Modern, minimalist rooms with excellent amenities, plus a huge underground bar with live DJs. Helpful staff.

Dylan $$
52 East 41st St, 10017
Tel (212) 338-0500 **Map** 9 A1
W dylanhotel.com
Set in a Beaux Arts building, with handsome walnut furnishings and a steakhouse restaurant.

Eventi Hotel $$
851 6th Ave, 10001
Tel (212) 564-4567 **Map** 8 E3
W eventihotel.com
Warm and colorful rooms, floor-to-ceiling windows, and great service in the heart of Chelsea.

Hotel Americano $$
518 West 27th St, 10001
Tel (212) 216-0000 **Map** 7 C3
W hotel-americano.com
Part of the hip Mexican chain, this hotel has sleek, minimalist

rooms. Charming rooftop bar and pool.

Ink 48 $$
653 11th Ave, 10036
Tel (212) 757-0088 **Map** 11 B5
W ink48.com
Brightly colored rooms with skyline views. Sip cocktails under the stars in the rooftop bar.

Kimberly Hotel $$
145 East 50th St, 10022
Tel (212) 755-0400 **Map** 13 A5
W kimberlyhotel.com
This low-profile hotel should not be under estimated; great value for money, with well-appointed and spacious rooms.

The Maritime $$
363 West 16th St, 10011
Tel (212) 242-4300 **Map** 8 D5
W themaritimehotel.com
Trendy hotel with a nautical theme. Porthole windows in the rooms have views of the Hudson River.

Morgans $$
237 Madison Ave, 10016
Tel (212) 686-0300 **Map** 9 A8
W morganshotel.com
Chic hotel with New York taxi-inspired black-and-white checkered pattern throughout. Complimentary continental breakfast.

DK Choice

The Standard High Line $$
848 Washington St, 10014
Tel (212) 645-4646
Map 3 B1
W standardhotels.com
Soaring, ultra-trendy hotel with fabulous views of the Hudson River. Impeccable rooms, floor-to-ceiling wall-to-wall windows, and exceptional service standards.

For more information on types of hotels *see pp282–3*

Eye-catching art adorns the walls at the Ace Hotel, Midtown

The Strand $$
33 West 37th St, 10018
Tel (212) 448-1024   **Map** 8 F2
🔲 thestrandnyc.com
Fashionable hotel with vintage
Condé Nast prints on the walls
and a breezy rooftop bar.

Ace Hotel $$$
20 West 29th St, 10001
Tel (212) 679-2222   **Map** 8 F3
🔲 acehotel.com
A chic, rock-and-roll hotel, with
over 200 rooms, most featuring
art by local and international artists.

Andaz 5th Avenue $$$
485 5th Ave, 10017
Tel (212) 601-1234   **Map** 8 F1
🔲 newyork.5thavenue.andaz.hyatt.
com
Enjoy a charming stay at this
hypoallergenic hotel with state-
of-the-art air purification system.

Casablanca Hotel $$$
147 West 43rd St, 10036
Tel (212) 869-1212   **Map** 8 E1
🔲 casablancahotel.com
Moroccan-themed hotel with
complimentary nightly cheese-
and-wine receptions.

The Chatwal $$$
130 West 44th St, 10036
Tel (212) 764-6200   **Map** 12 E5
🔲 thechatwalny.com
Art Deco meets contemporary
decor in this sophisticated hotel
filled with eye-catching art.

Library Hotel $$$
299 Madison Ave, 10017
Tel (212) 983-4500   **Map** 9 A1
🔲 libraryhotel.com
A library theme drives the decor,
with books running throughout.
A poetry garden features.

The Nomad Hotel $$$
1170 Broadway, 10001
Tel (212) 796-1500   **Map** 8 F3
🔲 thenomadhotel.com

Beautifully restored Beaux Arts
hotel with a very popular bar
and lounge.

**St. Giles New York –
The Court & The Tuscany** $$$
120–130 East 39th St, 10016
Tel (212) 686-1600   **Map** 9 A1
🔲 stgiles.com/new-york
Matched set of well-appointed
hotels with elegant, spacious
rooms, and stylish lounges.

Upper Manhattan

6 Columbus $$
6 Columbus Circle, 10019
Tel (212) 204-3000   **Map** 12 D3
🔲 sixtyhotels.com
Colorful 1960s Modernist decor,
original artwork, a rooftop lounge,
and an excellent sushi bar.

Bentley Hotel $$
500 East 62nd St, 10065
Tel (212) 644-6000   **Map** 13 C2
🔲 bentleyhotelnyc.com
Towering hotel with stellar views of
the East River. Rooms are comfortable with designer amenities.

NYLO New York City $$
2178 Broadway, 10024
Tel (212) 362-1100   **Map** 15 C5
🔲 nylohotels.com
Stylish rooms, many of which
have balconies. Beautiful views of
the city skyline. There are also two
great on-site restaurants to enjoy.

Budget
Downtown

Blue Moon Hotel $
100 Orchard St, 10002
Tel (212) 533-9080   **Map** 5 A3
🔲 bluemoon-nyc.com
A former tenement, this hotel
offers cozy rooms with modern
amenities. Complimentary
continental breakfast included.

Gatsby Hotel $
135 East Houston St, 10002
Tel (212) 358-8844   **Map** 5 A3
🔲 gatsbyhotelnyc.com
Snug, clean, and well-maintained
rooms, with sturdy furnishings
and flatscreen TVs.

Hotel 17 $
225 East 17th St, 10003
Tel (212) 475-2845   **Map** 9 B5
🔲 hotel17ny.com
Small but clean rooms with tidy
bathrooms. It was featured in a
Woody Allen movie in the 1990s.

Hotel 31 $
129 East 31st St, 10016
Tel (212) 685-3060   **Map** 9 A3
🔲 hotel31.com
Sister property to Hotel 17, with
simple but well-kept rooms and
cable TV.

Larchmont $
27 West 11th St, 10011
Tel (212) 989-9333   **Map** 4 D1
🔲 larchmonthotel.com
Simple, well-maintained
rooms in the West Village.
Basic amenities and TVs.

Off Soho Suites $
11 Rivington St, 10002
Tel (212) 979-9808   **Map** 5 A3
🔲 offsoho.com
Well-maintained budget
suites with either private or
shared kitchens.

Union Square Inn $
209 East 14th St, 10003
Tel (212) 614-0500   **Map** 4 F1
🔲 unionsquareinn.com
Basic but clean apartments and
rooms, most with kitchenettes.
Lower rates for extended stays.

Midtown

American Dream $
168 East 24th St, 10010
Tel (212) 260-9779   **Map** 9 A4
🔲 americandreamhostel.com
This friendly, well-located hostel
offers complimentary Wi-Fi and
good continental breakfast.

Americana Inn $
69 West 38th St, 10018
Tel (212) 840-6700   **Map** 8 F1
🔲 theamericanainn.com
Basic rooms with shared
bathrooms. Each floor has
a communal kitchenette.

Belvedere Hotel $
319 West 48th St, 10036
Tel (212) 245-7000   **Map** 12 D5
🔲 belvederehotelnyc.com
Family-friendly, spacious rooms
in soothing earthy colors. Lively
Brazilian restaurant.

Chelsea International Hostel $
251 West 20th St, 10011
Tel (212) 647-0010   **Map** 8 D5
W chelseahostel.com
One of the city's best hostels – a
variety of accommodations from
dorms to private rooms.

Chelsea Lodge $
318 West 20th St, 10011
Tel (212) 243-4499   **Map** 8 D5
W chelsealodge.com
This restored town house has
small rooms with wood floors,
and clean, shared bathrooms.

Colonial House Inn $
318 West 22nd St, 10011
Tel (212) 243-9669   **Map** 8 D4
W colonialhouseinn.com
Gay-friendly townhouse inn
with modern rooms, some with
private bathrooms and fireplaces.

**Fitzpatrick Grand
Central Hotel** $
141 East 44th St, 10017
Tel (212) 351-6800   **Map** 13 A5
W fitzpatrickhotels.com
Warm and inviting rooms, some
with canopied beds. Check out
the bustling on-site pub.

Hotel NYMA $
6 West 32nd St, 10001
Tel (212) 643-7100   **Map** 8 E3
W applecorehotels.com
Tasteful rooms in shades of
soothing brown and beige, with
flatscreen TVs and coffeemakers.

Pod 39 $
145 East 39th St, 10016
Tel (877) 358-0617   **Map** 9 A1
W podhotel.com
Snug but smartly furnished
rooms with flatscreen TVs and
bathrooms with rain showers.

DK Choice

Pod 51 $
230 East 51st St, 10022
Tel (212) 355-0300   **Map** 13 B4
W podhotel.com
One of New York City's best
budget hotels – rooms are
small and "pod-like" but savvily
outfitted with colorful furnishings,
comfortable beds, and flatscreen
TVs. The lobby features bright
murals, communal tables, a
friendly concierge, and a café/bar
with a daily happy hour. Relax
on the rooftop, surrounded by
the skyscrapers of Midtown.

La Quinta Manhattan $
17 West 32nd St, 10001
Tel (212) 736-1600   **Map** 8 E3
W applecorehotels.com
Comfortable rooms with coffee

machines. Complimentary
breakfast; lovely rooftop bar.

Riff Hotel Chelsea $
300 West 30th St, 10011
Tel (212) 244-7827   **Map** 8 D3
W riffchelsea.com
With interiors inspired by the
New York party scene of the
1980s, this quirky hotel offers
guests an interesting stay. Both
private and shared bathrooms
are available.

Vanderbilt YMCA $
224 East 47th St, 10017
Tel (212) 912-2500   **Map** 13 B5
W ymcanyc.org/vanderbilt
Small, quiet hostel accommo-
dation close to Grand Central.
Amenities include a launderette,
gym, and swimming pool.

Yotel $
570 10th Ave, 10036
Tel (646) 449-7700   **Map** 7 C1
W yotel.com
A massive hotel with snug rooms
and jaunty, space-age decor.
Automated check in/ checkout.

Upper Manhattan

Astor on the Park $
465 Central Park West, 10025
Tel (212) 866-1880   **Map** 21 A5
Snug, clean rooms with cable TV
and marble bathrooms. Snack
machines and laundry services
are available.

**Chic & Budget Rooms
& Apartments** $
269 West 131st St, 10027
Tel (917) 464-3528   **Map** 21 A1
W chicandbudget.com
These comfortable, well-
maintained apartments have
been built in historic brownstones in Harlem. The rooms
come with modern amenities.

Snug rooms and classy wooden flooring,
Chelsea Lodge, Midtown

**Hostelling International
New York** $
891 Amsterdam Ave, 10025
Tel (212) 932-2300   **Map** 20 E5
W hinewyork.org
A vast building resembling a
campus dorm, with a cafeteria,
game room, and picnic tables.

Jazz on the Park $
36 West 106th St, 10025
Tel (212) 932-1600   **Map** 21 A5
W jazzhostels.com
A lively, arty, hostel with simple
dorm rooms, complimentary
breakfast, and a coffeehouse
with live music.

Mount Morris House $
12 Mt Morris Park West, 10027
Tel (917) 478-6214   **Map** 21 B2
W mountmorrishouseandb.com
Originally built in 1888, this
elegant brownstone has five
cozy suites. The interiors are
decorated with period antiques.
Although the stay doesn't
include breakfast, there is
fresh cake on offer daily.

Brooklyn

**Best Western Gregory Hotel
Brooklyn** $
8315 Fourth Ave, 11201
Tel (718) 238-3737   **Map** 23 B4
W bestwestern.com
Comfortable, well-appointed
rooms, complimentary breakfast,
and an old-fashioned bar with
reasonably priced cocktails.

Business

Downtown

Holiday Inn Lower East Side $
150 Delancey St, 10002
Tel (212) 475-2500   **Map** 5 B4
W ihg.com
Simple but comfortable rooms
with plush beds and ergonomic
desk chairs.

**Best Western Seaport Inn
Downtown** $$
33 Peck Slip, 10038
Tel (212) 766-6600   **Map** 2 D2
W seaportinn.com
Splendid views of Brooklyn
Bridge from the terrace rooms.
Traditional decor, and a 24-hour
fitness center.

Marriott Downtown $$
85 West St, 10006
Tel (212) 385-4900   **Map** 1 B3
W marriott.com
Business-oriented hotel with
elegantly decorated rooms.
Some rooms have great views
of the Statue of Liberty.

For more information on types of hotels *see pp282–3*

Wyndham Garden Chinatown $$
93 Bowery, 10002
Tel (212) 329-3400   **Map** 5 A5
W wyndham.com
Contemporary rooms and all modern amenities, such as free Wi-Fi and a gym. Good location.

Midtown

Millennium Broadway $
145 West 44th St, 10036
Tel (212) 768-4400   **Map** 12 E5
W millenniumhotels.com
Choose from over 700 spacious and comfortable rooms at this hotel; popular with corporates.

Four Points by Sheraton $$
160 West 25th St, 10001
Tel (212) 627-1888   **Map** 8 42
W starwoodhotels.com
Plush, well-maintained rooms, some with balconies. Cozy restaurant and bar.

Hyatt 48 Lex $$
517 Lexington Ave, 10017
Tel (212) 838-1234   **Map** 13 A5
W hotel48lexnewyork.com
Great for corporate travelers, this high-end hotel has suites with landscaped terraces. Great on-site restaurant.

Metro Apartments $$
440 West 41st St, 10036
Tel (212) 706-2082   **Map** 7 C1
Comfortable aparthotel with fully equipped kitchenettes. Located 15 minutes from Times Square.

Murray Hill East Suites $$
149 East 39th St, 10016
Tel (212) 661-2100   **Map** 9 A1
W murrayhillsuites.com
Residential-style accommodations with suites, each with a fully equipped kitchenette. The minimum stay here is 30 days.

Radio City Apartments $$
142 West 49th St, 10019
Tel (212) 730-0728   **Map** 12 E5
W radiocityapts.com
Cozy accommodations, from studios to one-bedroom suites, most with kitchenettes. Penthouse options available. There is a great on-site Italian restaurant for guests.

Radisson Martinique on Broadway $$
49 West 32nd St, 10001
Tel (212) 736-3800   **Map** 3 F3
W radisson.com
Historic French-Renaissance building with an ornate lobby and sophisticated rooms. Sink into elegance and enjoy superlative service at this upscale hotel.

Affinia Dumont $$$
150 East 34th St, 10016
Tel (212) 481-7600   **Map** 9 A2
W affinia.com
Upscale rooms that resemble apartments, with full kitchenettes. Get pampered in the spa or work out at the fitness center.

Renaissance New York Hotel 57 $$$
130 East 57th St, 10022
Tel (212) 753-8841   **Map** 13 A3
W newyorkhotel57.com
Trendy hotel with impeccably kept spacious rooms, hardwood floors, and spotless marble bathrooms.

Farther Afield

Sheraton LaGuardia East Hotel $$
135–20 39th Ave, Queens, 11354
Tel (718) 460-6666
W sheratonlaguardiaeast.com
This 16-story hotel features simple but well-maintained rooms with coffee makers.

Luxury
Downtown

Gansevoort Meatpacking $$
18 Ninth Ave, 10014
Tel (212) 206-9700   **Map** 3 B1
W gansevoorthotelgroup.com
Well-appointed rooms with plush feather beds. The rooftop pool is a popular draw.

Gramercy Park Hotel $$
2 Lexington Ave, 10010
Tel (212) 920-3300   **Map** 9 A4
W gramercyparkhotel.com
Drawing heavily on its Bohemian heritage, this opulent hotel is filled with original artwork.

Exterior of The Greenwich Hotel, Downtown

The Greenwich Hotel $$$
377 Greenwich St, 10013
Tel (212) 941-8900   **Map** 1 B1
W thegreenwichhotel.com
Eclectic global style, from Moroccan tiles to Tibetan rugs. Snug rooms and inviting decor.

Ritz-Carlton Battery Park $$$
2 West St, 10004
Tel (212) 344-0800   **Map** 1 B4
W ritzcarlton.com
Elegant and modern rooms, complete with telescopes for views of the Statue of Liberty.

Soho House $$$
59 Ninth Ave, 10014
Tel (646) 253-6122   **Map** 3 B1
W sohohouseny.com
The New York branch of London's exclusive private club. Rooftop pool, library, and spacious rooms.

Trump SoHo $$$
246 Spring St, 10013
Tel (212) 842-5500   **Map** 4 D4
W trumpsohohotel.com
Rise above Manhattan in Trump's looming luxury hotel. Handsome rooms and a pool deck.

Midtown

Hilton Times Square $$
234 West 42nd St, 10036
Tel (212) 840-8222   **Map** 8 E1
W hiltonhoteltimessquare.com
Great service and elegant, well-equipped rooms offer a respite from the bustle of the city.

Lotte New York Palace $$
455 Madison Ave, 10022
Tel (212) 888-7000   **Map** 13 A4
W lottenypalace.com
A lavish hotel that lives up to its name. Set in an 1882 landmark building with a lovely courtyard.

DK Choice
Omni Berkshire Place $$
21 East 52nd St, 10022
Tel (212) 753-5800   **Map** 12 F4
W omnihotels.com
Superlative service and modern, well-equipped rooms with marble bathrooms make this an ideal choice for business travelers and families. Work out in the fully equipped fitness center with a sun deck, followed by creative cocktails and delicious cuisine in the Fireside Restaurant.

Key to Prices *see p284*

Le Parker Meridien $$
118 West 57th St, 10019
Tel (212) 245-5000 **Map** 12 E3
W parkermeridien.com
Spacious designer rooms, great service, and a rooftop pool. Serves some of the best burgers in town.

Sofitel $$
45 West 44th St, 10036
Tel (212) 354-8844 **Map** 12 F5
W sofitel-new-york.com
A warm blend of the contemporary and classic fills this 30-story building. Rooms on higher floors feature splendid views.

W Times Square $$
1567 Broadway, 10036
Tel (212) 930-7400 **Map** 12 E5
W wnewyorktimessquare.com
Upscale yet personable, with well-equipped rooms, a popular restaurant, and a lively bar scene.

**Waldorf-Astoria/
Waldorf Towers** $$
301 Park Ave, 10022
Tel (212) 355-3000 **Map** 13 A5
W waldorfnewyork.com
Presidents and heads of state have all graced this luxury hotel. Come here to experience great sophistication. The lobby is gorgeous.

Algonquin Hotel $$$
59 West 44th St, 10036
Tel (212) 840-6800 **Map** 12 F5
W algonquinhotel.com
Home of the famous 1920s literary "Round Table." Cozy, refurbished rooms.

**Four Seasons
New York** $$$
57 East 57th St, 10022
Tel (212) 758-5700 **Map** 13 A3
W fourseasons.com
The crown jewel in the Four Seasons chain, this luxury masterpiece has stunning views of Central Park.

Kitano $$$
66 Park Ave, 10017
Tel (212) 885-7000 **Map** 13 A5
W kitano.com
Great for corporate guests. Superlative Japanese service and complimentary green tea.

Langham Place $$$
400 5th Ave, 10018
Tel (212) 695-4005 **Map** 8 F2
W langhamhotels.com
A classy hotel with spacious suites filled with all modern amenities, including espresso machines and rain shower. Views of the Manhattan skyline.

The London NYC $$$
151 West 54th St, 10019
Tel (212) 307-5000 **Map** 2 E4
W thelondonnyc.com
A mural of London's Hyde Park defines this grand hotel. Gordon Ramsay's restaurant is on site.

Peninsula New York $$$
700 Fifth Ave, 10019
Tel (212) 956-2888 **Map** 12 F4
W newyork.peninsula.com
The Asian chain's Big Apple outpost offers well-appointed, plush rooms and an indulgent spa to unwind in after a long day.

The Plaza $$$
768 5th Ave, 10019
Tel (212) 759-3000 **Map** 12 F3
W theplazany.com
This magnificent 1907 grande dame effortlessly combines traditional decor with modern facilities. Exceptional service.

DK Choice

**Ritz-Carlton
Central Park** $$$
50 Central Park South, 10019
Tel (212) 308-9100 **Map** 12 F3
W ritzcarlton.com
This luxury hotel maximizes its proximity to Central Park at every turn – each floor features great views of the greenery. The stylish rooms and white-glove service are signature Ritz-Carlton – this hotel is among the very best in the city.

St. Regis $$$
2 East 55th St, 10022
Tel (212) 753-4500 **Map** 12 F4
W stregisnewyork.com
A 1904 Beaux Arts building, with a butler for every floor. Don't miss the Bloody Mary, a signature cocktail of the St. Regis group.

Upper Manhattan

Carlyle $$$
35 East 76th St, 10021
Tel (212) 744-1600 **Map** 17 A5
W rosewoodhotels.com
Frequented by celebrities and royalty, this esteemed hotel – with sophisticated interiors and ultra-elegant decor – offers phenomenal service and a wonderful afternoon tea.

Mandarin Oriental $$$
80 Columbus Circle, 10023
Tel (212) 805-8800 **Map** 12 D3
W mandarinoriental.com
A dramatic hotel with Asian-inspired opulence. Over 200 luxuriously appointed rooms and a trendy bar. Enjoy stellar views of Central Park and get pampered in the spa.

The Pierre $$$
2 East 61st St, 10021
Tel (212) 838-8000 **Map** 12 F3
W tajhotels.com
A grand lobby gives way to impeccable rooms with gracious interiors. Service is sophisticated and includes a special room-service menu for pets.

Sherry-Netherland $$$
781 5th Ave, 10022
Tel (212) 355-2800 **Map** 12 F3
W sherrynetherland.com
An old-world hotel with enormous and well-appointed suites. Indulge in luxury living and top-of-the-line service.

The Surrey $$$
20 East 76th St, 10021
Tel (212) 288-3700 **Map** 17 A5
W thesurrey.com
Check into one of this luxurious hotel's suites, many of which have kitchens. Features a roof garden, fitness center, and great, personalized service.

Spacious outdoor seating area at The Surrey, Upper Manhattan

For more information on types of hotels *see pp282–3*

WHERE TO EAT AND DRINK

New Yorkers love to eat well, and in the five boroughs there are more than 25,000 restaurants. City dwellers avidly read restaurant reviews in magazines and websites such as *New York* (www.nymag.com), to ensure that they are seen in the latest fashionable place. "In" restaurants and cuisines change with great regularity, while some haunts remain perennially popular. The restaurants cited in our listings have been selected as the best that New York can offer across a wide price range. While the information on pages 294–305 will help you to select a suitable restaurant, there are details of lighter refreshments on pages 306–8. *New York Bars* on pages 309–11 suggests some of the city's best drinking spots.

Shake Shack *(see p295)*, bustling with people at Madison Square Park

Restaurant Menus

Meals in most of the better restaurants consist of three courses: an appetizer (starter), an entrée (the main course), and a dessert. In some fine restaurants you may be offered a few complimentary extras. Appetizers at the better restaurants are sometimes the chef's most creative dishes. Coffee or tea and a dessert ordinarily conclude the meal in restaurants above the coffee-shop level. Some also offer a cheeseboard.

Traditional Italian menus offer antipasti (hot and cold appetizers), a first course – often a pasta dish, the main course – usually meat or fish, and a dessert.

To get a sense of a restaurant's cuisine, visit www.menupages.com, which features the menus of many New York eateries. Other local websites, including the weekly *New York* magazine's (www.nymag.com), often have links to restaurant menus.

Prices

You will always find a restaurant in New York to suit your budget. At inexpensive coffee shops, diners, and fast-food chains, $10–$15 will buy you a filling meal. There are also many acceptable, even first-rate, restaurants where you can eat well at a moderate cost – around $25 per person for a decent, filling meal, not including drinks – in attractive surroundings.

For dinner at a trendy New American venue with a star chef, the bill could be upward of $100 to $200 per person, excluding drinks. Many top restaurants do, however, offer fixed-price (or, as they are known in New York, prix-fixe) meals. This is a cheaper way of enjoying a good meal than choosing dishes from the à la carte menu. Lunch is less expensive than dinner in such places and, because of the profusion of business diners, lunch is often the busiest period of the day.

Taxes and Tipping

The New York City and state sales tax of 8.875 per cent will be added to your bill. Service is not usually included. Tipping can run from 10 per cent at a coffee shop to 20 per cent at the fanciest places, with 15 per cent an average fair tip. Many just double the sales tax to work out a tip.

The bill is known as the "check" in the US. The most commonly accepted credit cards are Visa,

The popular Red Hook Lobster Pound *(see p305)*

MasterCard, and American Express. Traveler's checks in US dollars are taken in some restaurants. Diners and coffee shops may accept cash only. In fast-food chains, you order at the counter and pay cash in advance.

Elegant interiors of the Venetian-inspired al di la trattoria *(see p305)*

Dining on a Budget

Despite the tales of $200 business lunches, there are ways to stretch a meal budget in New York. Order fewer courses than you would normally. American portions are huge, and an appetizer is often big enough for a light main course. You could share one with your companion or choose two appetizers and no entrée.

Ask your waiter if there is a prix-fixe menu. Many of the more expensive restaurants offer this at lunch and dinner – in the early evening it may be called the pre-theater menu. Or try a prix-fixe lunch buffet. These are popular in Indian restaurants and are reasonably priced.

Other options for a quick and tasty meal are the less expensive Chinese, Thai, and Mexican restaurants. Pizzerias and French bistros, as well as places that serve hamburgers or sandwiches, also offer good value. Alternatively, go to bars featuring "happy hours." They often offer hors d'oeuvres, which can make a meal in themselves.

If you simply want to see inside the restaurants every visitor has heard about, such as Gotham Bar and Grill or Four Seasons, just go to have a drink and soak up the atmosphere. Many restaurants post their menus or will let you see them before you are seated, which is good for checking prices in advance. During Restaurant Week (held in Jan/Feb and Jun/Jul), you can dine in some of the city's restaurants for a fraction of the usual cost – visit www.nycgo.com.

Minimalist interiors of the Italian restaurant, Hearth *(see p297)*

Hours

Breakfast hours are usually from 7 to 10:30 or 11am. Sunday brunch, a popular meal, is served at many restaurants between around 11am and 3pm. Lunch runs from 11:30am or noon to 2:30pm at most places, but the busiest time of the day is 1pm. Dinner is usually served from 5:30 or 6pm onward. The most popular time is around 7:30 or 8pm.

Some restaurants stop serving at 10pm during the week, or 11pm on Friday and Saturday. Certain informal restaurants are open from 11:30am to 10pm. Coffee shops are open long hours, from 7am to midnight or even 24 hours.

Dress Codes

Few restaurants demand that male diners dress formally, though a jacket or a jacket and tie might be required. At most restaurants, for both men and women, smart "business casual" suffices.

Women tend to dress up when dining at the more expensive restaurants. If you are unsure, check what the dress code is when you make your reservation.

Reservations

It is wise to make reservations at any restaurant above the diner/fast-food level, especially on weekends. Some of the trendiest restaurants won't accept bookings, or won't take them less than two months in advance. Make reservations for lunch at a Midtown restaurant as places here are popular with business diners.

Waits of an hour at the most popular spots are not unusual.

Smoking

Smoking is illegal in all bars and restaurants. The only exceptions are owner-operated bars that have special smoking rooms.

Children

When eating out with children, ask if there's a child's menu with half-portions. The prices are reduced, often by half. Dining out in the more formal New York restaurants is certainly not a family affair but children are accepted in more casual restaurants. Many family-friendly restaurants have facilities for babies or toddlers.

Wheelchair Access

While many restaurants may be able to accommodate a wheelchair, always mention your requirements when making your reservation. Many of the smaller places cannot cater to disabled customers due to lack of space.

Celebrity Chefs

New York has numerous celebrity flagships – traveling food connoisseur Anthony Bourdain runs Les Halles; Mario Batali helms several restaurants, such as Babbo and Eataly; David Chang is behind the Momofuku phenome-non; and Amanda Freitag (Empire Diner), Daniel Boulud (Daniel), Bobby Flay (Bar Americain), and Eric Ripert (Le Bernardin), all call the city home.

A meal in a top restaurant will not come cheaply, but it can be worth the splurge. Booking a

table can be difficult, and reservations should be made as early as two months in advance. Many reservations can be made online through Opentable (www.opentable.com).

Recommended Restaurants

New York City offers an amazing array of cuisines *(see The Flavors of New York, pp292–3)*, from Spanish, Greek, and Italian to local New York fare, along with a wide range of dining establishments. Our restaurants are divided into five geographical areas: **Downtown** encompasses Lower Manhattan and the Civic Center, the Lower East Side, Chinatown, Little Italy, SoHo and TriBeCa, Greenwich Village, the East Village, and Gramercy and the Flatiron District. **Midtown** covers both Lower and Upper Midtown, as well as Chelsea and the Garment District and Midtown West and the Theater District, which offers a host of restaurants with menus for the Broadway-bound. **Upper Manhattan** includes the Upper East Side, which features many upscale restaurants, the Upper West Side, Morningside Heights, and Harlem. **Brooklyn** also boasts an inventive culinary scene while **Farther Afield** includes restaurants in Queens, which often have an international flavor.

Throughout our listings, we've marked recommended restaurants as DK Choice. We've chosen these restaurants because they offer a special experience – either for the superb cuisine, for enjoying a uniquely New York night out surrounded by locals, for the excellent value, or a combination of these.

The Flavors of New York

Few cities can match the diversity of New York's restaurants. Reflecting the city's melting pot of nationalities, foods range from the "hautest" of French and continental cuisine to arguably the freshest sushi outside of Tokyo. Caribbean, Mexican, Thai, Vietnamese, Korean, Greek, Indian – all are well represented, and every block seems to have an Italian restaurant. The quality of the city's top restaurants is unsurpassed, and their chefs are superstars, as well known and revered as movie idols. So many nationalities are represented in the city's culinary culture, however, that only a few foods are actually native to it.

Dim sum

Fresh, local produce on display at the Greenmarket

Deli Dining

A large Jewish population has given rise to some of New York's best known specialties, now enjoyed by all – overstuffed corned beef and pastrami sandwiches, dill pickles, matzo-ball soup, herrings, blintzes, and bagels served with cream cheese and smoked salmon. The bagel, once synonymous with New York, has become a universal American food, but a true New York bagel is nothing like the bready imitations found in the hinterlands. It is shaped by hand, and the dough is cooked briefly in boiling water before being baked, resulting in a unique firm and chewy texture. A relative, and another New York specialty, is the bialy, a flat, chewy flour-dusted roll with a center indentation filed with toasted onions. The finest examples of each are to be found in the kosher bakeries of the Lower East Side (see pp86–95).

The Greenmarket

You may well find yourself next to a well-known chef browsing at New York's greenmarkets, open-air

Blintzes

Pastrami on rye

Dill pickles

Bagels with smoked salmon and cream cheese

Pickled herrings

Selection of classic foods available at any New York deli

New York Specialties

While New York dining may span all nations, a few special dishes are closely associated with the city. Manhattan Clam Chowder, prepared with tomatoes rather than cream, has been popular ever since it was introduced at Coney Island beach stands in the 1880s. In the city's many

Pretzels

steakhouses, a prime selection is the "New York strip steak," a boneless sirloin cut from the short loin, the tenderest portion of beef. Italian cuisine has often been given a New York spin. Rich and creamy New York cheesecake is made with cream cheese rather than the Italian ricotta. And, since traditional wood-burning ovens were impractical in New York, the first Italian immigrant chefs used coal ovens. Though these are rare today, purists still insist they are necessary for a true New York pizza.

Manhattan clam chowder This is a rich blend of potatoes, onions, tomatoes, oyster crackers, crumbs, and clams.

Fast food cart on a Manhattan street corner, selling hot dogs and sodas

markets where farmers from upstate New York sell freshly picked fruits and vegetables, as well as meat, poultry, and dairy products. Dozens of chefs patronize the greenmarkets, so you'll find ultra fresh local produce on many menus in the city. As many as 70 vendors attend the biggest of the markets in Union Square on Monday, Wednesday, Friday, and Saturday (see p125).

Street Food

Street food is a favorite choice in a fast-moving city. Hot dogs and oversized soft pretzels are classic New York choices, along with some surprisingly good food-cart specialties, from falafel to soup to barbecue to Texas chili, all ready to eat on the run. In winter, vendors all over town offer hot roasted chestnuts.

Soul Food

Harlem is America's most famous African-American community, and restaurants here are the place to sample specialties from the Deep South, such as fried chicken, ribs, collard greens, yams, and cornbread. A popular Harlem dish, fried chicken and waffles,

An Asian produce store in New York's Chinatown

is said to have originated to serve musicians leaving jazz clubs in the wee hours.

Asian Food

Chinese restaurants and dim sum parlors have long been found throughout the city, but lately they have been challenged by the arrival of many excellent Thai and Vietnamese restaurants. All these, however, take second place to the multiplying sushi bars and high-profile, highly praised Japanese chefs.

DELICATESSEN CLASSICS

Babkas Slightly sweet, yeasted coffee cakes.

Blintzes Crêpes filled with sweetened soft white cheese and/or fruit and sautéd.

Chopped liver Chicken livers mashed with minced onion, hard-cooked eggs and *schmaltz* (chicken fat).

Gefilte fish Minced white fish dumplings poached in fish broth. A holiday dish.

Knishes Soft dough shells filled with onion, mashed potatoes.

Latkes Grated potato, onion, and matzo-meal pancakes.

Rugelach Rich, cream-cheese-dough pastries filled with jam, chopped nuts, and raisins.

New York-style pizza Thin-crusted, a true New York pizza must be baked in a coal-fired oven.

New York strip steak Typically served with creamed spinach, fries, or hash-browns, this tender steak is hard to beat.

New York cheesecake This is a dense, rich, baked cake with a crust of pastry or graham crackers.

Where to Eat and Drink

Modern decor at Dirt Candy, popular for its vegetarian fare, Downtown

Downtown

Adrienne's Pizza Bar $
Pizza   **Map** 1 C4
54 Stone St, 10004
Tel (212) 248-3838
Munch on thin-crust square pizzas at this neighborhood favorite. Also try the antipasti.

Angelica Kitchen $
Vegetarian   **Map** 5 A1
300 East 12th St, 10003
Tel (212) 228-2909
Try innovative vegetarian cuisine, from aromatic soups and fresh salads to creatively prepared pasta dishes. All ingredients on the menu are grown organically, and bottled beverages of any kind are not offered.

Il Bagatto $
Italian   **Map** 5 B2
192 East 2nd St, 10009
Tel (212) 228-0977   **Closed** *Mon*
Friendly eatery that draws the crowds. There's a festive atmosphere at all times, with dim lights and candles. The inexpensive red wine is an added incentive.

Caracas Arepa Bar $
Venezuelan   **Map** 5 A2
93½ East 7th St, 10009
Tel (212) 228-5062
Small but perennially packed joint with flavorful Venezuelan fare. The specialty is *arepas* (corn cakes with a variety of savory fillings). Have them as a snack or a meal.

Congee Village $
Chinese   **Map** 5 A4
100 Allen St, 10002
Tel (212) 941-1818
Bustling restaurant specializing in congee, a hot rice porridge with meat or fish and spices. The fragrant noodle dishes are good too.

Corner Bistro $
American   **Map** 3 C1
331 West 4th St, 10014
Tel (212) 242-9502
Some of the best burgers in the city make this dive bar a cult favorite. After your meal, choose from the extensive menu of local beer.

Dirt Candy $
Vegetarian   **Map** 5 A3
86 Allen St, 10009
Tel (212) 228-7732   **Closed** *Sun*
High-concept vegetarian cuisine, from mint and tarragon zucchini pasta to portobello mushroom mousse. Everything on the menu can be made vegan on request.

Dumpling Man $
Chinese   **Map** 5 A1
100 St. Mark's Place, 10009
Tel (212) 505-2121
Tiny eatery serving classic northern Asian-style dumplings: fried or steamed, and stuffed with pork, chicken, tofu, or veggies. Soups and salads also available.

Great Jones Cafe $
American   **Map** 4 F2
54 Great Jones St, 10012
Tel (212) 674-9304   **Closed** *Mon*
An Elvis likeness draped with Mardi Gras beads sets the tone for this eatery. Enjoy the cocktails sat the bar. Sample the Cajun Mary, and play some vinyl, old-school style, on the jukebox.

Ippudo $
Japanese   **Map** 4 F1
65 Fourth Ave, 10003
Tel (212) 388-0088
Fukuoka-based Shigemi Kawahara, also known as the "Ramen King", set up this popular ramen shop, with its communal tables and booths. Enjoy the steaming bowls of classic *tonkotsu*-style (pork bone broth) noodles.

Ivan Ramen $
Japanese   **Map** 5 B3
25 Clinton St, 10002
Tel (646) 678-3859
Adorned with a massive papier-mâché mural, this charming eatery serves favorites such as dandan noodles and red chili ramen.

Joe's Shanghai $
Chinese   **Map** 4 F5
9 Pell St, 10013
Tel (212) 233-8888
A downtown institution, this bustling restaurant makes delectable dumplings stuffed with everything from pork to vegetables. Be sure to try the special soup dumplings.

DK Choice

Katz's Delicatessen $
Deli   **Map** 5 A3
205 East Houston St, 10002
Tel (212) 254-2246
A New York institution, this Jewish deli serves towering pastrami or corned-beef sandwiches, and other local delicacies. Vegetarians can relish the fat *knishes* (potato, meat, and cabbage dumplings), split pea soup, and potato latkes.

Lil' Frankies $
American   **Map** 5 A2
19–21 First Ave, 10003
Tel (212) 420-4900
Hip neighborhood pizzeria with a backyard garden for alfresco dining. Pizzas are made in a wood-fired brick oven.

Lombardi's $
American   **Map** 4 F4
32 Spring St, 10012
Tel (212) 941-7994
One of the top pizzerias in the city, with thin, charred, brick-oven-baked pizzas topped with everything from eggplant to pepperoni. Home-made meatballs and clam pie are also popular dishes.

Mighty Quinn's Barbeque $
American   **Map** 4 F2
103 Second Ave, 10003
Tel (212) 219-2000
This Texas-inspired slow-smoked barbecue joint has a lip-smacking

menu of brisket, ribs, and pulled pork, accompanied by burnt-end baked beans.

Mission Cantina $
Mexican   Map 5 A3
172 Orchard St, 10002
Tel (212) 254-2233
A whimsical menu with three types of dishes: raw, sharing, and plates. Try the masa-fried fish burritos, yellowfin tuna ceviche, and the mole spiced chicken wings.

Mission Chinese Food $
Chinese   Map 5 B5
171 East Broadway, 10002
Tel (212) 529-8800
This landmark fusion joint, started by Danny Bowien, offers dishes such as spicy Mapo tofu, the popular thrice-cooked bacon, and Char Siu Pig Ear Terrine.

Moustache $
Middle Eastern   Map 3 C2
90 Bedford St, 10014
Tel (212) 229-2220
Hugely popular, casual eatery with flavorful grilled lamb and chicken and delicious, crisp Turkish "pizzas" – pizzas made with pita dough.

Nom Wah Tea Parlor $
Chinese   Map 4 F5
13 Doyers St, 10013
Tel (212) 962-6047
An elegant, old-fashioned dim sum parlor from the 1920s with an inventive menu. Enjoy a variety of snacks, from taro and shrimp dumplings to egg rolls and salt-and-pepper shrimps.

Pho Pasteur $
Vietnamese   Map 4 F5
85 Baxter St, 10013
Tel (212) 608-3656
Sample excellent Vietnamese rolls and hot noodle soup with beef brisket or fish balls at this tiny, but very popular, eatery.

Shake Shack $
American   Map 9 A4
Southeast corner of Madison Square Park, near Madison Ave and East 23rd St, 10010
Tel (212) 889-6600
Sink your teeth into juicy burgers and crinkle-cut fries at this perennially popular shack, where guests can eat under the cool shade of trees. Delicious shakes.

Aquagrill $$
Seafood   Map 4 D4
201 Spring St, 10012
Tel (212) 274-0505
Calling all seafood lovers: this lovely restaurant, with an airy

outdoor patio, serves the freshest fish and shellfish in town, accompanied by aromatic sauces. Great seafood platter.

DK Choice

Balthazar $$
French   Map 4 E4
80 Spring St, 10012
Tel (212) 965-414
This bistro's hopping atmosphere is hard to resist, especially once you've caught a glimpse of it through the large windows overlooking Spring Street. Restaurateur Keith McNally's brasserie empire is crowned by this stylish place, which rolls out French favorites – steak frites, oysters, and Bordeaux wine – for a lively crowd, from SoHo literati to fashionistas in stilettos.

Battery Gardens $$
American   Map 1 C4
Opposite 17 State St, 10004
Tel (212) 809-5508
This eatery's unique waterside location makes it worth a visit. The Mediterranean-influenced American fare is decent, but the phenomenal views of the Statue of Liberty also merit a visit.

Beauty & Essex $$
American   Map 5 B3
146 Essex St, 10002
Tel (212) 614-0146
Extremely elegant, sophisticated, and spacious. Serves global small plates and offers an elaborate pre-selected menu for large groups.

Blue Hill $$
American   Map 4 E4
75 Washington Place, 10011
Tel (212) 539-1776
This restaurant uses the freshest ingredients sourced from local farms. Try the smoked salmon with beet purée, and check

out the elaborate five-course "Farmer's Feast" tasting menu, based on the week's harvest.

Blue Ribbon Bakery $$
American   Map 4 D3
35 Downing St, 10014
Tel (212) 337-0404
A small plates menu of excellent locavore cuisine, from barbecued pork to organic salads. Wash it down with the excellent selection of local beers.

Blue Smoke $$
American   Map 9 A3
116 East 27th St, 10016
Tel (212) 447-7733
Esteemed restaurateur Danny Meyer delivers authentic pit BBQ at its finest. Try the ribs or pulled pork sandwiches, both dripping with juices. There is an excellent jazz club downstairs with two sets every evening.

Boqueria $$
Spanish tapas   Map 4 D4
171 Spring St, 10012
Tel (212) 343-4255
Taste Barcelona-style tapas along with sangria, in this lively, vibrant place. Try grilled squid, lamb meatballs, and creamy croquettes with ham. The restaurant works closely with local farmers to get fresh, local ingredients.

Bubby's $$
American   Map 4 D5
120 Hudson St, 10013
Tel (212) 219-0666
Bubby's offers hearty traditional fare and famous pies that are rolled by hand and made with locally grown ingredients. Try the Arkansas red velvet cake or apple pie with creamy ice cream. Arguably the best place to sample established American recipes.

Elegant interiors at Aquagrill, Downtown

For more information on types of restaurants see p291

Low lighting and rustic decor at Da Silvano, Downtown

Craft
American   **Map** 9 A5 $$
43 East 19th St, 10003
Tel (212) 780-0880
Creative chef Tom Colicchio offers a "deconstructed" menu that celebrates fresh ingredients. Try the roasted swordfish or rabbit loin, or braised beef short ribs. Be sure to taste the mouthwatering desserts.

Da Silvano
Italian   **Map** 4 D3 $$
260 Sixth Ave, 10014
Tel (212) 982-2343
A Tuscan restaurant that's better known for its celebrity clientele than its cuisine. Coveted outdoor tables and gently lit interiors make for a great ambience.

Dirty French
French   **Map** 5 A3 $$
180 Ludlow St, 10002
Tel (212) 254-3000
Contemporary French bistro that offers a tweak on classics, such as duck *à l'orange* with preserved oranges, and brook trout with dried apricots and sesame.

Dos Caminos
Mexican   **Map** 4 F3 $$
475 West Broadway, 10012
Tel (212) 277-4300
Fresh Mexican cuisine, such as thick guacamole served with warm tortilla chips and grilled chicken, as well as potent tequilas, draw daily crowds to this rather boisterous restaurant. Popular for brunch.

L'Ecole
French   **Map** 4 E4 $$
462 Broadway, 10012
Tel (212) 219-3300
Delightful restaurant where students of the French Culinary Institute prepare all the exquisite

meals for customers – from seared fish to rich meats.

Edi & the Wolf
Austrian   **Map** 5 B2 $$
102 Ave C, 10009
Tel (212) 598-1040
This rustic restaurant is inspired by the casual neighborhood taverns in Austria. Feast on traditional fare such as pork schnitzel and delicious pastry desserts. Good choice of wines.

Empellón Cocina
Mexican   **Map** 5 A2 $$
105 First Ave, 10003
Tel (212) 780-0999
Innovative, but rooted in authentic Mexican style, this restaurant blends the classic and the contemporary. Try the lamb sweetbreads with pumpkin seeds.

Fatty Crab
Malaysian   **Map** 3 B1 $$
643 Hudson St, 10014
Tel (212) 352-3590
Chef Zak Pelaccio delights tastebuds with fragrant,

The bar area at Freemans restaurant, Downtown

Malaysian-inspired cuisine. Try classics such as beef rendang, and do not miss the delicious cocktails flavored with elderflower, honey, and Thai basil.

Fraunces Tavern
American   **Map** 1 C4 $$
54 Pearl St, 10004
Tel (212) 968-1776   **Closed** *Sun*
Historic 18th-century tavern with classic American steak and fish dishes. The place offers 18 craft beers on tap.

Freemans
American   **Map** 5 A3 $$
Freeman Alley, near Rivington, 10002
Tel (212) 420-0012
This fashionable restaurant, hiding at the end of an alley, has a menu reminiscent of a 1950s supper party, with rum-soaked ribs and stiff cocktails. Old-world American tavern-style decor.

DK Choice

Gramercy Tavern
American   **Map** 9 A5 $$
42 East 20th St, 10003
Tel (212) 477-0777
Acclaimed chef Michael Anthony creates superlative, market-fresh fare in this rustic yet elegant restaurant. Do not miss the chocolate bread pudding.

Les Halles
French   **Map** 1 C2 $$
15 John St, 10038
Tel (212) 285-8585
A lively brasserie with top-notch fare, from succulent steak with Béarnaise sauce to tasty grilled salmon to fresh salads with tangy dressings. There is a fine selection of French wine on the menu.

Hearth $$
Italian   Map 5 A1
403 East 12th St, 10009
Tel (212) 602-1300
Feast on Tuscan-American fare at this popular bohemian-chic restaurant. Signature dishes include marinated sardines, pan-seared skate, and stuffed cabbage. Top off the meal with olive-oil cake.

Hundred Acres $$
American   Map 4 D3
38 MacDougal St, 10012
Tel (212) 475-7500
Tuck into farm-to-fork cuisine, such as juicy lamb and fried green tomatoes, at this cozy spot. There is a lovely garden at the back of the restaurant.

Jane $$
American   Map 4 E3
100 West Houston St, 10012
Tel (212) 254-7000
Casual neighborhood bistro with a loyal following thanks to tasty unpretentious dishes made with fresh, local produce. Welcoming environs are packed for the popular weekend brunch service.

Jewel Bako $$
Japanese   Map 4 F2
239 East 5th St, 10003
Tel (212) 979-1012   **Closed** Sun
This tiny but impeccable restaurant serves exquisite sushi. Also check out the wide range of sashimi on offer. Note that the prices of dishes can quickly add up – but it's well worth it.

Kesté $$
Pizza   Map 4 D2
271 Bleecker St, 10014
Tel (212) 243-1500
This acclaimed Italian pizza-maker churns out some of the city's most delicious wood-fired, Neapolitan-style pizzas. Inventive toppings, as well as gluten-free, vegetarian, and vegan options.

Contemporary interior of Hearth, Downtown

The Little Owl $$
American   Map 3 C2
90 Bedford St, 10014
Tel (212) 741-4695
Charming neighborhood joint with innovative, market-fresh, Mediterranean-style cuisine. Try their signature pork chops and gravy meatball sliders.

DK Choice

Locanda Verde $$
Italian   Map 4 D5
379 Greenwich St, 10013
Tel (212) 925-3797
Enjoy family-style, impeccably crafted Italian cuisine, from pasta to seafood, at this stylish restaurant in actor Robert De Niro's hotel. Try the specialty Italian beers and cocktails.

Lupa $$
Italian   Map 4 F3
170 Thompson St, 10012
Tel (212) 982-5089
Celebrity chef Mario Batali serves superb pasta and grilled meats at this Italian *trattoria*. It is busy most nights of the week, so book

ahead. Enjoy a cocktail at the bar while waiting for your table.

The Mermaid Inn $$
Seafood   Map 5 A2
96 Second Ave, 10003
Tel (212) 674-5870
With its New England-style chowder, and lobster sandwiches, this casual place draws a trendy crowd. Wash the seafood down with a Brooklyn beer.

Momofuku Noodle Bar $$
Asian   Map 5 A1
171 First Ave, 10003
Tel (212) 475-7899
Celebrated Korean-American chef David Chang offers innovative ramen and other Japanese classics. Try the pork buns, and the fried chicken, which comes with pancakes.

Odeon $$
French   Map 1 B1
145 West Broadway, 10013
Tel (212) 233-0507
This bistro offers great steak tartare and spicy chicken dumplings. Enjoy the dessert wines and cocktails on offer. Online reservations only.

Otto $$
Italian   Map 4 E1
1 Fifth Ave, 10003
Tel (212) 995-9559
Buzzing, upscale pizzeria from chef Mario Batali. The creative wine list features excellent vintages from Italy. Reasonable prices and friendly service.

La Palapa $$
Mexican   Map 5 A1
77 St. Mark's Place, 10003
Tel (212) 777-2537
Colorful restaurant with regional Mexican cooking such as baked catfish, plus tart Margaritas, and other tequila drinks.

Attractive table settings at The Little Owl, Downtown

For more information on types of restaurants *see p291*

Pardon My French $$
French   Map 5 B2
103 Ave B, 10009
Tel (212) 358-9683
A buzzing bistro that serves
wholesome classics such as
moules frites (mussels) and duck
with apricots. The small backyard
offers a chance to experience a
relaxing dinner under the stars.

Pearl Oyster Bar $$
Seafood   Map 4 D4
18 Cornelia St, 10014
Tel (212) 691-8211   **Closed** *Sun*
This longtime favorite has a raw
oyster bar and sinfully tasty lobster
rolls. Very popular, so be prepared
to wait.

Prune $$
American   Map 5 A3
54 East 1st St, 10003
Tel (212) 677-6221
Small and rustic, this delightful
place does offshoots of American
favorites such as bacon and eggs
atop a tangle of peppery spaghetti.

Public $$
Australian   Map 4 F3
210 Elizabeth St, 10012
Tel (212) 343-7011
Experience cuisine from Down
Under with a classy twist at this
hip restaurant. One of the highlights featured on the menu is
the grilled kangaroo paired with
a New Zealand wine.

Red Farm $$
Chinese   Map 3 C2
529 Hudson St, 10014
Tel (212) 792-9700
Local and seasonal produce drive
this contemporary Chinese joint.
The menu includes playful dim
sum creations, such as the Pac
Man shrimp dumplings, and
delicious mains, such as the
crisp-skin smoked chicken.

Russ & Daughters Cafe $$
Jewish   Map 5 A4
127 Orchard St, 10002
Tel (212) 475-4880
Incredible hand-rolled bagels
with smoked salmon, knishes,
pickled herring, and other Yiddish
classics. The original Manhattan
gourmet branch opened this
charming café in 2014.

Sammy's Roumanian $$
Eastern European   Map 5 A4
157 Chrystie St, 10002
Tel (212) 673-0330
Feast on steak, latkes, ruby-red
pastrami, and chopped liver at
this old-world restaurant. Have a
local beer to top off the meal.
There is a party room upstairs for
those looking to shake a leg.

Ethnic interiors of Spice Market, which
serves Southeast Asian food, Downtown

DK Choice

Saravanaa Bhavan $$
Indian/Vegetarian   Map 9 A4
81 Lexington Ave, 10016
Tel (212) 679-0204
Inexpensive, all-vegetarian
menu, which incorporates a
dizzying assortment of South
Indian specialties such as
Rasam, a spicy lentil soup. Good
selection of Indian desserts.
Friendly service matches the
casual ambience.

Spice Market $$
Southeast Asian   Map 3 B1
403 West 13th St, 10014
Tel (212) 675-2322
This sensuous restaurant serves
Southeast Asian "street food" and
fusion cocktails. Check out the
vinegar-infused pork vindaloo
(a spicy curried dish).

The Spotted Pig $$
British   Map 3 B2
314 West 11th St, 10014
Tel (212) 620-0393
Upscale pub with excellent wine
list plus, of course, plenty of stout
and ale. Try the "5 veg" – a five-
course vegetarian platter.

Spring Street Natural $$
Vegetarian   Map 4 F4
62 Spring St, 10012
Tel (212) 966-0290
Wholesome dishes made with
fresh natural ingredients have
been a neighborhood staple for
decades. Choices include vegan
macrobiotic plates.

The Standard Grill $$
American   Map 3 B1
848 Washington St, 10014
Tel (212) 645-4100

Bustling farmhouse-chic bistro
with grilled steaks and burgers,
locally sourced salads, and an
excellent assortment of ales. The
grilled Mayan shrimp is popular.

Stanton Social $$
American   Map 5 A3
99 Stanton St, 10002
Tel (212) 995-0099
The party atmosphere and
creative cocktails overshadow
the small plates designed for
sharing at this trendy spot.
There is a DJ on weekends.

SUteiShi $$
Sushi   Map 2 D2
24 Peck Slip, 10038
Tel (212) 766-2344
Top-notch sushi and other
Japanese offerings in a stylish,
high-ceilinged space. Creative,
locally themed rolls include the
"King of NY" and "Peck's Peak."

Tamarind $$
Indian   Map 4 D5
99 Hudson St, 10013
Tel (212) 775-9000
Feast on excellent curries and
succulent lamb at this vibrant
restaurant. Offers great value for
money, with generous portions
and a wide range of Indian
dishes to choose from.

Tertulia $$
Spanish tapas   Map 4 D2
359 Sixth Ave, 10014
Tel (646) 559-9909
Sample smoked mussels and
steaming paella heaped with
shrimp at this vibrant tapas bar.
The menu also features an
excellent selection of tapas dishes.

I Trulli $$
Italian   Map 9 A3
122 East 27th St, 10010
Tel (212) 481-7372
Romantic, upscale restaurant
specializing in southern Italian
cuisine. Strict policy of sourcing
all ingredients locally.

Veselka $$
Ukranian   Map 1 B1
144 Second Ave, 10003
Tel (212) 228-9682
An East Village institution since
1954, this Ukrainian diner serves
the finest home-made *borscht*
(beetroot soup), veal goulash,
pierogi (savory dough dumplings),
and kielbasa sausages.

The Waverly Inn and Garden $$
American   Map 3 C1
16 Bank St, 10014
Tel (917) 828-1154
The homespun name belies the
scene within: celebrities and

fashionistas dine on classic American fare such as juicy pork chops. Popular weekend brunch. Reservations are a must.

Westville $$
American   **Map** 3 C2
210 West 10th St, 10014
Tel (212) 741-7971
Hearty traditional fare, from mac 'n' cheese to cod po'boys, at this casual, narrow eatery. The food is simple but wholesome, and the domestic beer list is top-notch too.

Zum Schneider $$
German   **Map** 5 B2
107 Ave C, 10009
Tel (212) 598-1098
It's Oktoberfest all year round at this boisterous beer garden with super sausages. Traditional Bavarian-German menu. Be warned: there are big crowds on the weekend.

Aldea $$$
Mediterranean   **Map** 8 F5
31 West 17th St, 10011
Tel (212) 675-7223   **Closed** *Sun*
Portuguese-American chef George Mendes is at the helm of this intimate Mediterranean-inspired spot. Do not miss the suckling pig with truffle purée.

Babbo $$$
Italian   **Map** 4 D2
110 Waverly Place, 10011
Tel (212) 777-0303
Famous chef Mario Batali's flagship restaurant, with superlative pasta, grilled meats, and offal. The wine list is extensive and bound to make wine lovers happy.

DK Choice

Bouley $$$
French   **Map** 1 C1
163 Duane St, 10013
Tel (212) 66-5829   **Closed** *Sun*
A high-profile restaurant by chef David Bouley; exquisite, pricey fare – but more than worth it. The emphasis is on both taste and nutritional value.

The Dutch $$$
American   **Map** 4 D3
131 Sullivan St, 10012
Tel (212) 677-6200
Oysters and traditional US cuisine, are highlights at this trendy tavern. Also enjoy an American bourbon, straight up. Great food in a lively, atmosphere.

Eleven Madison Park $$$
American-French   **Map** 9 A4
11 Madison Ave, 10010
Tel (212) 889-0905   **Closed** *Sun*

Contemporary cuisine is served in this beautiful Art Deco restaurant. The food is exquisite but it comes at a price. Don't forget your credit card.

Gotham Bar & Grill $$$
American   **Map** 4 E1
12 East 12th St, 10003
Tel (212) 620-4020
A stately restaurant that has become a respected New York institution. The Greenmarket fixed-price lunch menu offers excellent value for money.

Megu $$$
Japanese   **Map** 1 B1
62 Thomas St, 10013
Tel (212) 964-7777
Fabulous Japanese fare, including freshly caught fish, in this massive and trendy restaurant. The focus is on organic dining. Don't miss the kobe beef skewers.

Minetta Tavern $$$
Italian   **Map** 4 D2
113 McDougal St, 10012
Tel (212) 475-3850
Sink your teeth into juicy steaks at this bistro that is both casual and celebrity-friendly. The dark-wood bar serves top-notch cocktails and bourbons.

Nobu $$$
Japanese   **Map** 4 D5
105 Hudson St, 10013
Tel (212) 219-0500
One of NYC's best-known Japanese restaurants. Chef Nobu Matsuhisa has designed a superlative menu, but be prepared to splurge. Try the lobster with wasabi pepper sauce.

One if by Land,
Two if by Sea $$$
American   **Map** 3 C3
17 Barrow St, 10014
Tel (212) 228-0822

One of the most romantic restaurants in NYC, set in Aaron Burr's famous carriage house. Nightly three-course fixed-price menu with live piano music. Try the seven-course tasting menu.

Strip House $$$
American   **Map** 4 E1
13 East 12th St, 10003
Tel (212) 328-0000
A bordello-inspired steakhouse with plush banquettes. Don't miss the dry-aged strip steak with goose-fat potatoes, and the delectable 24-layer chocolate cake.

Tocqueville $$$
French   **Map** 8 F5
1 East 15th St, 10003
Tel (212) 647-1515   **Closed** *Sun*
Inconspicuous gem Tocqueville offers French cuisine with a Japanese twist, including lavender Arctic char. Excellent wine list.

Midtown

Burger Joint at
Le Parker Meridien $
American   **Map** 12 E3
119 West 57th St, 10019
Tel (212) 708-7414
Kitschy spot with mouthwatering burgers, shakes, and beers. It is tucked away behind the curtains in the lobby of Le Parker Meridien hotel.

Carnegie Deli $
Deli   **Map** 12 E4
854 Seventh Ave, 10019
Tel 800-334-5606
Huge pastrami and corned beef sandwiches are served at this classic New York deli. Also worth trying are the delicious knishes (dumplings).

Stately red-brick entrance to One if by Land, Two if by Sea, Downtown

For more information on types of restaurants *see p291*

Chic dining room at Pampano restaurant, Midtown

Ali Baba $$
Turkish   Map 9 B2
212 East 34th St, 10016
Tel (212) 683-92-6
Dine on babaganoush and stuffed grape leaves at this traditional eatery. Mouthwatering grilled meats are also on the menu.

Becco $$
Italian   Map 11 D5
355 West 46th St, 10036
Tel (212) 397-7597
Homely restaurant most famous for its pasta tasting menu and excellent Italian wine list.

Bottino $$
Italian   Map 7 C4
246 Tenth Ave, 10001
Tel (212) 206-6766
Housed in a century-old hardware shop, this northern Italian restaurant offers great food and a boutique wine list. It also has a beautiful patio and garden.

Cho Dang Gol $$
Korean   Map 8 F2
55 W 35th St, 10001
Tel (212) 695-8222
Beyond crammed 32nd Street,

with its array of Korean joints, lies this place. Try the home-made tofu.

Cookshop $$
American   Map 7 C5
156 Tenth Ave, 10011
Tel (212) 924-4440
Part of the Marc Meyer chain, with street-side tables and seasonal American fare. The menu includes pheasant pasta and Vermont lamb shoulder.

Dawat $$
Indian   Map 13 B3
210 East 58th St, 10022
Tel (212) 355-7555
Experience fragrant and delicious Indian fare. The salmon rubbed with coriander chutney is a highlight, or go for the popular chicken tikka masala.

Estiatorio Milos $$
Greek   Map 12 E4
125 West 55th St, 10019
Tel (212) 245-7400
Seafood palace with everything from grilled lobster to traditional Greek fish soup. Try the Mediterranean meze plate, or the grilled Canadian

scallops, and sample the selection of Greek wines.

Felidia $$
Italian   Map 13 B3
243 E 58th St, 10022
Tel (212) 758-1479
TV star and chef Lidia Bastianich serves upscale Italian cuisine in this refined town house. The wine list is top-notch.

Hill Country $$
Barbecue   Map 8 F4
30 W 26th St, 10010
Tel (212) 255-4544
This spot honors Texan barbecue by using a meat-smoking room to yield tender brisket, sausages, and ribs, plus there is a choice of sides. Live music most nights.

Marseille $$
French-Moroccan   Map 12 D5
630 Ninth Ave, 10036
Tel (212) 333-2323
This inviting restaurant with tiled floors features classic dishes such as duck cassoulet and tagines.

Norma's $$
American   Map 12 E3
119 West 56th St, 10019
Tel (212) 708-7460
One of Midtown's best-known brunch spots, serving massive omelets and pancakes.

Osteria al Doge $$
Italian   Map 12 E5
142 West 44th St, 10036
Tel (212) 944-3643
Northern Italian specialties, from hearty grilled meats to fresh home-made pasta, are served at this friendly, rustic spot. Do not miss the thin-crust pizzas.

DK Choice

Pampano $$
Mexican   Map 13 B2
209 East 49th St, 10017
Tel (212) 751-4545
A chic restaurant from chef Richard Sandoval. Signature dishes include smoked swordfish, grilled halibut, and guacamole. Good selection of desserts.

Quality Meats $$
American   Map 12 F3
57 W 58th St, 10019
Tel (212) 371-7777
Serves top-notch beef steaks, and excellent appetizers and sides. Great double rib steak too.

The Red Cat $$
American   Map 7 C4
227 Tenth Ave, 10011
Tel (212) 242-1122

Exposed brick and low-lighting at Quality Meats, Midtown

New England-style barnhouse setting, and professional service. Offers delectable dishes such as fried oysters. Sample the wild bass in white-wine butter.

Rue 57 $$
French fusion **Map** 12 F3
60 West 57th St, 10019
Tel (212) 307-5656
The unlikely pairing of French cuisine and Japanese sushi draws the crowds here. Or enjoy authentic bistro cuisine – it also dishes out American classics.

Shun Lee Palace $$
Chinese **Map** 13 A4
155 East 55th St, 10022
Tel (212) 371-8844
This upscale restaurant serves traditional Chinese mainland cooking. The Grand Marnier shrimps are sinfully good.

Taboon $$
Middle Eastern **Map** 11 C4
773 Tenth Ave, 10019
Tel (212) 713-0271
Middle Eastern meets Mediterranean at this inviting rustic eatery. Excellent wine list.

Tia Pol $$
Spanish tapas **Map** 7 C4
205 Tenth Ave, 10011
Tel (212) 675-8805
An infectious spirit pervades this tiny tapas bar. Sample fried chickpeas, squid in its own ink, and fresh fruit jugs of sangria, and check out the comprehensive all-Spanish wine list.

Trestle on Tenth $$
Swiss **Map** 7 C4
242 Tenth Ave, 10001
Tel (212) 645-5659
Dine on Swiss specialties, including rosti and pork, at this charming spot. In the summer, opt for the charming shaded garden.

Virgil's Real Barbecue $$
American **Map** 12 E5
152 West 44th St, 10036
Tel (212) 921-9494
Fill up on juicy pork ribs, chicken wings, hunks of cornbread, and collard greens at this noisy BBQ joint. Offers a variety of authentic Mexican, Creole, and Cajun classics.

DK Choice

Aquavit $$$
Scandinavian **Map** 13 A4
65 East 55th St, 10022
Tel (212) 307-7311
This high-end restaurant serves inventive cuisine in a sleek and minimalist dining room. Try Scandi classics such as Swedish meatballs, gravlax, and toast skagen. Enjoy signature cocktails in the comfortable bar lounge.

Artisanal $$$
French **Map** 9 A2
2 Park Ave, 10016
Tel (212) 725-8585
Dashing bistro with elegant interiors. Try the elaborate cheese platter and the fondues. Superb selection of cocktails. Great desserts.

Aureole $$$
American **Map** 8 F1
135 West 42nd St, 10036
Tel (212) 319-1660
Chef Charlie Palmer offers inventive cuisine at this handsome restaurant, which also features a popular pre-theater menu and an excellent selection of wines.

Le Bernardin $$$
French **Map** 12 E4
155 West 51st St, 10019
Tel (212) 554-1515
Chef Eric Ripert turns out French masterpieces at this elegant restaurant. Favorite dishes include red snapper with smoked paprika. Great for seafood lovers.

Stylish decor at Buddakan, an Asian fusion eatery in Chelsea, Midtown

BLT Steak $$$
American **Map** 13 A3
106 East 57th St, 10022
Tel (212) 752-7470
Trendy Bistro that serves up fat, succulent steaks with a variety of tangy sauces, including a creamy Béarnaise and a tart three-mustard one. The signature warm popovers and oversized onion rings are great.

Buddakan $$$
Asian fusion **Map** 8 D5
75 Ninth Ave, 10011
Tel (212) 989-6699
Enjoy modern Asian cuisine and cocktails at Buddakan, with its soaring ceilings and incredible decor. The spacious dining room is ideal for large groups.

DB Bistro Moderne $$$
French **Map** 8 F1
55 West 44th St, 10036
Tel (212) 391-2400
Famed chef Daniel Boulud is at the helm of this comfortably noisy bistro with excellent fare. There are two dining rooms, linked by a paneled wine bar. The French wine list is excellent.

Stylish and minimal styling at Aquavit, Midtown

Dining in style at Grand Central Oyster Bar, Midtown, famed for its seafood

Esca $$$
Italian   Map 8 D1
402 West 43rd St, 10036
Tel (212) 564-7272
Chef Mario Batali achieves
greatness again in this excellent
Southern Italian *trattoria*. Try the
superb whole sea bass for two,
cooked in sea salt.

Four Seasons $$$
American   Map 13 A4
99 East 52nd St, 10022
Tel (212) 754-9494   **Closed** *Sun*
Thanks to its impressive
longevity and stunning decor,
this restaurant is one of New
York's most famous. Experience
a relaxing lunch by the poolside.
There is a dedicated grill room
and a wooden bar that is a
popular draw. The art collection
is excellent.

DK Choice

Grand Central Oyster Bar $$$
Seafood   Map 9 A1
*Lower Level, Grand Central
Terminal, 89 East 42nd St,
10017*
Tel (212) 490-6650
Sample fresh oysters at this
seafood palace, which is
crowned by grand, vaulted
ceilings. The chefs opt for
simple preparation – a squirt
of lemon or a hand-plucked
garnish – allowing the fresh
fish and shellfish to shine on
its own delectable merit.

La Grenouille $$$
French   Map 12 F4
3 East 52nd St, 10022
Tel (212) 752-1495   **Closed** *Mon*
A classic French restaurant,
ideal for a romantic dinner.
The intimacy factor is magnified
by the soft banquettes and
flickering candles.

Key to Prices *see p294*

Marea $$$
Seafood   Map 12 D3
240 Central Park South, 10019
Tel (212) 582-5100
Dine on razor clams and sea
bass at this seafood oasis,
or enjoy the wide variety
of oysters and antipasti.
Excellent weekend brunch.

**Michael Jordan's
Steakhouse NYC** $$$
American
*23 Vanderbilt Ave, Grand Central
Terminal, 10017*
Tel (212) 655-2300
The chances of seeing the
celebrity basketball player
are slim, but the steaks are
perfectly charred. Ideal for
a power lunch.

Molyvos $$$
Greek   Map 12 E4
871 Seventh Ave, 10019
Tel (212) 582-7500
Superb Greek fare, from steaming
moussaka to juicy lamb. There is
also a fish display showcasing
what the kitchen has to offer.
Nice, spacious dining rooms.

Morimoto $$$
Japanese   Map 7 C5
88 Tenth Ave, 10011
Tel (212)-989-8883
Choose anything from fresh sushi
to "Kentucky Fried" blowfish. A
sake sommelier will act as your
guide to the exceptionally
extensive sake menu.

Russian Tea Room $$$
Russian   Map 12 E3
150 W 57th St, 10019
Tel (212) 581-7100
Although nowhere near its
famous original counterpart,
this opulent Russian restaurant
still knocks out a delicious
stroganoff (sautéd beef) and
an even better chicken kiev.

Classic burger at Michael Jordan's
The Steak House NYC , Midtown

The Sea Grill $$$
Seafood   Map 12 F5
19 West 49th St, 10020
Tel (212) 332-7610   **Closed** *Sun*
An elegant temple to seafood,
with superb grilled fish and
shellfish. Modern setting with
spectacular views.

Smith & Wollensky $$$
American   Map 13 B5
797 Third Ave, 10022
Tel (212) 753-1530
Bite into quality steaks at this
clubby steakhouse. Equally
hearty are the appetizers,
including split-pea soup
and seafood cocktails.

Upper Manhattan

Amy Ruth's $
Southern American   Map 21 B3
113 West 116th St, 10026
Tel (212) 280-8779
Soul food at its most comforting,
from delicious fried chicken to
ham hocks.

Beyoglu $
Turkish   Map 17 B5
1431 Second Ave, 10028
Tel (212) 650-0850
This whimsically decorated
place offers delicious and
authentic meze, including
stuffed grape leaves and *borek*
(filo pastry parcels stuffed with
feta cheese).

Café Frida $
Mexican   Map 16 D5
368 Columbus Ave, 10024
Tel (212) 712-2929
Chomp on Mexican favorites
such as fajitas and tacos at
this lively spot, and wash
them down with the tangy,
potent Margaritas.

Shanghai Pavilion $
Chinese   Map 17 B5
1378 Third Ave, 10021
Tel (212) 585-3388
Extensive menu of Shanghai
specialties, including top-
notch dim sum. Also offers
unique seafood dishes, such
as lobster tropicana. Great
food overall.

Sisters Cuisine $
Caribbean   Map 21 C2
47 E 124th St, 10035
Tel (212) 410-3000
Sample some of the best
Caribbean food in Harlem here.
The menu includes incredible
Jamaican jerk chicken, Trinidad-
style callaloo, and Guyanese
bread pockets.

Bar Boulud $$
French Map 12 D2
1900 Broadway, 10023
Tel (212) 595-0303
Famed chef Daniel Boulud opened this "peasant" restaurant with rustic French fare. The decor is sleek and modern, and there is an outdoor terrace area.

Brother Jimmy's BBQ $$
American Map 17 B5
1485 Second Ave, 10021
Tel (212) 288-0999
Carnivores will swoon at this rowdy restaurant with "finger-lickin'" BBQ. Thanks to the generous portions, it offers great value for money.

Café d'Alsace $$
French Map 17 B3
1695 Second Ave, 10128
Tel (212) 722-5133
A cheery slice of French Alsace, with tiled floors, flowing red wine, and crisp *tartes*. Opt for a sidewalk table to watch the crowds stream by.

Café Boulud $$
French Map 16 F5
20 East 76th St, 10021
Tel (212) 772-2600
Enjoy chef Daniel Boulud's impeccable creations in a casual setting. Seasonal dishes include duck breast with Brussels sprouts and apple cider.

Café Fiorello $$
Italian Map 12 D2
1900 Broadway, 10023
Tel (212) 595-5330
Tuck into an array of dishes from the antipasto bar at this cheerful joint. Don't miss the signature thin-crust pizza. Sit outside in warm weather

and watch the Lincoln Center crowds stream by.

Café Luxembourg $$
French Map 11 C1
200 W 70th St, 10024
Tel (212) 873-7411
An Art Deco Parisian bistro that is popular with business diners. Charmingly traditional, with antique mirrors and a zinc-topped bar.

Café Sabarsky $$
Austrian Map 16 F3
1048 Fifth Ave, 10028
Tel (212) 288-0665 **Closed** *Tue*
Classic Viennese café with aromatic coffees and hearty specialties from goulash to strudel. Lovely dining room lined with Austrian art.

Calle Ocho $$
Cuban Map 16 D4
45 W 81st St, 10024
Tel (212) 873-5025
It's a never-ending party at this colorful restaurant. Feast on a range of spicy Latino dishes, from *ceviche* to yucca fries, or try the marinated Aji tuna and cured salmon.

The Cecil $$
African-American Map 21 A3
210 W 118th St, 10026
Tel (212) 866-1262
Visit this stylish brasserie for its creative fusion menu, influenced by the African diaspora. Try the oxtail dumplings and the mussels with roti.

Dinosaur Bar-B-Que $$
American Map 20 D1
700 West 125th St, 10027
Tel (212) 694-1777
Started by avid bike enthusiasts, this rowdy BBQ joint dishes out

massive ribs, crispy chicken wings, and American beers. Come by on the weekends for live jazz and comedy shows.

Flex Mussels $$
Belgian Map 17 A4
174 E 82nd St
Tel (212) 717-7772
Be charmed by this delightful seafood bistro. Delicious mussels in a rainbow of flavors, from prosciutto and caramelized onion to blue cheese and bacon. The wine list is good too.

DK Choice

Gennaro $$
Italian Map 15 C2
665 Amsterdam Ave, 10025
Tel (212) 665-5348
Delectable cuisine, and a reasonably priced wine list. The lamb shank braised in red wine is quite a hit. There is a no-reservation policy at this popular restaurant, so be prepared to wait during peak times.

Loeb Boathouse Restaurant Central Park $$
American Map 12 E1
East 72nd St and Park Drive North, Central Park, 10023
Tel (212) 515-2233
Lovely setting by Central Park's lake. Popular with couples on a romantic date. Decent American fare and an outdoor bar area.

Maya $$
Mexican Map 13 C2
1191 First Ave, 10021
Tel (212) 585-1818
Come here for Mexican specialties – try the flavorsome guacamole and freshly made tortillas. Don't miss the drinks, from tangy margaritas to tequilas.

Penrose $$
American Map 17 B4
1590 Second Ave, 10028
Tel (212) 203-2571
Don't miss the delicious Pat LaFrieda Penrose burger, and the divine Irish breakfast, at this popular gastropub. A great lunch excursion from Museum Mile.

Pio Pio $$
Peruvian Map 15 C2
702 Amsterdam Ave, 10025
Tel (212) 665-3000
Try the signature crispy rotisserie chicken here. The hearty combo platters are a great way to save money – they're easily big enough to feed two.

Lovely outdoor seating at Cafe Boulud, Upper Manhattan

For more information on types of restaurants *see p291*

DK Choice

Red Rooster   **$$**
American   **Map** 21 B1
310 Malcolm X Ave, 10027
Tel (212) 792-9001
Clever, Southern-style comfort food is on offer at Red Rooster. Try the succulent steak with fried green tomatoes, tasty roast pork loin, or fiery jerk chicken. The restaurant's name pays homage to the original Red Rooster, a Harlem speakeasy where liquor was sold illicitly during Prohibition.

Stylish dining room at Daniel, Upper Manhattan, a great place for delightful French cuisine

Rosa Mexicano   **$$**
Mexican   **Map** 12 D2
61 Columbus Ave, 10023
Tel (212) 977-7700
This trendy restaurant serves sparkling sangrias and chunky guacamole. Try dishes such as tacos with achiote-seasoned pork, or spicy enchiladas. Gluten-free lunch and dinner are also on offer.

Sfoglia   **$$**
Italian   **Map** 17 A2
1402 Lexington Ave, 10128
Tel (212) 831-1402
A small and rustic eatery with Italian farmhouse fare such as duck with apricots. The menu changes bimonthly, and the Italian wine list is excellent.

Sylvia's   **$$**
Southern American   **Map** 21 B1
328 Malcolm X Ave, 10027
Tel (212) 996-0660
Soul food at its finest, from fried chicken with waffles to Carolina-style catfish. The breakfast spread is quite elaborate. The Southern desserts, including the peach cobbler, are divine.

Telepan   **$$**
American   **Map** 12 D1
72 West 69th St, 10023
Tel (212) 580-4300
Chef Bill Telepan sources local ingredients to create innovative dishes such as heirloom tomato gazpacho salad. There is a prix-fixe brunch menu, as well as a four-course tasting menu.

Asiate   **$$$**
Asian   **Map** 12 D3
80 Columbus Circle, 10019
Tel (212) 805-8881
Stellar views are matched by creative Asian cuisine. Popular dishes include Wagyu beef with oxtail sauce, pan-seared foie gras, and

butter-poached lobster. Three-course fixed-price brunch menu on weekends.

DK Choice

Daniel   **$$$**
French   **Map** 13 A2
60 East 65th St, 10021
Tel (212) 288-0033   **Closed** Sun
If splurging in the city is the objective, this is the place to do it. The opulent French restaurant of acclaimed chef Daniel Boulud offers a superlative sensory experience, from the first step into the grand dining room and the rich forkful of foie gras to the final bite of the sinful chocolate mousse. Excellent wine list and seamless service make the Daniel experience truly worthwhile.

Jean-Georges   **$$$**
French   **Map** 12 D3
1 Central Park West, 10023
Tel (212) 299-3900   **Closed** Sun
The jewel in the crown of famed French chef Jean-Georges Vongerichten. For an optimal overview, choose one of the exquisite tasting menus. The stress is on organic ingredients.

Elegant interiors at the well-reviewed Per Se, Upper Manhattan

Masa   **$$$**
Japanese   **Map** 12 D3
10 Columbus Circle, 10029
Tel (212) 823-9800   **Closed** Sun
Chef Masa breaks the record for the most expensive tasting meal ever at $450, but it is well worth every cent. Take a seat at the sushi bar to watch the chefs in action.

Per Se   **$$$**
American   **Map** 12 D3
10 Columbus Circle, 10019
Tel (212) 823-9335
Chef Thomas Keller has introduced superlative Californian-influenced cuisine to New York. There are two unique nine-course tasting menus to indulge in, and a great selection of wines, plus spectacular views of Central Park.

Picholine   **$$$**
French   **Map** 12 D2
35 West 64th St, 10023
Tel (212) 724-8585   **Closed** Sun
Popular with those attending a concert at Lincoln Center, Picholine offers superb French-Mediterranean cuisine and artisanal cheeses. Sample the diver sea scallops or the steamed black sea bass.

Sasabune   **$$$**
Sushi   **Map** 13 C1
401 East 73rd St, 10021
Tel (212) 249-8583
At this outpost of the famed Los Angeles and Honolulu sushi shrines the only option is the nightly *omakase* (chef's tasting) menu, freshly prepared to order.

**Tavern on
the Green**   **$$$**
American   **Map** 12 D2
Central Park West & 67th St, 10023
Tel (212) 877-8684
Central Park's most famous restaurant serves modern fare to well-heeled locals and visitors, many of whom come here to celebrate special occasions.

Brooklyn

Pies-n-Thighs $
American
166 South 4th St., Brooklyn, 11211
Tel (347) 529-6090
Classic American, from the dining to the decor. Try shrimp and grits, fried chicken, pulled pork, and butter biscuits. Delicious breakfast spread, and the weekend brunch menu is great.

al di là $$
Italian
248 Fifth Ave, 11215
Tel (718) 783-4565
Try the braised rabbit with black olives at this whimsical Venetian-inspired joint. Don't miss the mouthwatering desserts, including tangy gelato.

Fette Sau $$
American
354 Metropolitan Ave, 11211
Tel (718) 963-3404
Juicy BBQ, from ribs to pork belly, served in a rustic former garage. Wash the meal down with robust beer or a glass of wine.

Frankie's 457 Spuntino $$
Italian
457 Court St, 11231
Tel (718) 403-0033
Trendy neighborhood favorite with brick walls, hearty food, and stiff cocktails. Seasonal dishes include giant meatballs and eggplant crostini.

Grimaldi's $$
Italian
19 Old Fulton St, 11201
Tel (718) 387-7400
One of New York's most famous pizzerias. The coal-fired oven pizzas, with creamy mozzarella and fresh tomato sauce, are worth the long lines.

Marlow & Sons $$
American
81 Broadway, 11211
Tel (718) 384-1441
Wonderfully eccentric, with communal tables and Mediterranean-influenced American fare. The menu leans towards organic, and includes delicacies such as a tart of goat's cheese and wild leeks.

Pok Pok NY $$
Thai
117 Columbia St, 11231
Tel (718) 923-9322
Portland chef Andy Ricker has created quite a buzz with his showcase of northern Thai cuisine, with the sticky wings and pork ribs with mustard greens special favorites.

Prime Meats $$
American
465 Court St, 11231
Tel (718) 254-0327
A delight for carnivores, this friendly restaurant offers all kinds of meat from pork schnitzel to grass-fed beef. There's also a strong domestic beer list and potent cocktails.

Red Hook Lobster Pound $$
Seafood
284 Van Brunt St, 11231
Tel (646) 326-7650   **Closed** Mon
Fresh lobster meat is served every which way at this seafood shack. Choose a Maine lobster from the saltwater tank and have it cooked. The flexible catering service includes a specialized "lobster" truck that delivers door to door.

Rye Restaurant $$
American
247 South 1st St, 11211
Tel (718) 218-8047
Taste the succulent meatloaf sandwich and wash it down with a creative cocktail at this former factory.

DK Choice

Peter Luger Steak House $$$
American
178 Broadway, 11211
Tel (718) 387-7400
Since 1897, this New York institution has been satisfying carnivores with massive juicy slabs, from porterhouse to prime rib and pot roast. The sauce is rather too delectable, and the good news is that it can be taken home – it's bottled and for sale.

Farther Afield

Elias Corner $
Greek
24–02 31st St, Queens, 11102
Tel (718) 932-1510
Hugely popular restaurant with the freshest fish in town. The large garden is perfect for groups.

Jackson Diner $
Indian
37–47 74th St, Queens, 11372
Tel (718) 672-1232
Spacious cafeteria with one of the best buffets in town. Classic North Indian appetizers; try the tandoori chicken (cooked in a clay oven), samosas (fried stuffed pastries), and thick lassis (yogurt-based drinks).

Sripraphai $
Thai
64-13 39th Ave, Queens, 11377
Tel (718) 899-9599   **Closed** Wed
Locals swear by this place, said to serve the best Thai in the city. There is an elaborate menu dedicated to vegetarian food – try the sauteed drunken noodles with tofu, vegetables, chili, and basil leaves. Wash it down with some black Thai ice tea.

Agnanti Meze $$
Greek
19-06 Ditmars Blvd, Queens, 11105
Tel (718) 545-4554
Lively place with filled grape leaves and filo pastry stuffed with cheese on the menu. There is an outdoor patio for the summer, and a fireplace for winter.

Il Bambino $$
Italian
34–08 31st Ave, Queens, 11106
Tel (718) 626-0087
Solid Italian-American cuisine, such as fat paninis, and affordable wines on the extensive wine list. Try their popular peanut butter hot chocolate. Casual atmosphere and sharp service.

Peter Luger Steakhouse, a haven for meat lovers, Brooklyn

For more information on types of restaurants *see p291*

Light Meals and Snacks

You can get a snack almost anywhere and anytime in Manhattan. New Yorkers seem to eat endlessly – on street corners, in bars, luncheonettes, delis, before and after work, and long into the night. Casual eating in New York might include soft pretzels or char-roasted chestnuts from a corner stand; a huge sandwich from a deli; a Greek gyro sandwich (roasted lamb in pita bread) from street vendors; a pre-theater snack at a café or coffee bar; or a post-party binge at an all-night diner or bistro. While street fare is generally cheap, the quality and culinary skills vary greatly.

Food Halls and Markets

With the success of Mario Batali's **Eataly** (see p125), and **Smorgasburg**, the Brookyn food fair that debuted in 2011, gourmet food halls and markets are fiercly popular in New York. **Le District** is a French-themed hall in Brookfield Place (see p71), while **Chelsea Market** occupies the old Nabisco factory on the edge of the Meatpacking District. **The Pennsy** opened its doors in 2016 atop Manhattan's Pen Station and offers high end fast food from famous New York chefs. Celebrity chef Anthony Bourdain is due to open **Bourdain Market** – a farmers' market with, oyster bar, rooftop beer garden and Singaporean hawker-style food stalls – on Pier 57 in Chelsea by the end of 2016.

Delis

Delicatessens are a New York institution, not to mention a great source for a hefty lunch-time sandwich. Any visitor to the city should definitely try a deli's wonderful corned beef and pastrami sandwiches. While **Carnegie Delicatessen** in the Theater District is perhaps New York's most famous deli, **Katz's Deli** on the Lower East Side is much more authentic – and cheaper. Also deservedly popular is **Second Avenue Deli**, with its superb pastrami on rye.

Most deli business is takeout, and, as a result, delis are bustling places serving huge sandwiches at relatively cheap prices. Counter staff are typically surly, but to many that is part of the charm of these old-school establishments. **Mile End** provides a more modern deli experience. For New York ethnic Jewish flavor, try **Barney Greengrass**, on the Upper West Side. In operation since 1929, the "Sturgeon King" serves up lox, salmon, pastrami, and, of course, sturgeon. **Zabar's** is a takeout heaven for yuppies who put up with the crowds for superb smoked fish, pickles, and salads.

Cafés, Bistros, and Brasseries

Cafés, bistros, and the larger brasseries have become "in" places in New York. Try the upscale **Balthazar** on Spring Street for "brilliantly faux" everything except the menu, which is stellar. In the Meat-packing District, **Kava Cafe** serves gourmet sandwiches and expertly prepared coffees to a stylish crowd. The **Café Centro**, above Grand Central, is busy and noisy during lunchtime, and is a favorite with business types. The Centro's Provençal/Mediterranean fare includes fish soups and some succulent desserts. **Brasserie** on East 53rd, a longtime landmark, has had an elegant remodeling. **Benoit**, Alain Ducasse's casual bistro, is a classy destination offering familiar French fare to the Midtown lunch crowd. Down-town, **Odeon** is a TriBeCa favorite for its brasserie menu and late hours. **Raoul's** in SoHo is a French bistro with a relaxed ambience that keeps artists coming back for reliable, informal food.

Elephant and Castle, a minimally decorated café, is a Greenwich Village standby for soup-salad-omelet lunches. Its real forte is breakfast and brunch, served in ample portions at modest prices. The bar scene is lively too. Tiny **Chez Jacqueline** is also a favored Village spot. Its French bistro fare and proximity to several off-Broadway theaters make it popular with the young, and international crowd for a moderately priced dinner.

In the Theater District, try the Cuban **Victor's Café**. Large, lively, and Latin, it is known for authentic Cuban food served in giant portions at medium prices. **Chez Josephine** is an exuberant bistro-cabaret with live jazz piano playing. The scene is the main attraction here, and the French food is excellent.

La Boite en Bois, small but delightfully French, serves delicious French bistro food and is conveniently close to Lincoln Center. **P. J. Clarke's** is a welcoming bar famous for its burgers; it is also an affordable spot for a pre-theater meal.

Sarabeth's, on the Upper West Side, defies categorizing, but might best be dubbed a café. Breakfast or weekend brunch is the best time to try waffles, French toast, pancakes, and omelets.

The Gramercy Park area's **Les Halles** is about as all-out French bistro as New York gets. At its late-night peak, the decibel level is high, but regulars think the *frites* and beef dishes are worth the noise and crowds.

Pizzerias

Pizza is available all over New York, from street stands and fast-food places that sell it by the slice to a traditional Neapolitan pizzeria.

Some pizzerias offer some-thing more. **Arturo's Pizzeria** uses a coal oven for crisp, thin-crusted bases with the added inducement of live jazz. **Mezzogiorno** has a Tuscan menu and wonderful pizzas with unusual toppings. **Lombardi's** oven-baked pizzas are among the finest in Manhattan. The busy **Mezzaluna** also specializes in brick-oven, thin- crusted pizza,

as does **John's Pizzeria**, whose
fans, including Woody Allen,
consider it Manhattan's best. At
Two Boots, specialty pies are
named for characters in movies
and TV shows, such as The
Newman, from *Seinfeld*, and The
Dude, from *The Big Lebowski*.

Brooklyn boasts a top pizzeria
in Coney Island's **Totonno
Pizzeria**, which is well worth the
trip for real pizza aficionados.
Joe's Pizza has made a name for
itself in Manhattan. It's often
busy, but the lines move quickly.

Generally, pizza parlors are
good places to go for a cheap,
simple meal, particularly with
children. Most places won't take
reservations, so the popular
ones may have long lines.

Burger Joints

Apart from the hot-dog stands
on the street, New York has
many places selling better-
quality burgers, even though
prices for a top-notch gourmet
burger can often top $20.

Burgers have even gone
"upscale" with famed New
York restaurateur Danny Meyer
creating the **Shake Shack**,
which has several locations
around Manhattan, including
one at Madison Square Park. It
offers good-value eats all year
round. In Midtown, the stylish
Le Parker Meridien Hotel houses
the **Burger Joint**, which looks
like a truck-stop, and has some
of the best burgers in town.

Bright and basic, the five outlets
of **Jackson Hole** offer juicy, meaty
burgers in 28 varieties that are
popular with kids. Adults might
prefer smarter decor, but they
will like the low prices. Alternatively, sink your teeth into the
burgers at the **Five Guys** chain.

The **Corner Bistro** in Greenwich
Village offers great burgers,
which are tasty and reasonably
priced. The beer selection is good,
too, and the 4am closing makes
this a great late-night stop.

Diners and Luncheonettes

Diners and luncheonettes, also
called sandwich or coffee shops,
can be found all over the city.

Food is sometimes bland but
served in huge, cheap platefuls.
They are usually open from
breakfast until evening, and you
can stop in at almost any hour.

A favorite trend with diners
has seen 1990s replicas of the
old 1930s cheap-eats places.
One such retro diner is **Chock
Full o' Nuts**, a relaunch of a
chain of coffee-branded cafés.
A brighter, higher-energy option
can be found near Carnegie Hall,
in the **Brooklyn Diner**.

Theatergoers love **Junior's**
diner in Brooklyn, which is
famous for its delicious cheesecake. In the heart of Brooklyn's
hip Williamsburg neighborhood,
Diner offers an upscale take on
the NYC diner experience. **The
Coffee Shop** in Union Square
serves Brazilian-American fare
and is open all night.

On the Upper East Side, Eli
Zabar's **E.A.T.** sells excellent
but pricey Jewish favorites –
such as mushroom-barley soup
and challah bread, as well as
some sinful desserts. Another
popular spot in this area is **EJ's
Luncheonette**, offering classic
kid-friendly meals in a retro
1950s setting.

Veselka, not the usual New
York sandwich shop, serves
Polish/Ukrainian food at rock-
bottom prices to an eclectic
local crowd 24 hours a day.

Tea Rooms

Enjoy top-notch service, a range
of gourmet teas, and delightful
bites at a formal, prix-fixe
afternoon tea in a lounge at one
of New York's pricier hotels,
usually offered from 3 to 5pm.

For an extra-stylish tea, on
Chippendale furniture, visit
Carlyle in the Upper East Side.
Another good buy in hotel prix-
fixe tea is **Hotel Pierre**. Tea at the
Waldorf-Astoria comes with
Devonshire cream, while the
elegant tea at the Palm Court at
The Plaza has been an NYC
tradition for more than a century.

A variation on tea themes can
be found in a chain of teahouses
called **Saint's Alp**. These
delightful spots, serving frothy,
flavored, colorful tea drinks
poured over crushed ice, can be

found in the East Village and
Williamsburg areas. Teatime
can also be enjoyed at **Tea &
Sympathy**, in the Village, on
Greenwich Avenue.

Coffee and Cakes

You can get a decent cup of
coffee for as little as a dollar or
two, with endless free refills, at
most diners, luncheonettes,
and coffee shops. There is a
popular trend for coffee bars
that serve a variety of specialty
coffees, such as cappuccino,
espresso, and caffè latte. Ice-
cream parlors and patisseries
also serve good coffee, along
with sinfully luscious pastries.

People wait in lines out the
door at **Magnolia Bakery**'s
original Greenwich Village
location. There are also several
other outposts across the city
selling decadent cupcakes
and delicious cookies. **Joe**, the
self-proclaimed master of
"the art of coffee," maintains
numerous locations around
the city, while **Ferrara Bakery
and Café**, going strong since
1892, has moderately priced
Italian pastries, good coffee,
and outdoor seating.

**The Hungarian Pastry
Shop** has a range of Austro-
Hungarian delights and views
of St. John the Divine. **Sant
Ambroeus** is a luxurious
outpost of the Milanese
pasticceria selling sumptuous
desserts. In addition to home
delivery of pies or cakes,
Dessert Delivery has a nifty
café for tasting the pastries
and coffee. Try **Serendipity 3**,
famous for its Victoriana, ice-
cream creations – if you're an
ice-cream aficionado don't
miss the frozen hot chocolate
– as well as coffee, and mid-
afternoon snacks.

Barnes & Noble Café is a
happy refuge for coffee and
a pastry while browsing the
bookstore. **Mudspot** is the
permanent counterpart to the
mobile, bright orange
"Mudtrack" van that sells
potent coffee. And, like them
or not, you can't ignore
Starbucks, which has dozens
of locations around town.

DIRECTORY

Lower Manhattan and the Civic Center

Le District
Brookfield Pl, West St.
Map 1A2.

Lower East Side

Ferrara Bakery and Café
195 Grand St.
Map 4 F4.

Katz's Deli
205 E Houston St.
Map 5 A3.

Saint's Alp
39 3rd Ave.
Map 4 F1.

Two Boots
42 Avenue A.
Map 5 B2.

SoHo and TriBeCa

Lombardi's
32 Spring St.
Map 4 F4.

Mezzogiorno
195 Spring St.
Map 4 D4.

Odeon
145 W Broadway.
Map 1 B1.

Raoul's
180 Prince St.
Map 4 D3.

Starbucks
72 Spring St.
Map 4 F4.
One of many branches.

Greenwich Village

Arturo's Pizzeria
106 W Houston St.
Map 4 E3.

Balthazar
80 Spring St.
Map 4 E4.

Chelsea Market
75 9th Ave.
Map 3 A1.

Chez Jacqueline
72 MacDougal St.
Map 4 D2.

Corner Bistro
331 W 4th St.
Map 3 C1.

Elephant and Castle
68 Greenwich Ave.
Map 3 C1.

Five Guys
296 Bleecker St.
Map 3 C3.

Joe
141 Waverly Place.
Map 3 C1.

Joe's Pizza
7 Carmine St.
Map 4 D3.

Kava Cafe
803 Washington St.
Map 3 B1.

Magnolia Bakery
401 Bleecker St.
Map 3 C2.
200 Columbus Ave.
Map 12 D1.

Sant Ambroeus
259 W 4th St.
Map 3 C1.

Tea & Sympathy
108 Greenwich Ave.
Map 3 C1.

East Village

Mile End
53 Bond St. Map 4 F2.

Mudspot
307 E 9th St. Map 4 F1.

Veselka
144 2nd Ave. Map 4 F1.

Gramercy and the Flatiron

The Coffee Shop
29 Union Square West.
Map 9 A5.

Eataly
200 Fifth Ave. Map 8 F4.

Les Halles
411 Park Ave South.
Map 9 A3.

Shake Shack
Madison Square Park.
Map 8 F4.

Chelsea and the Garment District

Bourdain Market
Pier 57. Map 7 B5.

Chock Full o' Nuts
119 E 23rd St.
Map 9 A4.

The Pennsy
2 Pennsylvania Plaza.
Map 8 E2.

Midtown West and the Theater District

Carnegie Delicatessen
854 7th Ave. Map 12 E4.

Chez Josephine
414 W 42nd St. Map 7 B1.

John's Pizzeria
260 W 44th St.
Map 12 E5.
One of three branches.

Junior's
Shubert Alley, enter on
45th St. Map 12 E5.

Victor's Café
236 W 52nd St. Map 11 B4.

Lower Midtown

Second Avenue Deli
162 E 33rd St. Map 9 B2.

Café Centro
Grand Central Station, E
42nd St at Park Ave.
Map 9 A1.

Upper Midtown

Barnes & Noble Café
Citicorp Building, 160 E
54th St. Map 13 A4.

Brasserie
100 E 53rd St.
Map 13 A4.

Brooklyn Diner
212 W 57th St.
Map 12 E3.

Burger Joint
Le Parker Meridien Hotel,
118 W 57th St.
Map 12 E3.

Waldorf-Astoria
301 Park Ave. Map 13 A5.

Upper East Side

Benoit
60 W 55th St. Map 12 F3.

Carlyle
35 E 76th St. Map 17 A5.

Dessert Delivery
350 E 55th St.
Map 13 B4.
Tel 838-5411.

E.A.T.
1064 Madison Ave.
Map 17 A4.

EJ's Luncheonette
1271 3rd Ave. Map 13 B1.

Hotel Pierre
2 E 61st St.
Map 12 F3.

Jackson Hole
232 E 64th St.
Map 13 B2.
One of several branches.

Mezzaluna
1295 3rd Ave.
Map 17 B5.

The Plaza
768 5th Ave.
Map 12 F3.

Serendipity 3
225 E 60th St.
Map 13 B3.

Upper West Side

Barney Greengrass
541 Amsterdam Ave.
Map 15 C3.

La Boite en Bois
75 W 68th St.
Map 11 C1.

P.J. Clarke's
44 W 63rd St.
Map 12 D2.

Sarabeth's
423 Amsterdam Ave.
Map 15 C4.

Zabar's
2245 Broadway.
Map 15 C2.

Morningside Heights and Harlem

The Hungarian Pastry Shop
1030 Amsterdam &
109th St. Map 20 E4.

Brooklyn

Diner
85 Broadway, Brooklyn
Map 23 B2.

Smorgasburg
90 Kent Ave.
Map 23 B1.

Totonno Pizzeria
1524 Neptune Ave.

New York Bars

New York bars play a huge role in the life and culture of the city. Many New Yorkers spend the evening in a succession of bars, because each usually offers something more than just alcohol. There may be additional inducements, such as excellent food, live music, dancing, or a particularly large selection of beers. Brew pubs, which serve meals and brew beer on the premises, are also popular. Bars suiting every taste and budget are to be found on most corners.

Rules and Conventions

Bars generally remain open from around 11am until 2am. The majority stay open to 4am, when they must close by law. Many bars have a "happy hour," usually between 4 and 6pm, when they offer deals such as two drinks for the price of one and free snacks. Bartenders can refuse to serve anyone they consider having had too much to drink. Smoking is banned and is only allowed outside or in specially ventilated rooms.

The legal minimum drinking age is 21; if the bartender suspects you are younger, you'll be "carded," or asked for identification. Children aren't usually allowed in.

It is common to "run a tab" by giving the bartender a credit card and paying your bill just before you leave. Tipping the bartender is expected – 15 per cent of the bill or at least $1 per drink. Shots are not pre-measured, so if you want a bigger drink, it can help to "belly up" to the bar and tip the bartender accordingly for his or her generosity. You may even be poured a free drink if you tip handsomely. If you sit at a table, you'll be served there and charged more. A round of drinks can be expensive. Save money by buying a quart (95 cl) or a half-gallon (190 cl) pitcher of beer.

Many bars have obtained liquor licenses under an obscure cabaret law that prohibits dancing. Bars are regularly closed down for ignoring this rule, so if staff ask you to refrain from dancing to music, they are serious and should be obeyed.

What to Drink

Mainstream bars serve standard beers from big producers, such as Budweiser, Coors, and Miller, as well as high-profile imports including Becks, Heineken, and draft Guinness. Old pubs and chic bars have a much wider variety of beers, imported and small domestics. These include flavorful beers, usually based on traditional European styles, made by some of New York's microbreweries. The locally brewed Brooklyn Lager is highly rated.

Other popular drinks include "designer," or "fusion," cocktails, rum and coke, vodka and tonic, gin and tonic, dry Martinis, and Scotch or bourbon – either "straight up" (without ice) or "on the rocks" (with ice). The "Cosmopolitan" is very New York – vodka, cranberry juice, triple sec, and lime. Most of the bars serve a range of Martinis made with vodka.

Wine is widely available at bars, and the "wine bar" concept has made a comeback, with options all over the city.

Food

Some bars serve food such as burgers, fries, salads, sandwiches, and spicy chicken wings throughout the day. If you are visiting the bar of a popular restaurant, you can often order bar snacks. The majority of bar kitchens stop serving food around midnight.

Fashionable Bars

To get into a hip bar, you might need to look glamorous and be prepared to wait in line, unless you arrive early.

The Meatpacking District is lined with lively bars, including **Cielo**, a strobe-lit bar and club with potent cocktails and a soundtrack with everything from 1980s pop to hip hop. Hidden away in the trendy West Village is **Employees Only**, a stylish hangout that has won a cult-like following due to its expert cocktails and intense waitstaff. Many of its staff depart to run cocktail programs around the world. The bar's famed Bloody Mary mix can be purchased at fine specialty shops across the city. **Tao Bar**, located in a former theater next to the Four Seasons Hotel, is spread over three floors: the top two are devoted to pan-Asian cuisine and overlook the bar below. The nightlife in the Lower East Side (LES) is growing in leaps and bounds, with numerous bars and clubs opening their doors. Enjoy cocktails and conversation at the lively **Schiller's Liquor Bar**. Formerly the Bowery Bar, the **B-Bar** still attracts a stylish crowd, though some claim its glory days are over. In the summer, the enormous outdoor space can't be beaten. **Pravda** is another favorite in nearby NoLIta. Subdued lighting creates a degree of calm in this subterranean spot decorated in Soviet chic. **The Odeon** on Broadway captures the lively SoHo-TriBeCa scene.

Bars with Views

The Rooftop Bar, on top of the Pod 39 hotel, offers sensational views of Lower Manhattan and the Empire State. Also with great views are the **Rooftop Bar and Lounge** at the Empire Hotel, **Parkview Lounge** in the Time Warner Center, and, for views of the expanding World Trade Center skyline, the **Living Room Terrace** at the W Downtown. In warm weather, **Bryant Park Café** is a popular Midtown scene. Also with you can sip cocktails and soak up the dazzling views on **230 Fifth**'s vast wrap-around terrace.

Historic and Literary Bars

If you sample only one New York bar, it should probably be **McSorley's Old Ale House**, an Irish saloon often dubbed "McSurly's" because of its staff. It claims to have opened in 1854, and is one of the city's oldest bars.

The Ear Inn dates from 1890, when the first tavern opened on this SoHo site. Its cramped interior and long wooden bar ooze authenticity. Another SoHo favorite is **Fanelli's Café**, a former speakeasy that opened its doors in 1922 (though locals have been visiting the watering hole on this site since 1847).

Greenwich Village has some of the city's oldest bars, such as Dylan Thomas's favorite, the **White Horse Tavern**, an 1880s landmark still crowded with literary and collegiate types. It also has an outdoor café for warm weather. **Peculier Pub** is a beer-lover's paradise, with over 360 varieties of beer.

A good, if touristy, place for a drink in the financial district is **Fraunces Tavern**, first built in 1719 *(see p80)*.

Pete's Tavern in the Gramercy Park area dates to 1864. Busy until 2am, it is known for Victoriana and the house beer called Pete's Ale. The typical Irish pub **Old Town Bar** has been serving stout since 1892, and is now favored largely by advertising types. No longer the celebrity scene it once was, **Sardi's** still appeals to *New York Times* reporters, and serves generous portions.

Hidden away in the balcony of Grand Central Terminal is **The Campbell Apartment**, the former private office of 1920s tycoon John W. Campbell. The spectacular space resembles a 13th-century Florentine palace. On the Upper East Side, the **Uptown Lounge** offers potent cocktails, tasty nibbles, and lively dance tunes.

A bustling saloon with Irish bartenders, **P. J. Clarke's** has been New York's favorite since the 1890s. Dating back to 1930, the **21 Club** remains one of the city's most atmospheric haunts, complete with a ceiling crammed full of antique toys.

Near Carnegie Hall is **P. J. Carney's**, a watering hole for musicians and artists since 1927. It serves Irish ales and a good shepherd's pie.

Microbreweries

Since the 1990s America has been undergoing a craft beer-brewing renaissance, with mostly small and independant breweries producing small, exclusive batches of hoppy, tasty ales in a variety of styles. Though New York has arguably been a little slow developing a truly local microbrew scene, the situation is rapidly changing thanks in part to state legislation, with small-batch brewers, and bars that stock a variety of micro-brews, flourishing.

Founded in 1987, the **Brooklyn Brewery** pioneered the modern movement here, though it only started making beer at its Williamsburg headquarters in 1996. Today you can hang out in the brewery's cafeteria-style beer hall or take a tour. It's just $5 for a beer, and offerings include seasonal brews that you can't find in stores or restaurants.

Up in Greenpoint, Danish import **Tørst** serves 21 draughts in an appropriately sleek, barn-wood lined bar, including its own label, Evil Twin Brewing. Other Brooklyn spots to seek out are **Threes Brewing**, the Gowanus-based brewery with a full bar and 20 of its own beers on tap, and **Other Half Brewing** in Carroll Gardens, which offers a vast array of IPAs (India Pale Ales) and farmhouse ales.

Over in Queens there's **SingleCut Beersmiths**, a lager specialist, and **Transmitter Brewing**, producer of tasty farmhouse ales.

In Manhattan, **d.b.a** in the East Village features 14 draft beers on tap, while the West Village's **Blind Tiger Ale House** – for serious ale connoisseurs – boasts 28 rotating draughts.

Gay and Lesbian Bars

Gay bars can be found in Greenwich Village, Chelsea, and the East Village with a few on the Upper East and West Sides. Lesbian bars are mostly in Greenwich Village and the East Village. For current listings, check the free weekly gay publication *Next* (www.nextmagazine.com).

Hotel Bars

The **Algonquin Hotel** was a famous literary haunt in the 1920s and early 1930s, and its Lobby Lounge and Blue Bar remain atmospheric places for a drink.

The minimalist **Bar 44** in the Royalton Hotel is a perfect spot for a Martini while watching the theatrical crowds drifting in and out. Also in the Theater District, the **Paramount Bar** has floor-to-ceiling windows and is usually frequented by theater types.

The **Bull and Bear** in the Waldorf-Astoria, dating back to the Prohibition era, exudes comfort, charm, and a sense of history.

The stylish **King Cole Bar** at St. Regis Hotel is named after the colorful mural behind the bar, by Maxfield Parrish. The Bloody Mary is reputed to have been invented here.

The swanky **Grand Bar** at the SoHo Grand is one of New York's trendier nightspots, while the Roxy Hotel also draws a crowd to its **Church Lounge**.

The **Sky Terrace** at the Hudson Hotel offers scintillating views of the Hudson River. The **Rose Bar** and **Jade Bar**, in Gramercy Park Hotel, are filled with fashionistas drinking in the "eclectic-Bohemian" vibe.

The Upper East Side features **Bar Pléiades**, The Surrey's stylish Art Deco homage to Chanel, and **Bemelmans Bar** in the Carlyle, adorned with the whimsical murals of Ludwig Bemelmans.

DIRECTORY

Lower Manhattan and the Civic Center

Fraunces Tavern
54 Pearl St.
Map 1 C4.
w frauncestavern.com

Living Room Terrace
W Downtown,
123 Washington St.
Map 1 B3.

SoHo and TriBeCa

Church Lounge
Roxy Hotel, 26th Ave.
Map 4 D4.
w tribecagrand.com

The Ear Inn
326 Spring St.
Map 3 C4.
w earinn.com

Fanelli's Café
94 Prince St.
Map 4 E3.

The Grand Bar
SoHo Grand, 310
W Broadway.
Map 4 E4.
w sohogrand.com

The Odeon
145 W Broadway.
Map 1 B1.
w theodeonrestaurant.
com

Pravda
281 Lafayette St.
Map 4 F3.
w pravdany.com

Greenwich Village

Cielo
18 Little W 12th St.
Map 3 B1.
w cieloclub.com

Employees Only
510 Hudson St.
Map 3 C2.
w employeesonly
nyc.com

Peculier Pub
145 Bleecker St.
Map 4 D3.
w peculierpub.com

White Horse Tavern
567 Hudson St.
Map 3 C1.

East Village and Lower East Side

B-Bar
40 E 4th St. Map 4 F2.
w bbarandgrill.com

d.b.a.
41 1st Ave. Map 5 A1.
w drinkgoodstuff.com

McSorley's Old Ale House
15 E 7th St.
Map 4 F2.
w mcsorleysnewyork.
com

Schiller's Liquor Bar
131 Rivington St.
Map 5 B3.

Gramercy

Jade Bar
Gramercy Park Hotel,
2 Lexington Ave.
Map 9 A4.
w gramercypark
hotel.com

Old Town Bar
45 E 18th St. Map 8 F5.
w oldtownbar.com

Pete's Tavern
129 E 18th St.
Map 9 A5.
w petestavern.com

Rose Bar
Gramercy Park Hotel,
2 Lexington Ave.
Map 9 A4.
w gramercypark
hotel.com

Midtown West and the Theater District

The Algonquin Hotel
59 W 44th St.
Map 12 F5.
w algonquinhotel.com

Bar 44
Royalton Hotel,
44 W 44th St.
Map 12 F5.

Bryant Park Café
Bryant Park.
Map 8 F1.
w bryantpark.org

Paramount Bar
Paramount Hotel,
235 W 46th St.
Map 12 E5.

P. J. Carney's
906 7th Ave. Map 12 E3.
w pjcarneys.com

Sardi's
234 W 44th St.
Map 12 F5.
w sardis.com

Sky Terrace
Hudson Hotel,
356 W 58th St.
Map 12 D3.
w hudsonhotel.com

Lower Midtown

230 Fifth
230 Fifth Ave.
Map 8 F3.

Bookmarks
The Library Hotel, 299
Madison Ave.
Map 9 A1.

The Campbell Apartment
Grand Central Terminal,
15 Vanderbilt Ave.
Map 9 A1.

Upper Midtown

21 Club
21 W 52nd St.
Map 12 F4.
w 21club.com

Bull and Bear
Waldorf-Astoria Hotel,
Lexington Ave.
Map 13 A5.
w bullbearbar.com

King Cole Room
St. Regis Hotel,
2 E 55th St.
Map 12 F5.

P. J. Clarke's
915 3rd Ave.
Map 13 B4.

Parkview Lounge
10 Columbus Circle,
4th Floor.
Map 12 D3.
w gerberbars.com

Rooftop at Pod 39
Pod 39, 145 East 39th St.
Map 9 A1.
w thepodhotel.com

Tao Bar
42 E 58th St.
Map 13 A3.
w taorestaurant.com

Upper East Side

Bar Pléiades
20 E 76th St.
Map 17 A5.

Bemelmans Bar
The Carlyle,
35 E 76th St.
Map 17 A5.

Uptown Lounge
1576 Third Ave.
Map 17 B3.
w uptownlounge
nyc.com

Upper West Side

Rooftop Bar and Lounge
Empire Hotel,
44 W 63rd St.
Map 12 D2.
w empirehotelnyc.com

Brooklyn

Brooklyn Brewery
79 North 11th St,
Williamsburg.
Map 23 B1.
w brooklynbrewery.
com

Other Half Brewing
195 Centre St,
Carroll Gardens.
Map 23 A5.
w otherhalfbrewing.
com

Threes Brewing
333 Douglass St.
Map 23 B4.
w threesbrewing.com

Tørst
615 Manhattan Ave,
Greenpoint
Map 23 B1.
w torstnyc

Farther Afield

SingleCut Beersmiths
19–33 37th St, Astoria
w singlecutbeer.com

Transmitter Brewing
11th St, Long Island City
w transmitterbrewing.
com

SHOPPING

Visitors to New York inevitably include shopping in their plans. The city is the consumer capital of the world: a shopper's paradise and a constant source of entertainment, with dazzling window displays and a staggering variety of goods for sale. Anything can be found here, from high fashion to rare children's books, state-of-the-art electronics, and a truly mouthwatering array of exotic food. If you are looking for a personal hovercraft, read-in-the-dark eyeglass attachments, a designer bed for your pet gerbil, or a Wurlitzer jukebox, this is the city of your dreams. Whether you have $50,000 or $5, New York is the place to spend it.

The 1920s-style Henri Bendel store

Best Buys

New York is a bargain hunter's dream, with huge discounts on anything from household goods to designer clothes. Some of the best shops are on Orchard Street and Grand Street on the Lower East Side, where designer goods are sold at considerably lower than the retail price. You can find just about every imaginable item of clothing here, in addition to tableware, shoes, home furnishings, and electronics. Some shops in this area are closed on Saturday – the Jewish Sabbath – but are usually open all day Sunday.

Another great area for fashion bargain hunters is the Garment District, roughly between Sixth and Eighth avenues from 30th to 40th Street. The main hub, Seventh Avenue, was renamed Fashion Avenue in the early 1970s. Several designers and manufacturers have their showrooms here, some of which are open to the public. Many of their samples are put up for sales, which are announced on notices posted around the area. The best time to visit them is just before one of the major gift-giving holidays. Top Button (www.topbutton. com) has comprehensive sales listings.

Sales

One word you'll come across all over the city, anytime of the year, is "sale." So check the sale goods before you pay full price for any purchase. The best sales are during New York's main sale seasons, which generally run from June until the end of July and from December 26 until February. Look up the local papers for ads. Along Fifth Avenue in Midtown you'll see signs announcing "Lost Our Lease" sales. Avoid them, as these signs have been up for years at many shops. Also keep your eyes peeled for "Sample Sales," where the top designers sell to the public the sample outfits they have created to show store buyers. Sample sales occur at different locations throughout the city, and are generally not advertised, so your best bet is to keep a lookout for signs announcing sample sales, particularly on Fifth Avenue and on Broadway.

The Bulgari entrance at Hotel Pierre
(see p289)

How to Pay

Most shops accept major credit cards, although there will often be a minimum purchase price. If you want to use your traveler's checks, identification will be needed. Personal checks drawn in another currency will be refused. Some stores only take cash, especially during sales.

Opening Hours

Most shops are open from 10am to 6pm, Monday to Saturday. Many department stores are open through Sunday, and until 9pm at least two nights a week. Lunch hours (noon to 2:30pm), Saturdays, sales, and holidays will be the most crowded times in stores.

Clothes on display at Barney's New York

Taxes

The New York City sales tax is 8.875 per cent, although clothing and shoes under $110 are exempt. However, sales tax will be waived if the goods are shipped home.

Shopping Tours

If you dread braving the stores alone, shopping tours are a good, reasonably priced option. Apart from the main department stores, you could visit private designer showrooms, auction houses, or fashion shows. Some operators will customize tours to suit your requirements.

Bloomingdale's on 3rd Avenue

Department Stores and Malls

Most of the large – and best – department stores are located in midtown Manhattan. Explore them at your leisure, since all these stores tend to be enormous, with a great range of goods. If possible, avoid weekends and vacation times, when the crowds can be overwhelming. Prices are often high, but it is possible to find some bargains during sales.

Stores such as Saks Fifth Avenue, Bloomingdale's, and Macy's provide a diverse and extraordinary range of shopping services, including actually shopping for you.

One of the biggest malls in Manhattan is the **Shops at Columbus Circle** in the Time Warner Center. Its stores include Williams-Sonoma, Coach, and Hugo Boss. **Century 21** is a legendary Downtown department store selling designer

clothes and gifts at discount prices.

Barney's New York, favored by young professionals, specializes in excellent, though expensive, designer clothes.

Luxurious, elegant, and understated, **Bergdorf Goodman** sells contemporary clothes by European designers at high prices. The men's store is across the street.

Bloomingdale's *(see p177)* is the Hollywood film star of the department stores, with many eye-catching displays and seductive goods. New Yorkers young and old come here to seek out the latest in fashion. The linen and fine china departments have a reputation for quality, and the gourmet food section features a shop devoted entirely to caviar. Extensive shopping services and amenities include a noted restaurant, Le Train Bleu, with its view of the Queensboro Bridge. There is also a SoHo branch on Broadway. Though much smaller than the main store, it stocks a similar selection of luxury goods.

At the exclusive **Henri Bendel**, everything from the Art Deco jewels to beautiful handmade shoes is displayed as a priceless work of art. The store, laid out in a series of 1920s-style boutiques, sells an excellent range of innovative women's fashions.

Lord & Taylor is renowned for its classic and much more conservative fashions for men and women, with an emphasis on US designers.

Macy's, the self-proclaimed largest store in the world *(see pp130–31)*, has 10 floors selling everything imaginable from can openers to antiques. **Saks Fifth Avenue**, known for style and elegance, has long been considered one of the city's best department stores,

Exterior of the Century 21 department store

with service to match. It sells stunning designerwear for adults as well as children.

Directory

Shopping Tours

Elegant Tightwad
Tel (800) 808-4614.
W theeleganttightwad.com

Shop Gotham
Tel (866) 795-4200 or (212) 209-3370 to purchase tour tickets
W shopgotham.com

Department Stores and Malls

Barney's New York
660 Madison Ave. **Map** 13 A3.
Tel (212) 826-8900.

Bergdorf Goodman
754 5th Ave. **Map** 12 F3.
Tel (212) 753-7300.

Bloomingdale's
1000 3rd Ave. **Map** 13 A3.
Tel (212) 705-2000.
504 Broadway. **Map** 4 E4.
Tel (212) 729-5900.

Century 21
22 Cortland St. **Map** 1 C2.
Tel (212) 227-9092.

Henri Bendel
712 5th Ave. **Map** 12 F4.
Tel (212) 247-1100.

Lord & Taylor
424 5th Ave. **Map** 8 F1.
Tel (212) 391-3344.

Macy's
151 W 34th St. **Map** 8 E2.
Tel (212) 695-4400.

Saks Fifth Avenue
611 5th Ave. **Map** 12 F4.
Tel (212) 753-4000.

Shops at Columbus Circle
Time Warner Center. **Map** 12 D3.
Tel (212) 823 6300.

New York's Best: Shopping

In a city where you can shop 24 hours a day, the best plan is to tackle it the way New Yorkers do: by neighborhood. Each has its own character and specialties. Here are highlights of the best shopping districts – where they are and what you will find in each. If time is very tight, head for one of the huge department stores (see p313), or, if window shopping is your preference, stroll along Fifth Avenue, home to Manhattan's most glittering stores (see opposite). For great bargains in a truly ethnic area, try the Lower East Side.

Greenwich Village and the Meatpacking District
Quaint, eclectic, and antique choices in the Village, and gourmands will enjoy the myriad specialty food stores. Meander over to Meatpacking District for high-fashion shopping (see pp104–5).

Midtown West and the Theater District

SoHo
The area bordered by Sixth Avenue, Lafayette, Houston, and Canal streets is bustling with accessories, footwear, and clothes from designer flagships. It can get extremely crowded on weekends, especially along Broadway. Cross Broadway to NoLIta for even trendier, cutting-edge fashion (see pp98–9).

Chelsea and the Garment District

Hudson River

Greenwich Village

Gramercy and the Flatiron District

SoHo and TriBeCa

East Village

East Village and Lower East Side
Explore around St Mark's Place for shoes, avant-garde fashions, and ethnic goods (see pp114–15). Bargains are becoming harder to find in the Lower East Side, but trendy options are increasing (see pp88–9).

Lower Manhattan and the Civic Center

Lower East Side

Herald Square and the Garment District
Here you will find Macy's, a store that occupies an entire block. The surrounding area (especially Seventh Avenue) is the fashion wholesale center with major discounts during sales – but some stores accept cash only (see pp128–9).

Columbus and Amsterdam avenues
These are New York hot spots for exclusive but trendy designer clothes, quirky antiques, esoterica, and upscale gift shops *(see pp206–7)*.

Madison and Lexington avenues
Shoppers come here for classics in art and antiques, designer clothes, and shoes *(see pp180–81)*.

East 57th and 59th streets
Exclusive antiques and high fashion are found on 57th Street – and be sure not to miss Bloomingdale's *(see p177)*.

Fifth Avenue's Prestigious Stores

From Saks to Tiffany's Leading retailers have their flagship store on famous Fifth Avenue *(see pp164–6)*.

Harry Winston
(see p322)

New York Originals

New York is a city where just about any kind of shop, no matter how esoteric, will always attract customers. Dozens of tiny stores scattered around the city specialize in unusual merchandise, from butterflies and bones to traditional Tibetan treasures and shamrock sprigs from Ireland. Coming across these in some tucked-away corner is what makes shopping in New York such an entertaining and invigorating experience.

Specialty Stores

For every type of pen, the **Fountain Pen Hospital** stocks an enormous range, including such names as Mont Blanc and Scheaffer. For those with a bit more energy, **Blades** sells and rents out skates and also the trendiest skateboards plus all the safety equipment. **Mason's Tennis Mart** is the city's only remaining tennis specialty store – they let you try out all rackets.

If you're looking for different or unusual buttons, a visit to **Tender Buttons**, which stocks millions, is a must. Whether you want enamel, wood, or Navajo silver buttons – or perhaps want your own ones made into cuff links or earrings – here you'll find just what you want – and more. **Trash and Vaudeville** has been supplying punk and Goth gear to New Yorkers for decades and is the HQ of Astor Place clothing.

Leo Kaplan Ltd. is the place to go if you are a keen collector of paperweights. **C. O. Bigelow**, which dates back to 1838, is the country's oldest apothecary. Today the shop attracts fashionistas thanks to its fine, hard-to-find beauty products.

For the true romantic who wants to impress, everything sold by **Only Hearts** is heart-shaped, including pillows, soap, and jewelry. If you are artistic, or if you wish to buy a present for someone who is, visit **Blick Art Materials**, which stocks everything you could need, from easels and brushes to modeling clay. **Forbidden Planet** is a science-fiction megastore with everything from comics to models for the true fan.

Carrying anything one could want for their NYC apartment,

Gracious Home is chock-full of well-made goods, from Caswell-Massey Ltd. soaps to the trendiest lighting fixtures. This Upper West Side staple is a store that one can easily get lost in.

Guitar gurus will want to visit **Rudy's**, Matt Umanov's, or Sam Ash's guitar stores. Here you can find the widest and best choice of musical instruments in the city.

Bibliophiles will find a range of gifts in both the **New York Public Library Shop** *(see p142)* (such as bookends of the lions guarding the main entrance) and **The Morgan Library Shop** *(see pp160–61)*, including bookmarks and writing paper.

University logos and college colors dominate the many knickknacks and accessories for sale at the **NYU Bookstore** and the **Columbia University Bookstore.**

New York's basketball shrine, the **NBA Store**, offers merchandise for all the NBA teams. Then there is the **Yankees Clubhouse Shop**, that sells all imaginable things related to the legendary basketball team.

The Cathedral Shop at the Cathedral of St. John the Divine on Amsterdam Avenue is a large store selling books, artworks, herbs, jewelry, and religious items made locally.

In the East Village, **Obscura Antiques and Oddities** specializes in rare taxidermy, artifacts, and antiques. The shop once even had its own show on the Discovery Channel. **Posteritati** contains over 9,000 movie posters, with those of classics from *20,000 Leagues Under the Sea* to *Goldfinger*, to contemporary hits such as *Avatar*. In the West Village, the **Little**

Lebowski Shop has a cult following, thanks to its tribute to the movie, *The Big Lebowksi*. The owner of this eccentric theme store really does wander around in his dressing gown.

Memorabilia

At Lincoln Center, the **Metropolitan Opera Shop** has records, cards, librettos, small binoculars, and many other opera-related items. For theater fans, everything from scripts and vocal scores to CDs can be found at **One Shubert Alley**. For thousands of rare and classic film stills and posters visit **Jerry Ohlinger's Movie Material Store** on 216 W 30th Street.

The **Carnegie Hall Shop** carries musically themed cards, T-shirts, games, posters, tote bags, and much more. For something truly original and very American, be sure to visit **Lost City Arts** in the East Village and **Urban Archaeology** in Midtown. Between these two shops, you'll unearth all sorts of relics from America's past, from Barbie Doll lunch boxes to salvaged furniture, including antique, claw-footed bath tubs.

Toys, Games, and Gadgets

The **Children's General Store** is one of the city's smarter toy stores, with a focus on educational and classic goods, while a trip to the **American Girl Place** doll store could entertain a youngster all day, with options such as a café, photo studio, and hair salon. **Myplasticheart** is a quirky shop selling a dizzying assortment of designer toys and limited-edition collectibles. **Red Caboose** is for fans of model railways. On three floors, the **Toys 'R' Us** flagship glass building on Broadway is the largest toy store in the world, with a 60-ft (18-m) ferris wheel. There are several **Disney** and **Lego** stores around the city as well, guaranteed to thrill the young ones.

Dinosaur Hill on Second Avenue offers handmade puppets and toys, mobiles, and beautifully made children's clothes. It's expensive but worth it. Since 1848, **Hammacher Schlemmer** have been encouraging shoppers to buy gadgets that they didn't know they wanted for home, office, and recreation. The wacky **Toy Tokyo Shop** draws in a range of customers for its ensemble of cult memorabilia and Asian toys, largely from Japan.

Museum Shops

Some of New York's best souvenirs can be found in the city's many museum shops. In addition to the usual range of books, posters, and cards, there are reproductions of the exhibits on display, including jewelry and sculpture. The **Museum of Arts and Design** (see p145) has an excellent selection of American crafts as well as original works for sale. In addition to realistic model dinosaurs, rubber animals, minerals, and rocks, the **American Museum of Natural History** (see pp210–11)

has a variety of recycled products and earth-awareness gifts, which include posters, bags, and T-shirts with environmental messages, and a large selection of Native American handicrafts. There is also a kids' store with reasonably priced items such as shell sets, magnets, and toys.

The **Asia Society Bookstore and Gift Shop** (see p183) has a striking selection of Oriental prints, posters, art books, toys, and jewelry. Items related to interior design are offered at the **Cooper Hewitt, Smithsonian Design Museum** (see p182). One of New York's largest collections of Jewish ceremonial objects, including menorahs and Kiddush cups, books, and jewelry, is found in the small shop at the **Jewish Museum** (see p182).

For reproduction prints of famous paintings and other exquisite gifts, a visit to the **Metropolitan Museum of Art** (see pp186–93) gift store is a must. There is also an enormous book department and a children's gift shop. The traditional **American Folk Art Museum** (see p213)

prides itself on its American country crafts, including wooden toys, quilts, and weathervanes, which are mostly original. Works by craftspeople who currently have pieces on display in the museum are also sold. The **Museum of the City of New York** (see p195) specializes in pictures of old New York as well as books and unique prints and posters. The **Museum of Modern Art/MoMA Design Store** (see pp168–71) has a highly praised selection of innovative home furnishings, toys, and kitchenware inspired by international designers such as Frank Lloyd Wright and Le Corbusier.

The **Whitney Museum Shop** (see pp108–9) stocks American-made items, including jewelry, wooden toys, books, and posters complementing current exhibitions. The **Museum of Jewish Heritage** (see p76) has a shop with an unusual array of gifts, souvenirs, and educational material about Jewish life. Open to ticketed visitors only.

The Best of the Imports

The city of New York is a massive melting pot of ethnic groups, nationalities, and cultures. Many ethnic shops specialize in food or goods of a particular group. **Alaska on Madison** has a collection of Inuit art and Northwest prints and hangings. Situated in Chelsea Market, **Imports from Marrakesh** is jam-packed with inviting home-decor pieces that are custom-made by Moroccan artisans. The **Chinese Porcelain Company** sells exquisite Chinese decorative arts and furniture. **Himalayan Crafts and Tours** stocks everything from paintings to Tibetan rugs. **Sweet Life**, on the Lower East Side, is a tiny, old-fashioned candy shop with sweet delicacies from around the world. **Surma** is a Ukrainian general store that sells hand-painted eggs and linens. **Astro Gallery of Gems** has a

large collection of stunning jewelry and mineral specimens from Africa and Asia. Nearby, Chinatown is packed with shops selling everything from souvenirs to leather goods, all at low prices.

The folk art store, **La Sirena**, sells a variety of items from Mexico. Their products typically range from museum-quality pieces to the multicolored, traditional merchandise often found solely in marketplaces such as serapes, sombreros, and religious idols.

Addresses

Alaska on Madison
1065 Madison Ave.
Map 17 A4.
Tel (212) 879-1782.

Astro Gallery of Gems
417 5th Ave.
Map 8 F2.
Tel (212) 889-9000.

Chinese Porcelain Company
232 E 59th St.
Map 13 B3.
Tel (212) 838-7744.

Himalayan Crafts and Tours
2007 Broadway.
Map 11 C1.
Tel (212) 787-8500.

Imports from Marrakesh
88 10th Ave.
Map 7 C5.
Tel (212) 675-9700.

La Sirena
27 E 3rd St.
Map 4 F2.
Tel (212) 780-9113.

Sweet Life
63 Hester St.
Map 5 B4.
Tel (212) 598-0092.

Surma
11 E 7th St.
Map 4 F2.
Tel (212) 477-0729.

DIRECTORY

Specialty Stores

Blick Art Materials
1–5 Bond St.
Map 4 F2.
Tel (212) 533-2444.

Blades
120 W 72nd St.
Map 12 D1.
Tel (888) 552-5233.
One of two branches.

The Cathedral Shop
Cathedral of St. John the
Divine, 1047 Amsterdam
Ave. **Map** 20 E4.
Tel (212) 316-7540.

C. O. Bigelow
414 Avenue of the
Americas.
Map 4 D1.
Tel (212) 533-2700.

**Columbia University
Bookstore**
2922 Broadway.
Map 20 E3.
Tel (212) 854-4131.

Forbidden Planet
840 Broadway.
Map 4 E1.
Tel (212) 473-1576.

**Fountain Pen
Hospital**
10 Warren St.
Map 1 C1.
Tel (212) 964-0580.

Gracious Home
1992 Broadway.
Map 12 D1.
Tel (212) 231-7800.

Leo Kaplan Ltd.
114 E 57th St.
Map B A3.
Tel (212) 355-7212.

Little Lebowski Shop
215 Thompson St.
Map 4 E2.
Tel (212) 388-1466.

Mason's Tennis Mart
56 E 53rd St.
Map 13 A4.
Tel (212) 755-5805.

**The Morgan
Library Shop**
Madison Ave at 36th St.
Map 9 A2.
Tel (212) 685-0008.

NBA Store
545 5th Ave. **Map** 12 F5.
Tel (212) 515-6221.

**New York Public
Library Shop**
5th Ave at 42nd St.
Map 8 F1.
Tel (212) 930-0869.

NYU Bookstore
726 Broadway.
Map 4 E2.
Tel (212) 998-4678.

**Obscura Antiques
and Oddities**
207 Ave A.
Map 5 A1.
Tel (212) 505-9251.

Only Hearts
386 Columbus Ave.
Map 15 D5.
Tel (212) 724-5608.

Posteritati
239 Centre St. **Map** 4 F4.
Tel (212) 226-2207.

Rudy's
461 Broome St.
Map 4 E4.
Tel (212) 625-2557.

Tender Buttons
143 E 62nd St.
Map 13 A2.
Tel (212) 758-7004.

Trash and Vaudeville
4 St. Mark's Pl.
Map 5 A4.
Tel (212) 982-3590.

**Yankees Clubhouse
Shop**
245 W 42nd St. **Map** 8 D1.
Tel (212) 768-9555.

Memorabilia

Carnegie Hall Shop
881 7th Ave.
Map 12 E3.
Tel (212) 903-9610.

**Jerry Ohlinger's
Movie Material Store**
216 W 30th St.
Map 8 E3.
Tel (212) 989-0869.

Lost City Arts
18 Cooper Square.
Map 4 F2.
Tel (212) 375-0500.

**Metropolitan
Opera Shop**
Metropolitan Opera
House, Lincoln Center,
136 W 65th St.
Map 11 C2.
Tel (212) 580-4090.

One Shubert Alley
1 Shubert Alley.
Map 12 E5.
Tel (212) 944-4133.

Urban Archaeology
239 E 58th St.
Map 13 B3.
Tel (212) 371-4646.

Toys, Games, and Gadgets

American Girl Place
609 Fifth Ave.
Map 12 F5.
Tel (877) 247-5223.

**Children's General
Store**
168 E 91st St.
Map 17 A2.
Tel (212) 426-4479.

Dinosaur Hill
306 E 9th St, 2nd Ave.
Map 4 F1.
Tel (212) 473-5850.

Disney Store
1540 Broadway,
Times Square.
Map 12 E5.
Tel (212) 626-2910.
One of several branches.

**Hammacher
Schlemmer**
147 E 57th St.
Map 13 A3.
Tel (212) 421-9000.
One of two branches.

Lego Store
200 5th Ave.
Map 8 F4.
Tel (212) 255-3217.
One of several branches.

Myplasticheart
210 Forsyth St.
Map 5 A3.
Tel (646) 290-6866.

Red Caboose
23 W 45th St.
Map 12 F5.
Tel (212) 575-0155.

Toy Tokyo Shop
91 2nd Ave.
Map 4 F2.
Tel (212) 673-5424.

Toys 'R' Us
1514 Broadway,
Times Square.
Map 8 E2.
Tel (646) 366-8800.

Museum Shops

**American Folk
Art Museum**
2 Lincoln Square.
Map 12 D2.
Tel (212) 595-9533.

**American Museum
of Natural History**
W 79th St at Central
Park W. **Map** 16 D5.
Tel (212) 769-5100.

**Asia Society
Bookstore and
Gift Shop**
725 Park Ave.
Map 13 A1.
Tel (212) 288-6400.

**Cooper Hewitt,
Smithsonian
Design Museum**
2 E 91st St.
Map 16 F2.
Tel (212) 849-8400.

Jewish Museum
1109 5th Ave.
Map 16 F2.
Tel (212) 423-3200.

**Metropolitan
Museum of Art**
5th Ave at 82nd St.
Map 16 F4.
Tel (212) 535-7710.

**Museum of
Arts and Design**
40 W 53rd St.
Map 12 F4.
Tel (212) 956-3535

**Museum of the
City of New York**
5th Ave at 103rd St.
Map 21 C5.
Tel (212) 534-1672.

**Museum of
Jewish Heritage**
18 1st Place,
Battery Park City.
Map 1 B4.
Tel (646) 437-4200.

**Museum of
Modern Art/MoMA
Design Store**
44 W 53rd St.
Map 12 F4.
Tel (212) 767-1050.

**Whitney Museum
Shop**
99 Gansevoort St.
Map 3 B1.
Tel (212) 570-3614.

Fashion

Whether you're looking for a secondhand pair of 501s or the kind of ballgown a Hollywood actress would be proud to wear, you're sure to find it in New York. The city is the fashion capital of America and an important center of clothing manufacture and design. New York's clothing stores, like its restaurants, reflect the city's dramatically different styles and cultures. To save time it's probably best to visit one area at a time and wander from store to store. Alternatively, visit one of the major department stores for an excellent selection of fashion for everyone.

American Designers

Many American designers sell their creations in boutiques within the large department stores, or have exclusive shops of their own. One of the most famous is Michael Kors, known for sophisticated looks that are classic and comfortable.

The designs of Bill Blass, one of the kings of American fashion, feature an array of different colors, wild patterns, innovative shapes, and a lot of wit. Liz Claiborne's designs are always elegantly simple, casual, and reasonably priced, including everything you could possibly need from tennis whites to casual professional wear for women.

Marc Jacobs, popular with the fashion crowd, has his own label and store in Greenwich Village. James Galanos is an exclusive designer for the rich and famous, making one-of-a-kind couture clothes, and Betsey Johnson is popular with women able to wear figure-hugging fashions in fabulous fabrics.

Since the late 1990s, Donna Karan has become a name that appears everywhere. Her simple, stylish, and great-looking designs work for everything from work-out clothes to black-tie wear. Calvin Klein now has his name on place settings and sunglasses in addition to underwear, jeans, and a whole range of clothes. He is renowned for comfortable, sensuous, and well-fitting – as well as very hip – looks. Ralph Lauren is very well known for his aristocratic and expensive clothes, a "look" favored by the exclusive and posh Ivy League,

horsey set. For those with a taste for more experimental designs, Joan Vass specializes in moderately priced but exciting, colorful, and innovative knitwear.

Vera Wang offers a wonderful ready-to-wear collection, but it is her lavish wedding gowns that are enduringly popular. Among younger designers, both Alexander Wang and Anna Sui have boutiques in SoHo.

Discount Designer Clothes

If you're on the lookout for discount designer clothes, **Designer Resale**, **Encore**, and **Michael's** sell a wide range. Oscar de la Renta, Ungaro, and Armani are just some of the leading labels available. Clothes are either new or worn but should be near-perfect.

The designer discount emporium **Century 21** in Lower Manhattan sells European and American designer fashions discounted up to an amazing 75 per cent off regular retail prices. Bustling Union Square is flush with shopping options, including **Nordstrom Rack**, the discount offshoot of the famous Nordstrom department store.

Men's Clothes

In the center of midtown, you'll find two of the city's most highly regarded menswear stores: **Brooks Brothers** and **Paul Stuart**. Brooks Brothers is something of a New York institution, famous for its traditional, conservative clothing such as smart button-down shirts and Chinos. There's an

ultra-conservative women's line too. Paul Stuart prides itself on its very British look and offers a stylish array of superbly tailored fashions. Go to the high-quality department store **Bergdorf Goodman Men** to find beautifully made Turnbull & Asser shirts and marvelous suits by Gianfranco Ferré or Hugo Boss.

Barney's New York has one of the most comprehensive men's departments in America, with a truly massive range of clothes and accessories.

Uniqlo, the hip Japanese chain known for its modern, well-made, inexpensive casual clothes, has a flagship store on Fifth Avenue. Go to **Burberry Limited** if you are looking for classic British trenchcoats and traditional outdoor wear.

John Varvatos is famous for luxurious, sporty designs with superb detail. Uptown designer menswear boutiques include the renowned **Beau Brummel** with a selection of very stylish European clothes and **Thomas Pink**, whose bright colors and fine fabrics make this store a celebrity favorite. Many of these men's stores also carry striking women's fashions. The **Hickey Freeman** store on Fifth Avenue sells a wide range of men's traditional clothing.

Children's Clothes

In addition to an excellent selection within the large department stores, there are several shops around the city that sell children's clothing exclusively. A good example is **Bonpoint**, which has a world of French-style charm. Also stocked with delightful outfits and gifts is **Pink Olive**, in the East Village.

GapKids and **BabyGap**, often set within **Gap** stores, have comfortable, long-lasting cotton overalls, sweat pants, denim jackets, sweatshirts, and leggings. Actress Phoebe Cates has opened a hip kids' clothing store on Madison Avenue called **Blue Tree**. **Space Kiddets** has everything from booties to Western wear.

Women's Clothes

Women's fashion is subject to seasonal design trends, and New York stores keep pace with them all. Most of the city's most fashionable shops are found in Midtown around Madison and Fifth Avenues. These include some of the major department stores (see p313), which stock a range of American designers, including Donna Karan, Ralph Lauren, and Bill Blass.

Leading international names such as **Chanel** and **Valentino** also have shops here, as does one of the outstanding American designers, **Michael Kors**. There is also a handful of popular ready-to-wear stores, including **Ann Taylor**, which is much favored by young, busy professionals looking for stylish, comfortable clothing. **Banana Republic** is a Fifth Avenue crowd-magnet that sells sleek, smart casualwear and blue jeans cut in the trendiest styles. Right at the heart of this area stands the pink-marbled Trump Tower, which houses a selection of exclusive shops.

Madison Avenue is packed with designers for the smart set, who have everything you could ever need, including **Ralph Lauren**; **Givenchy**, who sells show-stopping formal gowns at phenomenal prices; Valentino, who has classic Italian clothes; and **Missoni**, famous for richly textured sweaters in sumptuous wools and colorful patterns. In SoHo, **Yves St Laurent Rive Gauche** has evening gowns, one-of-a-kind jackets, silks and extravagant blouses, and beautifully cut pants suits; **Vera Wang** has a stunning collection of bridal gowns, along with chic everyday outfits.

Sophisticated Italian looks are also available from Italian style kings **Giorgio Armani** and **Gianni Versace**. **Dolce & Gabbana** sells unique, one-of-a-kind Italian clothing. **Gucci**, one of the oldest Italian shops in America, is only for the wealthy and status-conscious.

The Upper West Side has many shops competing for attention with contemporary fashions. **Calvin Klein** now has a store on the East Side, specializing in hip, yet casual fashions. **French Connection** is known for its affordable separates, both casual and for the office. **Scoop** is *the* place to get a little black dress.

The villages – the East Village in particular – are the best places to go for secondhand clothing and 1950s rock 'n' roll gear, with ever-changing interesting shops run by new and young designers and art school graduates (see pp324–5). For a range of affordable, well-cut clothes from classic to casual, try **APC**, and for stylish, high-end designer clothes head to **Kirna Zabete**.

No Relation Vintage carries a huge selection of secondhand Levi's as well as hundreds of denim and leather jackets. **Screaming Mimi's** is where you could

unearth that pair of velvet bell-bottoms or go-go boots you've always dreamed of having. A more mainstream shop is **The Gap**, a chain store selling lots of moderately priced, casual and comfortable clothes for men, women, and children.

SoHo and NoHo/NoLita rival Madison Avenue for designer boutiques specializing in expensive but interesting clothes – the fashions here are far more avant-garde. The playful boutique Kirna Zabete, for example, features a unique range of clothes as well as accessories. You'll also find **Y-3 New York** in this area, among other exclusive stores. **Comme des Garçons** in Chelsea sells minimalist Japanese chic.

Cynthia Rowley is a prominent New York designer who sells flirty fashions for women, and **What Comes Around Goes Around** on West Broadway is the place to go for vintage jeans.

Size Chart

For Australian sizes follow the British and American conversions.

Children's clothing								
American	2–3	4–5	6–6x	7–8	10	12	14	16 (size)
British	2–3	4–5	6–7	8–9	10–11	12	14	14+ (years)
Continental	2–3	4–5	6–7	8–9	10–11	12	14	14+ (years)

Children's shoes								
American	7½	8½	9½	10½	11½	12½	13½	1½ 2½
British	7	8	9	10	11	12	13	1 2
Continental	24	25½	27	28	29	30	32	33 34

Women's clothing, single sizes							
American	2	4	6	8	10	12	14 16
British	6	8	10	12	14	16	18 20
Continental	34	36	38	40	42	44	46 48

Women's clothing, dual sizes				
American	XXS	XS	S	M L
British	XS	S	M	L XL
Continental	XS	S	M	L XL

Women's shoes						
American	5	6	7	8	9	10 11
British	3	4	5	6	7	8 9
Continental	36	37	38	39	40	41 44

Men's suits							
American	34	36	38	40	42	44	46 48
British	34	36	38	40	42	44	46 48
Continental	44	46	48	50	52	54	56 58

Men's shirts							
American	14	15	15½	16	16½	17	17½ 18
British	14	15	15½	16	16½	17	17½ 18
Continental	36	38	39	41	42	43	44 45

Men's shoes							
American	7	7½	8	8½	9	9½	10 10½
British	6	7	7	7.5	8	8½	9 9.5
Continental	39	40	40.5	41	42	42.5	43 44

DIRECTORY

Discount Designer Clothes

Century 21 Department Store
22 Cortland St.
Map 1 C2.
Tel (212) 227-9092.

Designer Resale
324 E 81st St.
Map 17 B4.
Tel (212) 734-3639.

Encore
1132 Madison Ave.
Map 17 A4.
Tel (212) 879-2850.

Michael's
1041 Madison Ave.
Map 17 A5.
Tel (212) 737-7273.

Nordstrom Rack
60 E 14th St.
Map 9 A5
Tel (212) 220-2080.

Men's Clothes

Barney's New York
660 Madison Ave.
Map 13 A3.
Tel (212) 826-8900.

Beau Brummel
484 Broome St.
Map 4 E4.
Tel (212) 219-2666.
One of several branches.

Bergdorf Goodman Men
754 5th Ave.
Map 12 F3.
Tel (212) 753-7300.

Brooks Brothers
346 Madison Ave.
Map 9 A1.
Tel (212) 682-8800.

Burberry Limited
9 E 57th St.
Map 12 F3.
Tel (212) 757-3700.

Hickey Freeman
543 Madison Ave.
Map 13 A4.
Tel (212) 586-6481.

John Varvatos
122 Spring St.
Map 4 E4.
Tel (212) 965-0700.

Paul Stuart
350 Madison Ave.
Map 13 A5.
Tel (212) 682-0320.

Thomas Pink
520 Madison Ave.
Map 13 A4.
Tel (212) 838-1928.

Uniqlo
666 5th Ave.
Map 12 F4.
Tel (877) 486-4756.

Children's Clothes

Blue Tree
1283 Madison Ave.
Map 17 A2.
Tel (212) 369-2583.

Bonpoint
1269 Madison Ave.
Map 17 A3.
Tel (212) 722-7720.

GapKids/BabyGap
60 W 34th St.
Map 8 F2.
Tel (212) 760-1268.
One of several branches.

Pink Olive
439 E 9th St.
Map 5 A1.
Tel (212) 780-0036.

Space Kiddets
26 E 22nd St.
Map 8 F4.
Tel (212) 420-9878.

Women's Clothes

Ann Taylor
330 Madison Ave.
Map 9 A1.
Tel (212) 949-0008.
One of several branches.

APC
131 Mercer St.
Map 4 E3.
Tel (212) 966-9685.

Banana Republic
626 5th Ave.
Map 12 F4.
Tel (212) 974-2350.

Calvin Klein
654 Madison Ave.
Map 13 A3.
Tel (212) 292-9000.

Chanel
15 E 57th St.
Map 12 F3.
Tel (212) 355 5050.

Comme des Garçons
520 W 22nd St.
Map 8 F3.
Tel (212) 604-9200.

Cynthia Rowley
376 Bleecker St.
Map 3 C2.
Tel (212) 242-3803.

Dolce & Gabbana
717 5th Ave.
Map 12 F3.
Tel (212) 965-8000.

French Connection
700 Broadway
Map 4 E2.
Tel (212) 897-9653.
One of several branches.

The Gap
277 W 23rd St.
Map 8 D4.
Tel (646) 336-0802.
One of many branches.

Gianni Versace
647 5th Ave.
Map 12 F4.
Tel (212) 317-0224.

Giorgio Armani
760 Madison Ave.
Map 13 A2.
Tel (212) 988-9191.
717 5th Ave.
Map 12 F3.
Tel (212) 207-1902.

Givenchy
747 Madison Ave.
Map 13 A2.
Tel (212) 688-4005.

Gucci
685 5th Ave.
Map 12 F4.
Tel (212) 826 2600.

Kirna Zabete
477 Broome St.
Map 4 F4.
Tel (212) 941-9656.

Michael Kors
790 Madison Ave.
Map 13 A2.
Tel (212) 452-4685.

Missoni
1009 Madison Ave.
Map 13 A1.
Tel (212) 517-9339.

No Relation Vintage
204 1st Ave.
Map 5 A1.
Tel (212) 228-5201.

Ralph Lauren
888 Madison Ave at 72nd St. **Map** 13 A1.
Tel (212) 606-2100.

Scoop
475 Broadway (near Spring St).
Map 4 E4.
Tel (212) 925-2886.
One of three branches.

Screaming Mimi's
382 Lafayette St.
Map 4 F2.
Tel (212) 677-6464.

Valentino
821 Madison Ave.
Map 13 A1.
Tel (212) 772-6969.

Vera Wang
158 Mercer St.
Map 4 E3.
Tel (212) 382-2184.

What Comes Around Goes Around
351 W Broadway.
Map 4 E4.
Tel (212) 343-9303.

Y-3 New York
92 Greene St.
Map 4 E4.
Tel (212) 966-9833.

Yves St Laurent Rive Gauche
80 Greene St.
Map 13 A1.
Tel (212) 431-3240.

Accessories

In addition to the following shops, all of the major Manhattan department stores have extensive accessory departments stocking a range of hats, gloves, bags, jewelry, watches, scarves, shoes, and umbrellas.

Jewelry

Midtown Fifth Avenue is where to find the most dazzling jewelers. By day, windows glisten with gems from around the world; by night they are empty – the jewels safely locked away. The most sensational shops are all within a couple of blocks of one another and include the museum-like **Harry Winston**, which showcases its coveted jewels from around the world. **Buccellati** is well respected for its innovative Italian creations and excellent workmanship. **Bulgari** has an impressive collection that ranges in price from a couple of hundred to over a million dollars.

Housed in a Renaissance-style palazzo, **Cartier** is a jewel in itself and sells its beautiful baubles at what, to most, are unthinkable prices. **Tiffany & Co**. has 10 floors of crystal, diamonds, and other jewels waiting to be packed up for you and taken away in the store's signature sky-blue boxes.

The Diamond District, a one-block area on 47th Street (between Fifth and Sixth avenues), is lined with shops displaying hundreds of thousands of dollars' worth of diamonds, gold, pearls, and other exotic jewels from around the world. The largest private jewelry vendor in the district is **Rafaello and Co.** Here, the staff pride themselves on reading a customer's personal style while making recommendations.

Hats

New York's oldest hat shop is **Worth & Worth**, which also has the largest collection of hats in the city. You can get anything here, from original Australian bush hats to silk toppers, to slouch hats and boaters. **Suzanne Millinery** is the hatmaker to the stars, as she has proved very popular with

celebrities such as Meryl Streep and Kate Hudson. **Lids** sells baseball caps in dozens of varieties, with logos ranging from sports teams to the evergreen "I HEART NY". For a wide range of fabulous headgear, stop by **The Hat Shop**, where you can find everything from classic to contemporary styles.

Umbrellas

The minute it starts to rain in New York, hundreds of street vendors selling umbrellas seem to sprout like mushrooms. Their umbrellas, which sell at just a few dollars, are without doubt the cheapest in the city, but unlikely to last much longer than the downpour itself.

For good-quality umbrellas, you'll find a fine selection of Briggsof London at **Worth & Worth**. There is a wide range of different sizes, trendy patterns, and traditional tartans and stripes at **Barney's New York**, and there's always **Macy's** *(see p130–31)* for the usual sizes and styles. World-famous **Gucci** has umbrellas to match its ties. Subway-themed ones can be found at the **NY Transit Museum Store**.

Handbags and Briefcases

From its convenient location near Union Square, **The Bag House** has been selling a varied assortment of travel gear and luggage since 1969. This neighborhood mainstay carries one of the city's largest selections of backpacks, messenger bags, and luggage from top brands such as Victorinox, Zero Halliburton, Rimowa, The North Face, Eagle Creek, and many more.

Elsewhere in the city are such exclusive shops as **Bottega Veneta**, and **Prada**, where

handbags are displayed like precious art, with prices to match. Younger and trendier places include **Jeffrey New York**, well respected for its on-trend designs, and the stylish **Il Bisonte**. **The Coach Store** is known for its simple, classic leather handbags. Designer **Kate Spade's** stylish yet practical rectangular handbags, in a plethora of prints and colors, have become modern classics, and add a chic touch to any woman's wardrobe.

For discount designer handbags try the legendary **Nordstrom Rack**, and for bargain briefcases from slim envelopes to thick lawyer's bags, a visit to the **Altman Luggage Company** is a must.

Shoes and Boots

Manhattan shoe stores are famous for their extensive selections of shoes and boots, and, if you shop around, you are sure to find what you want at a reasonable price.

Most of the large department stores in New York also have shoe departments, where you can find designer-label shoes in addition to other brands. **Bloomingdale's** *(see p177)* has a huge women's footwear department, and **Brooks Brothers** has one of the best selections of traditional men's shoes in the city.

For both men's and women's shoes, the most exclusive shops are around the midtown area. **Ferragamo** sells classic styles crafted in Florence. Go to **Botticelli** for whimsical shoe fashions. For stylish shoes at decent prices, head for **Sigerson Morrison** in NoLita. There's also **John Fluevog** with its selection of inventive, quirky shoes, that offer a variety of buckles, bright colors, and intricate designs.

Jutta Neumann has a cult following in the East Village, thanks to her incredibly comfortable, custom-made sandals. She also has a popular range of leather handbags. **MooShoes** is an all-vegan shoe and accessory store, that sells

100 per cent cruelty-free shoes. For beautiful handcrafted boots, try **E. Vogel Custom Boots & Shoes**.

Sneaker collectors should make a stop at **Alife Rivington Club** on the Lower East Side, which stocks several hard-to-find styles.

The **Jimmy Choo** boutique offers a plethora of sexy, stylish heels. Popular among Manhattan's chic set are the beautiful women's shoes, particularly the flattering heels, at **Manolo Blahnik**. **Christian Louboutin** rounds out the stiletto heavyweights. **Kenneth Cole** is another iconic designer of classic and contemporary shoes, along with beautiful, full-grain leather bags. Spain's most popular brand, **Camper**, has an airy SoHo store featuring their signature comfy, funky, and colorful shoes for women and men.

For the best in children's shoes, **Shoofly** has imported shoes in all styles.

For discounted shoes, go to West 34th Street and West 8th Street between Fifth and Sixth avenues, and Orchard Street on the Lower East Side. The **DSW** store, on the third floor of 40 East 14th Street, sells brand-name shoes and boots at a fraction of the regular price.

Lingerie

Expensive imports from Europe, which are sexy yet elegant, can be found at **La Petite Coquette**. More affordable is **Victoria's Secret** on Fifth Avenue or SoHo, which offers beautifully made lingerie in satin, silk, and many other fine fabrics. **Henri Bendel's** lingerie department offers a sumptuous array of lingerie, from naughty to nice. The Italian **La Perla** brand features seductive lingerie and undergarments in sensual fabrics from tulle and chiffon to satin.

DIRECTORY

Jewelry

Buccellati
714 Madison Ave.
Map 13 A2.
Tel (212) 308-2900.

Bulgari
730 5th Ave. **Map** 12 F3.
Tel (212) 315-9000.

Cartier
653 5th Ave. **Map** 12 F4.
Tel (212) 753-0111.

Harry Winston
718 5th Ave. **Map** 12 F3.
Tel (212) 245-2000.

Rafaello and Co.
22 W 47th St. **Map** 12 F5.
Tel (212) 840-0780.

Tiffany & Co
727 5th Ave. **Map** 12 F3.
Tel (212) 755-8000.

Hats

The Hat Shop
120 Thompson St.
Map 4 D3.
Tel (212) 219-1446.

Lids
239 W 42nd St. **Map** 8 E1.
Tel (212) 575-1711.

Suzanne Millinery
136 E 61st St. **Map** 13 A3.
Tel (212) 593-3232.

Worth & Worth
45 W 57th St, 6th Floor.
Map 12 F3.
Tel (212) 265-2887.

Umbrellas

Barney's New York
See p313.

Gucci
See p321.

NY Transit Museum Store
Grand Central Terminal.
Map 9 A1.
Tel (212) 878-0106.

Worth & Worth
See Hats

Handbags and Briefcases

Altman Luggage Company
135 Orchard St. **Map** 5 A3.
Tel (212) 254-7275.

The Bag House
797 Broadway. **Map** 4 E1.
Tel (212) 260-0940.

Il Bisonte
120 Sullivan St. **Map** 4 D4.
Tel (212) 966-8773.

Bottega Veneta
849 Madison Ave. **Map** 13
A1. **Tel** (212) 879-4182.

The Coach Store
595 Madison Ave. **Map** 13
A3. **Tel** (212) 754-0041.

Jeffrey New York
449 W 14th St. **Map** 3 A1.
Tel (212) 206-1272.

Kate Spade
454 Broome St. **Map** 4 E4.
Tel (212) 274-1991.

Nordstrom Rack
60 E 14th St. **Map** 9 A5.
Tel (212) 220-2080.

Prada
575 Broadway. **Map** 4 E3.
Tel (212) 334-8888.

Shoes and Boots

Alife Rivington Club
158 Rivington St. **Map** 5
B3. **Tel** (212) 375-8128.

Botticelli
666 5th Ave. **Map** 12 F4.
Tel (212) 586-7421.

Brooks Brothers
See p321.

Bloomingdale's
See p313.

Camper
110 Prince St. **Map** 4 E3.
Tel (212) 343-4220.

Christian Louboutin
967 Madison Ave. **Map** 17
A5. **Tel** (212) 396-1884.

DSW
40 E 14th St. **Map** 9 A5.
Tel (212) 674-2146.

E. Vogel Custom Boots & Shoes
63 Flushing Ave, Unit
331, Brooklyn Naval Yard.
Tel (718) 852-2887.

Ferragamo
655 5th Ave. **Map** 12 F3.
Tel (212) 759-3822.

Jimmy Choo
645 5th Ave. **Map** 12 F4.
Tel (212) 625-1820.

John Fluevog
250 Mulberry St. **Map** 4
F3. **Tel** (212) 431-4484.

Jutta Neumann
355 E 4th St. **Map** 5 C2.
Tel (212) 982-7048.

Kenneth Cole
595 Broadway. **Map** 4 E3.
Tel (212) 965-0283.

Manolo Blahnik
31 W 54th St. **Map** 12 F4.
Tel (212) 582-3007.

MooShoes
78 Orchard St. **Map** 5 A4.
Tel (212) 254-6512.

Shoofly
42 Hudson St. **Map** 1 B1.
Tel (212) 406-3270.

Sigerson Morrison
28 Prince St. **Map** 4 F3.
Tel (212) 219-3893.

Lingerie

Henri Bendel
See p313.

La Perla
434 W Broadway. **Map** 4
E3. **Tel** (212) 219-0999.

La Petite Coquette
51 University Place. **Map**
4 E1. **Tel** (212) 473-2478.

Victoria's Secret
115 5th Ave. **Map** 8 F5.
Tel (212) 477-4118.
591–593 Broadway.
Map 4 E3.
Tel (212) 219-3643.

Vintage Shops and Markets

As might be expected of one of the world's capitals of fashion, New York's thrift and secondhand scene is a huge industry. Every season the city's fashionistas replenish their wardrobes, passing on their old outfits, and local fashion houses donate clothing. The quality is typically high – vintage stores are frequented by local designers as much as shoppers looking for a bargain. There's a heavy concentration of stores in the Lower East Side, especially around Ludlow and Rivington streets, but good deals can be found all over the city. Better quality items are found in the Upper East Side.

New York flea markets are also good hunting grounds for vintage clothes, crafts, lingerie, jewelry, and collectibles. Store holders sell their wares in parking lots, playgrounds, and street fairs, especially around summer and spring. In December, Union Square and Bryant Park are filled with Christmas and craft markets.

Vintage Clothes and Shoes

Consignment stores on the Upper East Side are among the city's best-kept secrets for vintage designer clothes. Madison Avenue stalwarts **Michael's Consignment** and **Encore Consignment** – the latter Jackie Kennedy's favorite – have both been going strong since 1954. **BIS Designer Resale** is also good for used designer womenswear, offering brands such as Louis Vuitton. Downtown, **INA** is a designer resale shop crammed with end-of-season pieces, while the owners of **Amarcord** make regular trips to Italy in search of discarded fashion. **Tokio 7**, on the other hand, sells a slightly more flamboyant selection of secondhand and vintage items.

Well-curated emporium **Edith Machinist** specializes in trendy vintage shoes, while the best spot for high-end vintage and classics from the 1960s to the 1980s is **Resurrection**. **AuH20 Thriftique** offers a handpicked selection of 1980s and 1990s thrift and vintage, with everything priced at $30 or less. Also at the cheaper end, **Gabay's Outlet** is packed with remaindered merchandise

from Midtown's popular department stores, while **Screaming Mimi's** sells low-cost costumes, bags, shoes, and even housewares. **What Comes Around Goes Around** is another well-loved downtown vintage store. With its extensive collection of vintage designer clothing on offer, the store also sells classic items and collectibles. **Monk Vintage Thrift** offers women's and men's clothing, along with costume jewelry and satin bow ties. **Buffalo Exchange**, established in Arizona in the 1970s, allows visitors to bring in old clothes for a trade-in, or cash on the spot.

Thrift Stores

Many of the cheaper secondhand stores, such as **Angel Street Thrift**, help charities – in this case the non-profit Lower East Side Service Center. The proceeds of **Housing Works Thrift Shop** go to Housing Works, an AIDS charity, while **Cure Thrift Shop**, which stocks jewelry and vintage furniture as well as clothes, donates all of its proceeds to the Diabetes Research Institute. Non-profit **Vintage Thrift**, and its equally well-stocked offshoot, **Vintage**

Thrift West, fund the United Jewish Council of the East Side. Thrift chain shop **Goodwill** has a major presence in New York, with everything from old prom dresses to funky housewares usually available. The **Salvation Army** operates three secondhand stores in Manhattan, with clothes at rock-bottom prices.

On the other side of the East River, Brooklyn is home to **Beacon's Closet**, a massive used-clothing warehouse that specializes in modern fashion and vintage attire. **Domsey Express** is another monster store, with five floors full of everything, from boutique outfits to cheap Old Navy wear. Northern California's **Crossroads** is another clothing exchange that also sells cheap shoes and accessories, and **Brooklyn Junk** is a trove of vintage furniture, art, books, dishes, photographs, vinyl records, clothes, and accessories. **Eleven Consignment Boutique** sells high-end fashion, such as Ralph Lauren, Diane von Furstenberg, Louis Vuitton, and Hermes, at almost half the original prices, with discounts going up to 50 per cent.

Flea Markets

Hell's Kitchen Flea Market is the fastest-growing fair in New York, with over 170 vendors hawking antiques, furniture, vintage clothes, and bric-a-brac every weekend. **Chelsea Flea Market** boasts around 135 vendors selling antiques, decorative arts, vintage clothing, and costume jewelry. The largest market in the city, however, the Upper West Side's **Green Flea**, is divided into an antiques-and-collectibles section, and a farmers' market every Sunday. **Hester Street Fair** is the Lower East Side's fashionable summer flea and craft market (Saturdays only), though it's best known for its creative food stalls. It offers visitors some of the best home goods, artisanal food, jewelry, vintage clothing, and much more, in its bustling outdoor space. The relatively small **Nolita Market** features bargain jewelry and hand-printed T-shirts, and the bazaar-like **Malcolm Shabazz Harlem Market** contains an array of West African cloth, jewelry, masks, outfits, Ashanti dolls, and beads.

Across the East River, the weekend **Brooklyn Flea**, with locations in Fort Greene and Williamsburg, has become a major event, with over 200 stalls, artisanal food, and high-quality arts and crafts. There are also traditional secondhand offerings available for sale. Between the months of December and March, the market moves indoors – more information can be found on the website. If you have time to venture deeper into Brooklyn, the **Bushwick Flea** offers a more relaxed scene with fewer crowds, while **Shwick** market hosts more than 100 vendors, most of whom are local artisanal cooks and artists. Over in Queens, the **LIC Flea & Food** features heaps of vintage clothing, bags, furniture, prints, and accessories from local artists. The market also offers a variety of foodstalls, with live music and games for visitors.

DIRECTORY

Thrift and Vintage

Amarcord
252 Lafayette St.
Map 4 F3.
Tel (212) 431-4161.

Angel Street Thrift
118 W 17th St.
Map 8 E5.
Tel (212) 229-0546.

AuH20 Thriftique
84 E 7th St.
Map 5 A2.
Tel (212) 466-0844.

Beacon's Closet
74 Guernsey St,
Greenpoint, Brooklyn.
Tel (718) 486-0816.

BIS Designer Resale
1134 Madison Ave.
Map 17 A4.
Tel (212) 396-2760.

Brooklyn Junk
567 Driggs Ave,
Williamsburg.
Map 23 B1.

Buffalo Exchange
332 E 11th St.
Map 5 A1.
Tel (212) 260-9340.

Crossroads
24 W 26th St.
Map 8 F4.
Tel (646) 398-7917.

Cure Thrift Shop
111 E 12th St.
Map 4 F1.
Tel (212) 505-7467.

Domsey Express
431 Broadway,
Williamsburg.
Map 23 B2.
Tel (718) 384-6000.

Edith Machinist
104 Rivington St.
Map 5 A3.
Tel (212) 979-9992.

Eleven Consignment Boutique
70 5th Ave, Brooklyn.
Map 23 B4.
Tel (718) 399-7767.

Encore Consignment
1132 Madison Ave.
Map 17 A4.
Tel (212) 879-2850.

Gabay's Outlet
195 Ave A.
Map 5 A1.
Tel (212) 254-3180.

Goodwill
44 W 8th St.
Map 4 D2.
Tel (212) 477-7024.

Housing Works Thrift Shop
143 W 17th St.
Map 8 E5.
Tel (718) 838-5050.

INA
15 Bleecker St.
Map 4 F3.
Tel (212) 228-8511.

Michael's Consignment
1041 Madison Ave.
Map 17 A4.
Tel (212) 737-7273.

Monk Vintage Thrift
496 Driggs Ave,
Williamsburg.
Map 23 B1.
Tel (718) 384-6665.

Resurrection
217 Mott St.
Map 4 F4.
Tel (212) 625-1374.

Salvation Army
208 E 23rd St.
Map 9 B4.
Tel (212) 532-8115.

Screaming Mimi's
382 Lafayette St.
Map 4 F2.
Tel (212) 677-6464.

Tokio 7
83 E 7th St.
Map 5 A2.
Tel (212) 353-8443.

Vintage Thrift
286 3rd Ave.
Map 9 B4.
Tel (212) 871-0777.

Vintage Thrift West
242 W 10th St.
Map 3 C2.
Tel (646) 371-9262.

What Comes Around Goes Around
351 W Broadway.
Map 4 E4.
Tel (212) 343-1225.

Flea Markets

Artists & Fleas, Chelsea Market
88 Tenth Ave.
Map 7 C5.
Tel (917) 488-0044.

Brooklyn Flea
176 Lafayette Ave,
Fort Greene. **Map** 23 C2.
50 Kent Ave,
Williamsburg. **Map** 23 B1.
Tel (212) 243-5343.

Bushwick Flea
52 Wyckoff Ave, Bushwick.
Tel (845) 707-3942.

Chelsea Flea Market
W 25th St, between Sixth
Ave and Broadway
Map 8 E2

Green Flea
Columbus Ave, between
W 76th and W 77th Sts.
Map 16 D5.
Tel (212) 239-3025.

Hell's Kitchen Flea Market
W 39th St, between Ninth
and Tenth Aves.
Map 7 C1.
Tel (212) 243-5343.

Hester Street Fair
Hester and Essex Sts.
Map 5 B4.
Tel (917) 267-9496.

LIC Flea & Food
5-25 46th Ave, Long
Island City.
Map 14 E5.
Tel (718) 224-5863.

Malcolm Shabazz Harlem Market
52 W 116th St.
Map 22 D3.
Tel (212) 987-8131.

Nolita Market
Prince St, between
Mulberry and Mott Sts.
Map 4 F3.

Shwick
6 Charles Place, Brooklyn.
W shwick.us

Books and Music

As the publishing capital of America, it's not surprising that New York has the country's best selection of bookstores. These range from vast general interest stores to hundreds of esoteric places specializing in everything from sci-fi to suspense, selling new books and old. Music lovers will also find sounds for all tastes at reasonable prices, plus thousands of rare recordings.

General Interest Bookstores

One of the best-known New York superstore chains is **Barnes & Noble**, though it has closed many of its branches in recent years. The Union Square outpost remains one of its biggest and most attractive, with a large café and regular readings by touring authors. **Book Culture** is the largest independent bookstore in the city, boasting a fine selection of literary fiction, while friendly **McNally Jackson** stocks classics and contemporary fiction, and also has a café. Founded in 1977, **St Mark's Bookshop** is an East Village icon, stocked with titles on contemporary art, politics, gender studies, literary criticism, and the environment. **Shakespeare & Co.** offers a sensational selection of titles and is open late every night.

Thanks to inviting indie bookstores such as **Word** and **BookCourt**, Brooklyn is emerging as the literary capital of the nation. **Powerhouse Arena**, an airy space in Dumbo, frequently hosts events ranging from sedate author readings to wild literary-themed parties.

Secondhand Bookstores

New York's famous **Strand** book store, founded in 1927, contains an astonishing 2.5 million copies of secondhand and heavily discounted new books, spread out over several floors of crowded bookshelves and passageways. There is also a large, rare book room for first editions. **Housing Works Bookstore Café** is a lovely, high-ceilinged bookstore-café with a wide range of used books. **Westsider Bookshop** is as comprehensive as its music counterpart, as it stocks an enormous collection of used books, and country/bluegrass LPs. Brooklyn is represented by **Spoonbill & Sugartown**, specializing in used, rare, and new books on contemporary art, art history, architecture, and design.

Specialty Bookstores

The city's largest selection of theatrical books and publications is found at **Drama Book Shop**. Books that involve murder and suspense abound at the **Mysterious Bookshop**, while Jewish books and music are plenty at **J. Levine Books & Judaica**. **Kinokuniya Bookstore**, the largest Japanese bookshop in New York, offers English books on Japan, while the branch of prestigious Italian bookstore chain and publisher **Rizzolis**, specializes in European publications. **Bank Street Book Store** has one of the best selections of current children's books, and **Books of Wonder** stocks a variety of hardcover and rare children's books. Educational toys and their book tie-ins can also be found in the bright **Scholastic Store**, below Scholastic's SoHo offices.

The acclaimed publisher of volumes on art and architecture, **Taschen**, maintains a handsome store in SoHo. Cookbooks are on the menu at **Kitchen Arts & Letters**, with many out-of-print books and first editions. **Idlewild** is a travel-centric bookstore, where everything is arranged by destination.

Try **Forbidden Planet** or the venerable East Village stalwart, **St. Mark's Comics**, for a huge range of science-fiction books and comics. **Midtown Comics** has three spacious locations and offers a good range of comics at affordable prices. Vintage collectors might prefer **JHU Comic Books**, across from the Empire State Building. Collectible merchandise is available here at reasonable prices, as well as those at "ask Santa" rates. **Desert Island** draws Brooklyn's hipsters and artists with its selection of comics and graphic novels. Visit **Bluestockings** for new and used titles on a variety of subjects: from gender studies and homosexuality to capitalism and the prison system.

Music

For out-of-print records, **Westsider Records** is a collector's treasure trove, with an excellent choice of classical, jazz, and opera recordings. In the West Village, **House of Oldies** has a massive stock of deleted and rare records to suit all tastes. **Bleecker Street Records** is crammed with hip, hard-to-find treasures, while **Generation Records** has an assortment of hardcore, metal, and punk. True music enthusiasts should head to **Other Music**, which stocks obscure gems, from hot electronica to 1970s free jazz. **Academy Records** is another excellent choice, with second hand CDs, LPs, and DVDs.

DJs and vinyl lovers still have options for deep house, breakbeat, and electronica, such as **Turntable Lab** in Manhattan or the lively **Halcyon** in Dumbo. In the heart of trendy Williamsburg there is **Earwax** or the London-based **Rough Trade NYC**, a firm favorite among the hipster set. For jazz, seek out **Downtown Music Gallery** or the **Jazz Record Center**, which sells rare and out-of-print jazz LPs, books, videos, and music memorabilia. The bookstore of the **Juilliard School**, one of the world's most respected music schools, sells sheet music, books, and recordings.

DIRECTORY

General Interest Bookstores

Barnes & Noble
33 E 17th St.
Map 9 A5.
Tel (212) 253-0810.
One of several branches.

BookCourt
163 Court St,
Brooklyn.
Tel (718) 875-3677.

Book Culture
2915 Broadway.
Map 20 E3.
Tel (646) 403-3000.

McNally Jackson
52 Prince St.
Map 4 F3.
Tel (212) 274-1160.

Powerhouse Arena
37 Main St, Brooklyn.
Tel (718) 222-1331.

St. Mark's Bookshop
136 E 3rd Ave.
Map 5 A2.
Tel (212) 260-7853.

Shakespeare & Co.
716 Broadway.
Map 4 E2.
Tel (212) 529-1330.
One of several branches.

Word
126 Franklin St,
Brooklyn.
Tel (718) 383-0096.

Secondhand Bookstores

Housing Works Bookstore Café
126 Crosby St.
Map 4 F3.
Tel (212) 334-3324.

Spoonbill & Sugartown
218 Bedford Ave,
Williamsburg.
Tel (718) 387-7322.

Strand
828 Broadway.
Map 4 E1.
Tel (212) 473 1452.

Westsider Bookshop
2246 Broadway.
Map 15 C4.
Tel (212) 362-0706.

Specialty Bookstores

Bank Street Book Store
2780 Broadway.
Map 20 E5.
Tel (212) 678-1654.

Bluestockings
172 Allen St.
Map 5 A3.
Tel (212) 777-6028.

Books of Wonder
18 W 18th St.
Map 8 E5.
Tel (212) 989-3270.

Desert Island
540 Metropolitan
Ave, Brooklyn.
Tel (718) 388-5087.

Drama Book Shop
250 W 40th St.
Map 8 E1.
Tel (212) 944-0595.

Forbidden Planet
840 Broadway.
Map 4 E1.
Tel (212) 473-1576.

Idlewild
12 W 19th St.
Map 8 F5.
Tel (212) 414-8888.

JHU Comic Books
32 E 32nd St.
Map 8 F2.
Tel (212) 268-7088.

J. Levine Books & Judaica
5 W 30th St.
Map 8 F3.
Tel (212) 695-6888.

Kinokuniya Bookstore
1073 Sixth Ave.
Map 8 E1.
Tel (212) 869-1700

Kitchen Arts & Letters
1435 Lexington Ave.
Map 17 A2.
Tel (212) 876-5550.

Midtown Comics
200 W 40th St.
Map 8 E1.
459 Lexington Ave.
Map 13 A5.
64 Fulton St.
Map 2 D2.
Tel (212) 302-8192.

Mysterious Bookshop
58 Warren St.
Map 1 B1.
Tel (212) 582-1011.

Rizzoli
1133 Broadway.
Map 8 F4.
Tel (212) 759-2424.

St Mark's Comics
11 St Mark's Place.
Map 4 F1.
Tel (212) 598-9439.

Scholastic Store
557 Broadway.
Map 4 E4.
Tel (212) 343-6166.

Taschen Store
107 Greene St.
Map 4E3.
Tel (212) 226-2212.

Music

Academy Records
12 W 18th St.
Map 7 C5.
Tel (212) 242-3000.
One of several branches.

Bleecker Street Records
188 W 4th St.
Map 3 C2.
Tel (212) 255-7899.

Downtown Music Gallery
13 Monroe St.
Map 2 E1.
Tel (212) 473-0043.

Earwax
167 N 9th St, Brooklyn.
Tel (718) 486-3771.

Generation Records
210 Thompson St.
Map 4 E2.
Tel (212) 254-1100.

Halcyon
57 Pearl St at Water St,
Dumbo, Brooklyn.
Map 2 F2.
Tel (718) 260-WAXY.

House of Oldies
35 Carmine St.
Map 4 D3.
Tel (212) 243-0500.

Jazz Record Center
236 W 26th St.
Map 8 D4.
Tel (212) 675-4480.

Juilliard Store
144 W 66th St.
Map 11 C2.
Tel (212) 799-5000.

Other Music
15 E 4th St.
Map 4 F2.
Tel (212) 477-8150.

Rough Trade NYC
64 N 9th St, Brooklyn.
Map 6 F1.
Tel (718) 388-4111.

Turntable Lab
120 E 7th St.
Map 5 A2.
Tel (212) 677-0675.

Westsider Records
233 W 72nd St.
Map 11 D1.
Tel (212) 874-1588.

Art and Antiques

Any art-loving visitor to New York could easily spend days gallery-hopping around the several hundred galleries found throughout the city. Antiques lovers can find an exciting variety of goods, and many bargains, at the innumerable flea markets *(see p324–5)*; or they can browse through European and American fine antiques in one of the more exclusive antiques centers.

Art Galleries

One of the city's best-known art dealers is the **Castelli Gallery**, an important showcase for Pop Art during the early 1960s and now spotlighting new artists. **Mary Boone Gallery** features Neo-Expressionist artists such as David Salle and Julian Schnabel. **Pace Gallery** exhibits former and current stars, especially painter-photographers. **Postmasters** features impressive changing shows of emerging artists. **Marian Goodman Gallery** focuses on the European avant-garde.

In Chelsea, the **Matthew Marks Gallery** and **Marianne Boesky Gallery** are worth a visit. **Paula Cooper** often hosts controversial shows in her beautiful loft space. The **Gagosian Gallery** exhibits paintings by modern masters, with great works by Johns and Lichtenstein. Don't miss the exceptional shows of twentieth-century greats at the **Robert Miller Gallery**. **Hirschl & Adler Galleries** in Midtown is another option for high-profile exhibitions. **Lehmann Maupin Gallery** is the spot to see up-and-coming artists working in innovative forms. **Gladstone Gallery** is another heavy hitter in the art scene, and the influential **David Zwirner Gallery** lures crowds with its progressive, big-name exhibitions. The airy **Agora Gallery** shows local and international works, including Art Nouveau pieces.

In SoHo, **Artists Space** is a respected alternative gallery, with frequently changing theme-based exhibits, film screenings and installations, while the **Drawing Center** presents shows of contemporary and historical works on paper.

In the Lower East Side, **47 Canal** is a non-commercial, artist-run space for very experimental projects. Other fashionable galleries down here include **Frosch & Portmann**, **Salon 94 Bowery** (the offshoot of an Upper East Side gallery), and **Sperone Westwater**, housed in a building designed by Norman Foster.

In the West Village, **Gavin Brown's Enterprise** features young, highly experimental mixed-media artists, while the influential **White Columns** focuses on emerging talent.

Some of the most vibrant galleries in the city are found in Brooklyn; **Front Room** is a good place to get a sense of the Williamsburg scene, while **WAH Center** concentrates on painting and sculpture. Over in Dumbo, **Smack Mellon Gallery** displays multidisciplinary work by lesser-known artists.

American Folk Art

The **American Primitive Gallery** sells a variety of folk art curiosities, from Ozarks' antique wooden dolls to modern glass art.

Antiques Centers and Secondhand Antiques

In addition to hundreds of small shops selling everything from tiger teeth to multimillion-dollar paintings, Manhattan is home to **The Manhattan Art & Antiques Center**, which has over 70 dealers under one roof. The **Showplace Antique and Design Center** in Chelsea, featuring four floors of antiques, retro furnishings, and memorabilia, is also well worth a visit.

American Furniture

For furniture from the 17th, 18th, and 19th centuries, try **Bernard & S. Dean Levy** or **Circa Antiques** (now online and viewable by appointment only). Alternatively, go to **Woodard & Greenstein** for a truly wonderful selection of Shaker pieces, hooked rugs, and quilts.

Collectors of Art Deco or Art Nouveau furniture should pay a visit to **Alan Moss**, which is full of furniture and decorative items of all kinds. **Macklowe Gallery** on Madison Avenue has a massive collection of fine Art Nouveau furniture. Just a few blocks away, **Lillian Nassau** specializes in Tiffany lamps and many Art Nouveau and Art Deco pieces.

New York has a handful of retro shops, including **Adelaide**, which stocks treasures from the 1930s through to the 1960s.

International Antiques

If you're looking for English antiques, try **Florian Papp**. For European pieces, you'll have plenty of choices; try **Eileen Lane Antiques** (a major importer of Swedish antiques) and **Linda Horn Antiques**. **La Belle Epoque** stocks antique posters. Oriental dealers include luxury **Doris Leslie Blau** and **Flying Cranes Antiques** (inside the Manhattan Art and Antiques Center).

Auction Houses

Manhattan's two most celebrated auction houses are **Christie's** and **Sotheby's**, selling collectibles ranging from coins, jewels, and vintage wines to fine and decorative arts.

Also worth a try are **Doyle New York** and **Phillips**, both well-respected names for fine art, jewelry, and antiques. Bear in mind that items for sale are previewed several days before the auctions, so check the Friday and Sunday *Times* beforehand to see what's coming up. The venerable **Swann Galleries** auctions prints, books, maps, posters, autographs, and photographs.

DIRECTORY

Art Galleries

47 Canal
291 Grand St. **Map** 5 A4.
Tel (646) 415-7712.

Agora Gallery
530 W 25th St.
Map 7 C4.
Tel (212) 226-4151.

Artists Space
38 Greene St.
Map 4 E4.
Tel (212) 226-3970.

Castelli Gallery
18 E 77th St.
Map 17 A5.
Tel (212) 249-4470.

David Zwirner Gallery
525 W 19th St.
Map 7 B3.
Tel (212) 727-2070.

The Drawing Center
35 Wooster St.
Map 4 E4.
Tel (212) 219-2166.

Front Room
147 Roebling St,
Williamsburg.
Map 7 B3.
Tel (718) 782-2556.

Frosch & Portmann
53 Stanton St.
Map 5 A3.
Tel (646) 266-5994.

Gagosian Gallery
555 W 24th St.
Map 7 C4.
Tel (212) 741-1111.
One of several galleries.

Gavin Brown's Enterprise
620 Greenwich St.
Map 3 C3.
Tel (212) 627-5258.

Gladstone Gallery
515 W 24th St.
Map 7 C4.
Tel (212) 206-9300.

Hirschl & Adler Galleries
730 5th Ave, 4th Floor.
Map 12 F3.
Tel (212) 535-8810.

Lehmann Maupin Gallery
536 W 22nd St.
Map 7 C4.
Tel (212) 255-2923.

Marian Goodman Gallery
24 W 57th St.
Map 12 F3.
Tel (212) 977-7160.

Marianne Boesky Gallery
509 W 24th St.
Map 7 C4.
Tel (212) 680-9889.

Mary Boone Gallery
745 5th Ave.
Map 12 F3.
Tel (212) 752-2929.
One of two galleries.

Matthew Marks Gallery
523 W 24th St.
Map 7 C4.
Tel (212) 243-0200.

Pace Gallery
534 W 25th St.
Map 7 C4.
Tel (212) 929-7000.
One of several galleries.

Paula Cooper
534 W 21st St.
Map 7 C4.
Tel (212) 255-1105.

Postmasters
54 Franklin St.
Map 4 E5.
Tel (212) 727-3323.

Robert Miller Gallery
524 W 26th St.
Map 7 C3.
Tel (212) 366-4774.

Salon 94 Bowery
243 Bowery.
Map 4 F3.
Tel (212) 979-0001.

Smack Mellon Gallery
92 Plymouth St, Dumbo.
Tel (718) 834-8761.

Sperone Westwater
257 Bowery.
Map 4 F3.
Tel (212) 999-7337.

WAH Center
135 Broadway,
Williamsburg.
Tel (718) 486-6012.

White Columns
320 W 13th St.
Map 3 B1.
Tel (212) 924-4212.

American Folk Art

American Primitive Gallery
49 E 78th St, Suite 2B.
Map 17 A5.
Tel (212) 628-1530.

Antiques Centers and Secondhand Antiques

The Manhattan Arts & Antiques Center
1050 2nd Ave.
Map 13 A3.
Tel (212) 355-4400.

Showplace Antique and Design Center
40 W 25th St.
Map 8 F4.
Tel (212) 633-6063.

American Furniture

Adelaide
702 Greenwich St.
Map 3 C2.
Tel (212) 627-0508.

Alan Moss
436 Lafayette St.
Map 4 F2.
Tel (212) 473-1310.

Bernard & S. Dean Levy
24 E 84th St. **Map** 16 F4.
Tel (212) 628-7088.

Circa Antiques
374 Atlantic Ave,
Brooklyn.
Tel (718) 596-1866.
By appointment only.

Lillian Nassau
220 E 57th St. **Map** 13 B3.
Tel (212) 759-6062.

Macklowe Gallery
667 Madison Ave.
Map 13 A3.
Tel (212) 644-6400.

Woodard & Greenstein
303 E 81st St. **Map** 17 B4.
Tel (212) 988-2906.

International Antiques

La Belle Epoque
115a Greenwich Ave.
Map 3 C1.
Tel (212) 362-1770.

Doris Leslie Blau
306 E 61st St,
7th Floor.
Map 13 B3.
Tel (212) 586-5511.
By appointment only.

Eileen Lane Antiques
236 E 60th St.
Map 13 B3.
Tel (212) 475-2988.

Florian Papp
962 Madison Ave.
Map 17 A5.
Tel (212) 288-6770.

Flying Cranes Antiques
1050 2nd Ave.
Map 13 B4.
Tel (212) 223-4600.

Linda Horn Antiques
1327 Madison Ave.
Map 17 A2.
Tel (212) 772-1122.

Auction Houses

Christie's
20 Rockefeller Plaza.
Map 12 F5.
Tel (212) 636-2000.

Doyle New York
175 E 87th St.
Map 17 A3.
Tel (212) 427-2730.

Phillips
450 Park Ave.
Map 13 A3.
Tel (212) 940-1300.

Sotheby's
1334 York Ave.
Map 13 C1.
Tel (212) 606-7000.

Swann Galleries
104 E 25th St.
Map 9 A4.
Tel (212) 254-4710.

Gourmet Groceries, Specialty Food, and Wine Shops

New York's striking cultural and ethnic diversity is reflected in its food – the city's food shops provide a truly international feast. There is also a dazzling array of coffee stores and wine shops available almost everywhere you turn.

Gourmet Groceries

Scattered around town are several food emporiums that are tourist attractions in themselves. Remember, too, to visit the department stores, which often rival the specialty food stores.

At **Dean & DeLuca** on Broadway, a chic market and culinary destination, food has been elevated to an art form – don't miss the huge selection of take-out food. **Russ & Daughters** on Houston Street, one of the oldest gourmet shops, is known as an "appetizing" store, full of Jewish specialties and famous for smoked fish, cream cheese, chocolates, and bagels. The **Gourmet Garage** on Broome Street sells all kinds of delicious fresh food, in particular organic produce. **Zabar's** on Broadway is perhaps the finest food store in the world, with huge crowds jostling for the excellent smoked salmon, bagels, caviar, nuts and candies, cheese, and coffee. **William Poll** on Lexington Avenue offers picnic hampers as well as a great variety of prepared dishes.

Whole Foods, famed for their superb selection of natural, organic, wholesome foods, draws devoted shoppers throughout the city. The Whole Foods in Columbus Circle is one of the largest supermarkets in Manhattan, with row upon gleaming row of quality food "in its purest state," with no artificial additives. There's also a popular central Whole Foods on Union Square. **Fairway Market** on Broadway offers premium groceries from fresh produce to smoked fish and baked goods.

Specialty Food

Fabulous bread and cake shops abound, but one of the best is **Poseidon Greek Bakery,**

renowned for its filo pastry. **Ess-a-Bagel** operates two locations, both of which churn out some of the city's highest-rated bagels. Try the delicious Chinese pastries at **Golden Fung Wong Bakery,** or the pretzel croissants and great tarts at **City Bakery. Magnolia Bakery** is famed for its beautifully decorated and superb-tasting cupcakes. It has three locations in Manhattan.

Great confectionery shops include **Li-Lac Chocolates** for handmade truffles and **Mondel Chocolates** for chocolate animals. **Economy Candy** has a huge range of dried fruit and old-fashioned sweets, but for a real treat go to **Teuscher Chocolates,** which has fresh champagne truffles flown in direct from Switzerland. For pâté de foie gras, Scottish smoked salmon, beluga, and caviar, pay a visit to **Caviarteria.**

Myers of Keswick imports English food. For something more exotic, **New Kam Man Market** is a grocery store selling Chinese, Thai, and other Asian products. The sprawling **Eataly** (*see p125*) has fine imported Italian goods; you can take their fine cheeses and pastas home or dine at one of the numerous eateries within the complex. Go to **Lobel's** (open since 1840) for fine cuts of meat and game, and **Citarella** for fine seafood. For exotic spices and teas, visit **Sullivan Street Tea & Spice Co.,** in Greenwich Village, or the Middle Eastern shop **Kalustyan's.**

For a wide choice of cheese, as well as olives and charcuterie, visit **Murray's Cheese Shop.** Named New York's Best Cheese Shop by many of the city's newspapers, it is heaven for cheese-lovers, with over 250 types of cheese from around the world, from bloomy rinds

such as Camembert to moist ricotta. The friendly staff happily offers tastings from the mind-boggling selection. Make a picnic out of it, and pick up some of their fresh breads and olives to accompany your purchases.

If you are looking for true old Eastern European pickles, try **The Pickle Guys.** They also store pickled tomatoes, mushrooms, olives, hot peppers, sweet kraut, sauerkraut, herring, and sun-dried tomatoes.

For fruit and vegetables at reasonable prices, visit a farmers' greenmarket, but be sure to get there early for the pick of the crop. Among the most popular are **79th Street Greenmarket, TriBeCa Greenmarket,** and **Union Square.** For more information on the city's markets, phone (212) 788-7476.

Coffee Stores

New York also has many fine coffee stores. Among the best are **Oren's Daily Roast** and **Porto Rico Importing Company,** each with a mouth-watering selection. **The Sensuous Bean** features a superb range of gourmet coffees and teas, as does the cozy **McNulty's Tea & Coffee Company,** one of the nation's oldest coffee stores.

Wine Shops

Acker Merrall & Condit have been selling wines since 1820 and have an excellent selection. Go to **Garnet Wines & Liquors** for fine wines and champagnes at bargain prices. **Spring Street Wine Shop,** in the heart of SoHo, is a convenient, well-stocked spot to pop in for a bottle of fine wine. **Sherry-Lehmann Wine & Spirits** is among New York's leading wine merchants. **Astor Wines & Spirits,** New York's largest wine store, features a massive selection of premium and discount wines and spirits. Every month they highlight their Top 10 choices under $10 – great for superb bargains. **Union Square Wines and Spirits** offers a terrific variety of wines, and features tastings every week.

DIRECTORY

Gourmet Groceries

Dean & DeLuca
560 Broadway.
Map 4 E3.
Tel (212) 226 6800.
One of several branches.

Fairway Market
2127 Broadway.
Map 15 C5.
Tel (212) 595-1888.
One of several branches.

Gourmet Garage
489 Broome St.
Map 4 E4.
Tel (212) 941-5850.
One of several branches.

Russ & Daughters
179 E Houston St.
Map 5 A3.
Tel (212) 475-4880.

Whole Foods
10 Columbus Circle.
Map 12 D3.
Tel (212) 823-9600.
One of several branches.

William Poll
1051 Lexington Ave.
Map 17 A5.
Tel (212) 288-0501.

Zabar's
2245 Broadway.
Map 15 C4.
Tel (212) 787-2000.

Specialty Food

79th Street Greenmarket
Columbus Ave between
78th & 81st Sts.
Map 16 D5.
Open Sun.

Caviarteria
75 Murray St.
Map 1 B1.
Tel (212) 791-7777.

Citarella
2135 Broadway.
Map 15 C5.
Tel (212) 874-0383.
One of several branches.

City Bakery
3 W 18th St.
Map 8 F5.
Tel (212) 366-1414.

Eataly
200 5th Ave.
Map 8 F4.
Tel (646) 398-5100.

Economy Candy
108 Rivington St.
Map 5 A3.
Tel (212) 254-1531.

Ess-a-Bagel
831 3rd Ave.
Map 13 B4.
Tel (212) 980-1010.

Golden Fung Wong Bakery
41 Mott St.
Map 4 F3.
Tel (212) 267-4037.

Kalustyan's
123 Lexington Ave.
Map 9 A3.
Tel (212) 685-3451.

Ll-Lac Chocolates
40 Eighth Ave.
Map 3 C1.
Tel (212) 924-2280.

Lobel's
1096 Madison Ave.
Map 17 A4.
Tel (212) 737-1372.

Magnolia Bakery
401 Bleecker St.
Map 3 C2.
Tel (212) 462-2572.
One of several branches.

Mondel Chocolates
2913 Broadway.
Map 20 E3.
Tel (212) 864-2111.

Murray's Cheese Shop
254 Bleecker St.
Map 4 D2.
Tel (212) 243-3289.
One of two branches.

Myers of Keswick
634 Hudson St.
Map 3 C2.
Tel (212) 691-4194.

New Kam Man Market
200 Canal St.
Map 4 F5.
Tel (212) 571-0330.

The Pickle Guys
49 Essex St.
Map 5 B4.
Tel (212) 656-9739.

Poseidon Greek Bakery
629 9th Ave.
Map 12 D5.
Tel (212) 757-6173.

Sullivan Street Tea & Spice Co.
208 Sullivan St.
Map 4 D3.
Tel (212) 387-8702.

Teuscher Chocolates
25 E 61st St.
Map 12 F3.
Tel (212) 751-8482.
620 5th Ave.
Map 12 F4.
Tel (212) 246-4416.

TriBeCa Greenmarket
Greenwich St, between
Chambers and Duane Sts.
Map 1 B1.
Open Wed & Sat.

Union Square Greenmarket
E 17th St & Broadway.
Map 8 F5.
Open Mon, Wed, Fri,
and Sat.

Coffee Stores

McNulty's Tea & Coffee Company
109 Christopher St.
Map 3 C2.
Tel (212) 242-5351.

Oren's Daily Roast
1144 Lexington Ave.
Map 17 A4.
Tel (212) 472-6830.
One of several branches.

Porto Rico Importing Company
201 Bleecker St.
Map 3 C2.
Tel (212) 477-5421.
One of several branches.

The Sensuous Bean
66 W 70th St.
Map 12 D1.
Tel (212) 724-7725.

Wine Shops

Acker Merrall & Condit
160 W 72nd St.
Map 11 C1.
Tel (212) 787-1700.

Astor Wines & Spirits
399 Lafayette St.
Map 4 F2.
Tel (212) 674-7500.

Garnet Wines & Liquors
929 Lexington Ave.
Map 13 A1.
Tel (212) 772-3211.

Sherry-Lehmann Wine & Spirits
505 Park Ave.
Map 13 A3.
Tel (212) 838-7500.

Spring Street Wine Shop
187 Spring St.
Map 4 D4.
Tel (212) 219-0521.

Union Square Wines and Spirits
140 4th Ave.
Map 4 F1.
Tel (212) 675-8100.

Electronics and Housewares

From flatscreen TVs and top-of-the-line sound systems to swanky designer home furnishings, New York City abounds with electronics and housewares stores. Perhaps the most competitive retailers in New York are the ones that sell electronics, so it pays to shop around. Be particularly careful with electronics stores on the heavily touristed streets and those around the major tourist sights, such as Fifth Avenue near the Empire State Building. Many of these stores sell mediocre, sometimes faulty equipment at inflated prices, and it's a hassle or near impossible to get a refund once you've returned home. If you're buying electronic goods to take to Europe, make sure they have compatible voltages and formats (many in the US are made to different standards).

Sound Systems and Equipment

For the latest in cutting-edge stereo equipment, head to **Sound by Singer**. While **J&R Music World** is undergoing a a major renovation, **J&R Express** (inside Century 21) still sells a good selection of stereo and computer equipment. The Danish **Bang & Olufsen** showcases a range of sleek, minimalist sound systems that can dress up even the humblest flat. **Hammacher Schlemmer**, a New York mainstay since 1848, carries the "best, the only, and the unexpected" and has friendly, informative staff. Browse the quality systems at **Lyric HiFi & Video**, a favorite that's been around since 1959. The perennially jam-packed **Sony Store** delivers on its wide range of top-shelf sound systems and plenty of impulse-buy gizmos. True to its name, the chain store **Best Buy** does offer some of the best buys on an assortment of stereo systems and home-entertainment products – the Union Square branch is open 24 hours. For high-end stereo equipment and components, check out **Innovative Audio Video Showrooms**. Also stop to look around at the wide range of both used and new stereos at the friendly **Stereo Exchange**.

Photography

B & H Photo Video is where amateur and professional photographers and filmmakers can find everything they need. Open since 1898, **Willoughby's** has pretty good sales on photographic equipment and supplies. Those looking to immerse themselves in the world of analog photography make a beeline for the stylish **Lomography Gallery Store**. Head to Chelsea's **Foto Care** for a wide range of cameras and accouterments. **Print Space Photo Lab** offers a variety of services, including digital rentals, film processing, and both color and black-and-white darkrooms. Make for **Adorama** in the Flatiron District, and browse the spectacular displays of digital cameras and accessories, point-and-shoots, and disposables, and also affordable prices on film developing and processing. Don't miss the quality, high-end cameras and equipment at the elegant **The Photo Village**. The **Leica Store Soho** is a stylish showcase for the German camera-maker, with artsy photographic exhibits and special-edition cameras.

Computers

There are several Macintosh meccas in Manhattan, including the immense, airy **Apple Store SoHo** and the gleaming cube of a store on **5th Avenue**, which is open 24 hours a day. Neither quite matches the branch within Grand Central Terminal, a spectacular space. Mac-philes flock to all three to peruse and test-drive the latest models, plug in to iPods, and attend seminars geared to both novices and experts. If you brought your Mac from home and find that you need a repair, head to **Tekserve**, where a tech whiz should be able to fix the problem. All models and products are serviced, and the staff offers tips on new technologies; you can also get a free estimate and browse for upgrades. Conversely, the **Microsoft Store** is dedicated to all the best Microsoft products, including the popular Surface, Lumia phone and Xbox.

Kitchenware

Most of the department stores offer a wide range of household goods. For a specialized shop, try **Broadway Panhandler** on Eighth Street, a cook's heaven with outstanding baking and pastry-making equipment. Chain store **Williams-Sonoma** has kitchenware, utensils, and cookbooks. The East Village, particularly on and around Bowery Street, has long been the nucleus for restaurant supply stores, and you can find top-quality kitchenware at bargain prices here. The popular **MTC Kitchen** shop sells professional Japanese cooking tools, from ceramics and high-end knives to soba-making machines and sushi supplies.

Housewares and Furnishings

Baccarat, **Lalique**, and **Villeroy & Boch** are where you'll find the finest crystal, china, and silverware. **Orrefors Kosta Boda** has beautiful Swedish glassware, from vases to candlesticks, and **Tiffany & Co.** is also, of course, a fashionable spot. For the best of inexpensive, utilitarian china, visit **Fishs Eddy**. The esteemed **Joan B. Merviss** gallery sells fine, imported Japanese ceramics, and **La Terrine** and **Mackenzie-Childs** stock hand-painted ceramics. Browse the hip SoHo showcase of designer **Jonathan Adler**, whose eye-catching pottery in natural shades and primitive and organic shapes will stand out from everything else in your living room. His collection includes a "family" of playful decanters in the forms of man, woman, and child, plump vases of smiling suns and fish plates, and a menagerie of pottery animals, including bookends shaped like the front and back of a charging bull. **ABC Carpet & Home** on Broadway has an enviable reputation for home furnishings.

For elegant furniture, from soft leather sofas to luxurious beds and sleek tableware, try Giorgio Armani's posh **Armani Casa**. **Dune** on Lexington

Avenue in Lower Midtown offers chic furniture by contemporary designers, including wool sofas and convertible lounges. **Design Within Reach** is the source for fully licensed classics, such as Saarinen, Eames, and Bertoia. If you lean toward retro, head to **Restoration Hardware**, where you can choose from updated Art Deco furnishings, lighting fixtures, and patinated bronze accessories.

Linens

Linens can be found in most department stores, but for silk sheets and luxurious linens visit **D. Porthault** and **Pratesi**. The Italian **Frette**, on Madison Avenue, sells thick towels and robes and wonderfully soft cotton sheets and bedding. **Bed, Bath & Beyond** offers a varied selection of bed linens, kitchen, and bath accessories.

DIRECTORY

Sound Systems and Equipment

Bang & Olufsen
927 Broadway. **Map** 8 F4.
Tel (212) 388-9792.

Best Buy
52 E 14th St. **Map** 4 E1.
Tel (212) 466-4789.

Hammacher Schlemmer
147 E 57th St. **Map** 13 A3.
Tel (212) 421-9000.

Innovative Audio Video Showrooms
150 E 58th St. **Map** 13 A4.
Tel (212) 634-4444.

J&R Express
22 Cortlandt St
(Century 21). **Map** 1 C2.
Tel (212) 227-9092.

Lyric HiFi & Video
1221 Lexington Ave.
Map 17 A4.
Tel (212) 439-1900.

Sony Store
550 Madison Ave. **Map** 13 A4. **Tel** (212) 833-8800.

Sound by Singer
242 W 27th St. **Map** 8 D3.
Tel (212) 924-8600.

Stereo Exchange
627 Broadway. **Map** 4 E3.
Tel (212) 505-1111.

Photography

Adorama
42 W 18th St. **Map** 8 F5.
Tel (212) 741-0466.

B & H Photo Video
420 9th Ave. **Map** 8 D2.
Tel (212) 444-6615.

Foto Care
41 W 22nd St. **Map** 8 E4.
Tel (212) 741-2990.

Leica Store Soho
460 W Broadway. **Map** 4 E3. **Tel** (212) 475-7799.

Lomography Gallery Store
41 W 8th St. **Map** 4 D1.
Tel (212) 529-4353.

The Photo Village
369 W 34th St. **Map** 8 D2.
Tel (212) 989-1252.

Print Space Photo Lab
19 W 21st St, Suite 706.
Map 8 F4. **Tel** (212) 255-1919.

Willoughby's
298 5th Ave. **Map** 8 F3.
Tel (212) 564-1600.

Computers

Apple Store 5th Ave
767 5th Ave. **Map** 12 F3.
Tel (212) 336-1440.

Apple Store Grand Central
45 Grand Central Terminal. **Map** 9 A1.
Tel (212) 284-1800.

Apple Store SoHo
103 Prince St. **Map** 4 E3.
Tel (212) 226-3126.

Microsoft Store
Time Warner Center, 10 Columbus Circle. **Map** 12 D3. **Tel** (855) 270-6581.

Tekserve
119 W 23rd St. **Map** 8 F4.
Tel (212) 929-3645.

Kitchenware

Broadway Panhandler
65 E 8th St. **Map** 4 E2.
Tel (212) 966-3434.

MTC Kitchen
711 3rd Ave. **Map** 13 B5.
Tel (212) 661 3333.

Williams-Sonoma
10 Columbus Circle.
Map 12 D3.
Tel (212) 581-1146.
One of several branches.

Housewares and Furnishings

ABC Carpet & Home
888 Broadway. **Map** 8 F5.
Tel (212) 473-3000.

Armani Casa
979 3rd Ave, Suite 1424.
Map 13 B3.
Tel (212) 334-1271.

Avventura
463 Amsterdam Ave.
Map 15 C4.
Tel (212) 769-2510.

Baccarat
635 Madison Ave.
Map 13 A3.
Tel (212) 826-4100.

Design Within Reach
110 Greene St. **Map** 4 E3.
Tel (212) 475-0001.
One of several branches.

Dune
200 Lexington Ave. **Map** 9 A2. **Tel** (212) 925-6171.

Fishs Eddy
889 Broadway. **Map** 8 F5.
Tel (212) 420-9020.

Joan B. Merviss
39 E 78th St, 4th Floor.
Map 17 A5.
Tel (212) 799-4021.

Jonathan Adler
53 Greene St.
Map 4 E4.
Tel (212) 941-8950.

Lalique
609 Madison Ave.
Map 13 A3.
Tel (212) 355-6550.

Mackenzie-Childs
20 W 57th St.
Map 12 F3.
Tel (212) 570-6050.

Orrefors Kosta Boda
200 Lexington Ave.
Map 9 A2.
Tel (212) 684-5455.

Restoration Hardware
935 Broadway. **Map** 8 F4.
Tel (212) 260-9479.

La Terrine
1024 Lexington Ave.
Map 13 A1.
Tel (212) 988-3366.

Tiffany & Co.
See p166.

Villeroy & Boch
41 Madison Ave.
Map 9 A4.
Tel (212) 213-8149.

Linens

Bed, Bath & Beyond
620 Ave of the Americas.
Map 8 F5.
Tel (212) 255-3550.

D. Porthault
470 Park Ave.
Map 13 A3.
Tel (212) 688-1660.

Frette
799 Madison Ave.
Map 13 A1.
Tel (212) 988-5221.

Pratesi
829 Madison Ave.
Map 13 A2.
Tel (212) 288 2315.

ENTERTAINMENT IN NEW YORK CITY

New York City is a non-stop entertainment extravaganza, every day, all year round. Whatever your taste, you can be sure the city will satisfy it on both a grand and an intimate scale. The challenge is to take advantage of as many of the events on offer as possible. If it's theater, you can enjoy a mainstream success on Broadway or take a chance on an experimental production in a loft. If it's music, there's the magnificence of opera at the Met or a jazz group improvizing in a club in the Village. You can catch a spectacle of avant-garde dance in a café or try your own avant-garde dancing in one of the city's warehouse-sized clubs. Movie theaters abound. But perhaps best of all is wandering and watching the vast show that is New York.

TKTS discount ticket booth

Practical Information

Find out what events there are to choose from in the arts and leisure listings of *The New York Times* and the *Village Voice* newspapers and in *Time Out New York*, *New York*, and *The New Yorker* magazines. Listings are updated on the websites of these magazines, such as www.nymag.com and www.timeout.com/newyork. At your hotel ask for *Where*, a free weekly magazine with maps and information on the many attractions.

Hotel staff may be able to answer some of your questions and should also carry a wide selection of brochures and leaflets. In addition, they may be willing to reserve tickets for you. Some hotel TVs have a New York visitor information channel.

At **NYC & Company**, touch-screen kiosks provide information and sell tickets to the city's top attractions. Multilingual counselors, discount coupons, free maps, brochures, tour information, and ATMs are available. **Moviefone** gives online information

on all the films; and **ClubFone** has up-to-date information on nightlife.

Booking Tickets

Popular shows may be sold out for weeks ahead, so book early. Box offices are open daily, except Sundays, from 10am until 1 hour after the performance begins. You can either call in person, or telephone the box office directly. You can even speak to a ticket agency and order your seats by credit card. The biggest agencies are **Telecharge** and **Ticketmaster**; they charge a small fee for bookings. An independent ticket agent may also be able to find seats for you – numerous services, including many Broadway-focused ones, are listed online, as well as in the Yellow Pages. Fees usually vary according to demand.

Discount Tickets

Established in 1973, the non-profit **TKTS** company sells unsold tickets on the day of the performance for all Broadway shows. Discounts range from 25 to 50 percent, but the price will include a small handling fee and must be paid for in cash or by traveler's check.

The TKTS booth in Times Square (at Duffy Square under the red steps) sells matinée tickets from 10am to 2pm every Wednesday and Saturday, and from 11am to 3pm on Sundays; evening tickets are sold from 3 to 8pm (from 2pm on Tuesdays). The booths at Front and John streets, where lines are often shorter, sell evening tickets from 11am to 6pm daily (until 4pm on Sundays; closed Sunday in winter). Matinée tickets are sold the day before. There is also a TKTS booth in downtown Brooklyn.

You can purchase day-of-performance tickets from Ticketmaster at discounts of 10 to 25 per cent (with a small commission fee) by telephone. The **Hit Show Club** sells vouchers to its members (it's free to join), and these can be exchanged at box offices for discounted tickets. Some shows offer standing-room tickets on the day at a bargain price.

A band playing at a cozy New York jazz club

The Booth Theater on Broadway *(see p339)*

It's often the only way to catch a sold-out show on short notice, but you might not get the best view. You can also get discount tickets for shows at **Broadway.com**. **StubHub!** and **TicketsNow** are the largest ticket resale sites. Tickets for sports, music, and shows are e-mailed or couriered to you, and they come with a money-back guarantee.

"Scalpers" and Touts

If you buy from a "scalper" (a ticket tout), you risk getting tickets for the wrong day, counterfeit tickets, or paying outrageous prices. The police often monitor sports and theater venues for scalpers and their customers. If faced with no other options, insist on the seller escorting you to the entry gates to ensure that the tickets are genuine.

Free Tickets

Free tickets to concerts, TV shows, and special events are sometimes offered at NYC & Company (New York Convention & Visitors Bureau), which is open 8:30am–6pm Monday to Friday and 9am–5pm on weekends. Free or deeply discounted tickets to film or theater premieres are often advertised in *The New York Times*, *Daily News*, or *Time Out New York*. The "Cheap Thrills"

section in the *Village Voice* lists poetry readings, recitals, and experimental films. The Shakespeare Festival at the **Delacorte Theater** in Central Park offers free tickets – two per person – on a first-come, first-served basis (be prepared to queue).

Neon lights of theaters in the heart of Broadway

Disabled Access

Broadway theaters keep a few spaces and cut-price tickets for disabled spectators. Call Ticketmaster or Telecharge well in advance for information and to reserve your tickets. For Off-Broadway theaters, call their box offices. Some theaters offer special equipment for hearing-impaired patrons. **Tap** can arrange sign language for Broadway theaters.

Directory

Practical Information

ClubFone
Tel (212) 777-2582.
W clubfone.com

Movie Tickets Online
W fandango.com
W moviefone.com
W movietickets.com

NYC & Company
7th Ave, between 44th and 45th Sts. **Map** 12 E5.
Tel (212) 484-1222.
W nycgo.com

Booking Tickets

Telecharge
Tel (212) 239-6200, 800-432-7250.
W telecharge.com

Ticketmaster
Tel (212) 307-4100, 800-755-4000.
W ticketmaster.com

Discount Tickets

Broadway.com
226 W 47th St. **Map** 12 E5.
Tel (212) 398-8383, ext. 214.
W broadway.com

Hit Show Club
Tel (212) 581-4211
W hitshowclub.com

StubHub!
Tel (866) STUB-HUB.
W stubhub.com

TicketsNow
Tel 800-927-2770.
W ticketsnow.com

TKTS
Tel (212) 912-9770. Front & John sts. **Map** 2 D2. Duffy Square, Times Square. 47th St & Broadway. **Map** 12 E5.
W tdf.org/TKTS

Free Tickets

Delacorte Theater
Entrance via 81st St at Central Park W. **Map** 16 E4.
Tel (212) 539-8500.
W publictheater.org
Summer time only.

Disabled Tickets

Tap (Theatre Accessibility Program)
Tel (212) 221-1103 (Voice).
W tdf.org

New York's Best: Entertainment

New York is one of the great entertainment capitals of the world, with live music, theater, and comedy on every night of the year. Major sports events are a huge attraction too. Top names in every branch of the arts are drawn here to perform and often to live and work. In terms of nightlife, New York truly lives up to its reputation as "the city that never sleeps." From the huge choice offered, there are some venues and events that stand out; this selection has been chosen from the listings on pages 338 to 355 as among those not to be missed. Even if you experience only one of them, you will have been part of something as essentially New York as the Empire State Building or the Brooklyn Bridge.

Madison Square Garden
Top sporting action is found at "the Garden," including home games for basketball's New York Knicks and ice hockey's Rangers, plus other sporting events and big-name concerts *(see p354).*

Midto
West
the The
Distr

Chelsea and th
Garment Distri

Village Vanguard
The jazz clubs of Greenwich Village have played host to all the great names in jazz. Fans can catch the stars of today and tomorrow at the world-famous Village Vanguard and the Blue Note *(see p346).*

Hudson River

Gramercy a
the Flatiro
District

Greenwich Village

East Village

SoHo and TriBeCa

Lower East Side

Film Forum
At New York's most stylish art-house movie theater you can see the latest foreign and American independent releases or catch up with a classic in a wide range of retrospectives *(see p343).*

Lower Manhattan and the Civic Center

The Public Theater
Founded in 1954, The Public has a mandate to create theater for all New Yorkers. Its year-round Shakespeare Festival is part of a commitment to classical works, but new plays are also developed here *(see p116).*

Upper West
Side

Philharmonic Rehearsals
The Wednesday- and Thursday-morning
rehearsals at David Geffen Hall, previously
known as the Avery Fisher Hall, are often
open to the public at a fraction of the
normal ticket price *(see p344)*.

Upper East
Side

Central Park

| 0 kilometers | | 2 |
| 0 miles | 1 | |

Upper
Midtown

Lower
Midtown

Metropolitan Opera House
Reserve well ahead and prepare to
pay high prices to see the giants
of the opera world *(see p344)*.

East River

Shakespeare in Central Park
If you are a summer visitor, set aside a time
to get one of the rare free tickets for the
Delacorte Theater's open-air Shakespeare.
Shows feature top Hollywood and
Broadway names *(see p338)*.

Brooklyn

Carnegie Hall
Conveniently situated in the Theater District,
Carnegie Hall is famous the world over as a
showcase for the best in the musical arts.
A backstage tour gives a fascinating insight
into "the house that music built" *(see p344)*.

The Nutcracker
The Christmas event for children of every
age is performed each year at Lincoln Center
by the New York City Ballet *(see p340)*.

Theater and Dance

New York is famous for its extravagant musicals and its ferocious critics. It is one of the world's greatest centers for theater and dance, featuring every kind of production imaginable. Whether your preference is for the glitz and glamor of a Broadway blockbuster or something truly experimental, you'll find it here.

Broadway

The name Broadway has long been synonymous with New York's Theater District, but the majority of Broadway theaters are actually scattered between 41st and 53rd streets and from Sixth to Ninth avenues, with a few around the much-improved Times Square. Most were built between 1910 and 1930, during the heyday of vaudeville and the famous Ziegfeld Follies. The **Lyceum** *(see p140)* is the oldest theater still in operation (1903), the **American Airlines Theater**, permanent home of the Roundabout Theater Co., is one of the newest (1918).

Following a slump in the 1980s, many Broadway theatres have enjoyed a revival by using big names to draw in the crowds. This is where you will find the "power productions" – the big, highly publicized dramas, musicals, and revivals starring Hollywood luminaries in (it is hoped) sure-fire earners. Hits have included imports such as *Les Misérables;* New York originals such as *The Producers*; the popular children's favorite *The Lion King*; and great revivals including *42nd Street*. There have also been glitzy adaptations from movies, such as *Hairspray*; shows celebrating 1960s and 1970s pop favorites, such as ABBA in *Mamma Mia!* and Monty Python's *Spamalot*.

Off-Broadway and Off-Off-Broadway

There are around 20 Off-Broadway stages and 300 Off-Off-Broadway stages, whose productions will sometimes transfer to Broadway. Off-Broadway theaters have from 100 to 499 seats, and Off-Off-Broadway showplaces have fewer than 100. Both range from the well-appointed to the improvised, sited in lofts, churches, and even garages. Off-Broadway became very popular during the 1950s as a reaction to the commercialism of Broadway. It was also an ideal place for cautious producers to try out works considered too avant-garde for Broadway at lower operating costs. Since the mid-1990s, Off-Off-Broadway theaters have staged more experimental pieces by these same producers.

Off-Broadway theaters are found all over Manhattan, such as Central Park's open-air **Delacorte Theater** *(see p202)*, which opened in 1962. Some are even in the Broadway district, such as the **Manhattan Theater Club**. Farther afield are the **Brooklyn Academy of Music (BAM)** *(see p231)*, and the **92nd Street Y**. In these venues you will find lively, unusual, and experimental showcases for new talent as well as lots of uninhibited productions.

The Off-Broadway theaters mounted the first productions in New York of the works of playwrights Eugène O'Neill, Tennessee Williams, Eugene Ionesco, Sean O'Casey, Jean Genet, and David Mamet. Samuel Beckett's *Happy Days* premiered at the **Cherry Lane Theatre** in 1961, a venue that still promotes cutting-edge writing. Off-Broadway theaters also host modern and often irreverent treatments of the classics.

Sometimes a more intimate, smaller Off-Broadway stage suits a production better than a larger more established theater would, as proved by such long-running successes as *The Fantasticks* along with *The Threepenny Opera*, which shown at the **Lucille Lortel Theatre** between 1955 and 1961.

Performance Theaters

This extremely avant-garde art form can be found in several Off- and Off-Off-Broadway locations. Accurate descriptions and categorizations are almost impossible, but expect the bizarre and outlandish. The most likely venues to find this are **La MaMa Experimental Theatre Club, P.S. 122, HERE, Baruch Performing Arts Center, 92nd Street Y, Symphony Space**, and **The Public Theater** *(see p116)*. The latter is perhaps the most influential theater in New York. It was founded in the 1950s by the late director Joseph Papp, who introduced neighborhood tours to bring theater to people who had never seen it before.

The Public Theater created hits such as *A Chorus Line* and *Hair*; it is most famous for its free summer performances of Shakespeare at the Delacorte Theater in Central Park. It usually has several productions running, and at 6pm on the day of performance, rush standby (discounted) tickets (limited to two per person) are sold in the Public Theater lobby.

Theater Schools

New York is the best place in the country to see actors learning their trade. Foremost among the acting schools is **The Actors' Studio**. The late Lee Strasberg, the advocate of method acting – in which the actor aims for complete identification with the character being played – was its guru. His students included Dustin Hoffman, Al Pacino, and Marilyn Monroe. "In progress" productions feature trainees and are open to the public and free. Sandy Meisner trained many actors, including the late Lee Remick, at the **Neighborhood Playhouse School of the Theatre**. Its plays are not open to the public. The **New Dramatists** began in 1949 to develop new playwrights, helping the careers of the likes of William Inge. Play readings are open to the public and free.

Broadway Theaters

① Al Hirschfield
302 W 45th St.
Tel (212) 239-6200.

② Ambassador
219 W 49th St.
Tel (212) 239-6200.

③ American Airlines Theater
227 W 42nd St.
Tel (212) 719-1300.

④ August Wilson
245 W 52nd St.
Tel (212) 239-6200.

⑤ Barrymore
243 W 47th St.
Tel (212) 239-6200.

⑥ Belasco
111 W 44th St.
Tel (212) 239-6200.

⑦ Bernard B Jacobs
242 W 45th St.
Tel (212) 239-6200.

⑧ Booth
222 W 45th St.
Tel (212) 239-6200.

⑨ Broadhurst
235 W 44th St.
Tel (212) 239-6200.

⑩ Brooks Atkinson
256 W 47th St.
Tel (212) 307-4100.

⑪ Cort
138 W 48th St.
Tel (212) 239-6200.

⑫ Eugene O'Neill
230 W 49th St.
Tel (212) 239-6200.

⑬ Gerald Schoenfeld
236 W 45th St.
Tel (212) 239-6200.

⑭ Gershwin
222 W 51st St.
Tel (212) 307-4100.

⑮ Helen Hayes
240 W 44th St.
Tel (212) 239-6200.

⑯ Imperial
249 W 45th St.
Tel (212) 239-6200.

⑰ John Golden
252 W 45th St.
Tel (212) 239-6200.

⑱ Longacre
220 W 48th St.
Tel (212) 239-6200.

⑲ Lunt–Fontanne
205 W 46th St.
Tel (212) 307-4747.

⑳ Lyceum
149 W 45th St.
Tel (212) 239-6200.

㉑ Lyric
214 W 43rd St.
Tel (212) 556-4750.

㉒ Majestic
245 W 44th St.
Tel (212) 239-6200.

㉓ Marquis
1535 Broadway.
Tel (212) 307-4100.

㉔ Minskoff
200 W 45th St.
Tel (212) 307-4100.

㉕ Music Box
239 W 45th St.
Tel (212) 239-6200.

㉖ Nederlander
208 W 41st St.
Tel (212) 307-4100.

㉗ Neil Simon
250 W 52nd St.
Tel (212) 307-4100.

㉘ New Amsterdam
214 W 42nd St.
Tel (212) 307-4100.

㉙ New Victory
209 W 42nd St.
Tel (212) 239-6200.

㉚ Palace
1564 Broadway.
Tel (212) 307-4100.

㉛ Richard Rodgers
226 W 46th St.
Tel (212) 307-4100.

㉜ Samuel J. Friedman Theatre
261 W 47th St.
Tel (212) 239-6200.

㉝ St. James
246 W 44th St.
Tel (212) 239-6200.

㉞ Shubert
225 W 44th St.
Tel (212) 239-6200.

㉟ Studio 54
254 W 54th St.
Tel (212) 719-3100.

㊱ Walter Kerr
219 W 48th St.
Tel (212) 239-6200.

㊲ Winter Garden
1634 Broadway.
Tel (212) 239-6200.

For other theaters
see p341.

For keys to symbols *see back flap*

Ballet

At the heart of the dance world is Lincoln Center (see p208), where the New York City Ballet performs pieces in the **David H. Koch Theater**. This company was created by the legendary brilliant choreographer George Balanchine and is probably still the best in the world. The current director, Peter Martins, was one of Balanchine's best dancers and continues the strict policy of ensemble dancing rather than "star turns." The season runs from November to February and late April to early June. The ballet school at the **Juilliard Dance Theater** also presents a spring workshop every year, and this is a good chance to see budding stars.

The American Ballet Theater appears at the **Metropolitan Opera House**, which also hosts many visiting foreign companies, such as the Kirov, Bolshoi, and Royal ballets. Its repertoire includes classics, such as *Swan Lake,* and works by modern choreographers such as Twyla Tharp and Paul Taylor.

Contemporary Dance

New York is the center of many of the most important movements in modern dance. The **Dance Theater of Harlem** is world famous for its modern, traditional, and ethnic productions. Other havens of experimental dance include the **92nd Street Y** and the **Alvin Ailey American Dance Theater**. The unique **New York Live Arts** features contemporary dance and performance from around the world. **The Kitchen**, **La MaMa Experimental Theatre Club**, **Symphony Space**, and **P.S. 122** are all multimedia venues with the latest in contemporary dance, performance art, and avant-garde music. Choreographer Mark Morris's company performs at the **Mark Morris Dance Center** in Brooklyn; **New York City Center** (see p144) is a favorite spot for dance fans. It used to house the New York City Ballet and the American Ballet Theater before Lincoln Center was built. As well as once featuring the Joffrey

Ballet, City Center has held performances by all the great contemporary artists, including Alvin Ailey's blend of modern, jazz, and blues, and the companies of modern dance masters the late Merce Cunningham and Paul Taylor. Avoid the mezzanine, as the view is restricted.

The city's single most active venue for dance is probably the **Joyce Theater**, where such well-established companies as the Feld Ballet, along with bold newcomers and visiting troupes, perform.

Each spring the DanceAfrica Festival at the **Brooklyn Academy of Music (BAM)** (see p231) features everything from ethnic dance to hip-hop. During autumn the "Next Wave" festival of music and dance is held, celebrating international and American avant-garde dance and music. During winter, the American Ballet Festival is held here.

During June, the Tisch School of the Arts at **New York University** (see p111) holds a Summer Residency Festival with lecture-demonstrations, rehearsals, and performances, and **Dancing in the Streets** organizes summertime dance performances all over the city.

Throughout the month of August, **Lincoln Center Out of Doors** has a program of free dance events on the plaza, with such experimental groups as the American Tap Dance Orchestra.

The **Duke on 42nd Street** presents many contemporary dance companies and participates in events such as the New York Tap Festival.

At different times of the year, **Radio City Music Hall** holds several spectacular shows, with different companies from all over the world. At Christmas and Easter, it features the famously precise Rockettes dance troupe.

Choreographers and dance companies frequently present works-in-progress and recitals to the public. Among the most interesting venues for these is the **Joan Weill Center for Dance**, one of the country's

largest dance facilities and created by the Alvin Ailey American Dance Theater to promote black cultural expression. The **Hunter College Dance Company** performs new works by student choreographers, and the **Isadora Duncan Dance Foundation** recreates Duncan's original dances. To see contemporary choreographers, the best place to go is **Juilliard Dance Theater**.

Prices

Theater is extremely expensive to produce, and ticket prices tend to reflect this. Even Off- and Off-Off-Broadway tickets are not cheap anymore. Preview tickets are easier to get hold of, though, and it's fun to see a show before the reviews are in so you're able to make up your own mind.

For a Broadway theater ticket you can expect to pay $100 or more; for musicals, up to $200; Off-Broadway, $25 to $60. For dance, $20 to $50 is the usual range, with up to $125 for the American Ballet Theater.

Times of Performance

The general rules for theater-hours are: closed on Mondays (except for most musicals), with matinees on Wednesdays, Saturdays, and sometimes Sundays. Matinees usually begin at 2pm, with evening performances at 8pm. Be sure to check the correct dates and times of the performance beforehand, as tickets are usually non-refundable if you fail to turn up at the correct time.

Backstage Tours and Lectures

For those interested in the mechanics and anecdotes of the theater, your best bet is to go on one of the theater tours. The **92nd Street Y** organizes insider's views of the theater, with famous directors, actors, and choreographers taking part. Writers are invited along to read or discuss their current works. **Radio City Music Hall** also holds tours.

DIRECTORY

Off-Broadway and Off-Off-Broadway

92nd Street Y
1395 Lexington Ave.
Map 17 A2.
Tel (212) 415-5500.

Brooklyn Academy of Music
30 Lafayette Ave,
Brooklyn.
Tel (718) 636-4100.

Cherry Lane Theatre
38 Commerce St.
Map 3 C2.
Tel (212) 239-6200.

Delacorte Theater
Central Park. (81st St.)
Map 16 E4.
Tel (212) 539-8750.
Summer time only.

Lucille Lortel Theatre
121 Christopher St.
Map 3 C2.
Tel (212) 924-2817.

Manhattan Theater Club
311 W 43rd St.
Map 8 D1.
Tel (212) 399-3000

Vivian Beaumont
Lincoln Center.
Map 11 C2.
Tel (212) 362-7600.

Performance Theater

92nd Street Y
See Off-Broadway.

Baruch Performing Arts Center
55 Lexington Ave.
Map 9 A4.
Tel (646) 312-4085.

HERE Art Center
145 6th Ave.
Map 4 D4.
Tel (212) 647-0202.

La MaMa Experimental Theatre Club
74a E 4th St.
Map 4 F2.
Tel (212) 475-7710.

P.S. 122
150 First Ave.
Map 5 A1.
Tel (212) 477-5288.

Public Theater
425 Lafayette St.
Map 4 F2.
Tel (212) 539-8500.

Symphony Space
2537 Broadway.
Map 15 C2.
Tel (212) 864-5400.

Theater Schools

The Actors' Studio
432 W 44th St.
Map 11 B5.
Tel (212) 757-0870.

Neighborhood Playhouse School of the Theatre
340 E 54th St.
Map 13 B4.
Tel (212) 688 3770.

New Dramatists
424 W 44th St.
Map 11 C5.
Tel (212) 757-6960.

Ballet

David H. Koch Theater
Lincoln Center,
Broadway at 65th St.
Map 11 C2.
Tel (212) 870-5570.

Juilliard Dance Theater
60 Lincoln Center Plaza,
W 65th St.
Map 11 C2.
Tel (212) 769-7406.

Metropolitan Opera House
Lincoln Center,
Broadway at 65th St.
Map 11 C2.
Tel (212) 362-6000.

Contemporary Dance

92nd Street Y
See Off-Broadway.

Alvin Ailey American Dance Theater
405 W 55th St.
Map 11 C4.
Tel (212) 405-9000.

Brooklyn Academy of Music
See Off-Broadway.

Dance Theater of Harlem
466 W 152nd St.
Tel (212) 690-2800.

Dancing in the Streets
555 Bergen Ave, Bronx.
Tel (718) 292-3113.

Duke on 42nd Street
229 W 42nd St.
Map 8 E1.
Tel (646) 223-3000.

Hunter College Dance Company
695 Park Ave.
Map 13 A1.
Tel (212) 772-4490.

Isadora Duncan Dance Foundation
141 W 26th St.
Map 20 D2.
Tel (212) 691-5040.

Joan Weill Center for Dance
405 W 55th St.
Map 11 D4.
Tel (212) 405-9000.

Joyce Theater
175 Eighth Ave at 19th St.
Map 8 D5.
Tel (212) 242-0800.

Juilliard Dance Theatre
See Ballet.

The Kitchen
512 W 19th St.
Map 7 C5.
Tel (212) 255-5793.

Lincoln Center Out of Doors
Lincoln Center, Broadway
at 64th St.
Map 11 C2.
Tel (212) 362-6000.

La MaMa Experimental Theatre Club
See Performance Theater.

Mark Morris Dance Center
3 Lafayette Ave,
Brooklyn
Tel (718) 624-8400.

Martha Graham School of Contemporary Dance
55 Bethune St.
Map 3 B2.
Tel (212) 229-9200.

New York City Center
130 W 56th St.
Map 12 E4.
Tel (212) 581-1212.

New York Live Arts
219 W 19th St.
Map 8 E5.
Tel (212) 924-0077.

New York University
Tisch School of the Arts
(TSOA), 111 2nd Ave.
Map 4 F1.
Tel (212) 998-1920.

Paul Taylor Dance Company
551 Grand St.
Map 5 C4.
Tel (646) 214-5829.
W ptamd.org

P.S. 122
See Performance Theater.

Radio City Music Hall
50th St at Ave of
the Americas.
Map 12 F4.
Tel (212) 307-7171.

Symphony Space
See Performance Theater.

Backstage Tours

92nd Street Y
See Off-Broadway.

Radio City Music Hall
See Contemporary Dance.

Events Guide
W broadway.com
W playbill.com

Movies

New York is a film-buff's paradise. Apart from new US releases, which often debut here months in advance of other countries, many classic and foreign films are screened in the city.

New York has always been a testing ground for new developments in films, and it continues to be a hotbed of young and innovative talent. Many of Hollywood's best-known directors – Woody Allen, Martin Scorsese, and Spike Lee – were born and raised in New York, and the city's influence is perceptible in many of their films. They, and others, can often be seen filming on the streets of the city; many of New York's landmarks have become famous after appearing in films. Most of the TV networks based here offer free tickets to the recordings of their shows. Watching a show such as *The Tonight Show Starring Jimmy Fallon* is a popular activity for visitors.

First-Run Movies

New York reviews and box-office returns are so vital to a film's success that most major American films have their premieres in Manhattan's theaters. First-run films are shown mainly at the City Cinema chains, AMC Loews, United Artists, and Regal, which are scattered around the city. Some theaters have recorded information giving the names and duration of the different films showing, with starting times and ticket prices.

Programs start at 10am or 11am and are repeated every 2 to 3 hours until midnight. You should expect to line up for most evening and weekend performances of the more popular films. Making reservations using a credit card is possible at some theaters for an additional charge of about $2 per ticket. Matinees (usually before 4pm) are easier to get into. Senior citizens pay a reduced price for tickets: the required age may be over 60, 62, or 65 depending on the policy of the theater.

Film Festivals

A high point of the year for film buffs is the New York Film Festival, now in its third decade. Organized by the **Film Society of Lincoln Center**, the festival starts in late September and continues for two weeks at the many Lincoln Center theaters. Outstanding new films from the US and abroad are entered in a competition for the huge prestige of winning an award. Many of the films shown during the festival are later released and can usually be seen only in art houses.

The **Tribeca Film Festival**, created in part by director and actor Robert De Niro, was launched in 2002 to celebrate New York City as a filmmaking capital and to contribute to the long-term recovery of Lower Manhattan. The festival showcases a wide range of films, including classics, documentaries, and premieres, and usually takes place in late April and early May. Every November, **DOC NYC** presents a week's worth of film and video documentaries from around the world, followed by panel discussions.

Film Ratings

Films in the United States are graded as follows:

G General audiences; all ages admitted.

PG Parental guidance suggested; some material unsuitable for children.

PG-13 Parents strongly cautioned; some material inappropriate for children under age 13.

R Restricted. Children under 17 need to be accompanied by a parent or an adult guardian.

NC-17 No children under 17 and under admitted.

On Location

Many New York locations have played starring roles in films. Here are a few:

55 Central Park West will be remembered as Sigourney Weaver's home in *Ghostbusters*.

The Brill Building (1141 Broadway) contained Burt Lancaster's penthouse in *Sweet Smell of Success*.

The Brooklyn Bridge was a great backdrop in Spike Lee's *Mo' Better Blues*.

Brooklyn Heights and the **Metropolitan Opera** appeared in *Moonstruck*.

Central Park has shown up in countless films, including *Love Story* and *Marathon Man*.

Chinatown played a major role in *Year of the Dragon*.

The Dakota was where Mia Farrow lived in the classic *Rosemary's Baby*.

The Empire State Building is still standing after *King Kong*'s last battle. The observation deck is where Cary Grant waited in vain in *An Affair to Remember*; here Meg Ryan finally met Tom Hanks in *Sleepless in Seattle*.

Grand Central Terminal is famous for Robert Walker's meeting with Judy Garland in *Under the Clock* and for the magical ballroom sequence in *The Fisher King*.

Harlem hosted the jazz musicians and dancers in *The Cotton Club*.

Katz's Deli was the setting for the café scene between Billy Crystal and Meg Ryan in *When Harry Met Sally…*

Little Italy appeared in *The Godfather I* and *II*.

Madison Square Garden was the setting for the dramatic climax of *The Manchurian Candidate*.

Tiffany & Co. was Audrey Hepburn's favorite shop in *Breakfast at Tiffany's*.

The United Nations Building featured in *North by Northwest* and *The Interpreter*.

Washington Square Park was where Robert Redford and Jane Fonda walked *Barefoot in the Park*.

Foreign Films and Art Houses

For the latest foreign and independent films, go to the **Angelika Film Center**, which also has an upscale coffee bar. Other good places are the **Rose Cinemas** at the BAM, the **Film Forum**, and **Lincoln Plaza Cinema**. The Plaza has a busy program of art and foreign films. For Asian, Indian, and Chinese films, you should visit the **Asia Society**. The **French Institute** screens many French films with English subtitles on Tuesdays. The **Quad Cinema** shows a wide selection of foreign films, often quite rare. **Cinema Village** runs special film events, such as the Festival of Animation.

The **Walter Reade Theater** houses the Film Society of the Lincoln Center, offering retrospectives of international movies as well as celebrations of contemporary works, such as the popular annual Spanish Cinema Now festival.

Classic Films and Museums

Retrospectives of films by particular directors or featuring specific actors are shown at the Public Theater and the **Whitney Museum of American Art** *(see pp108–109)*. The **Museum of the Moving Image** *(see p257)* screens old films and also has many exhibits of memorabilia from the film industry. The **Paley Center for Media** *(see p167)* has regular screenings of classic films; you can also see or hear specific television or radio programs. Students interested in classic, new, and experimental movies will appreciate the collection of the **Anthology Film Archives**.

The shows at the Rose Center for Earth and Space at the **American Museum of Natural History** are worth a full day's visit.

On summer evenings in Bryant Park, you can watch free classic movies. On Saturday mornings, the **Film Society of Lincoln Center**, holds special children's shows.

Television Shows

A number of TV programs originate in New York. The popular *Tonight Show Starring Jimmy Fallon* and *Saturday Night Live* are almost impossible to get to see, but tickets for many other shows can be obtained online, by checking the **NBC**, ABC, and **CBS** websites, or sometimes on standby.

Another good source of free tickets is the Times Square Information Bureau *(see p365)*. On weekday mornings on Fifth Avenue around **Rockefeller Plaza**, free tickets for a number of TV programs are sometimes distributed by the program's production staff. There's absolutely no way that you can plan for this. It's simply a matter of good luck and being in the right place at the right time.

For those who want to get a glimpse behind the scenes of TV, NBC organizes tours of the studios, from 8:30am to 5:30pm Monday to Thursday, 8:30am to 6:30pm Friday and Saturday, and 9:15am to 4:30pm on Sunday (depart every 15 mins).

Choosing What to See

If you feel bewildered by the huge range of films offered in New York, check the listings in *New York* magazine, *The New York Times*, the *Village Voice*, and *The New Yorker*. The following Internet guides give show times and locations:
www.moviefone.com
www.movietickets.com

DIRECTORY

Film Festivals

DOC NYC
W docnyc.net

Film Society of Lincoln Center
Tel (212) 875-5367.
W filmlinc.org

Tribeca Film Festival
Tel (212) 941-2400.
W tribecafilm.com

Foreign Films and Art Houses

Angelika Film Center
18 W Houston St. **Map** 4
E3. **Tel** (212) 995-2000.

Asia Society
725 Park Ave. **Map** 13 A1.
Tel (212) 517-2742.

Cinema Village
22 E 12th St. **Map** 4 F1.
Tel (212) 924-3363.

Film Forum
209 W Houston St.
Map 3 C3.
Tel (212) 727-8110.

French Institute
22 E 60th St. **Map** 12 F3.
Tel (212) 355-6100.

Lincoln Plaza Cinema
1886 Broadway.
Map 12 D2.
Tel (212) 757-2280.

Quad Cinema
34 W 13th St. **Map** 4 D1.
Tel (212) 255-8800.

Rose Cinemas
Brooklyn Academy of
Music (BAM), 30 Lafayette
Ave, Brooklyn.
Tel (718) 636-4100.

Walter Reade Theater
70 Lincoln Center Plaza.
Map 12 D2.
Tel (212) 875-5600.

Classic Films and Museums

American Museum of Natural History
Central Park W at 79th St.
Map 16 D5.
Tel (212) 769-5100.

Anthology Film Archives
32 2nd Ave at 2nd St.
Map 5 C2.
Tel (212) 505-5181.

Film Society of Lincoln Center
See Film Festivals.

Museum of the Moving Image
35th Ave & 36th St.
Astoria, Queens.
Tel (718) 784-0077.

Paley Center for Media
25 W 52nd St. **Map** 12 F4.
Tel (212) 621-6600.

Public Theater
425 Lafayette St. **Map** 4 F4.
Tel (212) 539-8500.

Whitney Museum of American Art
99 Gansevoort St.
Map 3 B1.
Tel (212) 570-3600.

Television Shows

ABC
Tel (212) 580-5176.
W abc.com

CBS
Tel (212) 247-6497.
W cbs.com

NBC
30 Rockefeller Plaza at
49th St. **Tel** (212) 664-3056.
W thetouratnbc
studios.com

Rockefeller Plaza
47th–50th Sts, 5th Ave.
Map 12 F5.

Classical and Contemporary Music

New Yorkers have a voracious appetite for music. Live concerts by the world's most celebrated musical performers may be enjoyed at well-known halls throughout the year, and younger, newer artists, and exotic imports always find receptive audiences.

Tickets

Find out what you can choose from in New York by checking out the listings on the websites of NYC & Co., *The New York Times*, *Village Voice*, *Time Out New York*, and *The New Yorker*.

Classical Music

The orchestra in residence at David Geffen Hall in **Lincoln Center** *(see p208)* is the New York Philharmonic. It is also the annual site for the popular "Mostly Mozart" series and Young People's Concerts. Alice Tully Hall, in Lincoln Center, is an acoustic gem and home to the Chamber Music Society.

One of the world's premier concert halls is the revamped **Carnegie Hall** *(see p)*. Upstairs in the Weill Recital Hall there are quality performances for reasonable prices.

The **Brooklyn Academy of Music (BAM)** *(see p231)* is the home of the Brooklyn Philharmonic. Classical music, dance, opera, jazz, and world music all find an audience at the **New Jersey Performing Arts Center** in Newark.

The **Merkin Concert Hall** is host to some top chamber ensembles and soloists. For really excellent acoustics, go to the **Town Hall**. The Kaufmann Concert Hall at **92nd Street Y** also offers a lively menu of music and dance. There's also the **Frick Collection** and **Symphony Space**, both of which offer a varied program

Classical Radio

New York has three FM radio stations that broadcast classical music: WQXR at 96.3, the National Public Radio station WNYC at 93.9, and WKCR 89.9.

ranging from gospel to Gershwin, classical to ethnic. The beautiful Grace Rainey Rogers Auditorium in the **Metropolitan Museum of Art** is used for chamber music and soloists, while the well-equipped **Florence Gould Hall**, at the Alliance Française, presents a varied program of chamber music, orchestral pieces, concerts, and even classic French films.

The **Juilliard School of Music** and the **Mannes College of Music** are both considered excellent. Their students and faculties give free recitals, and there are shows by leading orchestras, chamber music groups, and opera companies. The **Manhattan School of Music** offers an excellent program of over 400 events per year, from classical to jazz.

At 9:45am on the Thursdays of the New York Philharmonic concerts, the evening show is rehearsed at the David Geffen Hall in Lincoln Center. Audiences are often admitted to listen, and rehearsal tickets are available at low prices. The **Kosciuszko Foundation** hosts the annual Chopin Competition. **Corpus Christi Church** has an active concert schedule, presenting such groups as the Tallis Scholars.

Opera

Dominating the city's operatic scene is Lincoln Center *(see p208–9)*, home to the New York City Opera, and the **Metropolitan Opera House**, which has its own opera company. The Met is the jewel in the crown, offering top international performers. More accessible and dynamic is the New York City Opera. Although the company went bankrupt in 2013, their shows

are now up and running at Jazz at Lincoln Center's Rose Hall. Lower-priced quality performances are staged by the up-and-coming singers at the **Village Light Opera Group**, the **Kaye Playhouse** at Hunter College, and the students at the **Juilliard Opera Center** in Lincoln Center.

Contemporary Music

New York is one of the most important places in the world for contemporary music. Exotic, ethnic, and experimental music is played in many first-rate venues. The Brooklyn Academy of Music (BAM) is the standard-bearer of the avant-garde. Each autumn the Academy holds a festival of music and dance called "Next Wave," which has helped launch many music careers.

An annual festival of serious modern music called "Bang on a Can" is performed at the **New York Society for Ethical Culture** and features works by Steve Reich, Pierre Boulez, and John Cage. Experimentalists, such as Italian musician Alessandro Sciarroni and Brooklyn-based performer Okwui Okpokwasili, feature at **New York Live Arts**.

Other venues include the **Asia Society** *(see p183)*, with its jewel of a theater for many visiting Asian performers, and **St. Peter's Church**.

Backstage Tours

Behind-the-scenes tours are offered by Lincoln Center and Carnegie Hall.

Religious Music

Few experiences are more moving than an Easter concert in the vast **Cathedral of St. John the Divine** *(see pp220–21)*. Seasonal music is also offered at many of the city's museums and in almost every other available space – from Grand Central Terminal's main concourse *(see pp152–3)* to bank and hotel lobbies. For jazz vespers in a stunning modern building, visit St. Peter's Church. Most of these concerts are free, but you are encouraged to make a contribution.

Alfresco

Free outdoor summer concerts take place in **Bryant Park**, **Washington Square**, and Lincoln Center's **Damrosch Park**. The annual concerts on Central Park's Great Lawn and in

Brooklyn's Prospect Park are performed by the New York Philharmonic and the Metropolitan Opera. In good weather, strolling musicians perform at South Street Seaport, on the steps of the Metropolitan Museum of Art *(see pp186–93)*, and in the area around Washington Square.

Music for Free

Free musical performances are given at **The Cloisters** *(see pp246–9)*. Sunday-afternoon recitals are held at Rumsey Playfield and the Naumburg Bandshell in

Central Park, as well as the Summerstage. Call **The Dairy** for more information. You will also find music in the **Federal Hall** *(see p70)*, while at Lincoln Center, don't miss the exciting free performances held in the Juilliard School of Music. Other venues include the **Greenwich House Music School** (free student recitals) and the **Winter Garden** at Brookfield Place *(see p71)*. Numerous free concerts and talks take place in the city's churches, including **St. Paul's Chapel**, **Trinity Church** *(see p71)*, and St. Thomas Church *(see p167)*.

DIRECTORY

Tickets

Internet Events Guide
w timeout.com/newyork
w nycgo.com
w nymag.com
w nytimes.com
w villagevoice.com

Classical Music

92nd Street Y
1395 Lexington Ave.
Map 17 A2.
Tel (212) 415-5500.

Brooklyn Academy of Music (BAM)
30 Lafayette Ave, Brooklyn.
Tel (718) 636-4100.

Carnegie Hall
881 7th Ave. **Map** 12 E3.
Tel (212) 247-7800.

Corpus Christi Church
529 W 121st St. **Map** 20 E2. **Tel** (212) 666-9350.

Florence Gould Hall (at the Alliance Française)
55 E 59th St. **Map** 13 A3.
Tel (212) 355-6160.

Frick Collection
1 E 70th St. **Map** 12 F1.
Tel (212) 288-0700.

Juilliard School of Music
Tel (212) 799-5000.

Kosciuszko Foundation
15 E 65th St. **Map** 12 F2.
Tel (212) 734-2130.

Lincoln Center
155 W 65th St. **Map** 11 C2.
Tel (212) 546-2656. For tours call: (212) 875-5350.
Alice Tully Hall: **Tel** (212) 875-5050. David Geffen Hall: **Tel** (212) 875-5030.

Manhattan School of Music
120 Claremont Ave. **Map** 20 E2. **Tel** (212) 749-2802.

Mannes College of Music
55 W 13th St. **Map** 4 D3.
Tel (212) 580-0210.

Merkin Hall
129 W 67th St. **Map** 11 D2.
Tel (212) 501-3330.

Metropolitan Museum of Art
1000 5th Ave at 82nd St.
Map 16 F4.
Tel (212) 535-7710.

New Jersey Performing Arts Center
1 Center St, Newark, NJ.
Tel 888-466-5722.

Symphony Space
2537 Broadway. **Map** 15 C2. **Tel** (212) 864-5400.

Town Hall
123 W 43rd St. **Map** 8 E1.
Tel (212) 997-1003.

Opera

Juilliard Opera Center
Tel (212) 769-7406.

Kaye Playhouse (Hunter College)
695 Park Ave.
Map 13 A1.
Tel (212) 772-4448.

Metropolitan Opera House
Map 11 C2.
Tel (212) 362-6000.

Village Light Opera Group
Perform at: Schimmel Center for the Arts at Pace University, 3 Spruce St.
Map 1 C2.
Tel (212) 346-1715.

Contemporary Music

Asia Society
725 Park Ave.
Map 13 A1.
Tel (212) 517-2742.

New York Live Arts
See Dance p341.

New York Society for Ethical Culture
2 W 64th St. **Map** 12 D2.
Tel (212) 874-5210.

St. Peter's Church
619 Lexington Ave.
Map 13 A4.
Tel (212) 935-2200.

Religious Music

Cathedral of St. John the Divine
1047 Amsterdam Ave & 112th St. **Map** 20 E4.
Tel (212) 316-7540.

Alfresco

Bryant Park
Map 8 F1.
Tel (212) 768-4242.

Damrosch Park
Map 11 C2
Tel (212) 875-5000.

Washington Square
Map 4 D2.

Music for Free

The Cloisters
Fort Tryon Park.
Tel (212) 923-3700.

The Dairy
Central Park at 65th St.
Map 12 F2.
Tel (212) 794-6564.

Federal Hall
26 Wall St. **Map** 1 C3.
Tel (212) 825-6888.

Greenwich House Music School
46 Barrow St. **Map** 3 C2.
Tel (212) 242-4770.

St. Paul's Chapel
Broadway at Fulton St.
Map 1 C2.
Tel (212) 233-4164.

Trinity Church
Broadway at Wall St.
Map 1 C3.
Tel (212) 602-0800.

Winter Garden
Brookfield Place, West St.
Map 1 A2.
Tel (212) 945-2600.

Rock, Jazz, and Live Music

There's every imaginable form of music in New York, from international stadium rock to the sounds of the 1960s, from Dixieland jazz or country blues, soul, and world music to talented street musicians. The city's music scene changes at a dizzying pace, with new arrivals (and departures) almost daily, so there's no way to predict what you may find when you arrive.

Prices and Venues

At clubs, expect to pay a cover charge and possibly a one- or two-drink minimum (at $8 or more) requirement. The prices for concerts typically range from $50 to $150 for the major venues. Many of the smaller concert venues offer seating in certain areas and dancing in others – often with different prices for each.

The top international bands are usually to be found on the huge stages at the **Barclays Center** or **Madison Square Garden** (see p131). Here the likes of Jay-Z, Bruce Springsteen, and Taylor Swift perform. Tickets for these events sell out very fast, unless you don't mind paying a lot for them through an agent or a scalper (see p335). During the summer, big (and usually free) outdoor concerts are held at **Central Park SummerStage** and at the **Prospect Park Bandshell**, found under the Celebrate Brooklyn umbrella.

Medium-sized venues for mainstream bands include the Art Deco palace of **Radio City Music Hall**, the **Hammerstein Ballroom**, and the **Beacon Theater**. Booking an impressive line-up of acts is the **Best Buy Theater** in Times Square. This state-of-the-art venue is known for its top-notch acoustics.

Rock Music

Rock comes in many forms: Gothic, industrial, techno, psychedelic, post-punk funk, indie, and alternative music are among the many genres. A lot of leading venues are basically bars with music. They will often book different bands every night, so check the listings in The New York

Times, Village Voice, or Time Out New York, or check websites to find out what's happening and at what time during that particular week. If you prefer to see more of a band than a giant video screen, the following venues tend to have a much more intimate, friendly atmosphere.

On the Lower East Side, the **Bowery Ballroom** boasts superior acoustics and sightlines and usually books well-known touring acts and local bands. A converted bodega, **Arlene's Grocery** attracts a loyal crowd thanks to acts ranging from rock to country and comedy. Its punk and heavy-metal karaoke on Monday nights (for free) is also popular. The **Mercury Lounge** is also one of the most happening music spots down here, featuring hot new bands being groomed for bigger stages.

Over the river, the **Knitting Factory** in Brooklyn is an intimate showcase for indie rock, while **Music Hall of Williamsburg**, set in an old factory, offers great acoustics and cheap prices. **The Rock Shop** is the best place to hear up-and-coming bands.

Jazz

The original Cotton Club and Connie's Inn, which were once crucibles of jazz, are long gone, as are the former speakeasies of West 52nd Street. However, many talented performers carry on the old traditions of Dave Brubeck, Les Paul, Duke Ellington, Count Basie, and other jazz bands. In Harlem, classic joints such as **Showmans Jazz Club** (which features veteran Hammond organ player Seleno Clarke) and **Minton's** are still going strong, while sax man

Bill Saxton still blows his horn Fridays and Saturdays at **Bill's Place**. No relation to the famous original (this version opened in 1977), the **Cotton Club** nevertheless offers good swing, blues, jazz, and a Sunday Gospel brunch.

In Greenwich Village, jazz temples from the 1930s survive and continue to foster great music. Foremost among them is the **Village Vanguard**, where some of the most highly revered jazz memories linger Sonny Rollins' A Night at the Village Vanguard was recorded here in 1957). **Blue Note** (open since 1981 and unrelated to the record label) hosts big bands at high prices but has a great atmosphere. **Smalls** offers cutting-edge jazz, with various acts every night often playing two or more sets each.

Smoke is an intimate Upper West Side nightspot offering a divergent roster of musicians, while Midtown's **Birdland** is an established supper club that hosts some big names, while sophisticated club and restaurant **Iridium** features progressive jazz.

Café Carlyle, an Upper East Side spot once famed for late jazz pianist and singer Bobby Short, now features clarinetist-filmmaker Woody Allen playing with Eddy Davis and his New Orleans Jazz Band most Monday nights (Jan–Jun only). **Jazz Standard**, with an ample underground performance space, showcases top-notch jazz performers most nights of the week. Part community center and café, part jazz and experimental music space, the **5C Café** is a throwback to old New York and has a laidback vibe.

Jazz at Lincoln Center events are scheduled throughout the year, including concerts by the renowned Lincoln Center Jazz Orchestra under the direction of Wynton Marsalis. It now has its own home since it moved into the world's first performing arts center specifically for jazz. It is housed in the Time Warner Center – a multi-venue facility on Columbus Circle perched above Central Park. If you're in New York in January, don't miss the annual **NYC Winter Jazzfest**, where famous jazz acts play at various clubs around Manhattan.

Folk and Country Music

Folk, rock music, and R&B (rhythm and blues) can be found at the rather faded **Bitter End**, which once showcased James Taylor and Joni Mitchell but now specializes in promising new talent (Lady Gaga got started here in 2007), as does the Lower East Side's **Rockwood Music Hall**. Also worth checking out is the **Sidewalk Café**, with its wide range of emerging performers and **Postscrypt Coffeehouse**, run by Columbia University students. In Brooklyn, the **Living Room** offers low-key folk and acoustic rock (Nora Jones started her career at the original location). The tiny Jalopy Theatre and School of Music has similar offerings.

Blues, Soul, and World Music

For blues, soul, and world music, options include the **Apollo Theater** in Harlem *(see p224)*. For more than 75 years the near-legendary Wednesday Amateur Nights have been responsible for discovering and launching stars, including the much-loved James Brown and Dionne Warwick. Also in Harlem, **Shrine** features Afro-beat, World Music and jazz.

The **B.B. King's Blues Club** lineup often features legendary jazz and gospel performers. Don't miss "After Work Fridays" at **SOB's** (Sounds of Brazil), a world music club specializing in Afro-Latin rhythms.

The blues artists that appear at **Terra Blues**'s range from authentic Chicago acoustic players to modern blues acts.

DIRECTORY

Music Venues

Barclays Center
620 Atlantic Ave, Brooklyn. **Map** 23 B4.
Tel(917) 610-6100.

Beacon Theater
2124 Broadway. **Map** 15 C5. **Tel** (212) 465-6500.

Best Boy Theater
2124 Broadway. **Map** 15 C5. **Tel**(212) 465-6500.

Central Park SummerStage
Rumsey Playfield.
Map 12 F1.
Tel (212) 360-2777.

Hammerstein Ballroom
311 W 34th St. **Map** 8 D2.
Tel (212) 279-7740.

Madison Square Garden
7th Ave & 33rd St. **Map** 8 E2. **Tel** (212) 465-6741.

Prospect Park Bandshell
62 West Drive, Prospect Park, Brooklyn **Map** 23 C5.
Tel (718) 683-5600.

Radio City Music Hall
See p341.

Rock Music

Arlene's Grocery
95 Stanton St. **Map** 5 A3.
Tel (212) 995-1652.

Bowery Ballroom
6 Delancey St. **Map** 4 F3.
Tel (212) 533-2111.

Knitting Factory
361 Metropolitan Ave, Brooklyn.
Tel (347) 529-6696.

Le Poisson Rouge
158 Bleecker St. **Map** 4 D3.
Tel (212) 505-3473.

Mercury Lounge
217 E Houston St. **Map** 5 A3. **Tel** (212 260-4700).

Music Hall of Williamsburg
66 N 6th St. **Map** 6 F1.
Tel (718) 486-5400.

The Rock Shop
249 Fourth Ave, Gowanus, Brooklyn. **Map** 23 B4.
Tel (718) 230-5740

Jazz

5C Café
68 Avenue C. **Map** 5 C2.
Tel (212) 477-5993.

Bill's Place
148 W 133rd St. **Map** 19 C3. **Tel** (212) 281-0777.

Birdland
315 W 44th St. **Map** 12 D5.
Tel (212) 581-3080.

Blue Note
131 W 3rd St. **Map** 4 D2.
Tel (212) 475-8592.

Café Carlyle
95 E 76th St. **Map** 17 A5.
Tel (212) 744-1600.

Cotton Club
656 W 125th St. **Map** 22 F2. **Tel** (212) 663-7980.

Iridium
1650 Broadway. **Map** 12 D2. **Tel** (212) 582-2121.

Jazz at Lincoln Center
150 W 65th St. **Map** 11 C2.
Tel (212) 258-9800.

Jazz Standard
116 E 27th St. **Map** 9 A3
Tel (212) 576-2232.

Minton's
206 W 118th St. **Map** 21 A3. **Tel** (212) 243-2222.

NYC Winter Jazzfest
W winterjazzfest.com

Showmans Jazz Club
375 W 125th St. **Map** 20 F1.
Tel (212) 864-8941.

Smalls
183 W 10th St. **Map** 3 C2.
Tel (212) 252-5091.

Smoke
2751 Broadway. **Map** 20 E5. **Tel** (212) 864-6662.

Village Vanguard
178 7th Ave S. **Map** 3 C1.
Tel (212) 255 4037.

Folk and Country Music

Bitter End
147 Bleecker St. **Map** 4 E3.
Tel (212) 673-7030.

The Living End
134 Metropolitan Ave, Brooklyn. **Map** 23 B1. **Tel** (718) 782-6600

Postcrypt Coffeehouse
2098 Broadway. **Map** 211 C1. W blogs.cuit.columbia.edu/postcrypt.

Rockwood Music Hall
196 Allen St. **Map** 5 A3.
Tel (212) 477-4155.

Sidewalk Café
94 Ave A. **Map** 5 B2.
Tel (212) 473-7373.

Blues, Soul, and World Music

Apollo Theater
253 W 125 St. **Map** 19 A1.
Tel (212) 531-5305.

B.B. King's Blues Club
237 W 42nd St. **Map** 8 E1.
Tel (212) 997-4144.

SOB's
204 Varick St. **Map** 4 D3.
Tel (212) 243-4940.

Terra Blues
149 Bleecker St. **Map** 4 E3.
Tel (212) 777-7776.

Clubs, Dance Halls, and Gay and Lesbian Venues

New York's nightlife and club scene is legendary, and deservedly so. Whatever your preference – be it a plush club with pricey bottle service, an old-school disco, or the soothing sounds and cocktails of a piano bar – you'll be amazed at the choice. There was a rash of big discos in the 1980s and 1990s, but few of these have survived and now the hip crowds tend to gravitate towards stylish, yet often casual, bars and lounges.

When and Where

The best and hippest time for clubbing is during the week – it's also a lot cheaper. Take a fair amount of money and some ID to prove your age (the legal minimum is over 21) – but beware: all the drinks are very expensive.

The trendiest clubs roll on until 4am or later. Fashions and club nights change all the time, so check club details in the listings magazines (see p334) and read the *Village Voice* to keep up to date with what's what. The most cutting-edge places nowadays are often popularized by word of mouth or Twitter, and organized by outfits that tend to move around. Your best bet is to move around, such as Blackmarket Membership (blkmarketrsvp@gmail.com), Tiki Disco (tikidisco.com), and Mister Saturday Night (www.mistersaturdaynight.com).

Dancing

New Yorkers thrive on music and dancing. The dance floors available all around the city range from the ever-popular **SOB's** – for jungle, reggae, soul, jazz, and salsa – to a few huge basketball-court-sized places, such as **Space** and **Pacha**. These legendary clubs, which started out in Ibiza, have opened swanky venues in Midtown and are consistently booking top international DJs to make the most of their colossal sound systems. These are the places for those who enjoy pounding music, sweaty dance floors, and a lively crowd.

To some, the formerly gritty Lower East Side is the city's most happening neighborhood, and the casual **bOb Bar** promises a hopping dance floor packed with diverse crowds grooving to old-school hip-hop and party tunes. Another venue that's always packed is **Webster Hall**, an elder statesman of NYC nightlife that offers four floors of R&B, pop, electro, or house (when it's not hosting a special event). By comparison, **Cielo** is embracing the 21st century. This sleek, upscale room aimed mostly at those who love electronica boasts a killer sound system that envelops dancers as they jostle in a sunken living-room dance floor.

Marquee is another A-list spot in Chelsea, with a glass-enclosed VIP mezzanine that draws Hollywood starlets. Check out also the monthly dance parties at the American Museum of Natural History's trippy space center, dubbed "One Step Beyond at the Rose Center."

Those who want to bop to 1980s classics head to the **Pyramid Room**, while **Santos Party House**, basically two large, square, and black-painted rooms, features wild hip-hop, Latin, and house music. Current trend-setters in Brooklyn include the popular Williamsburg venues **Output**, an industrial warehouse space, and underground dance specialist **Verboten New York**.

Piano Bars and Cabaret

New York piano bars and cabarets are less flashy than in the 1940s and 1950s but they still boast a wide variety of acts. Expect to pay a cover charge; many of the clubs also require that you have at least two drinks. More cabarets can be found on pages 350–51.

Marie's Crisis Café is a legendary Greenwich Village piano bar where patrons are invited and encouraged to sing cabaret standards and hit showtunes. **Uncle Charlie's** maintains a lively piano lounge and gay bar, giving patrons of the nearby Theater District a chance to belt out their own versions of Broadway favorites after a show. **Joe's Pub** at the Public Theater has decent food and a wonderful array of performances and musical acts.

Venues aimed at gay men include the trendy, traditional uptown **TownHouse**, a piano bar with restaurant, and **Don't Tell Mama**, a long-established gay bar that presents good musical revues along with spoofs. Popular gay cabarets include the **Duplex**, which has a mix of stand-up comics, comedy sketches and singers.

For raunchy neo-burlesque shows, a popular genre in New York, try the Slipper Room.

Gay and Lesbian Venues

The years since the mid-1990s have seen the arrival of clubs and restaurants specifically geared to gay and lesbian clientele. Magazines such as the *Village Voice* and *Time Out* have good listings of what's happening in the gay communities, and the *Gay Yellow Pages* generally covers the gay scene. If you need more information, you can phone the **Gay and Lesbian Switchboard.**

The Chelsea neighborhood, particularly around Eighth Avenue, is the bustling heart of New York's gay life. The Hell's Kitchen area, around the mid-40s between Eighth and 10th avenues, also thrums with gay nightlife – **Barrage** is a hopping bar featuring a popular Friday happy hour. The inviting and stylish **G Lounge** serves a potent selection of cocktails and flavored coffees, and is the perfect spot for a drink before hitting the clubs. Lively **Barracuda** features drag shows and draws a diverse crowd of regulars and newcomers, while **Gym** caters to those into sporting events. **Stonewall Inn**, meanwhile, is the famed site of the Stonewall riots, where the modern gay movement was effectively born, has undergone a multimillion-dollar refurbishment.

The comfy neighborhood lounge **Posh Bar & Lounge** pulls in a friendly crowd for its popular happy hour, 4–8pm, while **Lips**, in Midtown East, attracts hordes of people with what it proclaims is the "ultimate in drag dining." Often adorned with year-round Christmas lights, the long-running **Pieces** heats up most nights of the week with everything from drag shows to karaoke.

The gay and lesbian crowd can enjoy VIP treatment and bottle service at the upscale **XL Nightclub**. This Midtown haunt provides an assortment of cabaret performances, as well as colorful themed parties and drag bingo.

Henrietta Hudson in Greenwich Village caters solely to women, as does the imaginatively decorated **Cubby Hole**, a cozy lesbian bar where regulars often sing along to the jukebox.

DIRECTORY

Dancing

bOb Bar
235 Eldridge St.
Map 5 A3.
Tel (212) 529-1807.

Cielo
18 Little West 12th St.
Map 3 B1.
Tel (212) 645-5700.

Marquee
289 10th Ave.
Map 7 C4.
Tel (646) 473-0202.

Output
78 Wythe Ave,
Williamsburg.
Map 23B1.
www.outputclub.com .

Pacha
618 W 46th St.
Map 12 E5.
Tel (212) 209-7500.

Pyramid Club
101 Ave A.
Map 5 A2.
Tel (212) 228-4888.

Rose Center
Central Park West at
W 79th St.
Map 16 D4.
Tel ((212) 769-5200.

**Santos
Party House**
96 Lafayette St.
Map 4 F5.
Tel (212) 714-4646.

SOB's
204 Varick St.
Map 4 D3.
Tel (212) 243-4940.

Space
637 W 50th St.
Map 11 B4.
Tel ((212) 247-2447.

**Verboten
New York!**
54 N 11th St,
Williamsburg.
Map 23 B1.
Tel (347) 223-4732.

Webster Hall
125 E 11th St.
Map 4 F1.
Tel (212) 353-1600.

Piano Bars
and Cabaret

Don't Tell Mama
343 W 46th St.
Map 12 D5.
Tel (212) 757-0788.

Duplex
61 Christopher St.
Map 3 C2.
Tel (212) 255-5438.

Joe's Pub
425 Lafayette St.
Map 4 F2.
Tel (212) 539-8778.

**Marie's
Crisis Café**
59 Grove St.
Map 3 C2.
Tel (212) 243-9323.

Slipper Room
167 Orchard St.
Map 5 A3.
Tel (212) 253-7246.

TownHouse
236 E 58th St.
Map 13 B4.
Tel (212) 754-4649.

Uncle Charlie's
139 E 45th St.
Map 13 A5.
Tel (212) 661-9097.

Gay and
Lesbian Venues

Barracuda
275 W 22nd St.
Map 8 D4.
Tel (212) 645-8613.

Barrage
401 W 47th St.
Map 12 D5.
Tel (212) 586-9390.

Cubby Hole
281 W 12th St.
Map 3 C1.
Tel (212) 243-9041.

G Lounge
223 W 19th St.
Map 8 E5.
Tel (212) 929-1085.

**Gay and Lesbian
Switchboard**
Tel (212) 989-0999.

Gym
167 Eighth Ave.
Map 8 D5.
Tel (212) 337-2439.

**Henrietta
Hudson**
438 Hudson St.
Map 3 C3.
Tel (212) 924-3347.

Lips
227 E 56th St.
Map 13 B3.
Tel (212) 675-7710.

Pieces
8 Christopher St.
Map 4 D2.
Tel (212) 929-9291.

Posh Bar & Lounge
405 W 51st St.
Map 11 C4.
Tel (212) 957-2222.

Stonewall Inn
53 Christopher St.
Map 3 C2.
Tel (212) 488-2705.

XL Nightclub
512 West 42nd St.
Map 7 C1.
Tel (212) 239-2999.

Comedy, Cabaret, and Literary Events

From Jack Benny and Woody Allen to Chris Rock and Jerry Seinfeld, New York has spawned almost as many comics as it has jokes about itself, including the requisite quips: on crime – "In New York crime is getting worse. When I was there the other day, the Statue of Liberty had both hands up"; and, on driving – "Always look both ways when running a red light." Comedy is a cut-throat business here. This is good news for punters, because it means that no matter what comedy club you walk into, you'll be crying with laughter. NYC is also a consummate romancer, judging by its plethora of classic cabarets and lounges. An unforgettable New York experience is to be serenaded by a lounge singer in a dusky piano bar. New York also boasts a booming literary scene, with superb weekly readings and lectures.

Comedy Showcases

Many of New York's best current comedy clubs or showcases have evolved from earlier "improvisational" comedy. Part of the allure of New York comedy clubs is that you never know who might get behind the mic to deliver their spiel. Anyone from Louis C. K. and Roseanne Barr to Chris Rock could show up. A word of caution: if you don't want to be singled out and made fun of, sit away from the stage. Many of the larger comedy clubs offer meals, and at the more popular clubs, it's always a good idea to make reservations to ensure admission.

Leading the comedy club pack is the **Broadway Comedy Club** in the Theater District, which has formed from a merger of Chicago City Limits and NY Improv. As the city's largest club, it draws big names nightly. **Caroline's** also has big-name comics perform in elegant surroundings. The famous catchphrase of the bug-eyed New York comedian Roger Dangerfield was "I get no respect," but judging from the lasting fame of his **Dangerfield's Comedy Club**, which draws top acts from around the country, he seems to have gotten a fair amount of respect after all. The **Upright Citizens Brigade Theatre** has sassy, Chicago-style

improvisation on various days of the week.

Many of the UCB's weekly late shows are free. The **Gotham Comedy Club**, in the Flatiron District, presents a wide range of comics in an elegant setting. **Comic Strip Live**, on the East Side, has hosted a slew of talent, including Eddie Murphy, and continues to introduce many new comics to the scene. The basement-level **Comedy Cellar** in Greenwich Village presents a nightly lineup of new and established comics. Also good are **Stand-Up NY** and **New York Comedy Club**, which offer multiple comedy shows a night, as well as reasonably priced cocktails. **The West End Lounge** and **The Laugh Factory** are also good value. The biggest names often play multiple nights at places such as **The Theater at Madison Square Garden** and **Radio City Music Hall**.

Classic Cabarets and Piano Bars

Cabarets are a New York institution, synonymous with times gone by. Such cozy, just-for-listening places are often called "rooms" and are located in hotels. Most operate from Tuesday to Saturday (usually with a cover charge or a drink minimum), and most take

credit cards. Cabaret aimed at a predominantly gay scene can be found on pages 348–9.

Triad, on the Upper West Side, hosts a variety of shows, from stand-up comedy and burlesque to modern cabaret acts. A mixed crowd, including the talented staff, croons along at **Brandy's Piano Bar**, on the Upper East Side, while the "long-distance hummer" award goes to the late Bobby Short, who played his piano for over 25 years at the **Café Carlyle** in the Carlyle Hotel. Now Woody Allen plays there on select Mondays with Eddy Davis's New Orleans Jazz Band. Also in the Carlyle is **Bemelman's Bar**, with its whimsical murals; it attracts a relaxed crowd who enjoy first-class crooners.

Ars Nova, in Hell's Kitchen, is an informal, anything-goes cabaret where you may see show tunes and experimental comedy, and has attracted the likes of Liza Minnelli and Tony Kushner.

For a memorable evening of song and music, head to **Feinstein's/54 Below**, in Midtown West, where top-of-the-line performers entertain an appreciative crowd. Near the Flatiron, the **Metropolitan Room**'s intimate performance space hosts a wide range of shows, including cabaret acts and international jazz artists.

Literary Events and Poetry Slams

As the birthplace of some of the greatest American writers, from Herman Melville to Henry James, and the adopted home of countless others, New York City has long been a writer's city. The literary tradition is celebrated throughout the year, with readings and talks that take place at bookstores, libraries, cafés, and community centers across the city. Readings are usually free, but expect long lines for the better-known names.

The **92nd Street Y** hosts readings by some of the greatest writers to pass through New York, including many Nobel- and Pulitzer prize-winning authors. Most of the city's bookstores present a weekly or monthly reading series, including **Barnes & Noble** (the Fifth Avenue and Union Square branches usually attract high-profile authors). The **Mid-Manhattan Library** also presents readings, as does **Strand** book store. Enjoy spirited readings by playwrights at the **Drama Book Shop**. Check out *The New Yorker* magazine, available in book stores and at many newsstands, for current listings of readings and talks.

Poetry slams (also known as Spoken Word), are evenings of freeform poems, raps, and storytelling, usually raucous and entertaining, often unpredictable, and never boring. The **Nuyorican Poets Café**, in Alphabet City, is often heralded as the progenitor of spoken word in New York, and serves up a nightly mix of poetry slams, readings, and performances. Faculty members and staff at Columbia and CUNY, and writing professionals, can be found at **KGB Bar**'s series of literary events. **Bowery Poetry**, established as a performance space for spoken word in all its incarnations, presents an eclectic range of performances, from poetry jams to various performance arts. The **Poetry Project** at St. Mark's Church also hosts contemporary poetry readings, events, and even some workshops.

DIRECTORY

Comedy Showcases

Broadway Comedy Club
318 W 53rd St.
Map 12 E4.
Tel (212) 757-2323.

Caroline's
1626 Broadway.
Map 12 E5.
Tel (212) 757-4100.

Comedy Cellar
117 MacDougal St.
Map 4 D2.
Tel (212) 254-3480.

Comic Strip Live
1568 2nd Ave.
Map 17 B4.
Tel (212) 861-9386.

Dangerfield's
1118 1st Ave.
Map 13 C3.
Tel (212) 593-1650.

Gotham Comedy Club
208 W 23rd St.
Map 0 D4.
Tel (212) 367-9000.

The Laugh Factory
303 W 42 St.
Map 8 D1.
Tel (212) 586-7829.

New York Comedy Club
241 E 24th St.
Map 9 B4.
Tel (212) 696-5233.

Radio City Music Hall
50th St at Avenue of the Americas.
Map 12 F4.
Tel (212) 307-7171.

Stand-up NY
236 W 78th St.
Map 15 C5.
Tel (212) 595-0850.

The Theater at Madison Square Garden
7th Ave & 33rd St.
Map 8 E2.
Tel (212) 465-6741.

Upright Citizens Brigade Theatre
307 W 26th St.
Map 8 D4.
Tel (212) 366-9176.

The West End Lounge
955 W End Ave.
Map 20 E5.
Tel (212) 531-4759.

Cabarets and Piano Bars

Ars Nova
511 W 54th St.
Map 12 E4.
Tel (212) 489-9800.

Bemelman's Bar
Carlyle Hotel,
35 E 76th St.
Map 17 A5.
Tel (212) 744-1600.

Brandy's Piano Bar
235 E 84th St.
Map 17 B4.
Tel (212) 650-1944.

Café Carlyle
Carlyle Hotel,
35 E 76th St.
Map 17 A5.
Tel (212) 744-1600.

Feinstein's/ 54 Below
254 W 54th St.
Map 12 D4.
Tel (646) 476-3551.

Metropolitan Room
34 W 22nd St.
Map 8 F4.
Tel (212) 206-0440.

Triad
158 W 72nd St,
2nd Floor.
Map 11 C1.
Tel (212) 362-2590.

Literary Events and Poetry Slams

92nd Street Y
1395 Lexington Ave.
Map 17 A2.
Tel (212) 415-5729.

Barnes & Noble
555 Fifth Ave.
Map 12 F5.
Tel (212) 697-3048.
33 E 17th St.
Map 9 A5.
Tel (212) 253-0810.

Bowery Poetry
308 Bowery.
Map 4 F3.
Tel (212) 614-0505.

Drama Book Shop
250 W 40th St.
Map 8 E1.
Tel (212) 944-0595.

KGB Bar
85 E 4th St.
Map 4 F2.
Tel (212) 505-3360.

Mid-Manhattan Library
455 Fifth Ave at 40th St.
Map 8 F1.
Tel (212) 340-0833.

Nuyorican Poets Café
236 E 3rd St.
Map 5 B2.
Tel (212) 505-8183.

Poetry Project
St. Mark's Church,
131 E 10th St.
Map 4 F1.
Tel (212) 674-0910.

Strand
828 Broadway.
Map 4 E1.
Tel (212) 473-1452.

Late-Night New York

New York is indeed a city that never sleeps. If you wake up in the middle of the night – with a craving for pizza, a need to be entertained, or an urge to watch the sun rise over the Manhattan skyline – there are always plenty of options from which to choose.

Bars

The best and friendliest bars are often the Irish ones. **O'Flanagan's** or **Peter McManus Café** are both loud, have late-night entertainment, and cater to regulars. Go for a late-night dry Martini at the **Temple Bar**. The best piano bars are in the hotels: try the Café Carlyle or, for a less-expensive option, Bemelman's Bar, both in the **Carlyle Hotel**, or the legendary Feinstein's/54 Below *(see p351)*.

For hot American jazz until 4am, go to **Joe's Pub** or the **Blue Note**. **Cornelia Street Café** is a lively nook for literary readings. Poetry, theater, and Latin music can be found at the **Nuyorican Poets Café**. If you're in midtown, stop in at **Rudy's** for an eclectic late-night scene and a free hot dog with each drink purchase.

Midnight Movies

Special midnight showings and a youthful crowd can be found at the Angelika Film Center and Film Forum *(see p343)*. New multiplexes often show movies at midnight on weekends.

Shops

Shakespeare & Company booksellers on Broadway and the St. Mark's Bookshop are open until late. The **Apple Store** on Fifth Avenue is open 24 hours and well worth a visit at any time of the day. In the evening, DJs bring the store to life, while during the day more than 300 Mac specialists are available for training and consultations. In SoHo, **H&M** sells affordable fashion until 9pm Monday to Saturday and until 8pm on Sundays.

Among the many Village clothing stores that stay open late is **Trash and Vaudeville** (open to 8pm Mon–Thu, to 8:30pm Fri,

and to 9pm Sat); **Macy's** at Herald Square is open daily until 9:30pm. For health essentials, many **Duane Reade**, **CVS**, and **Rite Aid** pharmacies are open 24 hours.

Take-Out Food and Groceries

A few take-out food stores are open 24 hours a day, including numerous **Gristedes** emporiums and the **Westside Supermarket**. Many Korean greengrocers also stay open all night. The **Food Emporium** is a supermarket chain usually open until midnight. Liquor stores are usually open until 10pm and many deliver.

For the best in bagels, go to **Ess-a-Bagel**, **Bagels On The Square**, and **Jumbo Bagels and Bialys**. Many pizzerias and Chinese restaurants stay open late.

Dining

The trendy set often frequent **Balthazar**, and **Les Halles** for good French dishes. Twenty-somethings will seek out the **Coffee Shop** for late-night beer and Brazilian food. You'll find delicious and legendary sandwiches at the **Carnegie Deli**. **Caffè Reggio** in Greenwich Village has been a favorite for late-night coffee and desserts since 1927. Other good options include **Blue Ribbon** and **Odeon**. **The Dead Poet** is a real Upper West Side neighborhood hangout, with a jukebox, a lively bar, and late-night bar food. Downtown, the party crowds flock to **Artichoke Pizza**, which is open till 5am, for excellent pizza. There's also **Veselka**, a Ukranian diner in the East Village, open 24 hours a day.

Sports

There is late-night play at **Slate Billiards** until 4am on

weekends. Have late-night beers and burgers at **Bowlmor Lanes** bowling alley. Also popular is the **Lucky Strike Lanes and Lounge**, featuring cocktails, bowling, and music in a retro atmosphere. **24 Hour Fitness Club** offers a no-frill gym around the clock.

Services

Out in Queens, **Astoria Laundry** is open daily until 11pm for anyone who needs late-night laundry or dry-cleaning services. **Hair & Spa Party 24 Hours** stays true to its name by offering haircuts and manicures around the clock. Near Koreatown, **Red Market** is open for haircuts and coloring services until 11pm most nights. Mainly for women, the no-nonsense Korean **Juvenex Spa** provides massages and saunas at any time. If you're locked out, try **Mr Locks Inc**. For stamps, head to the General Post Office, open 24 hours. The UES and UWS branches of the popular grocery chain **Fairway Market** stay open until midnight.

Tours and Views

One of New York's most enjoyable walks is along the Hudson River at **Battery Park City**, open at all hours. Piers 16 and 17 at South Street Seaport attract strollers and revelers all night long, and **Watermark** bar and lounge on Pier 15 is often open until midnight for a late pick-me-up. Enjoy the city lights by taking a **Circle Line** 2-hour tour of the harbor at night.

Try the Riverview Terrace at Sutton Place: the benches offer a peaceful place to watch the sun rise over the East River, Roosevelt Island, and Queens. Two of the most sensational views with the Manhattan backdrop are (looking west) from the **River Café** and (looking east) from the **Chart House** restaurant.

Take a trip on the **Staten Island Ferry** *(see p76)* to see the

Statue of Liberty and the Manhattan skyline in the dawn light, or take a taxi across Brooklyn Bridge (see pp232–5) to watch the sun rise over New York Harbor. The ultimate view is from the Empire State Building: its observation decks (see pp132–3) stay open until

2am. **The Top of the Rock** at the observation decks (see p140) are open until midnight. The **Living Room Terrace** at the W Downtown offers expansive views of the Downtown skyline.

Château Stables offer rides in horse-drawn carriages, and **Liberty Helicopters** run flights

over the city at sunset. If you want something a little bit different, try **New York Food Tours'** multicultural bar-hopping tour. And if you still can't sleep, stroll along the Upper West Side and grab a couple of hot dogs at the famous **Gray's Papaya**.

DIRECTORY

Bars

Blue Note
See p347.

Carlyle Hotel
See p351.

Cornelia Street Café
29 Cornelia St. Map 4 D2.
Tel (212) 989-9318.

Joe's Pub
See p347.

Nuyorican Poets Café
236 E 3rd St. Map 5 A2.
Tel (212) 505 8183.

O'Flanagan's
1215 1st Ave. Map 13 C2.
Tel (212) 439-0660.

Peter McManus Café
152 7th Ave. Map 8 E5.
Tel (212) 929-9691.

Rudy's
627 9th Ave. Map 12 D5.
Tel (646) 707-0890.

Temple Bar
332 Lafayette St. Map 4
F4. Tel (212) 925-4242.

Shops

Apple Store
767 5th Ave. Map 12 F3.
Tel (212) 336-1440.

CVS Pharmacy
158 Bleecker St. Map 4 D3.
Tel (212) 982-3133.

**Duane Reade
Drugstores**
100 W 57th St. Map 12 E3.
Tel (212) 956-0464.
1279 3rd Ave at E 74th St.
Map 17 B5.
Tel (212) 744-2668.

H&M
558 Broadway. Map 4 E4.
Tel (212) 343-2722.

Macy's
See pp130–31.

RiteAid Pharmacy
See p367.

Trash and Vaudeville
See p318.

Take-Out Food and Groceries

Bagels On The Square
7 Carmine St.
Map 4 D3.
Tel (212) 691-3041.

Ess-a-Bagel
831 3rd Ave.
Map 13 B4.
Tel (212) 980-1010.

Food Emporium
810 8th Ave.
Map 12 D5.
Tel (212) 977-1710.
One of several branches

**Gristedes Food
Emporium**
262 W 96 St and
Broadway. Map 15 C2.
Tel (212) 663-5126.
One of many branches.

**Jumbo Bagels and
Bialys**
1070 2nd Ave. Map 13 B3.
Tel (212) 355-6185.

Westside Market
2171 Broadway. Map 15
C5. Tel (212) 595-2536.

Dining

Artichoke Pizza
328 E 14th St.
Map 5 A1.
Tel (212) 228-2004.

Balthazar
80 Spring St.
Map 4 E4.
Tel (212) 965-1414.

Blue Ribbon Bakery
See p295.

Caffè Reggio
119 MacDougal St.
Map 4 D2.
Tel (212) 475-9557.

Carnegie Deli
See p308.

The Coffee Shop
See p308.

The Dead Poet
450 Amsterdam Ave.
Map 15 C4.
Tel (212) 595-5670.

Les Halles
See p308.

Odeon
See p297.

Veselka
144 2nd Ave.
Map 5 A1.
Tel (212) 228 9682.

Sports

24 Hour Fitness Club
225 5th Ave.
Map 8 F4.
Tel (212) 271-1002.

Bowlmor Lanes
222 W 44th St.
Map 12 E5.
Tel (212) 680-0012.

**Lucky Strike Lanes
and Lounge**
624–660 West 42nd St.
Map 7 B1.
Tel (646) 829-0170.

Slate Billiards
See p355.

Services

Astoria Laundry
23–17 31st St, Queens.
Tel (718) 274-2000.

Fairway Market
2127 Broadway.
Map 15 C5
Tel (212) 595-1888.
One of several branches.

**Hair & Spa Party
24 Hours**
450 Park Ave S. Map 9 A3.
Tel (212) 213-0052.

**James A. Farley
Post Office Building**
See p131.

Juvenex Spa
25 W 32nd St, 5th Floor.
Map 8 F3.
Tel (646) 733-1330.

Mr Locks Inc.
Tel (866) 675-6257.

Red Market
13 E 13th St. Map 5 A1.
Tel (212) 929-9600.

Tours and Views

Battery Park City
West St. Map 1 A3.

Chart House
Lincoln Harbor, Pier D-T,
Weehawken, NJ.
Tel (201) 348-6628.

Château Stables
608 W 48th St. Map 15 B3.
Tel (212) 246-0520.

Circle Line
W 42nd St. Map 15 B3.
Tel (212) 563-3200.

Gray's Papaya
Broadway at 72nd St.
Map 11 C1.
Tel (212) 260-3532.

Liberty Helicopters
Tel (212) 487-4777.

Living Room Terrace
123 Washington St. Map
1 B3. Tel (646) 826-8600.

New York Food Tours
Tel (347) 281-6918.

River Café
1 Water St, Brooklyn. Map
2 F2. Tel (718) 522-5200.

Watermark
78 South St, Pier 15. Map
2 D2. Tel (212) 742-8200.

Sports

Many New Yorkers are ardent sports fans, and you'll find a range of sporting events, both to watch and participate in, going on throughout the year. The city boasts two professional baseball teams, two hockey teams, a basketball team, and two football teams. Madison Square Garden plays host to an extraordinary variety of spectator sports, including basketball, hockey, boxing, and track and field events. Tennis fans can take in the US Open tournament every August and September in Queens, and those who follow track and field events swarm to the Millrose Games, where top runners and other athletes compete.

Tickets

The easiest way to get hold of tickets is through **Ticketmaster**. For the big games, you may need a ticket agent or an online ticketing reseller such as **StubHub!**, which is far safer to use than a scalper (tout) outside the venue. You can also buy tickets at the stadium box office itself, though these tickets often sell out quickly. Finally, keep your eyes peeled for ticket offers in the free weeklies that are distributed throughout town.

Football

The city's two professional football teams are the New York Giants and the New York Jets. They both play their home games across the river in New Jersey at the **MetLife Stadium**, which hosted the 2014 Super Bowl – the first time the NYC area was the site of the big game. Tickets for the Giants, a team with many NFL and Super Bowl championships under their belt, are very difficult to obtain, but they may be available for the Jets, seen by some as perpetual also-rans but no less beloved by their fans. Their last championship win was in 1969.

Baseball

To capture the essence of this American institution, baseball fans should try to see the famed New York Yankees, who play at **Yankee Stadium**. The team's legendary accomplishments include winning the highest number of World Series titles and boasting such celebrated

players as Joe DiMaggio and Jackie Robinson. The New York Mets, the other major baseball team, play at **Citi Field** in Queens. Catching a game of "America's favorite pastime" on a crisp summer day is a memorable event. If you can, try and catch a game when the Yankees are playing their archrivals, the Boston Red Sox. The baseball season runs April–October.

Basketball

The NBA season runs from November–June. The New York Knicks play their home games at **Madison Square Garden**; tickets are pricey and difficult to attain, so reserve them far in advance through Ticketmaster or an online ticketing reseller. The Brooklyn Nets are the only major professional sports team in the borough; home matches are held at Brooklyn's gleaming **Barclays Center**. The ever-popular Harlem Globetrotters also play exhibition games at the Garden.

Boxing

Professional boxing matches are occasionally held at **Madison Square Garden** and the **Barclays Center**, which is home to the Daily News Golden Gloves in mid-April, the largest and oldest amateur boxing tournament in the US, with boxers from New York's five boroughs competing. Past Golden Glove winners, many of whom have gone on to become world champions, have included Sugar Ray Robinson and Floyd Patterson.

Horse Races

A day at the races may not be quite the lavish affair it once was, but the high-stakes races still draw the society crowd – hats, summer dresses, and all – along with lively crowds who have come to cheer, jeer, and bet on their lucky horse. Harness racing, in which horses pull sulkies (small carts), takes place year-round at the **Yonkers Raceway**. Flat races are held daily, except Tuesday, October to May, at the **Aqueduct Race Track** in Queens, and May to October at the **Belmont Park Race Track** in Long Island.

Ice Hockey

Fists and ice fly when the New York Rangers meet their competition at Madison Square Garden. Two other National Hockey League teams call the metro area home: the New York Islanders play in Brooklyn at the **Barclays Center**, and the New Jersey Devils play in the modern **Prudential Center** in Newark. The hockey season runs October–June, depending on playoffs.

Ice Skating

There are a variety of good places to go ice skating out of doors. One is the Rockefeller **Plaza Rink**, which looks beautiful at Christmas. The others are in Central Park: **Wollman Rink** and **Lasker Ice Rink**. For indoor sites, try the Sky Rink at **Chelsea Piers**.

Marathon

To be one of the 50,000-plus who enter the New York Marathon, you have to sign up six months in advance. The race is held on the first Sunday in November. Visit tcsnycmarathon.org for further information.

Tennis

The top tennis tournament in New York is the US Open, played each August at the **National**

Tennis Center. If you want to play tennis rather than watch it, look in the telephone directory under "Tennis Courts: Public and Private." For private courts, you can expect to pay about $50–70 an hour. The **Manhattan Plaza Racquet Club** offers both courts and lessons by the hour. For public courts, you will need a $15 single-play permit ($200 for full-season permits), available from the **NY City Parks & Recreation Department**. You will also need an identity card and a reservation coupon.

Track and Field

The Millrose Games, which draws top athletes from around the world, are normally held in early February at the **Washington Heights Armory**. The 100-meter sprint, pole vault, and high jump competitions are particularly exciting. **Chelsea Piers** also has a complete track-and-field complex, plus myriad activities such as bowling and a golf driving range.

Sports Bars

New York City is crammed with sports bars, often unmissable for their big screens, sports banners, and cheering (or booing), beer-guzzling patrons. For a slice of American sports life, step into a sports bar when a big game is on, and you'll soon be whooping it up with the rest of them. The **Village Pourhouse**, **Professor Thom's**, and **Croxley's Ales**, all in the East Village, offer a plethora of screens so that you can follow the action no matter where you are. **Bounce**, on the Upper East Side, is a boisterous sports lounge with drinks specials through the week. **Bar None** and **The Grafton** are also favorites, and for soccer try the amiable **Nevada Smith's** in the East Village, with friendly, Guinness-fueled crowds.

Other Activities

In Central Park, options include renting rowboats from **Loeb Boathouse** or playing chess – pick up the pieces from The Dairy (see p202). Rent rollerblades at **Blades** and have a free lesson on stopping at Central Park before making a circuit. Bowling is available at **Chelsea Piers** and a few other lanes throughout the city. **Slate Billiards** is one of the bars offering pool and darts.

DIRECTORY

Aqueduct Race Track
Ozone Park, Queens.
Tel (718) 641-4700.

Bar None
98 3rd Ave.
Map 4 F1.
Tel (212) 777-6663.

Barclays Center
620 Atlantic Ave,
Brooklyn.
Tel (212) 359-6387.

Belmont Park Race Track
Hempstead Turnpike,
Long Island.
Tel (718) 641-4700.

Blades
156 W 72nd St.
Map 12 D1.
Tel (212) 787 3911.

Bounce
1403 Second Ave.
Map 13 B1.
Tel (212) 535-2183.

Chelsea Piers Sports & Entertainment Complex
Piers 59–62 at 23rd St & 11th Ave (Hudson River).
Map 7 B4–5.
Tel (212) 336 6000.
w chelseapiers.com

Citi Field
126th St at Roosevelt Ave,
Flushing, Queens.
Tel (718) 507-8499.

Croxley's Ales
28 Ave B. Map 5 B2.
Tel (212) 253-6140.

The Grafton
126 1st Ave. Map 5 A2.
Tel (212) 228-8580.

Lasker Ice Rink
Central Park Drive East at 108th St. Map 21 B4.
Tel (212) 534-7639.

Loeb Boathouse
Central Park. Map 16 F5.
Tel (212) 517-2233.

Madison Square Garden
7th Ave at 33rd St. Map 8 E2. Tel (212) 465-6741.
w thegarden.com

Manhattan Plaza Racquet Club
450 W 43rd St.
Map 7 C1.
Tel (212) 594-0554.

MetLife Stadium
1 MetLife Stadium Dr,
East Rutherford, NJ.
Tel (201) 559-1515.
w metlifestadium.com
Tel (516) 560-8200.
w newyorkjets.com

National Tennis Center
Flushing Meadow Park,
Queens.
Tel (718) 595-2420.
w usta.com

Nevada Smith's
100 3rd Ave. Map 4 F1.
Tel (212) 982-2591.

NY City Parks & Recreation Department
Arsenal Building,
64th St & 5th Ave.
Map 12 F2.
Tel (212) 408-0100.
w nycgovparks.org

Plaza Rink
1 Rockefeller Plaza, 5th Ave.
Map 12 F5.
Tel (212) 332-7654.

Professor Thom's
219 2nd Ave.
Map 4 F1.
Tel (212) 260-9480.

Prudential Center
25 Lafayette St, Newark.
Tel (973) 757-6000.
w prucenter.com

Slate Billiards
54 W 21st St.
Map 8 E4.
Tel (212) 989-0096.

StubHub!
w stubhub.com

Ticketmaster
Tel (212) 307-4100.
w ticketmaster.com

Village Pourhouse
64 3rd Ave.
Map 4 F1.
Tel (212) 979-2337.

Washington Heights Armory
216 Fort Washington Ave.
Tel (212) 923-1803.

Wollman Rink
Central Park,
5th Ave at 59th St.
Map 12 F2.
Tel (212) 439-6900.

Yankee Stadium
161st and 164th sts,
The Bronx.
Tel (718) 293-4300.

Yonkers Raceway
Yonkers, Westchester County.
Tel (914) 968-4200.

Fitness and Wellbeing

New York City may be (in)famous for its concrete, crowds, and cacophony, but the urban jungle is a boon for sports and fitness aficionados. A host of possibilities beckon, from pedaling on the sun-washed riverfront and jogging under the shadow of Manhattan's signature skyline at the Central Park Reservoir to scaling a soaring climbing wall at one of the city's many upscale gyms, indulging in a massage at a gorgeous spa strewn with rose petals, and finding your inner peace in the lotus position at a yoga class.

Cycling

There's nothing like being stuck in midtown traffic to make you long for pedaling the open road. While Manhattan may be one of the most crowded islands on the planet, it offers a surprising number of bike trails. At the last count, Manhattan boasted more than 110,000 everyday cyclists. One of the most pleasant places to cycle is in Central Park during the weekend, when it's closed to cars. Bikes may be rented from **Central Park Bike Rentals** on 57th Street.

If you would like to feel the river breeze in your hair, pedal the well-maintained bike path along the West Side Highway that runs parallel to the Hudson River, or hit the bike trails in Riverside Park. On summer weekends, the paths can get exasperatingly congested, but if you go early or late in the day, or in the winter months, you can often coast solo.

With thousands of bikes at stations across the city, **Citi Bike** offers a rental system that allows visitors to bike around using 24-hour or seven-day access passes.

Fitness Centers, Gyms, and Health Clubs

In New York, a weekly workout has become almost de rigueur for even the most extreme workaholics. Gyms and health clubs have sprouted across the city to accommodate the demand, and serious sweating goes on at all hours, day and night. The options are endless: get your aggression out with a punch bag, increase your heart rate on the stairmaster,

or pump iron. Most major hotels have fitness centers. Many commercial gyms and health clubs are open only to members, but an increasing number of gyms now offer day passes. Check out the **Chelsea Piers Sports & Entertainment Complex** on Piers 59–62 near the Hudson River; there's something for everyone at this enormous facility. It's one-stop shopping at the multilevel **May Center for Health, Fitness, and Sport at the 92nd Street Y**, with exercise studios, weight-training, racquetball courts, a boxing room, and an indoor track. Day passes start at around $35. With its well-maintained gym along with an array of personal diet and exercise programs, the **Julien Farel Restore Spa at the Regency Hotel** on Park Avenue lives up to its promise to be "your health and fitness oasis when you're away from home."

You can enjoy a wide range of activities at the **YMCA** (one on the West Side and the other on 47th Street) fitness centers. The state-of-the-art training equipment, a number of gymnasiams, swimming pools, aerobics studios, running/walking tracks, and various courts for different games, should add to your enthusiasm of working out. The center also has special programs for elderly people designed to suit their physical stature for a healthy life.

Golf

Practice your swing at **Randall's Island Golf Center** on Randall's Island, or the

Chelsea Golf Club at Chelsea Piers. The city owns several courses in the boroughs, such as **Pelham Bay Park** in the Bronx and **Silver Lake Golf Course** on Staten Island.

Jogging

Some parks are safe for joggers, others are not, so be guided by your concierge or advice from trusted locals. It is not encouraged to run after dark, at dusk or before dawn. The most popular and beautiful route is around the reservoir in Central Park. The **NY Road Runners** on 89th Street have weekly running clinics and races, as does Chelsea Piers Sports & Entertainment Complex.

Pilates

The philosophy behind Pilates is based on the premise that the body's core is the "powerhouse" for the peripheral parts of the body. Challenge your muscles at a **Grasshopper Pilates** class, which is taught by a professionally trained dancer in SoHo. **Power Pilates** also hold strengthening classes throughout the city.

Yoga

It's easier to get in touch your spiritual center when you can do it in a place like the airy **Exhale Mind Body Spa** on Madison Avenue, with its high ceilings and hard-wood floors. "Journey into the Core," "Ride the Vinyasa Wave," and "Dance into Trance" at a variety of yoga sessions, the ideal antidote to the city's madness. And, just in case you think yoga isn't enough of a workout, then you haven't tried the core fusion power pack abs session. **Fluid Fitness** on Sixth Avenue offers an introduction to Gyrotonic training, a workout that follows the principles of yoga while using fluid exercises and non-linear circular motion to strengthen the core.

Spas

Pamper yourself at one of New York City's choice spas and you'll emerge fresh as a daisy – and ready to take on the urban jungle once again. Most spas offer packages where you can enjoy several treatments at a lower price. If you're traveling with your significant other, bond over a couples' massage. The intoxicating wafts of incense that greet you at the front door of the fragrant, low-lit **CLAY Health Club + Spa** are just a hint of the luxurious massage that awaits within.

At the comfy, casual **Oasis Day Spa**, on Park Avenue, select from six aromatherapy massages in aromas of uplift, refresh, balance, passion, calm, or relief. Men's specials include a Dead Sea salt scrub, an algae facial, or a muscle meltdown massage. For a slice of heaven, Bali style, disappear into the **Acqua Beauty Bar** on 14th Street and enjoy a botanical purifying facial, orchid pedicure, or Indonesian ritual of beauty, where your skin is scrubbed with ground rice and kneaded with fragrant oils. Enter **Bliss** on 57th Street and you'll soon discover that there's nothing a carrot and sesame body buff or fully loaded facial can't cure. Top it off with a decadent double chocolate pedicure, accompanied by a cup of creamy cocoa. Pure bliss. Celebrities including Antonio Banderas and Kate Moss swear by **Mario Badescu** on 52nd Street, whose facials and body scrubs, including the fresh fruit body scrub, with plump raspberries and strawberries, are as legendary as the beauty products, which are perfect to bring home as gifts.

Swimming

Many Manhattan hotels have pools with free access during your stay. It is also possible to purchase a day pass to use a hotel swimming pool and facilities – for example, at Le Parker Meridien (see p289). You can also swim and surf at the Surfside 3 Maritime Center at **Chelsea Piers**.

Indoor Sports

Chelsea Piers has it all: roller rinks, bowling, indoor soccer, basketball, rock climbing walls, fitness centers, golf, a field house for gymnastics, sports medicine, spa centers, and, of course, swimming pools. This huge complex, which is spread over four old West Side piers, is open to everyone.

Apart from providing fitness centers, gymnasium facilities, and indoor sports activities, the **Vanderbilt YMCA** also offers exercise, balance, and flexibility classes; organizes day trips; hosts special events; and has sports and volunteer opportunities. If you are planning an adventurous day out for your children with fitness on the agenda, or looking to burn extra calories, then the club is worth a visit.

DIRECTORY

Cycling

Central Park Bike Rental
348 W 57th St.
Map 12 D3.
Tel (212) 664-9600.

Citi Bike
W citibikenyc.com

Fitness Centers, Gyms, and Health Clubs

Chelsea Piers Sports & Entertainment Complex
Piers 59–62 at 23rd St & 11th Ave (Hudson River).
Map 7 B4–5.
Tel (212) 336-6000.
W chelseapiers.com

Julien Farel Restore Spa at the Regency Hotel
540 Park Ave.
Map 13 A3.
Tel (212) 888-8988.

May Center for Health, Fitness, and Sport at the 92nd Street Y
1395 Lexington Ave.
Map 17 A2.
Tel (212) 415-5729.

YMCA West Side
5 W 63rd St.
Map 12 D2.
Tel (212) 912-2600.
One of several branches.

Golf

Pelham Bay Park
The Bronx, 870 Shore Rd.
Tel (718) 885-1461.

Randall's Island Golf Center
Randall's Island.
Map 22 F2.
Tel (212) 427-5689.

Silver Lake Golf Course
915 Victory Blvd,
Staten Island.
Tel (718) 447-5686.

Jogging

NY Road Runners
9 E 89th St.
Map 17 A3.
Tel (212) 860-4455.

Pilates

Grasshopper Pilates
151 Spring St.
Map 4 E4.
Tel (212) 431-5225.

Power Pilates
920 3rd Ave, 6th Floor.
Map 13 B3.
Tel (212) 627-5852.

Yoga

Exhale Mind Body Spa
980 Madison Ave.
Map 17 A5.
Tel (212) 561-6400.

Fluid Fitness
1026 6th Ave
Map 8 E1.
Tel (212) 278-8330.

Spas

Acqua Beauty Bar
7 E 14th St. **Map** 8 F5.
Tel (212) 620-4329.

Bliss
19 E 57th St. **Map** 12 F3.
Tel (212) 219-8970.
One of several locations.

CLAY Health Club + Spa
25 W 14th St.
Map 4 D1.
Tel (212) 206-9200.

Mario Badescu
320 E 52nd St.
Map 13 B4.
Tel (800) 223-3728.

Oasis Day Spa
1 Park Ave.
Map 9 A2.
Tel (212) 254-7722.
One of two locations.

Indoor Sports

Vanderbilt YMCA
224 E 47th St. **Map** 13 B5.
Tel (212) 756-9600.

CHILDREN'S NEW YORK CITY

Young visitors soon catch the contagious excitement in the air in New York. Attractions for all ages abound, and plenty are designed especially for children. More than a dozen theater companies, two zoos, and numerous imaginative museums are aimed at the young, backed up with special events at many museums and parks. The chance to visit a TV studio is a treat, and New York's own Big Apple Circus is a perennial delight. With more to do than can ever be squeezed into a single visit, you'll hopefully never hear the cry "I'm bored!" Best of all, there's no need to spend a fortune to have fun.

A young visitor imitating the Statue of Liberty

Practical Advice

New York is family-friendly. Many of its hotels allow children to stay in parents' rooms for free, and will supply cots or cribs if needed. Most museums charge half price or less for children, while others are free. Children under 44 in (112 cm) also ride free on subways and buses when accompanied by an adult. Travel between 9am and 4pm to avoid rush hours.

Supplies such as diapers and medicines are readily available, and the Rite Aid Pharmacy (see p367) is open 24 hours a day. Finding changing tables in public toilets is less easy, but no one usually objects if a washroom counter is used. Best bets are the facilities in libraries, hotels, and department stores. Most hotels will arrange babysitters; try **Baby Sitters' Guild** or **Pinch Sitters**.

To find out more about the range of current activities for children, pick up a copy of the free quarterly calendar of events from the New York Convention and Visitors Bureau (see p362). Weekly listings can be found in *New York* magazine or *Time Out New York*.

New York Adventures

The city can seem like a giant amusement park for youngsters. Elevators whisk you sky-high for bird's-eye views from atop the world's highest buildings. You can set sail on the classic **Circle Line** tour around Manhattan; the sailboat *Pioneer (see p84)*; or the free round trip on the Staten Island Ferry (see p80). The Roosevelt Island Tram (see p176–7) is a Swiss cable car offering an airborne ride over the East River. Central Park (see pp198–203) is a source of rides of every kind – from the old-fashioned charm of the carousel to real horseback and ponycart rides. Children who prefer a faster pace can join the skate-boarders and

in-line skaters who cruise around the traffic-free park every weekend.

People cooling off on a playground in Central Park

Museums

While many of New York's museums appeal to all ages, some are designed just for the young. High on the list are the Children's Museum of the Arts (see p101), where kids can paint and sculpt, and the Children's Museum of Manhattan (see p213), a multimedia world in which children produce their own videos and newscasts.

There's also the **Staten Island Children's Museum**, where a huge climb-through anthill is one of the favorite items, and the Brooklyn Children's Museum (see p236). The *Intrepid* Sea, Air & Space Museum (see p145) is a real aircraft carrier. Finally, don't miss the dinosaur display at the American Museum of Natural History (see pp210–11).

Outdoor Fun

In summer, all of New York comes out to play. Central Park is a child's wonderland, from skating rinks to boating lakes, bicycle

Skating with Santa at Rockefeller Center

paths to miniature golf. The park offers free entertainment – such as guided walks by park rangers on Saturdays, toy sailboat races and summer storytelling. The Central Park Zoo and the Tisch Children's Zoo are favorites.

Children of all ages will be fascinated by the Bronx Zoo/ Wildlife Conservation Park, which is home to over 650 species *(see pp254–5).*

Coney Island *(see p259)* is just a subway ride away. Winter brings the chance to skate at Rockefeller Center *(see p140)* or in Central Park on a rink fringed with views of skyscrapers.

Indoor Fun

New York children's theater is of a quality and variety matching that for adults. Some favorite companies are the **Paper Bag Players** and **Theaterworks USA**, whose shows sell out fast; get schedules and reserve seats early.

The **Swedish Cottage Marionette Theatre** in Central Park has shows at 10:30am and noon Tuesdays through Fridays, and Saturdays until 1pm.

The New York City Ballet's annual Christmas production of *The Nutcracker* at Lincoln Center *(see p208)* opens at the same time that the **Big Apple Circus** sets up its tent nearby. Ringling Brothers and Barnum & Bailey Circus is in action at Madison Square Garden *(see p)* each spring.

Opportunities for youngsters to work off energy in winter are many, from indoor skating rinks to mini-golf and bowling alleys at **Chelsea Piers**. Kids can create video games, movies, and music for free at **Sony Wonder Technology Lab**.

One of the daring performances by the Big Apple Circus

Shopping

There will be no complaints about shopping trips if they include the huge **Disney** store or **Toys 'R' Us** for a vast range of wonderful toys and other items. For more information on other toy stores, see *New York Originals* on pages 316–18. Youngsters are welcomed for storytelling sessions at **Books of Wonder**.

Eating Out

Hamburger-and-pasta joint **Ottomanelli's Café** is very popular with children, and even adults find it hard to finish their huge burgers. The colorful **S'Mac**, where the specialty is creamy macaroni and cheese, is also a hit with youngsters. The lively **Hard Rock Café** is also popular, and most children enjoy the foods sold around Chinatown and Little Italy. Drop into the **Chinatown Ice Cream Factory** for some strange and wonderful flavors. For a quick hot snack, try pizza by the slice or pretzels and hot dogs from street vendors.

The famous Hard Rock Café at Times Square

DIRECTORY

Practical Advice

Baby Sitters' Guild
Tel (212) 682-0227.

Pinch Sitters
Tel (212) 260-6005.

Adventures

Circle Line
Pier 83, W 42nd St. **Map** 7 A1.
Tel (212) 563-3200.

Museums

Staten Island Children's Museum
1000 Richmond Terr, Staten Is.
Tel (718) 273-2060.

Indoor Fun

Big Apple Circus
Tel (212) 268-2500.

Chelsea Piers
Tel (212) 336-6800.

Paper Bag Players
185 East Broadway. **Map** 5 B5.
Tel (212) 353-2332.

Sony Wonder Technology Lab
550 Madison Ave. **Map** 13 A3.
Tel (212) 833-8100.

Swedish Cottage Marionette Theatre
Tel (212) 988-9093.

Theaterworks USA
151 W 26th St. **Map** 8 E4.
Tel (800) 497-5007.

Shopping

Books of Wonder
18 W 18th St. **Map** 8 C5.
Tel (212) 989-3270.

Disney store
1540 Broadway. **Map** 12 E5.
Tel (212) 626-2910.

Toys 'R' Us
See p316.

Eating Out

Chinatown Ice Cream Factory
65 Bayard St. **Map** 4 F5.
Tel (212) 608-4170.

Hard Rock Café
1501 Broadway. **Map** 8 E1.
Tel (212) 343-3355.

Ottomanelli's Café
1626 York Ave. **Map** 17 C3.
Tel (212) 772-7722.

S'Mac
345 E 12th St. **Map** 5 A1.
Tel (212) 358-7912.

SURVIVAL GUIDE

PRACTICAL INFORMATION

New York is one of the most diverse and exciting cities in the world. The fast pace of Manhattan may seem daunting at first, but there are many services to help tourists, and you should find the city safe and easy to explore. Midtown streets are straight and mostly laid out in an easy-to-follow grid pattern. Buses and subway trains *(see pp382–5)*

are reliable and cheap; there are plenty of cash machines; and money can be easily exchanged at banks and hotels. The wide range of prices offered by the many hotels *(see pp284–9)*, restaurants *(see pp294–305)*, and entertainment venues *(see pp334–57)* in the city means that your New York trip can be both fun and affordable.

Skaters at an ice rink in Central Park

When to Go

September and October are the prize months in New York, offering warm days, cool nights, and colorful leaves in the city parks. Late spring is also appealing, when the city is less crowded and humid. Summers can be unpleasantly hot, but there are attractions such as outdoor concerts, plays, and sporting events to keep visitors busy. Christmas in the city is wonderful, although you will have to share your experience with thousands of other tourists. Weather-wise, any season can be unpredictable; always pack layers, and be prepared for changes.

Visas and Passports

All visitors to the United States require passports valid for at least six months after the dates of travel. Citizens of the UK, Australia, New Zealand, and 32 other countries, including most EU countries, do not need visas if they are staying in the US for 90 days or less. However, they must

apply and pay for entry online via the Electronic System for Travel Authorization (ESTA). The ESTA is valid for up to two years and can be used for multiple entries into the US (www.esta.cbp.dhs.gov).

Canadians must show their passports when entering the US by air, and a passport or an enhanced driver's license proving citizenship when arriving by land or sea.

Those visitors requiring a visa should apply in person at the nearest US embassy or consulate in their own country. It is vital to begin the process early, allowing sufficient time for processing the application. Some services will expedite the process for a fee. Visit www.travel.state.gov for more details.

Customs Information

Customs allowances per person when you enter the US are 200 cigarettes, 100 cigars, or 4.4 lb (2 kg) of tobacco; no more than 2 pints (1 liter) of alcohol; and gifts worth no more than $100. Many foods, including fruits and

vegetables, may be brought by visitors into the United States. Baked items, candy, chocolate, and cheese are permissible, as are canned goods (except those containing meat or poultry products) if being imported for personal use.

Upon arrival at one of New York's airports, follow signs stating "other than American passports" to immigration counters, where your passport will be stamped. Next, reclaim your bags from the appropriate area and proceed to a customs officer, who will examine the customs declaration that you should have received and filled in on your flight.

New York tourist information office

Tourist Information

Advice on any aspect of life in New York City is available from the New York Convention & Visitors Bureau, known as **NYC & Co.** Its 24-hour touch-tone telephone service *(see p365)* offers help outside office hours.

New York City has another free phone and Internet service, **311**, which provides government information and non-emergency general assistance. Calls are answered by a team 24 hours a day, with a translation service.

Smoking and Etiquette

It is illegal to smoke in any public place or building in New York, including restaurants, and this law is taken very seriously.

When boarding buses, New Yorkers generally form a line rather than pushing to enter. Subway boarders are not so polite at rush hours, but do stand aside to let passengers exit before rushing in. Turning off cell phones in theaters, cinemas, and museums is expected. Casual wear is accepted in many places in New York City, but some establishments may require formal dress; check when you make a reservation.

The entrance to the Solomon R. Guggenheim Museum (see pp184–5)

Admission Prices

New York can be expensive for visitors, though you may often find a way to avoid high charges. Museum prices can run from $12 to $25, but some galleries, such as the Metropolitan Museum, call their charge a "suggested

Many stores have late opening hours to accommodate workers

The New York Pass and CityPASS

donation," leaving it to the visitor to decide what to pay. On Friday evenings (Saturdays for the Guggenheim), the Museum of Modern Art, Whitney Museum, and Folk Art Museum are open late and are free or have a "pay what you wish" policy. The Jewish Museum is free all day Saturday, while the Brooklyn Museum offers free art and entertainment on the first Saturday of the month (5–11pm). Consult local listings for museums of interest to you. The **New York Pass** and **CityPASS** (see p364), offer discounted entry to some 50 attractions.

Opening Hours

Business hours are generally from 9am to 5pm, with no lunchtime closing. Many Midtown stores stay open until 7pm to accommodate people in full-time jobs, and they may close even later on Thursdays, at 8:30 or 9pm. Most stores are also open from noon to 6pm on Sundays.

Typical banking hours run from 9am to 6pm, Monday to Friday; some banks also open on Saturdays from 9am to 4pm. ATM machines are available 24 hours for credit and debit card cash withdrawals (see p368).

Closing days vary for the major museums, as do the evenings they are open late, although most tend to be closed on a Monday. The Guggenheim, however, closes

on Thursdays. Phone ahead of your visit, or check the website, before planning your itinerary.

New York's traffic rush hours extend roughly from 8 to 10am and 4:30 to 6:30pm, Monday to Friday. During these times, every form of public transportation will be crowded.

Public Bathrooms

New York City does not provide many public bathrooms. Free restrooms can be found at city information centers, department stores, large bookstores (such as Barnes & Noble), and big restaurant chains (Starbucks, McDonald's), as well as at hotels. Bathrooms are also available in train and bus stations, but these are not usually the most pleasant options.

Taxes and Tipping

Sales tax in New York is 8.875 per cent, and it is added to all purchases (including meals), except for clothing and shoes under $110. Tipping is an integral part of New York life: taxi drivers expect 10–15 per cent; cocktail waiters 15 per cent; hotel room service 10 per cent (when not added to the bill); coat check $1; hotel maids $1 or $2 per day after the first day; hotel bellhops about $1 per bag; hairstylists 15–20 per cent, and barbers 10–20 per cent,. Waiters generally receive 15–20 per cent, of the bill, not including tax. A quick way to calculate restaurant tips is simply to double the tax, adding up to about 18 per cent.

City bus with access ramp lowered for a disabled passenger

Travelers with Disabilities

All city buses have ramps for easy access. Subways, however, are a challenge for the disabled, as most stations are accessed via steps from the street. Only the busiest stops and stations, such as Grand Central and Penn stations and the Port Authority Bus Terminal, have elevators. A list of accessible stations is available on the Metropolitan Transit Authority website (www.mta.info).

Most hotels, restaurants, and attractions are equipped for disabled visitors, but do check in advance. It is also wise to ask about accessibility to the restrooms.

Some museums offer tours for deaf, blind, or other disabled visitors, and all Broadway theaters have devices for the hearing-impaired. The *Official Accessibility Guide*, available free from the **Mayor's Office for People with Disabilities**, is a great resource, as is *Access for All*, published by **Healing Arts Initiative**. Both detail disabled access at public places such as museums, landmarks, theaters, and stadiums.

Senior Travelers

Seniors are welcomed in New York, and they are eligible for many offers. They travel half-fare on all subways and buses and get discounted prices at museums, movie theaters, and many sightseeing attractions. Drivers of city buses can lower the entry steps to make it easier for older passengers to board.

Gay and Lesbian Travelers

New York has a large gay and lesbian population. Gay Pride Week in June brings celebrants from around the world for a big parade, and the Halloween parade in Greenwich Village also has a large gay following. The **Lesbian, Gay, Bisexual & Transgender Community Center** is a good first stop for general information. Christopher Street in Greenwich Village is the proud birthplace of New York's gay scene. Eighth Avenue around Chelsea is the epicenter of activity today, with Hell's Kitchen and the East Village increasingly popular; Park Slope in Brooklyn is a hot spot for the lesbian community. **Next** (www.next magazine.com) is a free weekly publication that can be found in these areas. The monthly **GO Magazine** (www.gomag.com) covers the lesbian scene, and *Time Out New York (see p371)* and the *New York* magazine website (www.nymag.com) have gay and lesbian listings.

Sign for the Lesbian, Gay, Bisexual & Transgender Community Center

Student Travelers

Many museums and theaters in New York offer discounted admission for students. To receive this, however, you will need to show proof of your student status. Provided you have the right credentials, an **International Student Identity Card (ISIC)** can be purchased quite cheaply from **STA Travel**, which has a branch in New York. At the same time, ask for a copy of the *ISIC Student Handbook*, which lists places and services that offer discounts to card-holders, including selected accommodations, various museums, tours, theaters, attractions, nightclubs, and restaurants.

Although it is very difficult to obtain permission to work in the US, students are eligible to work as part of exchange programs or as interns. Again, STA Travel can provide you with further details.

Note that the minimum age for drinking in New York is 21, and patrons may be asked for proof of age.

International Student Identity Card

Traveling on a Budget

There are many ways to take advantage of the best of New York while on a budget. The **TKTS** booth *(see p334)*, near Times Square, offers half-price admission to same-day Broadway shows, while pre-theater prix-fixe meals save on dining. The David Rubenstein Atrium, across from Lincoln Center *(see p208)*, offers discount tickets for same-day performances, in addition to a free concert in the Atrium itself on Thursdays at 8:30pm. The New York Philharmonic invites visitors to rehearsals for just $20 on Thursdays, and the Juilliard School also presents free concerts. In summer, free Shakespeare plays and music by the Philharmonic and the Metropolitan Opera are performed in Central Park. Many TV shows produced in the city are free to watch live if you request tickets in advance. The **New York Pass**, while not cheap, is good value for those who plan to do a lot of sightseeing. It offers free entry to over attractions, from museums to the Empire State Building and river cruises. The **New York CityPASS** gives holders admission to six must-see sights in the city.

Time

New York is on Eastern Standard Time from late October to mid-March. Eastern Daylight

Time moves the American clock forward 1 hour the rest of the year.

Add 5 hours for the time in London, 8 hours for Moscow, 14 hours for Tokyo, and 16 hours for Sydney.

Electrical Appliances

All American electric current flows at a standardized 110 to 120 volts AC (alternating current). You will need an adapter plug and a voltage convertor that fits standard US electrical outlets. US plugs have two flat prongs.

Most New York hotels provide wall-mounted electric hairdryers in bathrooms. In addition, some hotels have wall plugs capable of powering both 110- and 220-volt electric shavers, but little else – not even radios. It can, in fact, be dangerous to connect anything more powerful.

Some New York hotel rooms provide coffeemakers; however, most have radios and clocks, and a large number have iPod docking stations. If you require an iron and ironing board, but they are not in the room, ask room service.

Conversion Chart

Bear in mind that 1 US pint (0.5 liter) is a smaller measure than 1 UK pint (0.6 liter).

Imperial to Metric
1 inch = 2.5 centimeters
1 foot = 30 centimeters
1 mile = 1.6 kilometers
1 ounce = 28 grams
1 pound = 454 grams
1 US pint = 0.5 liter
1 US gallon = 3.8 liters

Metric to Imperial
1 millimeter = 0.04 inch
1 centimeter = 0.4 inch
1 meter = 3 feet 3 inches
1 kilometer = 0.6 mile
1 gram = 0.04 ounce

Responsible Tourism

New York is increasingly aware of "green issues." Proper recycling bins, with separate areas for paper and plastic, are widely available. Most hotels encourage guests to be ecologically aware and not request fresh towels every day. Shoppers tend to carry reusable cloth shopping bags, which are sold in almost every department store and

Fresh local produce for sale at one of New York's greenmarkets

supermarket. Most markets carry organic foods, and the city's many neighborhood greenmarkets are popular sources of locally grown produce. The **Greenmarket at Union Square** (Mon, Wed, Fri, and Sat) is one of the best. Opening times vary.

You can contribute to these green efforts by patronizing restaurants that use locally grown produce. **Hearth** and **Gramercy Tavern** are two popular restaurants that have been given the **Slow Food NYC** seal of approval.

DIRECTORY

Embassies and Consulates

Australia
150 E 42nd St.
Map 9 A1.
Tel (212) 351-6500.
W newyork.consulate.gov.au

Canada
1251 Sixth Ave at 50th St.
Map 12 E4.
Tel (212) 596-1628.
W can-am.gc.ca/new-york

Great Britain
845 Third Ave.
Map 13 B4.
Tel (212) 745-0200.
W gov.uk

Ireland
345 Park Ave.
Map 13 A4.
Tel (212) 319-2555.
W dfa.ie

New Zealand
37 Observatory Circle, NW, Washington, DC, 20008.
Tel (202) 328-4800.
W nzembassy.com/usa-washington

Tourist Information

311
Tel 311. W nyc.gov/311

New York CityPASS
W citypass.com/

New York Pass
W newyorkpass.com

NYC & Co.
Seventh Ave at 44th St.
Map 12 E4. **Tel** (212) 484-1222. W nycgo.com

Travelers with Disabilities

Healing Arts Initiative
Tel (212) 575-7676.
W hainyc.org

Mayor's Office for People with Disabilities
Tel (212) 788-2830.
W nyc.gov/mopd

Gay and Lesbian Travelers

Lesbian, Gay, Bisexual & Transgender Community Center
208 West 13th St.
Map 3 C1.
Tel (212) 620-7310.
W gaycenter.org

Student Travelers

International Student Identity Card (ISIC)
W isic.org

STA Travel
722 Broadway.
Map 4 E1.
Tel (212) 473-6100.
W statravel.com

Budget Travel

W nycgo.com/free

Responsible Tourism

Gramercy Tavern
42 East 20th St.
Map 9 A5.
Tel (212) 477-6777.
W gramercytavern.com

Greenmarket at Union Square
Union Square.
Map 9 A5.
W cenyc.org

Hearth
403 E 12th St.
Map 5 A1.
Tel (646) 602-1300.
W restaurant hearth.com

Slow Food NYC
W slowfoodnyc.org

Personal Security and Health

New York is one of the US's safest large cities. There is a good level of security in the city, the transportation system, and at airports, and the city's police force is very much in evidence around Manhattan. As in any major metropolis, there are places where travelers should avoid venturing after dark alone, such as city parks and quiet streets. But if you keep your wits about you and stick to the following guidelines, you should enjoy a trouble-free and pleasant visit to New York City.

New York City police officers patrolling the streets

Travel Safety Information

Visitors can get up-to-date travel safety information from the **Foreign and Commonwealth Office** in the UK, the **State Department** in the US and the **Department of Foreign Affairs and Trade** in Australia (see *Directory box*).

Police

The New York City Police Department has around-the-clock foot, horse, bike, and car patrols. These are concentrated in specific areas at critical times – for instance, the Theater District aftershow times. There is also a police presence on the subways and buses, and this is reflected in the dramatic drop in crime statistics.

Lost and Stolen Property

There is no city-wide lost-and-found service, but the Metropolitan Transit Authority

(MTA) *(see p385)* has a lost-and-found department for city buses and subways, and the Taxi & Limousine Commission *(see p381)* will assist passengers who have left belongings in a cab. The lost-and-found rooms at Grand Central and Penn train stations are well managed, with helpful staff. If you don't know who to contact, phone 311 for guidance.

In the event of loss or theft of valuables, report all missing items to the police, or **Crime Victims Hot Line** and make sure you get a copy of the police report for your insurance claim. Keep the receipts of expensive items as proof of possession.

If your passport is stolen, report the theft immediately to your consulate *(see p365)*. Lost or stolen credit cards should also be reported promptly so that your account can be blocked. American Express *(see p369)* has offices in the city where new cards can be processed quickly, and other card companies can often provide replacements. It is always a good idea to separate your credit and debit cards, so that if a wallet is lost, you have a backup card.

What to be Aware of

Manhattan has become quite a safe place to roam, but pickpockets do operate and common sense still rules, as in any big city. Be alert, and walk as if you know where you're going. If someone asks you for money, be careful and avoid conversation.

It is better to avoid deserted locations late at night, even if there is no obvious danger. Parts of the Lower East Side, Chinatown, or Midtown west of Broadway bustle through dinner hours but feel empty after 10pm or so. The Financial District is deserted after business hours, and even the very trendy TriBeCa and SoHo areas are empty late at night. Subways stay crowded until around 11pm, but may not be advisable later. If you can't find or afford a taxi, try to travel with a group and keep to the main streets.

Parks are not recommended after dark, unless there is a concert or other event. If you want to go for a jog, ask your hotel concierge for a map of safe routes. In crowds, take precautions to avoid pickpockets.

When in the street, keep your wallet in an inconspicuous place, never in a back pocket, and have your MetroCard or change handy for bus fares – it's best not to

Be aware of pickpockets when exploring the city

Police car

Ambulance

Fire engine

have to dig into your purse or wallet in public. Never stop to count your money, and be aware of strangers at bank ATMs. Guard against purse snatchers by carrying your bag with the clasp facing toward you and the shoulder strap across your body.

Leave valuables at home or stored at the hotel in a locked suitcase or a closet safe. Do not allow anyone except hotel and airport personnel to carry your luggage or parcels.

In an Emergency

If you are involved in a medical emergency, proceed at once to a hospital emergency room. Dial 411, and ask the operator to give you the number of the nearest hospital. Should you need an ambulance, telephone 911. If you have time, avoid the crowded city-owned hospitals. Instead, choose a private hospitals listed in the Yellow Pages (see also *Directory box*). If your travel medical insurance is in order, you won't have to worry about costs, but remember that national insurance in other

countries is not valid in the US.

If the situation is not urgent, ask your hotel to call a doctor or dentist or to recommend one. You can find one yourself through the **NY Hotel Urgent Medical Services** or **NYU Dental Care**. The **Beth Israel Medical Center** has an excellent walk-in clinic. For general advice and information, call **Travelers' Aid**, which is geared to helping travelers. Note that the cost of prescriptions may be higher than in your home country.

Hospitals and Pharmacies

If you must visit a doctor or hospital, be prepared to undergo an expensive experience: some of the city's practitioners and facilities are among the best in the country, and they charge accordingly. The best way to protect yourself against large medical costs is with comprehensive travel insurance. Note that you will have to pay and then reclaim the money. All hospitals accept credit cards, as do most physicians and dentists. The city has many 24-hour pharmacies; some will often fill a prescription while you wait.

Travel Insurance

Travel insurance is highly recommended, mainly because of the high cost of medical care. There are many types and levels, with prices dependent on the length of your trip and the number of people covered.

A 24-hour pharmacy, one of many in the city

Among the most important features are emergency medical and dental care, trip cancellation, baggage and travel-document loss, accidental dismemberment and death. Many policies will cover all of these items.

DIRECTORY

Travel Safety Information

Department of Foreign Affairs and Trade (Australia)
W dfat.gov.au/
W smarttraveller.gov.au/

Foreign and Commonwealth Office (UK)
W gov.uk/foreign-travel-advice

US Department of State (US)
W travel.state.gov/

Police

All Emergency Services
Tel 911 (or 0).

Crime Victims Hot Line
Tel (212) 577-7777.

In an Emergency

Beth Israel Medical Center
55 E 34th St. **Map** 8 F2.
Tel (212) 252-6000.
One of three branches.

NY Hotel Urgent Medical Services
Tel (212) 737-1212.

NYU Dental Care
345 E 24th St/First Ave. **Map** 9 B4.
Tel (212) 998-9800, (212) 998-9828 (weekends and after 9pm).

Travelers' Aid
JFK Airport, Terminal 410.
Tel (718) 656-4870.

Hospitals and Pharmacies

Duane Reade
4 Times Square, near Broadway.
Map 8 E1. **Tel** (646) 366-8047.

Mount Sinai Roosevelt
58th St and Tenth Ave.
Map 12 D3. **Tel** (212) 523-4000.

NYU Medical Center
560 First Avenue at 33rd Street.
Map 9 C3. **Tel** (212) 263-5550.

Rite Aid
50th St/Eighth Ave. **Map** 12 D4.
Tel (212) 247-8384.

Banks and Currency

New York is the nation's banking center. It has a wealth of local, regional, and major national banks, plus many retail branches of the leading foreign banks. HSBC is well represented in the city; the banks of Australia, Canada, Ireland, Japan, and Turkey also all have offices or branches. Exchange bureaux are located in airports, the major train stations, and in various locations throughout the city.

American Express credit cards

Banking

New York banks are generally open weekdays from 9am to 6pm. Several banks open earlier or close later to suit commuters' needs, and many now stay open on Saturday 9am–4pm. Tellers are available to help customers in the bank, or you can use a cash withdrawal machine (ATM). Not all retail banks exchange foreign currency or cash traveler's checks. Your best bet for the latter is American Express Travel Services.

ATM for cash withdrawal

ATMs

Automated teller machines (ATMs) can be found in most bank lobbies. They enable you to obtain American currency 24 hours a day from your bank account using a debit or credit card. ATMs usually issue American bank notes in $20 denominations. Among the many advantages of ATMs is the swift, secure exchange of your money at the wholesale rate used between the banks. Bank fees are generally much lower than those charged by money-exchange offices (typically $3 per withdrawal). Before you leave for New York,

ask your bank which New York City banks and ATM systems will accept your bank card and what fees and commissions will be charged on each transaction. Most ATMs are part of either the Cirrus or the Plus network. They accept various US bank cards, MasterCard and Visa cards, and certain others.

Always be aware of your surroundings when using an ATM. Make sure you shield your PIN and, if available, use a machine located within the bank. Be careful when removing your card at the machine.

Credit Cards, Traveler's Checks, and Currency Exchange

MasterCard, **American Express**, **Visa**, and **Diners Club** cards are widely accepted throughout the United States, regardless of which company or bank issued them. These cards can also be used for purchases, as well as to obtain cash advances from ATMs. Before you travel, it is a good idea to phone your card provider and inform them that you will be abroad, or you may find that your card gets blocked when you start using it in New York. Charges may be higher when using a credit card – again, check with your bank before you leave. Most credit cards charge a foreign transaction fee between 1 and 3 per cent, when you buy something overseas.

In the United States, you can use a credit card to pay for most purchases in store and online. Major expenses such as tours, travel packages, and expensive rentals are all best paid for by credit card. Using a card also means that

you can avoid carrying large sums of money around with you.

Though traveler's checks are no longer widely used and cannot be cashed easily, even in US dollars (other currencies, including sterling, are almost never accepted in the US), many department stores, shops, hotels, and restaurants in New York still take them. **Thomas Cook** no longer issues checks (it prefers preloaded travel cards), though you can still cash American Express checks without a fee at Amex branches in New York.

Exchange rates for foreign currency are printed daily in *The New York Times* and *The Wall Street Journal* and may be posted in bank windows; you can also check www.xe.com.

Among the most well-established foreign-exchange brokers are **Travelex Currency Services Inc.** and American Express. When you use the services of a foreign-exchange broker, you will have to pay a fee, which will vary widely from one place to the next. There will also be a commis-sion. Unless it is necessary, avoid changing money at hotels or the airport, where rates are poor and fees, high.

Banking company **Chase** has over 400 locations where you can usually exchange money, and **TD Bank** also has branches throughout Manhattan, many of which are open on Saturdays and until 8pm on weekdays.

Wiring Money

In emergencies, you can arrange to have money wired to you through **MoneyGram** or **Western Union**, though there is a considerable fee.

Coins

American coins come in 1-, 5-, 10-, 25- and 50-cent pieces. A gold-tone $1 coin is also in circulation, as are the state quarters, which feature a historical scene on one side. One-dollar coins are not popular, however, and you will receive them mainly as change from vending machines. Each value of coin has a popular name: 25-cent pieces are called quarters, 10-cent pieces are called dimes, 5-cent pieces are called nickels, and 1-cent pieces are called pennies.

1-cent coin
(a penny)

5-cent coin
(a nickel)

10-cent coin
(a dime)

25-cent coin
(a quarter)

1-dollar coin

Bank Notes (Bills)

The units of currency in the United States are dollars and cents. There are 100 cents to a dollar. Bank notes come in the following denominations: $1, $5, $10, $20, $50, and $100. Security features include subtle color hues and fraud-busting color-shifting ink in the lower right-hand corner of the face of each note.

1-dollar bill ($1)

5-dollar bill ($5)

10-dollar bill ($10)

20-dollar bill ($20)

50-dollar bill ($50)

100-dollar bill ($100)

Communications and Media

New York is the headquarters of almost all the major television news organizations and book and magazine publishers in the country. The variety of readily available local newspapers and magazines makes it easy for visitors to keep up with world news as well as the latest dining and entertainment options in the city. The wide use of cell phones and the Internet has changed the communications picture in most of the world, and New York is no exception. Though some public telephones may still be found in hotel lobbies and on some streets, they have largely been replaced by cell phones. When it comes to the Internet, Wi-Fi is available for free all over the city, with the number of Internet cafés dwindling.

Using a laptop in the New York Public Library

Reaching the Right Number

- Six area codes are used in New York: 212 and 646 in Manhattan; the other boroughs use 929, 718, and 347; and 917 is for cell-phones citywide. Calls to 800, 888, 866, and 877 numbers are free.
- To call any number in Manhattan, even in your same area code, you must first dial 1.
- To make an international direct call, dial 011 followed by the country code (Australia: 61; New Zealand: 64; UK: 44), then the city or area code (minus the first 0) and the local number.
- International directory Enquiries are on 00. International operator assistance is on 01.

Internet

Visitors will find many ways to access the Internet in New York, but you will have a lot more freedom using your own device. Almost all major hotels offer the use of computers, but some hotel business centers can be expensive. There are now very few Internet cafés in New York; dependable options include **Internet Garage** in Brooklyn. Another alternative is to stop by a branch of the **New York City Public Library**, where free Wi-Fi (network NYPL) and free computer internet access are available. To use the computers, you need to get a guest pass at the main library building, which can be acquired by bringing proof of your identity and current home address. With the pass, you can reserve time slots for computers at any branch, in person or via nypl.org.

There are free Wi-Fi hotspots in most subway stations and places such as Times Square and Bryant Park, and complimentary connections at most hotels and cafés such as Starbucks.

Cell Phones

Visitors who wish to use their own cell phone in the US will need a tri-band phone and a SIM card that has been set up for "roaming." Ask your cellphone provider if you are unsure whether your phone is ready to be used abroad; all iPhones should be usable.

Roaming charges, especially for data, can be extortionate. Note that you are charged for the calls you receive as well as for the calls you make; even checking voicemails can result in a hefty charge. However, some cell-phone companies offer "bundles" of calls to save costs while you are away.

If you have a compatible, unlocked GSM phone and intend to use it a lot, it would be cheaper to buy a local SIM card. **AT&T** is your best option. Some networks also sell basic phones (with minutes; no paperwork or ID required), which means you will get a US number. **Cellhire** offers rentals at competitive rates, with multiple pricing options for phone, data, and overseas usage.

Public Telephones

If you can find a public telephone, you will see that the setup is standard. Most phones are coin-operated and take 5-, 10-, and 25-cent coins. A local call within New York costs 25 cents for three or four minutes, depending on the carrier. Calls elsewhere within the US, are usually 25 cents for one minute; overseas long-distance rates are pricier and it is better to use a prepaid calling card ($5, $10, and $20), which you can buy at most grocery stores and newsstands. Regulations require each public pay phone to post information about charges, toll-free numbers, and how to make calls using other carriers.

US Postal Service logo

US Postal Service logo

Postal Services

The city's main **General Post Office** *(see p131)* is open 24 hours a day. Stamps can be bought here, from branch offices, and from some drugstores and newsstands. As well as at post offices, letters can be mailed at your hotel's concierge desk (which usually sells stamps too); in letter slots in office-building lobbies; and in street mailboxes. These are usually painted blue, or red, white, and blue. The mail is generally not picked up on Sundays. Post offices are shown on the Street Finder maps *(see pp386–419)*.

All letters are sent first class. The post office also offers several special-delivery services: Priority Mail Express service, for next-day delivery; Global Express Guaranteed, which delivers overseas in one to three business days; and Priority Mail Express International, with delivery in three to five days. Private courier services such as **FedEx**, **UPS**, or **DHL** can be arranged through hotels. Online services are available.

Newspapers and Magazines

New York has two major daily newspapers, *The New York Times* and *The Wall Street Journal*, and two colorful tabloids, The *Daily News* and the *New York Post*. Two free morning tabloids are also available, *AM New York* and *Metro*. Both are useful for local events and a brief rundown of the news. The best entertainment listings are found in the Friday and Sunday editions of *The New York Times* and in weekly magazines such as *Time Out New York* (free on Wednesdays), *New York*, and *The New Yorker*. *The Village Voice*, a free weekly newspaper, also has entertainment listings, geared largely to a younger audience.

The free weekly *Where New York Magazine*, distributed through hotel concierges, lists major museums, their opening hours, and any exhibitions.

You can buy foreign newspapers at **Around the World**, **Barnes & Noble** bookstores, airports, and some hotels.

Television and Radio

TV program schedules for each day can be found in the local dailies. The *Daily News* on Sunday has a useful pull-out section of the next week's programs. The choice of TV stations in New York is vast. Major networks include CBS on channel 2, NBC on channel 4, ABC on channel 7, and WNYW (Fox) on channel 5. PBS offers cultural and educational fare on channel 13. Cable TV offers everything from the Arts & Entertainment Network to sports on ESPN and public-access programs.

AM radio stations include WCBS News (880AM), WINS News (1010AM), and WFAN Sports (660AM). Some FM stations are: WWFS – contemporary (102.7FM); WBGO – jazz (88.3FM); and WQXR – classical (105.9FM). It is possible to get BBC World Service programs on WNYC (93.9FM or 820AM).

Express Mail

Priority Mail

Standard Mail

GETTING TO NEW YORK CITY

A lot of global airlines run direct flights to New York. The city is also very well served by charter and domestic services. Price wars among airlines have reduced fares, and domestic flights are a relatively affordable form of travel. Early reservation and seat selection are good ways to ensure a more comfortable flight. New York City is also a regular docking point for many cruise ships.

The train network across the United States is not as extensive as the ones found in Europe, but Amtrak, the national carrier, has several comfortable and clean long-distance trains that run from New York. Interstate and long-distance buses are a cheaper way to travel and usually have air conditioning and on-board toilets. For information on arriving in New York, see the map on pages 376–7.

Taxis heading into LaGuardia airport

Air Travel

New York can be reached by air direct from most major cities. The flight from London takes about 8 hours; however, there are no direct flights from Australia or New Zealand. Instead, the airlines fly to the West Coast or Asia, which takes around 10–14 hours, land, refuel, and then continue on to New York.

Allow extra time at the airport, for both arriving and departing, and for the careful passport and security checks in the United States.

Among the main airline carriers to New York are **Air Canada**, **Delta**, **British Airways**, **American Airlines**, **Virgin Atlantic**, and **United Airlines**. All international flights arrive at either JFK or Newark airports.

Tickets and Fares

APEX (Advance Purchase Excursion) tickets for the scheduled airlines are usually the cheapest return fares apart from package tours. They must be bought at least 14 days in

advance and are valid for a stay of 7–30 days. The least expensive international air fares to and from Europe are found from November to March, excluding holiday periods. Budget airlines flying within the US – such as **Southwest Airlines**, **JetBlue**, and **Frontier** – often have better fares than the major airlines.

Booking online can help save money. Websites such as www.lastminute.com, www.priceline.com, and www.expedia.com have flight-and-hotel deals that tend to be cheaper than booking the two separately. Search engines including www.kayak.com are useful for comparing the costs of all the different airlines and online travel stores.

On Arrival

Be prepared for lengthy security precautions when you visit the United States. Make sure that you leave ample time for checking in – ask your flight carrier what time you need to arrive at the airport for your flight. They can also give you details about any restrictions on hand luggage.

The airline you are flying with will give you a US Customs form to fill out before you land. It asks simple questions such as your name, birth date, country of citizenship, passport number, and current address. Have this form and your passport ready

for the Customs and Border Protection officer who will inspect your documents (get in the line that says "non-US passports"). The officer may ask you questions such as why you are visiting and how long and where you will stay. Your fingerprints will be taken, and you will be photographed with a digital camera. After you've collected your baggage, you must meet the customs inspectors once again and leave the customs form with them.

AirTrain en route to JFK

John F. Kennedy Airport (JFK)

Every year, over 50 million passengers pass through New York's main airport, JFK. It serves over 100 airlines in nine terminals and is the main New York entry for international flights. JFK lies 15 miles (24 km) southeast of Manhattan, in the borough of Queens, about 45–60 minutes from Midtown. However, airport traffic is often heavy, so the trip can take longer.

Larger carriers such as American Airlines, British Airways, Delta, and United Airlines have their own arrivals and departure terminals, which they may share with some of their partners. Terminal 4 is the main arrival area for over

Planes standing at Newark airport

50 international airlines, and Terminal 1 serves many foreign carriers, including Air China, Air France, Alitalia, and Japan Airlines.

Foreign-exchange offices and ATMs are located in all terminals, and each terminal has a service desk to help book hotels and answer any transportation questions. Courtesy phones are also provided by car-rental companies.

Dispatchers regulate the line for the yellow taxis waiting outside each terminal. There is a flat fee of $52, plus tolls and tip. NYC Airporter buses go to Grand Central, Penn Station, and the Port Authority; tickets start at $17. **SuperShuttle** runs shared vans that will go to specific addresses for about $25 for the first guest and $10 for each additional passenger. Advance reservations are needed for the trip back to the airport. Go Air-Link has a similar service for $25. Round-trip fares are cheaper.

A light-rail system, AirTrain JFK, connects to the A train at Howard Beach, and to the E, J, and Z trains and Long Island Rail Road (for Penn Station) at Jamaica. The AirTrain costs $5; the subway, $2.75 with a (MetroCard).

If you are feeling super rich, **Helicopter Flight Services** offer a 10-minute helicopter ride for over $1,600 to East 34th Street.

Newark Liberty Airport (EWR)

Newark, New York's second-largest International airport, is about 16 miles (26 km) southwest of Manhattan, in New Jersey.

Most international flights into Newark arrive at Terminal B. Baggage trolleys are free for passengers arriving on inter-national flights. Foreign-exchange desks and ATMs can also be found in the terminal, but there is no left-luggage room.

The Ground Transportation Services desk can help arrange private onward travel. Courtesy phones are provided by limousine and car-rental firms. Many of these have a free shuttle service to their rental offices.

As with JFK, there are taxi stands located outside most arrival areas, and uniformed taxi dispatchers will help you hail a cab. The taxi ride into Manhattan takes about 40–60 minutes and will cost you between $50 and $70, plus tolls and tip.

Newark Airport Express buses to Manhattan stop at the Port Authority Bus Terminal, 42nd Street near 5th Avenue, Penn Station, and Grand Central Terminal. The journey time is no longer than a cab, but the fare is only $16. Round-trip fares bring about an additional discount.

AirTrain Newark takes approximately 10 minutes to link to NJ Transit and Amtrak trains, which then take around 25 minutes to arrive at Penn station. The total journey costs about $12 on NJ Transit, or around $32 on Amtrak.

Hotels can be booked on arrival in all terminals at Newark through courtesy phones that link directly to various Manhattan hotels. Staff are on hand to help you make the best choice.

LaGuardia Airport (LGA)

LaGuardia is a busy airport serving domestic carriers from all over the US. It lies 8 miles (13 km) east of Manhattan, on the north side of Long Island, in Queens. The trip to Manhattan averages 30 minutes.

Upon arrival, you can rent luggage trolleys from the baggage-claim area next to the luggage carousels. Sky-caps, people who check in your luggage for you, are on hand to assist you. Baggage can also be left in the Tele-Trip business center on the departure level. A foreign-currency exchange desk and ATMs are located in the Central Terminal. A free bus service runs between each of the terminals and parking areas from 5am to 2am.

Buses and taxis into the city and its suburbs depart from the front of the terminal buildings. If you are approached by other taxis offering you transportation, do not accept. These drivers have no insurance, and you will be overcharged. A taxi fare starts at $3.30 and increases by $0.50 every fifth of a mile. A single bus ride is $2.75. The cost of tolls, plus a peak-hour surcharge of $1 (4–8pm) weekdays or a night surcharge of 50 cents (8pm–6am), will be added to the taxi fare shown on the meter.

Terminal at LaGuardia airport

RMS *Queen Mary 2* cruise liner docked in Brooklyn

Arriving by Sea

Cruising past the Statue of Liberty into New York harbor is a thrilling experience. The city's three cruise ports are popular stopping-off points for many major cruise lines sailing to the Caribbean, Bermuda, Canada, and Europe.

The main **New York Cruise Terminal**, on 12th Avenue between 46th and 54th streets, serves Carnival, Silversea, Holland America, MSC, and NCL lines. Taxis are available at the vehicle entrance, located at 55th Street and 12th Avenue. The M57 and M31 crosstown buses provide convenient, inexpensive access to midtown, and it is only a 15–20-minute walk to the heart of Manhattan.

The state-of-the-art **Brooklyn Cruise Terminal** was opened in 2006 in Red Hook. It is the port of choice for Cunard and Princess Cruise lines and the home port of the *QM2*, which sails to New York from Southampton several times a year. You can also take the *QM2* from New York to Australia and New Zealand. Taxis from the terminal can drop you in Manhattan or at convenient subway stops into the city.

Royal Caribbean and Celebrity cruise ships use the **Cape Liberty Cruise Port** in Bayonne, on the New Jersey side of New York Harbor. It is 7 miles (11 km) from New York City and about 15 minutes from Newark International Airport. The Hudson–Bergen Light Rail station at 34th Street, an easy taxi ride just 2 miles (3.2 km) from the port, connects to PATH trains,

New Jersey Transit at Hoboken, and ferry services to and from New York. Visit www.njtransit.com for more information.

Passengers arriving by ship who remain in New York receive the same US Customs form as air passengers and go through the same procedures; *see p372*.

Arriving by Long-Distance Bus

Long-distance buses from all over the US arrive at the **Port Authority Bus Terminal**, on Eighth Avenue, between 40th and 42nd streets. The location is convenient to Midtown, and many hotels are within walking distance. Taxis can be found on the Eighth Avenue side of the terminal; the A and C subway stops are located on the lower floors in the terminal; and a one-block-long tunnel leads to Times Square station and other subway connections. The M42 crosstown bus stops at the corner of Eighth Avenue and 42nd Street, and uptown buses are available on Eighth Avenue. Buses from the Port Authority connect with all three airports, and the terminal also serves many busy commuter bus lines to New Jersey. With over 6,000 buses arriving and departing daily, the atmosphere can be hectic at rush hour.

Buses can be an economical way to see the US. **Greyhound Lines** and other companies such as **BoltBus** offer exceptionally inexpensive rates, particularly when booked in advance. Buses are comfortable and air conditioned, and they have reclining

seats, ample legroom, and, usually, bathrooms. Greyhound **NeOn** buses – available from New York to Philadelphia (2 hours), Washington, DC (4 hours), Boston (4.5 hours), Toronto (11.5 hours), Montreal (8.5 hours), and other cities – offer free Wi-Fi and plug-ins for devices such as iPads.

Greyhound has a ticket office in the Port Authority Bus Terminal, but it is cheaper to buy tickets over the phone or online. APEX tickets save 25 per cent off the regular price on shorter trips purchased at least 14 days in advance, and 10 per cent (or more) for tickets bought seven days in advance. "Friends and family" rates offer savings of 50 per cent for up to three companions with the purchase of a regular adult fare. Seniors, students, and military personnel have special discounts.

Arriving by Train

Amtrak, the US passenger rail service, connects New York with the rest of the country and Canada. Amtrak trains use **Penn Station** as their New York headquarters. The Metro-North train service and the daily commuter service from upstate New York and Connecticut arrive at Grand Central Terminal.

Amtrak has its own section in Penn Station for ticket sales and separate waiting rooms for coach and high-speed passengers. Tickets can be bought in advance by phone or online and picked up at the station at the ticket window or at automated kiosks. If you pick up tickets at the window, a photo ID will be requested.

The imposing entrance hall of Grand Central Terminal

Taxis are available from the station, and buses run downtown on Seventh Avenue and uptown on Eighth. The Lexington and Broadway lines also serve the station.

Amtrak trains are very comfortable, with ample legroom and snack-bar services, as well as dining cars on longer routes. Sleeping compartments are available on long-distance trips, some with showers and toilets en suite.

Amtrak's USA Rail Pass allows eight journeys over a 15-day period for $459; children pay half-fare. The most used train service from New York is Amtrak's Northeast Corridor route between Boston, New York, Philadelphia, and Washington, DC. Most of the trains on this route have unreserved seating, but high-speed Acela Express trains offer an hourly service with reserved first-class and business-class seating plus electrical outlets for laptops.

Arriving by Car

Manhattan is an island, so it must be approached via bridge or tunnel. From the south, the

Brooklyn Bridge, which connects Manhattan and Brooklyn across the East River

entries are from New Jersey via the Holland Tunnel to the Financial District, or the Lincoln Tunnel to Midtown. A more scenic approach is the George Washington Bridge, which arrives at 178th Street to the north of the city.

The Robert Kennedy Bridge (formerly known as the Tri-borough Bridge) has branches from two boroughs connecting to Manhattan. The bridge from Queens, east of the city, is used by those arriving at LaGuardia or JFK airports. The second branch, from the Bronx, approaches Manhattan from the north.

The two bridges merge into one and offer a striking view of the city skyline on the approach.

Those driving in from Queens can avoid tolls by taking the 59th Street Bridge. Queens is also connected to Manhattan by the Midtown Tunnel, which feeds into the Long Island Expressway.

The most famous approach to New York is via the Brooklyn Bridge, with its vistas of the skyscrapers of the downtown Financial District. Brooklyn is also connected to the city by the Brooklyn Battery tunnel.

Bridge and Tunnel Tolls

Most of the major access routes in and out of New York City levy tolls. Tolls for the tunnels to and from Long Island and Brooklyn cost $8, as does the Robert Kennedy Bridge. The Lincoln Tunnel, Holland Tunnel, and the George Washington Bridge between New York and New Jersey are free for those leaving New York, but they charge $14 coming into the city. Tolls must be paid in cash. Avoid E-Z Pass lanes, marked with purple signs, which are only for holders of pre-paid passes.

DIRECTORY

Air Travel

Air Canada
Tel (888) 247-2262.
W aircanada.com

Airport Information Service
Tel JFK: (718) 244-4444.
EWR: (973) 961-6000.
LGA (718) 533-3400.
W panynj.gov/airports

American Airlines
Tel (800) 433-7300.
W aa.com

British Airways
Tel (800) AIRWAYS.
W britishairways.com

Delta
Tel (800) 241-4141.
W delta.com

Frontier Airlines
Tel (801) 401-9000.
W flyfrontier.com

Helicopter Flight Services
Tel (212) 355-0801.
W heliny.com

JetBlue
Tel (800) 538-2583.
W jetblue.com

Newark Airport Express
Tel 877-863-9275.
W coachusa.com

Southwest Airlines
Tel (800) 435-9792.
W southwest.com

SuperShuttle
Tel (212) 209-7000.
W supershuttle.com

United Airlines
Tel (800) 241-6522.
W united.com

Virgin Atlantic
Tel (800) 862-8621.
W virgin-atlantic.com

Arriving by Sea

Brooklyn Cruise Terminal
Pier 12, Building 112,
Bowne Street,
Red Hook.
Tel (718) 246-2794.
W nycruise.com

Cape Liberty Cruise Port
14 Port Terminal Blvd,
Bayonne.
Tel (201) 823-3737.
W cruiseliberty.com

New York Cruise Terminal
Pier 90, 711
12th Avenue.
Map 11 B4.
Tel (212) 246-5450.
W nycruise.com

Arriving by Long-Distance Bus

BoltBus
W boltbus.com

Greyhound Lines
Tel (800) 231-2222.
W greyhound.com

NeOn
W neonbus.com

Port Authority Bus Terminal
Eighth Ave and W 40th St.
Map 8 D1. Tel (212) 564-8484. W panynj.gov

Arriving by Train

Amtrak
Tel (800) 872-7245.
W amtrak.com

Penn Station
Eighth Ave & 31st St. Map
8 F3. W amtrak.com

Arriving in New York

This map shows the links between New York's three airports and the center of Manhattan. It also illustrates rail connections linking New York to the rest of the United States and Canada. Travel information, including times for bus and rail services, and connections to subway lines, is listed in each information box. The passenger ship terminal, New York's key point of arrival for the flood of postwar immigrants, is located on 55th Street. Port Authority Bus Terminal, on the West Side, provides services across the city.

Ships at the passenger terminal

🚢 **Passenger Ship Terminal**
Piers 88–92 for some cruise ships. Cunard and Princess services use Brooklyn Cruise Terminal.

Key

- ▬ New York Airport Service and SuperShuttle *see p373*
- ▬ Long Island Rail Road
- ▬ NJ Transit trains
- ▬ Newark Airport Express *see p373*
- ▬ AirTrain *see p373*
- ▬ Subway A *see p383*

🚌 **Port Authority Bus Terminal**
All long-distance buses arrive and depart here; links to all city airports.

🚉 **Penn Station**
Long-distance trains serve the US and **Canada**; commuter trains to **Long Island** and **New Jersey**; NJ Transit to **Newark Airport**.
🚉 Amtrak, Long Island Rail Road, and New Jersey Transit services.
Ⓜ A, C, E, 1, 2, 3.

Passenger Ship Terminal 🚢
○ Midtow
West an
the Thea
Distric

Port Authority Bus Terminal 🚌
○

Chelsea and the Garment District

Penn Statio
○

Super Shuttle buses take passengers to any point between Battery Park and 227th St.

Greenwich Village

East Village

SoHo and TriBeCa

Lower East Side

✈️ **Newark**
🚌 **Newark Airport Express** 4am–1am, every 15–30 mins to **Penn Station, Grand Central**, and **Port Authority**.
🚉 **New Jersey Transit or Amtrak to Penn Station** 5am–midnight, every 5–20 mins Mon–Fri; every 50 mins Sat & Sun.

Lower Manhattan and the Civic Center

0 kilometers 2
0 miles 1

The Port Authority of New York and New Jersey, operator of JFK, Newark, and LaGuardia airports, has invested in the AirTrain, a rail link that connects JFK and Newark to the city subway system.

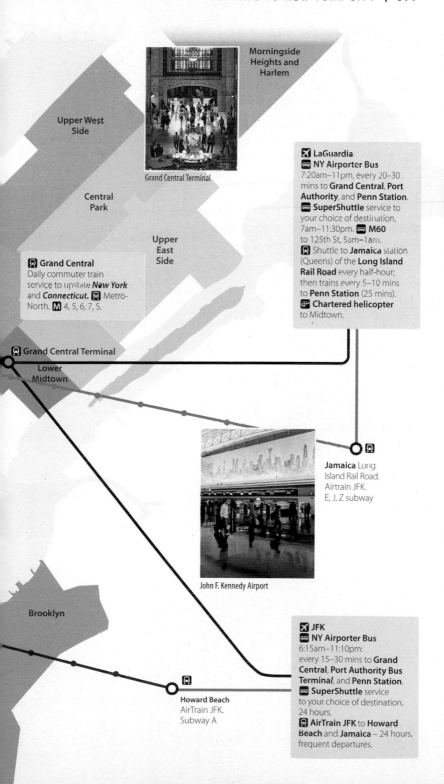

Morningside
Heights and
Harlem

Upper West
Side

Grand Central Terminal

Central
Park

Upper
East
Side

🚆 **Grand Central**
Daily commuter train
service to upstate *New York*
and *Connecticut*. 🚇 Metro-
North. Ⓜ 4, 5, 6, 7, S.

🚆 **Grand Central Terminal**

Lower
Midtown

✈ **LaGuardia**
🚌 **NY Airporter Bus**
7:20am–11pm, every 20–30
mins to **Grand Central**, **Port
Authority**, and **Penn Station**.
🚐 **SuperShuttle** service to
your choice of destination,
7am–11:30pm. 🚌 **M60**
to 125th St, 5am–1am.
🚆 Shuttle to **Jamaica** station
(Queens) of the **Long Island
Rail Road** every half-hour;
then trains every 5–10 mins
to **Penn Station** (25 mins).
🚁 **Chartered helicopter**
to Midtown.

Jamaica Long
Island Rail Road.
Airtrain JFK.
E, J, Z subway

John F. Kennedy Airport

Brooklyn

🚆 **Howard Beach**
AirTrain JFK.
Subway A

✈ **JFK**
🚌 **NY Airporter Bus**
6:15am–11:10pm:
every 15–30 mins to **Grand
Central**, **Port Authority Bus
Terminal**, and **Penn Station**.
🚐 **SuperShuttle** service
to your choice of destination,
24 hours.
🚆 **AirTrain JFK** to **Howard
Beach** and **Jamaica** – 24 hours,
frequent departures.

GETTING AROUND NEW YORK

With more than 6,000 miles (9,650 km) of streets, getting around New York might seem a problem, but the city is actually a network of small neighborhoods that are connected via subway or bus. Each one is also quite walkable or easy to get around on public transportation. Midtown Manhattan, for example, with many of the major sights, runs 25 blocks from 34th to 59th streets, and, if you should tire, you can hop on a bus that goes down Fifth Avenue or up Sixth.

Subways are the quickest way to get around. Service is frequent, inexpensive and reliable, and the trains make stops throughout Manhattan. The city's bus service is also reliable and convenient but can be slow in traffic. Weekly or unlimited MetroCards, valid for all public transportation, provide excellent value. Taxis are the best option for door-to-door transit, but they can be expensive if you are held up by traffic.

Green Travel

New York is working hard to be more energy-efficient for those traveling around town. Back in the 1990s, the city was a pioneer in launching an alternative-fuel vehicle program aimed at cutting emissions and making its bus fleet one of the cleanest in the world. It was the first in the US to switch all diesel buses to ultra-low-sulfur fuel. Cleaner-burning engines have been installed, and buses have been equipped with filters, cutting emissions by as much as 95 per cent. The MTA currently has around 2,000 hybrid-electric buses in operation. Numerous bicycle lanes have also been added around town for those brave enough to use them amid the heavy city traffic.

When it comes to leaving the city, the US train system is quite limited, but New York has some of the better connections, especially Amtrak's East Coast Metroliner and Acela trains *(see p374–5)*.

Cyclist in Central Park

Finding Your Way Around New York

Manhattan's avenues run north to south; New Yorkers say "uptown" and "downtown." Streets (except in the older areas) run east to west, and are referred to as "cross-town." Fifth Avenue is the divider between East and West street addresses.

Most streets in Midtown are one-way. In general, traffic is eastbound on even-numbered streets and westbound on odd-numbered streets. Avenues also tend to be one-way. First, Third (above 23rd Street), Madison, Avenue of the Americas (Sixth), Eighth, and Tenth avenues are northbound, while Second, Lexington, Fifth, Seventh, and Ninth avenues, and Broadway below 59th Street, are south-bound. There is two-way traffic

Finding an Address

A useful formula has been devised to help pinpoint any avenue address. By dropping the last digit of the address, dividing the remainder by 2, then adding or subtracting the key number given here, you will discover the nearest cross street. For example: to find No. 826 Lexington Avenue, you have to drop the 6; divide 82 by 2, which is 41; then add 22 (the key number). Therefore, the nearest cross street is 63rd Street.

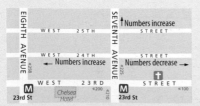

Avenue Address	Key Number
1st Ave	+3
2nd Ave	+3
3rd Ave	+10
4th Ave	+8
5th Ave, up to 200	+13
5th Ave, up to 400	+16
5th Ave, up to 600	+18
5th Ave, up to 775	+20
5th Ave 775–1286, do not divide by 2	-18
5th Ave, up to 1500	+45
5th Ave, up to 2000	+24
(6th) Ave of the Americas	-12
7th Ave below 110th St	+12
7th Ave above 110th St	+20
8th Ave	+10

Avenue Address	Key Number
9th Ave	+13
10th Ave	+14
Amsterdam Ave	+60
Audubon Ave	+165
Broadway above 23rd St	-30
Central Park W, divide full number by 10	+60
Columbus Ave	+60
Convent Ave	+127
Lenox Ave	+110
Lexington Ave	+22
Madison Ave	+26
Park Ave	+35
Park Ave South	+8
Riverside Drive, divide full number by 10	+72
St Nicholas Ave	+110
West End Ave	+60

Walking through Chelsea

on York, Park, 11th, and 12th avenues and on Broadway above 60th Street.

The grid of streets is rectangular rather than square, so crosstown blocks are longer than north–south avenue blocks. To gauge distances, 20 north–south city blocks equal about 1 mile (1.6 km); it takes only about five to eight crosstown (east–west) blocks to make up that distance.

Some streets have more than one name – for example, Avenue of the Americas is better known as Sixth Avenue. Park Avenue is called Park Avenue South below 34th Street and Fourth Avenue below 14th Street. The maps in this guide give the names most often used.

Planning Your Journey

Buses and subways are busiest during the rush hours: 8–10am and 4:30–6:30pm, Monday to Friday. Throughout these periods, it may be easier to face the crowds on foot than attempt any journey by bus, taxi, or subway. At other times of day and during certain holiday periods, the traffic is often much lighter, and you should reach your destination more quickly.

There are, of course, a few exceptions. When the president or other political celebrities visit, security measures can cause major disruption to the traffic. The area around Seventh Avenue, south of 42nd Street, is likely to be busy during the day with the truck and handcart traffic of New York's garment industry.

Avoid Fifth Avenue on parade days, which often take place in

spring and fall. On these days, and during the New York Marathon, it is difficult to get across town, as bus services are disrupted. If such events are scheduled during your visit, plan to see other areas of the city on that day. Subway traffic will not be affected, though trains may be more crowded than usual.

Driving in New York

Heavy traffic, lack of parking, and expensive rental cars make driving in New York a frustrating experience. If you decide to drive, you must wear a seat belt by law. Driving is on the right, and the speed limit is usually 30 mph (48 km/h) in Midtown. Most streets are one-way, and there are traffic lights at almost every corner. Unlike the rest of New York State, you can never turn right on a red light unless there is a sign indicating otherwise.

To rent a car, you must be at least 25 years old. You will need a valid driver's license, a passport, and a credit card.

Car Insurance

Unless you are adequately covered by your own insurance policy, you should take out damage and liability protection when renting a car. Check with your insurance company before you travel. Your car-rental agency will be able to provide you with a policy if necessary.

Parking

Finding a parking space in Manhattan is costly and difficult. You can use parking garages, or see if your hotel includes overnight parking, but both options are very expensive.

The busiest streets in Midtown do not allow parking. Other streets may have curbside meters for short-term (20–60 minutes) parking. Yellow street and curb markings mean no parking.

"Alternate-side" parking applies on most of the city's side streets. Cars may usually be left all day and night, but they must be moved to the other side of the street before 8am the next day. For specific information, call **311**.

Car-rental logos

Penalties

If you receive a parking ticket, you have seven days to pay the fine or to appeal. If you have any queries about your ticket, call the **Parking Violations Bureau**. If you cannot find your car, call 311 to find out if it has been towed. The **Traffic Department Tow Pound** is open 24 hours a day, Monday to Saturday. Redeeming your car will incur a $185 towing fee, $70 execution fee, and a $20-per-day storage fee. Traveler's checks, certified checks, money orders, and cash are accepted. If you have rented the car, the contract must be produced, and only the authorized driver may redeem the vehicle.

Vibrant Times Square with its neon billboards

Taxis driving through an intersection in SoHo

Taxis

There are more than 13,000 yellow cabs in New York, easily identified by their color, the distinctive logo on the door, and the light on top. A taxi can carry up to four passengers, with a single fare covering everyone on board. All taxis are metered and can issue printed receipts. Taxis can be hailed anywhere on the street, but taxi stands are scarce. Boro taxis operate in areas that aren't commonly served by yellow cabs, such as Brooklyn and Staten Island, but they need to be booked. The best places to find waiting cabs are outside Penn Station and Grand Central Terminal. Cabs indicate that they are available by turning on the top light. This goes off if the cab is occupied or if the side lights indicate "off duty."

Licensed taxis undergo periodic inspections and are insured against accidents and losses. Non-licensed, or "gypsy," cabs are unlikely to have these safeguards. They will have no meters and charge what they please.

Once the cab driver accepts a passenger, the meter starts ticking at $2.50, plus a state tax surcharge of 50 cents and an improvement surcharge of 30 cents. The fare increases 50 cents after each additional one-fifth of a mile or every 60 seconds of waiting time. There is an additional 50-cent charge from 8pm to 6am, and a $1 extra charge from 4 to 8pm on week days. It is customary to tip the driver about 15 percent. Taxi drivers will accept credit cards.

Make sure your driver understands where you want to go before you start your ride. If you have a map of the area, mark the locations you want. A driver should not ask you your destina-tion until after you've sat down, and by law must take you anywhere in the city. They must follow your requests not to smoke or talk on a cell phone, to open or close a window, and to pick up or drop off passengers as you direct. Each yellow cab displays the driver's photograph and registered number next to the meter. If drivers don't comply with your requests, you can report them to the **Taxi & Limousine Commission**.

The use of taxi apps has increased, with Uber overtaking yellow cabs in 2015. The base fare for an Uber is $3, with an additional $2.15 per mile. Lyft and Gett offer similar rates.

Walking

All intersections have lamp-posts with clearly marked street names; most have electric traffic signals. The lights show red (stop) and green (go) for vehicles, and "Walk/Don't Walk" signals for pedestrians. Crossing while the "Don't Walk" sign is showing is not recommended, nor is crossing mid-block, referred to in the US as "jay-walking."

Vehicles in the US drive on the right, and there are no road markings for pedestrians indicating the direction of traffic. It is best to look both ways before you cross, and beware of vehicles turning the corner behind as you cross.

Signs in Midtown

Midtown has several small parks and plazas where visitors can rest. In the Broadway area you can have a rest with a Times Square view on the high tier of steps behind the TKTS booth (Broadway and 47th St). Some of the surrounding blocks are traffic-free and furnished with chairs. The traffic islands around the Lincoln Center also offer seating.

Ferries

The 24-hour **Staten Island Ferry**, also from Battery Park, travels the channel and offers splendid views of lower Manhattan, the Statue of Liberty, Ellis Island, the bridges, and Governors Island. The round trip is the best bargain in New York, since it's free.

Water Taxis

The **New York Water Taxi** is mainly a commuter service, but it also offers various tours and a weekend hop-on/hop-off sightseeing boat (mid-Apr–mid-Oct). The route is around New York harbor, between West 44th and East 34th streets, with stops including Chelsea Pier, Battery Park, South Street Seaport, the Brooklyn riverfront, and Long Island City. In summer, water taxis provide a service to a couple of man-made beaches in Long Island City and on Governors Island.

Guided Tours

Whichever way you choose to see New York – with the help of a knowledgeable

A water taxi crossing New York harbor

guide, a photographer, a pre-recorded walk, or an exciting trip in a helicopter, boat, or horse-drawn carriage – organized sightseeing trips can save a lot of time and effort. Walking tours give in-depth background information about specific neighborhoods and the city's history and architecture that you might not get on your own. The **Municipal Art Society** is renowned for its knowledge-able guides. Fascinating behind-the-scenes tours are available for the New York Public Library, Metropolitan Opera, and Radio City Music Hall.

Bus tours are also a great way to see the city, as you can hop on/hop off as you please *(see also p385)*. The **Circle Line** runs several ferry services a day to the Statue of Liberty and Ellis Island from Battery Park, at the southern tip of Manhattan.

Cycling

Hoping to cut down on auto traffic, the city is making a real effort to create bike paths, which are a great way to see the city. . It takes courage to travel beside heavy traffic on busy Midtown streets; however, trails along the East River and far west side are pleasant and very popular, as are the many roads for bikers in Central Park, where auto traffic is banned on weekends. Visit www.nycbikemaps.com for bike routes. You can rent bikes at Columbus Circle or through the Citi Bike scheme *(see p356)*.

DIRECTORY

Car-Rental Agencies

Avis
Tel (800) 331-1212.
W avis.com

Budget
Tel (800) 527 0700.
W budget.com

Hertz
Tel (800) 654-3131.
W hertz.com

National
Tel (800) CAR RENT.
W nationalcar.com

Parking

Alternate Side Parking Information
Tel 311.

Parking Violations Bureau
Tel (718) 802-3636.

Parking Violations and Towing Information
Tel 311.

Police
Tel 911.

Traffic Department Tow Pound
Pier 76, W 38th St and 12th Ave. **Map** 7 B1.
Tel 311.

Taxis

Taxi & Limousine Commission
Tel 311.

Taxi Lost and Found
Tel 311.

Transportation Department
Tel 311.

Ferries

Staten Island Ferry
W siferry.com

Water Taxis

New York Water Taxi
Tel (212) 742-1969.
W nywatertaxi.com

Guided Tours

Big Apple Greeters
1 Centre St, Suite 2035.
Map 4 F4.
Tel (212) 669-8159.
W bigapplegreeter.org

Big Onion Walking Tours
476 13th St, Brooklyn.
Tel (212) 439-1090.
W bigonion.com

Bike the Big Apple
Tel (347) 878-9809.
W bikethebig apple.com

Boat Tours: Circle Line Sightseeing Yachts
Pier 83, W 42nd St.
Map 7 A1.
Tel (212) 563-3200.
W circleline42.com

Building Tours: Grand Central Terminal
E 42nd St at Park Ave.
Map 13 A5.
Tel (212) 883-2420.
W grandcentral terminal.com

Bus Tours: Gray Line of New York
42nd St and Eighth Ave.
Map 8 D1, Tel (212) 397-2620. W newyorksight seeing.com

Carriage Tours

59th St at Fifth Ave and along Central Park S.
Map 12 F3.
W nycarriages.com

Circle Line Downtown
W circlelinedown town.com

Harlem Spirituals, Inc.
690 Eighth Ave, **Map** 8 D1. Tel (212) 391-0900.
W harlemspirituals.com

Helicopter Tours: Liberty
Downtown Manhattan Heliport, 6 East River Piers. **Map** 2 D4.
Tel (800) 542-9933.
W libertyhelicopter.com

Heritage Trails
Federal Hall, 26 Wall St.
Map 1 C3.
W nps.gov/feha

Lower East Side Tenement Museum
108 Orchard St. **Map** 5 A4.
Tel (212) 431-0233.
W tenement.org

Metropolitan Opera Tours
Lincoln Center. **Map** 11 C2.
Tel (212) 769-7020.
W metoperafamily.org

Municipal Art Society
488 Madison Ave. **Map** 13 A4. Tel (212) 935-3960.
W mas.org

Museum at Eldridge Street
12 Eldridge St. **Map** 5 A5.
Tel (212) 227-8780.
W eldridgestreet.org

NBC Studio Tour

30 Rockefeller Plaza.
Map 12 F5. **Tel** (212) 664-7174 W thetouratnbc studios.com

New York Public Library
Fifth Ave and 42nd St.
Map 8 F1. **Tel** (917) 275-6975. W nypl.org

Radio City Music Hall Stage Door Tours
Sixth Ave. **Map** 12 F4.
Tel (212) 247-4777.
W radiocity.com/tours

Spirit of New York
W 23rd and Eighth Ave.
Map 8 D4. **Tel** (866) 211-3805. W spiritcruises.com

Walkin' Broadway
239 W 49th St. **Map** 11 C5.
Tel (212) 997-5004.
W walkinbroadway.com

Walking Tours: Adventures on a Shoestring
300 W 53rd St. **Map** 12 E4.
Tel (212) 265-2663.

Wall Street Walks
Tel (212) 209-3379.
W wallstreetwalks.com

World Yacht, Inc.
Pier 81, W 41st St. **Map** 7 A1. **Tel** (212) 630-8100.
W worldyacht.com

Cycling

Central Park Bike Rental
892 9th Ave. **Map** 12 E3.
Tel (212) 664-9600.
W bikerental centralpark.com

Traveling by Subway

The subway is the quickest and most reliable way to travel in the city. The vast system extends over 233 route miles (375 km) and has 469 stations. Most routes operate 24 hours a day throughout the year. The trains are air conditioned, well lit, safe, and (unless you are riding at rush hour) comfortable. Since the 1980s, a portion of all station-improvement funds has gone to the Arts for Transit project, with some notable results. Keep an eye out for the mosaics, sculptures, and artworks that decorate many subway and commuter rail stations.

Entrance to Times Square 42nd Street subway station

Tickets and Fares

A MetroCard must be purchased to enter the subway. The fare is $2.75 no matter how far you travel; if you buy a single-use ticket, though, the price rises to $3. If you are making several trips, buy a weekly unlimited ticket, and the cost per journey will work out to be less. Or, if you get a Pay-Per-Ride MetroCard and put $5.50 or more on it, you will receive an 11 per cent bonus credit. Metro-Cards, which can also be used on buses (see pp384–5), are sold at newsstands, drug-stores, and other locations around the city, as well as at all subway stations, where you can pay with cash. The machines take cash and debit and credit cards. One transfer per ride is allowed between the subway and bus; it must be used within 2 hours.

Using the Subway

Enter the subway by swiping your MetroCard at the turnstiles; the card is not needed to exit. Look for signs for uptown (northbound) and downtown (southbound) trains. Note that there are two types of trains: local trains stop at all stations, while faster express trains make fewer stops. Express lines have different letters or numbers than local ones; both types of stops are distinguished on every subway map.

Subway Stations

Many subway entrances are marked by illuminated spheres: green where the station booth is manned around the clock, red where there is restricted entry. Others are marked simply by a sign bearing the name of the station and the numbers or letters of the routes passing through it. Although the subway system runs 24 hours a day, not all routes operate at all times, though each station is still served. The basic service is between 6am and midnight. The most crowded periods are the week-day rush hours (6–8:30am and 4:30–6:30pm); it is best to avoid these times if you can. If not,

New York City Subway

New York subway logo

Reading the Subway Map

Each route is identified on the subway map (see inside back cover) by color, by the names of the stations at each end of the line, and by a letter or number. Local and express stops and interchange points are also identified. The letters and numbers below the station names indicate which routes serve that particular station. A letter or number in heavy type indicates that trains on that route stop there between 6am and midnight; letters in lighter type mean that the route is served by a part-time service only; a boxed letter or number shows the last stop on the line. Express trains are indicated on subway maps with a white (rather than solid) circle. The maps posted in all the subway stations have a comprehensive guide that explains the trains and timetable of each route. Note that New Yorkers refer to subway lines by letter or number, not by color.

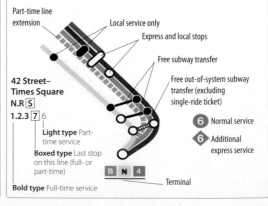

Traveling by Subway

Subways run north–south up and down the city; the N, R, E and F trains run east–west from Midtown to Queens. See below for the most useful routes.

1 There is a map of the subway system on the back inside cover of this book. Large-scale maps are also positioned in prominent areas in every station. Maps are also available at www.mta.info and at subway stations.

3 Use MetroCard to pass through the turnstile onto the platform.

6 On every platform, you will find a large subway map, while on each train there is a system map next to the door on both sides of the car. Newer trains have electronic route maps for that line that light up overhead. Stops are announced on the public address system, and you will see station names at each platform. The doors are operated by the conductor.

2 Buy a MetroCard from a station subway booth or MetroCard vending machine. The machines accept most credit and debit cards and bills up to $50, but no pennies. Vending machines can also be used to refill MetroCards.

4 Follow the directions for the train you want. For safety, stay in sight of the booth as you wait for your train; at night, stay in one of the yellow off-hours waiting areas.

5 Each train displays its route number or letter in the appropriate color and the names of the terminal stations.

7 After leaving the train, look for signs giving directions to the exit. If you need to change trains, just follow the signs to the connecting platforms.

during crowded times the first and last cars are usually less busy.

The subway is generally quite safe, but visitors may feel more secure riding during the day and until around 10pm, when there are many other passengers around. If you feel unsure, stand in the "Off-Hours Waiting Area" on the platforms. In an emergency, contact either the station agent in the station booth or a member of the train crew, who are located in the first car and in the middle of the train.

Subway Lines

Subways run north–south on Lexington, Sixth Avenue, Seventh Avenue, Broadway, and Eighth Avenue, with trains mostly running along one avenue. The #7 train runs west–east into Queens, while the E, F, M, N, Q, and R travel south–north until around Midtown, and then east into Queens. A shuttle train connects Grand Central–42nd

Street to Times Square–42nd Street. Some stations, such as those at Times Square, Union Square, and Columbus Circle, are convenient transfer points, where several lines converge.

Each subway line has a distinct color, while the routes on each line are identified either by letter or number. For example, the Lexington Avenue line is green and the #6 is a local train, while #4 and #5 run express. The Eighth Avenue line is blue, and the A train is the express, while C and E are local trains. First and last stops are posted on track signs and on each car. Large system maps are posted in all stations. Free individual subway maps are usually available from booth attendants.

Some lines are especially useful for visitors. The Lexington Line is the only one serving the East Side and its many museums. The #6 train stops near the Guggenheim, the

Metropolitan Museum of Art, and the Frick Collection. The red #1 Broadway/Seventh Avenue line on the West Side takes you to Lincoln Center, MoMA, Times Square, Greenwich Village, SoHo, the Financial District, and South Ferry, where you can catch a ferry to the Statue of Liberty.

Track work at weekends can cause changes to the schedule. When you enter, ask the booth attendant about changes that may affect your journey.

DIRECTORY

MTA Automated

Travel Planner

W tripplanner.mta.info

Subway Information

Tel 511.

W mta.info

Traveling by Bus

Traveling by bus is a good way to take in many of New York's sights. The city's 4,000-plus blue-and-white buses cover more than 200 routes in the five boroughs. Many run 24 hours a day, every day. The buses are modern, clean, air-conditioned, and energy-efficient. They are also quite safe and tend not to get crowded, except during rush hours. Smoking and eating are forbidden on all public buses, and only service animals (guide dogs) are allowed on board.

Bus stop in Midtown Manhattan

Tickets and Fares

You can pay the $2.75 fare on a bus using a MetroCard (see p382), or exact change in coins. Bus drivers cannot make change, and fare boxes do not accept dollar bills, half-dollars, or pennies. You can buy a Metro-Card at any subway station booth or machine and at many other outlets around the city.

If you need to take more than one bus to reach your destination, you are eligible for a free transfer. If you pay your fare with a MetroCard, transfers to bus or subway are automatically placed electronically on the card. If you use cash, ask the driver for a transfer ticket when you pay. Transfers are good for 2 hours.

Senior citizens with proof of age and the disabled pay half-fare. All buses can "kneel," lowering the steps to help elderly people to board (see p364). They are also accessible to wheelchairs via a lift with ramp, at the rear or front depending on the bus design.

Bus Stops

Buses will stop only at designated bus stops. They follow north–south routes on the major avenues, stopping every two or three blocks. Crosstown buses run east–west and usually stop at every block, with the exception of Park Avenue, which is skipped by some lines. Many routes run a 24-hour daily service.

Bus stops are marked by red, white, and blue signs, and yellow paint along the curb. Most also have bus shelters; newer shelters provide seating and helpful signs giving the location. A route map and schedule is posted at each stop. Buses use letters to indicate the boroughs they serve: M for Manhattan, B for Brooklyn, Bx for the Bronx, and Q for Queens. Bus stops often serve several routes, so check the maps at the stop for your route, then look for that route number posted on the lighted strip above the windshield on the front of the bus.

Some buses will be marked "Limited," indicated by a flashing sign in the route number space and by a card in the front window. These buses are faster since they make fewer stops, but be sure the stops they do make are near your destination. Limited buses do stop at streets connecting to crosstown buses.

Free city bus maps are often available on board; ask the driver for a copy.

Using Buses

Most buses run every 3–5 minutes during the morning and evening rush hours, and every 7–15 minutes from noon to 4:30pm and from 7 to 10pm. Bad traffic or adverse weather conditions can cause delays. Service is reduced on weekends and holidays.

Enter the bus at the front door. If you are unsure of your route, ask the driver if they will be stopping at your destination or close to it. The majority of New York's bus drivers are helpful and will call out your stop if you ask when you board. Put your MetroCard in the slot or drop the correct coins in the fare box, then look for a seat.

To request a stop when traveling on the bus, press the yellow vertical call strip between the windows. Some newer buses also have stop buttons on center poles. A "Stop Requested" sign near the driver will then light up. If the bus is crowded, it is wise to start moving toward the exit door when you are a few blocks from your stop.

Leave through the double door located toward the rear of the bus. The driver will activate the door release as soon as the bus has stopped, and a green light will go on above the door. You then push the yellow stripe on the door, and the doors will open automatically; they will stay open long enough for everyone to leave. If the strip does not work properly, just push the door and then hold it open for the passenger behind you as you leave.

The M86 crosstown bus traveling through Central Park

Night Buses

Most lines run 24 hours, but be sure to check the schedule posted at your stop. After 10pm, many buses run every 20 minutes or so. From midnight to 6am, expect to wait 30–60 minutes for a bus.

Bus Tours

One of the most popular ways to see the sights is aboard a hop-on/hop-off bus tour that allows you to get off wherever you like, stay as long as you want, and catch another bus when you are ready. Gray Line (see p381) is the best-known company offering these tours aboard double-decker buses. Routes include a Downtown Loop, Uptown Loop, Brooklyn Loop, and Night/Holiday Lights Tour (not hop-on/hop-off). Buy a 48- or 72-hour pass, and you can see a great deal of New York. While you ride, narration is available in several languages through rented headsets.

MTA Trip Planner

The MTA website has a useful feature known as the Trip Planner, which provides a map and directions by bus and/or subway between any two points in New York. Enter your starting and ending points, the time you expect to travel, preferred mode of transportation, how far you are willing to walk, and whether you need accessible vehicles, and you will get clear directions. Visit www.tripplanner.mta.info to access the planner.

DIRECTORY

MTA Travel Information

Tel 511.

ⓦ mta.info

Route Maps

Available from MTA/NYCT, Customer Service Center, 3 Stone St, Lower Manhattan. **Map** 1 C4.

Sightseeing Buses

For a pleasant and cheap alternative to a tour bus, hop on a city bus and see New York with the New Yorkers. Recommended bus routes include route M2, which runs down Fifth Avenue alongside Central Park and stops near the Guggenheim and the Met Museum. It then returns north on Madison Avenue (via the Empire State Building and the Rockefeller Center), where it runs alongside the M5, which continues south to SoHo and Greenwich Village. From Broad Street, head north on the M15 to visit Brooklyn Bridge and the United Nations, or take route M7 or M20 along Eighth Avenue for Times Square and Madison Square Garden.

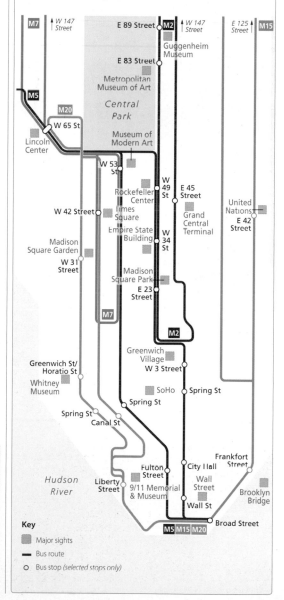

Key

■ Major sights

— Bus route

○ Bus stop (selected stops only)

STREET FINDER

The map references given with all sights, hotels, restaurants, shops, and entertainment venues described in this book refer to the maps in this section *(see How the Map References Work, opposite)*. These maps cover the whole of Manhattan and a key section of Brooklyn. A complete index of street names and all places of interest marked on the maps can be found on pages 411–19. The map *(below)* shows the areas covered by the *Street Finder*, within the various districts. The maps include all of Manhattan's sight-seeing areas (which are color-coded), with all the districts important for hotels, restaurants, bars, shops, theaters, and entertainment.

Shoppers in the neighborhood of Little Italy, on the Lower East Side

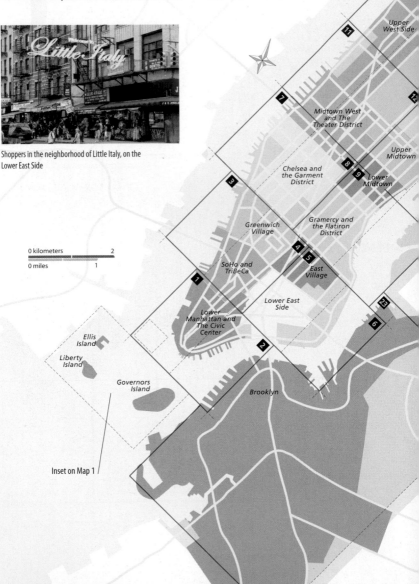

Key to Street Finder

- 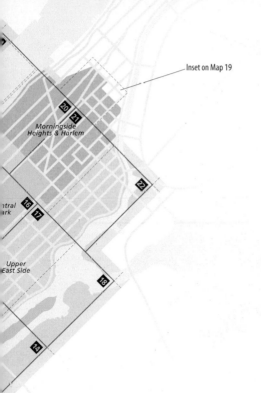 Major sight
- Other sight
- Railroad station
- M Subway station
- Heliport
- Ferry terminal
- Bus terminal
- Aerial tramway
- i Tourist information office
- Hospital with emergency room
- Police station
- Church
- Synagogue
- Railroad line
- Pedestrian street

Scale of map pages 1–22

0 meters	200	
0 yards	200	1:11,500

Scale of map page 23

0 meters	800	
0 yards	800	1:40,000

Inset on Map 19

Morningside
Heights & Harlem

Central
Park

Upper
East Side

How the Map References Work

The first figure tells you which Street Finder map to turn to.

❼ Theodore Roosevelt Birthplace

28 E 20th St. **Map 9 A5. Tel** 260-1616. **M** 14th St–Union Sq–23rd St. **Open** 9am–5pm Tue–Sat (last adm: 4pm). **Closed** public hols. hourly. Lectures, concerts, films, videos. **w** nps.gov/thrb

A letter and number give the grid reference. Letters go across the map's top and bottom; numbers, on its sides.

The map continues on map 5 of the Street Finder.

3

A

B

C

1

2

3

4

5

A

B

C

PIER 54

Fire Boat Station

PIER 53

PIER 52

PIER 51

PIER 46

PIER 45

PIER 40

PIER 34

PIER 26

Whitney Museum
of American Art

Hudson River

Tunnel

Holland

WEST STREET

THE HIGH LINE

LITTLE HIGH LINE

WEST 13TH STREET

WEST 12TH STREET

*The Meatpacking
District*

GANSEVOORT STREET

HORATIO STREET

JANE STREET

BETHUNE STREET

BANK STREET

WEST 11TH STREET

PERRY STREET

CHARLES LANE

CHARLES STREET

WASHINGTON STREET

WEHAWKEN STREET

BARROW STREET

MORTON STREET

LEROY STREET

CLARKSON STREET

HUDSON RIVER PARK

WASHINGTON STREET

WEST HOUSTON STREET

KING STREET

CHARLTON

VANDAM

SPRING STREET

RENWICK STREET

WEST STREET

CANAL STREET

WATTS STREET

DESBROSSES

VESTRY

LAIGHT

HUBE

GREENWICH STREET

WEST STREET

GREENWICH STREET

HUDSON STREET

GREENWICH STREET

WEST STREET

GREENWICH STREET

HUDSON STREET

HUDSON STREET

HUDSON STREET

HUDSON STREET

WASHINGTON STREET

TENTH AVENUE

ELEVENTH AVE

BLOOMFIELD STREET

JANE STREET

HUDSON STREET

EIGHTH AVENUE

GREENWICH AVENUE

WEST 12TH STREET

WEST 11TH STREET

WEST 4TH STREET

WAVERLY PLACE

SEVENTH AVENUE SOUTH

JACKSON SQUARE

St. Vincent's
Hospital

MULRY SQUARE

McCARTHY SQUARE

ABINGDON SQUARE

BANK STREET

BLEECKER STREET

PERRY STREET

CHARLES STREET

WEST 10TH STREET

Christopher St-
Sheridan Sq 1

SHERIDAN SQUARE

CHRISTOPHER STREET

BEDFORD STREET

GROVE STREET

COMMERCE ST

Grove
Court

75 1/
Bedfo
Stree

St. LUKE'S
GARDEN

Isaacs-
Hendricks
House

St. Luke's
Place

ST LUKE'S PLACE

JAMES J.
WALKER
PARK

HOUSTON STREET

Children's
Museum
of the Arts

GREENWICH STREET

HUDSON

Manhatta
Communi
Colleg

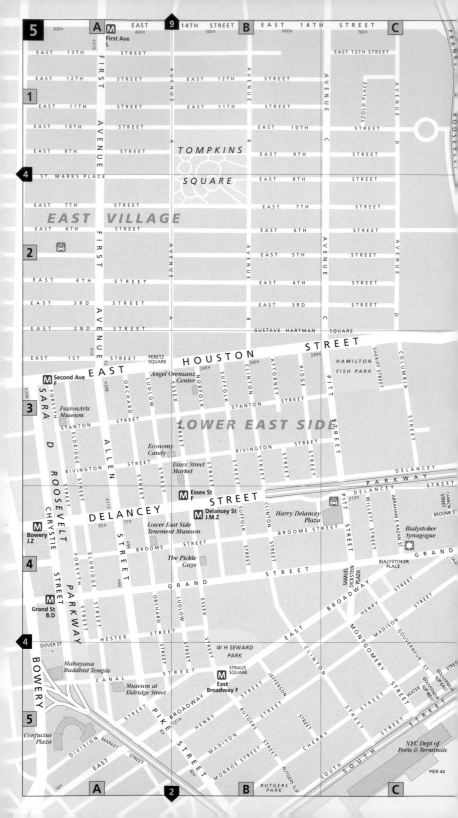

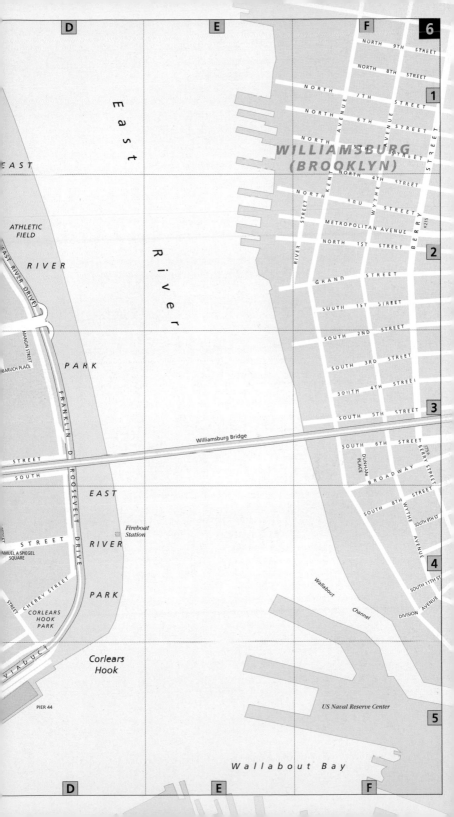

D

E

F

6

1

NORTH 9TH STREET

NORTH 8TH STREET

NORTH 7TH STREET

NORTH 6TH STREET

NORTH 5TH STREET

WILLIAMSBURG
(BROOKLYN)

NORTH 4TH STREET

NORTH 3RD STREET

METROPOLITAN AVENUE

NORTH 1ST STREET

GRAND STREET

SOUTH 1ST STREET

SOUTH 2ND STREET

SOUTH 3RD STREET

SOUTH 4TH STREET

SOUTH 5TH STREET

SOUTH 6TH STREET

BROADWAY

SOUTH 8TH STREET

E a s t

EAST

ATHLETIC
FIELD

RIVER

R i v e r

PARK

EAST RIVER DRIVE

MANGIN STREET

BARUCH PLACE

FRANKLIN D ROOSEVELT DRIVE

Williamsburg Bridge

STREET

SOUTH

EAST

RIVER

PARK

STREET

SAMUEL A SPIEGEL
SQUARE

STREET

CHERRY STREET

CORLEARS
HOOK PARK

VIADUCT

Corlears
Hook

PIER 44

Fireboat
Station

AVENUE 7TH

AVENUE

KENT AVENUE

WYTHE AVENUE

BERRY STREET

RIVER STREET

#215

DUNHAM PLACE

BERRY STREET

WYTHE AVENUE

SOUTH 9TH ST

SOUTH 11TH ST

DIVISION AVENUE

Wallabout
Channel

US Naval Reserve Center

Wallabout Bay

2

3

4

5

D

E

F

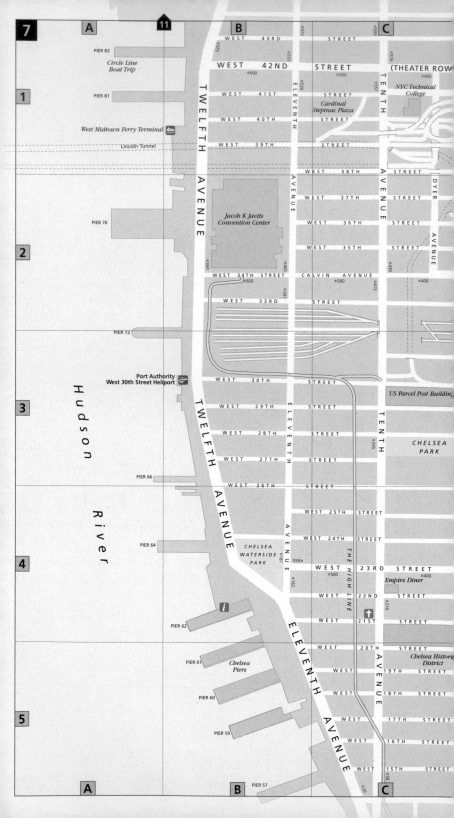

7

11

A | B | C

1

2

3

4

5

PIER 83

Circle Line
Boat Trip

PIER 81

West Midtown Ferry Terminal

Lincoln Tunnel

PIER 76

PIER 72

Port Authority
West 30th Street Heliport

PIER 66

PIER 64

CHELSEA
WATERSIDE
PARK

i

PIER 62

PIER 61

Chelsea
Piers

PIER 60

PIER 59

PIER 57

H u d s o n

R i v e r

WEST   43RD   STREET

WEST   42ND   STREET   (THEATER ROW)

WEST   41ST   STREET

NYC Technical
College

WEST   40TH   STREET

WEST   39TH   STREET

WEST   38TH   STREET

Jacob K Javits
Convention Center

WEST   37TH   STREET

WEST   36TH   STREET

WEST   35TH   STREET

WEST   34TH   STREET   CALVIN   AVENUE

WEST   33RD   STREET

US Parcel Post Building

WEST   30TH   STREET

WEST   29TH   STREET

WEST   28TH   STREET

CHELSEA
PARK

WEST   27TH   STREET

WEST   26TH   STREET

WEST   25TH   STREET

WEST   24TH   STREET

WEST   23RD   STREET

Empire Diner

WEST   22ND   STREET

WEST   21ST   STREET

WEST   20TH   STREET

Chelsea Historic
District

WEST   19TH   STREET

WEST   18TH   STREET

WEST   17TH   STREET

WEST   16TH   STREET

WEST   15TH   STREET

TWELFTH   AVENUE

ELEVENTH   AVENUE

TENTH   AVENUE

DYER   AVENUE

ELEVENTH   AVENUE

THE HIGH LINE

A | B | C

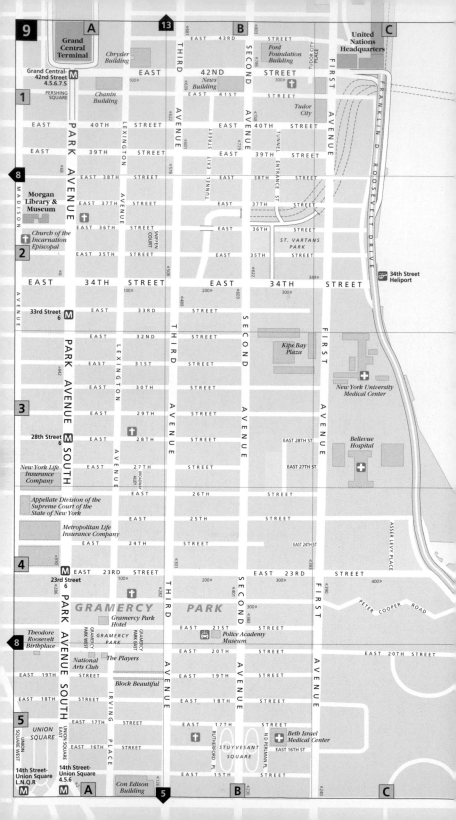

10

GANTRY
PLAZA
STATE PARK

49TH   AVENUE

Belmont
Island

50TH   AVENUE

5TH   STREET

VERNON   BLVD

JACKSON   AVENUE

11TH   STREET

Queens - Midtown Tunnel 495

51ST   AVENUE

AVENUE

BORDEN   AVENUE

M Vernon Blvd-
Jackson Ave
7

1

2ND   STREET

(FRONT)

Long Island City
Station

54TH (FLUSHING)   AVENUE

QUEENS
(LONG ISLAND CITY)

55TH   AVENUE

5TH   STREET

Newton Creek

MANHATTAN   AVENUE

STREET

BOX

45TH   STREET

2

56TH AVENUE

COMMERCIAL   STREET

CLAY   STREET

DUPONT   STREET

FRANKLIN   STREET

EAGLE   STREET

E   a   s   t

GREENPOINT
(BROOKLYN)

WEST   STREET

FREEMAN   STREET

GREEN   STREET

STREET

3

HURON   STREET

STREET

R   i   v   e   r

INDIA   STREET

JAVA STREET

Manhattan
Marina

KENT STREET

GREENPOINT
AVENUE

4

PIER 70

PIER 69

FRANKLIN D ROOSEVELT DRIVE (EAST RIVER DRIVE)

AVENUE C

PIER 68

PIER 67

5

AVENUE   C

EAST 16TH STREET

EAST 15TH STREET

A **15** B C

1

WEST 72ND STREET
«300 «200

VERDI
SQUARE
M 72nd Street
1.2.3

SHERMAN
SQUARE

The Dorilton

WEST 71ST STREET

WEST 70TH STREET

FREEDOM PLACE

WEST END AVENUE

UPPER
WEST SIDE

AMSTERDAM

BROADWAY

WEST 66TH STREET

The
Juilliard
School

Ac
Tr
Hi

2

CONRAIL
PIERS
(ABANDONED)

WEST 65TH STREET

WEST 64TH STREET

HENRY HUDSON PARKWAY

MILLER HIGHWAY

Lincoln
Center

Metropolitan
Opera House

Da
Geff
He

AMSTERDAM AVENUE

DAMROSCH
PARK
Guggenheim
Bandshell

Hudson

WEST 61ST STREET

WEST 60TH STREET

Fordham
University

3

River

PIER 99

PIER 98

PIER 97

New York City
Downtown Boathouse

PIER 96

WEST 59TH STREET

WEST 58TH STREET

WEST 57TH STREET
«600 «500 «400

WEST 56TH STREET

ELEVENTH AVENUE

«823

TENTH AVENUE

Roosevelt
Hospital
Center

PIER 95

WEST 55TH STREET

PIER 94

WEST 54TH STREET

DE WITT
CLINTON
PARK

WEST 53RD STREET

4

PIER 92

WEST 52ND STREET

N.Y.C. Passenger Ship Terminal
(Port Authority)

WEST 51ST STREET

PIER 90

WEST 50TH STREET

TWELFTH AVENUE

WEST 49TH STREET

ELEVENTH AVENUE

TENTH AVENUE

PIER 88

WEST 48TH STREET

HELL'S KITCHEN

WEST 47TH STREET

5

PIER 86

WEST 46TH STREET

Intrepid Sea, Air &
Space Museum

WEST 45TH STREET

AVENUE

PIER 84

«505 «589 «614

A **7** B WEST 44TH STREET C

15

A

20

B

C

RIVERSIDE
PARK

RIVERSIDE DRIVE EAST

RIVERSIDE DRIVE WEST

HUDSON PARKWAY

9 A

WEST 102ND ST
WEST 101ST STREET
WEST 100TH STREET
WEST 99TH STREET
WEST 98TH STREET
WEST 97TH STREET

BROADWAY

WEST END AVENUE

AMSTERDAM

1

96th Street
1.2.3

WEST 96TH STREET Ⓜ

WEST 95TH STREET
POMANDER WALK
WEST 94TH STREET
WEST 93RD STREET
WEST 92ND STREET
WEST 91ST STREET

AVENUE

UPPER
WEST
SIDE

2

JOAN
OF ARC
PARK

WEST 90TH STREET
WEST 89TH STREET ✤
WEST 88TH STREET
WEST 87TH STREET

BROADWAY

WEST END AVENUE

AMSTERDAM

Jewish
Center ✤

3

WEST 86TH STREET Ⓜ 86th Street
1
WEST 85TH STREET

EDGAR ALLAN POE STREET

WEST 83RD STREET
WEST 82ND STREET
WEST 81ST STREET
WEST 80TH STREET

RIVERSIDE DRIVE

AVENUE

Children's
Museum of
Manhattan

4

Hudson River

HENRY HUDSON PARKWAY

RIVERSIDE
PARK

Boat
Basin

WEST 79TH STREET ✝ Ⓜ 79th Street
1
WEST 78TH STREET
WEST 77TH STREET
WEST 76TH STREET
WEST 75TH STREET

BROADWAY

AMSTERDAM AVENUE

✝

5

WEST 74TH ST
Ansonia
Hotel

A

11

B

C

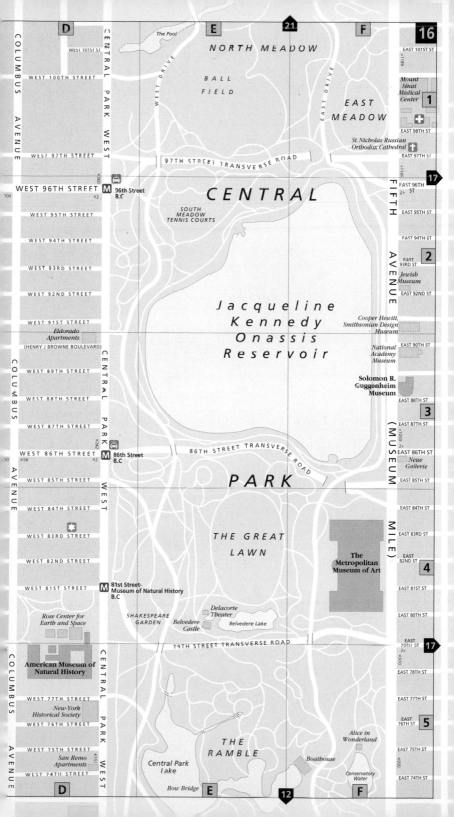

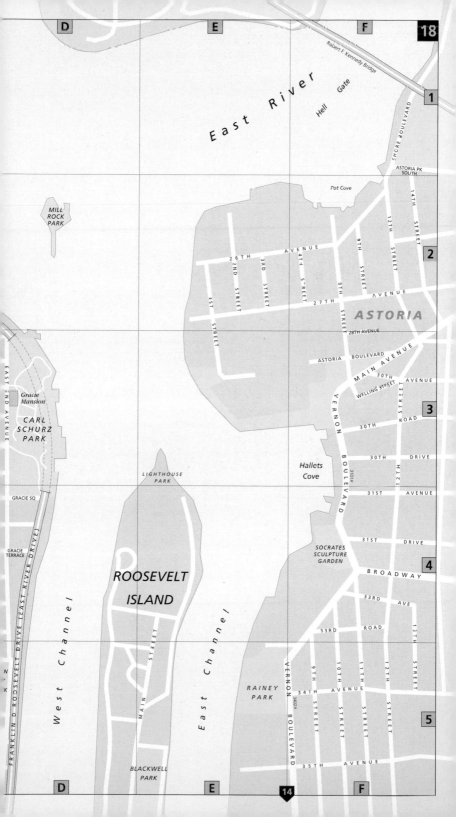

D · E · F · **18**

Robert F. Kennedy Bridge

E a s t   R i v e r   Hell   Gate

1

SHORE BOULEVARD

ASTORIA PK
SOUTH

Pot Cove

14TH
STREET

12TH
STREET

MILL
ROCK
PARK

2

9TH
STREET

26TH
STREET

2ND
STREET

3RD
STREET

4TH
STREET

A V E N U E

5
STREET

8TH
STREET

27TH

A V E N U E

ASTORIA

1ST
STREET

28TH AVENUE

ASTORIA   BOULEVARD

M A I N   A V E N U E

30TH

3

EAST END AVENUE

*Gracie
Mansion*

**CARL
SCHURZ
PARK**

WELLING STREET

A V E N U E

VERNON

30TH

STREET

ROAD

GRACIE SQ

LIGHTHOUSE
PARK

*Hallets
Cove*

30TH

DRIVE

12TH
STREET

310 ST

31ST

A V E N U E

GRACIE
TERRACE

B O U L E V A R D

31ST

DRIVE

**SOCRATES
SCULPTURE
GARDEN**

4

FRANKLIN D ROOSEVELT DRIVE (EAST RIVER DRIVE)

W e s t   C h a n n e l

**ROOSEVELT
ISLAND**

E a s t   C h a n n e l

B R O A D W A Y

33RD   AVE

33RD   ROAD

13TH
STREET

MAIN
STREET

**RAINEY
PARK**

VERNON

9TH
STREET

10TH
STREET

11TH
STREET

12TH
STREET

34TH   A V E N U E

340 ST

5

B O U L E V A R D

35TH   A V E N U E

**BLACKWELL
PARK**

D · E · **14** · F

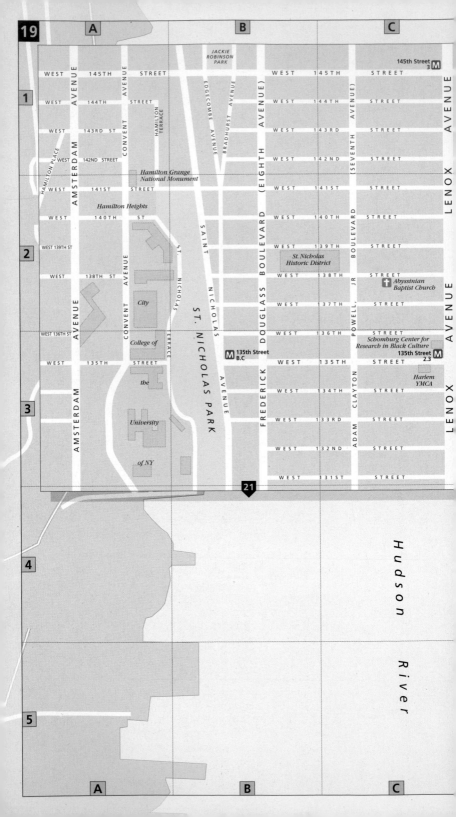

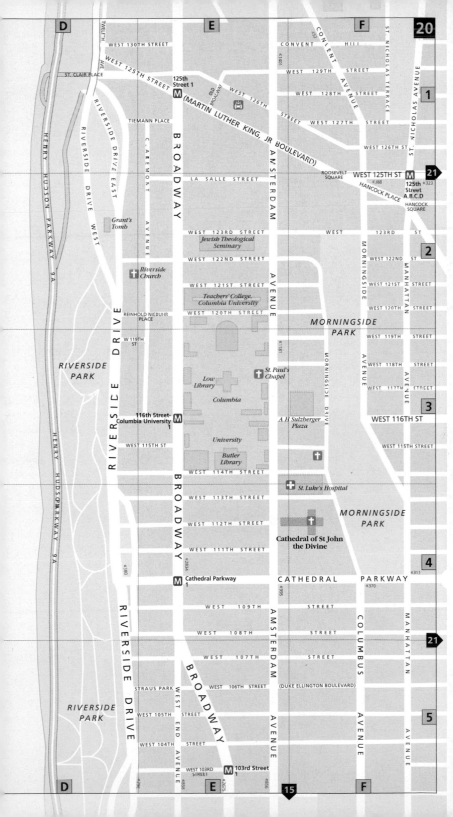

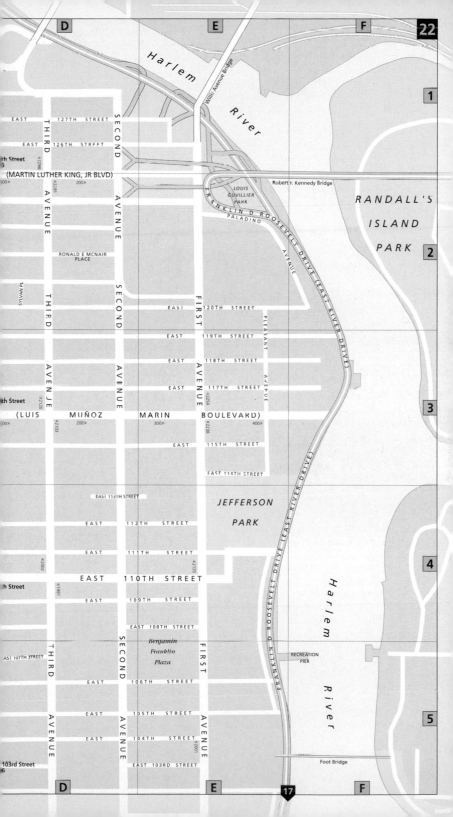

Street Finder Index

Each place name is followed by its borough (unless in Manhattan) and then by its Street Finder reference

Each place name is followed by its borough (unless in Manhattan) and then by its Street Finder reference

Each place name is followed by its borough (unless in Manhattan) and then by its Street Finder reference

General Index

Acknowledgments

Dorling Kindersley would like to thank the many people whose help and assistance contributed to the preparation of this book.

Main Contributor
Eleanor Berman has lived in New York for around 40 years. Her travel articles are widely published and she is the author of *Away for the Weekend: New York*, a favorite since 1982. Her other books include *Away for the Weekend* guides for the Mid-Atlantic, New England, and Northern California, *Travelling on Your Own* and *Reflections of Washington, DC*.

Other Contributors
Stephen Keeling.

Museum Contributors
Michelle Menendez, Lucy O'Brien, Heidi Rosenau, Elyse Topalian, Sally Williams.

Dorling Kindersley wishes to thank editors and researchers at Websters International Publishers: Sandy Carr, Matthew Barrell, Sara Harper, Miriam Lloyd, Ava-Lee Tanner, Celia Woolfrey.

Additional Photography
Rebecca Carman, Rachel Feierman, Steven Greaves, Michelle Haimoff Andrew Holigan, Edward Hueber, Eliot Kaufman, Karen Kent, Dave King, Norman McGrath, Howard Millard, Michael Moran, Ian O'Leary, Rough Guides/ Greg Roden, Rough Guides/Nelson Hancock, Rough Guides/Angus Oborn, Susannah Sayler, Paul Solomon, Chuck Spang, Chris Stevens, Peter Wilson.

Additional Illustrations
Peter Bull, Steve Gyapay, Arshad Khan, Kevin Jones, Dinwiddie MacLaren, Janos Marffy, Chris D. Orr, Nick Shewring, John Woodcock.

Cartography
Maps: Uma Bhattacharya, Andrew Heritage, Suresh Kumar, James Mills-Hicks, Chez Picthall, John Plumer (Dorling Kindersley Cartography), Kunal Singh. Advanced Illustration (Cheshire), Contour Publishing (Derby), Europmap Ltd (Berkshire). Street Finder maps: ERA-Maptec Ltd (Dublin) adapted with permission from original survey and mapping by Shobunsha (Japan).

Cartographic Research
Roger Bullen, Tony Chambers, Ruth Duxbury, Ailsa Heritage, Jayne Parsons, Laura Porter, Donna Rispoli, Joan Russell, Jill Tinsley, Andrew Thompson.

Design and Editorial
Managing Editor Douglas Amrine
Managing Art Editors Stephen Knowlden, Geoff Manders
Senior Editor Georgina Matthews
Series Design Consultant Peter Luff
Editorial Director David Lamb
Art Director Anne-Marie Bulat
Production Controller Hilary Stephens
Picture Research Susan Mennell, Sarah Moule
DTP Designer Andy Wilkinson
Revisions and Relaunch Team Keith Addison, Namrata Adhwaryu, Umesh Aggarwal, Asad Ali, Emma Anacootee, Lydia Baillie, Kate Berens, Eleanor Berman, Vandana Bhagra, Subhashree Bharati, Shruti Bahl, Jon Paul Buchmeyer, Ron Boudreau, Linda Cabasin, Rebecca Carman, Michelle Clark, Sherry Collins, Carey Combe, Diana Craig, Maggie Crowley,

Guy Dimond, Vidushi Duggal, Nicola Erdpresser, Rhiannon Furbear, Fay Franklin, Tom Fraser, Anna Freiberger, Jo Gardner, Camilla Gersh, Alex Gray, Eric Grossman, Michelle Haimoff, Marcus Hardy, Mohammad Hassan, Sasha Heseltine, Rose Hudson, Pippa Hurst, Kim Inglis, Jaqueline Jackson, Stuart James, Claire Jones, Bharti Karakoti, Priya Kukadia, Rahul Kumar, Rakesh Kumar Pal, Mathew Kurien, Maite Lantaron, Jude Ledger, Jason Little, Shahid Mahmood, Nicola Malone, Alison McGill, Susan Millership, Jane Middleton, Nancy-Jane Maun, George Nimmo, Todd Obolsky, Clare Peel, Helen Partington, Helen Peters, Pollyanna Poulter, Leigh Priest, Pamposh Raina, Nicki Rawson, Alice Reese, Marisa Renzullo, Amir Reuveni, Lucy Richards, Ellen Root, Liz Rowe, Azeem Siddiqui, Sands Publishing Solutions, Anaïs Scott, Ankita Sharma, Shailesh Sharma, Rituraj Singh, Beverly Smart, Meredith Smith, AnneLise Sorensen, Anna Streiffert, Clare Sullivan, Avantika Sukhia, Andrew Szudek, Alka Thakur, Hollie Teague, Shawn Thomas, Nikky Twyman, Conrad Van Dyk, Vinita Venugopal, Ajay Verma, Ros Walford, Catherine Waring, Lucilla Watson, Ed Wright.

Special Assistance
Beyer Blinder Belle, John Beatty at the Cotton Club, Peter Casey at the New York Public Library, Nicky Clifford, Linda Corcoran at the Bronx Zoo, Audrey Manley at the Morgan Library, Jane Fischer, Deborah Gaines at the New York Convention and Visitors Bureau, Dawn Geigerich at the Queens Museum of Art, Peggy Harrington at St. John the Divine, Pamela Herrick at the Van Cortlandt House, Marguerite Lavin at the Museum of the City of New York, Robert Makla at the Friends of Central Park, Gary Miller at the New York Stock Exchange, Laura Mogil at the American Museum of Natural History, Fred Olsson at the Shubert Organization, Dominique Palermo at the Police Academy Museum, Royal Canadian Pancake House, Lydia Ruth and Laura I. Fries at the Empire State Building, David Schwartz at the American Museum of the Moving Image, Joy Sienkiewicz at the South Street Seaport Museum, Barbara Orlando at the Metropolitan Transit Authority, the staff at the Lower East Side Tenement Museum, Msgr. Anthony Dalla Valla at St. Patrick's Cathedral.

Research Assistance
Christa Griffin, Bogdan Kaczorowski, Steve McClure, Sabra Moore, Jeff Mulligan, Marc Svensson, Vicky Weiner, Steven Weinstein.

Photographic Reference
Duncan Petersen Publishers Ltd.

Photography Permissions
Dorling Kindersley would like to thank the following for their kind permission to photograph at their establishments: American Craft Museum, American Museum of Natural History, Aunt Len's Doll and Toy Museum, Balducci's, Home Savings of America, Brooklyn Children's Museum, The Cloisters, Columbia University, Eldridge Street Project, Federal Hall, Rockefeller Group, Trump Tower.

Picture credits
a = above; b = below/bottom; c = center; f = far; l = left; r = right; t = top.
Works of art have been reproduced with the permission of the following copyright holders: © ADAGP, Paris and DACS, London 2011: April 1971–July 1972, by Jean Dubuffet 69tc, donated by the Norwegian Government, 1952 158tr, 184cla, 185cra, 185crb; © ARS, NY and DACS, London 2011:181cr; © 2015 Calder Foundation, New York/DACS, London: 109br; Jose de Creeft ©DACS, London/VAGA, New York 2011: 55cl, 201cla; © DACS, London 2011: 157crb, 159tc; Walter De Maria

Broken Kilometer 1979 98cl; *Charging Bull* © Arturo Di Modica 1998 76tl; DK IMAGES: Judith Miller/Wallis & Wallis, Sussex 60br; © Kingdom of Spain, Gaia – Salvador Dali Foundation, DAC2S, London 2011: 170cla; © Marisol Escobar/DACS, London/VAGA, New York 2011: 57bc; Milton Hebald *Romeo and Juliet* 337cr. © Jasper Johns/DACS, London/VAGA, New York 2011: 108cl; ©The Estate of Roy Lichtenstein/DACS, London 2011: 171tl, 108clb; Georg John Lober *Hans Christian Andersen* 1956, 200br; © Sucession Picasso/DACS, London 2011: 38tr, 111tl, 169cb, 170cr, 184clb, 185hl, 188cl; Printed by permission of the Norman Rockwell Family Trust © 1961 the Norman Rockwell Family Trust: 159br; © Licensed by The Andy Warhol Foundation for the Visual Arts, Inc/ARS, New York and DACS, London 2011. 109c; © The Whitney Museum of American Art: 39br, 108bl; Yu Yu Yang: *Untitled*, 1973, 59br.

The Publishers are grateful to the following museums, companies and picture libraries for permission to reproduce their photographs:

9/11 Memorial Museum: Jin Lee 37cr, 74tl, 74bc, 75br. **Ace Hotel:** Lyle Thompson 285tr. **Akwaaba Mansion:** 282tc. **Al Di La:** Paul Thorburn 290cr. **Alamy Images:** AA World Travel Library 135c; Ambient Images Inc/Joseph A. Rosen 167c; Sandra Baker 364tl; Patrick Batchelder 204; Business 154clb; Peter Cavanagh 367cla; Robert K. Chin 296t; Comstock Images 293c; Wendy Connett 90ca, 112; Songquan Deng 360–6; Randy Duchaine 256cr; Eye Ubiquitous/Jon Hicks 129cb; Kevin Foy 75tl; Jeff Greenberg 270cla; David Grossman 47bl; Jean Hubert 230bl; Kuttig - Travel - 2 229cr; Ian Marlow 367cl; Patti McConville 278-9; Ellen McKnight 372cla; Eric Nathan 114clb; PCL 293tl; Alex Segre 292cla; Lana Sundman 367tl; thkmedia de 334bc; Hugh Threlfall 366cla, ZUMA Press, Inc. 141tc. **American Museum-Hayden Planetarium, NY:** D. Finnin 212tc. **American Museum of the Moving Image:** Carson Collection © Bruce Polin 257tl. **American Museum of Natural History, NY:** 41clb, 210ca; D. Finnin 210bl. **Angel Orensanz Center:** Laszlo Regas 95cl. **Aquagrill:** Tim Gerasimou 295br **Aquarius, UK:** 167tr. **Aquavit restaurant:** 301b. **The Asia Society, NY:** 183cl. **Avery Fisher Hall:** © N McGrath 1976 337tr. **Avis Budget Group:** 379crb. **Bargemusic:** Etienne Frossard 228cl. **The Bettmann Archive, NY:** 20clb, 21cla/cr/bl, 22cl, 24cb/bl, 24–5cb, 27br, 28cla/cra/crb, 32clb, 33tl, 33c, 47br, 51c, 56–7b, 73tl, 78cla, 83crb, 83br, 105bl, 173cl, 181br, 203tl, 206cl, 219c, 225tc, 251tr, 271tr. **Bettmann/UPI:** 29bc, 31br, 32bl, 33tl, 48cl, 50cla, 51bl, 82clb, 149ca, 159cr, 270br, 271cr. **Big Apple Circus:** Maike Schulz 359tc. **Bloomingdale's:** 313cl. **Boqueria:** 296bc. **British Film Institute:** © Roy Export Company Establishment 171tr. **The British Library, London:** 18. **Brooklyn Children's Museum:** Bruce Cotler 236tl. **Brooklyn Historical Society:** detail 235tl. **Brooklyn Historical Society:** John Halpern 229br. **The Brooklyn Museum:** 40bl, 41c, 238–9 all, 240–41 all; Lewis Wick Hine, *Climbing Into The Promised Land*, 1908 – 38clb. **Brown Brothers:** 69br, 84tr, [...]br. **Camera Press:** 30crb/bl, 33crb, 123crb; R Open 50tr. **Carlyle Hotel, NY:** 283tr. **Carnegie Hall:** © H. Grossman [...] Allan Cash: 32br. **Cathedral of St. John The Divine:** [...]yatt Peace Fountain 1985, 221tl. **CBS Entertainment/ [...]too:** "Vacation from Marriage" 167br. **Chelsea Lodge:** [...]hildren's Museum of the Arts: 101cl. **Christ [...] United Methodist:** 194c. **CityPASS:** 363c. **Colorific!:** [...] Black Star: 83cr. T. Cowell 217cr. R. Fraser 78tr. D. [...]81bl. **Corbis:** Alan Schein Photography 214; AS400 DB [...]tmann 32cra, 33br, 133cl, 277ca; Jacques M. Chenet [...]motix / Andy Katz 35crb; Randy Duchaine 93tl; EPA / [...]ne 35bl; Kevin Fleming 275tl; Todd Gipstein 79tl; Bob [...]a; David Lehman: 134bl; Mascarucci 300tl; Gail [...] 201bl, 273tr, 275br; Michael Setboun 260, 272tr; [...]ews / Doug Meszler 104tr; Steven E. Sutton 53br;

Ramin Talaie 37cra; David Turnley 34cl; VIEW/Nathan Willock 86; Michael Yamashita 277cb; Bo Zaunders 370cl. **Culver Pictures, Inc:** (inset) 9, 21crb, 22clb, 23bl, 25tl/br, 29cb, 50br, 78cb, 79cr/cb, 76tl, 83bl, 117bl, 120tc, 123bl, 133cr, 143c, 145clb, 223tl/bc/crb, 263cb. **Daily Eagle:** (detail) 91clb. **The Dinex Group:** Eric Laignel 303b; B Milne 302tl. **Dirt Candy:** 294tl. **Dollar Thrifty Automotive Group, Inc.:** 379cra. **Dorling Kindersley:** Courtesy of National Museum of the American Indian/ Steven Greaves 41tl, 77t; Courtesy of The Jewish Museum/ Steven Greaves 180tr; Morgan Library and Museum/ Steven Greaves 29tr. **Dreamstime.com:** Aleksandra Alimova 110tl; Alexpro9500 379br; Valentin Armianu 164tc; Rafael Ben-ari 77br; Bigapplestock 80tl, 128bl, 224c; Jon Bilous 134tr; Ryan Deberardinis 105br; Demerzel21 230tl, 231tr; Alexandre Fagundes De Fagundes 377cb; Julie Feinstein 145br, 228bl; Prochasson Frederic 148cl; Leo Bruce Hempell 228cr; Wangkun Jia 359bl; Anthony Aneese Totah Jr 256bl; Daniel Kaesler 375tc; Andrew Kazmierski 315tr; massimo lama 56cl; Nicole Langener 133tl; Leungphotography 91bl; Littleny 33tr, 250b; Tatiana Morozova 382cl; Newphotoservice 35tl; Johannes Onnes 35cr, 108tc; Rolf52 10bl; Sangaku 258cr; Ulf Starke 107cr; Starstock 51tr; Tupungato 386cl; Victorian: 166tl; Hilda Weges 37br; Zhukovsky 374tl. **Esto:** P Aaron 336clb. **Four Seasons Hotel:** Peter Vitale 283cr. **Fraunces Tavern Museum, NY:** From the exhibit "Come All You Gallant Heroes" The World of the Revolutionary Soldier December 4, 1991 to August 14, 1992: 24cla. **The Frick Collection, NY:** *St Francis In The Desert* by Giovanni Bellini 39bl, 196-7 all. **Garrard The Crown Jewellers:** 141c. **© The George Balanchine Trust:** *Apollo*, choreography by George Balanchine, photo by P Kolnik 5bl; George Balanchine's *The Nutcracker*, SM, photo by P Kolnik 337br. **Getty Images:** AFP/Stan Honda 384cla; age fotostock 82, /José Fuste Raga 13br; AWL Images /Gavin Hellier 64–5, / Jon Arnold 2–3; FilmMagic 242; Mitchell Funk 335cb; Glow Images, Inc 266–7; Michael Grimm 380tl; The Image Bank/ Siegfried Layda 36, / Riou 13tl; Lonely Planet Images/Angus Oborn 1; Neos Design – Cory Eastman 198; Photodisc/ Thomas Northcut 136; Photolibrary/Barry Winiker 12br, 148clb; Stone/Hiroyuki Matsumoto 178; Vetta/S. Greg Panosian 66; Barry Winiker 141tl. **Greenmarket Farmers Market:** 365tr. **The Greenwich Hotel:** 288bc. **Hearth:** 291tr, 297tr. **IStockphoto.com:** Ken Brown 33cb; JayLazarin 231br; ovidiuhrubaru 35br. **Jacques Marchais Center of Tibetan Art:** 258bc. **Alan Kaufman** 94bl. **Robert Harding Picture Library:** Harpers New Monthly Magazine: 233tl. **The Image Bank:** 17clb, 235br; P. Miller 377tc; A. Satterwhite 79bc. **Japan Society:** © Jack Vartoogian, NY 63bc, 154tc. **The Jewish Museum, NY:** 180tr, 182c. **Juliana's Pizza:** Biz Jones 229tl. **The Kobal Collection:** 207tc. **Lebrecht Music:** Toby Wales 145tl. **The Leisure Pass Group:** 363cla. **The Lesbian, Gay, Bisexual, & Transgender Community Center:** 364c. **Frank Leslie's Illustrated Newspaper:** 232br, 233cra. **Library of Congress:** 22bc, 25cla, 28br. **Library Hotel Collection:** 280bl. **The Little Owl:** Jon Selvey 297bl. **Leonardo Media Ltd:** 280br/cla, 281br/tl. **The Lowell Hotel, NY:** 283cl. **Macy's:** 314bl. **Madison Square Garden:** 131cr, 336tr. **Magnum Photos:** © H. Cartier-Bresson 171c. **Mary Evans Picture Library:** Library of Congress 8-9, 26br, 233br, 100bl. **Metro-North Commuter Railroad:** F. English 152tr/ca. **The Metropolitan Museum of Art, NY:** 186cla/clb/bc, 187 all, 188br/tr/c/bl/br, 189tl/tr, 190–91 all, 192–3 all, 246 all, 247ca/ cr/bl/br, 248tl/tr, 249tr/c/b; *Young Woman With A Waterjug* by Johannes Vermeer 37bl; *Figure of a Hippopotamus*, faience, Egypt, 12th Dynasty 39crb. **Metropolitan Transit Authority:** 382cr; MTA/Patrick Cashin all 383, 384tr/bl. **Michael Jordan's The Steak House N.Y.C.:** 302bc. **Collection of The Morgan Library, NY:** *Blanche of Castille and King Louis IX of France, author dictating to a scribe*, moralized Bible, c1230 38cr, 161bl, *Song of Los* David A. Loggie (gift of Mrs Landon K. Thorne)

160cla, *Biblia Latina* David A. Loggie 160clb, 160br, 161cb/tc/br. **Morris-Jumel Mansion, Inc NY:** 21tl; A Rosario 25crb. **Museum of American Finance:** Alan Barnett 70tr. **The Museum of the City of New York:** 19b, 20cra, 20–21, 21tr, 22ca, photo J. Parnell 23cb, 24cl, 26cla/clb, 27cb/crb/bc, 28c, 29c., 31tc/c, 39tr (silver porringer), 233crb (Talfour). **The Museum of Modern Art, NY:** 168ca, 175cr/crb/cb/bl, 170cla/cr, 171tl/b; *The Bather*, c. 1885, Paul Cézanne 170bc; Lillie P. Bliss Collection 169cra; © 2004 Photo Elizabeth Felicella, architectural rendering Kohn Pedersen Fox Associates, digital composite Robert Bowen 168tr; ©2005 Timothy Hursley 164c, 168clb; *The Goat* by Pablo Picasso, 1950, 38tr; *Portrait of the Postman Joseph Roulin* by Vincent van Gogh, 1889, 37ca. **National Baseball Library, Cooperstown, NY:** 4tr, 27bl, 30cl. **National Car Rental:** 377cr. **National Museum of The American Indian/Smithsonian Institution:** 20c. **National Park Service:** Ellis Island Immigration Museum 82ca, 82cb; Statue of Liberty National Monument 79clb. **New Museum of Contemporary Art:** Dean Kaufman 94tr. **New York Botanic Garden:** Tori Butt 252bc, 253t/ca; Jason Green 252crb; Muriel Weinerman 253bl. **The New Yorker Magazine Inc:** Cover drawing by Rea Irvin, © 1925, 1953, All rights reserved, 30bc. **New York Public Library:** Special Collection Office, Schomburg Center for Research in Black Culture 31cla; Stokes Collection 25tr. **New York Stock Exchange:** 73cra. **New York Transit Museum:** Black Paw Photo 230cr. **NYC & Company:** 362br, Julienne Schaer, 2009 366br; Stefano Giovannini 363tr; One If By Land, Two If by Sea: 298tl. **One World Observatory:** 35tr; 37clb; 75tl. **Pampano:** 301tr; **Per Se:** 304bl; **Performing Arts Library:** Clive Barda 206bl. **Peter Luger Steakhouse:** 305br. **The Pickle Guys:** 93tc. **Photolibrary:** Renaud Visage 160. **Popperfoto:** 31cra/cr, 73crb, 264cla. **Quality Meats:** Michael Weber 300bl. **Queen Elizabeth II September 11th Garden:** 58c. **The Port Authority Of New York & New Jersey:** 373br. **Collection of The Queens Museum of Art:** purchased with funds from the George and Mollie Wolfe World's Fair Fund 31crb; Official souvenir, purchase 34cb. **Red Hook Lobster Pound:** Daniel Krieger 290bc. **Rensselaer Polytechnic Institute:** 232–3c, 233bl. **Rex Features Ltd:** Sipa-Press 54cr/br; 369. **Rex Shutterstock:** CSU Archives / Everett Collection 32cr; Imagebroker 314cl; REX USA LTD 34tr. **The Ritz-Carlton New York;** Battery Park: 283tc. **Courtesy of the Rockefeller Center © The Rockefeller Group, Inc:** 30clb. **The St. Regis, NY:** 282c. **Scientific American:** 18 May 1878 edition 232tr; November 9, 1878 edition 234bl. **Shake Shack:** Peter Mauss / ESTO 290cl. **The Sherman Group/New York water Taxi:** 380br. **Skidmore, Owings & Merrill LLP, Chicago:** 56cr. **Skyscraper Museum:** Robert Polidori 57tl; 272bl. **The Society of Illustrators:** 194tl. **The Solomon R Guggenheim Museum, NY:** 184–5 all. **South Street Seaport Museum:**

R.B. Merkel 80bl. **Spice Market:** 298tc. **Frank Spooner Pictures:** Gamma 156clb; Liaison/Gamma/ Anderson 17tr, 157cla. Liaison/Levy/Halebian: 46tr, 49c. **sta travel group:** 364cra. **The Standard Hotel, New York:** Todd Eberle 286tl. **Starwood Hotels and Resorts Worldwide Inc.:** 138cl. **SuperStock:** age fotostock 96, 126, 162./ Nikhilesh Haval 92tl; Ambient Images Inc. 140tl; Jean-Pierre Lescourret 102; Robert Harding Picture Library 118; Tetra Images 146. **The Surrey:** 289tr. **Theater Development Fund:** David LeShay 334cl. **Top of the Rock:** 12tr. **Turner Entertainment Company:** 133br. **Union Square Hospitality Group:** Nathan Rawlinson 299br. **United Nations, NY:** 156cla, 157ca, 158tr/bc, 159tc/cla/br. **Collection of The Whitney Museum of American art, NY:** 108cl/c/clb, 109cr, purchase with funds from a public fundraising campaign in May 1982. One half of the funds were contributed by the Robert Wood Johnson Jr. Charitable Trust. Additional major donations were given by The Lauder Foundation; the Robert Lehman Foundation, Inc.; the Howard and Jean Lipman Foundation, Inc; an anonymous donor; The TM Evans Foundation, Inc.; MacAndrews & Forbes Group Incorporated; the DeWitt Wallace Fund, Inc; Martin & Agnes Gruss; Anne Phillips; Mr and Mrs Laurance S. Rockefeller; the Simon Foundation, Inc.; Marylou Whitney; Bankers Trust Company; Mr and Mrs Kenneth N Dayton; Joel and Anne Ehrenkranz; Irvin and Kenneth Feld; Flora Whitney Miller. More than 500 individuals from 26 states and abroad also contributed to the campaign 109crb; gift of an anonymous donor 58.65 109cr; **Wheeler Pictures:** 82tr; **Wildlife Conservation Society, Bronx Zoo:** Julie Maher 254tr/cl, 255bl/br. **Woodlawn Cemetery:** 250tr. **Robert Wright:** 16tr, 45tl, 138tr/c/bl; 139tl/br, 152br, 153tl/cr, 367tc.

Front Endpapers
Alamy Images: Patrick Batchelder Ltl; Wendy Connett Rbc; **Corbis:** Alan Schein Photography Lftl; VIEW/Nathan Willock Rbr; **Getty Images:** age fotostock Rfbr; Neos Design – Cory Eastman Rcr; Photodisc/Thomas Northcut Ltc, Lfcl; Stone/ Hiroyuki Matsumoto Rfcr; Vetta/S. Greg Panosian Lclb; **SuperStock:** age fotostock Lfclb, LFCL, Rcb; Jean-Pierre Lescourret LCL; Robert Harding Picture Library Rfcrb; Tetra Images Rcrb.

Cover
Front and Spine: 4Corners: Pietro Canali / SIME

Pull Out Map Cover
Pietro Canali / SIME 999
All other images © Dorling Kindersley.
See www.dkimages.com for further information.

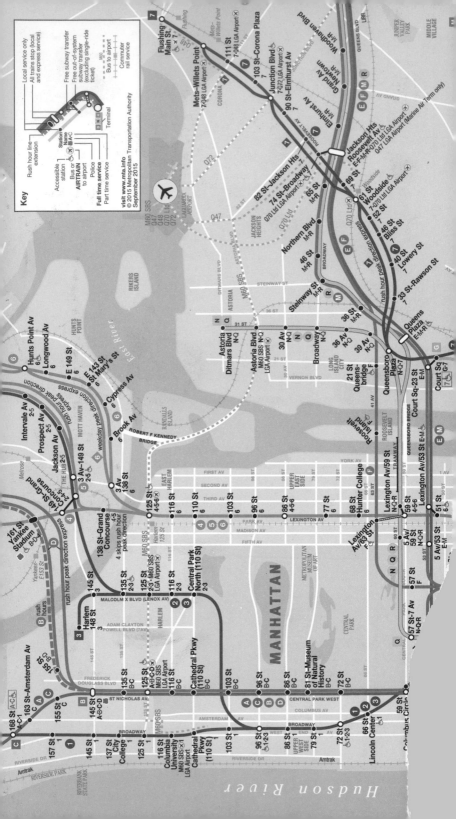